TRUST AND POWER ON THE SHOP FLOOR

D1617572

TRUST AND POWER ON THE SHOP FLOOR

An ethnographical, ethical, and philosophical study
on responsible behaviour in industrial organisations

Maarten Johannes Verkerk

HD
58.7
.V47
2004
West

Eburon Delft
2004

ISBN 90-5972-033-4

Eburon Academic Publishers
P.O. Box 2867
2601 CW Delft
The Netherlands
tel.: +31 (0) 15 - 2131484 / fax: +31 (0) 15 - 2146888
info@eburon.nl / www.eburon.nl

Lay-out: Wouter Vuurboom

Cover: Interior of a glass furnace
Cover design: Studio Hermkens, Amsterdam.

© 2004 M.J. Verkerk, Hoensbroek. All rights reserved. No part of this publication may be reproduced, stored in a retrieval system, or transmitted, in any form or by any means, electronic, mechanical, photocopying, recording, or otherwise, without the prior permission in writing from the proprietor.

"So Jesus called them all together (the twelve disciples) to him and said,
'You know that the men who are considered rulers of the heathen
have power over them,
and the leaders have complete authority.
This, however, is not the way it is among you.
If one of you wants to be great, he must be the servant of the rest;
and if one of you wants to be first, he must be the slave of all.
For even the Son of Man did not come to be served;
he came to serve and to give his life to redeem many people'."

Mark 10 : 41 – 45

Contents

Preface

Nowadays, the social responsibility of organisations is no longer disputed. Managers devote a lot of attention to codes of conduct and ethical programmes. This development is gratifying, because it shows awareness in today's companies of the social dimension of behaviour in organisations. It also shows that companies respect the ethical interests of various stakeholders. Attention given to social and ethical issues is related to the changing position of enterprises in today's society. Organisations increasingly have to account for their social and ethical behaviour.

The study of ethical issues in universities and enterprises shows a certain bias. Attention is given to big issues such as the Brent Spar affair of Shell, the production capacity of Heineken in Burma, and the Pinto fires of Ford. In other words, attention focuses on decision-making processes by managers. This bias has several undesirable side effects. It suggests that responsible behaviour is mainly concerned, first, with big issues in the boardroom rather than small issues on the shop floor; and, second, it is concerned with managerial decision making rather than with daily employee activities.

This study has a different focus. It deals with responsible behaviour of employees on the shop floor of an organisation. In my opinion, a responsible organisation requires responsible management *and* responsible employees. Therefore, a responsible organisation focuses on big issues in the boardroom *and* small issues on the shop floor, and deals with decision making of managers *and* daily activities of workers. The change in focus – from decision making in the boardroom to actions on the shop floor – places the responsibility of management in a new perspective. First, such a change stresses the importance of the primary process in that it recognises that the social responsibility of an organisation must be expressed first and foremost by the execution of the primary process by employees on the shop floor. Second, such a change emphasises that the management has to take the lead. The management has to create structural and cultural conditions for responsible behaviour of employees in the organisation. It has to take the first steps towards the formulation of normative principles and has to motivate employees to behave in accordance with these principles.

This thesis has been written from the perspective of a factory manager as a 'reflective practitioner'. It deals with responsible behaviour of employees in industrial organisations, and focuses on the structural and cultural conditions that have to be fulfilled by a manager so that operators on the shop floor can act in a responsible way. An investigation of processes of responsibility on the shop floor requires an analysis on three levels: phenomena on the shop floor, organisation design theory, and philosophy of organisation. The research question that integrates these levels is formulated as follows:

How can employees on the shop floor act in a responsible way?

This research question is investigated by way of an explorative expedition in manufacturing organisations, in which deep structures of organisational processes are studied. In a process of seeking and finding, paradoxes are identified, unexpected

13

data are reported, existing views are confirmed, ideas are falsified, and theories are re-interpreted. Organisational ethnography is used as the main research strategy.

This study has to be positioned at the crossroads of two different traditions. First, the Dutch tradition of Socio-Technical Systems Design developed by De Sitter, Dankbaar, Den Hertog, Van Eijnatten, and many others. This tradition emphasises the authority of employees to control their own workplace and advocates participation of employees in organisational processes. The second tradition is the reformational-philosophical tradition of social criticism developed by Van Riessen, Schuurman, Goudzwaard, and many others. It concentrates on a normative development of western society based on norms of technology, economy, justice, and love.

This thesis is organised as follows. The Prologue tells a story from the perspective of a manager about paradoxes on the shop floor. Operators are expected to carry out a production task but cannot do so due to failing conditions. Nevertheless, they are held accountable. To cope with such an impossible situation, employees often resort to irresponsible behaviour. In Chapter 1, paradoxes on the shop floor are explored in greater detail. It tells stories about the shop floor, reviews development in manufacturing, and discusses responsibility in a technological age. Further, the research questions and objectives are formulated. Chapter 2 investigates the research questions from a theoretical perspective, analysing the fundaments of Taylorism or Scientific Management, Socio-Technical Systems Design, Lean Production, Business Process Reengineering, and the Mini-Company Concept. Chapter 3 examines the research questions by outlining two ethnographical case studies. It describes the start-up of an actuator factory in Roermond and the turn-around of a glass factory in Aachen. In Chapter 4, the basic beliefs, social background, and intellectual development of the author are made explicit. Attention then focuses on answering the research questions. An evaluation of the main research strategy – ethnography by a manager – is given from a methodological and epistemological point of view. A detailed analysis of both cases shows that high-trust and high-power relations are essential conditions for responsible behaviour of employees on the shop floor. Further, a philosophical critique of industrial organisations reveals a complex normative structure in which different types of normativity are interlaced. These different types of normativity are identified and their mutual relations are indicated. A plea is made for an *ethics of responsibility*, expressing the fundamental responsibility of the human actor to fellow man, society, and natural environment. The idea of an ethics of responsibility implies a *normative reinterpretation of organisation theory* that respects dignity and vocation of employees, and develops sound trust and power relations. In other words, structural and cultural aspects of organisations must be developed not only through norms of technology and economy, but also through norms of power, social intercourse, justice, love (care), and trust. An ethics of responsibility implies nothing less than a *transformation of the organisational practice*. In this process, the factory manager is a key actor.

Prologue

I started my management career in a small factory in Eindhoven, the Netherlands, which produced several types of image intensifiers. The technical specifications of these products were quite strict, as a result of which the quality of the manufacturing process had to be given a lot of attention. The equipment was sophisticated, process instructions were present, and employees were trained to work with great precision. Despite these precautions, the manufacturing process was not stable. Repeatedly, something went wrong, as a result of which deliveries were put into danger.

> Story. The most critical step in the manufacturing process was the application of the light-sensitive layer by evaporation of inorganic materials from a dispenser. A dispenser is a thin metallic pipe with a diameter of 1 to 2 millimetres and a length of about 20 millimetres. The production process of these dispensers was not a very stable one, their quality varying from good to bad. The cause of the variations was not known. It was suspected that the employees did not work with sufficient accuracy. Therefore, they were asked to carry out the process with the utmost precision.

This story raises several questions. What does it mean if a process is not stable? Why did the management suspect that employees did not work with sufficient accuracy? Why didn't the management investigate the cause of the variations?

> Continued. At that time, a company-wide quality improvement programme was launched, in which our factory also had to participate. The management team formulated an improvement programme, which I presented to the entire crew. I emphasised that our employees were responsible for the quality of the products. I asked them to work in accordance with the instructions, to inspect semi-manufactured products meticulously, and to handle components, assemblies and products with great care. In other words, I invited them to take their own responsibility. In particular, I was drawing attention to the manufacturing of dispensers.

In retrospect, my presentation raises critical questions. What was behind the 'beautiful' words about employee responsibility? A well-defined view? A sympathetic idea without an organisational foundation? Keep in mind that the manufacturing process of dispensers was unstable.

> Continued. Six months later, the production process of dispensers destabilised again, and the employees that operated this process were called to account. It was suggested that the process had weakened due to diminished discipline, but no indications of this were found. For about two weeks, the firm was unable to make any product and a production stop threatened. Then all of a sudden, the process started again. Nobody knew why!

Later, the investigations of a technical laboratory revealed the cause.

> Continued. A technical laboratory was commissioned to investigate the production process of dispensers. It was found that the equipment operated at the limit of its

possibilities, as a result of which small variations in starting materials or equipment settings led to an unstable situation. The equipment was redesigned and new settings were defined. From that time on, the production process of dispensers was stabilised.

This story clearly shows a paradox. On the one hand, employees were made responsible for the production of dispensers – a process that was not stable. On the other hand, employees were called to account. In fact, they were blamed for the problems in the production of dispensers.

The character of this paradox can be better understood when we focus attention on the asymmetry of the manager-employee relation. A manager gives an employee the responsibility to perform a production task. The act of 'giving responsibility' implies that the basic conditions – e.g., good equipment, suitable tools, up-to-date process instructions and adequate training – have been fulfilled so that the employee can perform his or her tasks smoothly. In addition, a manager also calls an employee to account. The act 'calling to account' implies the tacit assumption that an employee can result in result without a hitch because the basic conditions to perform the tasks were indeed fulfilled. However, if the basic conditions are not fulfilled a paradox appears. The figure below illustrates and clarifies this paradox.

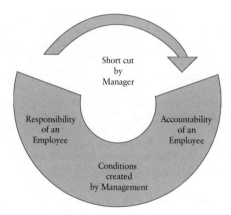

The figure shows that employee responsibility and accountability are inextricably connected with the conditions created by the management. Generally, a manager assumes that the conditions are fulfilled so that s/he can call an employee to account. However, if the conditions are not fulfilled a paradox arises: the employee has to carry out a certain manufacturing task, but is unable to do so due to failing conditions. In fact, the manager takes a short cut by calling the employee to account without considering the conditions. The problem of this short cut is its naturalness, it just happens.

The story about the production of dispensers clearly illustrates this short cut. I did not know that accidental variations in the starting materials could result in an unstable situation, nor did I know that the settings of the equipment were so critical. In addition, I did not investigate the required conditions for controlled manufacturing. Still, I called the employees to account: I took a short cut. Actually, I didn't give the operators the responsibility for the process but *I delegated the guilt* for the unstable situation. In other words, *I reduced responsibility to accountability*.

This story is not an exception. There are thousands of similar stories in manufacturing and this type of paradoxes can be found on the shop floor every single day. And every day, managers take a short cut, delegate guilt to employees, and reduce responsibility to accountability. Paradoxes and short cuts have a disastrous effect on organisations. Employees are caught an impossible position: they are forced to find a way-out to survive, e.g. by trespassing instructions, disregarding quality measurements, falsifying data, or creating non-transparency. In other words, they cope with paradoxes by showing irresponsible behaviour.

Paradoxes and short cuts occur not only in activities directly related to the manufacturing process. They are also present in other areas, e.g. safety aspects, environmental regulations, social intercourse, moral issues, and so on. The mechanism that produces the paradox is essentially the same. Employees have certain responsibilities in these areas. However, they cannot bear their responsibility due to failing conditions. Again, a short cut by the management will lead to irresponsible behaviour of employees. In these areas, however, the paradox and short cut are even less visible, particularly, because the technical and economical perspective that dominates industrial cultures obscures the specific character of these responsibilities.

CHAPTER 1

Paradoxes on the shop floor

The Prologue has shown that paradoxes are present on the shop floor of manufacturing organisations. Shop floor employees have the responsibility to execute various production activities, however, the conditions necessary to perform these activities are often lacking. The result is a paradox: employees are called to account for tasks they cannot perform. Paradoxes put employees in an awkward situation. They force them to take (illegal) actions to protect their own interests.

This chapter explores paradoxes on the shop floor of industrial organisations in more detail. Section 1 sketches the presence of paradoxes in the context of new production concepts. It is shown that three different levels of analysis are required to understand the development of paradoxes on the shop floor. Section 2 explores the first level of analysis: phenomena on the shop floor. The nature of paradoxes is then investigated from the perspective of the shop floor. Section 3 deals with the second level of analysis: organisation design theories. A short history of manufacturing is presented to enable the reader to understand the societal context of new production concepts. It is indicated that these concepts claim technical superiority and social innovation. Section 4 pays attention to the third level of analysis: the philosophy of organisation. A philosophical account of responsibility and accountability on the shop floor of manufacturing organisations is given. It is shown that the basic beliefs of a manager about man, labour, and organisation play a key role. In the last section, the motive, research questions and objectives of this study are formulated.

1 Introduction

I have managed factories in The Netherlands, Germany and Taiwan for more than fifteen years – small factories (30 employees) and large factories (850 employees). In all these factories, I have spent many hours on the shop floor. These hours have been spent talking with operators about their work, hobbies, and family (all factories), experiencing the pressure of the production (all factories), enjoying the silence of clean room (The Netherlands), encountering the humidity of the production areas (Taiwan), feeling the heat of the presses (Germany), drinking hot chocolate from a machine in the coffee corner (The Netherlands), eating home-made food of undefined composition in an empty corner of the production area (Taiwan), and drinking fresh coffee in a control cabinet of a large glass furnace (Germany).

Being on the shop floor evoked many feelings in me; not only feelings of astonishment, but also feelings of bewilderment. I have met employees who were very motivated, who did their job with joy and enthusiasm, who took initiatives to control the technical processes, and who made proposals to improve the working environment. The day-to-day contact with these employees has been one of the most motivating experiences in my career. However, I have also met employees who were not motivated at all, who had a lack of interest, who were frustrated, discouraged and apathetic, and who showed a lot of fear and mistrust. Some of these employees told me that they only worked for the money. They told me that their real life started after working hours. I always got down after a chat with these employees. I never got such experiences out of my mind.

Through the years, I have learned to 'read' the shop floor. Gradually, I began to understand that there is large difference between the 'world of management' and the 'world of employees'. I found that processes on management level and processes on the shop floor each have their own dynamics. I discovered some underlying mechanisms. Further, it occurred to me that these differences between the world of management and the world of employees might play a key role in the development of paradoxes.

During my career I have experienced power and powerlessness, relaxation and stress, happiness and distress, and trust and mistrust. I have experienced all these phenomena within my own body. I am absolutely sure that the employees with whom I have worked together have experienced the same phenomena.

Fear, mistrust, domination, dehumanisation, and alienation in manufacturing organisations have been investigated thoroughly.[1] It is widely acknowledged that these phenomena are strongly related to the extreme division of labour that has dominated western industries since the introduction of Scientific Management by the American engineer Frederick Taylor. A number of new production concepts

---

[1]   See for example Walker and Guest (1952), Gouldner (1954), Dalton (1959), Blauner (1964), Crozier (1964), Braverman (1974), Fox (1974), Edwards (1979), Karasek and Theorell (1979), and Runcie (1980).

have been developed to overcome the social consequences of the Tayloristic approach, among other things. These concepts offer an alternative approach to the design of production lines and organisation of labour. Further, they offer different tools and methods to improve the performance of the factory. For example, Socio-Technical Systems Design, Lean Management, Business Process Reengineering and the Mini-Company Concept are widely applied in modern industrial organisations.

Philips Electronics N.V. was one of the leading companies in the development of new production concepts.[2] The company stood at the cradle of the Dutch approach to socio-technical thinking, developed a world-wide manufacturing programme, and introduced the mini-company concept. In my first manufacturing position in Philips, I was 'initiated' in socio-technical thinking and the promise of a 'new world of work'. Later on, I was trained in improvement techniques and the mini-company concept. Through the years, I experienced that new production concepts did work and that the promise of a 'new world of work' could be realised in modern factories. All this changed, however, after taking up a management position in a glass factory in Aachen, Germany. In this organisation socio-technical principles and continuous improvement were implemented. However, I discovered that the 'old' problems of Taylorism were still present. I found that the shop floor was troubled with paradoxes and managerial short cuts. I met a lot of apathy, frustration, fear, and mistrust on the production line. Furthermore, I experienced the negative influence of these phenomena on my own body and my own job satisfaction. The Aachen factory made me doubtful. After all, I had to conclude that new production concepts – 'espoused theories of action' (Argyris[3]) – did not prevent the development of paradoxes and managerial short cuts on the shop floor. I also had to conclude that the promise of a 'new world of work' did not hold for the production lines in Aachen.

These conclusions raised a lot of different questions. Do we make the right observations? Do we have to change our way of looking? Do we use production concepts with serious shortcomings? Have we come to the limits of our design theories? Are we overlooking fundamental characteristics of industrial organisations? Are we ignoring the meaning of labour?[4]

A closer look shows that these questions operate on different levels.[5] The first two questions refer to *concrete phenomena on the shop floor*, the third and fourth

---

[2]   Den Hertog (1977) and De Weerd (2001).

[3]   Argyris (1991, p103).

[4]   The English word 'meaning' has two different senses. Firstly, it is used in sentences like 'the meaning of this word' or 'the meaning of that symbol'. In these sentences, it refers to the interpretation of a word or a symbol. Secondly, it is used in sentences like 'the meaning of life' and 'the meaning of work'. In these sentences, it refers to a deeper significance that transcends activities of human beings. The German language has two different words for it: 'Bedeutung' and 'Sinn'. Mostly, the meaning of the word 'meaning' in this study will be clear from the context. If that is not the case, the German word will be added in parenthesis.

[5]   Compare Jochemsen and Glas (1997, p102 ff.).

to the *basics of organisation design theory*, and the fifth and sixth to *fundamental features of man and organisation (the philosophy of organisation)*. Therefore, an in-depth knowledge of paradoxes and managerial short cuts as well as a fundamental understanding of a 'new world of work' requires an integrative analysis of these different levels.

Are we making the right observations? Industrial managers are trained to make plans, to measure progress according to formal criteria, and to evaluate implementation on the basis of technical and financial data. Sometimes surveys are done to measure employee satisfaction. However, do formal criteria, technical and financial data, and survey results provide us with the right information? One step further, do major projects like the implementation of new production concepts require different ways of looking at phenomena on the shop floor? In literature, technical data, financial results, and development of employee satisfaction during the implementation of new production concepts have been investigated thoroughly.[6] However, these studies do not give a rich description of the behaviour of and the interaction between operators, engineers and managers. These studies also do not map meticulously what these concepts bring about in terms of social mechanisms on the shop floor. For that reason, another research strategy is required. A detailed study of phenomena on the shop floor asks for an ethnographical approach.[7] Ethnographical studies on organisational change within modern factories are scarce.[8] Further, ethnographical studies during the implementation of new production concepts are even scarcer.[9] Within these studies, the 'partial perspective' (Roosen[10]) of a factory manager is completely absent.

The first level of analysis – describing phenomena on the shop floor – will be very helpful. However, to understand why new production concepts fail in many factories, we have to investigate these concepts themselves.[11] The implementation of new production concepts has to be placed against the background of company-wide improvement programs. Training in these new concepts is obligatory for all managers. In a short period of time, the essentials of new approaches are explained and the main steps for implementation are outlined. In addition, an implementation plan for all factories is made. However, critical questions have to be asked. Are these concepts 'universally' applicable? Do they require special attention

---

6   See for example De Sitter (1981), Schonberger (1986), Hall (1987), Hayes et al. (1988), Ohno (1988), Davenport and Short (1990), Womack et al. (1991), Goldman and Nagel (1993), Hammer and Champy (1993), Kidd (1994), De Sitter (1994), Hammer (1996), Hooft (ed.) (1996), Schonberger (1996), Womack and Jones (1997), Monden (1998), Van Breukelen et al. (1998), Purser and Cabana (1998) and Eijbergen (1999).

7   See for example Dalton (1959), Graham (1984), Rosen (1985, 1988) and Watson (1994).

8   Exceptions are Kamata (1982) and Delbridge (1998).

9   The study of Hennestad (2000) contains some ethnographical observations.

10 Roosen (1991, p2).

11 See for example Argyris (1991), Hayes and Pisano (1994), Hammer and Stanton (1995), Pruyt (1996), Argyris (1998), Breukelen et al. (1998), Carter (1998), and Hennestad (2000).

during implementation? Do they have serious shortcomings? In literature, many studies describe the improvement of performance upon implementing new production concepts in manufacturing organisations.[12] However, the whole process of implementation is still an under-researched area.[13] The relation between the basics of new concept, specific manufacturing context, local 'colour' of the shop floor, and nature of the change in progress is not investigated.[14] In conclusion, to understand the failure of new production concepts we have to investigate the phenomena on the shop floor and the nature of new production concepts in an integrative analysis.

The first and second level of analysis is very important in understanding the complex dynamics during the implementation of new production concepts. However, it is also very important to understand the nature of these new concepts. We have to ask ourselves whether we are digging deep enough. After all, factories are human organisations through and through. It cannot be taken for granted that new production concepts match with the humanity of human beings. All new production concepts claim to offer an integral or holistic alternative to Taylorism. However, none of these approaches plausibly justify this claim by offering a philosophical view on organisational reality, for example. In literature, critical management studies have been published.[15] These studies indicate that organisations cannot be seen as neutral structures but have to be considered as highly complex social phenomena. The value of these critical studies is limited because they do not offer a cosmology or ontology of organisations. In addition, the critical tone drowns out the organisational content. In conclusion, to under-stand the nature and character of new production concepts, we have to do a philosophical analysis in order to reveal structural limitations of these concepts and to discover normative dimensions of human responsibility in an organisational context.

It has to be emphasised that these different levels of analysis – *concrete phenomena on the shop floor*, *basics of organisation design theory*, *fundamental features of man and organisation (the philosophy of organisation)* – are strongly related. They influence each other and they are mutually dependent. An ethnographical description of phenomena on the shop floor is required to develop theories about human behaviour in organisations. Also, an in-depth understanding of new production concepts is essential to develop a philosophy of organisation. On the other hand, a philosophical analysis of organisations is of the utmost importance in analysing the strengths and limitations of different theoretical approaches and to set up a framework within which concrete phenomena can be interpreted. In the following sections these levels of analysis will be elaborated upon.

---

[12] See for example De Sitter (1981), Schonberger (1986), Womack et al. (1991), Hammer and Champy (1993), De Sitter (1994), Schonberger (1996), Womack and Jones (1997), Purser and Cabana (1998), Van Breukelen et al. (1998), and Eijbergen (1999).

[13] Voss (1988), Hennestad (2000).

[14] Exceptions are Beers (1996) and Hennestad (2000).

[15] See for example Alvesson and Wilmott (1996) and Alvesson and Willmott (eds) (1999).

2 The shop floor in stories

In the previous section the presence of paradoxes on the shop floor is sketched in the context of the introduction of new production concepts in modern factories. It is argued that a deeper insight into this type of phenomena requires an analysis at different levels: phenomena on the shop floor, organisation theory, and philosophy of organisation. In this section the first level – phenomena on the shop floor – is elaborated upon. Stories from the past – which are branded on my memory – are retold to get a sharper picture of short cuts by managers, and different aspects of employee responsibility and accountability on the shop floor. These stories are written from the perspective of a factory manager as 'reflective practitioner'.

2.1 Logistical problems

Paradoxes on the shop floor are often difficult to recognise. Sometimes they are woven in 'unwritten rules' (Scott-Morgan[16]) or 'behaviours and attached meaning systems' (Rosen[17]). This story from the sintering unit of the actuator factory in Roermond is an example of this.

> *Story.* An important step in the production of ceramic multilayer actuators is the sintering process. This process consists of four sub-processes: binder burn-out, pre-sintering, sintering, and flat-sintering. Every sub-process consists of several activities: for example, preparing the plates, building a pile, loading the furnace, starting the program, performing quality measurements, unloading the furnace, removing the plates from the pile, and cleaning the plates. 4 to 8 furnaces were available for each step of the process.
>
> In this unit, there were many problems. Firstly, there were severe logistical problems. The output of every shift had to be about six batches. However, some shifts delivered (to the next production station) only three batches and other shifts about ten batches. This difference was caused by an irregular logistical flow. Sometimes, the foregoing shifts had filled all furnaces so a regular logistical flow was guaranteed. However, in other cases the foregoing shifts had focused their attention on emptying the furnaces, removing the plates from the pile, and cleaning the plates. As a consequence, many furnaces were empty and the logistical flow stagnated. Secondly, there were a lot housekeeping problems. Everywhere in the unit, piles of products could be seen. Employees stood in each other's way. The unit was also dirty. Finally, there were many frictions between the shifts, especially due to the last step: the cleaning of the plates. Nobody liked that work. Preferably, this step was left over to the next shift. During the shift changeover, the presence of a large amount of batches before cleaning caused a lot of quarrelling.

---

[16]   Scott-Morgan (1994).
[17]   Rosen (1991).

Line management told the employees to mind the logistical process, to pay attention to the housekeeping, and to clean a certain number of batches every shift. However, nothing changed. Line management increased their efforts. Nothing changed.

At the same time, a project to decrease the throughput time in the factory was launched. Special attention was given to the sintering unit. A short analysis showed that the logistics in this unit was fully out of control. A university student investigated the logistical problems in this unit. After several weeks of analysis, making proposals, and rejecting proposals, a breakthrough was realised. The total logistical chain was broken down into in four cycles. The activities of every cycle were described in detail. Once a cycle was started, it had to be finished. Preferably, a total cycle had to be finished in the same shift. At the shift changeover, unfinished cycles had to be passed to the new shift. These cycles had to be finished first. At the same time, a number of rules were made to set priorities between the different cycles. Finally, visual tools were made to judge the logistical flow at one single glance, e g by colour coding the furnaces.

The implementation of these cycles, priority rules, and visual tools was guided intensively by line management. Firstly, all shifts were trained extensively. Secondly, over a two-week period one of the line managers was present at every shift changeover to check the cycles, priority rules, and visual tools. If necessary, corrections were made. After this period, the new method of working ran without any problems.

The results of the new working method were amazing. The combination of cycles, priority rules, and visual tools led to a continuous logistical flow. Every shift delivered five to seven batches to the next station. In addition, the housekeeping problems were solved. The definition of the cycles meant that the work in progress was greatly reduced. This reduction made the regular cleaning of the unit possible. Finally, the atmosphere between the different shifts improved strongly. The main causes for frictions were taken away. The cycles resulted in a continuous flow. The annoying activities like cleaning of the plates were done as an integral part of the cycle.

There are some remarkable issues in this story. There were many problems with logistics, housekeeping, and relations between shifts in this unit. Initially, management only paid some attention to these problems. They told the employees how to handle the logistics, how to keep the unit clean, and how to cooperate between the shifts. However, no tools were developed to control the logistics. These actions did not result in any improvements. Later, a project was started to reduce the throughput time of the factory. It has to be noted that this project was not initiated to solve the specific problems in the sintering unit but to reduce the overall throughput time. The project resulted in a redesign of the logistical processes in the sintering unit. The redesign resulted in defined work cycles, priority rules and visual tools. This redesign appeared to be a condition for the employees to manage the logistical processes on the shop floor and to keep their workplace clean. At the same time, the redesign took away the points of friction between the shifts, resulting in improved social relations.

In conclusion, this story indicates that paradoxes on the shop floor are often difficult to identify. At first sight, the problems in this unit were caused by bad employee behaviour. However, a serious investigation showed that the problems in this unit originated from a bad design – or better: no design – of the processes on the shop floor. It illustrates that management has to create the conditions for responsible employee behaviour.

2.2 Packing faults

Some problems in a factory are easy to identify and the solution often speaks for itself. Nevertheless, such problems can be difficult to solve. The next story, which comes from the Glass Factory in Aachen, addresses this type of paradox.

> *Story.* In the glass factory, television screens were produced for the television industry. A part of the production of these screens had to be packed on pallets for transport to a customer in France. We regularly received complaints about the packing. The first layer of products was often damaged. The cause of this problem was easily found: nail heads rising above the wooden parts of the pallet caused the broken packing material. One out of ten pallets had to be repaired. It was decided that every pallet would be visually inspected just before use. The bad ones had to be repaired directly by the packing operator. Repair took only two to three minutes. The problems were discussed with the employees. They were told about the complaints, cause, and solution. Photographs of the damaged products were shown, new packing material and hammers were made available, and brief instruction was given. Management oversaw the implementation of the inspection and repair. Regularly, the shift leader, department manager and factory manager checked the quality of the pallets and explained to the employees why this was so important.
>
> At the same time, a packing document was made on which the operator had to stamp his number. This document had to be attached to the pallet. In this way, packing problems could be traced back to individual employees. The original plan was to implement the use of the stamp together with the check and the repair of the pallets. However, the delivery time of the stamps appeared to be much longer than expected. Therefore the decision was taken to begin with the inspection and repair of the pallets and implement the use of the stamp later.
>
> For the first few weeks there was no improvement at all. Pallets were still found with damaged products in the first layer. We decided to re-instruct the operators. Again, no clear improvement was observed. Some weeks later, the stamps came in – we implemented them directly. One week after implementation, we got a call from our customer. The problem was still present. The pallets contained damaged products. The operator numbers, which were stamped on the packing document, were given to us. The department manager had a talk with the packing operators concerned. They were told individually that the quality of their work was not acceptable and moreover, that a strong improvement was expected. This feedback appeared to be crucial in changing the behaviour of the employees. After three weeks the problem was solved. The customer no longer reported damaged products in the first layer.

This story shows some unusual items. Firstly, no improvement was observed after showing the employees the photographs and giving them the instructions. Clearly, the highlighted need of the customer did not lead to a change in the behaviour of the employees as the faulty pallets were still used. Secondly, management supervised the implementation of the visual inspection and repair. Management visited the shop floor and talked with the employees. Obviously, these visits led only to a temporal change in behaviour: the pallets were only repaired when management was present and when management disappeared, the bad pallets were not repaired. Thirdly, the implementation of the stamp as such did not result in a change in behaviour. A breakthrough only took place after individual feedback was given to the packing operators. All employees unambiguously interpreted these talks as 'Now it is serious'. I would like to make a personal remark. It was a shock for me that showing photographs, instructing employees, and management supervision were not enough to change employee behaviour. It is noteworthy that individual feedback, including the threat of disciplinary consequences, appeared to be necessary to force employees to serve the customer.

This story reveals a different kind of paradox. Namely, that it is difficult to implement a simple solution for a well known problem. This paradox raises a lot of questions. Why did employees not change their behaviour after receiving the instructions? Why were personal feedback and the threat of disciplinary consequences required to implement the solution? These questions can only be answered by investigating the context in which events occur and by providing a rich description of the social context of this paradox. An ethnographical approach seems to be inevitable to reveal the 'deep structure' (Dyer and Wilkins[18]) of this behaviour. Further, it has to be remarked that this story suggests that calling to account is a basic condition for bearing responsibility. This means that the relation between 'responsibility' and 'accountability' has to be investigated in more detail.

2.3 Quality of antimony balls

The development, identification, and dismantling of paradoxes are strongly influenced by the behaviour of employees and engineers. This influence is illustrated by a story from the image intensifier factory in Eindhoven.

> *Story.* A development engineer approached me. He was angry. He asked me to act immediately. What had happened? In the shop, antimony balls with a diameter of one to two millimetres were produced. These balls were leaded with metallic wires, which were about 20 millimetres long. The manufacturing of these products was rather simple. In the first stage of production, small holes in a metal jig were filled with antimony powder. By means of electrical current the powder in the jig was heated, began to melt, and small, round, shiny antimony balls appeared. In the second stage these balls were melted down again and bonded to a tungsten wire. In the first step of the process, Joyce and Ann, female employees in their mid forties, saw some deviations. The formation of the antimony balls was different. In addition,

---

[18]   Dyer and Wilkins (1991).

the shiny appearance of the balls was not the same. In their opinion, there was something wrong with the powder. Joyce and Ann discussed this phenomenon with a factory engineer. However, the factory engineer did not listen. He was irritated and refused to react. He said to them: "When I order you to make balls, then you have to make balls. No discussion." After having said this, he left the shop floor. The operators were shocked. Fifteen minutes later, a development engineer came on the shop floor. Joyce and Ann told him about the problem and about the reaction of the factory engineer. The development engineer told the operators to stop production. In his opinion, the deviating formation and appearance indeed indicated a powder problem. The powder was investigated thoroughly. A contamination was found and the powder was rejected for production.

This story gives more insight into the social context of paradoxes. Evidently, the factory engineer was of the opinion that the responsibility of employees was restricted to the execution of technical tasks. He did not expect them to use their knowledge and experience to manufacture good products. His message to the employees was clear: "I need your hands. I don't need your brains". On the contrary, the development engineer took the view that employees have a lot of expertise concerning the manufacturing process. He supported them in their responsibility: the production of good products. He listened to their comments. He took some time to look at the phenomena. At the end, the customer was saved a quality problem.

This story shows the importance of the behaviour of employees and engineers in the identification and dismantling of paradoxes. It suggests that a culture that respects the knowledge and experience of employees on the shop floor is a basic condition for responsible behaviour.

2.4 Lead-containing materials

The attitude and behaviour of managers is a decisive factor in the social context of the shop floor. In an improvement culture there are many possibilities to identify and to dismantle paradoxes. It is also possible to anticipate the views of employees: a story from the actuator factory in Roermond in the Netherlands illustrates this.

Story. In this factory, electronic components for the printer industry were produced. These components were made of lead-containing materials. The use of these materials was subjected to strict legal regulations due to health risks and environmental pollution. We largely fulfilled these regulations

In this factory, an improvement culture had been developed. That means a culture in which all employees – including the operators of the shop floor – were involved in a process of continuous improvement. Management had indicated explicitly in which area improvements had to be introduced: quality, costs, deliveries, safety and environment, morale, and housekeeping. Part of these improvements was realised by means of interdisciplinary improvement teams. These teams were allowed – within certain limits – to set their own priorities.

An improvement team decided to reduce the waste of lead-containing materials in their own unit. Their basic motivation was to contribute to a reduction of environmental pollution. Management respected this choice. After several weeks, the team came up with a proposal. To implement this proposal, financial and technical resources were required. It appeared that the payback time of this proposal was longer than one year. From an applied economics point of view, the investment should have therefore been rejected. Nevertheless, the required resources were made available. The team reduced the waste of lead-containing materials by more than fifty percent.

This story has several important characteristics. In this factory an improvement culture was present. Environmental problems were indicated as a possible area of improvement. Management supported the wishes of the employees to reduce the waste of materials and made resources available. Such a context offers employees good opportunities to bear responsibility with respect to the natural environment.

2.5 Closing the factory

Do employees feel that their activities lead to significant value for other people? Do employees experience meaning ('Sinn') in their work? How is this experience related to the whole context of the shop floor? The next story about the closure of the actuator factory in Roermond touches upon these questions.

> *Story*. In the dicing department of the actuator factory about 7 people worked per shift. Each shift had a first operator. In the starting-up period, the dicing process was quite problematic. The process had to be developed. The yields were low and the quality not very stable. The dicing stage of the process had caused production to stop two or three times. It took about two to three years to control the dicing process. Several breakthroughs were realised by an intensive co-operation between operators, first operators, factory engineers, development engineers, and management.
>
> One of the first operators was named Peter – a very committed employee. He had joined several improvement teams. He had assisted in the layout of the unit, had contributed to the control of the process, and had improved the housekeeping. He knew why quality was important. He had also met several representatives of the customer. On the one hand, Peter had been weighed down by quality problems; and on the other hand, he had enjoyed the breakthroughs. Consequently, the dicing unit was his unit.
>
> One incident was characteristic of Peter's attitude. In summer holidays, students were hired to continue production. Preferably, these positions were offered to children of our own employees. Peter's daughter also came to our factory to work. She was a friendly girl. I met her several times on the shop floor. Once, I had a longer discussion with her. I said to her: "Please, let me guess. Before you had your first day in the factory, your father gave you instructions. He told you how to behave and how to handle the products. He told you about the critical aspects of our produc-

tion." My guess appeared to be right. Peter had instructed his daughter in detail. He had told her to do a very good job. She did …

At that time, Peter had been at the company for twenty-five years. This called for a celebration and during the celebration, he told me about his background. He was raised in a small family. He had one brother, a sea captain. For many years, he had been jealous of his career. However, not anymore. He was proud to be a first operator. He was proud to assist the development of the dicing process. He was proud to organise his own shift well.

Then, five years after the opening of the factory, I had to tell the crew that the factory had to be closed. Market developments and lack of investment money had brought higher management to this decision. Several days later, in an evening shift, I had a long talk with Peter. He was very down. He told me about the improvements to which he had contributed: solving quality problems, controlling the process, and organising the unit. The factory was his factory. Now, his factory had to be closed. Tears came into his eyes. The job in our factory did mean a lot to him. It was more than earning money. It was something like his life's work.

Peter was one of the (many) employees who had contributed strongly to the start-up of the factory. He felt ownership of the processes on the shop floor. He felt responsible for it. He experienced meaning in his daily work. This story indicates that the three levels of analysis – phenomena on the shop floor (discussions, closure of a factory), organisation design theory (socio-technical design, improvement culture) and the philosophy of organisation (experiencing meaning) – have to be discussed integratively.

2.6 Evaluation

The stories above deal with paradoxes, short cuts by managers, and (ir-)responsible behaviour of employees on the shop floor. Every story shows that technology, organisation, the manufacturing activities of employees, process development by engineers, and conditions created by management are strongly interlaced. Thus important questions arise. What types of different paradoxes are present? How do these paradoxes develop? How can these paradoxes be identified? How do the (ir-)responsible behaviour of employees relate to conditions created by management? How is behaviour linked to the whole organisational system?

Managers habitually pass the buck for production problems to others. All too often they blame employees for the bad performance of the organisation. The stories told in this section show that the organisational reality of the shop floor is much more complex. These stories also show that it is much too simplistic to see this issue either as a problem of rotten apples (bad employees) or as a problem of rotten barrels (bad organisation). The stories in this section show that the fundamental meaning of the notions of 'responsibility' and 'accountability' is quite problematic. An analysis on the level of the phenomena of paradoxes on the shop floor, organisation theory, and the philosophy of organisation is required to understand the meaning of these notions.

The notions of 'responsibility' and 'accountability' belong to normal management language. They appear in job descriptions and organisational procedures. They are used in official meetings and informal discussions. They are applied to employees who are working on the shop floor. It is taken for granted that if a word is used that the meaning of this word is known. It is also taken for granted that if different people use the same word that the meaning is the same. However, that is not always the case. The stories told above show that the meaning of the notions 'responsibility' and 'accountability' is unclear, untransparent and ambiguous.[19]

The frequent use of the notions 'responsibility' and 'accountability' suggests that everybody in the organisation behaves according to the intended meaning of these words. It is assumed that the employees follow job descriptions and quality procedures. It is also assumed that supervisors lead their people accordingly. Everyday practice shows that these suggestions are false. The alignment between expected and actual behaviour is sometimes far from close. It appears that day-to-day behaviour in organisations is driven by informal rules. Scott Morgan calls these rules 'unwritten rules'.[20] It appears that bad behaviour and power structures undermine the effectiveness and efficiency of an organisation.

The notions of 'responsibility' and 'accountability' refer to individuals. He or she is responsible. He or she is accountable. However, in the reference to individuals, the context of individual behaviour is ignored and conditions that are required to bear responsibility and to render accountability are out of the picture. Ignorance of the context is worrisome. Neglecting the conditions for responsibility and accountability is unacceptable. The reason is that the primary cause of most of the problems on the shop floor lies in the context or in conditions not being met. Rightly, Victor Fitzsimmons, Vice President of a manufacturing company, characterised the shop floor as the place where all the 'sins of the whole organisation' are collected.[21]

In addition, it has to be noted that the notions of 'responsibility' and 'accountability' reveal a certain bias or preference. These notions are often used to characterise the job of a manager. The expression 's/he has a responsible job' is mostly applied to managerial functions and not to executory functions. This usage suggests that managers bear real responsibility and employees on the shop floor do not. In other words, managers are responsible actors and employees are passive instruments.

In many factories, technical and organisational systems are not only designed to control production but also to control the behaviour of individual employees. Inherently, these systems themselves tell their own message: namely, that employees cannot be trusted and have to be controlled by technical means and organisational systems. Generally, this message is well understood by employees on the shop floor. In turn, they re-interpret this message by believing that management cannot be trusted. As a result, they resist management initiatives in order to guar-

---

[19] See also Dalton (1959) and Watson (1994).
[20] Scott-Morgan (1994).
[21] Suzaki (1993, p 428).

antee their own interests. In other words, the design of a production line and the development of the organisation tell their own story and initiate their own dynamics.

Finally, the notions of 'responsibility' and 'accountability' transcend the activities of employees on the shop floor. They are connected to questions about the meaning of work and the meaning of life as illustrated by the story 'Closing the factory' (section 2.5.). In industrial practice, these type of questions are seldom discussed as they do not match with the technological and economic perspective of an industrial organisation and because there is a certain embarrassment with respect to this subject.

Paradoxes and managerial short cuts make up the world of employees on the shop floor. It is clear that the notions of 'responsibility' and 'accountability' are quite problematic. It appears that the meaning of these notions strongly depends on the whole technical and organisational context. Managers believe that they can control the behaviour of employees without being aware of the dynamics they initiate with their own behaviour. Managers believe that they can exert power by procedures and systems without being aware of the counter-powers that are set free.[22] All these observations make it plausible that an investigation of paradoxes and short cuts on the shop floor requires an analysis on three levels: description of phenomena on the shop floor, analysis of the basics of organisation design theories, and philosophical study of the relation between man, labour and organisation.

---

[22] Milgram's bewildering experiments show the influence of hierarchical power on the behaviour of individuals (Milgram, 1992).

3 A 'new world of work'

In the beginning of this chapter, the presence of paradoxes on the shop floor has been sketched in the context of new production concepts in modern factories. It has been argued that a study on the mechanisms and dynamics of paradoxes requires an analysis on different levels. In the previous section, telling and examining stories from the shop floor illustrated concrete phenomena i.e. the first level of analysis. In this section the second level will be outlined, namely organisation design theory.

To understand the development of organisational design in modern companies a brief history of manufacturing will be presented. It will be argued that societal developments urge modern companies to abandon classical methods and to introduce new production concepts. These new concepts promise a 'new world of work' that combines technical superiority with social innovation. In practice, every manager struggles with the implementation of these new concepts. Paradoxes and managerial short cuts prevent the development of a world class organisation.

3.1 Introduction

The current business environment is very dynamic.[23] The needs of customers change continuously. Competition always increases. New technologies have to be implemented. Employees expect challenging careers and professional education. Society presses for stringent measures with respect to the safety of products and the pollution of the natural environment. Stockholders require a high return on investment. The changing environment makes heavy demands on modern organisations, from chief executive officer at the top to the workers on the shop floor. Traditional organisational concepts that are based on the methods and techniques of the American engineer Frederick Taylor are not workable anymore. A number of new production concepts have been developed to meet the requirements of present-day society. These concepts are adorned with flowery words like 'manufacturing excellence' or 'world class manufacturing'.

3.2 The rise of Taylorism

The American engineer Frederick Taylor laid the foundation of western industry. In the beginning of the twentieth century, he introduced scientific methods in the factory in order to improve the efficiency of production processes. The organisation of labour became a field of activity of engineers. The objective was to control labour by means of scientific methods, technological means and management tech-

---

[23] See for example Porter (1980, 1985), Peters (1987), Bolwijn and Kumpe (1991) and d'Aveni (1994, 1995).

niques.[24] Throughout his life, Frederick Taylor has been at the centre of bitter controversies.[25] On the one hand, industries and universities warmly welcomed his ideas. On the other hand, unions and politicians strongly opposed his ideas.[26] Despite the opposition, Taylor's ideas spread quickly.[27] In 1919 a French poet described the progress in post-war Europe as a march 'from Taylorisation to Taylorisation'.[28]

In the same period, Henry Ford started the mass production of automobiles. The most characteristic element of his production technology was the moving assembly line. Extreme division of labour and sophisticated design of the parts made the assembly line possible.[29] Furthermore, Ford introduced various methods to increase discipline. A social department was established to support the private life of the workmen. Although Ford has strongly influenced the development of western industry, the influence of Taylor has been estimated as greater than that of Ford.[30]

Tayloristic principles formed the basis of American industry.[31] Large scale and highly efficient factories were developed. Manufacturers like Ford, Singer, Du Pont, and AT&T became masters in mass production. The United States became the leading nation in the industrial world.[32] World War II pushed American industry to its limits. Many products, which were previously produced in small volumes, had to be produced in large quantities, e.g. guns, jeeps, tanks and aeroplanes. The tools of scientific management were refined and renewed to realise a quick spurt in production. After World War II, the United States made the financial resources and know-how available for a quick recovery of western industry.[33] European and Japanese organisations were modelled according to the American example. Van Breukelen et al. conclude[34]:

"By copying the U.S. firms which until then had been so successful, the up-and-coming European and Japanese firms were largely modelled on Tayloristic principles, making Taylorism the dominant form of industrial organisations in the world."

The principles of Taylor have been criticised from the beginning. As early as 1911, a special committee of the American congress concluded that the "Taylor system

---

[24] In section 2 of Chapter 2 the ideas of Taylor will be elaborated in more detail.
[25] Guillén (1994) and Kanigel (1997).
[26] The opposition against the Taylor system has to interpreted against the background of changes in the American society (Jacques, 1996).
[27] Guillén (1994) and Kanigel (1997, p485 ff.).
[28] Kanigel (1997, p486).
[29] Womack et al. (1991, p26 ff.).
[30] Kanigel (1997, p495).
[31] The ideology of Scientific Management was not widely accepted. By contrast, its techniques were generally accepted (Guillén, 1994, p267).
[32] Hayes et al. (1988).
[33] Hayes et al. (1988, p 51).
[34] Van Breukelen et al. (1998, p22).

appears to be of such a character and nature as to be detrimental to the best interests of American working men".[35] Throughout the years, it became clear that this committee was right. Mass production resulted in absenteeism, high sickness, a lack of motivation, apathy, and low morale. In other words, mass production resulted in dehumanisation and alienation.[36]

3.3 Working man as social being

It was increasingly understood that the scientific management of industrial organisations had proceeded at the expense of the well-being of the employee. During and after World War I, research projects were started in England and the United States to investigate the psychological and social aspects of this.

Elton Mayo and his co-workers investigated the influence of working conditions on productivity in the Hawthorne factory of General Electrics in Chicago.[37] It was believed that – in accordance with the principles of scientific management – an improvement in the physical conditions would lead to an improvement in productivity. However, these investigations led to contradictory results, which could only be explained by assuming a strong influence of social processes on productivity. Consequently, the attention was shifted from technical to social aspects of manufacturing organisations. The impact of the Hawthorne investigations was tremendous. The foundations of industrial sociology were laid. Eyes were opened for the working man as a social being. A new movement in organisational science was born: the Human Relations movement.[38] Personnel departments were called into being, conditions of employment were described, training and education were stimulated, and worker participation was advocated. Despite all these adaptations however, the Tayloristic basis of manufacturing organisations was kept intact.

The ideas of the Human Relations movement stimulated a lot of research in the field of work satisfaction and work motivation. The attention shifted from the character of social relations to the idea of self-actualisation of individual employees. The essence of management was defined as creating the possibilities for personal growth. This shift took place under the influence of the work of Maslow, McGregor, Herzberg and others.[39] However, this approach also did not take formal leave of the principles of Frederick Taylor.

A real breakthrough in organisational thinking took place after World War II. Eric Trist and Ken Bamforth of the Tavistock Institute of Human Relations in London investigated the psychological, social, and economic consequences of

---

[35]   Kanigel (1997, p448).
[36]   See for example Walker and Quest (1952) and Karasek and Theorell (1979).
[37]   Roethlisberger and Dickson (1967) describe the original account of these experiments. The best available history is Gillespie (1991).
[38]   Van Assen and Den Hertog in Galan et al. (1983, p51 ff.), Gillespie (1991), Guillén (1994), and Mok (1994, p93 ff.).
[39]   Maslow (1954), McGregor (1985), and Herzberg et al. (1959). See also De Galan et al. (1983), Handy (1985), Guillén (1994), Mok (1994), and Pugh and Hickson (1996).

different production technologies and organisations of work in coal mining.[40] They concluded that the production process has to be characterised as a socio-technical system. Consequently, the choice of the production technology has a strong influence on the social characteristics of a manufacturing organisation. In other words, the detrimental effects of Tayloristic organisations only can be prevented by rejecting the Tayloristic principles for designing manufacturing organisations and by applying fundamentally different design principles. These principles are characterised by the idea of a 'whole task' and the idea of 'authority to coordinate one's own labour'. This new approach was named Socio-Technical Systems Design. The pioneering work of Trist, Emery and Bamforth led to a number of new initiatives. In Scandinavia, Australia, The Netherlands, and the United States comparable approaches were developed.[41] However, the diffusion of these ideas happened slowly.[42]

3.4 Technical superiority and social innovation

In about 1960 the business environment changed significantly. The implementation of new technologies, the breaking down of trade barriers, increased competition from Japanese companies, and increasing requirements of customers challenged western industry. It appeared that the Tayloristic factories could not meet the expectations of this new environment. Western industry was in a crisis. Western industry was designed for efficiency. However, the market required quality and flexibility.[43]

Originally, western industry answered these new challenges with technological innovations.[44] Computer Aided Design was seen as a powerful tool to reduce the lead-time to develop new products. Computer Integrated Manufacturing was expected to increase the control of the production process. The un-manned factory was presented as a realistic vision. Huge amounts of money were invested in these technological innovations. However, the gap between western and Japanese companies did not decrease. Gradually, it became clear that a purely technological approach was not the right answer to cope with the changing environment. In an article in the *Harvard Business Review* Skinner criticised the technological dream of Computer Integrated Manufacturing. He concluded[45]:

> "Before we should dream of instituting Computer Integrated Manufacturing – and we should – we must consider how the world of business is moving (...) What is most lacking is not technique but practitioners who develop innovative ideas under com-

---

[40] Trist and Bamforth (1951).
[41] Van Eijnatten (1993).
[42] Pruijt (1996).
[43] Bolwijn and Kumpe (1986, 1991). See also Van Breukelen et al. (1998, p24 ff.)
[44] Van Breukelen et al. (1998, p27 ff.).
[45] Skinner (1988, p16).

petitive duress. Just-in-Time or Total Quality Control won't make a business competitive, MEN and WOMEN will."

In other words, the secret of a world-class factory is not found in its technological superiority but in the know-how and attitude of its employees. At the same time, he concluded that the future of the un-manned factory was still quite a way off.

Towards 1970 it became clear that the efficiency, quality, and flexibility of the Japanese factories appeared to be much higher than that of America and Europe. The consequences were considerable. Some industries in the United States and in Europe were completely wiped out, e.g. the camera industry and the consumer electronics industry. Other industries lost a large amount of their market share, e.g. the motorcycle and the car industry. For example, in 1960, about 50 percent of all cars were produced in the United States, about forty percent in Europe and about three percent in Japan. In 1985, these three regions each accounted for about thirty percent of car production![46]

A lot of studies were done to understand the secret of the Japanese approach. Western studies have identified production technology[47], managerial superiority[48], social organisation[49], and shared values[50] as differentiating factors. Japanese authors emphasise the importance of improvement techniques.[51] Japanese production techniques have drawn their insight both from Scientific Management and Human Relations. The ideas of work division, short cycle times, and time-and-motion study were taken from the former, and the ideas of participation, cooperation, and teamwork from the latter. An unambiguous judgement about Japanese production techniques is lacking, however. Some authors believe that lean production is the future for western industry.[52] Others conclude that lean production is an extension of Taylorism.[53] In western countries Japanese techniques are known as Lean Management or Lean Production.[54]

In the same period socio-technical approaches were presented as an alternative to Taylorism. Socio-Technical Systems Design proposes fundamentally different design principles for manufacturing organisations (see also section 3.3).[55] In addition, participative change strategies have been elaborated in detail.[56] The Mini-Company concept combines socio-technical ideas with continuous improvement.[57]

---

[46]   Womack et al. (1991).
[47]   Pascale and Athos (1981), Schonberger (1982, 1986, 1996), and Womack et al. (1991).
[48]   Pascale and Athos (1981), Hayes et al. (1988), and Womack et al. (1991).
[49]   Hayes et al. (1988), Womack et al. (1991), and Besser (1996).
[50]   Pascale and Athos (1981) and Besser (1996).
[51]   Sasaki and Hutchins (1984), Imai (1986), Ohno (1988), and Monden (1998).
[52]   E.g. Womack et al. (1991).
[53]   E.g. Conti and Warren (1993).
[54]   Womack et al. (1991) and Womack and Jones (1997).
[55]   De Sitter (1981), De Sitter et al. (1986), Van Eijnatten (1993), Taylor and Felten (1993), De Sittter (1994), De Sitter et al. (1997), and Purser and Cabana (1998).
[56]   Gustavsen (1992) and Emery (ed.) (1993).
[57]   Suzaki (1993).

The discussion about 'world class manufacturing' intensified in the period between 1980 and 1990. Special attention was paid to the strategic role of manufacturing, the development of human capabilities, and social innovation. Wheelwright and Hayes have made an important contribution to this debate. In the *Harvard Business Review* they wrote an article entitled 'Competing through manufacturing'.[58] In this article they analysed the changing position of the manufacturing function in the present business environment. To understand the changing position they distinguish four stages in the strategic role of manufacturing:

> The first stage is called 'internally neutral'. In this stage the manufacturing function is considered to be 'neutral' with respect to the competitive success of the company. Attention is focused on minimising the negative impact of manufacturing on the business. Stage 1 companies consider manufacturing as a simple and straightforward process that can be done without a lot of management care.
>
> The second stage is called 'externally neutral'. In this stage the manufacturing function is also considered to be 'neutral' with respect to the competitive success of the company. In this stage an external yardstick is used: the organisation has to follow 'industrial practice'. Stage 2 companies are characterised by a defensive approach. They invest in manufacturing in order to prevent falling behind the competition.
>
> The third stage is called 'internally supportive'. In this stage the manufacturing function is expected to support and to strengthen the competitive position of the company. The manufacturing strategy is derived from the overall business strategy. Long-term developments and trends in manufacturing are addressed carefully. Investments in manufacturing are screened for consistency with the overall strategy.
>
> The fourth stage is called 'externally supportive'. In this stage the manufacturing function contributes significantly to the competitive position of the company. The manufacturing strategy is an integral part of the business strategy. Business decisions are made based on marketing, development and manufacturing considerations. Long-term manufacturing programs are developed to secure the strategic objectives of the company. Efforts to anticipate the potential of new manufacturing technologies are made. In other words, stage 4 organisations see manufacturing as a strategic resource.

Wheelwright and Hayes stress that the shift to the fourth stage – an externally supportive factory or world-class factory – is a radical one.[59] It requires a different type of organisation, a different style of management, and a different calibre of employees. Key words are teamwork, creative experimentation and organisational learning. Three years later, this view was elaborated on in the book entitled *Dynamic Manufacturing. Creating the Learning organisation* by Hayes, Wheelwright and Clark.[60] In their opinion, the new factory is characterised by four unifying principles: (1) management makes the difference, (2) the importance of adopting a holistic perspective, (3) the whole organisation must relentlessly pursue customer value and competitive advantage, and (4) the centrality of continual

---

[58] Wheelwright and Hayes (1985).
[59] Wheelwright and Hayes (1985, p105).
[60] Hayes et al. (1988).

learning and improving. [61] It goes without saying that the view of Hayes, Wheelwright and Clark do imply a break with the principles of Taylorism.

Other authors advocate comparable views. For example, Quinn emphasises in his book *Intelligent Enterprise* that every company has to be 'best in class' in specific competencies, services and know-how. [62] He shows that this approach requires an 'ad hoc', 'fluid', 'cross-disciplinary' and 'co-operative' organisation. Hayes and Pisano write provokingly that a 'beyond world-class' strategy is required to cope with the business environment. [63] In their opinion, the approach of American industry to world-class manufacturing was too technical and too little attention was given to the development of human capabilities. In other words, the human side of the organisation has been ignored. Forward and others introduced the idea of *mentofacturing*. [64] In their view, manufacturing has to be replaced by mentofacturing. Manufacturing means 'made by hand', and mentofacturing 'made by mind'. The change from manufacturing to mentofacturing has to be based on the development of employees and the learning of the organisation. In accordance with this, Leonard-Barton characterises the factory as a 'learning laboratory'. [65] Warnecke introduced the idea of the *fractal* company. [66] He emphasises the self-organising capability of a learning organisation. Goldman, Nagel, and Kidd introduced the idea of *agile* manufacturing. [67] This idea implies an integral design of people, organisation, and technology. Pfeffer stressed the human side of the company. [68] His ideas are clearly expressed by the title of his book: *Competitive advantage through people*.

In the early nineties Hammer and Champy proposed fundamentally redesigning western industries by the use of advanced information technologies. [69] In their view companies must not be built around simple tasks but around business processes. Reenginering the basic processes of an organisation should lead to a 'new world of work'.

3.5 Conclusion

In the first section of this chapter it has been noted that phenomena like paradoxes and short cuts appear in organisations that have adopted new production concepts. This chapter has explored the background of these concepts.

---

[61]   Hayes et al. (1988, p340 ff.).
[62]   Quinn (1992).
[63]   Hayes and Pisano (1994).
[64]   Forward et al. (1991).
[65]   Leonard-Barton (1992).
[66]   Warnecke (1993).
[67]   Goldman and Nagel (1993) and Kidd (1994).
[68]   Pfeffer (1994).
[69]   Hammer (1990), Hammer and Champy (1994), Champy (1995), Hammer and Stanton (1995), and Hammer (1996).

Societal developments urge international companies to introduce new production concepts. These new concepts are often indicated by the term 'world-class manufacturing'. It has been shown that world-class manufacturing involves not only a set of sophisticated manufacturing technologies but also an inspiring working environment in which human capabilities are developed continuously. That means world-class manufacturing implies social innovation.[70]

World-class manufacturing is a container idea that includes a number of different tools, techniques, theories and views. From a distance, a monolith of methods and ideas can be observed. However, a closer look reveals fundamental differences in approach.

In manufacturing practice four different production concepts have been espoused as a reliable guide to world-class level. These concepts are Socio Technical Systems Design, Lean Management, Business Process Reengineering, and the Mini-Company Concept. All these approaches promise a 'new world of work'. All these approaches claim technical superiority and social innovation. In the next chapter these claims will be studied. Particular attention will be given to the design of the workplace, structural characteristics of responsibility and accountability, and processes of interaction between employees and management.

<hr />

[70] Looise (1996).

4 Responsibility in a technological age

In section 1 it has been argued that a study of paradoxes and managerial short cuts requires an analysis on different levels. In section 2, the first level – concrete phenomena – has been illustrated by telling and analysing stories from the shop floor. In section 3, the second level – organisation design theory – has been outlined by sketching the industrial and societal background of new production concepts. In addition, the promise of a 'new world of work' that combines technical superiority with social innovation was discussed. In this section, the third level – the philosophy of organisation – is addressed.

Philosophical considerations urge us to take a step down from organisation design theory in order to reflect on the position of human beings in industrial organisations. Philosophical reflections force us to view the relation between man, technology, and organisation from different angles. It offers an intellectual context to discuss fundamental dimensions of alienation and meaning ('Sinn'). It motivates us to re-consider the concept of employee responsibility and accountability in manufacturing organisations. It gives elbow room to discuss the development of individual employees in a standardised context.

All new production concepts claim to present an integral or holistic alternative to Taylorism. All new concepts claim technical superiority and social innovation. However, there are fundamental differences between these concepts. Therefore, a philosophical analysis is required to understand the strengths and limitations of each of these new production concepts. The question that forces itself upon us is which organisational concept does justice to the humanity of the human worker.

4.1 Moral and religious considerations

In a technological age, moral and religious considerations belong not only to the speciality of theologians and philosophers but are inherent to the field of organisational science. These types of considerations can help us to dig one level deeper in industrial organisations to understand phenomena on the shop floor.

In western industry, the dominant view is that management is first and foremost a rational activity. Technological models, mathematical calculations, and economic considerations play the first fiddle. In addition, moral and religious dimensions are pushed into the background. This view on management is an expression of the enlightened idea on man and reality. I reject this view from the bottom of my heart. Let me start with a personal statement. I have been raised in the Calvinistic tradition. This tradition has shaped my views on man, morality and meaning ('Sinn'). A key notion is the idea of stewardship. Man is seen as a responsible being. He has to develop the earth in honour of God. My parents have set the example. My father taught me about the ethic of work and my mother about respect for people. This background has influenced my thinking and my actions.

In management circles, moral and religious arguments do not seem to play a (large) role. The impression given is that reality consists of markets and customers, budgets and profits, technology and innovation. The suggestion is that technological and economic discourse is morally neutral. Is this impression true? Is this suggestion right? These questions in particular have been discussed extensively in theology and philosophy.[71] However, to prevent the idea settling that theologians and philosophers have crossed the boundaries of their discipline and introduced questions that are alien to organisational science, I would like to show 'from within' that moral and religious considerations belong inherently to the field of management and organisation. I would like to pay attention to the work of Nijhof, Guillén, and Watson who have shown that decision processes, the adoption of organisational theories, and management activities, are strongly influenced by moral and religious considerations.

André Nijhof has studied decision processes in organisations.[72] He shows that change processes often lead to paradoxical situations. On the one hand, managers have to strive for the objectives of the organisation. On the other hand, they have to care for the employees that are affected by the organisational change. Nijhof has investigated how managers deal with conflicting interests. He has shown that managers use different strategies to cope with their moral responsibilities, e.g. ethical displacement, cooperation with other parties and deliberation with employees. He concludes that managers take their moral responsibilities seriously[73] [74]:

> "We noticed in the case studies that moral responsibilities do play an important role in conducting organisational change."

Mauro Guillén has done a comparative study on the adoption of three major models of organisational management: Scientific Management, the Human Relations movement, and structural analysis.[75] The main thesis of his study is that adoption of these models does not necessarily follow from their scientific credibility. Also, it is not solely determined by economic and technological factors. He found that institutional factors play an important role, e.g. the mentality of the business elite, influence of professional groups, support of the state, and response of the workers. Amongst others, Guillén concludes that religion affects the adoption of an organisational paradigm[76]:

---

[71] See for example Van Riessen (1949), Van Riessen (1953), Dooyeweerd (1963), Dooyeweerd (1969), Goudzwaard (1979), Schuurman (1980), Wolters (1984), Woltersdorff (1984), and Hinkelammert (1986).

[72] Nijhof (1999).

[73] Nijhof (1999, p220).

[74] Nijhof (1999, p220) also found that in the process of justifying decisions, there is 'only limited reference to moral responsibilities'. See also Bird and Waters (1989).

[75] Guillén (1994).

[76] Guillén (1994, p296, 297).

"Religious differences have been used (...) to understand the adoption of Scientific Management and Human Relations as paradigms of organisation by the management intellectuals (...) This book, however, has presented systematic evidence that Catholicism and Protestantism have different effects on the kind of organisational paradigm that is adopted. Catholicism has generally emphasised the community, self-actualisation, paternalism, and organicism, while Protestantism has emphasised individualism, instrumentalism, independence, and contractualism. In Germany, Protestant management intellectuals generally supported the Scientific Management paradigm, while Catholic ones took side with the Human Relations school. In Spain, the dominant Catholic background played a key role in the reception, adoption, and adaptation to local conditions of American ideas about Human Relations at work. In Britain, Christian humanistic ideals similar to those proposed by the Roman Catholic Church prompted management intellectuals to accept Human Relations."

Tony Watson has done an extensive case study on management.[77] He worked for more than one year alongside managers of an electronics company in Britain. He has reported his findings in his book *In Search of Management. Culture, Chaos & Control in Managerial Work*. Watson closes with the following conclusion[78]:

"The image which has taken shape is one of management as essentially and inherently a social and moral activity; one whose greatest successes in efficiently and effectively producing goods and services is likely to come through building organisational patterns, cultures and understandings based on relationships of mutual trust and shared obligation among people involved with the organisation. Management is essentially a human social craft. It requires the ability to interpret the thoughts and the wants of others − be these employees, customers, competitors or whatever − and the facility to shape meanings, values and human commitments."

Watson's final conclusion includes several notable points. Firstly, he does not characterise management primarily as a rational or economic activity. In his view, management is *essentially* a social and moral activity. Secondly, he does not consider social and moral aspects as 'additional'. In his view, management is *inherently* a social and moral activity.

In conclusion, Nijhof, Guillén and Watson have shown that moral and religious arguments do play an important role in managerial activities. Therefore, the influence of the basic beliefs of managers cannot be ignored in the adoption of a new production concept and the dynamics of the interaction between managers and employees.

---

[77] Watson (1994).
[78] Watson (1994, p223).

4.2 The theory of responsibility

Developments in western society ask for a fundamental reflection on the responsibility of man. Western society has a high standard of living, well-developed health care, and an extensive educational system. However, western society is also threatened by pollution of the environment, shortage of materials, social dichotomies, crisis of meaning ('Sinn'), and so on. Against this background, the questions about responsibility of man do take on an existential slant.

What about the responsibility of man? What about *my* responsibility? These questions have been asked penetratingly by the philosopher Hans Jonas in his book *The Imperative of Responsibility. An Ethics for the Technological Age.*[79] Jonas indicates that mankind has come into a new situation. The development of modern science and technology has increased the power of man considerably. Man uses this power to fulfil the needs of modern society. Consequently, natural resources are consumed at a high speed, the burdening of nature with the waste materials of human consumption is enormous, and finally, the human body is manipulated to improve quality of life. This development raises a lot of questions.[80]

In former times, man could foresee the consequences of his actions. The goal of an intervention was proximate. The range of the action was small. The time span involved was limited. The effects and the side-effects were surveyable. The use of the non-human world was considered more or less as ethically neutral. Ethics focused on the dealing of man with man, including the dealing with himself or herself. At that time, ethics was *anthropocentric*.

All this has changed. Modern technology has given mankind enormous powers. The goal of human interventions is far-reaching. The range of action is large. The time span involved is unlimited. The effects and the side-effects are not surveyable. The actions of man do lead to irreversible changes in the biosphere.

---

[79] Jonas (1984).

[80] Hans Jonas discusses human responsibility against the background of developments of western society. Therefore, I will elaborate his thoughts in more detail. In literature other attempts are made to investigate the notion 'human responsibility'. For example, Van Weers (1977) has given an extensive philosophical account. He emphasises the 'evocative' aspect: man has to be enabled to render accountability. This enabling process includes both the execution of tasks of sufficient importance and the development of the qualities of man. Bovens (1990) distinguishes in his book *Verantwoorde-lijkheid en organisatie* (Responsibility and Organisation) five different meanings of the word 'responsibility': responsibility as cause, responsibility as liability, responsibility as ability, responsibility as role, and responsibility as virtue. To understand responsibility in complex organisations, Bovens focuses his investigations on 'responsibility as liability' and 'responsibility as virtue'. He refers to these forms as 'passive responsibility' and 'active responsibility'. Bovens emphasises that it is not allowed to oppose passive and active responsibility sharply with each other. In his opinion these basic forms are related with 'responsibility as role' as the connecting piece. Van Zuthem (1993) notices that in modern organisations the responsibility of employees is often reduced to functional aspects. He speaks about 'damaged' responsibilities. He stresses that the responsibility of employees has to be integral (covering all aspects) and substantial (normative character).

Even irreversible changes take place in the human body. The danger is that human existence is at stake. In view of these developments, Jonas states that we have to rethink the basic principles of ethics. New dimensions of responsibility have to arise. He states that our supreme duty is to preserve 'human transcendence'.[81] The basic principle of ethics has to be that the existence of man must never be put 'at stake'.[82] We have to say an 'ontological yes' to man.[83]

Jonas has developed a theory of responsibility. In his view, ethical theory has to deal with two aspects.[84] The first aspect covers the normative principles for human behaviour. The second aspect covers the attitude of the individual to behave according to these normative principles. Jonas characterises the first aspect as the 'objective side' of ethics because it focuses on the rational validation of the moral claim. He characterises the second aspect as the 'subjective side' of ethics because it handles the emotional attachment to the moral claim. Jonas emphasises that these two aspects are 'mutually complementary'. For example, the most cogent demonstration of the right of normative principles would be powerless if humans are not motivated to respond to these principles. The objective and subjective side are also 'integral to ethics itself'. In other words, ethics has to address both sides.

Hereafter, Jonas mentions three conditions that are necessary to bear responsibility.[85] The first condition is the presence of 'causal power'. That means it must be possible for an action to have an impact on the world. The second condition is that the actor has the authority to execute this action. The third condition is that the actor can foresee the consequences of his or her actions to some extent. Unfortunately, Jonas does not elaborate on these conditions systematically.

4.3 The context of responsibility

Jonas has given us a cultural-philosophical framework to discuss ethical questions. It is questionable whether this framework can be used within this study. At the very least, a detailed analysis of the ontology of Jonas is required. It would be going too far to perform such an analysis in this study.

Jonas' view about responsibility has some interesting consequences for the agenda of managers and management intellectuals. It means an extension of the agenda of organisation theory with normative principles, motivation to behave according to these principles and conditions for responsibility. Jonas' view about responsibility defines a context of responsibility for employees on the shop floor. It also offers a 'tool' to ask critical questions about new production concepts. Especially the following questions have to be addressed:

---

[81]   Jonas (1984, p33).
[82]   Jonas (1984, p37).
[83]   Jonas (1984, p82).
[84]   Jonas (1984, p85).
[85]   Jonas (1984, p90).

1. Which normative principles play a role on the shop floor?
2. Which organisational conditions have to be fulfilled so that employees on the shop floor are motivated to behave according to these principles?
3. Which organisational conditions have to be fulfilled so that employees on the shop floor can actively bear responsibility and can render accountability for their day-to-day activities?

The first question has to do with a structural analysis of the workplace. This analysis will be done in the last chapter of this study. Here, I would like to point to the multidimensionality of the organisation of a factory. For example, on the shop floor, technological, social, economic, juridical, and moral dimensions play a role.[86] Each dimension has its own characteristics and own normative principles. Techni cal norms are related to the operation of equipment, execution of measurements, and adjustment of processes; social norms have to do with co-operation between employees, relationships with management, and celebration of anniversaries; economic norms focus on the reduction of waste, decrease in costs, and increase in efficiency; juridical norms refer to the contractual relations between employer and employee, safety requirements of equipment, and environmental standards; and moral principles are related to behaviour on the shop floor, quality of working life, and management of environmental problems. All these different norms play a role on the shop floor.

The second question has to do with attitude and motivation. The attitude and motivation of employees are determined by internal and external factors. Internal factors are personality, education, abilities, past experiences, and basic beliefs. External factors are labour conditions, payment, training, design of the workplace, style of management, and organisational culture. Management can influence the external factors. Therefore, attention has to be focused on organisational conditions. Generally, attitude and motivation are positively influenced by a participative style of management.

The third question has to do with the organisational conditions relating to bearing responsibility and to rendering accountability on the shop floor. The conditions mentioned by Jonas have to be specified.[87] The first condition has to do with causal power. Does execution of the production equipment result in suitable products? Does application of an out-of-control instruction result in an improvement of the process? The second condition has to do with control and authority. Do employees receive all information that is required to operate the production line? Do they have the authority to stop the production process in the case of quality problems? Do they participate in discussions about the social responsibility of the company? The third condition has to do with foreseeing the consequences of an action. Are the employees well trained in the technical aspects of the manufacturing process? Are they familiar with the different safety aspects of the production line? Are they aware of environmental consequences in case of emergencies? These conditions have to be fulfilled by the factory manager. After all, s/he is responsible

---

[86] Dooyeweerd (1969) distinguishes fifteen different dimensions.
[87] Jonas (1984, p90).

for the strategy, technical design, organisational structure, and personnel policy of the factory.

To understand the context of responsibility, attention has to be given to the asymmetrical relationship between a manager and an employee. This asymmetry clearly comes to the fore in sentences like 'The manager gives responsibility to an employee' and 'A manager calls an employee to account'. It has to be emphasised that the organisational context of 'giving responsibility to an employee' and 'calling an employee to account' is quite different. First, this difference lies in the time orientation of the discussion. The act of 'giving responsibility to an employee' is oriented to the future. The manager describes what s/he expects from the employee. On the contrary, the act of 'calling an employee to account' is oriented to the past. The manager refers to agreements made in the past.[88] Second, this difference lies in the content of the discussion. The act of 'giving responsibility to an employee' requires an in-depth discussion about the (new) assignment. Particular attention has to be given to training, supervision, authority, coaching, and so on. The act of 'calling an employee to account' also requires an in-depth discussion about the results. Here, attention is especially focused on realised production, quality of products, professional attitude, and so on. In a formal context, the distinction between 'giving responsibility' and 'calling to account' is quite clear. In everyday practice, the distinction is easily blurred with the result that employees are confronted with paradoxes and managerial short cuts.[89]

However, what happens if a manager cannot fulfil these conditions? What happens if a manager is pressed to accept tough targets for his or her organisation which leads to these conditions not being met? In an article in the *Harvard Business Review*, Thomas Teal touches on these types of problems.[90] He states that managers serve 'two masters': an organisational one (the boss) and a moral one (their own conscience). He emphasises that a manager sometimes has to follow the moral one. I would like to tell you one story in which I felt a strong tension between these two bosses. Eventually, I made my choice for the moral one – with severe consequences, which appeared later.

---

[88] Hogenhuis (1993) highlights the differences in time orientation. He defines the act of 'giving responsibility' as 'prospective responsibility' and 'calling to account' as 'retrospective responsibility'.

[89] In Christian thought, the asymmetry in the manager-employee relationship has been emphasised. It is especially stressed that a manager has authority over employees and that employees have to stand in awe of the manager. However, the authority of the manager and the awe of the employee are restricted. Their limits lie in the freedom and responsebility of the individual employee (Van Riessen, 1962). From the perspective of paradoxes on the shop floor and short cuts by managers, it is fruitful to define the asymmetry of the employment relation in a 'reversed' direction. Namely, employees have 'authority' over a manager – i.e. to create the conditions for responsibility – and a manager has 'to stand in awe' of employees – i.e. to respect the calling of employees.

[90] Teal (1996).

Story. Every year a new budget is made. An important part of this budget is the yield of the production. In the Glass Factory in Aachen, a target yield of xx % was proposed for the production of raw cones in the coming year. However, the actual yield was more that 10 % lower.

During the discussion about the budget, I referred to technical problems in the manufacturing process of raw cones. I told my boss that the development group had concluded that that process was not under control. In addition, they concluded that know-how to improve the yield in the short term was not present. I proposed a target yield for the coming year of about 3 to 5 percent higher than the actual yield. I also explained the reasons underlying this proposal. My boss did not accept my proposal. He stated that the low yield in the cone department was a management problem and not a technical problem. He overruled me: the target yield of xx % came in the budget

Reflection. The budget proposal had been discussed earlier in the management team of the factory. It was concluded that an increase in yield of 3 to 5 % would be a challenge. In other words, the budget proposal was not realistic. Acceptance of this proposal would put the department manager and the crew concerned in an impossible position: severe budget losses every month. For that reason, I could not accept the yield of xx %. In my view, the remark that the yield problem was a managerial problem and not a technical problem was ridiculous. After all, no development engineer could tell management how to produce these products with a target yield of xx %. In addition, the responsibility for a controlled manufacturing process lies with the development group. And ... the manager of this group reported hierarchically to my boss! I was quite surprised that he closed the (short) discussion by overruling me.

End of the story. The discussion about the budget yield appeared to have severe consequences. Six weeks later, the department manager was replaced. At the same time I was discharged from my responsibilities for this department. The change in management did not result in any improvements. One year later, the yield was still at the same value (about 10 % below the target of xx %).

This story emphasises the responsibility of management to fulfil the conditions for responsibility and accountability. Moreover, it shows that management easily takes a short cut by delegating the guilt for uncontrolled processes to lower managerial levels.

4.4 Freedom, labour, and authority

Marxist theories have extensively described the domination of labourers in the industrial system. Yves Schwartz acknowledges the value of these theories for understanding the phenomena of oppression, dehumanisation, and alienation in his book *Travail et Philosophie*. However, he also identifies a contradictory tension.

He points out that employees are not only determined by the system but (can) also create room for self-development within the system. Schwartz writes[91]:

> "Ainsi, à l'intérieur des contraintes matérielles et sociales et travaillant celles-ci, s'ouvre l'espace d'une gestion différenciée de soi-même. Charge de travail, fatigue cessent d'être des données objectives agressant de l'extérieur l'individu, elles se négocient en une alchimie subtile où tout dépend de la manière dont l'individu, dans ses virtualités singulières et ses limites, rencontre l'objectif à réaliser comme point d'appui ou au contraire comme restriction de ses possibles."

In his view, a production line, for instance, has a double character. It is not only a condition for production, but also a place where individuals seek to express themselves[92]:

> "Ainsi, d'un côté l'équipe a un double caractère: nécessité technique, condition de la productivité, variable souvent occultée mais déterminante des calculs de rentabilité et, de l'autre, lieu d'une alchimie toujours aléatoire où des histoires et des vies singulières cherchent à s'exprimer positivement dans les actes collectifs informels requis par ces industries de process. Deux éléments hétérogènes et pourtant inséparables."

He continues to state that the success of modern industry depends on employees feeling 'at home' in a high-tech environment[93]:

> "Toute réussite micro-industrielle suppose ici que s'instaure comme un succédané de vie familiale. Cela veut bien dire que des questions subjectives sont posées au travailleur posté : si 'famille' il y a, y 'prendre sa place' renvoie à l'individu et à son histoire."

The double character of a production line can result in a paradoxical consciousness of employees[94]:

> "Dans un premier temps – avant que l'entreprise ne soit coopérative –, il [l'ouvrier] rapportait comment certains disaient: 'Moi, je fais ce qu'on me dit'. Mais dans un second qui réfutait de façon très profonde le schématisme de ce propos, il affirmait au contraire : 'Jamais un ouvrier ne reste devant sa machine en pensant: je fais ce qu'on me dit'. Ce qui était dire que les possibles individuels cherchent toujours à prendre pied dans une configuration industrieuse, fût-elle en apparence la plus désespérée."

Especially the struggle for self-development holds for Tayloristic and neo-Tayloristic factories. However, numerous studies have shown that division of

---

[91] Schwartz (1992, p47).
[92] Schwartz (1992, p49).
[93] Schwartz (1992, p49, 50)
[94] Schwartz (1992, p48).

work, bureaucratic procedures, and continuous observation can never hold human freedom in a definitive grip.[95]

What about new production concepts? It cannot be taken for granted beforehand that these concepts – despite all rhetoric about social innovation – will leave room for the humanity of the labourer. In my opinion, the crux of this problem could be present in what Schwartz calls the 'double character' of a production line. If this is true, then a radical reinterpretation of the Marxist view is required to liberate labour. The key actor in this reinterpretation has to be the factory manager. S/he has to use his or her room for self-development for the benefit of self-realisation of subordinates. S/he has to design production lines so that the humanity of employees will be secured. S/he has to develop procedures so that the self-expression of employees will be realised. S/he has to interact with employees on the shop floor so that they feel at home on the production line. This reinterpretation implies that managers use their authority to create conditions for freedom for employees. It also implies that organising has a normative character.

The philosopher Van Riessen has fundamentally investigated the problems of technology and society.[96] He positions human responsibility in the perspective of human freedom. In his article 'Respect for human being in cooperation' he emphasises that managers have to use their authority to create freedom *towards* responsibility. He writes[97]:

> "Dat wij respect moeten hebben voor de medemens met wie wij leven en werken, berust niet op een vage intuïtie, maar op de heldere overtuiging, dat deze naaste door God geschapen is, naar *Zijn beeld* en tot *Zijn dienst* in de schepping. En dit respect is niet een gereserveerde achting of een afgedwongen eerbied voor de naaste; het vloeit voort uit de *liefde* tot de naaste (...) Wat wij daarin willen respecteren is zijn *vrijheid*, die uitzonderlijke menselijke gave (...) Wij moeten ons ervan onthouden in die vrijheidsruimte binnen te dringen en de vrije verantwoordelijkheid van de naaste

---

[95] See for example Bendix (1956) and Dalton (1959).
[96] Van Riessen (1949, 1953, 1962, 1971).
[97] "That we have to respect fellow man with whom we live and work, does not rest on a vague intuition, but on a clear belief that this neighbour is created by God, in *His image* and to *His service* in the creation. And this respect is not a distant regard or a wrung esteem for fellow man; it results from *love for* the neighbour (...) What we have to respect is his *freedom*, that unique human gift (...) We have to abstain from breaking into the room of freedom and from harming the free responsibility of fellow man against God. We are not allowed to deprive him of his calling, it is an infringement of his humanity if we take someone's place in thinking and acting, that his freedom becomes superfluous (...) As far as within our ability and our authority, we have to create, to develop and to defend the conditions that his freedom needs (...) *The authorities have* to exercise – in order to coordinate, to stimulate and to protect the community – *as much power over their subordinates so that their freedom to responsibility in their societal calling is maximal* (...) This human being has not alone his own place in the whole of cooperation, he also should bear immediate responsibility for the whole. Here, one could use with some reservations the word 'democracy' (translation M.J.V.)". Van Riessen (1962, p50-62). Italics by Van Riessen.

52

tegenover God aan te tasten. Wij mogen hem niet van zijn roeping beroven, het is een aantasting van zijn menselijkheid als wij zo voor hem in de plaats denken en doen, dat zijn vrijheid overbodig wordt (…) Voor zover in ons vermogen en binnen onze bevoegdheid ligt moeten wij de voorwaarden scheppen, ontwikkelen en verdedigen die zijn vrijheid behoeft (…) *Het gezag moet* voor het coördineren, stimuleren en beschermen van de gemeenschap *zoveel macht over de ondergeschikten uitoefenen, dat hun vrijheid tot verantwoordelijkheid in hun gemeenschapsroeping maximaal is* (…) Deze mens heeft niet alleen zijn eigen plaats in het geheel der samenwerking, hij behoort ook onmiddellijke verantwoordelijkheid voor het geheel te dragen. Men zou hier met enige reserve het woord 'democratie' kunnen plaatsen."

Van Riessen emphasises respect for the human being. He also emphasises that authority of management is restricted by the freedom of employees. This view implies that organisations – i.e. design of the production line, development of organisational procedures, and style of management – have a normative character.

4.5 Experience of meaning

Everybody longs for meaning in work ('Sinn'). Every employee wants his or her work to have a deeper significance. Every operator desires his or her activities to have a deeper significance. The experience of meaning goes beyond the technical activities themselves. It is more than operating a machine or performing a quality inspection. To formulate it philosophically: what brings about the experience of meaning is transcendent with respect to that experience.[98] In accordance with that, work is not a means to experience meaning; meaning can be experienced in the act of working. Modern mass production has resulted in alienation. Employees have lost sight of the meaning in their work. In my opinion, this phenomenon can not be seen as separate from the scientific basis of western industry. Tayloristic organisations give employees the idea that they are a cog in the industrial system; a cog that can easily be replaced by somebody else. In addition, Tayloristic organisations give employees the idea that they can only execute their tasks if they are controlled by direct checks, technical systems, and bureaucratic procedures. In addition, Tayloristic principles are detrimental to human self-esteem. Division of work blocks an individual's overview. Separation of thinking and execution harms human dignity. Functional management erodes human responsibility.

The fathers of the new production concepts claim that a 'new world of work' also implies the experience of meaning. However, this claim cannot be taken for granted. In the previous section it has been concluded that managers have to use their authority to secure the freedom of employees. It also has been concluded that organisations have a normative character. As a hypothesis I would like to suggest that experience of meaning is related to the normative character of industrial organisations.

---

[98]   Burms and De Dijn (1990, p28).

4.6 Conclusion

The considerations in this section offer different perspectives on analysing concrete phenomena and organisation design theories from a philosophical point of view. It has been shown that moral and religious views play a role in the adoption of new concepts and in the interaction between managers and employees. It has been indicated that the context of responsibility requires reflection on normative principles, the motivation to behave according to these principles, and the realisation of conditions for responsibility. Finally, it has been argued that organisations have a normative character.

5 Motive, research questions, and objectives

In the Prologue of this study I have identified paradoxes that arise on the shop floor of industrial organisations. On the one hand, employees are made responsible for the manufacturing of products. On the other hand, they cannot make these products with the required quality. The problem of this paradox is not the existence as such, but the naturalness with which a manager takes a short cut and calls employees to account without wondering whether the conditions are fulfilled. These types of paradoxes also arise with respect to the safety, environmental, social, and moral responsibilities of employees. Paradoxes have a disastrous effect on organisations. Employees try to find a way out to survive. Often they cope with paradoxes by showing irresponsible behaviour. In this chapter the existence of paradoxes and managerial short cuts on the shop floor has been investigated in the context of new production concepts in modern factories.

5.1 Motive

Why write a second thesis? Why spend many hours in isolation in the study?

The first personal motive to write a second thesis is a professional one. I have managed factories for more than fifteen years. In this period, I have met happy and motivated employees, but also frustrated and apathetic employees. I have experienced trust and certainty, but also mistrust and fear. I have developed factories to a world-class level, but I have also failed to identify paradoxes and to prevent short cuts. These experiences have left a deep mark on myself. They urged me to question new production concepts critically and to think about underlying mechanisms of motivation, frustration, trust and fear.

The second personal motive to study the processes on the shop floor is a religious one. I have been raised in the Calvinistic tradition. This tradition holds specific ideas about man, labour and organisation. The idea of man as responsible being is a cornerstone. Man is responsible for ruling the world as a good steward under the authority of God. Labour is considered as a part of good stewardship. I have devoted myself to organising factories in such a way that all employees, including operators on the shop floor, can perform their work as good stewards.

5.2 Research questions and objectives

The objective of this study is to reinterpret existing theories and to develop new theories. To realise this objective, a research question is required that guides us in gathering data, evaluating design theories, and reflecting on man, labour and organisation.[99]

---

[99] Strauss and Corbin (1990, p33-40).

The story in the Prologue provided the initial questions of this study. How can we prevent paradoxes on the shop floor? How can we prevent operators from being caught in an impossible position? How can we prevent operators from resorting to irresponsible behaviour? During the research process these initial questions were refined and specified for the different levels of analysis. The research question on the level of 'phenomena on the shop floor' is as follows:

How do paradoxes evolve on the shop floor?

The objective of this level of analysis is to identify and to investigate the mechanisms that lead to the development of paradoxes on the shop floor. An ethnographical research strategy is used to provide a 'rich description' of the social context and to reveal the 'deep structure' of the behaviour of employees and managers (Dyer and Wilkins[100]).

The research question on the level of 'organisation design theory' is as follows:

Why do new production concepts fail in many modern factories?

The objective is to investigate why new production concepts – 'espoused theories of action' (Argyris[101]) – fall short in preventing the development of paradoxes on the shop floor. It also has to be understood why the implementation of a new production concept does not necessarily lead to a 'new world of work'. To realise these objectives, the relation between the basics of new concepts, specific manufacturing context, sub-culture on the shop floor, and the implementation process has to be studied in detail.

The research question on the level of the 'philosophy of organisation' is as follows:

How can employees on the shop floor act in a responsible way?

The objective is to develop a theory and practice of responsibility with respect to employees on the shop floor. Special attention will be given to conditions that have to be fulfilled by a factory manager so that employees on the shop floor can bear responsibility and can be held accountable. Realisation of these objectives implies a philosophical analysis of industrial organisations. It has to be noted that this research question includes the first two research questions.

The research questions will be studied from the perspective of a factory manager. The objectives will be realised by a multi-disciplinary approach: a theoretical analysis of new production concepts (Ch. 2), an ethnographical study of two cases (Ch. 3), and an ethnographical, organisational, ethical and philosophical evaluation (Ch. 4).

---

[100] Dyer and Wilkins (1991).
[101] Argyris (1991).

Note on language

Generally, I will refer to managers and employees as 'he' and 'she' (or 's/he'). There are two exceptions. First, in cases where the original literature refers explicitly to a male expression, in which case this usage will be respected. Second, in the Glass Factory in Aachen all employees and managers in manufacturing operations were male, so it is more appropriate to use male expressions only.

In this study, the expressions 'ethics' and 'ethical' will be used to indicate a normative theory of responsible behaviour of human beings. The expressions 'morality' and 'moral' will be used to indicate one dimension of this normative theory. Namely, that dimension of responsible behaviour that reflects the care a human being shows to him/herself, to others, to society as a whole or the natural environment. These distinctions will be elaborated on in section 5 and 6 of Chapter 4.

CHAPTER 2
New production concepts

In the first chapter of this thesis, it has been indicated that societal developments have urged modern industries to abandon classical manufacturing methods and to introduce new production concepts. These new concepts promise a 'new world of work' that combines technical superiority with social innovation. In practice, new production concepts fall short in preventing the development of paradoxes and managerial short cuts. Additionally, the promise of a 'new world of work' is often not realised.

In the previous chapter, it has been shown that an analysis on three levels is required to understand the failure of new production concepts. These levels consist of concrete phenomena on the shop floor, the basics of organisational design theory, and the philosophy of organisation. For each level, a research question has been formulated. These questions are:

How do paradoxes evolve on the shop floor?

Why do new production concepts fail in many modern factories?

How can employees on the shop floor act in a responsible way?

An integrative analysis of these questions requires an in-depth study of the new production concepts in modern factories. Particular attention has to be paid to the design of the workplace, the responsibility of employees, and the implementation strategy.

This chapter is structured in the following way. Section 1 introduces the topic of this chapter. Section 2 summarises the principles of the American engineer Frederick Taylor, who has laid the foundations of western industry. Sections 3 to 6 present alternative production concepts: Socio-Technical Systems Design, Lean Production, Business Process Reengineering, and the Mini-Company Concept are described respectively. Section 7 evaluates the different concepts.

1 Introduction

At the end of the nineteenth century, the American engineer Frederick Taylor introduced scientific methods in the factory. He believed that the development of the 'one best way' and the 'one best implement' on the shop floor would solve the labour problem and would bring prosperity for both the employee and the employer. Frederick Taylor laid the foundations of the tradition of Scientific Management.

In the course of time, a number of alternatives – New Production Concepts – have been proposed. All these concepts claim to propose a more efficient, more effective and/or more human approach than Scientific Management. These concepts have different backgrounds, present different methodologies to design organisations, offer different tools and techniques to improve the performance of a factory, and express different views with respect to man and organisation.

The Dutch engineer Ulbo de Sitter criticised extreme division of labour. In his view, simple and repetitive tasks had to be replaced by complex and meaningful tasks. To realise this objective a detailed design theory and design methodology were developed. The approach of De Sitter is part of the paradigm of the so-called Socio-Technical Systems Design.

The Japanese engineer Taiichi Ohno refined the approach of Taylor. He introduced a number of techniques to reduce waste and to increase efficiency. The key concepts here are standardisation and continuous improvement. Rightly, Ohno is named the father of the Toyota Production System or Lean Production.

The consultants Michael Hammer and James Champy also criticise the division of labour. They state that corporations have to be built around business processes. That means simple and repetitive tasks have to be placed within a 'coherent business process'. This approach is named Business Process Reengineering.

Finally, the Japanese consultant Kiyoshi Suzaki emphasises that people have to form the centre of the shop floor. In his view, the expertise and the creativity of the employees have to be used to improve the technical, social and moral aspects of production. To realise this, the so-called Mini-Company Concept was developed.

It has to be noted that Taylor, De Sitter, Ohno, Hammer, Champy, and Suzaki have experienced the factory from different perspectives. Taylor is the only one who has worked for several years as an employee on the shop floor. Taylor, De Sitter, Ohno, and Suzaki have all worked as engineers and/or managers in an industrial environment. Furthermore, Taylor, De Sitter, Ohno, Hammer, Champy, and Suzaki have worked as consultants for (manufacturing) companies.

In this chapter, Scientific Management and the various new production concepts are studied from the original texts. The main reason for this is that I prefer to interpret these texts from the point of view of a factory manager as 'reflective practitioner'. I would like to pay attention to the design of the workplace, the responsibility of employees, and the implementation strategy. In addition, I would like to point out specific parts in these texts that reveal underlying views.

2 Frederick Taylor: The 'One best way'

Frederick Taylor has been named as the father of Scientific Management. He introduced scientific methods in the factory. He proposed new methods of management. The influence of Taylor upon the development of western industry cannot be overestimated. Many engineers have developed his principles further. His concepts have formed several generations of managers. His views have been exported to Europe, Russia and the Far East. And his thoughts have stood the test of time.

The New Production Concepts discussed in this chapter are in one way or another an extension of or a reaction to the ideas of Frederick Taylor. Therefore, his approach has to be outlined in more detail. Taylor has summarised his views is several papers and books. This section is based on the following key texts: *Shop Management* (1903), *Principles of Scientific Management* (1911), and *Taylor's Testimony Before the Special House Committee* (1912).[1]

This section has the following set-up: the background of Frederick Taylor (2.1), the principles of Scientific Management (2.2), illustration of these principles using four (famous) examples (2.3), the responsibility of management (2.4), the responsibility of workmen (2.5), the 'very essence' of Scientific Management (2.6), and an evaluation (2.7).

2.1 Background

Frederick Winslow Taylor was born in 1856 in a cultured and well-to-do family in Philadelphia.[2] He was, in the words of his father, a person of 'gentle breeding'.[3] He had a carefree youth. At the age of sixteen, Fred entered the Philips Exeter Academy to prepare himself for the Harvard entrance examinations. He belonged to the top of his class. At Exeter, Fred suffered from serious headaches and his doctors advised him 'to go easy on his eyes'. Therefore, he left the academy in the beginning of 1874.[4] Later, Fred continued the preparations for Harvard. He passed the examinations with honours. However, he did not enrol.

In those days, it was obvious and natural to start a career in mechanical engineering with an apprenticeship in a machine shop. So this is what Taylor did. In 1874, he began an apprenticeship as a pattern maker and machinist in a small shop

---

[1] In his testimony, Taylor (1912, p172) states that his 'exact views' are 'much more nearly' expressed in *Principles of Scientific Management* than in *Shop Management*. The reason is that he had to reduce the original text of *Shop Management* by about one-third before it was accepted for publication by the American Society of Mechanical Engineers. He published *Principles of Scientific Management* at his own expense to prevent any reduction.

[2] Bibliographical data is based on Kanigel (1997).

[3] Kanigel (1997, p31).

[4] The eye problems would be later diagnosed as astigmatism (Kanigel, 1997, p87-91).

in Philadelphia named Enterprise Hydraulic Works, also known as Ferrell & Jones. In early 1878 Taylor finished his apprenticeship. In the same year, he got a job at Midvale Steel Company. He started as an ordinary worker on the shop floor of the machine shop. Within a period of eight years, he progressed through the stages of ordinary labourer, timekeeper, machinist, gang boss, foreman, assistant engineer, and chief engineer of the works.

In the 1870s, steel making was still fussy and temperamental. All steel making companies suffered from serious problems in the production process. At Midvale Steel Company, it was believed that "... more accurate chemical knowledge of the difference between good and bad steel ..." was needed.[5] In the beginning of the 1870s Brinley and Davenport, chemists by trade, joined Midvale to improve the steel making process. So Midvale became one of the first companies in which a scientific approach prevailed to solve industrial problems. This meant that in 1878, Fred Taylor started to work in a company in which a scientific approach was welcomed. It was in this company that he carried out experiments on metal cutting.

In early 1881, Taylor enrolled at Stevens Institute of Technology. Special arrangements were made to finalise this study. In the academic year of 1882-83, he enrolled as a special student at the chemistry department of the University of Pennsylvania. His work and his studies completely filled his time.

Taylor left Midvale in the autumn of 1890 to become manager of a paper mill in Maine. However, the production process appeared not to be under control. The paper mill venture turned into a debacle. Taylor resigned from his position; and from 1893 onwards he earned his living as a management consultant.

In 1885, Taylor became a member of the American Society for Mechanical Engineers. At that time, it was believed that the paying system would be the key to productivity improvement in manufacturing. Taylor did not agree with this view. In 1895, he presented his ideas about management and paying systems to the American Society for Mechanical Engineers. His paper was entitled 'A Piece Rate System. A Step toward Partial Solution of the Labour Problem'. Taylor's paper has to be seen in the context of the bloody Homestead strike of July 1892 where the loss of ten deaths had to be mourned. Taylor claimed that his proposal would solve the "... antagonism between employers and men ...[and would promote] a most friendly feeling between the men and their employers, and so render unions and strikes unnecessary."[6] In the discussion following his presentation, all attention went to the paying system and the new management techniques were ignored.

In 1898, Taylor became employed at the Bethlehem Steel Works. There he continued his metal-cutting experiments. As a part of these studies, he investigated the hardening of cutting tools. At the end of 1899 and beginning of 1900, Fred Taylor and Maunsel White, a Bethlehem metallurgist, discovered high-speed steel. Tools made from this type of steel could cut at speeds that doubled, tripled or even quadrupled the old speeds. A patent application was granted. The discovery of high-speed metal made Taylor famous in the industrial world and brought him a lot of money.

---

[5]   Kanigel (1997, p157).
[6]   Kanigel (1997, p281).

At Bethlehem Steel Works, Taylor also performed a number of time studies. These studies focused particularly on pig iron handling and shovelling. In this period, Henry Noll, (Taylor gave him the name Schmidt), appeared on the world stage. He became the most famous labourer in history because he could handle 45 tons of pig iron a day.

The management at Bethlehem Steel Works was not very satisfied with Taylor's efforts, however. He was blamed for the limited increase in output of the machine shops. Taylor stopped his activities on May 1, 1901. A month later Bethlehem Steel was sold. The new owner threw out all the tools and techniques implemented by Taylor.

From 1901 onwards Fred Taylor again became a consultant. He devoted all his time to the propagation of his ideas. He lectured around the world. He was 'Mr. Scientific Management'. In 1903, Taylor presented his views at a conference of the American Society of Mechanical Engineers. His paper was entitled *Shop Management*. The paper was received well (the text has been published in a book of the same name).

In spring 1904, the Taylors removed to a new house on the old Sherwood estate in Chestnut Hill. From this house, named Boxly, he continued to spread the 'new gospel of industrial enlightenment'.[7] They came in their hundreds to listen to him. In a two-hour, non-stop dialogue, he presented the principles of Scientific Management. After lunch, he took the attendants to two companies that had installed his system: Link-Belt and the Tabor Manufacturing Company. In 1911, Taylor presented his ideas in a more systematic manner in *Principles of Scientific Management*. This book was an edited version of his Boxly talks by a guest writer.

In the same year, a wave of criticism came about. The application of the principles of Scientific Management at the government arsenal in Watertown resulted in serious labour troubles. The first strike against the Taylor system broke out. The strike as such is not worth mentioning: a handful of men who went back to work after one week. However, its impact was huge: big headlines in the papers, alarmed unions, and petitions in Congress. In August, the House of Representatives passed a resolution to investigate Taylor and other systems of shop management. A Special Committee, presided by W.B. Wilson, was set up. In January 1912, this committee interviewed Fred Taylor. In his opening speech, which was a revised version of the Boxly talks, he emphasised that Scientific Management involves a complete mental revolution.

Shortly after the investigations of the House of Representatives, Taylor's wife, Louise, became ill. Taylor tenderly and lovingly cared for her. Taylor died in 1917.

---

[7] Kanigel (1997, p412).

2.2 What is Scientific Management?[8]

In the first chapter of *Principles of Scientific Management,* Taylor expresses his belief that the interests of employers and employees are basically the same. In his view, harmonious cooperation is required to realise prosperity for both parties. He writes[9]:

> "The principal object of management should be to secure the maximum prosperity for the employer, coupled with the maximum prosperity for each employee. The words 'maximum prosperity' are used (...) to mean not only large dividends for the company or the owner, but the development of every branch of the business to its highest state of excellence, so that the prosperity may be permanent. In the same way maximum prosperity for each employee means not only higher wages than are usually received by men of his class (...) it also means the development of each man to his state of maximum efficiency, so that he may be able to do, generally speaking, the highest grade of work for which his natural abilities fit him (...) prosperity for the employer cannot exist through a long term of years unless it is accompanied by prosperity for the employee, and *vice versa*."

What prevents maximum prosperity for the employer and the employee? Taylor asserts that productivity in industry is too low. He suggests three causes for this.[10] The first is the fallacious belief of the workmen that any increase in output would result in unemployment. The second is the defective system of management, which makes it necessary for workmen to work slowly or to soldier in order to protect their interests. The third is the use of inefficient rule-of-thumb methods that lead to a waste in effort. Taylor believed that application of the philosophy and the techniques of Scientific Management could overcome these obstacles. In his opinion, it is the duty of management to do a systematic study of the work and to develop the 'one best way' and the 'one best implement'. He also believed that management has to help and to guide the labourer in working according to the developed methods. Such a close and personal cooperation of management and workmen would bring a great increase in efficiency and with it prosperity for all parties. As Taylor put it[11]:

> "What the workmen want from their employers beyond anything else is high wages, and what employers want from their workmen most of all is a low labour cost of manufacture. These two conditions are not diametrically opposed to one another as would appear at the first glance. On the contrary, they can be made to go together in all classes of work, without exception, and in the writer's judgement the existence or

---

[8] Taylor characterised his approach as 'scientific'. Presently – taking into account the development of science and technology – his approach has to be labelled as 'scientific-technological'.

[9] Taylor (1911, p9, 10).

[10] Taylor (1911, p15-24).

[11] Taylor (1903, p22).

absence of these two elements forms the best index to either good or bad management."

But how could high wages and low labour costs be united? Taylor emphasises that management has to take the lead to realise these objectives. In *Shop Management* he proposes the following principles[12]:

"(a) A Large Daily Task. Each man in the establishment, high or low, should daily have a clearly defined task laid out before him. This task should not in the least degree be vague nor indefinite, but should be circumscribed carefully and completely, and should not be easy to accomplish.

(b) Standard Conditions. Each man's task should call for a full day's work, and at the same time the workman should be given such standardised conditions and appliances as will enable him to accomplish his task with certainty.

(c) High Pay For Success. He should be sure of large pay when he accomplishes his task.

(d) Loss In Case Of Failure. When he fails he should be sure that sooner or later he will be the loser by it."

In *Principles of Scientific Management* Taylor emphasises that both workmen and management have to do their fair share. The workmen have to show 'initiative', ingenuity, good will, and work hard. The management has to take on new burdens, new duties and "... responsibilities never dreamed of in the past."[13] He mentions[14]:

"*First*. They develop a science for each element of a man's work, which replaces the old rule-of-thumb method.

Second. They scientifically select and then train, teach, and develop the workmen, whereas in the past he chose his own work and trained himself as best as he could.

Third. They heartily cooperate with the men so as to insure all of the work being done in accordance with the principles of the science which has been developed.

Fourth. There is an almost equal division of the work and the responsibility between the management and the workmen. The management take over all work for which they are better fitted than the workmen, while in the past almost all of the work and the greater part of the responsibility were thrown upon the men."

In his testimony, Taylor calls these four elements the 'principles of Scientific Management'.[15]

Taylor declares that the application of these principles is not limited to industrial activities. They can also be applied to social activities like the running of our

---

12 Taylor (1903, p63, 64).
13 Taylor (1911, p36).
14 Taylor (1911, p36, 37). These duties are found in comparable wording in Taylor (1912, p40- 45).
15 Taylor (1912, p40).

homes, the governing of our churches, and the management of our philanthropic institutions.[16]

2.3 Examples of Scientific Management

Taylor was absolutely convinced that the principles of Scientific Management could be applied to all types of work. He wanted to show that "… every single act of every workman can be reduced to a science."[17] I would like to illustrate these principles by the use of four examples: shovelling, the inspection of bicycle balls, the overhauling and cleaning of boilers, and metal-cutting.

At the works of Bethlehem Steel Company, a lot of shovelling had to be done. One could question whether there is much of a science in the work of shovelling. However, Taylor investigated this process in detail[18]:

> *The science of shovelling.* The most important materials that were shovelled at the yard were rice coal and ore. The load to the shovel was about 3 ½ pounds for rice coal and about 38 pounds for ore. This difference raises an important question. What is a proper shovel load? Is it 3 ½ pounds? Is it 38 pounds? Something in between? To answer this question a careful scientific investigation was started.
>
> Taylor selected some 'first-class' shovellers from the yard. He offered them a double salary to participate in his investigations. He told them to work continuously and to avoid any slow working and soldiering. At the same time, an assistant with a piece of paper, a pencil and a stopwatch would observe their work. The experiments started. The influence of the shovel load was investigated. The number of shovel loads that each man handled in the course of the day was counted and written down. At the end of the day, the total tonnage of material handled by each man was weighed. In this way the average shovel load and the total load were known. For example, with an average shovel load of 38 pounds a man could handle about 25 tons a day. Then the shovel was made a bit shorter so that the average shovel load would be reduced from 38 pounds to about 34 pounds. Now it was found that with an average shovel load of 34 pounds a man could handle 30 tons a day. The shovel was again shortened. The load was reduced to approximately 30 pounds, and again the tonnage handled per day increased. It was found that the highest amount of material was shovelled with a load of 21 ½ pounds. If the shovel load was cut below this figure, the total tonnage handled per man per day decreased.
>
> Taylor also investigated the force to drive the shovel into the pile. He found out that most workmen used the wrong method. For example, in shovelling refractory material most of the workers used the muscular force of their arms. However, it requires much less exertion if the workmen use the weight of their body. These investigations led to the 'one best method' to force the shovel into a pile.

---

[16] Taylor (1911, p8).
[17] Taylor (1911, p64).
[18] Taylor (1911, p64-68) and Taylor (1912, p50-65 and p222-225).

These investigations led to many changes. Firstly, a special shovel was designed for every particular material; a small shovel for heavy materials and a large one for light materials. Each shovel could contain a load of approximately 21 ½ pounds. Secondly, the yard workers were selected. The shovelling work had to be done by first-class men and by labourers who were well suited to their job. These workmen were offered a 60 % increase in salary. Thirdly, the organisation of the work was changed. Clerks planned the work at least one day in advance. In the morning, the workman got two pieces of paper. The first piece of paper informed him about the material to be shovelled, the type of shovel to be taken from the shovel room, and the part of the yard where he had to work. The second piece of paper informed the workman about his results of the day before. A white piece of paper meant that he had performed according to the standard and had earned his bonus of 60 %. A yellow piece of paper meant that he had failed to meet the standard and had not earned his bonus. Finally, if a workman received a yellow piece of paper three of four times, a teacher would be sent from the labour office to train him again in the science of shovelling.

The introduction of the new system led to high efficiency. The number of shovellers was reduced from 400-600 to 140 men. The average number of tons per man per day was increased from 16 to 59. The average earnings increased from $ 1.15 to $1.88. The average cost of handling a ton decreased – despite the additional costs for clerks, foremen and teachers – from $ 0.072 to $ 0.033.

The second example concerns the inspection of bicycle balls. "When the bicycle craze was at its height ...", several million small balls of hardened steel were used annually in bicycle bearings.[19] The last important step in the production process was the visual inspection of the balls. Taylor got the assignment to reorganise the visual inspection of the largest bicycle ball factory in the States[20]:

The inspection of bicycle balls. About one hundred and twenty girls worked in the visual inspection process. These girls were 'old hands' and skilled in their jobs. They worked 10 ½ hours per day; with half a Saturday as holiday. The girls applied the following inspection procedure. They placed a row of small polished steel balls on the back of their left hand, in the crease between two of the fingers pressed together. The balls were rolled repeatedly, and were minutely examined in a strong light. With the aid of a magnet held in the right hand, the defective balls were picked out and thrown into special boxes. This type of inspection required the closest attention and concentration.

Observation of the inspecting girls showed that a considerable part of the working day was spent in idleness because the working day was too long. It was decided to shorten their working hours in successive steps from 10 ½ to 10, to 9 ½, to 9, and finally to 8 ½ hours, with the pay per day remaining the same. Taylor found that with each shortening of the working day the output increased instead of decreased.

The next step was the scientific selection of the inspectors. The inspection of bicycle balls requires the combination of a quick perception followed by a quick action. It

---

[19]   Taylor (1911, p86).
[20]   Taylor (1903, p85-91) and Taylor (1911, p86-98).

was found that these characteristics were present in inspectors with a so-called low 'personal coefficient'. The measurement of this coefficient was developed in the laboratory of a university. This method was used to select the first-class inspectors. Many of the (hard-working and motivated) girls did not met the selection requirements and were laid off.

The quality of the visual inspection was an important factor. By means of a second inspection, the quality of the inspection process was measured. The results of this second inspection were fed back to the individual inspectors. A teacher was sent to the girls who were falling behind to find out what was wrong, and to encourage and to help her to catch up.

Finally, it was found that after about an hour and a half of consecutive work the girls became nervous. They evidently needed a rest. Therefore, a ten minute period for recreation was arranged at the end of every hour and a quarter.

What were the overall results? The girls received an increase in salary of 80 to 100 %. Their working day was decreased from 10 ½ to 8 ½ hours. During the day, they received four recreation periods of ten minutes to prevent overworking. Finally, they received two additional days of rest per month (without loss of pay). The number of girls involved decreased from one hundred and twenty to thirty five. The quality of the inspection was increased by two-thirds.

The third example has to do with quite a different type of work: the overhauling and cleaning of boilers. Taylor writes that he asked one of his assistants to write a complete instruction card for this type of work. However, the assistant was not experienced in this field and failed. Therefore Taylor decided to do the work himself.[21]:

> *The overhauling and cleaning of boilers.* Taylor did all the work of overhauling and cleaning a set of boilers by himself. He carried out a careful time study of each of the elements of the work. The time study showed that a great part of the time lost was due to the constrained position of the workman. Thick pads were made for the elbows, knees and hips and special tools and appliances were made for the various elements of the work. An instruction card was also made, outlining the use of the required tools and appliances.
>
> After training and implementation, it appeared that all the trouble taken was justified. The time needed for overhauling and cleaning one boiler decreased by a factor of five. The quality of the operation also improved.

The last example has to do with the science of metal-cutting. Taylor was asked to improve the efficiency of a machine shop by the introduction of Scientific Management[22]:

> *The science of metal-cutting.* One lathe was selected for investigation. A careful record was made of the time needed to finish each of the parts the mechanic worked

---

[21] Taylor (1903, p181, 182).
[22] Taylor (1903, p178-180), Taylor (1911, p98-112) and Taylor (1912, p78-108).

upon. Relevant parameters like speed and feeds were also noted. A careful analysis of every element of the machine was made. Its pulling power at its various speeds, its feeding capacity, and its proper speeds were determined by using some general slide-rules. After that, changes were made in the countershaft and driving pulleys so that it could run at its proper speed. Tools were made from high-speed steel. These tools were properly shaped, dressed, treated and ground. For this special lathe, a slide-rule was made so that the mechanic could adjust the equipment. These investigations resulted in a gain in operating time of two and one-half times to nine times the speed.

Taylor continued investigating the science of cutting at Midvale Steel Company. In total, he did 30.000 to 50.000 experiments. During these experiments, he used more that 800.000 pounds of steel. Taylor determined twelve independent parameters that influence the cutting process. Each of these parameters was investigated in detail. One of the biggest problems was to keep eleven parameters stable during the investigation of the twelfth parameter. Finally, he succeeded in describing the influence of each of these parameters in a pattern.

Taylor concluded that in the machine shops under investigation not one machine in a hundred had the correct cutting speed.[23]

Taylor also investigated psychological questions. For example, he studied the motives that influence workmen.[24] He identified two important factors: a daily task and a bonus.

2.4 Responsibility of management

In *Principles of Scientific Management*, Frederick Taylor broke down the responsibilities of management into four principles: the development of a science, the scientific selection and training of workmen, heartily cooperation between management and workmen, and the equal division of work and responsibility between management and the workmen.[25]

Principle 1: Development of a science
The first responsibility of management is the development of a science to replace the old rule-of-thumb knowledge of the workmen. To realise this objective, management has 'to gather' the traditional knowledge of the workmen. This knowledge has to be translated into rules, laws and formulae to help the workmen in their daily work.[26]

In his *Shop Management* paper, Taylor gives a lot of attention to the various paying systems that were in use at the time. He points out that these systems have one weak point in common: the determination of a standard or a 'fair day's work'.

---

[23]   Taylor (1911, p112).
[24]   Taylor (1911, 119-122).
[25]   Taylor (1911, p36, 37).
[26]   Taylor (1911, p36) and Taylor (1912, p40).

Under the ordinary piecework system, the employer tries to find out the quickest time in which a job can be done. The employer uses this standard to force the workmen to realise a high output. Under the premium system, the employees determine the quickest time and receive a premium when they produce above that standard. In the system the workmen try to set the 'quickest time' which enables them to easily exceed this standard and earn a premium. In other words, under the ordinary piecework system, management tries to secure their interests, and under the premium system, the workmen try to do the same. He concludes that the piecework system and the premium system are founded upon 'deceit' and a 'lack of justice'.[27] Under these systems there is no heartily cooperation between management and workmen and the result is low productivity. Taylor proposes that paying systems should be founded on a just basis. Arbitrariness from the side of the employer and soldiering and slow working from the side of the employee should be excluded. In his view, a just foundation can be provided by an accurate and scientific study of unit times.[28] Such a study has to result in an objectively determined 'daily task' or 'fair day's work'. Taylor emphasises that time studies have to be done in close and friendly cooperation with the workmen.[29] He states that the time standards have to be "… accepted both by the workmen and the management as correct."[30] In the case of injustice, the workmen have to bring the case to the attention of the management and an impartial and careful scientific investigation has to be done.[31]

The methods of performing times studies are described extensively.[32] Every operation is divided into its elementary units that are studied in detail. Taylor proposes the following general method[33]:

"The general steps to be taken in developing a simple law of this class are as follows:
First. Find, say, 10 or 15 different men (…) who are especially skilful in doing the particular work to be analysed.
Second. Study the exact series of elementary operations or motions which each of these men uses in doing the work, which is being investigated, as well as the implements each man uses.
Third. Study with a stopwatch the time required to make each of these elementary movements and then select the quickest way of doing each element of the work.
Fourth. Eliminate all false movements, slow movements, and unless movements.
Fifth. After doing away with all unnecessary movements, collect into one series the quickest and best movements as well as the best implements.
(…) This best method becomes standard and remains standard."

---

[27] Taylor (1903, p41).
[28] Taylor (1903, p58).
[29] E.g. Taylor (1912, p166).
[30] Taylor (1912, p143).
[31] Taylor (1912, p145, 150, 226). Taylor emphasises that absolute justice to the workmen characterises Scientific Management (Taylor, 1912, p145).
[32] Taylor (1903, p149-177), Taylor (1911, p116-118) and Taylor (1912, p108-111).
[33] Taylor (1911, p117-118). See also Taylor (1912, p109-110).

These general steps were applied in the examples described above – shovelling, inspecting balls, overhauling and cleaning boilers, and metal-cutting. The time required for each individual step was determined, unnecessary movements were eliminated, tools were developed and the 'best method' was determined; resulting in a 'complete standardisation of all details and methods'.[34]

In the hearings before the Special Committee, Taylor was asked whether specialisation is not one of the characteristics of Scientific Management. Taylor answered that division of work already took place under the older types of management and it 'undoubtedly' would continue under Scientific Management.[35] In his view, a workman becomes more productive when he works in his speciality.[36]

Taylor also discusses the various paying systems. He stresses that a 'proper task' has to be determined through studying unit times. The particular paying system adopted, is "… merely one of the subordinate elements."[37]

Principle 2: Scientific selection and training of workmen
The next responsibility of management is the scientific selection of the workmen to ensure that they have the physical and intellectual qualities to achieve the required output. After that, they have to be trained to work according to the developed laws and the fixed standards to become 'first-class'. Taylor believes that every worker could be first-class at some job[38]:

> "In the past the man has been first; in the future the system must be first (…) The first object of any good system must be that of developing first-class men; and under systematic management the best man rises to the top more certainly and more rapidly than ever before (…)
>
> It would seem to be the duty of employers, therefore, both in their own interest and in that of their employees, to see that each workman is given as far as possible the highest class of work for which his brains and physique fit him (…)
>
> [One of the duties of management] is the scientific selection and then the progressive development of the workmen (…) And then as deliberately and as systematically to train and help and teach this workman, giving him, wherever it is possible, those opportunities for advancement which finally enable him to do the highest and most interesting and most profitable class of work for which his natural abilities fit him

---

[34] Taylor (1903, p123).
[35] Taylor (1912, p203-205).
[36] Taylor (1912, p203-204) refers to one example of division of work. He was told that in a shoe factory the manufacturing of an 'upper' consists of more than 450 operations; a different man doing each of these operations. Taylor presents this example without any comment. One page later, he writes 'there is no question about it, there are various elements in this specialisation that are deplorable'.
[37] Taylor (1911, p34).
[38] Taylor (1911, p7), Taylor (1903, p28), and Taylor (1912, p42). See also Taylor (1903, p183), Taylor (1911, p9, 12) and Taylor (1912, p154-156, 204, 246).

(...) This scientific selection of the workman is not a single act; it goes from year to year and is the subject of continual study on the part of the management."

Taylor emphasises that all the workmen "... rise to a better class of work and to higher pay under scientific management."[39] As evidence, he refers to the development of the salaries of the workmen in the Tabor Manufacturing Company.[40]

Principle 3: Heartily cooperation between management and workmen

The third responsibility of management is to ensure that all the work is done according to the principles and laws of science.[41] This requires heartily cooperation between management and workmen. Such a cooperation implies a 'mental revolution' on both sides.[42] Management has to take care that[43]:

> "(...) the work may be done in accordance with scientific laws (...) And each man should be daily taught by and receive the most friendly help from those who are over him (...) This close, intimate, personal cooperation between management and the men is of the essence of modern scientific or task management."

Throughout all his works, Taylor continuously stresses the importance of the mental revolution on the side of management. He warns that in no instance should a change from the old to the new type of management take place unless the directors of the company fully understand and believe in the fundamental principles of Scientific Management.[44] The wrong attitude on the part of management or a misunderstanding of the philosophy of the system will result in failure in implementation.[45]

Taylor emphasises in nearly every example the importance of hearty and harmonious cooperation between management and workmen.[46] However, such

---

[39] Taylor (1912, p156).

[40] Taylor (1912, p276, 277). In discussing the duties of management, Taylor (1903, p105) states that the possibilities of functional foremanship will not be realised 'until almost all of the machines in the shop are run by men who are of smaller calibre and attainments, and who are therefore cheaper than those required under the old system'. Braverman (1974, p118) interprets the quotation as: 'the purpose was to cheapen the worker by de creasing his training and enlarging his output'. Wrongly, Braverman does not recognise that these men of 'smaller calibre' were originally labourers. They were trained and promoted to machinist working in a machine shop (Taylor, 1903, p106). Compare also Taylor (1912, 245). And, under the new system the salaries were increased by 30 to 100% in comparison with the old system. Taylor (1903, p146) stresses that under Scientific Management workers can be promoted to machinists, and machinists to foremen. Both have the opportunity to earn a higher salary and to rise to a higher class of work.

[41] Taylor (1912, p42).

[42] Taylor (1911, p131, 140) and Taylor (1912, p27-30).

[43] Taylor (1911, p26).

[44] Taylor (1903, p128, 129) and Taylor (1911, p135).

[45] Taylor (1911, p28, 128, 129) and Taylor (1912, p34, 252, 284).

[46] E.g. Taylor (1911, p85) and Taylor (1912, p77).

cooperation cannot be taken for granted. Taylor concludes that there is a lot of opposition from the side of management. In his experience, nine-tenths of the problems are due to management and only one-tenth due to the workmen.[47] He condemns the behaviour of directors who are willing to pay for new machines but refuse to invest in their organisation.[48] Taylor's expectation of management is that they develop a relationship of trust with their workmen. He rejects the behaviour of an employer who goes "...through his works with the kid gloves on ... is never known to dirty his hands or clothes and who either talks to his men in a condescending or patronising way, or else not at all...".[49] Taylor says that it is desirable for each man to have the opportunity to 'airing his mind freely' with management.[50]

Principle 4. Equal division of work and responsibility between management and workmen

Taylor remarks that under the old systems of management the workman bears the whole responsibility for his work. He does the planning, he develops his own skills, and he designs his own tools. In the opinion of Taylor, management has to take over all the work for which they are better suited than the workmen, e.g. determination of the quickest methods, development of laws and slide-rules, design of implements, continuous training and help, and supervision and control of the workmen[51]:

> "An almost equal division of the work and responsibility between the workman and the management. All day long the management work almost side by side with the men, helping, encouraging, and smoothing the way for them, while in the past they stood one side, gave the men but little help, and threw on to them almost the entire responsibility as to methods, implements, speed, and harmonious cooperation (...) under this new type of management there is hardly a single act or piece of work done by any workman in the shop which is not preceded and followed by some act on the part of one of the men in the management."

Taylor stresses that perhaps[52]:

> "(...) the most prominent single element in modern Scientific Management is the task idea. The work of every workman is fully planned out by the management at least one day in advance, and each man receives in most cases complete written instructions, describing in detail the task which he is to accomplish, as well as the means to be used in doing the work."

---

[47] Taylor (1912, p43, 153, 195).
[48] Taylor (1903, p62).
[49] Taylor (1903, p184).
[50] Taylor (1903, p184).
[51] Taylor (1911, p85) and Taylor (1912, p44, 45).
[52] Taylor (1911, p39). See also Taylor (1912, p6).

Taylor discusses the duties of management in detail. For example, a gang boss who is in charge of the lathes needs the following qualities: he must be a good machinist, he must be able to read the drawings, he must plan ahead, he must see that each man keeps his machine clean, he must check the quality of the products, he must see that his men work at a proper speed, he must constantly check that the parts are made in the right sequence, he must control the timekeeping, and he must take care of discipline. Taylor concludes that it is impossible to find gang bosses who possess all these qualities. For this reason, he proposes introducing "... two broad and sweeping changes in the art of management."[53] The essence is to remove the 'brainwork' from the shop floor and to introduce functional management[54]:

> "(a) As far as possible the workmen, as well as the gang bosses and foremen, should be entirely relieved of the work of planning, and of all work which is more or less clerical in its nature. All possible brain work should be removed from the shop and centred in the planning or laying-out department (...)
>
> (b) Throughout the whole field of management the military type of organisation should be abandoned, and what may be called the 'functional type' substituted in its place. 'Functional management' consists in so dividing the work of management that each man from the assistant superintendent down shall have as few functions as possible to perform. If practicable the work of each man in the management should be confined to the performance of a single leading function."

Taylor proposes four types of executive functional bosses: (1) gang bosses, (2) speed bosses, (3) inspectors, and (4) repair bosses. Additionally, four representatives of the planning department have to guide the workmen: (1) order of work and route clerk, (2) instruction card clerk, (3) time and cost clerk, and (4) shop disciplinarian. That means every workman receives his daily orders and help directly from these eight different bosses.[55]

2.5 Responsibility of the workmen

Taylor emphasises that Scientific Management entails a complete revolution of the workmen's mental attitude toward their employer and their work[56]:

> "(...) the men must be brought to see that the new system changes their employers from antagonists to friends who are working as hard as possible side by side with them, all pushing in the same direction (...) All but a few of them will come to understand in a general way that under the new order of things they are cooperating with their employers to make as great a saving as possible and that they will receive their fair share of this gain."

---

[53] Taylor (1903, p98).
[54] Taylor (1903, p98, 99).
[55] Taylor (1903, p99-104).
[56] Taylor (1903, p130-132).

It is the responsibility of the workmen "... to change from their old easy-going ways to a higher rate of speed, and to learn to stay steadily at their work, think ahead and make every minute count."[57] In other words, he has to work according to the 'one best way' and use the 'one best implement'.[58] Taylor remarks that there is 'comparatively little opposition' on the part of the workmen to cooperate with the management.[59] He states that under Scientific Management the labourer works harder and better than under the old system.[60] Taylor commends the contribution of the workmen highly[61]:

> "Nine-tenths of the improvements that have come under Scientific Management have come from this friendly cooperation on the part of the workmen with the management. Almost all of the best suggestions for improvement come from intelligent workmen who are cooperating in the kindliest way with the management to accomplish the joint result of producing a big surplus which can be divided between the two sides equitably."

Taylor remarks that some workmen, despite their best intentions, fail to work within the new system. Others are so 'balky' and 'lazy' that teaching and kind treatment does not lead to any improvement in behaviour.[62]

2.6 The 'very essence' of Scientific Management

What is the 'very essence' of Scientific Management? Taylor answers this question extensively during his testimony. This 'very essence' consists of two principles: first, a complete mental revolution on the side of the workmen and the management; and second, a scientific investigation of the job to determine the 'one best way' and the 'one best implement'. In Taylor's words[63]:

> "Scientific Management is not any efficiency device, nor a device of any kind for securing efficiency; nor is it any bunch or group of efficiency devices. It is not a new system of figuring costs; it is not a new scheme of paying men; it is not a piecework system; it is not a bonus system; it is not a premium system; it is no scheme for paying men; it is not holding a stop watch on a man and writing things down about him (...) It is not divided foremanship or functional foremanship (...)
> Now, in its essence, Scientific Management involves a complete mental revolution on the part of the workingman engaged in any particular establishment or industry –

57	Taylor (1903, p132).
58	For references see under 2.4. See also Taylor (1911, p83, 123).
59	Taylor (1912, p43).
60	Taylor (1911, p36).
61	Taylor (1912, p148). See also Taylor (1912, p196).
62	Taylor (1903, p132) and Taylor (1912, p174).
63	Taylor (1912, p26-31).

a complete mental revolution on the part of these men as to their duties toward their work, toward their fellow men, and toward their employers. And it involves the equally complete mental revolution on the part of those on the management's side – the foreman, the superintendent, the owner of the business, the board of directors – a complete mental revolution on their part as to their duties toward their fellow workers in the management, toward their workmen, and toward all of their daily problems. And without this complete mental revolution on both sides Scientific Management does not exist (…)

This, gentlemen, is the beginning of the great mental revolution which constitutes the first step toward Scientific Management. It is along this line of complete change in the mental attitude of both sides; of the substitution of peace for war; the substitution of hearty brotherly cooperation for contention and strife; of both pulling hard in the same direction instead of pulling apart; of replacing suspicious watchfulness with mutual confidence; of becoming friends instead of enemies; it is along this line, I say, that Scientific Management must be developed (…) this new outlook – this new viewpoint – is of the very essence of Scientific Management.

There is, however, one more change in viewpoint which is absolutely essential to the existence of Scientific Management. Both sides must recognise as essential the substitution of exact scientific investigation and knowledge for the old individual judgement or opinion.

These are the two absolutely essential elements of Scientific Management."

In *Principles of Scientific Management* Taylor states that the "… philosophy of Scientific Management is just beginning to be understood …."[64] In the course of the testimony, Taylor was asked how many companies use his system in its entirety. His answer is humiliating: "In its entirety – none; not one."[65]

2.7 Evaluation

At the time Fred Taylor started his apprenticeship at Ferrel & Jones the conditions for industry were very bad. An economic depression had arisen like none before. The unemployment rates were high. The wages were low. In addition, many families were starving. In this situation, Taylor developed his views about the joint interests of employers and employees; an interest that would result in high profits for the employer, and secure jobs and high wages for the employees. Against this background, it can be understood that Taylor was seen as 'Mr. Progressive' who criticised the evil of the existing industrial system and offered a way out under the guidance of science.[66]

Taylor was a man of immense spirit and intelligence. He managed to extract the best from everybody in his environment. He became a zealous purveyor of the

---

64 Taylor (1911, p27).
65 Taylor (1912, p280).
66 Kanigel (1997, p504).

'new gospel of the industrial enlightenment'.[67] In his Boxly talks and factory tours he convinced large groups of managers of the truth of his approach.

Taylor was also a controversial person. Many saw him as a maker of the modern world. Others viewed him as a modern slave driver. Many adored him as a saint. Others viewed him as a devil. Taylor deserved his controversial position not least due to his difficult personality. Kanigel describes him as a "… volcano that could erupt at any time, for any reason."[68] He fought with everyone. He had a genius to make enemies. He even managed to irritate his best friends. Taylor proclaimed that Scientific Management would substitute peace for war. However, he did not have the ability 'to walk the talk'.

Scientific basis

As a child, technical and scientific matters already moved Fred Taylor. In his holiday diaries, many mathematical problems can be found. An old friend remembers that Fred constantly experimented with his legs "… to discover the step which would cover the greatest distance with the least expenditure of energy."[69] At Midvale, this aptitude was challenged. Taylor found himself in a company in which scientific methods were used to solve metallurgical problems. In this environment, he started scientifically studying cutting processes and other production processes.

Adam Smith had already propagated the division of work in *The Wealth of Nations* (1776) to improve the efficiency of manufacturing processes. Taylor continued this track. His position in history will be marked by the *scientific study* of manufacturing processes. That means, breaking down the work into elementary units, determining the one best way, developing the one best implement, and implementing the scientific standard. Contemporaries and disciples have added a number of comparable methods and techniques. For example, Frank Gilbreth invented motion studies and Henry Ford designed the assembly line. Without a doubt, Taylor laid the fundamentals of a new mode of manufacturing: mass production. For many decades, this mode has been superior.

Taylor was an engineer in heart and soul. He investigated the problems of manufacturing from a technical perspective. He believed that this perspective would solve the 'labour problem' definitively. In his testimony, he stated repeatedly that a strike had never broken out in shops that were managed according to his methods.[70] Taylor cannot be blamed for choosing a technical perspective. However, he has to be blamed for not realising the limitations of his perspective. For example, in *Shop Management* Taylor remarks that "Through generations of bitter experiences working men as a class have learned to look upon all change as antagonistic to their best interests."[71] He did not realise that the workmen would also include his methods within the category of changes that would be 'antagonis-

---

[67]   Kanigel (1997, p412).
[68]   Kanigel (1997, p354).
[69]   Kanigel (1997, p104).
[70]   Taylor attributed the strike at Watertown to a wrong application of his methods (Kanigel, 1997, p450).
[71]   Taylor (1903, p137).

tic' to their best interests. He did not understand that the workers did not share his belief in science. [72] He did not grasp that trust cannot be bought by paying a high bonus.

The Mental Revolution

Taylorism is more than a bundle of tools and techniques. It is above all a vision that industrial conflict could be resolved scientifically for the good of all. This vision arises strongly from his testimony. He describes the 'very essence' of Scientific Management as a complete mental revolution (section 2.6). He believed that science as a neutral arbiter could align the interests of employees and employers. He was absolutely convinced that a scientific approach could prevent any labour unrest.

Taylor fought bitter wars to introduce scientific methods in the factory. He urged employees to work according to his ways. He dismissed workers who did not obey him immediately. He used hierarchical power to implement Scientific Management. He conveyed the message – with his own behaviour – that management, power and Scientific Management were closely related. Through this, Taylor confirmed the existing power relations as present in the employer-employee relationship. He did not take any additional measures to guarantee that both the interests of the employer and employee would be served. He did not define any special conditions to limit the arbitrariness and misuse of power from the side of the employer. He did not implement any new organisational structures to support the mental revolution. In conclusion, he believed that such a mental revolution could be realised without a change in the existing power relations.

This issue was also raised during the hearings. Mr. Wilson, Chairman of the Special Committee, compared the mental revolution with "... the lion and the lamb laying down together ..."[73] Taylor rejected this comparison. He replied that Scientific Management could not exist in shops with lions at the head. He stated that "Injustice is typical of some other management, not of scientific management."[74] Taylor must have realised that the chairman touched a weak spot. In a letter to a potential witness, he wrote that the statement that injustice is incompatible with Scientific Management is "... the most effective weapon (...) against inconvenient questions."[75]

---

[72] From the beginning, the scientific basis of Scientific Management has been questioned. Already in 1911 an engineer wrote an article with the title 'Has Scientific Management science?' (Kanigel, 1997, p508). During the hearings the scientific content of his approach was also questioned critically (Taylor, 1912). In practice, Taylor did not always follow his own instructions. For example, he introduced a piece-rate system at the paper mill without time studies. Furthermore, scientific experts appeared to be falible. For example, in the shovelling experiments, a serious mistake was made (Kanigel, 1997, p254, 511, 512).

[73] Taylor (1912, p152).

[74] Taylor (1912, p152, 153).

[75] Kanigel (1997, p477).

Complete control

The objective of Taylor was to control the manufacturing process completely. All elements of his system – scientific study of the manufacturing process, standardised processes, standardised tools, training of the workmen, functional bosses, hierarchical control, and payment system – were focused on completely controlling the production organisation. This complete control also involved a domination of the employee. This idea is strongly expressed in the Introduction of *The Principles of Scientific Management* where Taylor writes that "In the past man has been first; in the future the system must be first."[76] Precisely this statement shows that in the philosophy of Scientific Management the employee has to be shaped in such a way that s/he fits into the scientifically designed system. This statement shows – using the words of the critical management studies – that Scientific Management 'produces' its own labourers.[77]

There is an inherent contradiction in Taylor's thinking. His system is based on two pillars: (1) a complete mental revolution and (2) scientific control of the manufacturing process (see section 2.6). However, these pillars are incompatible with each other. A complete mental revolution excludes scientific control of the manufacturing process; complete scientific control of the manufacturing process rules out a complete mental revolution. Scientific Management has focused its attention on the complete control of the manufacturing process, including the complete control of the employee. Consequently, the dignity and freedom of the employee is fundamentally affected.

Humanity

Most of the issues raised against the principles of Taylor were already present in an embryonic form in the resolutions in Congress, in the hearings of the Special Committee, and in the articles of the papers at the time. For example, in House Resolution 90 it was stated that under Taylor only the strongest could survive[78]:

> "(...) the said 'Taylor system' appears to be of such a character and nature as to be detrimental to the best interests of American workingmen, being in its essential parts a 'high-speed' process, where none but the strong survive and they being crowded constantly to the maximum point of physical exertion."

In the hearings, Taylor denied that Scientific Management demanded more arduous labour. He emphasised that the job was actually easier due to the improved working methods. However, in one of his talks he stated that you have to pay a bonus to a first-class man "... to get him work like the devil.".[79] The experiments done by Taylor and his co-workers showed that this statement appeared to be true.

---

[76] Taylor (1911, p7).

[77] Jacques (1996) has investigated the industrialisation process in the United States of America. He has shown that in the course of this process the 'industrial employee' replaced the 'federalist citizen'. See also Alvesson and Willmott (1996, 1999).

[78] Kanigel (1997, p448).

[79] Kanigel (1997, p209).

During the pig iron handling experiments it was remarked that it was considerably difficult to get men who were able to stand this work.[80] In addition, during the inspection of bicycle ball experiments "...many of the most intelligent, hardest working, and most trustworthy girls' were laid off."[81]

In the papers, the inhuman aspects of the Taylor system were criticised. For example, the head of the American Federation of Labour wrote[82]:

> "[The Taylor system makes] every man merely a cog or a nut or a pin in a big machine, fixed in the position of a hundredth or a thousandth part of the machine, with no need to employ more than a few mechanical motions nor any brain power except the little required in making those motions."

Taylor emphasised that all brainwork had to be removed from the shop floor[83], which meant that the main task of the employee was to execute the physical operations. Informally, he also stressed that the workmen were only hired for their mechanical ability and that he did not care for their initiative.[84]

Taylor prided himself on his intimate contact with the workers on the shop floor. Repeatedly, he reminded his listeners that he started his career as a labourer. Nevertheless, his empathy with the workmen did not run so deep. Taylor cherished his freedom and independence. He would never have worked under his own system.

Industrial utopia

One question remains. Why would a man who did not need to work at all devote his life to create an industrial utopia? Robert Kanigel has tried to answer this question in his book *The One Best Way*. He remarks that there was a natural split between Taylor's early period as an apprentice at the pump works and his second period as a gang boss at Midvale. The first period was characterised by the warmth and friendship of his colleagues, and the second one by hate and bitterness of his subordinates. Kanigel suggests that Fred was determined to get back what he once had: friends in the shop. He wanted 'to reclaim Eden'.[85]

Conclusion

Frederick Taylor caused a revolution in management thinking. He declared that the principal object of management should be to secure maximum prosperity for both the employer and the employee. He redefined the responsibilities of management. He pleaded for a mental revolution from the side of the employer. He advocated the development of a manufacturing science. Taylor developed the foundations of a new mode of factory management: mass production. He discovered new

---

[80]   Taylor (1911, p61) and Kanigel (1997, p322, 323).
[81]   Taylor (1911, p90).
[82]   Kanigel (1997, p446).
[83]   Taylor (1903, p98).
[84]   Kanigel (1997, p226, 391).
[85]   Kanigel (1997, p215 ff.).

tools and techniques. He invented methods to manage a factory scientifically. Rightly, he can be named the father of Scientific Management.

An unambiguous conclusion about the principles of Taylor is not possible. On the one hand, Scientific Management contributed strongly to the development of the western economy. Both employers and employees reaped the fruits of this approach. On the other hand, Scientific Management resulted in dehumanisation and alienation. At the hearings, the detrimental effects of this system were already pointed out. Later studies in mass production confirmed that these phenomena are inherent to this approach. On the one hand, Scientific Management values the contribution of the workmen to the standardisation and improvement of the manufacturing process. Taylor writes positively about this contribution regularly. On the other hand, Scientific Management did not develop any methods and techniques to give this contribution an organisational foundation. Furthermore, in daily practice and informal discussions Taylor stressed that he hired the workmen only for their strength and mechanical ability and that he did not care for their initiative. On the one hand, Scientific Management advocates a different style of management, a style that is characterised by cooperation with and continuous support of the workmen. On the other hand, Scientific Management did not change the hierarchical relations in the manufacturing organisation, which meant that the new style of management could not develop.

The spirit of Taylor is about everywhere in industrial practice. Manufacturing organisations are still dominated by a technological approach and a hierarchical style of management. Scientific Management has been replaced by Industrial Engineering. Continuous improvement has been incorporated (Lean Production). However, the tensions between science and humanity, domination and freedom, and power and trust are still present; with all their consequences. From my perspective, the following characteristics of Scientific Management are the most problematic: the extreme division of labour, the one-sided technical approach in the design of industrial organisations, the hierarchical power structure, instrumental view on the employee, the absence of attention paid to the influence of the environment, and a static view on organisations.

3 Socio-Technical Systems Design: Participative Democracy

In 1949, Ken Bamforth of the Tavistock Institute of Human Relations visited the Elsecar mine in South-Yorkshire, England. He discovered a new form of organisation of work .[86] Along with Eric Trist, he investigated this form thoroughly. This discovery led to a new organisation paradigm: Socio-Technical Systems Design.

Trist was a social psychologist. Ken Bamforth was an ex-miner. The Elsecar mine was his old pit. At that time, the mining process was organised in the following way. A group of about forty to fifty miners formed a production unit. The workmen were divided over three shifts. Every shift was specialised in certain activities. The first shift prepared the coal front. The second shift expanded the underground network. The third shift removed and transported the coal. The total production cycle took twenty-four hours. However, Trist and Bamforth discovered an unknown form of organisation of work during their visit. In a new seam, the usual technology used to mine coal could not be applied. Therefore, the technology was adapted to the new situation. This adaptation made a change in organisation of work possible. The division of labour was strongly reduced. A group of eight miners became responsible for the full cycle in coal extraction: preparing the coal front, expanding the network, and removing and transporting the coal. The 'new' form of organisation of work resembled the situation that existed before mechanisation. Trist and Bamforth investigated the psychological, social, and economic consequences of the different technologies and organisations of work used to mine coal. They concluded that the production process has to be characterised as a socio-technical system. Further, they emphasised that workers should have the authority to coordinate their own labour. These conclusions initiated the birth of a new paradigm.

The basic objective of the Socio-Technical Systems Design is to put an end to the extreme division of labour that has dominated industrial work since the introduction of Scientific Management. Socio-Technical Systems Design implies a fundamental redesign of the organisation. This redesign is focused on the design of the workplace, design of the factory, control of labour, and communication. The aim of Socio-Technical Systems Design is – according to the essential objectives as described in the Dutch approach – to improve the quality of work, quality of organisation, and quality of work relations.

In modern Socio-Technical Systems Design, different schools can be distinguished. I will focus my attention on the Dutch approach as developed by Ulbo De Sitter and others. The main reasons to highlight this approach – which is also named Integral Organisation Renewal – is that it offers a detailed design theory and design methodology. At the same time, participative change strategy is proposed. In addition, some attention will be given to the Australian approach (Participative Design) and the Scandinavian approach (Democratic Dialogue). These approaches are focused on the change process.

---

[86]   Trist and Bamforth (1951).

The approach of Socio-Technical Systems Design will be explored using the following key texts. The background and key characteristics are described using the solid study *The Paradigm that changed the Work Place* (1993) by Frans van Eijnatten. The approach of Integral Organisation Renewal will be introduced based on the article 'From Complex Organisations with Simple Jobs to Simple Organisations with Complex Jobs' (1997) by Ulbo de Sitter, Friso den Hertog and Ben Dankbaar. The methods of Participative Design will be outlined using the volume *Participative Design for Participative Democracy* (1993) by Marilyn Emery, Fred Emery and Alan Davies; and the approach of Democratic Dialogue will be summarised using the study *Dialogue and Development* (1993) by Björn Gustavsen.

This section has the following set up: it starts with the background of Socio-Technical Systems Design (3.1), followed by the key characteristics of Socio-Technical Systems Design (3.2), a description of Integral Organisational Renewal 3.3), an outline of Participative Design (3.4), a portrayal of Democratic Dialogue (3.5), and an evaluation (3.6).

3.1 Background

Van Eijnatten distinguishes three main phases in the development of Socio-Technical Systems Design[87]:

- o   Phase I (1949 - 1959+) : The period of the Socio-Technical Pioneering Work;
- o   Phase II (1959 - 1971+): The period of Classical Socio-Technical Systems Design;
- o   Phase III (1971 - xxxx) : The period of Modern Socio-Technical Systems Design.

The first phase of Socio-Technical Systems Design is closely coupled with the pioneering work of the Tavistock Institute.[88] From the start, the policy of this institute was to investigate social phenomena in real-life settings. The aim was to understand these phenomena by changing them. In other words, action research was chosen as the main strategy. The discoveries of Trist and Bamforth initiated a number of experiments in British coalmines. Semi-autonomous working groups were introduced at various locations. In the pioneering phase, the experimental results were explained using psychoanalytical theory, group theory, and systems theory.

The second phase of Socio-Technical Systems Design is related to the 'Industrial Democracy' programme in Norway.[89] In this country, a favourable climate was present to start large-scale experiments. Employers, employees, and government formed a joint committee to study problems of industrial organisations. The

---

[87]   Van Eijnatten (1993, p17).

[88]   Van Eijnatten (1993, p22-32). See also Trist and Murray in Trist and Murray (1993, p1-34).

[89]   Van Eijnatten (1993, p32-44).

Trontheim Institute of Industrial Social Research did the research. This institute called in the help of their British colleagues. Einar Thorsrud of the Norwegian Work Institute and Fred Emery of the Tavistock Institute designed the Industrial Democracy project. The most important objective was to study "… the roots of industrial democracy under the condition of personal participation in the work-place."[90] The program included a number of field experiments in which alternative forms of organisation of work were developed. These experiments were concentrated mainly around semi-autonomous groups. The change process was systematically elaborated. The starting point was a socio-technical analysis of the business situation, followed by a description of the company policy. After that, a change program was formulated. A number of methods and techniques were developed to guide this program. In this period a number of basic concepts were elaborated in more detail; amongst others the concept of the changing environment, the definition of a socio-technical system, and the main socio-technical design principles.

In the third phase of Socio-Technical Systems Design, the tools and techniques of the socio-technical approach were elaborated on in detail and the theoretical framework was given a solid foundation. Four 'schools' can be identified in this phase of the Socio-Technical Systems Design[91]:

- o   School A (1971 - xxxx): Participative Design;
- o   School B (1973 - xxxx): Integral Organisational Renewal;
- o   School C (1979 - xxxx): Democratic Dialogue;
- o   School D (1971 - xxxx): North-American Consultancy.

These schools share some fundamental orientation and assumptions. The first three schools emphasise that an effective organisation should have a 'development orientation' and have the 'characteristics of a learning environment'.[92] They reflect an image of man as a 'responsible actor'.[93] The fourth variant is a continuation of the first phase of Socio-Technical Systems Design.[94]

3.2 General characteristics of Socio-Technical Systems Design

Van Eijnatten characterises Socio-Technical Systems Design by means of six statements[95]:

- o   "Statement 1: Socio-Technical Systems Design involves a basic shift in organisational paradigm. Socio-Technical Systems Design adds as its basic philosophy a set of democratic values to organisation theory.

---

[90]   Quoted from Van Eijnatten (1993, p33).
[91]   Van Eijnatten (1993, p18).
[92]   Van Beinum in Van Eijnatten (1993, pxxii).
[93]   Van Beinum in Van Eijnatten (1993, pxxiii).
[94]   Van Eijnatten (1993, p76-80). See for example Taylor and Felten (1993).
[95]   Van Eijnatten (1993, p2).

- Statement 2: Socio-Technical Systems Design is neither a management approach, nor a workers seizure. As a holistic approach, Socio-Technical Systems Design tries to combine both interests.
- Statement 3: Socio-Technical Systems Design has strong roots in participation. With respect to organisational policy, Socio-Technical Systems Design adds to the usual technical and economic goals a set by relevant human goals.
- Statement 4: Socio-Technical Systems Design propagates a dual design orientation, creating both democratic structures ànd democratic social processes at the same time.
- Statement 5: Socio-Technical Systems Design is not exactly a theory-based sound academic discipline. Developed as an action research movement, Socio-Technical Systems Design is, above all, pragmatic, applied and problem-oriented. As such, it has acquired only a modest position in the formal system.
- Statement 6: Socio-Technical Systems Design as a field is not very homogeneous. Although, there is a lot of shared common ground, conceptual and methodological diversity has developed over the years, resulting in various approaches, applied in different areas."

These six statements express a paradigmatic change in organisational theory. The old organisation could be characterised with the words 'autocracy', 'bureaucracy' and 'hierarchy'. The new organisation has to be characterised with the words 'democracy', 'network', and 'participation'. In this context, the word 'democracy' does not refer to the representation of employees in decision-making processes on company level, but to the authority of employees to coordinate their own labour activities. Emery and Emery define democracy as "… locating responsibility for coordination clearly and firmly with those whose efforts require coordination …"[96]

---

[96]   F. and M. Emery in Emery (1993, p108).

The old and the new paradigm have been discussed extensively by Trist, Van Beinum, and Ketchum and Trist. Van Eijnatten gives the following summary[97]:

	Old paradigm	New paradigm
(1)	Redundancy of parts	Redundancy of functions
(2)	External coordination and control	Internal coordination and control
(3)	Autocracy	Democracy
(4)	Fragmented socio-technical system	Joint optimisation of the socio-technical system
(5)	Technological imperative – man as extension of machine, a commodity	Man is complementary to the machine and a resource to be developed
(6)	Organisational design based on total specification	Organisation design based on minimum critical specification
(7)	Maximum task breakdown, narrow skills	Optimum task grouping, multiple broad skills
(8)	Building block is one person – one task	Building block is self-managing social system
(9)	Alienation	Involvement and commitment

I would like to comment briefly on these characteristics. (1) In the new paradigm, the labour division is strong reduced. Every employee can perform several functions. (2) In the new paradigm, the control of the employee by a supervisor is reduced in favour of control by the employee him- or herself. (3) The new paradigm supports the participation of employees in the decision-making process with respect to their own workplace. (4) The new paradigm claims an integral approach to social, economic and technological aspects. (5) The new paradigm considers employees as a valuable resource for the organisation. (6) The new paradigm prefers to design the contours of an organisation and allow the details to be outlined by the workers themselves. (7) The new paradigm promotes limiting the breaking down of tasks and advocates multi-skilled employees who perform different tasks. (8) The new paradigm takes the group as starting point of the organisation. The employees in the group have the authority to control their own work. (9) Labour division leads to alienation. The involvement of employees and a labour system with 'whole tasks' leads to commitment.

---

[97] Van Eijnatten (1993, p10). See for example also Cherns (1987), and Trist and Murray (1993).

There is also a change in personal attitude between the old and the new paradigm. Van Eijnatten gives the following summary[98]:

	Old attitude	New attitude
(1)	Feeling of having learned it all	Learning never stops
(2)	Reductionist thinking	Systems thinking
(3)	Dependence on procedures	Focus on results
(4)	False simplicity	Complexity
(5)	It is 'they' who are to blame	Personal accountability
(6)	Virtue of being certain	Doubt
(7)	Belief in stability	Continuous change

(1) The new attitude is characterised by continuous learning. (2) The new attitude is based on thinking in wholes. (3) The new attitude is focused on attaining good results instead of adhering to standard procedures. (4) Personal assumptions and pre-conceptions should be made explicit in order to find real solutions. (5) Individuals should take responsibility themselves instead of blaming others. (6) In a rapidly changing world, it is not good to pretend certainty. A more doubtful attitude will stimulate learning and will result in better achievements. (7) Finally, the business environment is far from stable. Our world is characterised by continuous change.

The old and new paradigms differ strongly in their theoretical backgrounds.[99] The old paradigm is characterised by the machine approach. The organisation is seen as a machine that consists of clearly defined parts. The individual parts behave in a predictable way. Consequently, turning the right knobs can control the behaviour of the whole organisation. The new paradigm is characterised by a systems approach. The organisation is seen as an open system that interacts with the environment. The system will adapt itself to the changing environment. In the old paradigm, the researcher is seen as an objective investigator who tests clearly defined hypotheses. In the new paradigm, the researcher is seen as actor who influences the organisation under investigation.

3.3 Integral Organisational Renewal

3.3.1 Background

In the mid-seventies, many experiments in work design were set up in The Netherlands. The leading company in this field was Philips. The diffusion of new practices to other plants and other firms appeared to be slow. The redesign process was supported by a number of production managers and external experts. However,

---

[98] Van Eijnatten (1993, p10). See for example also Cherns (1987), and Trist and Murray (1993).

[99] Van Eijnatten (1993, p12-16, p81-111).

90

higher management and staff departments did not back up this process. The result was that the forces behind this process were not strong enough. In addition, it became clear that the organisational environment in which the new work forms were embedded limited the diffusion. The redesign process also had to include the design of the product, choice of the production technology, logistical structure of the factory, accounting system and so on.

A network of researchers, consultants, and managers, who were specialised in organisational design, started The Netherlands Institute for the Improvement of the Quality of Work and Organisation. The objective was to develop an integral framework for organisational redesign. The word 'integral' refers in this context to the quality of work (well-being of employees), the quality of the organisation (efficiency and effectiveness of the organisation), and the quality of work relations (social relations between management, employees, unions and so on).[100] The pioneering work of De Sitter was taken as a starting point.

The conditions for this framework were formulated as follows[101]:

o "The design theory must embrace concepts and principles which are generally applicable irrespective of the specific nature of the organisation.
o The design theory should focus on structural design as well as on the 'learning' aspects of organisational development.
o The theory must open possibilities to customise the design for specific organisations.
o The theory must be easily applicable and manageable in actual practice.
o The design theory should be easily communicable and provide a language in which managers and workers from different functional areas can talk effectively about the same organisational problems and solutions.
o The theory must incorporate active involvement of management and empowerment of the workers concerned.
o The theory cannot be partial in approach, but should deal with the organisation as a whole."

These efforts have resulted in Integral Organisational Renewal.

The Dutch approach is founded in the above theory. The organisation is seen as an open system. This means that every organisation interacts continuously with its environment. Therefore, the design of a production system depends strongly on the requirements of the environment, e.g. customers, labour market, legal regulations and so on.

The Dutch approach has resulted in a coherent set of design principles, design rules and design sequences. This approach has been elaborated on in a number of Dutch books.[102] The main publication in the English language is the article 'From

---

[100] De Sitter (1981, p77 ff.).
[101] De Sitter et al. (1997, p502).
[102] De Sitter discusses the development of labour in western society in *Op weg naar nieuwe fabrieken en kantoren (Developing new factories and offices)* (1981). In this book, he also sketches the contours of a new approach. De Sitter et al. elaborate on the

Complex Organisations with Simple Jobs to Simple Organisations with Complex Jobs' from Ulbo de Sitter, Friso den Hertog and Ben Dankbaar (1997).

3.3.2 Examples of socio-technical redesign

In the course of the years, several hundreds of industrial projects using the Dutch approach have been executed. Several of these projects have been documented well.[103] Two examples of socio-technical redesign will be described. The first example concerns the redesign of a silversmithing company.[104]

> *Example.* Zilverstad in Schoonhoven (The Netherlands) is a family-owned company, founded in 1875. This company produces and sells old premium and corporate gifts, jewellery, and souvenirs. About two third of the turnover comes from their own production and the rest from foreign production. In the seventies, they experienced a dramatic reduction in turnover as a result of severe competition from the Far East. They decided to change the strategic course of the company. They replaced their low-cost commodity products with high-quality special products. This change involved the introduction of several new production techniques. At the same time, they prepared to export to Germany, Belgium, and France.
>
> The new course appeared to be successful from the beginning; new markets were developed and sales increased strongly. Then customers started asking for shorter lead times and yet higher quality. The organisation could not cope with these requirements. The variety in products was too large; and the internal processes were too complex.
>
> In 1990, the organisation of Zilverstad was redesigned according to the ideas of Integral Organisation Renewal. At that moment, the company was organised functionally with a centralised staff and employed about 80 people. The redesign process resulted in an organisation with the following characteristics:
>
> o The manufacturing organisation was rearranged into three parallel groups: White Group, Blue Group and Yellow Group. The groups are characterised by differences in batch size and technology. The White Group manufactures large batches, mainly spoons. The Blue Group manufactures medium batches, mainly composite products. The Yellow Group manufactures small batches, mainly jewellery. Every group functioned as a self-managing team.

---

socio-technical design theory in *Het flexibele bedrijf (The flexible company)* (1986). De Sitter gives an extensive review of his approach in *Synergetisch produceren (Synergetic manufacturing)* (1994). Van Ewijk-Hoevenaars et al. present a practical guide to the design of organisations and the process of change in *Naar eenvoud in organisatie (To simplicity in organisation)* (1995). Van Eijnatten et al. examines the essence of the socio-technical approach in *Socio-technisch ontwerpen (Socio-technical designing)* (1996). This book also compares the Dutch approach with Lean Management and Business Process Reengineering.

[103] See for example De Sitter (1981), Van Eijnatten (1993), Roberts (1993), Hooft (1996), De Sitter et al. (1997) and Eijbergen (1999).

[104] Roberts (1993) has described this case.

- o A fourth group was introduced to manage the wholesale business. This group also functioned as a self-managing team.
- o In the whole task group, many management functions were integrated: planning, quality, the purchase of specific materials, the improvement of technologies, and budgetary control.

The new organisation led to rich rewards: higher productivity, shorter lead times, higher delivery reliability, less inventory, and an increase in turnover. In addition, absenteeism decreased.

The second example concerns the redesign of a company specialised in non-woven products.[105]

Example. The business unit: Industrial Non-wovens of Akzo Nobel, develops, manufactures, and sells non-woven floor covering, roofing, and other products. The unit employs about 250 people. At that time the business was quite profitable and competition was moderate. However, management did expect a change in the business environment. They anticipated demands from the market to increase: shortened lead times, improved quality, lower prices, and an increase in variety.

In 1989, the management decided to redesign the business unit according to the principles of Integral Organisational Renewal. It was concluded that the present organisation with its functional set-up had to be drastically changed. The redesign resulted in an organisation with the following characteristics:
- o Three parallel self-managing production teams were introduced. Each team covered a separate product/market combination.
- o The staff activities were decentralised and located in the self-managing teams.
- o A great effort was put into training, information systems, and employee flexibility.

The results of the redesign appeared to be very positive. Productivity greatly increased, costs per unit decreased considerably, and absenteeism was lowered by 2 %.

In the beginning of the nineties, it became clear that the changes that were anticipated by management appeared to be more severe than expected. Prices decreased dramatically and the speed of innovation became very high. The business unit was prepared to cope with these changes.

The Zilverstad and Industrial Non-wovens cases demonstrate two typical socio-technical characteristics. Firstly, the breaking up of the (production) organisation into parallel self-managing groups and secondly, the integration of staff functions in these groups. The new organisation led to a strong reduction in complexity and an increased control capacity.

---

[105] Bussemakers and Den Hertog in Van Ewijk-Hoevenaars et al. (1995, p221-223) describe details.

3.3.3 Basic concepts
The Dutch approach is based on four basic concepts[106]:

- o The concept of Integral Design;
- o The concept of Controllability;
- o The twin concepts of Production Structure and Control Structure;
- o The concept of Structural Parameters.

The concept of Integral Design states that a truly integral socio-technical design should include the different aspect systems and subsystems of an organisation. The word 'aspect-system' is understood as the different aspects of a subsystem or system. The word 'subsystem' is understood as a coherent part of a system. The distinction between these terms is fundamental. For example, we can distinguish between a production subsystem, development subsystem, and sales subsystem. These subsystems form identified parts of a system. Every subsystem is characterised by several inter-relating aspects, e.g. technical, social, economic etc.

The concept of Controllability refers to the structural conditions that have to be realised to improve the controllability of the system. 'Controllability' is understood as the ability of the system to cope with variations. For example, a production line has to handle variations caused by the breaking down of equipment or changes in demand. The objective of this concept is to identify the structural parameters of the organisation, which determine the control capacity of the system. The objective is to match the required control capacity of the system with the actual control capacity that is built into the system.

The twin concepts of Production Structure and Control Structure point to two basic aspect-systems. The first aspect-system involves the grouping and coupling of the performance or transformation functions of the production line. The second one involves the allocation and coupling of the control functions of the production line.

The concept of Structural Parameters refers to the fundamental structural parameters of the production and control structure. These parameters specify the design of the primary production process, primary control structure, and organisation of the supporting functions.

3.3.4 Design principles and design methodology
These basic concepts have resulted in a number of design principles, design strategies and design sequences. A summary is given in Figures 3.1 and 3.2. The red threads are reduction in complexity and increase in control capacity.

---

[106] De Sitter et al. (1997, p505).

Design Sequence

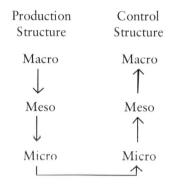

Figure 3.1 Design sequence

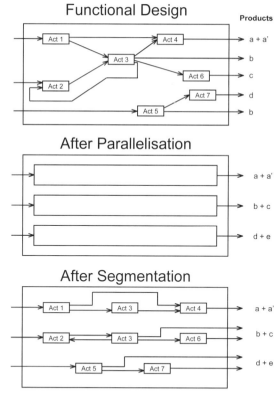

Figure 3.2 Reduction of complexity by parallelisation and segmentation (Van Ewijk-Hoevenaars (1995))

The main principles, strategies and sequence rules are[107]:

- o Design Sequence. First design the production structure and then the control structure. See Figure 3.1.
- o Design the Production Structure Top-Down. The design of the production structure starts at macro-level (see parallelisation below), proceeds to meso-level (see segmentation below), and concludes at micro-level (workstation). See Figure 3.1.
- o Parallelisation of the Production Structure. The complexity in manufacturing can be reduced strongly by designing parallel production lines. Every production line produces its own product or family of products. See Figure 3.2.
- o Segmentation of a Production Line. A production line can be split up into segments of relating production steps. The boundaries of the individual segments have to be clearly defined. Segmentation also leads to reduction in complexity. See Figure 3.2.
- o Design the Control Structure Bottom Up. The design of the control structure starts at micro-level (workstation), proceeds to meso-level (segmentation) and concludes at macro-level (parallel lines). See Figure 3.1.
- o Unity of time, Location and Action. The control structure can be defined as the allocation, selection, and coupling of control cycles. The basic elements of the control cycle are measuring a parameter, judging the result, and acting. The control cycle has to be designed successively for workstations, segments, and production lines. The leading principle of control is 'unity of time, place and action'. 'Unity of time' means directly after the measurement. 'Unity of place' means at the position where the measurement is taken. 'Unity of action' means that the employee who performs the measurement also takes action.

Application of these design principles, strategies and rules at the meso-level leads to the organisation of 'self-managing groups' or 'whole-task groups'. Such a group is responsible for a production unit, i.e. a segment of a production line or a whole production line. Examples of these groups are given in the cases described above (section 3.4.2). The members of the self-managing group or whole-task group are multi-skilled. They are trained to perform the various manufacturing activities within the unit. The members of the group execute the control functions within the production unit. These functions include logistical planning, measuring quality, repair and maintenance activities, and so on.

In the Dutch approach, the quality of work is a structural parameter. It refers to the amount of control capacity that is built into a task in relation to the required control capacity. The quality of work is high when this relation is positive and low when it is negative. De Sitter points out that a shortage of internal control capacity will lead to stress, and a shortage of external control capacity to alienation.[108]

---

[107] De Sitter et al. (1997, p508-516).
[108] De Sitter (1994, p5-39) has elaborated these elements in detail.

3.3.5 Change strategy

Integral Organisational Renewal also offers a participative change strategy. This strategy consists of the following steps[109]:

- o Step 1: Raising Awareness of the Need for Change. Management, staff, operators and works council have to be convinced that a change in the organisation is required in order to cope with the dynamic business environment.
- o Step 2: Strategic orientation. The strategy of the company has to be defined or redefined. This can be done for example by an analysis of the strengths, weaknesses, threats, and opportunities. The strategic study is carried out by a group of about twenty persons. These persons are chosen from various functions, different sectors, the works council and the management team. The minimum result of the strategic exploration is a document containing a list of external requirements and an overview of the current and required performance.
- o Step 3: Structural Exploration. The discrepancies between actual and required performance are investigated thoroughly. These discrepancies are related to the structure of the production system.
- o Step 4: On-the-Job Training in Self-Design. The members of the organisation are trained to design their own work organisation. The training has a strong on-the-job character: the members of the organisation provide the content and the material.
- o Step 5: Redesign. Firstly, the production structure is designed in a top-down process. Secondly, the control structure is designed in a bottom-up process. If necessary, the design is performed in an iterative process.

In conclusion, Integral Organisational Renewal has developed a detailed design theory for complex organisations. This approach has found its footing in Dutch universities: it is taught at the universities of Eindhoven, Groningen, and Nijmegen.

3.4 Participative Design

Fred Emery developed Participative Design. He was one of the architects of the Industrial Democracy project in Norway. In 1969, he returned to Australia where he was asked to lead similar projects. These activities resulted in the development of Participative Design.

Emery attributed the disappointing results of the Industrial Democracy project to the expert approach used by researchers. The expert approach neglects the knowledge and the involvement of the people who work on the shop floor. He found out that workers have many ideas on how to redesign their workplaces. *"This is the essence of participative design."*[110] In other words, the challenge is " ... to create optimal conditions for constructive utilisation of the mutual trust re-

---

[109] De Sitter et al. (1997, p520-524).
[110] M. Emery in Emery (ed.) (1993, p14). Italics by M. Emery.

quired to produce a genuine structural alternative…"[111] Participative Design has been developed to create these conditions.

Fred Emery positions the debate about the democratisation of the workplace within the framework of the developments of western culture. He notices a remarkable contradiction. On the one hand, western society is based on the principles of democracy. On the other hand, modern western enterprises still adhere to the principles of autocracy. [112] Moreover, he advocates a shift in the type of democracy in organisations: from a representative to a participative democracy.[113] In his view employees have to control their own job. Emery writes[114]:

> "The democratisation of work can only be achieved by allowing to those who are responsible for doing a job the power to decide how they can best coordinate their efforts."

Fred and Merrelyn Emery describe participative democracy as[115]:

> "(…) *locating responsibility for co-ordination clearly and firmly with those whose efforts require co-ordination if the common objectives are to be achieved.*"

Merrelyn Emery points to the fragility of democracy at the workplace. She emphasises that democratisation has to be rooted in a "… *widespread and contextualised conceptual and practical understanding if it is to stand a change against the forces of autocracy.*"[116]

Participative Design does not offer a design theory and design methodology. Instead, some standards are offered to judge the present workplace against and to give directions for change. In *Participative Design: Work and Community Life* Fred and Merrelyn Emery propose two major 'design principles': the six psychological requirements and the redundancy of functions.

The first design principle formulates the psychological requirements that the workplace and the social climate have to meet[117]:

- o "Adequate elbow room. The sense that they [the workers] are their own bosses and that except in exceptional circumstances they do not have some boss breathing down their necks (…).
- o Changes of learning on the job and going on learning. We accept that such learning is possible only when people are able to (a) set goals that are reasonable chal-

---

[111] M. Emery in Emery (ed.) (1993, p14).
[112] F. Emery in Emery (ed.) (1993, p35).
[113] F. Emery in Emery (ed.) (1993, p37).
[114] F. Emery in Emery (ed.) (1993, p95).
[115] F. and M. Emery in Emery (ed.) (1993, p108). Italics by F. and M. Emery.
[116] M. Emery in Emery (ed.) (1993, p21). Italics by M. Emery.
[117] F. and M. Emery in Emery (ed.) (1993, p100, 101).

lenges for them and (b) get a feedback of results in time for them to correct their behaviour.

o An optimal level of variety, i.e. they can vary the work so as to avoid boredom and fatigue (...).

o Conditions where they can and do get help and respect from their work mates (...).

o A sense of one's own work meaningfully contributing to social welfare (...) Meaningfulness includes both the worth and quality of a product, and having a perception of the whole product (...).

o A desirable future. Put simply, not a dead-end job; but hopefully one with a career path which will continue to allow personal growth and skills increase."

The second design principle has to do with redundancy.[118] To behave flexibly and adaptively an organisation must contain a certain degree of redundancy. In a bureaucratic or autocratic organisation, redundancy is built in by a 'redundancy of parts'. In such an organisation every person performs one task or one set of tasks. An overcapacity of employees is present to replace sick employees or to cope with increase in demand ('redundancy of parts'). This overcapacity needs control and coordination by a person who is located one level above the one where the work is done. In a democratic organisation, redundancy is built in by a 'redundancy of functions'. In such an organisation, the employees are trained to perform various tasks and to control and coordinate their own work.[119] The redundancy of functions results in an organisation built on self-managing groups who take responsibility for their own work.

Participative Design offers several concepts and methods for change. The main ones are the Participative Design workshop and the Search Conference.

The Participative Design workshop is the starting point of the redesign process.[120] This workshop is attended by 4 to 10 people and takes 2 to 3 days. The attendants are selected from all levels of the organisation (a so-called 'deep slice'): employees, middle management, and management. Union representatives are also invited. The members are brought together based on equality and are guided by a facilitator. They receive a short training in design concepts and design techniques. They analyse and evaluate their own work situation in terms of the psychological requirements mentioned above. In the redesign phase, the production flow is analysed in more detail and alternative designs are developed for the workplace. After that, these alternatives are evaluated with respect to the psychological requirements; one of the alternatives is chosen, and an implementation plan is made. The participants of the workshop guide the whole change process from the design to the implementation.

---

[118]   F. and M. Emery in Emery (ed.) (1993, p102-110).
[119]   F. and M. Emery in Emery (ed.) (1993, p105).
[120]   F. and M. Emery in Emery (ed.) (1993, p110-122).

Another important technique is the so-called Search Conference.[121] The objective of a Search Conference is to plan a new future for the organisation. This new future includes the goals and strategies for working in a democratic way. The Search Conference is attended by a 'deep slice' of the organisation who conferences for two or three days. The conference is focused on a joint learning process of the attendees. The Search Conference is also a suitable tool for planning at other levels, e.g. a local industrial level.

In conclusion, Participative Design aims to develop a democratic organisation. The basic characteristic of such an organisation is that employees decide about their own workplace. Participative Design does not offer a design theory or design methodology but focuses its attention on the change process.

3.5 Democratic Dialogue

The development of the Democratic Dialogue has to be understood against the background of the Industrial Democracy program in Norway.[122] This program included a number of field experiments in industrial companies. Methods, techniques and theories were elaborated to develop a new organisation of work. A comparable program was launched in Sweden. Through the years, the problems, difficulties and limitations of this approach emerged.

Björn Gustavsen, the father of the Democratic Dialogue, remarks that at the time of the Industrial Democracy program, the situation was far from clear. However, in the light of hindsight it is possible to identify some problem areas; he mentions the following [123]: the belief that organisations could be developed by using a single theory, the dominance of experts in the change process, the problems of diffusion, and finally the issue of legitimisation. To overcome these difficulties, Gustavsen breaks with the classical expert approach. He proposes a dialogue-based interactive approach, focusing both on the development of local theories and on the creation of networks within and between organisations. Gustavsen has elaborated on this approach in *Dialogue and Development* (1992).[124] The spearhead of this approach is open communication. This means that Gustavsen presents a theory of communication and not a theory of design.[125] He characterises his approach as 'management by dialogue'.[126]

---

[121] F. and M. Emery in Emery (ed.) (1993, p214-257)
[122] This program has been described briefly in section 3.1.
[123] Gustavsen (1992, p17-26).
[124] Gustavsen juxtaposes his approach with Socio-Technical Systems Design and Lean Production in Van Eijnatten (1993, p185-191).
[125] Gustavsen (1992, p69). See also Gustavsen in Van Eijnatten (1993, p189).
[126] Gustavsen (1992, p56).

The spearhead of Democratic Dialogue is changes in the pattern of communication.[127] These changes lead to new structures in the organisation of work and technology. This process follows the following cycle[128]:

Changes in patterns of communication	$\Rightarrow$	Changes in which issues are defined as subject to development and the way in which development work is performed
$\Uparrow$		$\Downarrow$
Changes in the selection and configuration of technological elements	$\leftarrow$	Changes in the organisation of work

In Democratic Dialogue, language plays the leading role. Gustavsen describes the objective of research as a 'restructuring of language'.[129] Such restructuring has to be done in a participative process with those who use this language daily.[130] Language is viewed as the joining mechanism between theory and practice.[131] Therefore, the essential feature of Democratic Dialogue is not only to explore theoretically the importance of dialogue, it is also aimed at 'creating dialogues'.[132] Gustavsen stresses that dialogues are important because they are the cradles of power. He states that power is found "... first and foremost *in* the discourses."[133] [134]

Democratic Dialogue is built on the experience gained in the 'LOM-programme' in Sweden in the period between 1985 and 1990.[135] 'LOM' is an abbreviation for the Swedish terms for 'Leadership, Organisation and Co-determination'. It is a tripartite workplace development programme.

The idea of democratic dialogue plays an essential role in the Swedish programme. It is operationalised according to the following criteria[136]:

1. "The dialogue is a process of exchange: ideas and arguments move to and fro between the participants.
2. It must be possible for all concerned to participate.

---

[127] Gustavsen (1993, p69).
[128] Gustavsen (1993, p70).
[129] Gustavsen (1993, p33).
[130] Gustavsen (1993, p55).
[131] Gustavsen (1993, p36).
[132] Gustavsen (1993, p34).
[133] Gustavsen (1993, 110).
[134] Nashold (1993, p39ff) describes the underlying hypothesis of the Democratic Dialogue as a 'linguistic-organisational infrastructure'.
[135] The LOM-program has been evaluated extensively by Nashold et al. (1993).
[136] Gustavsen (1992, p3, 4).

3. This possibility for participation is, however, not enough. Everybody should also be active. Consequently, each participant has an obligation not only to put forth his or her own ideas but also to help others to contribute their ideas.
4. All participants are equal.
5. Work experience is the basis for participation. This is the only type of experience which, by definition, all participants have.
6. At least some of the experience, which each participant has when entering the dialogue, must be considered legitimate.
7. It must be possible for everybody to develop an understanding of the issues at stake.
8. All arguments, which pertain to the issues under discussion, are legitimate. No argument should be rejected on the grounds that it emerges from an illegitimate source.
9. The points, arguments, etc. which are to enter the dialogue must be made by a participating actor. Nobody can participate 'on paper' only.
10. Each participant must accept that the other participants can have better arguments.
11. The work role, authority, etc. of all participants can be made subject to discussion - no participant is exempt in this respect.
12. The participants should be able to tolerate an increasing degree of difference of opinion.
13. The dialogue must continuously produce agreements, which can provide platforms for practical action. Note that there is no contradiction between this criterion and the previous one. The major strength of a democratic system compared to all other ones is that it has the benefit of drawing upon a broad range of opinions and ideas which inform practice, while at the same time being able to make decisions which can gain the support of all participants."

To realise the idea of democratic dialogue, four 'action parameters' are proposed[137]: the clustering of enterprises, conferences, broad-based deep-slice projects, and networks.

Clustering enterprises. The basic unit of change process is a cluster of four companies. Each participating company goes through the development cycle together with three other companies.

Conferences. In the starting phase, conferences are used to initiate the democratic dialogues between the participating companies of the cluster. Each of the four companies is represented by 8 to 10 people (vertical slice). The staff of the conference comes from the research organisation that participates in the programme. The conference discusses the following topics.[138] Firstly, how a company can become a good company which has good workplaces within five years time. Secondly, what problems will be encountered in trying to realise the vision of a good workplace. Then the participants are asked to develop ideas and suggestions on how the problems could be solved. Finally, the representatives of each company sit together to

---

[137] Gustavsen (1992, p4-9).
[138] Gustavsen (1993, p42, 43).

discuss possible steps to realise a good company and a good workplace. Conferences are also used to initiate the democratic dialogue within a company.

Broad-based, deep-slice projects. The democratic dialogue leads to a broad range of different development projects. Within each company, a 'project pattern' has to be developed which broadly spans the main issues, levels and interest groups. A number of actors are invited to participate in these projects. A loose set of topics and ideas will then emerge. The change process in the company can involve these successive steps[139]: the establishment of a central project group, a project development conference, the start of a 'limited' development process, broadly organised development work, constitution of the results, evaluation, and consolidation. In democratic dialogues about the workplace and the company, a number of different theoretical sources can be relevant. However, these sources can be used in the participative process but do not form the 'spearhead' of the change program.

Networks. The arranging of conferences, the clustering of enterprises, and broad-based project designs are used to create networks. These networks have to function as an infrastructure for change and development. The long-term aim is to establish a set of networks that cover most of the industries in a country.

Why apply a democratic method? Gustavsen reviews this question again at the end of his book *Dialogue and Development*. He writes[140]:

> "If we want to mobilise all concerned, to pool their insights, synchronise their actions and ensure loyalty and support towards decisions, there is no other social organisation comparable to participative democracy."

3.6 Evaluation

The initial discoveries of Eric Trist and Ken Bamforth led to the development of a new tradition: Socio-Technical Systems Design. This tradition gained a firm foothold in several countries, e.g. Norway, Sweden, England, Australia, The Netherlands, and the United States of America. However, this approach did not break through in other industrial countries. For example, in leading Japanese textbooks on manufacturing, no references are made to this approach.[141] Within the socio-technical tradition, there is a lively discussion about the basic principles; it also juxtaposes itself with Lean Production, Business Process Reengineering, and the Mini-Company Concept. However, an in-depth discussion between the followers of Socio-Technical Systems Design and the followers of other New Production Concepts is absent.

If the tradition of Socio-Technical Systems Design has to be characterised in one word, it could be described as 'participative democracy'. The essence of a democratic organisation is that employees have the power to decide how they can

---

[139] Gustavsen (1993, p39, 40).
[140] Gustavsen (1993, p120).
[141] E.g. Monden (1998).

best coordinate their own efforts. The basic belief is that people can make far better use of their talents in a democratic organisation. Negatively expressed, it is the belief that human resources cannot – even ought not – be managed by specifying every job in detail and by designing organisations hierarchically.

Let us first summarise the basic views of these approaches. Integral Organisation Renewal emphasises the structural design of an organisation. A detailed design theory and an explicit design methodology have been developed. De Sitter states that his approach gives "... micro-structural foundation of a democracy within the realm of work."[142] In his magnum opus *Synergetisch produceren* (*Synergetic manufacturing*) he states that mobilisation of human resources is 'in the first place' a question of the organisation of labour.[143] Van Eijnatten, Kuipers and Den Hertog conclude In a recent review that the strength of the Dutch approach is her kernel: a detailed design theory; her approach: an explicit design methodology; and her starting point: participative democracy[144] In conclusion, the 'essence' of Integral Organisational Design is 'design'. A number of rules and techniques to design organisations have been developed. Many organisations in The Netherlands have been organised according to these rules and techniques. Within the design process participation and communication play an important role. However, these aspects are not well developed.

Participative Design emphasises the participative process. In this school industrial democracy is defined as 'personal participation in the workplace'.[145] The key of the participative process is that the expertise of employees is used to design the workplace.[146] This design takes place in the so-called Participative Design workshop. In this workshop, the participants are given some tools to support the design process. However, Participative Design does not encompass a design theory, design methodology, or communication theory. Its 'essence' is the participative process.

Democratic Dialogue emphasises the communication process. The essential feature of this approach is to create dialogues.[147] Gustavsen states that the strength of a dialogue is "... its ability to engage many people, utilise their experience, bring in all relevant concerns, and create commitment to the efforts."[148] A dialogue implies participation. For that reason, the Democratic Dialogue approach shares many points of similarity with Participative Design. Gustavsen questions whether a democratic approach is possible in an industrial environment because democracy and power can easily conflict. He states – based on the writings of Foucault – that the dialogue form has to be used to uncover any power issues. Democratic Dialogue has not developed a design theory or design methodology. Its 'essence' is a communicative process.

---

[142] De Sitter in Van Eijnatten (1993, p172).
[143] De Sitter (1994, p38).
[144] Van Eijnatten et al. in Van Eijnatten (1996, p289).
[145] Emery and Thorsrud, quoted from Van Eijnatten (1993, p33).
[146] M. Emery in Emery (1993, p14).
[147] Gustavsen (1992, p34).
[148] Gustavsen (1992, p83).

In conclusion, Integral Organisational Renewal, Participative Design, and Democratic Dialogue offer different methods to realise a democratic organisation. Integral Organisational Renewal focuses on the design of the organisation (and offers some tools to achieve participative change), Participative Design on the participation of employees in the change process, and Democratic Dialogue on the dialogues between the participants.

How are the different approaches in the socio-technical tradition related to each other?

First, this question can be investigated from a theoretical point of view. De Sitter emphasises that a view of 'the whole' is required to understand the different aspects of organisations.[149] Generally speaking, we could state that a view of 'the whole' is required to understand the relation between different socio-technical approaches. An integral approach to organisations requires a holistic view based on the reality in which we live. In other words, a (philosophical) ontology or cosmology is needed to relate the different aspects or dimensions of an organisation to each other; especially the relation between technical, social, psychological, communicative, and economic aspects. In the Introduction to this study (Chapter 1), I have referred to the philosophical analysis of reality as developed by the Dutch philosophers Dooyeweerd and Vollenhoven. This approach will be used in Chapter 4 to analyse the essence of each approach and to relate the different approaches to each other.

Second, this question can be investigated from a practical point of view. I would like to emphasise the importance of a design theory and design methodology. A factory manager has to make many decisions about production technologies, production layouts, the control of the manufacturing processes, horizontal and vertical communication, and so on. Integral Organisational Renewal offers a detailed design theory and design methodology to help deal with these type of decisions. Participative Design and Democratic Dialogue do not offer this. Furthermore, a factory manager needs a change strategy. Integral Organisational Renewal offers some strategies and Participative Design and Democratic Dialogue pride themselves on their participative and communicative strategies. They come down to the same thing: participation and communication. Despite all the rhetoric, these strategies are not specific enough to support a self-managing team. Furthermore, they do not identiy the importance of continuous improvement. These shortcomings of Socio-Technical Systems Design are well compensated by the Mini-Company Concept (see section 6 of this chapter).

---

[149]   De Sitter in Van Eijnatten (1993, p160-166).

4 Lean Production: The elimination of waste

In the autumn of 1973, Japan was severely hit by the oil crisis. The growth of the economy dropped to zero. Japanese managers were suddenly confronted with a decrease in production. Many companies suffered heavy financial losses. The Toyota Motor Company however, came through this crisis very well. The Japanese industry attributed this remarkable success story to Toyota's production system. From that point on, the Toyota Production System received a lot of attention. Its improvement techniques spread through the country and beyond.

The Toyota Production System is characterised by a continuous drive to eliminate waste; waste caused by overproduction, inventories and defective parts, for example. The system is built on two concepts: 'Just-In-Time' and 'Autonomation' Just-in-time is an important tool which can be used to realise continuous flow in the factory: the parts reach the assembly line at the time and in the amount they are needed. Autonomation is described as 'automation with a human touch'. Autonomation means that the equipment stops automatically when defective parts are produced. These two concepts highlight waste. This waste can then be eliminated by the application of a number of improvement techniques.

In the United States of America, the publication *The Machine that Changed the World* (1990), drew attention to Japanese production techniques. James Womack, Daniel Jones, and Daniel Roos performed a world-wide study of the car industry. They claimed that the Japanese approach was superior to western methods. They also gave these production techniques a name: Lean Production. In the meantime, many studies have been published about Japanese production techniques. As there are considerable differences between Japanese car producers, the expression 'Japanese production techniques' is not unequivocal. Generally, the Toyota Motor Corporation is seen as the founding father of Lean Production. For that reason, the focus will be on the Toyota Production System. The following key texts are used: *Toyota Production System. Beyond Large-Scale Production* (1988)[150] by Taiichi Ohno, *The Toyota Production System* (1992) by the Toyota Motor Corporation, and *Toyota Production System. An Integrated Approach to Just-In-Time* (1998)[151] by Yasuhiro Monden. In addition, the findings of two Western studies on the Toyota Production System are given.

The following topics will be discussed respectively: the background of the Toyota Production System (4.1), the idea of waste (4.2), the just-in-time principle (4.3), the concept of autonomation (4.4), the approach to standardisation and

---

[150]   The original Japanese edition *Toyota seisan hōshiki* was published in 1978.

[151]   In the Preface to the Third Edition, Monden (1998, pxv, xvi) writes: "In the first edition of this book (1983), I explained how the rationale (...) of the Toyota Production System was developed over a period of 30 years. In the second edition (1993), I added elements relating to computer technologies that enhance conventional Just-In-Time system performance (...) In this third edition of the Toyota Production System, I explain the system's recent evolution; specifically, pursuing the goal of respect for humanity".

improvement (4.5), humanity in the Toyota system (4.6), western studies to the Japanese approach (4.7). This is followed by an evaluation (4.8).

4.1 Background

Sakichi Toyoda[152] (1867-1930) was the founder of the Toyoda Spinning and Weaving Company. In 1902, he invented a loom that would stop automatically if the thread broke or ran out. This invention opened the way for automated loom-works where a single operator could handle a large number of looms. This led to a strong reduction in the wastage of materials and improved the quality of the fabric. In 1930, Sakichi Toyoda sold his patent to the Platt Brothers in England for ¥ 1 million.

In 1930, Kiichirō Toyoda, the son of Sakichi Toyoda, visited Europe and the United States of America. He reported extensively about the state of the art automobile industry. Sakichi Toyoda decided to spend the money from the Platt Brothers on automobile research. He assigned his son Kiichirō Toyoda to this new activity.

Kiichirō Toyoda started to investigate the American automobile manufacturing systems. He developed production methods to manufacture the basic materials for car production in Japan. In 1933, Kiichirō Toyoda announced the goal to locally produce cars for the public[153]:

> "We shall learn production techniques from the American method of mass production. But we will not copy it as is. We shall use our own research and creativity to develop a production method that suits our own country's situation."

The American method of mass production was adapted to meet the requirements of the Japanese market. Large quantities of cars were produced in a few different types. To prevent production losses surplus inventories of parts were along the production lines. The various parts were produced in large lots to realise a high level of efficiency. On the other hand, the Japanese market demanded small quantities of cars in many types. To cope with this requirement the various parts had to be produced in small series. More specifically, the parts had to be produced in the sequence and at the moment needed. To realise this flexibility a quick die change over was necessary. These considerations led to the 'just-in-time' idea.

In 1943, Taiichi Ohno, a graduate from the mechanical department of the Nagoya Technical High School, joined the Toyota Motor Company. Ohno began his career as an engineer in the Toyoda Spinning and Weaving Company. After the

---

[152] In the Japanese culture, the family name appears first. In Japanese publications in the English language, this custom is often not practised, e.g. Toyota (1992). In this section, the western style is adopted.

[153] Ohno (1988, p91).

closure of this company, he was transferred to the automobile section of Toyota. Ohno comments on this transfer as follows[154]:

> "My textile experience was valuable. Whether in car or fabric production, the relationship between workers and machines is basically the same."

In 1947, Ohno became in charge of one of the manufacturing machine shops of the Koromo plant. To improve production, his first step was to establish a 'flow system'.[155] To realise this flow a radical change of the layout was required. Traditionally, in a manufacturing shop the machines with the same function are grouped together and large batches of parts are machined in one process and then forwarded to the next process. As an experiment, he rearranged the various machines to follow the processing sequence. In the flow system, one part is machined in one process and immediately forwarded to the next process. Later, the machines were arranged in parallel lines or L-shapes to enable workers to operate three or four machines along the production line. These changes meant that the 'one operator - one machine' system was abandoned for the 'one operator - many machines and different processes' system. To run these lines smoothly the machines had to be greatly improved.

In 1949 the Japanese government lifted restrictions on small passenger car production and abolished price controls. In 1952, the Toyota Motor Company went into full-scale operation. Ten years later, the flow line using the kanban concept was adopted worldwide in all Toyota factories.

As mentioned before, the Toyota Production System is based on two concepts. The first one is 'just-in-time' and the second one is 'autonomation'. Both concepts find their origin in the history of the Toyota corporation. The idea of 'just-in-time' came from Kiichirō Toyoda. He proposed that in a comprehensive industry such as automobile manufacturing, the best way to work would be "... to have all parts for the assembly at the side of the line just in time for their use."[156] Taiichi Ohno elaborated on this idea further. He was inspired by the American supermarket where "... a customer can get (1) what is needed, (2) when needed, and (3) in the amount needed."[157] The idea of 'autonomation' was taken from the experiences of the Toyoda Spinning and Weaving Company. Sakichi Toyoda invented machines with a 'human-like intelligence'. He equipped the looms with a device so that they would stop automatically when the thread broke or ran out.[158]

In the preface to the English edition of *Toyota Production System*, Taiichi Ohno expresses the objectives of the Toyota Production System as follows[159]:

---

[154] Ohno (1988, p76).
[155] Ohno (1988, p10).
[156] Ohno (1988, p75), and Toyota (1992, p5).
[157] Ohno (1988, p26), and Toyota (1992, p5).
[158] Ohno (1988, p77), and Toyota (1992, p4).
[159] Ohno (1988, pxiii). Italics by M.J. Verkerk.

"The most important objective of the Toyota system has been *to increase production efficiency* by consistently and thoroughly eliminating waste. This concept and the equally important *respect for humanity* that has passed down from the venerable Sakichi Toyoda (1867-1930), founder of the company and master of inventions, to his son Kiichirō Toyoda (1894-1952), Toyota Motor Company's first president and father of the Japanese passenger car, are the foundations of the Toyota Production System."

4.2 Waste

The basis of the Toyota Production System is the absolute elimination of waste. 'Waste' refers to all work carried out that does not add value to the product. To eliminate waste, we must understand its nature. Ohno lists the following categories[160]:

"Production waste can be divided into the following categories:
- o overproduction
- o waiting
- o transporting
- o too much machining (over-processing)
- o inventories
- o moving
- o making defective parts and products."

The Toyota Production System has been designed in such a way that waste is highlighted. All techniques – flow processes, just-in-time production, autonomation techniques, standardised work procedures, and continuous improvements – support the identification of waste. Ohno stresses that it is the responsibility of management to utilise materials, equipment, floor space and manpower effectively.

Particular attention is paid to the waste of human resources. Ohno distinguishes between waste, non-added-value work and value-added work.[161] Waste refers to the needless or repetitious movements of workers. These types of movements have to be immediately eliminated. Non-added-value work refers to walking to pick up parts, opening up packages of goods which have been delivered, pushing the buttons of machines and so forth. Non-value-added work may also be regarded as waste and as such have to be eliminated. Value-added work refers to types of processing which contribute to the production of the product. Such processing adds value. In accordance with this view, Ohno states that the value of work for employees is enhanced by the elimination of wasteful and meaningless jobs.[162]

---

[160] Ohno (1988, p19, 129). See also Monden (1998, p2, 3).
[161] Ohno (1988, p57).
[162] Ohno (1988, p20).

4.3 Just-in-time

The objective of the Toyota Production System is to shorten lead-times[163]:

> "The Toyota Production System, quite simply, is about shortening the time it takes to convert customer orders into vehicle deliveries. To do that, we have arranged the entire sequence from order to delivery in a single continuous flow."

How can lead-times be shortened? With this question, we arrive at the heart of the Toyota Production System. This system is based on flow. Flow means that value is added to the product within each process while the product flows along.[164] To realise flow, a just-in-time supply of parts and a levelled production are required.[165]

To realise flow, the first requirement is to supply the parts to the line just-in-time. A 'pull' system can achieve this. To understand this principle Ohno invites his readers to think 'in reverse'.[166] In a conventional line, each process sends its output to the next station regardless of the actual needs of that station. In a 'reverse' line, the latter station goes to a former process to deliver only the output that is needed. In the Toyota Production System, the production line is taken as a starting point. The production plan, indicating the quantity of the desired types of cars, is given to the assembly line. The assembly line withdraws from the former processes only the right parts in the quantity needed and at the time needed. The direction of the manufacturing process is in reverse: it 'starts' with the finished product and 'ends' with the production processes of the parts suppliers. The links in the just-in-time chain have to be connected and synchronised.

To manage the just-in-time flow of parts a *kanban* system is used. A kanban is a printed card in a plastic envelope. The card carries all details on the production and deliveries of parts. The kanban is used within Toyota itself and between Toyota and the cooperating firms. The kanban serves several functions and operates according to the following rules for use[167]:

Functions of the kanban	Rules for use
1. Provides pick-up or transport information.	1. The latter process picks up the number of items indicated by the kanban at the former process
2. Provides production information.	2. The former process produces items in the quantity and sequence indicated by the kanban.
3. Prevents overproduction and excessive transportation.	3. No items are made or transported without a kanban.

---

[163] Toyota (1992, p2). See also Monden (1998, p105-120).
[164] Ohno (1988, p130).
[165] Monden (1998, p15-88) gives a detailed description.
[166] Ohno (1988, p5).
[167] Ohno (1988, p30).

4. Serves as a work order attached to goods.

5. Prevents defective products by identifying the defective process.

6. Reveals existing problems and maintains inventory control.

4. A kanban is always attached to the goods.

5. Defective products are not sent on to the subsequent process. The result is 100 % defect-free goods.

6. Reducing the number of kanbans increases their sensitivity.

Toyota gives the following example to illustrate the use of a kanban [168]:

Example of kanban The operator takes a new box of parts. He removes the so-called 'withdrawal' kanban from the box and deposits it in a kanban mailbox. The team leader gathers the contents of the mailboxes at prescribed times and brings them to the sorting room. In this room, an automatic sorter places the kanban cards in separate boxes for the different suppliers. The driver that brings the parts in from the supplier picks up the kanban of his company after unloading the truck. He delivers the kanban at the sorting room of the production site of the supplier. At the site, a new box of parts is already prepared. The new box contains a so-called 'production' kanban. Then, the withdrawal kanban is placed onto the new box and the production kanban is removed. The supplier delivers the new box of parts to the plant as indicated on the withdrawal kanban. The production kanban goes back to the production area of the supplier as an order for a new box of parts. This cycle is repeated continuously.

A large assembly shop at Toyota has two or more kanban stations, each of which processes about ten thousand kanbans per shift. The kanban functions as an 'organic' link between the final assembly line and the parts suppliers (internal and external). The kanban also functions as a sensitive tool to prevent and to identify waste. Ohno calls a kanban the 'autonomic nerve' of an assembly line.[169]

The second rule of kanban use means that the latter process withdraws the parts evenly in terms of time and quantity. This is not only important for the synchronisation of each production process within the Toyota Motor Company, but also for the production processes of the cooperating firms outside. To limit fluctuations a balanced planning procedure is applied. At Toyota the production planning takes place on several levels: annual, semi-annual, quarterly, monthly, every ten days, and daily. The monthly plans are used to allocate personnel and materials for the coming month. The ten-day plans enable the factories to respond to changes in domestic demand. The daily plans determine the exact sequence of the cars to be produced. The different types are spread as much as possible over the day to prevent peaks in workload and peaks in withdrawal of parts. In this way, the production line is levelled.[170]

---

[168] Toyota (1992, p24, 25).
[169] Ohno (1988, p29).
[170] Ohno (1988, p36-40), Toyota (1992, p18-22), Monden (1998, p63-74).

The just-in-time principle and the production levelling extend far beyond the factory. They shape and streamline the whole organisation. Employing these principles means drastically changing logistics, purchasing, marketing and controlling. It requires total commitment from the whole organisation.

4.4 Autonomation

The second concept of the Toyota Production System is 'autonomation' or 'automation with a human touch'.[171] Autonomation means that the production equipment is fitted with devices that stop the machine automatically when an abnormality occurs. Autonomation has a number of advantages.[172] Firstly, it stops the machine from continuing to produce defective parts. Secondly, it prevents defective parts being fed to the next station. Thirdly, it illuminates the occurrence of problems. Finally, it eliminates the need for an employee to watch over each machine continuously.

Autonomation is an important tool to drive back waste. From Toyota's perspective, watching over a machine continuously is a waste of human resources. Autonomation can help us to eliminate that type of waste. Toyota writes[173]:

> "[The Toyota Production System] is oriented towards eliminating every minute and every second that is not absolutely necessary to generate value (...) [Autonomation] eliminates the need for an operator or operators to watch over each machine continuously (...) [Autonomation] thus is a humanistic approach to configuring the human-machine interface. It liberates employees from the tyranny of the machine and leaves him free to concentrate on tasks that involve exercising human judgement."

Autonomation also employs a number of techniques to visualise information, to prevent mistakes and to highlight problems. Toyota presents the following examples[174]:

> *Examples of autonomation.* A classical example is the 'fixed-position stop system'. In this system, the worker who notices an abnormality can stop the production flow by pulling a rope overhead or by pushing a button. Immediately, a numbered lamp lights up on a large *andon* signboard to call the attention of a supervisor to the problem. The line stops when the product reaches the next 'fixed-position', that is the point where a complete job is finished. The supervisor rushes to the station indicated on the signboard and helps to correct the problem.

---

[171] Monden (1998, p221-238) gives a detailed description.
[172] Autonomation has also been inspired by considerations about safety (Ohno, 1988, p7).
[173] Toyota (1992, p7, 10).
[174] Toyota (1992, p11-16).

Another example is visual information. Every vehicle on the assembly line carries sheets that prominently display all the information about the specification of the car. People working on the line can easily see what procedures and parts to use.

A further example is to redesign the equipment in such a way that tools or work pieces cannot be mounted wrongly on the machine, e.g. a lathe can be equipped with a positioning tool so that the product cannot be mounted backwards on the spindle.

The last example is to equip a pair of stamping dies with sensors. The sensors have to detect whether semi-manufactured products are positioned properly on the lower stamping die. These sensors prevent the (expensive) dies from cracking as a result of missing or wrongly positioned work pieces.

Autonomation covers a family of techniques that support employees in preventing, highlighting and solving problems. That means that quality is built into the production processes.

What is the relation between just-in-time and autonomation? To understand this relation Ohno uses the analogy of a baseball team.[175] Autonomation corresponds to the skill and talent of the individual players, and just-in-time to the teamwork. In other words, autonomation focuses on the quality of the individual processes, and just-in-time on gearing these individual processes towards a continuous production flow.

4.5 Standardised work and improvement

Just-in-time and autonomation are the pillars of the Toyota Production System. Standardisation and improvement continuously strengthen these pillars.[176] Standards and work procedures establish the processes in an organisation and everybody has to work according to them. Standards and work procedures are continuously improved with respect to efficiency, quality, and working conditions. This continuous improvement is called *kaizen*.

Standards and work procedures are described in worksheets. In Toyota's factories, three sheets are available at each workplace: a production capacity sheet, a standardised work flow combination table, and a standardised work chart. The production capacity sheet specifies the maximum capacity of the machines. The standardised work flow combination indicates the required manpower which is needed per step. The standardised work chart is a diagram that illustrates the work sequence. Standardisation is a condition for improvement.

In Toyota's factories, teams of employees establish – and implement – the standards and work procedures. These standards and work procedures are flexible and subject to continuous modification and improvement. Employees are encouraged to make suggestions for improvement. Teams ('quality circles') are invited to streamline the production flow, to improve the quality of the processes, and to

---

[175] Ohno (1988, p7, 8).
[176] Toyota (1992, p38-46), and Monden (1998, p177-197).

enhance productivity. Kaizen is one of the keys to shop floor management.[177] Toyota writes[178]:

> "The Toyota Production System is a framework for raising quality and productivity and for invigorating employee morale. But the continuing improvements of kaizen are what actually make those things happen.
>
> Ultimately, kaizen is about job ownership. It means giving employees full responsibility and authority for their jobs. They take responsibility for turning out products that will earn the satisfaction of customers. And they receive the authority to modify and shape their work in ways that raise quality and productivity and that improve working conditions."

Kaizen enables Toyota to realise cost reduction even in periods of low growth.

4.6 Humanity

Taiichi Ohno indicates 'respect for humanity' as one of the objectives of the Toyota system.[179] How is humanity anchored in the Toyota Production System? Two connected aspects play an important role.

Firstly, the employee manages his or her own work.[180] He or she operates the equipment, controls the logistics via the kanban system, executes quality measurements, identifies problems, and has the authority to stop the line. The daily work is done according to detailed instructions. Standardisation and improvement has led to equipment that can be operated easily. Even precision machining is as simple as attaching a tool and pushing a button.[181] Preferably, it takes several days to train new workers.[182] Monden remarks that in many manufacturing systems the productivity is increased and the costs are reduced by an increasing demand on the individual worker. He characterises such an approach as 'dehumanisation of the worker'. He claims that Toyota has solved the conflict between productivity and human concerns by the policy of continuous improvement.[183] [184]

Secondly, the employee is invited to make a positive contribution to the design and the improvement of his or her own workplace. The implementation of ideas

---

[177] In Japanese literature the improvement of the workplace is central, see for example the Japan Human Relations Association (1995) and Kobayashi (1995).

[178] Toyota (1992, p46).

[179] Ohno (1988, pxiii).

[180] Toyota (1992 (p4-8).

[181] Toyota (1992, p36).

[182] Ohno (1988, p22).

[183] Monden (1998, p177). See also Toyota (1992, p39).

[184] The idea that continuous improvement is an expression of respect for humanity is also written by Sasaki in Sasaki and Hutchins (1984, p121).

from employees contributes strongly to job satisfaction and the morale of the group. Toyota writes[185]:

> "Employees that participate in the system discover the satisfaction of designing their own jobs and managing their own work (...) Employees, meanwhile, harbour creativity and immense potential for ideas – often much more than even they themselves realise. Job satisfaction is a matter of having opportunities to exercise creativity. People enjoy their work when it involves trying out their own ideas, mastering new skills, and making a visible contribution. The Toyota Production System engenders job satisfaction by providing employees with opportunities to exercise judgement and creativity. Each team – about eight employees working under a team leader – has the responsibility and the authority to design their own jobs. Working together, the members of the team discover ways to smooth the flow of the production, to raise quality and to improve their working conditions."

Under the heading 'Stimulating or Stressful' Toyota continues[186]:

> "(...) responsibility and authority are motivational, while nothing is more demoralising over the long term than spending time in an unproductive manner (...) The Toyota Production System enforces a creative tension in the workplace. Employees don't coast. Just-in-time demands continuous vigilance. Continuing improvements in the name of *kaizen* demand unflagging efforts to find better ways of doing things. The overall result, however, is a stimulating workplace. A workplace where employees can take charge of their own destinies."

Monden makes a direct connection between humanity and the elimination of waste. He states that "... humanity is a matter of allying human energy with meaningful, effective operations by abolishing wasteful operations."[187] As he believes that morale and work will suffer if employees waste their time on 'insignificant jobs'; his plea is for workers to be given 'valuable jobs'.[188]

Monden also stresses the importance of open communication between employees and management. Such open communication is required to elaborate proposals for improvement and to implement them. He states that if management and engineers respect the proposals from the shop floor, that "No one will feel alienated, and every worker will feel that his work is an important part of his life.".[189] [190]

---

[185] Toyota (1992, p2, 3).
[186] Toyota (1992, p7).
[187] Monden (1998, p185).
[188] Monden (1998, p185).
[189] Monden (1998, p185, 186).
[190] It is interesting to note that Monden (1998, p185) refers to the article 'By days I make the cars' by John F. Runcie (1980) in the *Harvard Business Review*. He brings this case to the fore as a (bad) example of where there is no open communication between management and workers.

116

Monden suggests that stressful conditions have the upper hand in the old factories of Toyota and points out that Toyota has (only) been promoting further improvements in the workplace for a short time. In the Preface to the Third Edition of *Toyota Production System* he writes[191]:

> "In this third edition of *Toyota Production System*, I explain the system's recent evolution; specifically, pursuing the goal of respect for humanity. In other words, Toyota has developed an approach to boost morale in the assembly plant by (1) redesigning the assembly line into many split-lines and (2) improving working conditions by introducing ergonomic devices to alleviate fatigue. Toyota promotes these improvements to forestall labour shortages in its plants. The supply of young Japanese labour is expected to decrease because (...) Japanese youngsters are inclined to dislike working in shops. Most tasks are characterised as difficult, dirty, and dangerous (3D) (referred to in Japanese as 3K (*Kitsui, Kitanai, and Kiken*))."

Monden reports a change in the structure of the Toyota Production System to improve the morale of employees. The conventional assembly line of Toyota consists of about three or four sub-lines. The sub-lines are approximately 300 meters long and are connected together. In 1992, Toyota built a plant with a different production structure in Kyushu. In this plant, the assembly line is divided into 11 functional split-lines. The division between the lines is based partly on differences from a car design standpoint and partly on differences from an operational standpoint. These functionally divided lines are identified as 'self-containing lines'. The functional split-line is an organisational unit which consists of 10 to 20 employees and which is headed by a foreman.[192] Monden also reports the development of a scientific model to mitigate the workload of the operator.[193]

4.7 Western studies

The success of the Toyota Production System has stimulated a lot of scientific research on the secret of this approach. To make up the description of Lean Production it is worthwhile to mention two Western studies of this approach.

James Womack, Daniel Jones, and Daniel Roos have done an extensive study on Lean Production in the car industry. The have reported their findings in *The Machine that Changed the World. The Story of Lean Production*. This book is focused on the whole business system: running the factory, designing the product, coordinating the supply chain, dealing with customers, and managing the enterprise. In the chapter about manufacturing, they question why lean methods are superior to traditional ones.[194] In their view, manufacturability and automation play an important role. However, the key lies in two organisational features.

---

[191] Monden (1998, pxvi).
[192] Monden (1998, p349-362).
[193] Monden (1998, p379-382).
[194] Womack et al. (1991, p93-100).

Firstly, a maximum number of tasks and responsibilities are transferred to a team of assembly line workers. Secondly, there is a system in place that detects defects quickly and traces them back to their original cause.

Womack and Jones have elaborated on the principles of Lean Production in *Lean Thinking. Banish Waste and Create Wealth in Your Corporation*. They conclude that the essence of lean thinking can be summarised in five principles[195]:

> "After interactions with many audiences and considerable reflection, we concluded that lean thinking can be summarised in five principles: precisely specify *value* by specific product, identify the *value stream* for each product, make value *flow* without interruptions, let the customer *pull* value from the producer, and pursue *perfection*."

The starting point for lean thinking is value. Value is defined from the perspective of the customer: a specific product that meets the customer's needs at a specific price at a specific time. The next step is the identification of the value stream. This involves all the specific activities that are required to develop, to manufacture, and to deliver a product into the hands of a customer. The analysis of a value stream will reveal steps that unambiguously create value, steps that create no value but are unavoidable with the present technology, and steps which create no value and have to be avoided. The value-creating activities have to be setup in such a way that the product flows through the production area. Lean systems have to be designed so that they can make exactly what the customer wants: thus the customer 'pulls' the products from the supplier. The last principle is perfection. The production has to be perfect. All waste has to be removed from the operation.

Steven Spear and Kent Bowen have investigated the Toyota Production System extensively. They pretend that they have 'decoded the DNA' of this system. In their view, the key of the Toyota Production System is a 'rigorous problem-solving process'. The following basic rules are identified[196]:

> **Rule 1:** All work shall be highly specified as to content, sequence, timing, and outcome.
> **Rule 2:** Every customer-supplier connection must be direct, and there must be an unambiguous yes-or-no way to send requests and receive responses.
> **Rule 3:** The pathway for every product and service must be simple and direct.
> **Rule 4:** Any improvement must be made in accordance with the scientific method, under the guidance of a teacher, at the lowest possible level in the organisation."

These rules form the cornerstone of a learning organisation. All activities, connections, and flow-paths have built-in tests to automatically identify problems or deviations. Spear and Bowen conclude that the continual response to problems and deviations makes the production system so flexible and adaptable to the changing circumstances.

---

[195] Womack and Jones (1997, p10). Italics by Womack and Jones.
[196] Spear and Bowen (1999, p97-106).

4.8 Evaluation

Lean Production has unleashed a lively discussion in academic literature. Supporters and opponents have crossed swords with each other. The main points of this discussion will be reviewed. After that, the practical value of this approach is evaluated.

Womack et al. state that Lean Production will become the 'standard global production system' of the twenty-first century.[197] They conclude[198]:

> "Lean Production is a superior way for humans to make things. It provides better products in wider variety at lower cost. Equally important, it provides more challenging and fulfilling work for employees at every level, from the factory to headquarters. It follows that the whole world should adopt lean production, and as quickly as possible."

This conclusion seems to be confirmed by the study of Adler and Cole.[199] These scientists compared two automobile plants: New United Motor Manufacturing Inc. (NUMMI) in California (USA), a joint venture between Toyota and General Motors, and Volvo in Uddevalla (Sweden). The NUMMI plant is based on the Japanese 'lean production' model, and the Uddevalla plant on the socio-technical 'human-centred' model. In the NUMMI plant, the employees work in teams of four to five workers and are led by a team leader. Each team member performs a work cycle of about sixty seconds. In the final assembly department, the teams are linked in a traditional assembly line. In the Uddevalla plant, the assembly line has been abolished. Employees work in teams of about ten people. The team is fully responsible for assembling the car from the subsystems up. The work cycle takes about two hours and consists of a balance of tasks. The teams have a high level of autonomy. Adler and Cole found that the NUMMI plant was superior to the Uddevalla plant with respect to both performance and a motivational working environment. They attributed this difference to the potential for learning: in the NUMMI plant *organisational* learning is encouraged and in the Uddevalla plant *individual* learning. Adler and Cole conclude[200]:

> "(...) the combination of standardised work and more democratic management has proven potent at NUMMI in its ability to sustain both continuous improvement and worker morale. It might well represent the model for the next generation of labour-intensive, mass-production activities."

---

[197] Womack et al. (1991, p278).
[198] Womack et al. (1991, p225).
[199] Adler and Cole (1993).
[200] Adler and Cole (1993, p93).

Adler and Cole characterise NUMMI's organisation of work as a 'democratic Tayloristic model'.[201]

Williams et al. have studied the claims of Womack, Jones and Roos in detail.[202] They state that the difference between Lean Production and mass production is not empirically sustainable, that the 'half the human effort' claim exaggerates the Japanese advantage, and that they have not explained how the Japanese take labour out and control labour costs.

Berggren challenges the view of Lean Production as an omnipotent system and unequivocal blessing.[203] He states that the experience of Japanese automobile plants, such as NUMMI, cannot be generalised because it is not representative of Japanese manufacturing operations in the United States. In his opinion, the working conditions are contradictory.[204] The positives are: job security, the more egalitarian profile, the high quality of products, the exhaustive screening process of new employees, and problem solving on the shop floor. The negatives are: unlimited performance demands, long working hours, overtime demands, health and safety complaints, and the rigorous factory regime. Berggren points out that even the Japanese federation of unions within the car industry has criticised the 'san kei' as: difficult (Kitsui), dirty (Kitanai), and dangerous (Kiken). Berggren concludes that Lean Production is certainly not the 'ultimate station' of industrial development.[205]

Conti and Warner have investigated six factories in western Japan.[206] They also point out the contradictory character of the labour process in lean factories. They express this by saying that employees are working four hours a month in a 'very non-Tayloristic manner' to make their work for the rest of the month even 'more Taylor-like'.[207] They conclude that the Toyota Production System has to be seen as a 'legacy of Scientific Management'.[208] Delbridge has investigated the working conditions of two British factories that have adopted lean methods. He concludes that the Japanese model is little more than "… an extension of the principles of Taylor through the systematic standardisation and proceduralisation of tasks within the context of heightened managerial dominance and control."[209] Dankbaar draws a comparable conclusion.[210] He characterises Lean Production not as an alternative to Fordism but as its perfect form.

The working conditions in lean factories have been criticised by a number of authors. They point to: monotony and boredom, the speed of the line, work-related disabilities, the unfairness of team leaders, and so on.[211] Benders has

---

[201] Adler and Cole (1993, p89).
[202] Williams et al. (1992).
[203] Berggren (1993).
[204] Berggren (1993, p172-180).
[205] Berggren (1993, p185).
[206] Conti and Warner (1993).
[207] Conti and Warner (1993, p39).
[208] Conti and Warner (1993, p40).
[209] Delbridge (1998, p204).
[210] Dankbaar (1997).
[211] E.g. Runcie (1980), Kamata (1982), Berggren (1993), and Besser (1996).

pointed out that Japanese producers do recognise that the Lean Production system is the cause of various problems with respect to the quality of working life.[212] Therefore, changes in the production structure are proposed.

Various authors have discussed the team concept in lean factories. Mishina concludes that the Toyota team has no autonomy: it is a small organisational unit in a hierarchy-based organisation.[213] Kieser characterises Japanese teams as 'Klaglose Kooperation' ('cooperation without complaint') and German teams as 'Qualifizierte Gruppenarbeit' ('qualified teamwork').[214] Van Amelsfoort notes that Japanese teams have a low level of control capacity.[215]

Finally, we turn to the influence of culture. Meek mentions contradictory research findings coming from Japan.[216] On the one hand, turnover statistics, absenteeism, participation rates in improvement programs, and so on, all seem to suggest that Japanese employees are highly satisfied with and committed to their jobs. On the other hand, comparative studies in job and workplace satisfaction have shown that Japanese employees have invariably recorded low levels of job and workplace satisfaction. Meek concludes that this contradiction has to be understood against the background of the Japanese culture: the mentality to survive and to function effectively in a demanding work environment (*ganbatte*). Hard work, dedication, and loyalty are generated by feelings of gratitude and obligation toward the employer for protection, support and care. Besser suggests that Toyota has successfully transplanted this aspect of culture into their Camry plant in the United States.[217] She introduces the metaphor of the 'company team'. The company team is the shared belief in the 'community of fate'. It is a shared set of attitudes toward the organisation, work and other employees.[218] The 'community of fate' is the belief in a common destiny: that employees will all sink or swim together.

Now Lean Production will be evaluated from a practical point of view. Lean Production has developed a number of sophisticated production technologies. The most important techniques are the kanban, autonomation, and related methods. In addition, Lean Production has developed a number of techniques for continuous improvement. In a participative approach, all levels and all functions in the organisation cooperate to reduce waste. Consistent application of these techniques does lead to a learning organisation. In the 'best cases' high employee motivation is reported.[219] The lean production technologies are in many aspects superior to those developed by Taylorism. At the same time, they are not offered by other approaches, e.g. Socio-Technical Systems Design or Business Process Reengineer-

---

[212]   Benders (1996).
[213]   Mishina (1994).
[214]   Kieser (1993).
[215]   Van Amelsfoort (1992).
[216]   Meek (1999).
[217]   Besser (1996, p49-119).
[218]   Besser (1996, p87).
[219]   E.g. Adler and Cole (1993).

ing. For these reasons, the production technologies and improvement techniques of Lean Production will occupy an important place in modern factories.

On the other hand, Lean Production has to be characterised as a one-sided technological approach to the factory. The production structure, the control structure, the improvement structure, and socio-dynamic factors are focused on the primary production process. In the lean philosophy, respect for humanity is mainly defined in terms of efficiency: it is inhuman to perform a job where there are wasteful activities. The technological character of Lean Production leads a paradox. The one side of this paradox is that this philosophy contributes to a motivating working environment through the participation of employees in the continuous improvement of the workplace. The other side of this paradox is that this philosophy discards humanity as a separate value, giving rise to a number of social problems. For example, high levels of work division and short work cycles do lead to monotony, boredom, apathy, and alienation. The limitations of Lean Production come strongly to the fore when it is juxtaposed with the Dutch approach to Socio Technical Systems Design (see section 3 of this chapter). This approach aims for an integral design of the quality of the organisation (technical performance), the quality of working life (well-being), and the quality of labour relations (social relations).

5 Business Process Reengineering: The redesign of business processes

In 1990 Michael Hammer published an article entitled 'Reengineering Work: Don't Automate, Obliterate' in the *Harvard Business Review*. Hammer argued in this article that the approach American companies usually used to improve performance no longer worked. He called for a radical redesign of business processes; a redesign enabled by a creative application of modern information technology and telecommunication systems. This article set the ball rolling on a number of reengineering projects. Success stories were published and failures were reported.

In *Reengineering the Corporation. A Manifesto for Business Revolution* (1993), Michael Hammer and James Champy elaborate on the ideas of Business Process Reengineering. They emphasise that reengineering is focused on a redesign of the *business processes* of a company. Reengineering does not mean tinkering with what already exists. It does not mean making incremental changes that leave the basic structure of the company intact. It also does not mean a reorganisation of a department or organisational unit. Reengineering means nothing less than a radical and fundamental redesign of the core processes supported by advanced modern information technology. It means 'starting over'; it implies the 'creation' of a new company.

Reengineering the Corporation confirmed the rise of a new *hype* and the emergence of a new *business*. Market research estimated that in 1994 about 75 percent of America's largest companies had already begun reengineering; that the total amount of expenditures involved was over 30 billion dollars; and that reengineering consultation services came to anywhere between 1.4 to 2.6 billion dollars.[220] Hammer and Champy also profited from this hype. They sold more than 1.7 million copies of their book within a year and a half.[221]

Since the nineties, there have been a number of publications dedicated to Business Process Reengineering.[222] It appears that the objectives of this approach are quite clear. However, the basic concepts and techniques are less articulated. In practice, the application of these concepts and techniques is quite difficult. Hammer and Champy estimate that 50 to 70 percent of the organisations that undertake reengineering do not succeed.[223] Hammer and Stanton point out that "Organisations have an amazing ability to find new ways of making mistakes."[224] To prevent these mistakes they wrote the book *The Reengineering Revolution. A Handbook* (1995).[225] Notwithstanding the high number of failures, Hammer and Stanton are not afraid to use superlatives to describe the benefits of reengineering. They speak about the creation of a 'new company' and the emergence of a 'new

---

[220] Hammer (1995, pxi, 68).
[221] Hammer (1995, pxi).
[222] Davenport and Short (1990) have developed a comparable approach.
[223] Hammer and Champy (1994, p200).
[224] Hammer and Stanton (1995, p15).
[225] Hammer and Stanton (1995, pxiv).

world'.[226] In their view, our age will be remembered as 'the age of the Reengineering Revolution'.[227]

The following key texts are used to describe Business Process Reengineering: the article 'Reengineering Work: Don't Automate, Obliterate' (1990) by Michael Hammer; *Reengineering the Corporation. A Manifesto for Business Revolution* (1993) by Michael Hammer and James Champy; *The Reengineering Revolution. A Handbook* (1995) by Michael Hammer and Steve Stanton; *Reengineering Management. The Mandate for New Leadership* (1995) by James Champy; and *Beyond Reengineering* (1996) by Michael Hammer.

In this section the following topics are discussed: the background of Business Process Reengineering (5.1), the essence of reengineering (5.2), the main principles (5.3), a new world of work (5.4), and the role of modern information technology (5.5). The section ends with a review (5.6).

5.1 Background

Hammer and Champy observe that the achievements of American enterprises do not fulfil the requirements of the market. They attribute the poor performance of these companies to the structure and organisation. For more than two centuries, people have built companies around the philosophy of Adam Smith; that "... industrial work should be broken down into its simplest and most basic *tasks*.".[228] However, the division of labour does not work in the post-industrial age. Hammer and Champy state that "... corporations will be founded and built around the idea of unifying those tasks into coherent business *processes*."[229] They conclude that traditional companies were superbly suited to the conditions of an earlier era, but that they do not suit the dynamics of the present business climate. Advanced technologies, the disappearance of boundaries between markets, and the changed expectations of customers require a different structure and a new organisation.[230]

Traditionally, American managers boosted the performance of their organisations by process rationalisation and automation. However, this approach does not break away from outdated rules and fundamental assumptions that underlie the business processes. In practice, the existing operations were left intact and information technology was used to speed up processes. For that reason, a breakthrough in performance could not be realised. Hammer writes[231]:

> "It is time to stop paving the cow paths. Instead of embedding outdated processes in silicon and software, we should obliterate them and start over. We should 'reengineer' our businesses: use the power of modern information technology to radically

---

[226] Hammer and Stanton (1995, p320-321).
[227] Hammer and Stanton (1995, p320-322).
[228] Hammer and Champy (1994, p2). Italics by Hammer and Champy.
[229] Hammer and Champy (1994, p2). Italics by Hammer and Champy.
[230] Hammer and Champy (1994, p11).
[231] Hammer (1990, p104).

redesign our business processes in order to achieve dramatic improvements in their performance."

Business Process Reengineering advocates radical redesign and using information technology to enable new processes.[232] Reengineering means a break with the past. It means 'discontinuous thinking'.[233] Hammer and Champy warn that reengineering cannot be done in small and cautious steps. Reengineering is an 'all-or-nothing proposition'.[234]

Why do the old ways of doing business – which are characterised by the division of labour – not work anymore? Hammer and Champy mention three forces: customers, competition and change.[235] Since the beginning of the early eighties, the dominant force in the supplier-customer relationship has shifted. In the past, suppliers had the upper hand. Nowadays, customers take charge. Furthermore, competition has intensified. Niche competitors have changed the face of every segment of the market. Falling trade barriers led to an 'invasion' of foreign competitors. In addition, new companies gained market share by adopting an unconventional approach. Finally, change has become a constant factor. It is both pervasive and persistent. Moreover, the pace of change has accelerated. In *Reengineering the Corporation* Hammer and Champy conclude that[236]:

> "[The three forces] – customers, competition, and change – have created a new world for business, and it is becoming increasingly apparent that organisations designed to operate in one environment cannot be fixed to work well in another. Companies created to thrive on mass production, stability, and growth can't be fixed to succeed in a world where customers, competition and change demand flexibility and quick response (...) The core message of our book, then, is this: It is no longer necessary or desirable for companies to organise their work around Adam Smith's division of labour. Task-oriented jobs in today's world of customers, competition, and change are obsolete. Instead, companies must organise around *process*."

To organise companies around business processes a set of procedures and techniques have been developed. This set is called *business reengineering*.[237]

---

[232]   Hammer (1990, p108).
[233]   Hammer (1990, p107), and Hammer and Champy (1994, p3).
[234]   Hammer and Champy (1994, p5).
[235]   Hammer and Champy (1994, p17-24).
[236]   Hammer and Champy (1994, p24, 27, 28).
[237]   Hammer and Champy (1994, p5).

5.2 The essence of Reengineering

What is reengineering? Hammer and Champy give the following definition[238]:

> "Reengineering is the fundamental rethinking and radical redesign of business processes to achieve dramatic improvements in critical, contemporary measures of performance, such as cost, quality, service, and speed."

This definition contains four key words: fundamental, radical, dramatic, and processes. The words 'fundamental', 'radical', and 'dramatic' clearly show that Hammer and Champy do not opt for an improvement of the performance of the core-processes of the company. They choose for a fundamental rethinking and a radical redesign. They propose a 'reengineering revolution' to create a new company. The next key word is 'processes'. A process is defined as "... a related group of tasks that together create a result of value to a customer."[239] The key words in this description are 'value' and 'customer'. This means that every task in a process has to be judged from the point of view of value creation for the customer.

In the foreword to *Beyond Reengineering* Hammer emphasises that 'processes' are the most significant aspect of reengineering.[240] In the first place, processes have to be focused on the demands of customers. That means that a 'process perspective' is a customer's perspective.[241] In the second place, the focus on processes dissolves not only the boundaries between departments in a company, but also the boundaries between companies, i.e. between a company and its customers and suppliers.[242] In the third place, a process point of view obliges a company to rethink its strategy. Hammer emphasises that a company should not define themselves in terms of their currents markets, products or services, but in their processes. In Business Process Reengineering a company has to be world-class in its processes. Processes therefore define the core competence of companies.[243]

Hammer and Champy illustrate the essence of Business Process Reengineering in the radical changes that mainstream companies such as IBM Credit, Ford Motor, Kodak, Hallmark, Taco Bell, Capital Holding, Bell Atlantic, and many others, have made.

To illustrate the essence of business reengineering two well-known examples will be presented[244]:

> *Example.* The first case concerns IBM Credit Corporation. The process of deciding about a credit loan for a customer was divided into five main steps. An expert carried out each step. The entire process consumed six days on average, although it some-

---

238 Hammer and Champy (1994, p32).
239 Hammer (1996, p5). See also Hammer and Champy (1994, p35).
240 Hammer (1996, pxii).
241 Hammer (1996, p12).
242 Hammer (1996, p168-190).
243 Hammer (1996, p191-205).
244 Hammer (1990, p105-107), and Hammer and Champy (1994, p36-39, p44-46).

times took as long as two weeks. This process was much too long. It gave the customer six days to find another source of financing, or to consider buying another computer. In their efforts to improve this process, IBM Credit installed a control desk to answer the questions of the salespersons about the status of the deal. However, this solution did not solve the problem of the long turnaround. Two senior managers hit upon an idea. They took a financial request and walked themselves through all five steps, asking personnel in each office to process this request immediately. They learned from the experiment that performing the whole task took only ninety minutes in total. That means that the remainder of the time was consumed by passing the form on from one office to the next. In other words, the problem did not lie in the tasks and the people performing them, but in the structure of the process itself. In the end, IBM Credit decided to replace its specialists by generalists. Instead of sending a form from office to office, one person handled the entire application from beginning to end. Instead of five persons each executing one step of the process, one person executed all five steps of the credit loan process. The performance of the department greatly improved. The turnaround was reduced from six days to four hours. The number of deals handled increased by a factor of one hundred. These improvements were realised without an increase in headcount.

Example. The second case concerns the product development process at Kodak. In 1987, one of Kodak's competitors launched a new disposable camera. Kodak had no competitive product to offer. Its traditional product design process would take about seventy weeks to produce a comparable camera. Such a time delay would give this competitor an enormous advantage in the market. At that time, development processes at Kodak were partly parallel (e.g. the design of the different parts of a camera) and partly sequential (e.g. the design of the camera and the design of the manufacturing tools). Kodak reengineered its product development process using a Computer Aided Design and Computer Aided Manufacturing system. An integrated product design database was created which enabled a parallel development of the camera parts and the manufacturing tools. This new approach, called concurrent engineering, cut the development process from concept to production from seventy weeks to thirty-eight weeks. At the same time, it reduced its tooling and manufacturing costs for this camera by twenty-five percent.

Hammer and Champy characterise these examples as illustrations of *'true business reengineering'*.[245] They illustrate the four requisite characteristics of reengineering. They show that reengineering is " ... the *fundamental* rethinking and *radical* design of business *processes* to achieve *dramatic* improvements in critical, contemporary measures of performance, such as cost, quality, service, and speed."[246]

---

[245] Hammer and Champy (1994, p46). Italics by Hammer and Champy.
[246] Hammer and Champy (1994, p46). Italics by Hammer and Champy.

5.3 The principles of Reengineering

Business Process Reengineering proposes several general principles for redesigning an organisation. In the *Harvard Business Review* article Hammer identifies seven principles[247]:

HBR1.   *Organise around outcomes, not tasks.* The principle of this is that one person has to perform all the steps in a process.

HBR2.   *Have those who use the output of the process perform the process.* This principle suggests that an employee who needs the output of a process must perform that process himself or herself.

HBR3.   *Subsume information-processing work into the real work that produces the information.* This principle states that the employee who produces the information also processes that information.

HBR4.   *Treat geographically dispersed resources as though they were centralised.* This principle states that databases, telecommunication networks, and standardised processing systems can be applied to reap the benefits of centralisation (e.g. scale effects) while maintaining the benefits of decentralisation (e.g. flexibility).

HBR5.   *Links parallel activities instead of integrating their results.* The principle of this is that parallel processes have to be linked from the beginning to prevent sub-optimisation, mistakes, double work and so on.

HBR6.   *Put the decision point where the work is performed, and build control into the process.* This principle suggests that the people who do the work should make the decisions and that the process itself can be controlled through built-in controls.

HBR7.   *Capture information once and at the source.* Modern information technology makes it simple to collect, to store and to transmit information. This enables information to be collated at the source and then transferred to the required stations.

In *Reengineering the Corporation* the following principles are identified[248]:

RtC1.   *Several jobs are combined into one.* That means: formerly distinct jobs or tasks are integrated into one job.

RtC2.   *Workers make decisions.* That means: decision making becomes a part of the job.

---

[247] Hammer (1990, p108-112). The literal wording of the principle as outlined by Hammer is displayed in italics. The prefix 'HBR' in the numeration is used to refer to the principles as defined in the *Harvard Business Review* article.

[248] Hammer and Champy (1994, p50-64). The literal wording of the theme as outlined by Hammer and Champy is displayed in italics. The prefix 'RtC' in the numeration is used to refer to the principles as defined in the book *Reengineering the Corporation*.

RtC3. *The steps in the process are performed in a natural order.* After reengineering, the different steps of the process are sequenced in terms of what needs to follow what.

RtC4. *Processes have multiple versions.* To meet the demands of today's business environment, we need multiple versions of the same process. Each version has to be tuned to the specific requirements of the different markets.

RtC5. *Work is performed where it makes the most sense.* Work is shifted across organisational boundaries to improve the overall performance of the process.

RtC6. *Checks and controls are reduced.* Reengineered processes only use controls if they make economic sense.

RtC7. *Reconciliation is minimised.* Cutting back the number of external contact points means that the chance that inconsistent data will require reconciliation is reduced.

RtC8. *A case manager provides a single point of contact.* The case manager acts as a buffer between the complex process and the customer.

RtC9. *Hybrid centralised/decentralised operations are prevalent.* The advantages of centralisation and decentralisation are combined in one process.

There are several points of similarity between these lists, e.g. the principles HBR1, HBR4, and HBR6 correspond with the principles RtC1, RtC9, and RtC6, respectively. There are also several differences, e.g. principle HBR5 is not present in the list of *Reengineering the Corporation*, and principle RtC4 is not present in the list of the *Harvard Business Review* article. With a bit of creativity, the remaining principles in these lists are comparable with each other.

These lists present general principles rather than concrete design rules. They concern three main themes. Firstly, simple tasks in a business process have to be combined into one complex job (HBR1, HBR2, HBR3, HBR6, RtC1, RtC2, RtC5, and RtC8). Secondly, modern information technology and telecommunication have to be used to redesign the business process (HBR4, HBR7, and RtC9). Thirdly, the character of the newly designed business processes is indicated (RtC3, RtC4, RtC6, and RtC7).

Business Process Reengineering begins with redesigning the business process. This is the most important step. After that, the structure of the organisation will become 'apparent'.[249] Reengineering moves inevitably through all the facets of an organisation. It leads to an organisation that differs in all aspects from the old one.[250]

---

[249] Hammer and Champy (1994, p41).

[250] The approach of Davenport and Short (1990, p14) is comparable. They distinguish five steps in Business Process Reengineering:
(1) Develop Business Vision and Process Objectives
(2) Identify Processes to Be Redesigned
(3) Understand and Measure Existing Processes
(4) Identify Information Technology Leavers
(5) Design and Build a Prototype of the Process.

5.4 A new world of work

Business Process Reengineering leads to a 'new world of work'. Hammer and Champy write[251]:

> "When a process is reengineered, jobs evolve from narrow and task-oriented to multidimensional. People who once did as they were instructed now make choices and decisions on their own instead. Assembly-line work disappears. Functional departments lose their reasons for being. Managers stop acting like supervisors and behave more as coaches. Workers focus more on the customers' needs and less on their bosses'. Attitudes and values change in response to the new incentives. Practically every aspect of the organisation is transformed, often beyond recognition."

In *Beyond Reengineering* Michael Hammer gives some examples of the new world of work created by Business Process Reengineering. For example, the GTE Corporation of Florida reengineered the way it handled customers' requests for repairs and service. In the past, there was a supervisor for every eight to ten technicians. The supervisor did the planning, instructed the technicians, and handled every problem beyond technical repairs. In the new organisation the number of supervisory positions has been reduced. The technicians are divided into small teams that cover a specific geographical area. The team is responsible for the whole repair and service process. A technician described the changes as follows[252]:

> "In the old days, the supervisors used to encourage us to call them at the drop of a hat. "If you have any questions or doubts about what you're doing, give us a call and we'll be glad to jump in our truck and talk to the customer and you about the problem". They treated us like children. Sometimes they could help, but it usually wasn't necessary. For example, if we had an irate subscriber, we'd call our supervisor who would come out and calm the guy down. The customer responded to his 'shirt and tie and company vehicle'. Now we don't have the tie, but we can deal with them (...) We're also developing ongoing relationships with the customers. The fact that you've got four or five people zoned in a certain geographic area means that we get personally familiar with our customers' equipment and problems (...) There's much more pride in ownership. You have self-esteem and all those things. There's much more job satisfaction than there ever was, too (...) Some people think the new freedom and responsibility are more stressful, but not to me. I thought the old set-up was stressful because they didn't treat us with nearly as much trust and dignity as now (...)"

---

[251] Hammer and Champy (1994, p65).
[252] Hammer (1996, p26-28).

Hammer and Champy notice the following changes in work and organisation[253]:

1. *Work units change – from functional departments to process teams.* A process team is a group of people working together to perform an entire process.

2. *Jobs change – from simple tasks to multi-dimensional work.* The members of a process team share joint responsibility for the whole process. They perform a whole job, i.e. a process or a sub-process.

3. *People's roles change – from controlled to empowered.* Reengineered processes imply that employees get the authority to make decisions to manage the whole process.

4. *Job preparation changes – from training to education.* Reengineered processes require employees who have insight into the character of the process.

5. *Focus of performance measures and compensation shifts – from activity to results.* Performance and contribution are the primary bases for compensation.

6. *Advancement criteria change – from performance to ability.* Advancement to another job in the organisation is based on the ability of the person in question.

7. *Values change – from protective to productive.* Reengineering demands that employees believe deeply that they work for their customers and not for their bosses.

8. *Managers change – from supervisors to coaches.* Process teams need coaches to support the team in its work.

9. *Organisational structures change – from hierarchical to flat.* Reengineering leads to flat organisations because the teams take decisions and execute controls.

10. *Executives change – from scorekeepers to leaders.* Executives must be leaders who can influence and change the values and beliefs of the organisation by their words and their deeds.

These changes show that reengineering has an impact upon the whole company. It transforms (1) the business processes, (2) jobs and structures, (3) management and measuring systems, and (4) values and beliefs. Hammer and Champy call these four items the 'four points' of a 'business system diamond'.[254] These points are linked in a specific way. The business processes determine the jobs and the structure of an organisation. The way in which the work is organised determines management and measurement systems. Management systems are the primary shapers of the values and beliefs of an organisation. Finally, the reigning values and beliefs must support the design of the business processes. In a changing business environment, this cycle is continuously in motion.

In *Beyond Reengineering* Michael Hammer explores the new world of work in more detail. He states that the process-centred organisation creates a 'new economy' and a 'new world'.[255] 'Simple processes and complex jobs' will replace 'simple

---

[253] Hammer and Champy (1994, p65-82). The literal wording of the theme as given by Hammer and Champy is displayed in italics.

[254] Hammer and Champy (1994, p81).

[255] Hammer (1996, pxv).

jobs and complex processes'.[256] He speaks about 'reversing' the Industrial Revolution.[257] In process-centred organisations, there is no great divide between 'doing' and 'managing'. Management is no longer an activity of a special function. It becomes a part of *everyone's* job'.[258] The role of management changes fundamentally: from manager to process owner. The task of a process owner is to design the business process, to coach the process teams that execute the business process, and to advocate the interests of the business process in the corridors of power.[259] The change from the task-centred organisation to the process-centred organisation is drastic. It means the 'end of the organisational chart'.[260] A loose association of professionals replaces the structured hierarchy with bosses and subordinates. It also means a drastic change in the 'soul' of the company, i.e. the corporate culture.[261] Obedience and diligence are replaced by initiative; and job security by opportunity for development. The new organisation is a learning organisation characterised by an open inquiry, morale, humility, learning, and sustainability.[262]

In *Reengineering Management. The Mandate for New Leadership*, James Champy analyses the consequences of Business Process Reengineering for management. He states that a 'fundamental revolution' in actual management practice is required.[263] In his view, the main obstacle to such a revolution is management itself.[264] Champy points out that a power shift within the corporation is required to meet the changes in the market.[265] The hardest part of reengineering appears to be the sharing of power.[266] Champy identifies five key processes of management: (1) *mobilising* human resources, (2) *enabling* employees to exercise control, (3) *defining* the objectives of the organisation, (4) *measuring* the business performance, and (5) *communicating* about business processes, culture and behaviour, and standards and objectives.[267] Champy emphasises that the employees who are closest to the corporation's products and customers need to have greater authority and responsibility.[268]

The new world of work provides an opportunity for fulfilment and meaning. Hammer writes[269]:

> "Work should give substance, meaning, and value to our lives. It should make us feel that we are contributing to the world, that we are helping to make it a better place,

---

[256] Hammer (1996, p36).
[257] Hammer (1996, p49).
[258] Hammer (1996, p43). Italics by Hammer.
[259] Hammer (1996, p73-93).
[260] Hammer (1996, p116-137).
[261] Hammer (1996, p153-167).
[262] Hammer (1996, p251-253).
[263] Champy (1995, p5).
[264] Champy (1995, p1).
[265] Champy (1995, p20).
[266] Champy (1995, p26).
[267] Champy (1995, p111 ff.).
[268] Champy (1995, p150).
[269] Hammer (1996, p267).

that we are somehow leaving a legacy. Work should help us to focus not on ourselves but on others, the beneficiaries of our work, and, in so doing, free us from the relentless focus on our own concerns that eventually leaves the taste of ashes in our mouths."

Hammer points out that the recent spate of books and seminars about 'workplace spirituality' bespeaks a longing for transcendent meaning in our daily lives. Hammer himself is ambiguous about the spiritual meaning of work. On the one hand, he states that in our secular age we may no longer see our work as 'service to the Divine' but as 'service to humanity'.[270] On the other hand, he refers to papal encyclical about the spiritual meaning of work and says that its 'prophetic words' capture the essence of process-centred work.[271]

5.5 The role of Information Technology

Business Process Reengineering ascribes a crucial role to modern information technology. The role of this technology is not to accelerate or to automate the existing processes, but to enable the design of new processes. Information technology is characterised as an *essential enabler* that *permits* companies to reengineer their processes.[272]

Hammer and Champy point to the 'disruptive' power of modern information technology and modern communication systems.[273] These technologies can break the old methods of working and can enable a radical redesign of a business process. The following examples illustrate the disruptive power[274]:

> *Example.* "*Old rule:* Information can appear in only one place at one time.
> *Disruptive technology:* Shared databases.
> *New rule:* Information can appear simultaneously in as many places as it is needed."

> *Example.* "*Old rule*: Managers make all decisions.
> *Disruptive technology:* Decision support tools (database access, modelling software).
> *New rule:* Decision-making is a part of everyone's job."

> *Example.* "*Old rule:* Field personnel need offices where they can receive, store, retrieve, and transmit information.
> *Disruptive technology:* Wireless data communication and portable computers.
> *New rule:* Field personnel can send and receive information wherever they are."

---

[270]   Hammer (1996, p268).
[271]   Hammer (1996, p269).
[272]   Hammer and Champy (1994, p83). Italics by Hammer and Champy.
[273]   Hammer and Champy (1994, p91).
[274]   Hammer and Champy (1994, p92- 96).

Modern information technology and telecommunication systems break the classical unity of 'time, place, and action' and create new unities in redesigned processes.

5.6 Evaluation

Business Process Reengineering has created a new *hype*. The danger of hypes is that managers and consultants greet the new approach with open arms, apply the techniques as a tool of management, and finally miss the point. It is difficult to avoid the impression that this has happened to Business Process Reengineering. Hammer writes in the introduction of *The Reengineering Revolution. A Handbook* that not only a lot of reengineering successes can be reported but also a lot of reengineering failures. He remarks that reengineering is not an 'unqualified success'.[275] He writes that reengineering is a very difficult and hard undertaking.[276] Carter states that reengineering has failed to deliver its promised range of benefits. He attributes this failure to the fact that the practice of reengineering is too complex.[277]

To understand the large risk of failure it is worthwhile to summarise what Business Process Reengineering offers and what Business Process Reengineering does not offer. Hammer and Champy identify *why* traditional companies cannot meet the requirements of the market anymore. They point out that a process-oriented approach is required to overcome the limitations of the traditional organisation. They show that employees can be mobilised to serve the needs of the customers. Hammer and Champy describe *what* they want to realise: the rethinking of company strategy, the creation of a new organisation, the emergence of a new world of work, and a change in the behaviour of management and employees. The 'what' of Business Process Reengineering shows a lot of similarities to the Dutch approach of Socio-Technical Systems Design.[278] Both approaches focus on redesigning business processes, reorganising the company based on business processes, integrating different aspects into a 'whole task', and giving authority and responsibility to those who are close to the process. The 'what' of the new world of work intends to remove the division of labour and to mobilise the capabilities of employees.

From a theoretical and practical point of view, Business Process Reengineering has two main shortcomings. Firstly, Business Process Reengineering describes the 'why' and the 'what' of reengineering. However, Business Process Reengineering does not describe *how* these objectives can be realised. The cases which are described give some rough guidelines as to how the main business processes can be identified, how the boundaries between departments can be removed, how process-centred jobs can be outlined, and how the style of management and the culture of the organisation has to be developed. Rough guidelines are not enough. A detailed

---

[275] Hammer and Stanton (1995, pxiv).

[276] Hammer and Stanton (1995, pxiv).) and Carter (1998).

[277] Carter (1998).

[278] See for example Van Eijnatten et al. in Van Eijnatten et al. (1996, p261 ff.) and Simonse (1994).

design theory, a structured design methodology, and a detailed model to guide the change process are needed. Secondly, Business Process Reengineering is mainly a top-down approach. This approach leads to many tensions in the change process. On the one hand, a fundamental and radical change of an organisation within a short period of time requires an autocratic and hierarchical approach. On the other hand, self-management and participation are central in the new organisation. Business Process Reengineering does not offer tools and techniques to cope with this tension. The absence of a design theory and the paradoxical change strategy explains why reengineering is so extremely complex and difficult and why so many failures are reported.

6 The Mini-Company Concept: People make it happen

The shop floor is the heart of the factory. That is the place where the products are made. That is the place where responsibility and accountability are given form. World-class manufacturing requires the development of a vision on the shop floor. Kiyoshi Suzaki has contributed strongly to such a vision.

Kiyoshi Suzaki emphasises the turbulent character of the business environment. Today's companies have to cope with changing needs of customers, with increased pressure of international competition, and with development of new technologies. Suzaki states that survival in the present business world demands control of the processes 'closest to where the action is', and that is the shop floor.[279] He characterises the shop floor as the place where the 'most fundamental value-added activities' take place.[280] He describes the shop floor as the 'most crucial point' of conducting business.[281] For these reasons, he pleads for 'excellence in shop floor management'.[282] In Suzaki's view, the strategy of a company should reflect such thinking.

Suzaki advocates a humanistic approach. In his opinion, people are the centre of the shop floor. He writes[283]:

> "Instead of machines or systems, people must be considered to be at the centre of the shop floor."

And elsewhere[284]:

> "Systems make it possible; people make it happen."

Suzaki has worked out his ideas more or less systematically in *The New Manufacturing Challenge* (1987) and in *The New Shop Floor Management* (1993). These books will be used as key texts. In *The New Manufacturing Challenge*, Suzaki presents many techniques to improve the factory floor. Attention is given to the principles of flow production, methods to design workplaces, techniques to reduce waste, and tools for continuous improvement. In *The New Shop Floor Management* he addresses the key points for renewing an organisation. The following items are discussed: clarity of vision, customer orientation, involvement of all workers, continuous improvement, training of employees and a supportive management style. Suzaki's books have a strong 'how-to-do' character.[285]

---

[279] Suzaki (1993, p262).
[280] Suzaki (1993, p1).
[281] Suzaki (1993, p22).
[282] Suzaki (1993, p22).
[283] Suzaki (1993, p222).
[284] Suzaki (1987, p229).
[285] The ideas of Suzaki have not received a lot of attention in the scientific literature. To my knowledge, the Roermond case is the first case in which the application of the Mini-

137

The following aspects will be presented: the background of the vision of Suzaki (6.1), the importance of the production structure (6.2), the design of the organisational structure (6.3), people orientation (6.4), and evaluation (6.5).

6.1 Background

Kiyoshi Suzaki grew up in Japan. He started his career as an engineer and manager at Toshiba. After several years, he joined the *Boston Consulting Group* in Tokyo as a consultant. This gave him the possibility to take a look behind the scenes of many (industrial) companies in the Far East. Later, he migrated to the United States of America. He followed several business courses and worked for different American companies. Finally, he started his own consulting company. He provided seminars and consulting services to dozens of American, European and Asian companies. Among others, he has trained the management of Philips.

Suzaki is strongly influenced by the production philosophy of the Toyota Motor Corporation. In the acknowledgements of both books, he thanks Mr. Taiichi Ohno of Toyota.[286] Ohno has described the Toyota production system in his book *Toyota Production System. Beyond Large-Scale Production*. Ohno describes the following concepts and techniques in detail: flow production, just-in-time, line-stop, kanban, standard work procedures, visual control, waste recognition, waste elimination, teamwork, and work improvement. All these concepts and techniques return in the books of Suzaki.

In the acknowledgements of his books, Suzaki also thanks the American authors Richard Schonberger, Robert Hall and Steven Wheelwright.[287] Richard Schonberger has written the bestsellers *Japanese Manufacturing Techniques: Nine Hidden Lessons in Simplicity* and *World Class Manufacturing. The Lessons of Simplicity Applied*. In these books total quality control, just-in-time production, flow concepts, problem solving and people involvement are emphasised. Robert Hall has written the book *Attaining manufacturing excellence*. He advocates the philosophy of 'value added manufacturing'.[288] This means executing only those activities that really add value to the product or add value for the customer. Hall focuses on the concepts of total quality control, improving operations by means of the just-in-time approach, and total people involvement. Steven Wheelwright has co-authored the book *Dynamic Manufacturing. Creating the Learning Organisation*.[289] In this book, the following topics are emphasised: creating value for customers, the technical infrastructure of the factory, organisational structure, continuous improvement and the use of the full potential of all workers. One of

---

Company Concept has been evaluated scientifically (see Chapter 3 of this study). Verkerk et al. (1997) and De Leede (1997) published parts of this case earlier.

[286] Suzaki (1987, pxiv) and Suzaki (1993, p450).
[287] Suzaki (1987, pxiii) and Suzaki (1993, p452).
[288] Hall (1987).
[289] Hayes et al. (1988).

the chapters of this book bears the title 'People Make it Happen', showing a strong focus on people.[290]

In summary, Suzaki has developed his ideas about customer orientation, workplace organisation, continuous improvement and people involvement against the background of leading Japanese and American authors.

6.2 Flow production

Kiyoshi Suzaki emphasises the importance of the production structure. In many factories, a function-oriented or process-oriented layout is present. That means machines with the same function or machines that are part of a similar process are grouped together. Different orders are grouped in a large batch that is transferred at regular intervals from one step in the production to the other. In this approach, attention is primarily paid to the efficiency of the individual machines and the quality of the individual steps in the process. Less attention is given to linking the different production steps together. Generally, the function-oriented or process-oriented approach leads to an irregular flow in material and a long lead-time. Various types of waste will be found, e.g. labour-intensive production co-ordination and scheduling, long transportation lines, accumulation of in-process inventory, double or triple handling of materials, extremely long production lead-times, problems in identifying causes of defects, and difficulties in improvement due to lack of standardisation.[291]

Suzaki strongly advocates a product-oriented layout or flow production. In this approach, the different production steps are linked together: machines with different functions or processes are grouped together to produce one product or a family of products. The individual products 'flow' in a continuous stream from the beginning to the end of the line. A lot of attention is paid to the efficiency and the quality of the whole line. In addition, less attention is given to the efficiency of the individual machines and the quality of the individual processes. The product-oriented layout or flow production leads to well-defined material flows, short throughput times and short reaction times. Suzaki proposes parallel production lines for different types or families of types of products. He gives the following arguments[292]:

1. Waste. The flow concept makes a reduction of all kinds of waste possible in, for example, co-ordination, transportation, in-process inventory, handling, lead time, floor space, material consumption and so on.
2. Customer orientation. The flow concept makes a quick response to the changing wishes of the market possible; e.g. product diversification and short delivery times.

---

290   Hayes et al. (1988, p242).
291   Suzaki (1987, p46-49).
292   Suzaki (1987, p49-57).

3. Continuous improvement. The flow concept is a necessary condition for continuous improvement. In this concept, problems in the flow will lead directly to a line-stop. A line- stop means no production. The stop can only be removed by finding the root cause and solving the problem. This results in a continuous improvement of the flow. A lot of techniques to expose problems, to find root causes and to solve problems are described.[293]

The emphasis on flow production brings Suzaki to two 'unusual' statements. Firstly, he rejects the emphasis on the machine utilisation rate. In his view, the 'on-demand-utilisation factor' is much more important. Secondly, he rejects the development of large, efficient, and highly automated machines. These type of machines appear to not be flexible enough to meet the requirements of the market. He advocates improvements in machines and low-cost automation.[294]

Suzaki emphasises that the design of the parallel production lines requires an analysis of the product mix and process flow. The following (simplified) steps are proposed[295]:

1. Product-quantity analysis. The production volume per type is calculated.
2. Process route analysis. The process route for every type is systematically depicted.
3. Grouping. Identical and similar process routes are grouped together.
4. Idea generation. Design of parallel production lines for individual types or families of types.

Suzaki stresses that the design of the production structure has to be human-oriented or human-centred. This comes to the fore in two things. Firstly, he promotes all kinds of improvements that result in easier and more efficient production methods for operators. Secondly, he advocates the view that operators have to participate in projects to improve the machines, the processes and the flow of the production lines.

6.3 Company within a company

In *The New Shop Floor Management*, Suzaki gives a description of his vision on the shop floor. In this description technical, economical, organisational and cultural aspects are mentioned in an arbitrary order[296]:

---

[293] Suzaki (1987, p90 ff., p146 ff.). The systems to expose problems in the line are called the 'nerves and muscles' of the factory.
[294] Suzaki (1987, p57-62).
[295] Suzaki (1987, p73-89).
[296] Suzaki (1993, p38).

- o the shop floor is the core of the activity
- o mutual trust
- o belief in change
- o positive morale
- o working together
- o homogeneous groups
- o understanding internal customers
- o love of product
- o exposing problems
- o motivated people

- o open/transparent organisation
- o involvement of people
- o housekeeping
- o care for product
- o achieving total quality
- o ease of communication
- o learning
- o everything in its place
- o discipline in complying with procedures
- o responsible for own area

In this list, a description of the attitude of the individual operator and characteristics of the group dominate. How can such a 'dream list' of attitudes and characteristics be realised? How can such a vision be implemented? Before answering these questions, it is necessary to describe Suzaki's view on organisations in a changing world.

Organisational innovation
Suzaki compares the business world with the natural world. In the natural world, changes in environmental conditions form a direct threat to survival. Evolutionary processes make it possible for biological species to adapt to these changes. Species that adapt quickly will survive, whereas species that cannot adapt will die out. According to Suzaki, a comparable type of evolutionary process takes place in the business world. In order to cope with the changing environment, companies have to continuously adapt their organisations. In the words of Suzaki[297]:

> "In the business world, too, a company needs to adapt to changes in order to survive. Governed by the law of survival of the fittest as practised in our free market system, the bottom line is that everybody needs to be involved in serving the customer better with minimum waste."

A basic characteristic of organisational innovation is the involvement of all employees. Suzaki quotes with approval the words of Konosuke Matsushita, the founder of Matsushita Electric Industries[298]:

> "Only the intellects of all employees can permit a company to live with the ups and downs of and the requirements of its new environment."

Involvement of all employees means that top-down, bottom-up and cross-functional processes have to be managed.[299]

---

[297] Suzaki (1993, p87).
[298] Suzaki (1993, p27).
[299] Suzaki (1993, p263).

Another basic characteristic of organisational innovation is the continuous drive to produce value for the customer. This drive has to determine the organisational set-up. Barriers that hamper customer satisfaction have to be broken down.[300]

These two basic characteristics – involvement of employees and customer orientation – are connected. Empowered people will break down organisational barriers to serve the customer. A customer-oriented organisation requires empowered people.

Suzaki characterises the renewed organisation using the metaphors of a biological organism, the nervous system of the brain, and an orchestra.[301] These metaphors indicate essential qualities such as adaptability, flexibility, growth and wholeness. The following important points of organisational innovation are mentioned[302]:

o   Top management should clear their own minds in order to identify ways to explore the potential of people.
o   There must be a change from power-oriented thinking to people- and customer-oriented thinking.
o   The power base must shift from the top of the organisation to a lower level (the mini-company concept), so that each decision can be made at the lowest possible level.
o   Top management should help co-ordinate these activities and provide necessary support.
o   As each person in the organisation can be considered the president of a mini-company, everybody should go through the points mentioned above by themselves as well.
o   As we execute these ideas, everybody needs to try to eliminate his for her own job to create more room for growth for everybody else."

The implementation of these important points is the responsibility of top management.

Collection of mini-companies

Kiyoshi Suzaki promotes the idea of a 'company within a company' as the basis of organisational innovation.[303] He describes the organisation as a collection of 'mini-

---

[300] Suzaki (1993, p41 ff.). Compare also Suzaki (1987, p216 ff.).
[301] Suzaki (1987, p232, 237), Suzaki (1993, p49-51, 89, 295).
       Maslow has developed a hierarchy of needs to describe the development of the individual. This model is used by Suzaki to describe the development of an organisation (Suzaki, 1993, p88).
       Suzaki uses the brain metaphor not only to characterise the organisation of the factory but also to characterise the control points to monitor the production lines (Suzaki, 1993, p245, 252).
[302] Suzaki (1993, p89).
[303] Suzaki (1993, p65 ff.).

companies', which are networked by customer-supplier relationships. Every unit or department of a (larger) company is seen as a mini-company. Each mini-company should have its own mission. Employees who work in such a unit or department are the owners of the mini-company. They run their mini-company to serve the internal or external customers. They receive their materials from internal or external suppliers. They report regularly to the management of the company, who are considered as bankers who provide the mini-company with resources.

Suzaki indicates the following steps as essential for running the mini-company[304]:

1. "Name the mini-company.
2. Write a mission statement for the mini-company.
3. Make up a company profile by listing its people and describing its machines, etc.
4. Develop a customer-supplier relationship chart for the mini-company and discuss the meaning of the arrows (Suzaki indicates the strength and the character of customer-supplier relationships with different arrows in his figures, MJV).
5. Clarify the objectives of the mini-company.
6. Develop plans of action to achieve objectives, then execute plans.
7. Monitor the progress, and celebrate the accomplishment as appropriate.
8. Repeat this cycle at regular intervals."

All these steps have to be carried out by the employees of the mini-company. Naming the mini-company is important. It often gives people a 'sense of identity'.[305] Each mini-company should have its own mission or value statement.[306] In the view of Suzaki, the mission is more than a collection of words. It represents the 'will-power and creativity of the people'.[307] It is the result of a 'desire for self-expression'.[308] It should be something that we can 'identify with'.[309] It allows people to develop 'greater ownership and pride' in what they do.[310] It reflects the 'intrinsic values of the organisation'.[311] The company profile describes the mini-company: the machines, processes and employees. The customer-supplier relationships are charted to describe the relationships, to reduce barriers between units or departments, and to practice customer orientation.[312] The objectives of the mini-company are discussed to develop a joint vision within the mini-company. A

---

[304] Suzaki (1993, p70). See also Suzaki (1993, p264 ff.).
[305] Suzaki (1993, p74).
[306] The mission of the company is developed in a combined top-down and bottom-up process. The mission of the mini-company should be in-line with the mission of the company (Suzaki, 1993, p284-286).
[307] Suzaki (1993, p73).
[308] Suzaki (1993, p73).
[309] Suzaki (1993, p73).
[310] Suzaki (1993, p74).
[311] Suzaki (1993, p73).
[312] Suzaki (1993, p41 ff., 65 ff.).

combination of top-down and bottom-up processes is proposed to realise congruent objectives in the company.[313] The objectives have to be realised by the execution of the improvement cycle. This cycle consists of the following activities[314]:

- o plan (make a plan)
- o do (execute the plan)
- o check (measure whether the objectives have been achieved)
- o action (if the objectives are not met, analyse and develop new plan).

Monitoring forms an important part of the improvement cycle[315]. Without monitoring, there can be no improvement. The indicators for customer satisfaction, performance of the mini-company and health of the organisation have to be measured and displayed. White boards on the shop floor are used to share information and to celebrate progress. It is 'having fun' with 'show and tell'.[316] Suzaki uses the metaphor of glass wall management to indicate open communication throughout the organisation; open communication about the mini-company, its mission, its objectives, its performance and its health. [317] This cycle has to be repeated at regular intervals.

Continuous communication with the customers, suppliers and management is of utmost importance, especially with regards to formulating the mission, objectives and improvement plan of the mini-company. This communication is the responsibility of the president of the mini-company (supervisor).[318]

Mini-company as metaphor

The idea of a mini-company is applied in the first place to production units[319]. Suzaki does not explicitly discuss the relation between the production structure (parallel lines, production of parts or sub-assemblies in separate groups) and the organisational structure (different mini-companies). Based on the examples given in his books, a direct link can be expected. Every production unit should be able to manage its activities as a mini-company. The operators who are working in such a unit form the mini-company. The customers of the mini-company are internal customers (next production process) or external customers. The suppliers of the mini-company are internal suppliers (previous production process) or external suppliers. Finally, the mini-company reports on a regular basis to line management.

The idea of a mini-company is applied in the second place to auxiliary departments.[320] Auxiliary departments have to actively develop customer-supplier relationships with the production departments. Are the requirements of the customers

---

[313] Suzaki (1993, p77, 262 ff.).
[314] Suzaki (1993, p103 ff., 196 ff., 229 ff.).
[315] Suzaki (1993, p87 ff., 229 ff., 262 ff.).
[316] Suzaki (1993, p147).
[317] Suzaki (1993, p78 ff.).
[318] Suzaki (1993, p71).
[319] Suzaki (1993, p65 ff., 87 ff., 229 ff., 262 ff.).
[320] Suzaki (1993, p68 ff.).

144

clear? Are the customers satisfied with the service? How can we improve? Auxiliary departments have to function as a 'company'. All aspects of mini-companies can be applied: mission, customer relationships, supplier relationships, improvement program and so on.

The idea of a mini-company is applied in the third place to management and people on the shop floor. This means managers may see "… people at the shop floor as their customers, in conveying the idea to get things done. Also, people on the shop floor may view managers as customers, in proposing improvement ideas and getting resources for implementation."[321] In other words, the dependence between managers and workers is defined as a customer-supplier relationship.

The idea of a mini-company is applied in the fourth place to the activities of an individual in a mini-company. The mini-company idea relates to the idea of self management. Every person is the 'president' of his or her area of responsibility and must deal with customers, suppliers, employees, and bankers in running his or her mini-company.[322] In this context, Suzaki uses the word 'mini-mini-company' to characterise the activities of individuals in a mini-company.[323]

In conclusion, the idea of a mini-company is used by Suzaki to describe the activities and responsibilities of individuals and departments in organisations. This idea functions as a metaphor to describe processes and relations. Suzaki has worked out this metaphor in detail for production units. His ideas also can be applied to auxiliary departments. In addition, he indicates how this metaphor can be applied to the relationship between management and employees, and to the activities of individuals.

6.4 People make it happen

Suzaki really knows what the shop floor is. On every page of his books the love for employees can be felt. He writes sensitively and states that experiences on the shop floor make us 'feel humble'.[324] Suzaki interprets the factory as a human organisation. He places people in the centre of the shop floor.[325] He believes that systems make production possible and that people make it happen.[326]

Portrayal of man
Kiyoshi Suzaki regularly attacks the traditional or Tayloristic organisation.[327] He reproaches these organisations because employees are seen as tools or extensions of machines, because the creativity, skills and brains of employees are not used, and

---

[321] Suzaki (1993, p65).
[322] Suzaki (1993, p65, 86). See also Suzaki (1993, p262, 298). This idea has been worked out in detail for every job in an organisation (Suzaki, 1993, p73).
[323] Suzaki (1993, p269).
[324] Suzaki (1993, p10).
[325] Suzaki (1993, p222).
[326] Suzaki (1987, p229).
[327] Suzaki (1993, p4, 26-29, 61, 79-83, 200-202, 287-291, 296-299).

because the values of employees are not respected. Suzaki wants to pass the stage of Taylorism. He mentions 'respect for people' as one of the core values of shop floor management.[328]

Suzaki stresses the importance of the shop floor. He characterises the shop floor as the place where the action is, as the place where the wishes of customers are fulfilled. Suzaki states that the capabilities of every employee are needed to control and to improve the shop floor. He writes[329]:

> "In other words, a customer-oriented organisation should be a people-oriented organisation. Accordingly, a major role of managers in a people-oriented organisation is to develop people's capabilities."

The importance of training is emphasised in every chapter.[330] Suzaki quotes with approval the words of Konosuke Matsushita that we first have 'to make people' before 'making products'.[331] Making people means: stimulate the creativity, use the brains, and develop the skills of employees. It also means to develop 'pride and higher self-esteem' in their jobs.[332] Suzaki founds his idea of developing the capabilities of people on the hierarchy of needs as proposed by Maslow: addressing the higher needs of the employees.[333]

The views of Suzaki are sustained by the idea that development of people means development of the organisation[334]:

> "What we are addressing here is a way in which management can instil in each individual a belief that as he or she grows, the company grows as well. In other words, if each person has self-managing or autonomous capabilities while linked to the total organisation, we can create a system that is more humane, addressing the minds of people as opposed to simply viewing the business only in terms of financial position."

Suzaki connects the 'secret of man' with the activities of employees on the shop floor[335]:

> "I believe we all share something in common. Whether it is our willpower or creativity or something else (...) as soon as we try to describe (...) we may lose the essence (...) the analogy that comes to my mind is the moon shining in the sky and the dew on the grass reflecting the moon in each drop. The moon represents the core value. Since each human being is valuable, regardless of his fate, each of us is a dewdrop. Within each of us, we have something that is the core of our being. And perhaps, if

---

[328] Suzaki (1993, p297).
[329] Suzaki (1993, p67).
[330] See especially Suzaki (1993, p116 ff.).
[331] Suzaki (1993, p5, 66-67).
[332] Suzaki (1993, p31).
[333] Suzaki (1993, p88, 220).
[334] Suzaki (1993, p5).
[335] Suzaki (1993, p342-343).

we are attentive and our minds are not preoccupied, we might see evidence of this on our shop floor, too."

Suzaki ends *The New Shop Floor Management* by expressing his confidence in the capabilities of man[336]:

"I am sure that we can find a solid foundation [i.e. to cope with the turbulence of the market on the shop floor, MJV] within ourselves."

This statement raises many questions. Why does Suzaki believe in the individual? Why is he so positive about the capability of man to improve his situation? Why is he so positive that we hold destiny in our hands? Why does he expect management to accept a change in power? There are some indications that the belief of Suzaki in the individual is founded in the Buddhist doctrine of enlightenment and self-salvation.[337]

Style of management

The portrayal of man as pictured by Suzaki has a great influence on his view on management. In contrast with traditional or Tayloristic management he stresses an open and trusting management style, development of people, sharing of information, decentralised power structure and encouragement of self-management.[338] Suzaki states that development of trust relations between management and employees is the responsibility of management.[339] He writes that the level of an employee's morale depends on the leadership of management.[340] An important role of management is to upgrade the skills and to address the higher needs of people.[341] Suzaki puts the importance of management in perspective. He states that leadership is situational which means that "There are times when managers must lead, and times when individuals must lead."[342]

Suzaki stresses the need for a change in power. In his opinion, there must be a change from 'power-oriented thinking' to 'people- and customer-oriented thinking'.[343] He warns that managers should overcome the fear of losing control.[344]

---

[336] Suzaki (1993, p344).
[337] Suzaki emphasises continuously that one of the main hurdles to implementing shop floor management is our own attitude, our own beliefs, and our own ego. He emphasises continuously that we have to find our own solutions. These remarks match Buddhist thought which states that the cause of all evil and the power of salvation lies within the human individual. Furthermore, the epilogue of *The New Shop Floor Management* speaks volumes.
[338] Suzaki (1993, p201, see also p297).
[339] Suzaki (1987, p225).
[340] Suzaki (1987, p233).
[341] Suzaki (1993, p124, 220).
[342] Suzaki (1993, p202).
[343] Suzaki (1993, p89, see also p288).
[344] Suzaki (1993, p201), see also Suzaki (1987, p224).

Finally, he teaches that our ego, orientation to power, mind set, and hang ups is the 'ultimate hurdle' in realising this change.[345]

6.5 Evaluation

Suzaki is not a scientist. He does not work on a theoretical justification of his view. He does not provide a well-founded organisational theory. Suzaki is also not a philosopher. He does not present fundamental conceptions about man and organisations. He does not think in depth about the essence of man and the meaning of labour. Suzaki is a consultant. He tries to sell his ideas, advice and books. Suzaki has visited many factories within various industries. He has spoken with managers and employees. First and foremost, he knows the shop floor. He knows that workers on the shop floor in traditional factories are seen as production factors, as tools or extension of machines. He knows that workers on the shop floor in people-oriented factories are considered as talented beings and sources of creativity. Suzaki knows about de-humanisation and alienation in Tayloristic organisations. He knows about pride, self-esteem and ownership in participative organisations. Above all, Suzaki loves people. You can feel it on every page of his books. You can feel it if you listen to his presentations or if you speak to him personally.

Suzaki emphasises that the organisation of a factory has to be human-centred or human-oriented. This means that the technical structure and the organisational structure have to be designed in such a way that people can make it happen. Suzaki strongly advocates organisations in which people can develop their creativity, pride, and self-esteem. In the realisation of the human organisation, the Mini-Company Concept plays an important role.

The ideas of Suzaki have to be understood against the background of the Toyota Production System (see section 6.1). The elimination of waste is a cornerstone of his approach. He emphasises flow production, workplace organisation, design of equipment, reduction of waste, and continuous improvement. All these techniques originate from Taiichi Ohno.

Suzaki pays a lot of attention to the layout of the factory. He advocates a product-oriented production structure. This means that machines with different functions are grouped together to enable the manufacturing of (a family of) products. The individual products 'flow' in a continuous stream from the beginning to the end of the line. This approach entails the design of parallel production lines to manufacture different (families of) products. Suzaki gives some guidelines on redesigning the production into parallel lines. These guidelines are comparable with the Dutch approach of Socio-Technical Systems Design (see section 3.4). However, a detailed design theory and design methodology is not presented.

Suzaki links the organisation of the factory directly to the production structure. The employees who work in a parallel production line (or in an auxiliary unit) form a group. This group is responsible for all aspects of the production, e.g.

---

[345] Suzaki (1996, Annex p4).

production planning, quality, logistics, relations with suppliers and customers, the morale of the group, improvement activities, and so on. In this way, Suzaki locates the control capacity as low as possible in the organisation. Comparison with Socio-Technical Systems Design reveals two issues. First, in both approaches the control capacity is located as low as possible in the organisation. In the Dutch approach, the control structure has been built up in a systematic way. In the mini-company approach, this is done more qualitatively. Second, in the Dutch approach the control capacity is mainly limited to technical and logistic aspects of the production. However, in the mini-company approach 'all' aspects of a company are involved. The last issue relates to Suzaki's view on organisations. He considers a mini-company as an element in a network of relations. The different stakeholders of the mini-company, e.g. internal and/or external customers, internal and/or external suppliers, management, employees, and society as a whole, form the network.

In conclusion, in the Mini-Company Concept a technical approach and a human-oriented approach are combined. Suzaki presents a number of (Japanese) production techniques to realise flow production, to reduce waste, and to enable continuous improvement. At the same time, he proposes an organisation in which participation and communication is structurally anchored.

In the mini-company, the interests of the different stakeholders are balanced. This balancing process takes place by defining the mission and by drawing up the improvement program. Here, one of the strongest points of Suzaki's concept comes to the fore. He gives an organisational approach to combine continuous improvement, participation of employees and recognition of the interests of different stakeholders. These topics are combined in a program to run the company. Tools to execute the different steps of this program are given. Suzaki has worked out the participative processes of goal-setting and execution more structurally than Socio-Technical Systems Design, Lean Production, and Business Process Reengineering.

7 Evaluation

In this evaluation, Socio-Technical Systems Design, Lean Production, Business Process Reengineering, and the Mini-Company Concept will be related, compared, and reviewed against the background of Scientific Management. Particular attention will be given to the design of the workplace, the responsibility of employees, and the implementation strategy.

Design of the workplace

In his testimony before the Special House Committee, Frederick Taylor summarised the essence of Scientific Management in two principles. The first principle refers to a complete mental revolution from the side of both employees and employers to realise maximum prosperity for both parties. The second principle specifies a scientific investigation of the workplace to determine the 'one best way' and the 'one best implement'. These two principles return – in quite different shape – within the new production concepts. Figure 7.1 gives an overview of this.

In Scientific Management the 'mental revolution' is focused on 'heartily cooperation'. This cooperation is supported by the development of scientific methods and a hierarchical organisation. Lean Production follows the same track. The 'maximum prosperity' for both employees and employers as proposed by Taylor finds its counterpart in the 'community of fate' present in Japanese companies.[346] In Lean Production the scientific methods originally developed by Taylor and his disciples are refined and extended by the development of a coherent set of production technologies.[347] Lean Production deviates from Taylorism in its emphasis on continuous improvement and the participation of employees in the improvement process. In Lean Production a hierarchical organisation is also present.[348] In Scientific Management and Lean Production the scientific investigation of the workplace in focused on the technical aspects. A high division of labour and short work cycles is present.

In Socio-Technical Systems Design, Business Process Reengineering, and the Mini-Company Concept, the 'mental revolution' has structural-organisational characteristics. That means cooperation is supported by participative organisational structures. Socio-Technical Systems Design and the Mini-Company Concept offer a set of detailed methods and approaches to develop a participative organisation. Business Process Reengineering advocates the same track but does not give a

---

[346] Cole has done a comparative study in American and Japanese industry. He says that in Japanese companies the employees believe that they share a common destiny with each other. They will all sink or swim together. Cole termed this belief the 'community of fate', see Besser (1996, p14). The idea of a common destiny is strongly expressed in the publication of Toyota (Toyota, 1992, p1-3).

[347] Delbridge (1998). Conti and Warner (1993) and Kanigel (1997, p490-492) describe the diffusion of Taylorism in Japan.

[348] A 'simple' comparison between American Scientific Management and Japanese Lean Production is difficult because hierarchy has to be understood against the background of the whole culture, see Hofstede (1980) and Trompenaars (1993).

detailed method for change. In Socio-Technical Systems Design, Business Process Reengineering, and the Mini-Company Concept, a style of management is described (prescribed) that corresponds with the participative character of the organisation. In Socio-Technical Systems Design, Business Process Reengineering, and the Mini-Company Concept, the scientific investigation of the workplace is focused on the organisational aspects. Additionally, in the Mini-Company Concept a lot of attention is also paid to the technical aspects of the workplace and the continuous improvement of it. In the Mini-Company Concept the improvement techniques are not only applied to technical but also to social and moral issues. Generally, Socio-Technical Systems Design, Business Process Reengineering, and the Mini-Company Concept offer complete and whole tasks, and long work cycles.[349]

Responsibility of employees

The responsibility of employees in Taylorism and new production concepts will be compared according to three aspects. The first aspect covers functional responsibilities.[350] The second aspect refers to responsibilities with respect to the design of the workplace and continuous improvement. The last aspect has to do with social and moral responsibilities. Figure 7.2 gives an overview of this. (To prevent the repeated use of the word pair 'responsibility and accountability', the word 'responsibility' in this paragraph also includes 'accountability'.)

In the Taylor system the responsibility of employees is limited to one aspect of the whole production process: the execution of one or more short-cycled production steps or transformation processes. The responsibility for other functional aspects like planning, preparing the equipment, and quality measurements is located one level above the employee, i.e. the foreman. The responsibility of the employee is restricted to the execution of a transformation process. The responsibility for the controlling aspect is also located one level above the employee, i.e. the foreman. The responsibility for social and moral aspects is limited to disciplinary issues. Lean Production follows the Tayloristic track. The employee is responsible for the execution of one or more short-cycled production steps or transformation processes. The employee is also responsible for functional aspects like planning, preparing the equipment, and measuring quality. This responsibility is designed into the production structure as much as possible. Control aspects are also designed into the production structure as much as possible. Generally, the pace of the belt limits the possibilities for executive and control tasks, which are not fully integrated in the production line. In Lean Production, the employee has

---

[349] In the Dutch approach of Socio-Technical Systems Design, a structural approach is given to design the production process to longer work cycles, see De Sitter (1994).

[350] De Sitter (1994) has given a detailed analysis of the manufacturing process. He describes the manufacturing process as a sequence of relating sub-processes. Each sub-process can be characterised with a verb: to accept an order, to plan the production, to prepare the equipment, to execute the transformation processes, to perform the quality measurements, to deliver the product and to send the bill. Every process has an executive and a controlling aspect.

the responsibility to make suggestions and to participate in improvement teams. The improvement teams are mostly focused on the workplace. Social and moral responsibility is limited to legal and disciplinary issues.

In Socio-Technical Systems Design, Business Process Reengineering, and the Mini-Company Concept, the employee is responsible for the execution of a coherent part of the production process, a module, or a whole product. At the same time, the employee is responsible for other functional aspects like planning, preparing the equipment, measuring quality and for the control aspects of the different functional aspects. In Socio-Technical Systems Design and Business Process Reengineering, the functional responsibilities of employees with respect to the customer (and/or supplier) are not elaborated. In the Mini-Company Concept these responsibilities have been developed structurally. In Socio-Technical Systems Design, Business Process Reengineering, and the Mini-Company Concept the employee is jointly responsible for the design of the own workplace. In the Mini-Company Concept, the responsibility for continuous improvement is elaborated in detail. In Socio-Technical Systems Design, Business Process Reengineering, and the Mini-Company Concept, the employee is also responsible for social and moral aspects. In the Mini-Company Concept, the social and moral responsibility of the employee is well elaborated. At the same time, continuous improvement with respect to these aspects is emphasised.

Implementation strategy

The implementation strategies of the new production concepts vary greatly. Lean Production has developed no specific implementation methods and follows the hierarchical track of the Taylor system. Business Process Reengineering also has no implementation strategy. In practice, a hierarchical top-down process is used that is incompatible with the characteristics of the new organisation. Consequently, many failures are reported. In Socio-Technical Systems Design and the Mini-Company Concept participative change strategies have been developed. The advantage of a participative change strategy is that employees feel ownership of the change process.

Conclusion

Socio-Technical Systems Design, Lean Production, Business Process Reengineering, and the Mini-Company Concept offer different approaches to technical organisations. Lean Production follows the technical and hierarchical track of Scientific Management. The division of labour is high and the work cycles are short. Consequently, the responsibility and accountability of employees is limited to the functional aspects of one or more short-cycled production steps. Business Process Reengineering presents a challenging view of a new organisation. However, it is not described how this new organisation can be realised. Socio-Technical Systems Design, and the Mini-Company Concept follow a different track. The division of labour is greatly reduced and the work cycles are long(er). Participation of employees in the technical and organisational processes is a core value. The responsibility of the employees covers technical, customer-oriented, design and improvement, and social and moral issues.

The differences between Socio-Technical Systems Design, Lean Production, Business Process Reengineering, and the Mini-Company Concept are not only differences on the level of organisational theory. They reflect fundamentally different views on man, labour, and organisations. In Chapter 4 this subject will be elaborated on.

Figure 7.1 Comparison of Scientific Management and New Production Concepts: mental revolution and scientific focus

	Mental revolution	Scientific focus
Scientific Management	• appeal to employees and employers to cooperate heartily • appeal to employees is 'supported' by bonuses and the organisational hierarchy • appeal to employers is not supported by organisational measures • hierarchical organisation	• scientific investigation of the workplace is focused on technical aspects • expert approach • high division of labour, short work cycles, standardisation, and functional leadership
Socio-Technical System Design	• cooperation of employees and employers is a structural characteristic of the organisation • key characteristic of the organisation is the socio-technical design (Dutch school), participative structures (Australian school), and communicative processes (Scandinavian school) • participative organisation	• scientific investigation of the workplace is focused on organisational processes • participative design of the workplace • design of complete and whole tasks • long work cycles
Lean Production	• joint effort of employees and employers to reduce waste • idea of 'community of fate' • continuous improvement is a structural characteristic of the organisation; tools for technical improvements are well-developed • hierarchical organisation	• scientific investigation of the workplace is focused on technical aspects • improvement of the workplace • high division of labour, short work cycles, and standardisation
Business Process Reengineering	• employees and employers cooperate together in a process-oriented organisation • general principles for a process-oriented organisation are given • participative organisation	• scientific investigation of the workplace is focused on business processes • complete and whole tasks
The Mini-Company Concept	• employees and employers cooperate together in the mini-company process • participation is structurally anchored in the mini-company process; continuous improvement is focused on technical, social and moral issues • participative organisation	• scientific investigation of the workplace is focused on all aspects of a mini-company • participative design of the workplace • continuous improvement of the workplace • complete and whole tasks • short and long work cycles

Figure 7.2 *Comparison of Scientific Management and New Production Concepts: functional responsibility, responsibility for design and improvement, and social and moral responsibility of employees on the shop floor. (Note: For style reasons, the word 'responsibility' in this paragraph also includes 'accountability'.)*

	Functional responsibility	Responsibility for design and improvement	Social and moral responsibility
Scientific Management	• the employee is responsible for the execution of one or more short-cycled transformation processes • the responsibility for other functional aspects is located one level above the employee: the foreman • the responsibility for control aspects is located one level above the employee: the foreman	• the employee is stimulated to make suggestions for improvement	• the employee is responsible for the discipline
Socio-Technical Systems Design	• the employee is responsible for the execution of a complete task: coherent part, module, or whole product • the employee is responsible for other functional aspects of the whole-task group like planning, preparation of the equipment, and quality measurements • the employee is responsible for control aspects of the whole task	• the employee is jointly responsible for the design of the workplace	• the employee is responsible for the discipline • the employee is responsible for meeting legal regulations • the employee is responsible for the social and moral aspects of the whole-task group
Lean Production	• the employee is responsible for the execution of one or more short-cycled transformation processes • the employee is (partly) responsible for other functional aspects (which are mostly integrated in the production line) • the employee is (partly) responsible for control aspects (which are mostly integrated in the production line)	• the employee is stimulated to make suggestions for improvement • the employee has the responsibility to participate in improvement teams • improvement is focused on the workplace	• the employee is responsible for the discipline • the employee is responsible for meeting legal regulations

Business Process Re engineering	• the employee is responsible for the execution of a complete task: coherent part, module, or whole product • the employee is responsible for other functional aspects of the business process like planning, preparation of the equipment, quality measurements, and relations with the customer • the employee is responsible for control aspects of the business process	• the employee is jointly responsible for the design of the workplace	• the employee is responsible for the discipline • the employee is responsible for meeting legal regulations • the employee is responsible for the social and moral aspects of the process team
The Mini-Company Concept	• the employee is responsible for the execution of a complete task: coherent part, module, or whole product • the employee is responsible for other functional aspects of the mini-company like planning, preparation of the equipment, quality measurements, and relations with the supplier and the customer • the employee is responsible for control aspects of the mini-company	• the employee is jointly responsible for the design of the workplace • the employee is jointly responsible for improvement with respect to all functional aspects of the production • a structured approach for continuous improvement is given	• the employee is responsible for the discipline • the employee is responsible for meeting legal regulations • the employee is responsible for the social and moral aspects of the mini-company: structural approach is given • the employee is responsible for the improvement of the social and moral issues of the mini-company

CHAPTER 3
Case studies

Societal developments are urging modern industries to abandon classical manufacturing methods and to introduce new production concepts. These new concepts promise a 'new world of work' that combines technical superiority with social innovation. However, in practice, these new concepts fall short in preventing the development of paradoxes and managerial short cuts. Additionally, the promise of a 'new world of work' is often not realised.

To understand the failure of these new production concepts an integrative analysis on three levels is necessary. These levels are: concrete phenomena on the shop floor, the basics of organisational design theory, and the philosophy of organisation. For each level, a research question has been formulated. These questions are:

How do paradoxes evolve on the shop floor?

Why do new production concepts fail in many modern factories?

How can employees on the shop floor act in a responsible way?

The previous chapter presented an in-depth study of the new production concepts in modern factories. Particular attention was paid to the design of the workplace, the responsibility of employees, and the implementation strategy.

In this chapter these research questions are investigated on the basis of two ethnographical case studies in manufacturing. These cases are presented from the perspective of a factory manager as 'reflective practitioner'. The first case concerns the set-up of a new factory in Roermond (The Netherlands); and the second deals with the turning-around of a factory in Aachen (Germany). I was responsible for the manufacturing operation in both factories. The objective of these case studies is to investigate the research questions *from within*.

This chapter is structured in the following way. Section 1 summarises the methodology used in this study. Section 2 describes the Roermond case study. Section 3 outlines the Aachen case study. The last section compares the main similarities between these case studies.

1 Methodological approach

In the book *Onderzoek in organisaties. Een methodologische reisgids*, (*Research in Organisations. A methodological guide*) Friso den Hertog and Ed van Sluijs use the metaphor of a traveller to characterise the role of a researcher in organisational research.[1] They use this metaphor for two purposes. In the first place, they emphasise that the investigator has to travel to the organisation in order to understand the processes at hand. S/he has to leave the familiar environment of the university. S/he has to trek to a (partly) unknown terrain. S/he has to explore the new territory step by step. S/he has to experience the habits and customs of the organisation. S/he has to unravel the formal and informal patterns of behaviour that drive day-to-day behaviour.

In the second place, Den Hertog and Van Sluijs use this metaphor as a heuristic means. A traveller has to make an itinerary. The destination, the duration, the means of transportation and so on has to be determined. The same holds for the investigator. S/he has to make a design of the whole study. Firstly, the objective of the study has to be defined. This objective can be defined in detail, e.g. the testing of a specific hypothesis about the behaviour of employees in an organisation. The objective can also have an open character, e.g. the characterisation of a sub-culture in a technical organisation. Secondly, the researcher has to choose a set of instruments for his or her investigations. The instrument can be a questionnaire which reveals specific and detailed data about the subject under investigation. The instrument can also be the researcher him- or herself. For example, in action research and ethnography the researcher is one of the key observers. In this case, phenomenological data is gathered. It goes without saying that the methodology applied depends greatly on the objective of the study. Thirdly, the researcher has to choose a certain role. For example, the researcher can remain impartial during one of the key processes of a survey as an assistant can supervise the filling in of questionnaires by respondents. However, during an ethnographical study where the manager is ethnographer – as in this study – the researcher plays an active role in the change process. S/he is jointly responsible for the design and the course of the change process under investigation.

1.1 Research design

The development of a research design is an important part of a scientific study. It guides the researcher in ensuring that the initial research question will be addressed. Robert K. Yin gives the following definition of a research design[2]:

> "In the most elementary sense, the design is the logical sequence that connects the empirical data to a study's initial research questions and, ultimately, to its conclusions. Colloquially, a research design is *an action plan for getting from here to there*,

---

[1]   Hertog and Sluijs (1995).
[2]   Yin (1994, p19). Italics by Yin.

where *here* may be defined as the initial set of questions to be answered, and *there* is some set of conclusions (answers) about these questions. Between 'here' and 'there' may be found a number of major steps, including the collection and analysis of relevant data."

The following elements are important in a research design[3]:

- o   the research question of the study;
- o   the objective of the study;
- o   the research strategy (logical reasoning) to relate the 'here' (the initial questions) to the 'there' (the conclusions);
- o   the method of working (methods of collecting data);
- o   the products of the investigation;
- o   the planning and organisation of the project.

This first section looks at the first four elements in more detail.

1.2 Research questions of this study

The wording of a research question in a scientific study is crucial.[4] The research questions of this study have been formulated as follows:

How do paradoxes evolve on the shop floor?

Why do new production concepts fail in many modern factories?

How can employees on the shop floor act in a responsible way?

It took a long time to come up with the wording.[5] To understand the background of the research questions, I would like to give you a short outline of this process.

I started my career in production in a component factory in Eindhoven. I had some rough ideas about man and labour when I started. These ideas were formed during my college days at which point a discussion was taking place within our churches about the position of man in his environment. The discussion focused on the value of the cultural mandate in the present society. We invited various authors to our student union and discussed this subject extensively. This is why I studied the following books: *Christ and Culture* by K. Schilder, *Man: The Image of God* by G.C. Berkouwer, *De mens onderweg* (*Man on his way*) by H. Berkhof, *Algemene genade* (*Common Grace*) by J. Douma, and *Ethiek en pelgrimage* (*Ethics and*

---

[3]   Hertog and Sluijs (1995, p54-62) and Yin (1994, p18-53).
[4]   Strauss and Corbin (1990, p33-40), Yin (1994, p6 ff.) and Hertog and Sluijs (1995, p55-57).
[5]   In fact, this process can be characterised as 'explanation building', see section 1.4.4 of this chapter.

162

Pilgrimage) by W.H. Velema.[6] The cultural mandate emphasises that man is a responsible being; that man is an office holder; that man is placed on earth to develop nature and culture to the honour of God. Labour is an important part of that mandate. The idea of the cultural mandate appeared to be fruitful. In The Netherlands it has been diffused and elaborated on in various Christian political parties and Christian trade unions.[7]

I started my professional training in management within my first year as factory manager of the component factory in Eindhoven. I was trained in the Dutch approach to Socio-Technical Systems Design. This approach offers a detailed design theory for (industrial) organisations. It offers an integral approach to the quality of the organisation, the quality of work life and the quality of labour relations. I attended lectures by, among others, Ulbo de Sitter, the father of the Dutch approach. De Sitter brings back memories of commitment. He wanted to put an end to the extreme division of work in industrial organisations. He was moved by the phenomena of alienation and dehumanisation. De Sitter was also one of the few scientists in this field who connected the design of organisations to questions of meaning ('Sinn').[8] The Dutch approach to Socio-Technical Systems Design gave me a framework within which I could realise my 'tacit' ideas about man and labour.

Starting up a new factory in Roermond (for the production of ceramic multi-layer actuators) gave me a chance to develop my ideas further. In the initial phase, operators, engineers and managers worked together to solve problems and to realise production. A typical pioneering atmosphere was present. There was enthusiasm, commitment, a lack of organisational boundaries, limited hierarchical influence, a problem-oriented atmosphere, and participation within all functions and layers. Gradually, the organisation developed into a maturer phase. In this period I was faced with the question of how to carry forward the basic characteristics of the preceding phase (the pioneering phase) into the mature phase. This question arose both within the management team and on the shop floor. The Dutch approach to Socio-Technical Systems Design did not help me to answer this question. The production structure and the control structure were already designed according to this approach. Both an external consultant and a Philips director drew my attention to the *The New Shop Floor Management* book by Kiyoshi Suzaki. As soon as I started reading the book, I was enthusiastic about it. Suzaki's ideas about the shop floor matched my ideas about man and labour. Suzaki emphasises the integral responsibility of employees (e.g. responsibility for the deliveries, quality of products, use of scarce materials, environment, and morale in the group). At the same time, he offers a framework within which this integral responsibility can be realised. In a participative process with our employees we implemented the Suzaki model in our factory. This process has been described in the book *Marktgericht productie*

---

[6]   Schilder (1977), Berkouwer (1962), Berkhof (1969), Douma (1974) and Velema (1974). The meaning of the term 'man: the image of God' has been discussed in Verkerk and Vegter (1990).

[7]   See Boersema (1999).

[8]   De Sitter (1994). See also Eijnatten et al. (1995, 1996).

management. Van taakgroep naar mini-company (Market-oriented production management. From Work Group to Mini-Company) by myself, Jan de Leede and Henk van der Tas.[9] In this book a preliminary analysis of processes of responsibility and accountability on the shop floor has been given. The conditions that have to be realised by management were made explicit. This book also includes a philosophical analysis about responsibility and meaning.[10] This theme has been subsequently elaborated on in various articles.[11]

In my last year in the Roermond factory, the idea arose of doing a systematic investigation of responsibility and accountability on the shop floor. I discussed this idea with Dr. Ir. Egbert Schuurman, Professor of Reformational Philosophy and Philosophy of Technology. Provisionally, the focus was on the relation between technology and organisations. The basic assumption was that organisations are managed in a technological way. This view ignores the humanity of industrial organisations. Consequently, employees on the shop floor are dominated and their responsibility is limited to functional aspects. By then, I was put in contact with Dr. Friso Den Hertog, Professor of Technology, Organisational Design, and Organisational Policy. In his view, the 'competitive edge' of the study had to be the description of organisational processes through the eyes of a manager. He told me that these types of studies are scarce. In the meantime, I had started my job in the Aachen factory. During my training period, I realised that the processes on the shop floor had to be greatly improved. Paradoxes and managerial short cuts troubled the shop floor. Lack of discipline and process control had left deep marks in the factory. Deep-rooted mistrust and widespread frustration were present in the whole organisation. I had to conclude that new production concepts were not working in the Aachen factory. During an intensive discussion with Egbert Schuurman and Friso den Hertog it was concluded that – in one way or another – the relation between 'responsibility' and 'accountability' was pivotal. It was clear that particular attention had to be paid to the conditions which have to be fulfilled by the factory manager so that employees can bear responsibility and can render accountability. Furthermore, it was decided that a multi-level approach would be fruitful (ethnography, organisational design theory, and philosophy).

After this meeting, it took a period of two years to map paradoxes on the shop floor, to understand the managerial short cuts, and to identify the importance of fulfilling organisational conditions. Once the first versions of the Roermond and the Aachen case were written, the rough draft of the research questions was finalised.

In the final stage of the study, the research questions were 're-interpreted' by identifying trust and power as key conditions for enabling employee responsibility and accountability on the shop floor. In addition, the study was 're-positioned' due to the upcoming debate about the social responsibility of organisations.

---

[9]   Verkerk et al. (1997).
[10]   Verkerk et al. (1997, p173-183).
[11]   Verkerk and De Leede (1997), Verkerk (1998), and Verkerk and De Leede (1999).

1.3 Objective of this study

The investigations of this study were done when I was working as factory manager. In both cases I was jointly responsible for the development of manufacturing organisations. My first objective was to develop the manufacturing organisations so that they could become world-class.[12] The change processes to realise this objective were initiated and managed. This objective was in no way contradictory to the scientific study of this change process. In fact, exploration, application, and theory development went hand in hand. Scientific reflections during a change process are of the utmost importance in understanding observed phenomena and in deciding about the next steps to take.

In the Prologue, I have identified the paradox between responsibility and accountability that arises every day on the shop floor of industrial organisations. I have indicated that this paradox has a disastrous effect on organisations. It has a negative influence on the technical and economic performance of the organisation and it results in mistrust and fear in the whole organisation. For that reason, the most rudimentary objective of this study is to describe the phenomena that are related to paradoxes and managerial short cuts on the shop floor and to understand why the implementation of new production concepts often fails.[13] The integrative objective of this study is[14]:

> "To develop a theory and practice of responsibility with respect to employees on the shop floor."

This objective is specified with respect to my managerial responsibility[15]:

> "Special attention will be paid to the conditions that have to be fulfilled by a factory manager so that employees on the shop floor can bear responsibility and can render accountability."

The wording of this objective expresses two ideas. Firstly, the factory manager is indicated as the *key person* in charge of fulfilling the conditions. Secondly, s/he is indicated as the *key actor* in charge of fulfilling the conditions. A multi-level approach will help us to reveal the deep structures of the processes of responsibility and accountability on the shop floor and to see these processes in a wider context.

---

[12]   In 1994 Philips started a company-wide program to make their manufacturing operations world-class. Amongst others, the books of Suzaki (1987, 1993) were used as reference.

[13]   See section 5 of Chapter 1.

[14]   See section 5 of Chapter 1.

[15]   See section 5 of Chapter 1.

1.4 Research strategy

The research strategy has to serve the objective of the study. The initial questions have to lead to the final conclusions through logical reasoning. In the words of Yin[16], we have to connect the 'here' with the 'there'. The purpose of the research strategy is to lead to reliable and valid answers to the research question. That means the working method deals with a 'logical' problem.[17]

Yin identifies five key research strategies: the experiment, the survey, the archival analysis, the historical study and the case study.[18] Den Hertog and Van Sluijs also mention five different strategies: the experiment, the survey, the case study, action research and ethnography.[19] Yin, Den Hertog and Van Sluijs emphasise that the form of the research question is an important clue to selecting the research strategy.[20] The research questions are 'why', and 'how' questions. To study these types of questions we have to explore the field under investigation. The main research strategy chosen in this investigation is an ethnographical case study.

1.4.1 A call for organisational ethnography

Ethnography often has the character of an exploration in unknown territory. The ethnographer leaves his office and sets out to describe what he sees, hears, and feels. He or she does not take any instrument with him. He or she is his or her own tool. The ethnographer makes observations during his/her long-term presence in the field of investigation. He or she participates in the group under study. Organisational ethnography focuses on the culture of the organisation. The aim of organisational ethnography is to relate observable behaviour to patterns of meaning ('Bedeutung').

What is ethnography? The ethnographical research tradition has two historical roots: cultural anthropology and American sociology. Two things have always been at the heart of ethnographical research: spending a long period of time at the research site and participative observation by the researcher him- or herself. It is difficult to give a sharp definition of ethnography. Unequivocal definitions are absent in the literature. However, the following core elements are present[21]:

o   "The demarcation of a social entity which the research focuses on (...);

o   The description and interpretation of cultural phenomena with the objective of better understanding them ('Verstehen');

o   Data collection through participative observation, mostly during a long period of field research;

o   A vision of science and the enhancement of knowledge."

---

[16]   Yin (1994, p19).
[17]   Yin (1994, p20).
[18]   Yin (1994, p6).
[19]   Hertog and Sluijs (1995, p58).
[20]   Yin (1994, p6 ff.) and Hertog and Sluijs (1995, p55-57).
[21]   Hertog and Sluijs (1995, p185).

In recent decades several studies have been conducted in the organisational sciences which may be viewed as being ethnographical. There are the classical studies: *Patterns of Industrial Bureaucracy* by Alvin W. Gouldner (1954), *Men Who Manage* by Melville Dalton (1959), and *The Bureaucratic Phenomenon* by Michel Crozier (1964). More recent studies are 'Breakfast at Spiro's: Dramaturgy and Dominance' and 'You Asked for It: Christmas at the Bosses' Expense' by Michael Rosen (1985, 1988), and *In Search of Management* by Tony J. Watson (1994). However, ethnography is generally not very popular in organisational science.

Dalton criticises the theoretical approach in management science that has led to 'endless literature' and a 'flood of guidebooks',[22] In his view an ethnographical approach results in 'questions and hypotheses which stimulate insights among practitioners'.[23] His aim is to get 'as close as possible' to the world of managers and to interpret this world and its problems 'from the inside'.[24] Graham also criticises the research in the field of operations research and management science. He cites with approval Tinker and Lowe who characterise this field as 'all science and no management'.[25] He argues that the cultural-anthropological approach is 'putting management back into management science'.[26] Graham distinguishes between what we *think* happens and what is actually *done*. He states that what is actually done cannot be revealed by only interviews and surveys but has to be revealed by participative observation.[27] Rosen is worried by the lack of ethnographical studies. In his opinion, this lack is caused by the scientific community and the scientific journals that pressure scientists to limit themselves to 'short snapshots of organisational life', e.g. conference presentations and journal articles.[28] He states that this lack 'slows the refinement of theoretical formulations'.[29] Dyer and Wilkins also call for (ethnographical) case studies. In their view, an in-depth study of a single case may provide a 'rich description of the social scene', describe the 'context in which events occur' and reveal the 'deep structure of social behaviour'.[30] They state that theories, which are born out of such studies, will be both 'more accurate and more appropriately tentative' because the researcher must take into account the intricacies and qualifications of a particular context.[31] Watson argues that the 'ethnographer's hand' is required to understand the basic organisational activities and the processes in which managers are involved.[32] Scott-Morgan calls for managers themselves to take on the role of an ethnographer. He has shown that a large number of improvement processes in organisations get stuck in 'unwritten rules'. He states

---

[22]   Dalton (1959, p1).
[23]   Dalton (1959, p1).
[24]   Dalton (1959, p1).
[25]   Graham (1984, p527).
[26]   Graham (1984, p527, 536).
[27]   Graham (1984, p528-530).
[28]   Rosen (1991, p19).
[29]   Rosen (1991, p19).
[30]   Dyer and Wilkins (1991, p615).
[31]   Dyer and Wilkins (1991, p615).
[32]   Watson (1994, p1-8).

that managers have 'to decode' these unwritten rules and have to align the formal and informal rules of the organisation.[33] Finally, Bate strongly disapproves of the climate in organisational research that keeps investigators away from organisations because 'field work takes too long'.[34] He stresses that the 'right question' cannot be found in the textbook but has to be found in the field. Therefore, organisational studies and ethnography have to be put back together.

> *Reflection*. I fully agree with and would like to make some comments on these calls for ethnographical studies. Firstly, it is very difficult to understand the processes on the shop floor in detail. The interactions between technology and people, between employees, technicians and management, between behaviour and meaning ('Bedeu-tung') are so complicated that interviews or surveys alone cannot reveal them. Inten-sive participative observation is required to know *what* happens on the shop floor. At the same time, a lot of contextualised information is required to understand *why* this happens.
>
> Secondly, the shop floor cannot be studied in a 'one-shot' investigation. Knowing and understanding the shop floor is a long-winded process. In practice, the 'deep structure' of social behaviour is revealed step by step. I regularly had the feeling of 'now I know what's happening'. However, three months later I had the same feeling again! In my experience, it takes at least two to three years for a factory manager to understand the processes on the shop floor.
>
> Thirdly, I have read a lot of books about management and organisations. The books by Dalton, Watson and Scott-Morgan taught me more about social behaviour than any theoretical textbook. This experience confirms for me the value of ethnographi-cal studies.

The field under investigation – the processes of responsibility on the shop floor – requires a detailed understanding of the social environment of the shop floor and the whole organisational context within which this environment exists. The inter-action between employees, engineers, middle management, and management has to be investigated. The 'unwritten' codes that determine the interpretation of rules have to be studied. The social mechanism that underlies changes in behaviour has to be understood. The subtle processes by which meaning ('Bedeutung') is attached to behaviour have to be known. In my experience, one of the most important tasks of a factory manager is to give meaning.[35] He or she has to continually interpret and reinterpret the rules of the organisation and to give meaning to them. The same holds for management initiatives. A manager has to manage the interpretation of his or her initiative and has to give meaning to it. Rosen describes the goal of organisational ethnography as follows[36]:

---

[33] Scott-Morgan (1994).
[34] Bate (1997, p1151).
[35] Compare Weick (1995).
[36] Rosen (1991, p12).

"The goal of ethnography in general is to decode, translate, and interpret the *behaviours* and attached *meaning systems* of those occupying and creating the social system being studied. Ethnography, therefore, is largely an act of sense-making, the translation from one context to another of *action* in relationship to *meaning*, and *meaning* in relationship to *action*."

The field of investigation – the processes of responsibility and accountability on the shop floor – is not well defined. An in-depth investigation is required to identify the research questions and to understand the deep structure of social behaviour. For that reason, organisational ethnography has been chosen as the key strategy for studying the field of investigation. This strategy allows the investigator to 'follow where the problems lead' him or her.[37]

1.4.2 Epistemological and methodological questions

The development of ethnography as a scientific method has initiated a hot debate about its status. This debate has led to two divergent traditions. Den Hertog and Van Sluijs describe these traditions as follows[38]:

"The central question here has been whether ethnography involved a completely new view of scientific research, the gathering of knowledge and the development of theories, or that ethnography was 'merely' a method which can be fitted into the existing (positivistic) model of science (...) First, in the positivist paradigm, which focuses on discovering generalisable relations between quantifiable and directly observable variables through quantitative research. Standardisation of observation procedures and the independence of the researcher are important here. The second tradition, focusing upon the naturalistic paradigm, is not concerned with the objective reality, but views reality as a construction that people build around themselves by the meaning they attach to phenomena. The main objective of the research is to discover the 'meaning' of the social environment through research carried out in its natural environment. The researcher is part of the environment and cannot break away from that entirely. What's more, he cannot extricate himself from his own interests and, hence, he will always be biased to a certain extent. By contrast with the quantitative approach this type of research is referred to as 'qualitative'. The qualitative approach also resists reductionism in the positivist quantitative approach, which is concerned with the idea that problems will be better understood when they are reduced to the simplest elements that make them up. In the qualitative approach, insight is not gained until one looks at the whole."

---

[37] Graham (1984, p527) describes the advantages of the ethnographical approach as follows: "Thus I believe that we should follow where the problems lead us rather than lead the problems to follow us."

[38] Hertog and Sluijs (1995, p189).

The contrast between both lines of thought has been summarised by Easterby-Smith et al. as follows[39]:

	Positivist paradigm	Naturalistic paradigm
Basic beliefs	The world is external and objective.	The world is socially constructed and subjective.
	Observer is independent.	Observer is part of what is observed.
	Science is value-free.	Science is driven by human interests.
Researcher should:	Focus on facts	Focus on meaning
	Look for causality and fundamental laws.	Try to understand what is happening
	Reduce phenomena to simplest elements.	Look at the totality of each situation.
	Formulate hypotheses and test them.	Develop ideas through induction from data.
Preferred methods include:	Operationalising concepts so that they can be measured.	Using multiple methods to establish different views of phenomena.
	Taking large samples.	Small samples investigated in depth.

The differences between the positivist paradigm and naturalistic (or social-constructivist) paradigm are not only a matter of research strategy. There is a fundamental difference with respect to the views about the accessibility of reality (epistemology). In addition, there is a difference in world view (ontology).

The positivist paradigm acknowledges the existence of an objective reality. It is believed that the socio-cultural phenomena in this reality can be understood by the application of scientific methods. The researcher is seen as an independent observer who can grasp this objective reality. The social-constructivist paradigm, on the contrary, states that objective knowledge does not exist. It is believed that researchers construe their own reality by interpreting the observed phenomena. Consequently, scientific theories are seen as the outcome of a social construction process. The construction process is influenced by the cultural background of the researcher and is embedded in the place of investigation. Social processes, economic interests, political power, and ideological and religious beliefs, play a role in this place of investigation.

---

[39]   Quoted from Hertog and Sluijs (1995, p190).

In organisational ethnography the social-constructivist paradigm dominates. Most ethnographers believe that statistical data about behaviour does not generate a lot of insight into organisational processes. They believe that an in-depth investigation of the context has to be included to investigate the patterns of meaning ('Bedeutung') which are attached to certain types of behaviour.[40] Rosen writes[41]:

> "At the heart of organisational ethnography, therefore, lies the assumption that, because corporate culture is a concept about meaning and its construction, about ideas, values, beliefs and assumptions, it might be reasonable be studied from a social constructionist, interpretivist perspective, from a perspective exploring how the shared meaning system of the members of any particular organisation is created and recreated in relationship to the social processes of organisation (...) The aim of social constructionist research is to understand how members of a social group, through their participation in social process, enact their particular realities and endow them with meaning. The realm of meaning – the world of the symbol, and thus of culture – must be integrated with the realm of behaviour in this form of investigation. Thus while the meaning of behaviour is not problematic in positivist research – the important thing is that the object can be measured – meaning is *the* focus of investigation in the social constructionist case."

I would like to make some comments from my own perspective.

In the first place, in the positivist approach, organisational phenomena are operationalised into distinct, measurable and quantitative parameters. After that, these parameters are measured in a number of different organisations and relationships between these parameters are established. For example, Stainer and Stainer have carried out a survey in 480 organisations in order to investigate the relationship between productivity, quality, and ethics.[42] In this survey questions were asked about productivity programs, improvement programs, quality assurance programs, total quality management approaches, ethical cultures, and the existence of a codes of conduct. Furthermore, these organisations were asked about their opinion with respect to the relationship between the various parameters. Stainer and Stainer conclude that there is a close relationship between productivity, quality, and ethics. Furthermore, they recommend some guidelines to improve the management of technical organisations. The advantage of such a quantitative approach is that a large number of organisations are covered and that empirical relations can be identified. However, a disadvantage is that underlying mechanisms cannot be revealed because they are not directly visible and cannot be measured quantitatively. For example, it is very important to investigate the example set by management, the meaning ('Bedeutung') attached to ethical behaviour by management, and the influence of the philosophy of life as an internal motivator of employees and management. These underlying mechanisms cannot be identified in a quantitative

---

[40] In social-constructivistic studies the boundary between meaning as 'Bedeutung' and meaning as 'Sinn' is often diffuse.
[41] Rosen (1991, p6). Italics by Rosen.
[42] Stainer and Stainer (1995).

approach but need an ethnographical approach. More generally, the positivistic approach focuses on *directly observable* and *quantitative* aspects of complex organisational phenomena. This means that essential aspects of organisational phenomena which are *not* directly observable and which are *not* quantifiable are not taken into account. Therefore, it is not surprising that the quantitative approach *alone* does not lead to an in-depth understanding of behaviour in organisations. On the contrary, ethnographical methods discover the 'patterns of thinking' which underlie observable behaviour.[43] These considerations show that the positivist and social-constructivist approach cannot be seen as competing methods.[44] A detailed understanding of the possibilities and limitations of these approaches can only be achieved on the basis of an epistemology and ontology (see under 'finally').

In the second place, in the positivist approach, complex organisational phenomena are operationalised in a number of quantifiable parameters. These parameters are then measured in a number of organisations. However, the process of operationalising a phenomenon also implies that this phenomenon is investigated 'out of context' because the same set of parameters is used for every organisation. For example, let us take the phenomena of 'trust' and 'mistrust'. In the literature a large number of studies have reported on trust and mistrust in organisations. These studies show a large conceptual diversity. Shapiro laments that all these investigations have resulted in a 'confusing potpourri of definitions' applied to a host of units and levels of analysis.[45] Bigley and Pearce show in a review article that a general approach to the phenomena of 'trust' and 'mistrust' is not very productive.[46] They propose to investigate these phenomena in particular organisational settings. In their opinion, we have to shift from the question of 'what is trust?' to 'which trust and when?'[47] In other words, the meaning of the notions of 'trust' and 'mistrust' strongly depends on the context. Additionally, it has to be remarked that the 'essence' of a notion like 'trust' or 'mistrust' can never be understood by making a concept operational and by quantifying the different elements. To really understand what these notions mean, a researcher has to experience them in the field of investigation. Bate rightly speaks about 'being there'.[48] In addition, Dyer and Wilkins conclude that in-depth case studies are required to reveal the deep structure of organisational behaviour.[49] These considerations also show the limitations of the quantitative approach and the specific value of an ethnographical approach.

In the third place, the positivist approach presents the investigator as an objective and rational observer. Both philosophical considerations as well as empirical studies have shown that this characterisation is not right. A researcher is not an

---

[43] The term 'pattern of thinking' is from Graham (1984, p528).
[44] Graham (1984, p536) pleads for a synthesis of the positivistic and the social-constructivistic method.
[45] Quoted from Bigley and Pearce (1998, p405).
[46] Bigley and Pearce (1998).
[47] Bigley and Pearce (1998, p406).
[48] Bate (1997, p1163).
[49] Dyer and Wilkins (1991).

objective and rational observer but a human being with feelings, interests, and beliefs. These feelings, interests and beliefs cannot be switched-off at the research site.[50] Marx, Nietzsche and Freud have started the criticism of 'rational' man. Marx has shown that human thinking is strongly influenced by economic conditions. Nietzsche characterises human beings not by rational thinking but by the 'will to power'. Finally, Freud has stated that human ego is determined to a great extent determined by libidinal desires. The definite blow to the idea of rational man was dealt by postmodern philosophy (Foucault, Lyotard, Derrida, and others). Postmodern philosophy has shown the aggressive nature of the rationalistic paradigm that wipes out differences and excludes other perspectives. Around 1930, reformational philosophy fundamentally attacked the idea of rational observer by pointing out that all thinking has a religious root.[51] Recently, Geertsema has argued that knowledge is first and foremost 'human' knowledge.[52] Hoogland has stressed that all knowledge is dependent on the world view of the researcher.[53]

In the fourth place, criticism of the positivistic point of view does not imply a preference for the social-constructivist paradigm. The social-constructivist approach rightly acknowledges the influence of political, economic, and ideological and religious factors in organisational research. However, what is the consequence of this influence? Are the described phenomena *only* the result of political, economic, or ideological and religious factors? Are the theories *only* a human construct? Or are the described phenomena and theories developed a claim to reality; a claim that is inherently limited by the reductionist approach of science and/or by the partial perspective of the observer? A discussion of these questions also requires an epistemological and ontological basis.

Finally, I would like to make my own epistemological and ontological position clear. I have been educated in the tradition of reformational philosophy. Within this tradition questions about epistemology and ontology are discussed intensively.[54] Herman Dooyeweerd, the father of reformational philosophy in The Netherlands, has argued that all theoretical thought has a religious root.[55] This means that every analysis, interpretation and theory is embedded within a religious world view. This philosophy excludes the possibility of a neutral position in scientific investigations. In other words, 'value-free' science is impossible. With this basic assumption, I come close to the point of view of social constructivism. However, there is one fundamental difference. In reformational thought every scientific claim is – in the end – bound to the order of the created reality.[56] The background to this statement is the idea that everyday reality has a normative structure. In

---

[50] Latour (1987).
[51] Dooyeerd (1969). The Dutch original appeared in 1935/1936.
[52] Geertsema (1992).
[53] Hoogland (1998).
[54] See for example H. Hart in McIntire (1985, p143-166) and R. Woudenberg in (Woudenberg et al. (1996, p21-85).
[55] Dooyeweerd (1969, I, p3-165, II, p429-598). See also Woudenberg in Woudenberg et al. (1996, p21-85).
[56] See also Hoogland (1998).

positivistic thinking norms are no more than a rule or an agreement. In social-constructivist thinking norms are the result of an evolutionary process and therefore a human construct. In reformational thinking the created reality has a normative structure. This means that in organisational research the investigator tries to *discover* the normative structure of reality in a *particular* context. This particular context also contains the *human* investigator. What follows from this approach is that no investigator (either from positivistic, social-constructivist or reformational birth) can claim *ex cathedra* that his or her view is superior. Every scientific claim is a claim about the organisational reality. The question of to what extent a claim does justice to this reality has to be asked and can be discussed quite seriously.

It has to be emphasised that in the reformational approach epistemology is seen as an integral part of ontology,[57] However, explaining why this is the case is complex. The many-sidedness or multi-dimensionality of everyday reality is a cornerstone in the ontology of reformational thought.[58] Dooyeweerd has identified fifteen aspects or dimensions: arithmetic, spatial, kinematic, physical, biotic, conative (psychic), logical (analytical), historical (power), lingual (meaning ('Bedeutung')), social, economic, aesthetic, juridical, moral and belief or trust (religion). On the one hand, these aspects or dimensions cannot be reduced to each other. Every aspect or dimension has its own 'essence' or 'quality' (or, in the wording of Dooyeweerd: 'meaning-kernel'). On the other hand, these aspects or dimensions are closely connected and refer to each other. Furthermore, these aspects or dimensions are not 'separate' available. Every object, every structure and every subject functions in all aspects or dimensions.

The reformational view has three methodological consequences. Firstly, it portrays the investigator as a human being who functions in all fifteen dimensions – as a being with psychological feelings, social contacts, economic interests, a will to power, moral views, and religious beliefs. This means that an investigator is not an objective and rational observer. Secondly, it shows that our ability to understand reality is not external to reality but is an integral part of it (logical aspect or analytical dimension). Thus this view holds that it is possible to acquire knowledge about the world in which we live. In addition, the ability to understand reality is closely connected to the other aspects or dimensions of (particular) human beings. As a consequence, all knowledge is 'human knowledge'. Thirdly, these basic assumptions imply that the organisational phenomena under study are many-sided or multi-dimensional. The 'negative' consequence of this implication is that every operationalisation of organisational phenomena results in reducing the multi-dimensional reality to one or more aspects or dimensions. For example, the focus on the psychological or social aspects of an organisational phenomenon 'automatically' means that the coherence with other aspects of this phenomenon will be lost. Further, it means that an organisational phenomenon can never be understood by numerical data alone. For example, the members of an organisation can indicate their level of trust in management on a scale from one to ten. However, this number 'as such' does not say anything about trust. As a consequence, a positivistic

---

[57]   Dooyeweerd (1969, I, p3-165).
[58]   Dooyeweerd (1969, II, p3-426).

approach results in the loss of the 'essence' or the 'quality' of a phenomenon. In addition, the fine structure of the phenomenon is not understood. To interpret data of this type, the investigator has to experience what trust is in the particular organisational context. The social constructionist approach is more open to the many-sidedness or multi-dimensionality of reality. Therefore, the ethnographical method will give us more insight into the subtle coherence of the different dimensions of an organisational phenomenon.

1.4.3 The manager as ethnographer

Dalton, author of the ethnographical study *Men who Manage*, wrote extensively on the preconceptions and methods he employed in this study. [59] He identifies the following shortcomings of the ethnographical method[60]:

1. "closeness to unique detail may limit attempts to classify data, to formulate problems, and to generalise;
2. the researcher's peculiar personality may attract him to unrepresentative informants or lead him to identify with some inconsequential subgroup;
3. his presence may disturb the very situation he is seeking to freeze for study (...);
4. where he works in a disguised role, he may give associates false clues, for their responses are directed to his stimulated role and he may note them down as the *real* behaviour without knowing that he was duped by unintended distortions;
5. when very friendly with his informants, the researcher may unwittingly communicate the answers he wishes (...);
6. if the researcher is not long in, and around, the area he is studying, he may mistake an unusual event for a typical one and overstress its importance."

Item 3 is very important for managers who take on the role of ethnographer as employees regularly change their behaviour when a factory manager comes in. This observation would speak volumes about the culture of the organisation. However, employees regularly do not change their behaviour at all when a manager comes in. In this case, the situation can be studied without disturbance. Items 4 and 6 do not apply at all to a manager as ethnographer. There is one particular shortcoming of a factory manager playing ethnographer: every manager wants to see the positive effects of his or her actions. The phenomena on the shop floor can too easily be interpreted in relation to the actions of a manager.

Dalton lists the following advantages of an ethnographical method[61]:

1. "the researcher is not bound by fixed, and sometimes crippling, research plans (...);
2. the technique enables the inquirer to avoid pointless questions which often cause ridicule behind his back and injure the research in unconsidered ways;

---

[59] Dalton (1964). See also Dalton (1959, p273 ff.).
[60] Dalton (1964, p74).
[61] Dalton (1964, p75).

3. greater intimacy allows the investigator more correctly to impute motives;
4. he is also better able to get the best-informed informants (...);
5. the participant has a great advantage in getting at covert activity;
6. he has time to build superior rapport before he asks disturbing questions;
7. also, since he is not committed to treating the always dissimilar informants uniformly, he can select uniquely equipped 'specialists' in different areas of his problem;
8. finally, in many cases the established circulator is able to work his way to files and confidential data that the peripheral formalist usually never reaches."

Items 4, 5, 7, and 8 strongly apply to the manager as ethnographer. There is one special advantage of a factory manager as ethnographer. He or she is also an actor. He or she has the possibilities to change something in the organisation and to investigate the consequences of these actions. Within certain limits, a factory manager has the possibility to experiment in an organisation.

Dalton concludes that "the merits of participative observation do outweigh its defects, especially when the method is combined pragmatically with other methods as supplement or as an equal or major research arm".[62]

Rosen emphasises that every ethnographical study presents a 'partial perspective'.[63] The ethnographer interprets what he or she is observing, what he or she is experiencing, or what others tell him or her. Rosen states that an ethnographer interprets behaviour against a 'tableau of meaning structures' within his or her own imaginings.[64]

This study also presents a 'partial perspective': the 'partial perspective' of a factory manager. This perspective is of the utmost importance in investigating the research question of this study. Especially, a first order 'construction' is given of the feelings, intentions, meanings, and beliefs of a factory manager. Spooner states that ethnographers study others to find out more about themselves and about others.[65] He continues by saying that ethnographers, in doing so, change not only their own lives, but also change the lives of those studied.[66] The idea of this mutual influence doubly applies to the present study as the ethnographer is also a key actor and change agent.

> *Reflection.* I would like to underline these remarks by Spooner. This study forced me to reflect on my work and myself. For that reason, this study can be interpreted as an attempt to understand myself, to rethink my style of management, and to make my beliefs about man, organisation, labour and meaning explicit. This goes beyond what I would have done had I not done this study.

---

62   Dalton (1964, p75).
63   Rosen (1991, p2). See also Clifford in Clifford and Marcus (eds.) (1986, p1-26).
64   Rosen (1991, p2).
65   Quoted from Rosen (1991, p2).
66   Quoted from Rosen (1991, p2).

Watson has expressed the idea of mutual influence as the 'strategic exchange perspective'. He writes[67]:

"The strategic exchange perspective is a way of looking at individual and social human life in a way which draws on a range of ideas from social theory. It tries to deal with the essential two-sidedness of social life: the side in which individuals can be seen to initiate, choose and shape their world, and the side in which they can be seen as being constrained and shaped by influences external to themselves. Human actions, in the managerial context or any other, have patterns to them which arise from an interplay between deliberate choice or purpose and the social, political economic circumstance in which they find themselves - circumstance which involve a constant struggle to cope and survive."

The 'strategic exchange perspective' applies both to the relation between factory manager and higher management, and to the relation between factory manager and middle management/shop floor.

Rosen mentions four concerns in conducting organisational ethnography: working knowledge, organisational secrecy, trust, and role definition.[68] Before reviewing these concerns, I would like to pay attention to my role as ethnographer. In the Roermond case study, a lot of research was done in close cooperation with a university student and a university researcher. These investigations were formally approved by the management team and formally announced in the organisation. The Roermond case has been described in the book *Marktgericht productie management. Van taakgroep naar mini-company* (*Market-oriented production management. From Work Group to Mini-Company*) by myself, Jan de Leede and Henk van der Tas.[69] The text of this book was formally approved by the business manager. For the Aachen case study, I did not officially announce my study. Through time I asked several colleagues to tell me stories about the shop floor. I told them that I collected these stories for discussions with Professor Den Hertog at the University of Maastricht. I also hinted to my bosses that I regularly discussed the problems on the shop floor with scientists at the University of Maastricht. Finally, I used the report of the change process in the tool shop (see section 3.6 of this chapter) as a tool to bring the processes of responsibility up for discussion with my management team and with my boss. The existence of this report was also justified by referring to the University of Maastricht.[70]

Let us now return to Rosen's concerns. His first concern has to do with working knowledge. How much technical expertise does the ethnographer have? What about the emotional feelings which arise from doing a particular type of work?

---

[67] Watson (1994, p25).

[68] Rosen (1991, p17).

[69] About one year after the publication of this book it was decided that the Roermond case study would be used for this study.

[70] The references to the University of Maastricht did not cause further questions. It was known that I had a lot of connections in the scientific world. It was also known that I was co-author of a book about manufacturing excellence.

What about the social relations within which the task is embedded? In this study, the ethnographer is the factory manager who has to fulfil the conditions necessary so that employees on the shop floor can bear responsibility and can render accountability. That means, taking the partial perspective of a factory manager, the ethnographer of this study is 'as close as possible'.[71] There is a complete removal of the 'me-anthropologist-you-native' framework.[72] The factory manager has the highest degree of participation in investigating the research question of this study.

The second concern has to do with organisational secrecy. Outside observers have limited access to business information and meetings of the management team. A lot of organisational information is confidential, e.g. information about strategy, finances, market position, and so on. Also, a lot of meetings – especially workshops in which the strategy is discussed and the functioning of the management team is brought up – have a confidential character. In this study the ethnographer is a member of the management team: the factory manager. Generally, the factory manager plays a key role in the management team: the activity of manufacturing is the largest part of a business (both in financials and in number of employees). As a manager, I had access to all documents in the plant, was present in all relevant policy meetings, and attended all workshops of the management team.[73] In addition, I also took part in corridor chats.

The third concern has to do with trust. How much is the ethnographer trusted by the organisation he is investigating? Do the employees see him or her as an outsider? Or do they see him or her as a representative of the management team? In the first case the ethnographer can built up a relationship based on mutual trust. In the second case he or she will be viewed as a part of the political environment. In this study the ethnographer is the factory manager. As a manager, everybody knew my hierarchical position. Basically, all information that was told to me was 'coloured'. In the Roermond case study, politics played a minor role. My relationships with most employees and colleagues were based on mutual confidence. In the Aachen case study, politics was an important part of the management environment. Relationships based on mutual confidence were not 'natural'.

The last concern has to do with role definition. A participant observer has to switch from the 'participative' role to the 'observer' role and vice versa. Switching back and forth hinders both roles. This concern applies strongly to the factory manager as ethnographer. The pace of the manufacturing process has all employees firmly in its grip. A factory manager controlled by the organisation. Under stress it is difficult to make accurate observations and careful descriptions. The implication is that additional attention has to be paid to the quality of these investigations.

In conclusion, participative observation by a factory manager has several specific advantages, e.g. lengthy presence on the shop floor, 'working knowledge'

---

[71] Dalton (1959, p1). Compare also Graham (1984).

[72] Bate (1997, p1164).

[73] The future of a whole business is often discussed at higher management levels. I was not always involved in these discussions. For example, I do not know about the 'who' and 'when' of the decision to close the ceramic multilayer actuator activity in Roermond in 1997.

(Rosen), selection of reliable informants, access to all information, presence in confidential meetings, and possibility to change something (or to experiment). Specific measures are required to cope with the weaknesses of participative observation by a factory manager (see below).

1.4.4 Validity and reliability

There are four criteria for establishing the quality of empirical social research: the construct validity, internal validity, external validity and reliability.[74] We will now discuss the application of these criteria for this study.

The 'construct validity' criterion deals with the question of whether the operational measures and the observations carried out cover the variables and concepts under study. Yin describes three strategies to improve the construct validity. The first strategy is the use of triangulation or multiple sources of evidence.[75] In this study three types of triangulation are used: triangulation of data sources, investigators, and methods. Details are described in section 1.5 of this chapter. The second strategy is to maintain a chain of evidence.[76] This means that an external observer can follow the evidence that underpins the route from the initial research questions to the ultimate conclusions. The case studies are arranged in such a way that the chain of evidence is as clear as possible. The third strategy is that key informants review the draft report of the case study.[77] This strategy has been applied in both case studies.

The 'internal validity' criterion deals with the establishing of causal relationships between variables or events. Yin describes three strategies to guarantee internal validity. The first strategy is pattern matching.[78] This strategy involves comparing empirically observed patterns with predicted patterns (or with several alternative predictions). This strategy has been applied to the investigations within the Roermond case study and at the beginning of the Aachen case study.[79] The second strategy is explanation building.[80] Explanation building is a special type of pattern matching strategy. This strategy deals with building an explanation of a case and refining this explanation by means of an iterative process using data and observations from the case and other cases. This strategy has been applied to the first case study after analysing the second one. The third strategy is time series.[81] This means following a single of various variables as a function of time. This strategy has been

---

[74] Yin (1994, p33).
[75] Yin (1994, p90 ff.).
[76] Yin (1994, p98 ff.).
[77] Yin (1994, p144 ff.).
[78] Yin (1994, p106 ff.).
[79] In April 1999, after finishing the Roermond and Aachen case studies, I applied the strategy of pattern matching to phenomena in another factory (a ceramic multilayer capacitor factory). I made some predictions about processes of responsibility and accountability on the shop floor based on the patterns derived from the Roermond and the Aachen case studies. To my surprise, the same patterns were observed!
[80] Yin (1994, p110 ff.).
[81] Yin (1994, p113 ff.).

applied several times, as described in section 1.5 of this chapter and the case descriptions.

The 'external validity' criterion deals with the generalisation of the findings of the study beyond the investigated cases. Regularly it is argued that a large number of case studies are required for generalisation. Yin, however, argues that case-study research does not rely on *statistical* generalisation but on *analytical* generalisation.[82] That means that the analyst should try to generalise the results of one (or some) case studies in a 'theory'. Spooner follows the same line of thought. He states that ethnographical case studies deal with '*general* forms of organisation' and '*general* ways of thinking in particular contexts'.[83] In this study two cases are investigated. The use of two case studies hardly increases the external validity of this study from a statistical point of view (two samples instead of one). However, two case studies do increase the possibility to generalise the theory further (see paragraph 1 4 5 of this chapter). It has to be stressed that an *analytical* generalisation is made possible by the existence of an (implicit) worldview or cosmology.

The last criterion is reliability. Reliability relates to the quality of the reported data. The objective is to guarantee that if another investigator were to do the same case study and follow exactly the same procedures he should arrive at the same findings and conclusions. The question of reliability is very important to *this* study. After all, this study is done from the perspective of the factory manager. By definition, another investigator cannot perform this role (unless it is another manager/ethnographer with roughly the same views and roughly the same style of management). By definition, this ethnographer describes his own actions and the effect of his own decisions. This means that a bias in observation and interpretation is inherently connected to this study. However, a number of measures are taken to differentiate, to modify, to balance or to neutralise this bias.[84] Firstly, I have made use of other observers (investigator triangulation). Secondly, I have made use of quantitative and semi-quantitative data, including questionnaires and audits. Thirdly, I have made use of informants who gathered 'stories in context'. Finally, key persons within the respective organisations reviewed the case study report.

The different methods of collecting data that are used in this study are described in paragraph 1.5 of this chapter.

1.4.5 Selection of cases

The cases described in this study were not selected on the basis of formal criteria. They were the result of a combination of circumstances. Looking back, these cases can be characterised as opposite cases. In Roermond, a new factory had to be created. The whole organisation was strongly customer focused from the beginning on. I selected most of the middle management myself. We successfully implemented the most important aspects of world-class manufacturing. The relationship

---

[82]   Yin (1994, p36).

[83]   Quoted from Rosen (1991, p3). Italics by Rosen.

[84]   Scandura and William (2000) emphasise the importance of the application of triangulation and other sources.

between management and employees was based on mutual confidence. Within the period described, no changes in management occurred.

The Aachen Glass Factory was an existing factory. Management and middle management were strongly internally oriented. The relation between management and employees was characterised by deep-rooted mistrust. Many people in the organisation were frustrated due to events that had happened in the past. The factory was far from world-class. Furthermore, this factory 'suffered' from managers only staying for relatively short periods of time.

The choice of these cases was determined by the course of my career. And that course was not totally accidental. The decision to assign me as factory manager in the glass factory in Aachen was also inspired by my experience in manufacturing excellence and my participative style of management.

The study of two quite different factories is fruitful from a theoretical point of view. It enables the development of a richer theoretical framework.[85]

1.5 Methods of collecting data

In this study different methods of collecting data are applied. These methods will be briefly described.

Work diaries
It is my habit to make notes during meetings. In particular, I write down decisions, main arguments, evaluative remarks and special items. I am used to noting down the remarks of all attendees during evaluations of improvement programs, special meetings and workshops. After meetings, I regularly write down some evaluative comments. During the writing of the case studies I have read and reread my diaries to select information. In particular, the diaries gave me insight into the different opinions of the management team about world-class manufacturing and the strategic positioning of the factory. I also wrote down remarkable comments. I re-read more than 1000 diary pages for the Roermond case study and more than 500 pages for the Aachen case study.

Participant observation
I have made a lot of observations in both case studies – during meetings and workshops, in improvement teams, in personal discussions, in the corridors, in the coffee bars, on the shop floor, and during social events. For the Roermond case study I made some notes of these observations. For the Aachen case study, special notes were made with a view to this study.

In the Roermond case study, I spent many hours on the shop floor. In the start-up period, about twenty operators were present. I cooperated intensively with these operators to get the production process under control. If necessary, I put on working clothes to solve an equipment or process problem. I also visited the fac-

---

[85] Yin (1994, p46).

tory in the evenings and in the weekends. During these visits I had a lot of time to talk to (individual) operators. I continued to have a very good relationship with the operators from the start-up period. I got a lot of information about the way 'we operate around here' from them.[86] I also often got to the bottom of problems that were caused by blameworthy behaviour, e.g. a lack of discipline.

I also spent many hours on the shop floor in the Aachen factory, including evenings and weekends. I built up a relationship based on mutual trust with only a few operators. These were mostly the operators who explained the process during my training period. In the Aachen factory sometimes the operators gave me valuable information. In other cases the state of affairs stayed hidden.

My presence on the shop floor enabled me to gather a lot of information. I informally interviewed many employees, e.g. operators, middle management, repair and maintenance technicians, and engineers. I especially spoke with employees in critical situations, e.g. in the case of serious process problems I asked them about their feeling about a problem, the control of a process, and the support of engineering and management. I asked them 'five times why'.[87] In these type of situations I found out a lot of 'non-official' information; this means information that I was not supposed to know. For example, employees told me about the relationships in the shift, relationships with other shifts, and about the behaviour of individuals. For a manager it is difficult to use 'non-official' information in the right way (see below). I also asked the employees about the training they had got, the workshop they had attended, the improvements implemented, and so on. I particularly tried to find out how certain decisions were turned into practice, why certain problems arose and others did not, and why some improvements were implemented successfully and others were not.

It can also happen that an employee spontaneously tells a lot of information about the shop floor. For example, when he or she is upset by an incident that happened that day. These employees can be characterised as a 'once-only' informant. The information from this type of informants has to be handled carefully. The information given can be wrong. For example, if the employee is not well informed, if the employee has his own agenda, or if the employee gives a socially desirable answer. Also, events from the past are told as if they had happened the day before.

> *Example.* I would like to give one striking example. In the Aachen case study I asked some employees about the quality of the products which were delivered to the customer. They told me that in the weekends regularly rejected products were delivered. An employee of the customer confirmed this story. I checked this information in-depth. After a lot of interviews and checking of data I found out that this practice had stopped at least one year ago. However, in the opinion of the employees, the delivery of rejected products in the weekends still continued.

---

[86]   Graham (1984, p529).
[87]   'Five times why' is a Japanese expression for asking 'why' till the root cause of the problem has been found.

Therefore, more sources were used to check the information of 'once-only' informants.

Furthermore, in all organisations there are employees who say anything that comes to mind. These employees can give a lot of information if you take the time to speak with them. The information of these employees also has to be checked carefully.

> *Example.* In my first month in the Aachen factory an employee spontaneously told me the following. "Mr. Verkerk", he said, "it is always the same. A new manager is coming. He has a lot of new ideas. He wants to implement new working methods. And … we have to follow. Mostly, they stop checking after several days. Then we go back to the old working method. Or, we give the impression that we use the new working method but in practice continue using the old method." Later on, I realised that he had told me exactly how the employees operated in that department. Every time I met this employee on the shop floor, he told another story.

I sometimes used a 'trick' to get to the truth. I told the employees that I doubted their explanation and I suggested that I knew what really happened. For example, when I did not believe the explanation or when I had inside information from an informant. In some cases, this suggestion helped me to get to the bottom of the problem.

Informants

In an organisation it is normal practice for some employees to go to a manager and express their worries. When the manager takes time to listen to them and gives them the feeling that their information is used in a proper way, these employees become 'regular' informants. In the Roermond factory I had several of these informants. In the Aachen factory I only had a few.

From my point of view, an employee developed from being a 'once-only' informant into a 'regular' informant if the information transferred appeared to be reliable two or three times in a row. Furthermore, the information of a 'regular' informant was checked if his or her information was incompatible with other data.

Informants regularly indicated that the information they provided was more or less confidential, especially when there were frictions between employees, shifts, or departments. In such a case, it was often not possible to check the information openly or to act immediately. Generally, I discussed with the informant how I could use his or her information without revealing the source.

> *Example.* In the Roermond factory one of the maintenance technicians told me that in his shift the operators caused a lot of equipment breakdowns by careless work (in every shift there was one maintenance technician). He had discussed the method of working with the shift. However, his views were not accepted. He asked me to use this information very carefully to prevent a bad relationship between him and his shift. About two weeks later, I asked the maintenance manager to analyse the breakdowns of equipment: per type, per shift, and as a function of time. This data confirmed the confidential information of the maintenance technician. I asked the

manager of the maintenance department to discuss this data with all shifts (including the maintenance technicians). The causes of the breakdowns were identified and new rules of the game were agreed. Furthermore, the intervention of the maintenance manager appeared to be fruitful: the relationships between the shifts and their maintenance technicians were improved. In this case, the existence of an informant was never revealed.

Sometimes, an informant gave me a covert tip. For example, it was suggested that I read a certain logbook, look at the process control charts of a certain process, ask an operator about something that had happened, and so on. In practice, these tips appeared to be very fruitful.

> *Example.* In the Aachen case study, an engineer suggested that I ask an inspector of the morning shift about the slip through of bad products to the customer. In my daily tour, I met this operator and asked him about the quality of the products delivered to the customer. He was angry. He told me that in the night shift nearly no inspections were done, with the result that the quality of the products delivered to the customer was not guaranteed. He showed me the papers that proved his assertions.

The observations of the shop floor and the information from informants were often discussed in the management team of the factory. They were used to identify problems and to improve the working procedures. These experiences were also summarised in 'stories' that were told and retold in the corridors and in workshops.

Observation by thirds
In both case studies I have made use of observations by staff members, university students, university investigators, and external consultants. In the Roermond case study, a personnel officer and an external consultant supported the whole process of implementing mini-companies. After starting-up a mini-company the whole procedure was evaluated. Sometimes, they were asked to make some observations during a workshop. They also gave me feedback about my behaviour. In this case study we also used a university student and a university investigator as observers.

In the Aachen case study, internal and external consultants guided the project entitled 'Future'. The progress and the course of the process were followed in detail. I consulted them about the next steps to be taken. I also asked them to make notes about the body language of the participants, in particular to identify the presence of 'under-the-skin' resistance. The atmosphere of the social gathering after the workshop was also discussed.

Formal interviews

In the Roermond case study, a university investigator carried out formal interviews.[88] In the last few months I was at Aachen I carried out some semi-structured interviews. Then, notes were made during the interview.

Member checks

In Roermond, the case study description was discussed with the business unit manager, three middle managers, and one factory engineer. In Aachen, the case study description was discussed with two members of the management team of the Aachen Glass Factory, three members of the management team of the manufacturing department, and one external consultant. These member checks led to an extensive discussion about the 'why's', especially in Aachen. These discussions often resulted in a semi-structured interview.

Personal opinions, feelings and considerations

In both cases I was extremely personally involved. Part of my intentions, feelings and considerations have been written down in reports, plans, evaluations, and in my work diaries. Others are indelibly printed in my memory.

The main text of the case descriptions contains the 'official' information that is based on documents, minutes, and so on. Personal experiences, opinions, feelings and considerations are formatted in a smaller font size in indented passages. These passages are introduced with the word 'example', 'reflection', or something similar.

Documentation

In my capacity as factory manager, a lot of relevant documentation was brought to my attention. I had access to nearly all documents which did not arrive automatically on my desk. In the Roermond case study, all documents with respect to the structure of the organisation, the start of improvement teams, the start of mini-companies, evaluation of mini-companies, evaluation of questionnaires, results of audits, internal newsletters, and minutes of management team meetings have been studied. In the Aachen case study, all documents with respect to the 'Future' project, minutes of the management team meetings, minutes of the world-class manufacturing meeting, the Philips Quality Award process, and internal newspapers have been studied. Some critical information, like business plans and strategic data, has been studied too. In both cases I investigated enormous piles of minutes, reports, business plans, and other official documentation.

Surveys

In Philips a company-wide survey called the 'Employee Motivation Survey' was carried out in 1994, 1996, and 1999. A standardised questionnaire was used. This survey covered twelve subjects: customer orientation, cooperative working relationships, external yardstick, management support, immediate boss support, performance orientation, reward and recognition, personal growth and develop-

---

[88]   De Leede (1997).

ment, overall satisfaction, quality, financial awareness and entrepreneurial behaviour. In the Roermond case a survey was done on the social-dynamic aspects of teamwork and on the effects of mini-companies. The questionnaire of this survey is described in the thesis of Jan de Leede.[89]

Audits

Roermond and Aachen factories have been formally audited many times: by certified authorities using the ISO 9000 and ISO 14000 standards, by internal auditors using the ISO 9000 and ISO 14000 standards, and by peer audits using the Philips Quality Award standard. Customers regularly audited the factory. Sometimes a formal standard was used, and sometimes not. Audit reports have been used in this study. Personally, I am a certified auditor for ISO 9000 and the Philips Quality Award.

Archival records

No archival records were used in the Roermond case study as this case concerned the start-up of a new factory. Historical data of the plant was not investigated. In the Aachen case study some archival records were used. For example, I checked the development of the costs and the number of rejected plungers of the tool shop over a longer period.

---

[89]   De Leede (1997).

2 Case study: Ceramic Multilayer Actuators Roermond

In September 1990, I started my training period in a development laboratory in Eindhoven. The objective was to understand the basic principles of ceramic multilayer actuators and to learn the production technology. In January 1991, I went as an expatriate to Kaohsiung (Taiwan) to manage the development and to start up the pilot production. At the end of the year a serious problem came to the surface: the internal resistance of the products appeared not to be under control. In spring 1992 a contract was concluded with a Japanese customer to deliver multilayer actuators for the ink-jet printing market. In order to solve the problem of the internal resistance and to meet the contract with the Japanese customer the decision was taken to concentrate all actuator activities in Roermond. In August 1992 I started working as factory manager of the actuator operation in Roermond.

The decision to concentrate the actuator business in Roermond was not an arbitrary choice. In this plant the multilayer technology was available (ceramic multilayer capacitor factory). The decision was also taken to transfer the aforementioned development laboratory from Eindhoven to Roermond. This decision gave Roermond a new future. This plant would become the birthplace of new businesses based on multilayer technology. One of the first new 'babies' would be the Ceramic Multilayer Actuators business unit.

The Passive Components Business Group – to which the Ceramic Multilayer Actuators business unit belonged – considered the new baby as very important. One of the directors said that if the business group could not bring this baby to adulthood, then it would never be able to start a new business.

At that time, the ink-jet printing market appeared to be very erratic. Competition was tough and new models were launched every six months. The Ceramic Multilayer Actuators business unit had to cope with these challenges. Once – in a presentation to the whole crew – a representative of a Japanese customer characterised the dynamics of the business environment and its influence on the actuator business unit with the words 'When it blows in the market, there is a storm in the factory'. Indeed, there was often a 'storm' in the factory. Pro-active development and concurrent engineering were developed to cope with the 'blowing' in the market.

The factory organisation has been developed in a process of trial and error. The Dutch approach to Socio-Technical Systems Design and the Mini-Company Concept of Suzaki have been guiding principles. Furthermore, three red threads have run through this process: four-way communication, participation, and continuous improvement.

In the period between autumn 1992 to spring 1996, the business grew rapidly. The majority of the turnover was realised in one segment (ink-jet printing) and for one customer (a Japanese customer). However, the broadening of the customer base and application base went much more slowly than planned. In summer 1996, the sales to this Japanese customer collapsed. The business unit did not survive this 'storm'. The management of the Passive Components Business Group decided not to continue the activity. In April 1997, the actuator factory was closed. I then started as a factory manager in the Aachen Glass Factory.

The Ceramic Multilayer Actuators business unit was a part of Philips Electronics N.V. The Philips group has a divisional structure. In 1997, the main divisions were PolyGram, Business Electronics, Components, Sound & Vision, Semiconductors, Lighting, Medical Systems, and Domestic Appliances and Personal Care. Every division consists of different Business Groups. In 1997, the main Business Groups of the division Components were Display Components, Passive Components, Optical Storage, and Flat Display Systems. The Ceramic Multilayer Actuators Roermond business unit was a part of the Passive Components Business Group.[90]

The Passive Components Business Group identified the multilayer technology as one of its core technologies. This technology was in use for the production of capacitors and could be used for a number of innovative products in different applications. The multilayer actuator was the first new product based on this core technology that was introduced in the market. The business was based in Roermond. In August 1992, I started working there as the factory manager.

In the Roermond case three red threads can be identified: four-way communication[91], participation, and continuous improvement. These red threads were present in all phases of the development of the actuator organisation.

In the Philips group several company-wide programs were running in order to improve the performance of the whole organisation.[92] These programs were obligatory. The Ceramic Multilayer Actuators business unit was strongly involved in the so-called customer days. The role of these days in the development of the organisation will be described.

The case description has the following set-up: short introduction (2.1), start-up of the new factory (2.2), the mini-company process (2.3), Customer Day 1995 (2.4), investigations of the University of Twente (2.5), Customer Day 1996 (2.6), start-up of the second cycle of the mini-company process (2.7), first steps of the Philips Quality Award process (2.8), closure of the actuator factory (2.9), and evaluation (2.10). Figure 2.1 gives an overview of the main activities and milestones in the Roermond case.

---

[90] The Passive Components Business Group was dismantled in 1999-2000. The Components division was dismantled in 2002.

[91] Four-way communication is defined as a two-way vertical communication (between operators and management and vice versa) and a two-way horizontal communication (between operators and their customers or suppliers and vice versa).

[92] De Weerd (2001) has given an extensive description of the quality policy of the Philips organisation.

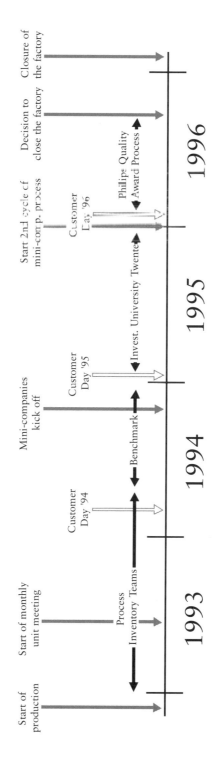

ROERMOND

Start of production

Start of monthly unit meeting

Mini-companies kick off

Customer Day '94

Customer Day 95

Start 2nd cycle of mini-comp. process

Decision to close the factory

Closure of the factory

Process Inventory Teams

Benchmark

Invest. University Twente

Customer Day '96

Phillips Quality Award Process

1993   1994   1995   1996

Figure 2.1 Main activities and milestones in the development process of the actuator organisation

189

2.1 Introduction

2.1.1 History

In the mid eighties, the Passive Components Business Group started the development of ceramic multilayer actuators in a laboratory in Eindhoven. The basic materials were developed, products for specific applications were designed, physical properties were measured, and an extensive market study was done. In the beginning of 1990 it was decided that the pilot production would be allocated to a Philips plant in Kaohsiung (Taiwan). This decision was made on the basis of the following arguments. The ceramic multilayer actuator technology was based on the multilayer technology that was developed for the production of capacitors. Therefore, it was natural to allocate the new business close to one of the multilayer capacitor factories of Passive Components. The factory in Kaohsiung (Taiwan) was chosen above the factory in Roermond (The Netherlands) due to the presence of cheap labour. Further, it was believed that the industrial process was stable enough to justify a pilot production abroad.

In January 1991 I went to Taiwan to start up the pilot production. In this period a serious problem came to light: the internal resistance of the products appeared to not be under control. This means that some production runs resulted in products with a high internal resistance and other runs in products with a low internal resistance. At that time, the root cause of this phenomenon could not be identified.[93] The investigations to find the root cause and to solve the problem failed. In spring 1992, a contract was agreed with a Japanese customer to deliver multilayer actuators for the ink-jet printing market. Taking into account the process problems in Taiwan and the contract with a Japanese printer company, it was decided in April 1992 that all actuator activities would be concentrated in Roermond.

The choice for Roermond was obvious. Firstly, the multilayer technology was available in the Roermond plant (ceramic multilayer capacitor factory). Secondly, the decision was taken to transfer the development laboratory of Passive Components in Eindhoven (including the actuator part) to Roermond in the course of 1992/1993. This decision supported the strategic view of Roermond as the birthplace of new businesses based on multilayer technology.

2.1.2 Market and products

A Japanese consulting company did a market study on actuators. Several applications of these components were investigated and samples were offered to selected customers. In all applications the ceramic multilayer actuators were used in the heart of the product. A piezo-electric material has two fundamental properties. The first one is that under the influence of an electric field the shape of the product changes, e.g. the product becomes longer or shorter. For example, this property can be used to control a valve or the head of an inkjet printer. The second one is that under the influence of a physical force, which results in a change in the shape

---

[93]   In 1996 it was proven that the problem of the internal resistance was inherent to the properties of the basic material.

of the product, an electrical field is generated. This property can be used in a crash sensor, for example.

To control the head of an inkjet printer the following design can be used. Under the influence of an electrical field the shape of the actuator changes. This change induces a pressure wave in the ink chamber of the printer head, resulting in the ejection of a small droplet of ink. After this, the original shape of the actuator is restored, and the ink chamber is refilled from a reservoir. In this design, the printer head contains a large number of (small) actuators, ink chambers, and ejection holes. The actuators are driven with a high frequency.

In the beginning of 1992, it was decided that the development and manufacturing of actuators would be concentrated on ink jet printers. At the time, the market for ink-jet printers was very turbulent. Dot-matrix printers were over the hill. Ink-jet printers were the new standard. The competition was very strong. Launching a new model on the market could change the relations between the different competitors from one day to the next. As a consequence, the market was characterised by a short time-to-market, high volume and high mix flexibility, and tough competition. The dynamics of the printer market had direct repercussions on the position of the Roermond factory: the factory had to keep up with the erratic developments in the market. An additional complicating factor was the complex technology used to manufacture actuators. The actuator was a new product. The manufacturing equipment and processes were still under development. This means that during this development process changes in specifications and generations of the product had to be incorporated. In fact, an intensive co-development process between the (Japanese) customer and our factory arose. Some of our suppliers were also involved in this process.

The characteristics of the market and the product implied high demands on the organisation. The solution had been sought in concurrent engineering (development and production at overlapping stages). This requires close cooperation between the development group and manufacturing organisation. In addition, continuous improvement was needed to ensure higher yields, better quality and punctual delivery. The production process included the processing of lead-containing materials. Environmental considerations urged the management to control the production process, the exhaust of gases, the drainage of waste water, and the handling of waste materials.

2.1.3 The manufacturing process and operator activities
The process of manufacturing ceramic multilayer actuators consists of six interrelating process steps:

1. *Foil casting*. The starting point is a ceramic powder. The powder is put in a mill. Water and chemicals are added. The powder is milled till the required fineness is achieved. The resulting mixture is called 'slurry'. In a two-step process the slurry is mixed with chemicals and a binder. The resulting mixture is called slib. The slib is taken up onto a metal belt to form a thin film. The film is dried in a heated tunnel. The foil is then rolled up on a reel.

2. *Screen-printing.* The foil is cut in pieces. These pieces are screen printed individually with a silver-palladium paste to form the required electrode pattern. The screen-printed layers are stacked and dried. After that, the stack is compacted to a plate.

3. *Sintering.* The pressed plates are heated up slowly to remove the organic binder. Then the plates are sintered at high temperatures to obtain a dense ceramic material.

4. *Dicing.* The sintered ceramic plates are glued on a support. The individual products are separated by means of a dicing process. After that, the glass plate is heated up and the individual products are removed manually. Glue residues are removed by a cleaning step involving acetone.

5. *Application of end terminations.* End terminations are applied by thin-film evaporation. After that, the products are polarised to obtain the piezo-electric properties. Then the electrical properties are measured.

6. *Packing.* Finally, the individual products are visually inspected and packed.

Generally, the operators run the equipment, execute the quality measurements, take action in the case of deviations, enter data in the electronic data system, do small repair activities, and organise the internal logistics. The following actions are carried out for each step of the process:

1. *Foil casting.* Firstly, slurry is made. The operator weighs the materials, fills the mill, starts the machine, takes a sample at the end of the process, measures the mean grain size, and takes a decision about the quality of the slurry. The whole cycle of slurry making takes about five hours. Secondly, a slib is made. The operator puts the slurry in another vessel, weighs the binder and the chemicals, adds them in a certain order, starts the mixer, weighs other chemicals, adds them, starts the mixer again, evacuates the mixture, and the resulting slib is put in a tank. The whole cycle of slib making takes about one hour. Thirdly, foil is casted. The operator connects the tank with the slib to the foil caster, measures the physical characteristics of the foil, adapts the settings of the equipment, checks the quality of the foil every half an hour, replaces a full reel by an empty one, measures the physical characteristics of the foil, and cleans the equipment at the end of the casting. The whole cycle of foil casting takes about fifteen hours. The operators manage the logistics of slurry making, slib making, and keeping the stocks at the required level. Most operators were certified to make slurry, to make slib, and to cast foil.

2. *Screen-printing.* Firstly, a screen-printed stack is made. The operator prepares the equipment, puts the reel with foil on it, adds the paste to the screen, starts the screen-printing process, measures the physical characteristics of the screen-printed layer, checks the quality of the screen printed layer, removes the cassette at the end of the order, cleans the equipment and prepares it for the next batch. The whole cycle takes about one hour for one batch. Secondly, the printed stack is dried. The operator puts the cassette in a drying furnace, starts the furnace, checks the drying cycle, and takes the cassette out. The whole drying cycle takes about sixteen hours. Thirdly, the stack is pressed. The operator

prepares the press, puts the cassette in the holder, starts the press, checks the visual quality of the pressed plates, cleans the pressing dyes regularly, and performs some measurements on a pressed plate. The whole pressing cycle takes about half an hour for one batch. Finally, the pressed plates are quartered. The operators place the pressed plates in a simple piece of equipment, press some buttons to quarter the plate, and check the quality of the quartered plates. This cycle takes about fifteen minutes per batch. The operators controls the logistics from screen printing to delivery to the next unit. Most operators were certified to perform all activities in this area.

3. *Sintering*. Firstly, the binder is burnt out. The operator places the quartered plate on a special support, makes a pile, fills the furnace, starts the furnace, checks the temperature cycle during the burn out process, empties the furnace, checks the whole temperature cycle again (via a recorder), and performs a physical measurement on a dummy. Secondly, pre-sintering is done. The operator places the burnt-out pile in the furnace, starts the furnace, checks the temperature cycle during the pre-sintering process, empties the furnace, removes the plates from the pile, and checks the whole temperature cycle again (via a recorder). Thirdly, sintering is done. The operator places the pre-sintered plate on a special support, makes a pile, fills the furnace, starts the furnace, checks the temperature cycle during the sintering, empties the furnace, checks the whole temperature cycle again (via a recorder), performs a physical measurement on a dummy, and removes the plates from the pile. Fourthly, flat sintering is done. The operator places the sintered plate on a special support, makes a pile, fills the furnace, starts the furnace, checks the temperature cycle during the flat-sintering process, empties the furnace, checks the whole temperature cycle again (via a recorder), removes the plates from the pile, and cleans the plates with water. The whole cycle of every furnace process takes about twenty-four hours. The operator time involved per furnace process varies between one to three hours per batch. The operators manage the logistics. Most operators were certified to execute all steps.

4. *Dicing*. Firstly, the flat-sintered plates are glued onto a glass plate. The operator places a glass plate in a small machine, adds glue by pressing a button, puts the ceramic plate on it, places the glass plate with the ceramic plate on a belt, and checks every glued plate visually. Every batch the operator measures the amount of glue added. Glueing one plate takes about fifteen seconds. A whole batch takes about one hour. Secondly, the glued plate is diced. The operator places the glued plate on a dicing machine, measures every plate at four points, starts the machine, removes the diced plate, checks the plate visually, and starts the next one. The cycle takes about one minute for one plate. A whole batch takes about four hours. In addition, for every batch several physical measurements have to be made on a diced plate. Thirdly, the individual products are removed manually ('de-glueing'). The operator puts the glass plate with the separated products on a heater, removes the individual products manually, puts them in a rack, places the racks in cleaning machine, and checks the cleaned products visually. The time to remove one product is several seconds. The whole cycle takes about four hours for one batch. The operators control the

logistics. Most dicing operators were also certified for glueing. Most de-glueing operators did not operate the dicing machine.

5. *Application of end terminations*. Firstly, the cleaned products are backed out. The employee takes the product manually from the rack, places the product on a ceramic plate, and places the ceramic plates on the belt of a furnace. The products are then transported to a clean room. The whole cycle takes about an hour for one batch. Secondly, the backed-out products are put in an evaporation jig. The operator takes the product from the plate, puts the product in a jig, closes the jig, places the jig in a cassette, puts the cassette in the cleaning equipment, and places the jig with the cleaned products in an evaporation jig. The whole cycle takes more than an hour for one batch. Thirdly, the cleaned products are evaporated. The operator places the evaporation jig in the equipment, starts the pumping process, starts the evaporation process, continually checks the evaporation process visually and electronically, removes the evaporation jig from the equipment, and measures some physical properties of the evaporated layer. The whole evaporation cycle takes about five hours. Fourthly, the evaporated products are polarised and measured. The operator removes the jigs from the evaporation jigs, places the jig in a robot, and starts the robot. The robot takes the products out of the jig and places them in a polarising jig. The operator takes the polarising jig out of the robot, places the polarising jig in a polarising machine, starts the process, removes the polarising jig from the machine and places it in the measuring equipment, and finally removes the products from the polarising jig and places them on a plate. The whole cycle takes about two hours for one batch. The operators manage the logistics. All operators were certified for handling the products and the jigs, and for operating the polarisation and measuring equipment. Some of the operators were also certified for operating the evaporation process.

6. *Packing*. Firstly, the products are visually inspected. The operator takes the plates with the products and inspects both sides visually using a binocular. This step takes about two hours for one batch. Secondly, the products are packed. The operator takes the products from the plate, puts the products manually in a taping machine, puts the label on the reel, and packs the reels in a box. This step takes about two hours for one batch. The operators control the logistics. All operators are certified both for visual inspection and taping.

2.1.4 Organisation

Figure 2.2 shows the organisation chart of the Ceramic Multilayer Actuators Business Unit. At full production, the business unit totalled about 175 employees.

Figure 2.3 presents the organisation chart of the production department. 6 employees were working in the foil casting unit, 12 employees in screen printing, 20 employees in sintering, 35 employees in dicing, 30 employees in end terminations, and 25 employees in packing. There were 8 employees in the Repair & Maintenance department, 3 employees in Factory Engineering, and again 3 employees in Quality Engineering.

194

The production ran non-stop: twenty-four hours a day, and seven days a week. A five-shift system was used.

Business Unit Ceramic Multilayer Actuators

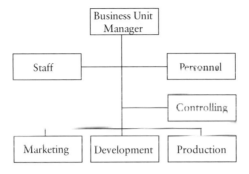

Figure 2.2 Organisation chart of the Business Unit Ceramic Multilayer Actuators

Production Department

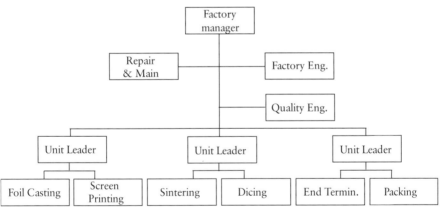

Figure 2.3 Organisation chart of the production department

2.1.5 Case description

The case description covers the period from August 1992 to December 1996. In December 1996 the management of the Components division of Philips decided not to continue the actuator business for marketing and strategic reasons. In April 1997 the business unit was closed.

Parts of this case have been described in the book *Marktgericht productie-management. Van taakgroep naar mini-company (Market-oriented production management. From semi-autonomous work group to mini-company)* (1997) by Maarten Verkerk, Jan de Leede, and Henk van der Tas. Five members of the actuator organisation read the first draft of this book: the business manager, three unit leaders and one factory engineer. Parts of this case have also been described in Jan de Leede's *theorie Innoveren van onderop, Over de bijdrage van taakgroepen aan product en procesvernieuwing (Bottom-up innovation; on the contribution of semi-autonomous work groups to product and process innovation)* (1997).

The case description has been re-written and elaborated on for this study in the period from October 2000 to December 2000. The words 'factory', 'production' and 'production department' are used as synonyms.

2.2 Start-up phase

The start-up phase roughly covered the period between summer 1992 and spring 1994. In this phase both technical and organisational processes were developed to a mature state.

2.2.1 Design of the new factory

Around June 1992, the layout of the new actuator factory was designed. The design was based on socio-technical principles.[94] The primary process was split-up into six segments or units. The boundaries of the segments were chosen in such a way that the dependencies within the segments were larger than the dependencies between the segments.

> *Detailed description of the socio-technical design.* In the Roermond team I was the most experienced manager in the (pilot) production of actuators. For that reason, I played a key role in designing the layout of the new factory. The design of the production structure was based on the principles of the Dutch approach to Socio-Technical Systems Design. These principles were applied 'covertly' because no one except myself was trained in this approach.
>
> The first step of the design of the production structure is parallelisation: the design of parallel lines. Basically, the product mix of actuators consists of two families: products which are large and thin (e.g. 18 x 6 x 0.5 mm^3) and products which are small and thick (e.g. 3 x 3 x 2 mm^3). Taking into account the line balance of a manufacturing line, designing two parallel lines was obvious: one for each family.

---

[94]   The Dutch approach to Socio-Technical Systems Design was used (see section 3.4 of Chapter 2).

However, due to the fact that only the large and thin products were in pilot production (contract with the Japanese customer) it was decided that the line for these products would be designed. Furthermore, from a technical point of view it was no problem to run both the small and thick products on this line.

The second step in the design of the production line is segmentation: the splitting up of the line into related production steps or segments. This step requires a mapping of the dependencies between the individual production steps. Schumacher has proposed the use of the following parameters: technical linkage, informational linkage, error linkage, and directional linkage.[95] In our case, technical and error linkage were important. In practice, the boundaries of the segments were chosen in such a way that every segment delivers a well-defined semi-finished product to the next segment. The segmentation process will be illustrated for the first two segments.

The first three sub-processes are slurry making, slib making and foil casting. Slurry and slib making are comparable activities. They are done in the same room under normal production conditions. Foil casting is a different type of activity. It is done in another room under special conditions (clean room: control of temperature, humidity and dust). From a quality point of view, however, the processes of slurry and slib making, and foil casting are strongly interdependent. The quality of the slurry and the slib to a great extent determines the quality of the foil. Therefore, the decision was taken to combine slurry making, slib making, and foil casting in one segment. In addition, this segment had a clearly defined product: a foil.

The next four sub-processes are screen-printing, drying, pressing, and quartering. Screen-printing and pressing are comparable activities: they involve the operation of high-tech equipment. The drying process can be seen as a preparatory step for the pressing operation. In addition, the screen printing, drying, and pressing steps have to be under special conditions (clean room: control of temperature, humidity and dust). Moreover, these steps are strongly dependent and the quality of the screen printing process can be judged well after pressing. Based on these arguments it was decided that the screen printing, drying, and pressing sub-processes should be combined in one segment. There were two possibilities for the quartering step. Firstly, to characterise it as the last step of the pressing operation. Secondly, to see it as the preparatory step for the sintering operation. The first possibility was chosen. The main argument was that technologically, the quartering step related more to its preceding steps that to the steps that followed. The 'Screen printing' unit had a clearly defined product: a quartered plate.

In the segmentation of the other sub-processes, the dependencies were analysed in the same way and comparable considerations played a role.

At that time, designing the factory was difficult due to the fact that the manufacturing process was in development. In some cases, the boundary of a segment was changed later on as a result of technological developments.

---

[95]   Schumacher (1983, p20-21).

2.2.2 Statistical Process Control

During the start-up of the actuator factory it was emphasised that the manufacturing processes should be (statistically) controlled. This meant that the development of a controlled process had to be one of the main objectives of the development group. In addition, the process should be monitored and improved during the pilot production and production.

> *Background.* The start up of a new factory implied a break-through in thinking about process control. It was decided that process control should be an integral part of the development process. This means that the development group had to shift its attention from *product control* to *process control*. In other words, the quality of the production process should be so high that the manufactured products 'automatically' meet the requirements. This approach means that quality is built into the process. In addition, it implies that critical parameters are identified, measurement tools are developed, and out-of-control-action-plans are defined. This means that employees can control the process.

The management team hired a consultancy company in order to train development engineers, factory engineers, and management in the principles of Statistical Process Control (September-October 1992).

2.2.3 Process Inventory Teams

In September 1992, the building was ready and the equipment was moved in. In October 1992 four Process Inventory Teams were started up. These teams were a direct result of and a part of the training in Statistical Process Control. The teams covered the main processes: foil casting, screen-printing, sintering, and dicing.[96] The objective of these teams was to make an inventory of the process and to bring this process under statistical control.

The Process Inventory Teams were cross-level and cross-functional[97]: they consisted of two operators, a unit leader, a factory or development engineer, a repair and maintenance technician, a member of the management team, and an external consultant. These teams met up weekly or fortnightly. The objective of each team was to identify the critical process steps, to determine the critical process parameters of these steps, to develop a method by which these parameters could be regularly measured, to bring the process under (statistical) control, and to agree on an out-of-control action plan. In practice, both process parameters as well as product parameters were measured and brought under control. The Process Inventory teams used a workbook that helped guide the members.

---

[96] At that time, a Japanese sub-contractor applied end terminations. Later on, this activity was carried out in Roermond.

[97] In the Scandinavian and Australian approach to Socio-Technical Systems Design, use is made of a 'deep slice' or 'vertical slice'. These expressions indicate the presence of various levels in a team. Within this analogy, a cross-level and cross-functional team can be referred to as a 'diagonal slice' (suggestion by J.F. den Hertog).

In practice, the Process Inventory Teams functioned not only as a team to control the process, but also as a platform for the discussion of all issues that arise in the starting-up phase of a factory. These issues varied from practical tools to fundamental process problems. Increasingly, operators, development engineers, and management used this platform to bring up issues and to get support for solving problems. The activities of these teams resulted in a number of actual improvements on the shop floor.

> *Reflection*. I coached two out of the four Process Inventory teams. These teams were my first experience with interdisciplinary improvement teams. I was really excited about it. Firstly, the *interdisciplinary* character appeared to be important. It regularly occurred that one member brought up important information about a problem that was not – or could not – be observed by one of the other members. For example, operators and repair and maintenance technicians made a lot of comments about process problems to the development engineers. Secondly, the discussion *as such* appeared to be important. One of the team members regularly let something slip that triggered one of the other team members. Often, the comment was wrong, but the (unintended) trigger was there. Thirdly, participation leads to *commitment*. The members of the Process Inventory Teams were very committed to implementing the decisions of the team. Finally, improving contributes to the development of *strong relationships* between the members of the team. As a factory manager, I have often made use of these relationships. When there was a problem in the factory, I often went to an employee who I knew from an improvement team to discuss the facts and possible causes. In the same way, employees used their relationship with me to get support for solving a problem or getting information about the business.

The Process Inventory Teams functioned for more than one year. In this period the equipment was made operational. The processes were brought under control. The process instruction cards were made. The employees were trained. Finally, a large number of small improvements were implemented. After that, the teams were disbanded.

In two departments, a so-called Process Action Team succeeded the Process Inventory Team. This team consisted of one operator, one factory engineer and one development engineer. The objective of this team was to improve the process control further.

Later, improvement teams were also started in the End Terminations and Packing units. The teams worked in a comparable way to the Process Inventory Teams.

2.2.4 Monthly unit meetings
The Process Inventory Teams mobilised a large part of the organisation. The results of the teams were communicated intensively and new methods and procedures were implemented quickly. However, with the growing organisation an important problem came to light. These teams only involved some of the employees. The team members participated actively, but the other members of the unit increasingly stood to one side. To cope with this problem a monthly unit meeting was started up.

The monthly unit meeting was done in a classical form. The meeting was focused on the exchange of information. The unit leader informed the employees - mostly per shift – about the financial results, outstanding orders, quality and quality problems, changes in the process instructions, safety and environment, discipline rules, and so on. Sometimes, a subject was discussed in detail. The employees got the opportunity to ask questions. Furthermore, every operator could ask questions about or comment on the reports and queries at the end of the meeting.

The monthly unit meeting was experienced as significant. The atmosphere was good. The information was relevant. However, both the management and the employees were not fully satisfied. Several problems came to the fore. Firstly, a lot of information was exchanged, but almost nothing was 'done'. Only some remarks from the reports and queries were placed on an action list and dealt with by management. Secondly, the information exchange was mainly one-sided: from management to employees. The other way around was only practised during the reports and queries at the end of the meeting. Thirdly, a unit structure requires that the activities of the different units are geared to one another. However, the relationships between the foregoing unit (the supplier) and the next unit (the customer) could not be managed via this meeting. Finally, the contribution of the information exchange to the know-how and the craftsmanship of the employees appeared to be low.

> *Reflection.* Personally, I have been the member of a large number of improvement teams and I have attended many monthly unit meetings. There is a big difference between 'being a member of a team' and 'attending a unit meeting'. A team member participates actively and an attendant consumes passively. Improvement team activities lead to involvement and ownership, and attending a unit team meeting satisfies only the demand for information. In my experience, a classical unit team meeting has to be interpreted as a 'hygiene factor' (Herzberg). The absence of such a meeting always results in dissatisfaction, but the presence of it will not cause satisfaction. Further, the symbolic meaning of both improvement teams and unit meetings has to be emphasised. They express respect for the employees. In unit meetings the need of employees to obtain relevant information and the right to ask questions is respected. In improvement teams the contribution of the employees to the improvement process is acknowledged. Needless to say the symbolic meaning of improvement teams is much larger than that of unit meetings.

In conclusion, the monthly unit meeting in its classical form satisfied the need for information but hardly contributed to involvement and ownership.

2.2.5 Quality Award

In March 1993, a Japanese customer honoured the Ceramic Multilayer Actuators business unit with a Quality Award. During the presentation it was remarked that the cooperation with the Dutch company was 'nearly as good as cooperation with a Japanese company'.[98]

2.2.6 Customer Day 1994

On January 10th, the Chief Executive Officer of Philips, Mr. Timmer, launched Philip's second Customer Day. The objective of this day was to help managers introduce the 'process way' and to teach the organisation to 'hear the voice of the customer'.[99] In this approach every delivery to a customer is seen as the result of a large number of processes within the company. To satisfy the customer all these processes have to be linked up.

Customer Day 1994 was used to discuss customer-supplier relationships within the factory. After all, every unit has an internal supplier and an internal customer.[100] The importance of customer-supplier relationships in the process of continuous improvement is highlighted by the following story.

Story. On the shop floor I met an employee who grumbled about the quality of the batches. I asked him what was wrong. He told me that the plates were contaminated. This contamination resulted in a lot of problems in the glueing process. He regularly had to stop the process in order to clean the plate. I asked him why he accepted this batch and did not return it to the Sintering unit (the supplier). He answered that it would cause a lot of additional work for his colleagues if he returned the batch. I took the contaminated batch and went to the first operator of the Sintering unit and explained the problem to him. It was decided that an operator of the Sintering unit would clean the batch. Furthermore, I told the employees of the Dicing unit that they had the right to return contaminated batches and told the employees of the Sintering unit that they had to improve the cleaning of the plates. During the following weeks I regularly discussed the quality of the batches both with the (first) operators of the Sintering unit as well as with the (first) operators of the Dicing unit. After some months, the problems were completely solved. I regularly intervened to solve these types of problems on the shop floor.

Reflection. In this story the problems between a supplier (sintering unit) and its customer (dicing unit) were solved after management intervention. This story is characteristic of the state of play at the time: the problems between units were only solved by intervention from management. In other words, self-management does not develop automatically. Both the experiences of this customer day (see below) and the mini-company process (see 2.3) shows that participation and continuous improvement are suitable processes for the development of self-management.

---

[98] *Print*, April 1993.
[99] Manual 'Customer first: the process way' by the Corporate Quality Bureau, p1, 3.
[100] Basically, the first unit has no internal supplier and the last unit has no internal customer. In these cases, purchasing was seen as the supplier for the first unit (Foil casting) and marketing as the customer of the last unit (Packing).

The units were informed about the topic of the customer day several weeks in advance. They were invited to suggest issues. Management collated and classified these issues, and composed the teams that would discuss them on the customer day. Generally, each team consisted of unit members, a representative of the internal supplier, a representative of the internal customer(s)[101], and an engineer or member of the management team. All employees were involved: in total there were 19 factory teams with 6 to 7 members.

> *Reflection.* The management team agreed the program of Customer Day 1994. It was believed that this program would contribute to an improvement of the performance of the business unit. All members of the management team participated in the discussions.

The program for the customer day was described in the booklet 'Customer Day 1994'.[102] In the foreword it was written that[103]:

> "To achieve satisfied customers we have to cooperate better (...) Our factory can be compared with a relay team: every member has to pass the baton on to the next person. If one person drops the baton, then the whole team loses. The same holds for the factory. If one employee does a bad job, then the whole actuator factory loses (...) If we want to satisfy our external customers, then we have to take care of the customers in our own factory. We have to ask the following questions:
> o   Is our customer in the factory satisfied?
> o   Do we ask our internal customer whether s/he is satisfied?
> o   How do we react when our customer comments on quality?
> During the 1994 Customer Day we will talk with our customers. Listen to them. Try to solve their problems. Try to make them satisfied. If your customer has many remarks: then you have a lot of possibilities to improve. Do not forget:
>
> THE CUSTOMER IS KING
> also in the factory!"

During the customer day each team discussed their own topics. As much as possible, solutions were discussed and agreements about implementation made. After the customer day, most of the teams gathered one or more times to finalise their assignment.

For example, team 14 discussed the relationships between the Dicing unit and the Packing unit.[104] This team consisted of three operators from the Dicing unit,

---

[101]   In several cases, more than one internal customer was identified. For example, in one customer day, the Sintering unit team and representatives of both the Dicing and Packing units were present. The reason was that certain types of quality problems that arose in the Sintering unit affected both the Dicing and Packing units.

[102]   The program did not cover all issues suggested by the employees. These items were also listed in the booklet. Management also indicated how to address these items.

[103]   Booklet 'Customer Day 1994', p1.

two operators from the Packing unit, and one assistant from the quality department. Their assignment was to answer the following questions[105]:

1. How can drying stains be prevented in the last cleaning step in the Dicing unit?
2. How can the products in the mould (in the Dicing unit) be oriented so that they can be easily packed with the right orientation (in the Packing unit)?
3. How can a regular supply of batches from the Dicing unit to the Packing unit be guaranteed (especially in the weekend)?

Several weeks after the customer day the team reported the following improvements[106]:

1. The cause of drying stains is contaminated solvent. To prevent drying stains the solvent in the cleaning unit will be renewed three times a week.
2. The Dicing unit will orient all products in the same way. This orientation will be done during the de-glueing process. The process instruction has been adapted. All employees have been instructed. At this moment, the products are delivered with the right orientation.
3. Every shift has to deliver three batches per shift to the Packing unit.

Furthermore it was agreed that[107]:

"The slip through of wrong products from the Dicing unit to the Packing unit has to be greatly decreased. Every plate has to be checked visually after dicing. In the case of strange phenomena or extensive chipping the deviating plates will be supplied separately".

The other teams reported comparable improvements. The results of all teams were summarised in the 'Evaluatie Customer Day 1994' booklet, which was distributed to all employees. Also, the remaining action points were listed and the follow-up described.

Reflection. Most teams worked intensively on their assignment. The atmosphere in the meetings was quite good. They were also satisfied with the results. In my opinion, the main reason for this enthusiasm was that the teams addressed and solved daily problems. The members of the management team were also enthusiastic about these teams. For most of them, it was their first experience in participating in a cross-level and cross-functional team.

---

[104] At that time, no end terminations were applied. This means that after dicing the products were transferred to the Packing unit, where they were visually inspected and packed.
[105] Booklet 'Customer Day 1994', p8.
[106] Booklet 'Evaluatie Customer Day 1994', p12, 13.
[107] Booklet 'Evaluatie Customer Day 1994', p13.

During the customer day several employees asked to start-up a kind of technical unit meeting. In their opinion, there were too few opportunities to discuss technical items. I promised that I would handle this question in the near future.

2.2.7 Benchmarking
The Process Inventory Teams required a structural follow-up; the limitations of the monthly unit meeting underlined the necessity of such a follow-up, and the request of several operators to organise a technical unit meeting expressed the same idea. However, how could such a follow-up be structured?

> *Reflection.* I wanted to continue with improvement teams in a structured way. However, I did not know how. At that time, I was familiar with the Dutch variant of the Socio-Technical Systems Design that is focused on the design of organisations. However, I was not familiar with Swedish and Australian variants of Socio-Technical Systems Design that focus on participative structures.

It was decided that several Philips factories would be benchmarked. From March to April 1994, we (an intern and myself) carried out a study. The objective of the benchmark was to learn about developing a 'learning organisation'. Three factories were visited: a lighting factory in Hamilton (UK), a component factory in Blackburn (UK), and a semi-conductor factory in Nijmegen (The Netherlands). In Hamilton the Japanese approach to improvement was explicitly applied. Quality circles attacked quality and production problems. In Blackburn a national improvement approach was applied. Improvements were made in multi-level and multi-disciplinary teams. In Nijmegen improvement teams were used to solve persistent problems. In these teams representatives from all shifts were present. In all factories the improvement process was strongly supported by management.

> *Reflection.* The visit to the lighting factory in Hamilton made a deep impression on me. The plant manager explained the role of improvement teams in the turn-around of the factory. He tried to convince us of his approach. It was clear beyond any doubt that he 'walked his talk' and that he was 'Mr. Improvement'. Looking back, this impression confirms my experience: the development of a learning culture starts with management. Management has to give meaning to improvement activities in their words (explaining the policy) and in their deeds (coaching a team).

In the report it was concluded that the factories visited showed a shift in organisational culture.[108] Firstly, this shift in culture was management driven. Secondly, the responsibility for the production was not given to individuals but to units. Thirdly, the improvement process was organised in multi-disciplinary teams. These teams solved problems that were present on the shop floor. Finally, it was observed that all factories focused on translation of the voice of the customer to the shop floor and a structural embedding of improvement teams in the organisation. The

---

[108]   E. van Riet, 'Benchmarking Industrial Organisations', March/April 1994.

benchmark report was closed with some recommendations.[109] It was emphasised that the management team of Ceramic Multilayer Actuators should declare itself openly in favour of continuous improvement and teamwork. Furthermore, the organisational conditions to develop such a culture should be fulfilled. Amongst others, the training of employees and the facilitation of teams was mentioned.

2.2.8 Consultancy

In November 1993, a two-day workshop was organised to discuss the strategy of the business unit, the objectives of the factory, the budget of the factory, and the organisational structure of the factory. The unit leaders, factory engineers, maintenance engineer, personnel officer, and myself attended this workshop. An external consultant (Mr. Henk van der Tas) coached the workshop. The production structure and the control structure were elaborated on, responsibilities were assigned, and improvement actions agreed.

During the benchmarking process, the external consultant was contacted. The following key questions were asked:

o   How can the voice of the customer reach the shop floor?
o   How can the improvement process be structurally embedded in a five-shift production organisation?

A prerequisite was that the chosen solution should be in accordance with the socio-technical organisation of the factory.

The external consultant referred to the book entitled *The New Shop Floor Management* by Kiyoshi Suzaki. He proposed that we take this book as a starting point to answer these questions. I read this book. I was very enthusiastic about Suzaki's ideas. However, a lot of questions remained. How can these ideas be applied in a five-shift system? Which responsibilities have to be delegated to the shop floor? How can a shift in influence and power from management to operators be realised?

> *Seminar.* In the same period, Philips offered me the opportunity to attend a seminar with Suzaki. I asked him how his ideas could be realised in a three or five-shift production system. His answer was as simple as disconcerting: 'That's your problem'. Later, I expressed my displeasure with this answer. He remarked that he had interpreted my question as an excuse not to implement his ideas. Further, he said that he never answered these kinds of questions. In his experience, managers have to find their own solution because managers do not follow advice, but only implement solutions they have found out themselves. This answer stresses the importance of the idea of ownership. However, it underestimates the importance of finding a practical form.

The main question of 'How to apply these ideas in a five-shift system?' was finally decided in a discussion with the external consultant. In accordance with the socio-

---

[109]   E. van Riet, 'Benchmarking Industrial Organisations', March/April 1994, p11, 12.

technical design of the organisation, the mini-company should be a socio-technical unit.

> *Reflection.* Looking back, it is quite obvious that the mini-company is a socio-technical or semi-autonomous work group. However, at that time it was not obvious to me. The main cause was that De Sitter and Suzaki present a quite different line of thought. De Sitter offers a design theory and design methodology. Suzaki offers many ideas and methods for continuous improvement. It took some time before I understood that these approaches were not contradictory but complementary. The socio-technical group designed according to the principles of De Sitter is the most natural unit to apply the mini-company concept of Suzaki.

The insight, to identify the boundaries of the mini company with the socio technical unit or semi autonomous group, appeared to be important. As a consequence, the unit was made responsible for delivering good products to the internal customer. In addition, shift-changeover problems were defined as an internal issue of the unit.

> *Reflection.* The practical importance of this decision was great. In developing customer-supplier relationships within a five-shift factory it is very important to known who the supplier is. The moment we started to implement the rule that a batch with (preventable) quality problems should be returned to the supplier, we often got this reaction: this batch was not made by our shift (as could be seen from the batch card). Deciding that the mini-company includes all five shifts prevented this kind of problem as each shift could be made accountable for the delivery of a batch with quality problems. Nevertheless, a lot of explanation and communication was needed before returned batches were accepted without grumbling.

2.3 The mini-company process

The improvement philosophy and mini-company concept were elaborated by middle management, the personnel officer, the factory manager, and an external consultant (Mr. Henk van der Tas). The essence of De Sitter's approach to Socio-Technical Systems Design[110], the mini-company philosophy of Kiyoshi Suzaki, and the improvement philosophy of Masaaki Imai were taken as starting points.

> *Reflection.* At that time, I understood the basic ideas of De Sitter's approach to Socio-Technical Systems Design, the Mini-Company Concept, and the improvement philosophy of Imai. However, I had not analysed them in detail (like I have done in Chapter 2). I used these three approaches in the following way. The Dutch approach

---

[110] The principles of the Dutch approach to Socio-Technical Systems Design were applied 'covertly' (see 2.2.1).

as used to design the production structure. The Dutch approach and the Mini-Company Concept were used to design the control structure. The Mini-Company Concept and the improvement philosophy of Imai were used to design the improvement structure (the improvement structure is defined as the tools, techniques, and procedures employed to ensure continuous improvement).

2.3.1 Creation of support

The management team, middle management, and the shop floor supported the mini-company process. The creation of support from these parties will be respectively described.

The management team took the view that the Process Inventory Teams had to be continued in a new structure. It was decided that other factories would be benchmarked (see section 2.2.7) for this purpose. In May 1994, I presented the results of the benchmark, the improvement philosophy of Imai, and the mini-company philosophy of Suzaki to the management team.[111] In July 1994 it was formally decided that these philosophies would partially shape the policy of the actuator factory. Furthermore, means were made available: a vacancy for a team facilitator and a budget of 100.000 Dutch guilders for training and consultancy were agreed upon.

> *Reflection.* Why did the management team agree with the conclusions of the benchmark? Why did the management team accept the improvement philosophy? Why did the management team support the implementation of mini-companies? In my opinion, the following arguments played a role. Firstly, it was common knowledge that participation had proven its worth in the start-up phase of the factory. The approach of the benchmarked organisations, the improvement philosophy of Imai, and the mini-company philosophy of Suzaki were in accordance with the approach of the start-up phase. Secondly, every member of the management team had experienced the value of continuous improvement him- or herself by coaching a team on the customer day (see section 2.2.6). Probably, this experience was decisive. Thirdly, everybody was convinced that the developments in the market required an improvement culture in the factory. Finally, Philip's Board of Management advocated the approach of Suzaki (This approach was introduced in a training course that was obligatory for management).
>
> It was not difficult to convince the management team of the mini-company philosophy. During the discussion the atmosphere was like 'yes, that's the way we have to go'. Several questions were asked about the total amount of money involved (facilitator, budget for training and consultancy, and hours of operators and man-

---

[111] In this presentation I did not refer to the Dutch approach to Socio-Technical Systems Design. The main reason was that the production and control structure were already de signed according to this approach. For the next step I did not need the design approach of De Sitter but I did need the improvement philosophy of Imai and the mini-company philosophy of Suzaki. Furthermore, nobody in the management team was familiar with the ideas of De Sitter whereas several members of the management team were familiar with the views of Imai and Suzaki.

agement). In practice, the management team supported the mini-company philosophy not only verbally but also visibly (see below).

The external consultant stressed the importance of support from middle management (unit leaders). He advised – under the slogan 'seeing is believing' – that the middle management should visit a factory with an improvement culture. In June 1994, the unit leaders, factory engineers, consultant, and myself visited a lighting factory in Middelburg (The Netherlands). Many improvement teams were running in this factory. These teams selected the issues to be improved, analysed the problem in detail, and proposed a solution to management. Middle management or the engineering department implemented the solution. The pros and the cons of the improvement approach in Middelburg were discussed extensively. An in depth comparison was made with the Process Inventory Teams. In the same period, I discussed the ideas of Suzaki with middle management. I showed them that the mini-company process would be a natural extension of our present way of working. Parallel to the discussion in the management team, it was decided by the unit leaders, factory engineers, and myself that the Mini-Company Concept had to be implemented in the factory.

> *Reflection.* Why did middle management support this process? Why was there no resistance? I would like to mention three aspects. Firstly, middle management had experienced first-hand the limitations of the monthly unit meetings, the advantages of the Process Inventory Teams, and the fruits of the development of customer-supplier relationships. I regularly emphasised these limitations, advantages, and benefits. In doing so, I intentionally gave meaning to the limitations of the present approach and the urgency to develop the organisation further. Secondly, middle management participated actively in the change process. The various aspects of the mini-company process were discussed. Potential problems and possible pitfalls were put on the table. All decisions were taken in consensus (Note: I am aware that a 'decision in consensus' does not mean that all members agree). Finally, in the recruitment and selection of middle management, special attention was paid to a participative management style and coaching capabilities.
>
> Middle management actively supported the mini-company process. I never felt any signs of resistance. Things regularly went wrong through inexperience or through insufficient understanding of the process or philosophy. Therefore, it was necessary to coach middle management intensively in this (difficult) process.

Finally, the development of support from the shop floor has to be addressed. The operators were very positive about the Process Inventory Teams and the improvement teams of the Customer Day 1994. The main reason was that these teams solved *their* daily problems. The request (see section 2.2.6) to organise a technical unit meeting has to be understood against this background.

The operators were informed about the findings of the benchmarking process. They were also told bit by bit about the ideas of Suzaki. The mini-company process was presented as the answer to the request for a technical unit meeting. This answer was accepted.

Reflection. The continuous formal and informal communication about the benchmarking process and its follow-up was crucial in the creation of support from the shop floor. Everybody knew that one of the objectives of this benchmark was to organise the improvement process structurally and find out how to shape a technical unit meeting. The moment the mini-company process was presented to the organisation, all employees had already heard of it and 'knew' that it was an answer to their wishes.

Generally, change processes create a lot of resistance. However, the introduction of the mini-company process went smoothly. Why is this?

Reflection. The Process Inventory Teams, monthly unit meetings, and the development of the customer supplier relationship (Customer Day 1994) can be interpreted as a 'prelude' to the mini-company concept. From this point of view, the implementation of mini-companies was not a radical change in the organisation, but could be characterised as the result of a long evolutionary process. In this period, I used all my rhetorical qualities to emphasise that the mini-company process was the 'logical' successor to the Process Inventory Teams, monthly unit meetings, and the improvement of customer-supplier relationships. At the same time, I projected the success of these 'preludes' onto the new mini-company process. The active support for the mini-company process only can be understood as a direct result of the presence of high-trust relations within the business unit (see Chapter 4).

In October 1994, I presented the improvement philosophy and the mini-company process to the crew of the whole business unit: operators, engineers and management. This presentation was done in groups of 5 to 10 people. During and after the presentation, there was room for questions and discussions.

Presentation. The presentation was named 'Improving and adapting in a turbulent environment'. The sub-title was 'Working together on improvement'. The presentation consisted of the following parts:
- the mission of the Ceramic Multilayer Actuators business unit
- the requirements of the market
- the consequences for the factory
- the kaizen philosophy ('kaizen' is the Japanese term for continuous improvement)
- the 7-jump (step-method to improve based on the PDCA-cycle)
- the identification of areas for improvement
- the 9-jump (step-method for the mini-company process)
- glass wall management.

In the presentation, the different areas of improvement were identified: quality, costs, deliveries, safety and environment, motivation or morale of the group, and housekeeping. It was stressed that improvement in all these areas was equally important.

The slides of the presentation were compiled in a booklet named *Verbeteren en aanpassen in een turbulente omgeving* (*Improving and adapting in a turbulent environment*).[112] This booklet was distributed to all members of the business unit.

> *Reflection.* Why did I compile the slides of the presentation in a booklet? My most important consideration was to give meaning to its content. I often referred to this booklet to emphasise the message. I also used this booklet to emphasise: 'It's our philosophy and I am accountable for it'.

> *Anecdote.* The presentation was conducted by an external agency. In my opinion, an important message has to be communicated professionally. However, the bill for the design of the presentation was quite high. I never succeeded in convincing my boss that these expenses were justified.

The atmosphere during the presentations was quite good. I therefore concluded that there was enough support to continue the mini-company process.

2.3.2 Starting-up a mini-company

The first mini-factories were started up in October-November 1994. The process of starting up a mini-company is summarised in Figure 2.4. The key elements were communication, training, and improvement cycles. The whole cycle took about one year. All members of the mini-company had to participate in this process. The first training course took one day. It was held in a meeting room within the plant. The second training course took two days. It was held in a hotel that was located ten kilometres away from the factory.

> *Reflection.* The decision to run the second training course in a hotel resulted in unpleasant discussions in the plant. It was questioned whether it was really necessary 'to put up' operators in a hotel. We had two arguments for holding this course in a hotel. Firstly, to strengthen the social relations between the members of the unit. Second, to give meaning to the whole mini-company process. In practice, both arguments appeared to be valid.

---

[112]   M.J. Verkerk (RSB-46-94 MV401, 04-10-1994).

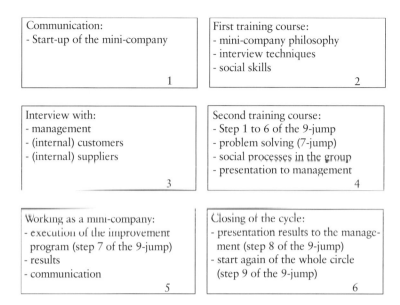

Communication: - Start-up of the mini-company 1	First training course: - mini-company philosophy - interview techniques - social skills 2
Interview with: - management - (internal) customers - (internal) suppliers 3	Second training course: - Step 1 to 6 of the 9-jump - problem solving (7-jump) - social processes in the group - presentation to management 4

Working as a mini-company:
- execution of the improvement
  program (step 7 of the 9-jump)
- results
- communication
5
	Closing of the cycle:
	- presentation results to the manage-
	  ment (step 8 of the 9-jump)
	- start again of the whole circle
	  (step 9 of the 9-jump)
	6

Figure 2.4 Schematic representation of the process of starting up a mini-company

The key cycle in this process is the so-called 9-jump. This 9-jump is based on a cycle given by Suzaki.[113] Figure 2.5 on the next page gives an overview of the different steps.

The most important activities of the cycle are the formulation of the mission statement, identification of suppliers and customers, design of the improvement program and the execution of this plan. The interviews with management, customers, and suppliers were important to gather information for these activities. It has to be emphasised that the mini-company itself formulated the mission statement and set the priorities of the improvement program.

> *Reflection.* The members of the management team were actively involved in the start-up of mini-companies. The business manager and the marketing manager were interviewed about ten to fifteen times by a group of two or three operators. The other members of the management team were interviewed about five times. The management team became very enthusiastic about the interviews. It gave them an excellent opportunity to communicate their view about the business and to tell the operators how their mini-company could support the business.

---

[113] Suzaki (1993, p70).

9-jump	
step 1	Name the mini-company
step 2	Write a mission statement for the mini-company
step 3	Make an overview of the employees of the mini-company and the most important machines
step 4	Make an overview of the customer-supplier relationships of the mini-company
step 5	Incorporate the results of the interviews with the management, the (internal) customers, and the (internal) suppliers
step 6	Make an improvement program for the coming period
step 7	Execute the improvement program with the 7-jump
step 8	Present the results to the management
step 9	Start the 9-jump again

Figure 2.5 An overview of the 9-jump

At the end of the second training course, the mission statement, the identified customers and suppliers, and the improvement program were presented to and approved by myself.

> *Approval.* The presentation of the mission statement, the identified customers and suppliers, and the improvement program was followed by an intense discussion. These elements were core-elements in the whole mini-company process. Therefore I paid a lot attention to them. In most cases, the presented proposals were approved. Although I never rejected or overruled one of the proposals, in some cases, I could convince the members of the mini-company that they had to extend the mission statement or to change the priorities of the improvement program. For example, one mini-company did not mention anything about quality in their mission statement. In the discussion it was admitted bashfully that a statement about quality was forgotten. The mission statement was adapted accordingly.

Figures 2.6 and 2.7 give an example of a mission statement and an improvement program, respectively.

Mission statement of The Plumbers (a mini-company)

To achieve satisfied (internal and external) customers in an efficient way by:

- working according to the process instructions;
- working as a team to realise improvements within the unit, and in relations with customers and suppliers;
- communicating well between all shifts by means of a systematic shift-changeover method and unit meetings;
- communicating informally with customers and suppliers about the quality of the deliveries;
- taking responsibility both individually and as a team for the housekeeping in the unit.

Roermond, February 1996

Note:
The unit defined the suppliers of the ceramic powder and the organic binder as their main (external) suppliers. The unit defined the Screen-printing, Sintering, and Packing units, and the development group (for trials), as their main (internal) customers.

Figure 2.6 Mission statement of the Foil casting unit

Improvement program of The Plumbers (a mini-company)

The following improvements have to be realised:

- update of the process instructions;
- development of a complaint procedure (complaints from customers);
- reduction of the number of complaints;
- improve the agenda of the monthly unit meeting, i.e. add delivery performance, complaints, information from factory engineering and development, and comments from the customers;
- reduce wastage of powder and foil;
- improve the ergonomics in the wet room.

Roermond, February 1996

Figure 2.7 Improvement program of the Foil casting unit

The seventh step of the 9-jump is to execute the improvement program. The members of the mini-company work together to realise the targets. Glass wall management and the monthly mini-company meeting are important elements in the mini-company process. These processes are described below.

2.3.3 Execution of the improvement program

Continuous improvement is an important element of the 9-jump. Different areas of improvement were identified: quality, costs, deliveries, safety and environment, motivation or morale of the group, and housekeeping. The improvement program had to cover these areas. The execution of this program was done step-by-step: the improvement actions were completed according to the agreed priority. An improvement team covers every element. A cross-level and cross-functional team ('diagonal slice') was taken. Generally, such a team consisted of five operators (one from every shift), a member of middle management or myself, and one or more technicians or engineers. Generally, the unit leader was the chairman. The team met every week or every two weeks. In addition, a facilitator supported the team.

The improvement teams used a short-term cycle, the so called 7-jump. This cycle is in fact an extended version of the Plan-Do-Check-Action circle, i.e. the planning stage is composed in four phases. The 7-jump is described in Figure 2.8.

7-jump

step 1	Describe the problem
step 2	Collect the data
step 3	Find the causes
step 4	Design a plan to solve the problem
step 5	Execute the plan
step 6	Check on desired results
step 7	Standardise the improvement

Figure 2.8 An overview of the 7-jump

In practise, the improvement programs covered all identified areas.

Examples of topics of improvement teams:
o   quality: improvement of the quality of the foil (reduction of loose particles), improvement of the quality of plates (no dirt, no broken edges), and the improvement of the quality of the dicing process;
o   costs: reduction of maintenance activities, reduction of material use, and reduction of registration procedures;
o   deliveries: improvement of the logistics between the mini-companies;
o   safety and environment: introduction of lifting tools, reduction of pollution to the environment, and the reduction of the use of water for cleaning;
o   motivation or morale of the group: improvement of the shift-change procedure, improvement of the communication between the shifts, adaptation of the agenda of the mini-company meeting, and standardisation of work procedures;
o   housekeeping: in all units the housekeeping was improved.

Reflection. Many daily problems were included in the improvement program of a mini-company. For example, insufficient housekeeping, problems with the shift changeover, and differences of opinion with the internal customer. The very starting of an improvement team already had a positive outcome: the friction caused by the problems decreased. After solving the problems, the atmosphere between the employees always greatly improved.

Reflection. In fact, this list shows how 'easy' improving is: put the right people around the table, give them some tools to analyse the problem, give them the means to solve the problem, and implement the proposals with management support. The only thing I had to do as a manager was to keep pressure on the whole improvement process. I also ceaselessly emphasised the importance of this process, i.e. by informally asking the members of the teams about the progress. I did not realise that it could not be taken for granted that this process would run so smoothly (see the Aachen case).

In the period between April 1995 and April 1996, twenty improvement teams successfully completed their activities. The improvement teams regularly reported their results within a meeting of the management team.

2.3.4 Working together as a mini-company

The 9-jump and the 7-jump formed the heart of the way the mini-company worked together. They both express the values developed in the mini-company process and influence the culture of the mini-company, which in turn influences the behaviour of its members. The 9-jump and the 7-jump have to be supported by an information and communication structure.

In his book *The New Shop Floor Management,* Suzaki introduces the term 'glass wall management'. He uses the metaphor of the glass wall to indicate that the organisation of the mini-company has to be as clear as glass. This means the production flow, cooperation patterns, and information exchange have to be structured in such a way that the state of play is clear at a single glance. In the actuator factory several short-cycle structures were used, i.e. the mini-company white board, the shift changeover procedure, and other forms. Also one long-cycle structure was present, i.e. the mini-company meeting.

The mini-company white board

The mini-company white board visualises the policy and the state of play. Figure 2.9 shows a photograph of the mini-company white board of the Screen-printing unit. This mini-company named themselves 'Archana'.

Background. In the groundwork to the start-up of the mini-company process, the employees of the Screen-printing unit decided to adopt a child via Foster Parents. This child was a girl, named Archana. This decision shows that the unit wanted to work as a team. The message was: we are a group; we will act as a group; we will stick up for this girl; and we identify ourselves with her. This decision also shows that in the experience of these employees, the mini-company process was more that just a part of their working life. Maybe the most important message of this decision was: there is more between heaven and earth than paid labour, i.e. there are people who need our care. The photograph of the girl was present on the mini-company white board, so, every shift they were reminded of their joint responsibility.

Figure 2.10 illustrates the set-up and the different elements of a mini-company white board

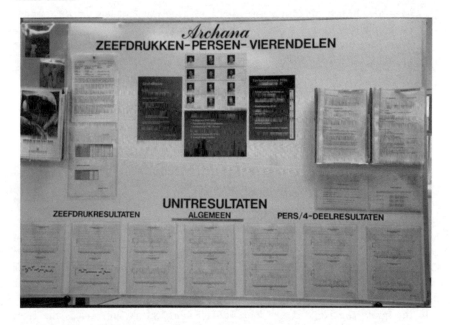

Figure 2.9 The mini-company white board of the 'Archana' unit

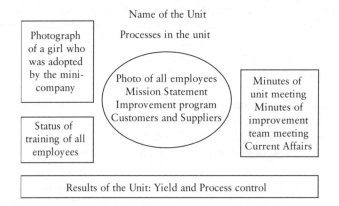

Figure 2.10 Set-up and elements of the mini-company white board of the 'Archana' unit

Generally, the mini-company white board was updated by the unit leader with the help of one or two operators. In practice, a lot of management attention was needed to keep these boards up-to-date.

Shift changeover procedure

A smooth shift changeover is an important condition for the cooperation between the five shifts in the unit. However, the shift changeover is often a cause for technical and social problems. Information about the work in progress is not transferred correctly, quality problems are not discussed, the equipment is left in a bad state, or the workplace is a mess. Shifts continuously complained about the previous shift. Generally, an improvement team in which representatives of all shifts were present solved these types of problems.

The shift changeover was mostly structured by means of a form that had to be filled in and signed by the shift that was ending and the shift that was starting. These forms were specified for the first operator and per workplace. An improvement team with the support of line management implemented the new procedure.

Other forms

Several other forms of short-cycle information and communication tools were used. For example, some information forms, a logbook, Statistical Process Control charts, and a Computer Aided Manufacturing System. There was regularly a short meeting to discuss serious problems or to pass on important messages at coffee time.[114]

The mini-company meeting

The mini-company meeting is a long-cycle structure for information and communication. Generally, these meetings were held every 4 to 6 weeks and were organised per shift. The (standardised) agenda is described in Figure 2.11.

Preferably, the minutes of the meeting were made by one of the operators with the support of the facilitator.

---

[114]   In a five-shift system this meeting has to be held five times to cover all shifts.

```
Agenda of the mini-company meeting
1.  Minutes and action points of the preceding meeting
2.  Announcements from the unit leader
      - market developments
      - new customers
      - financial results and so on
3.  Safety and environment
4.  Relations with the customers and suppliers of the unit
5.  Results of the mini-company
      • yield
        process control
        quality
        delivery performance and so on
6.  Progress of the improvement teams
7.  Reports and queries
```

Figure 2.11 The (standard) agenda of the mini-company meeting

2.3.5 Evaluation by management

At the end of the (9-jump) cycle, management formally visited the mini-company to evaluate the results. Figure 2.12 presents the criteria that were used.

```
Evaluation criteria
Quality of the mini-company process
•  execution of the mission statement
•  relationship with the (internal) customer
•  relationship with the (internal) supplier
•  discussion of the results
•  improvement process (use of 7-jump)
•  internal communication
```

Figure 2.12 Evaluation criteria for the mini-company process

Generally, the evaluation by management was presented in the mini-company meeting. This evaluation also functioned as the input for the next cycle (9-jump). If the results were good, the members of the mini-company were given a symbolic present such as a watch or a calculator. In December 1995 the mini-company called 'The Plumbers' was evaluated for the first time by management. The official report states[115]:

"**1. Execution of the mission statement.**
Positive points:
o   there is a lot of evidence that the operators of the unit work according to the process instructions;
o   the unit is a reliable supplier of foil to its customer;
o   the employees work neatly and the unit is clean;
Improvement opportunity:
o   the unit must regularly evaluate whether they are working according to their mission statement;
Judgement: 7 points (out of 10)
(...)
5. Continuous improvement.
Positive points:
o   several improvement teams have realised their targets;
o   in the mini-company meeting many small improvements were agreed on and then implemented;
Judgement: 8 points (out of 10)
(...)
Overall judgement:
The mini-company has performed tremendously well. 43 points have been awarded out of 60. We expect the mini-company to realise further improvements in the coming year without any problems".

The evaluation by management was considered a serious event, as can be understood from the following story.

Story. The management (factory manager, personnel officer, and efficiency engineer) evaluated the results of a particular mini-company. This mini-company received 38 out of 60 points. This result was seen as quite good. The result was communicated informally to the morning shift that was present. At twelve o'clock I left the factory for a training session somewhere nearby the factory. At exactly two o'clock, I was called to the reception desk because there was an urgent call for me. An operator of the afternoon shift (that started at two o'clock in the afternoon) was on the phone. He said that he was very angry about the judgement. He had expected more than 50 out of the 60 points. He ordered me to come directly to the factory and to discuss the result. I told him that I was in a training session and could not come directly. However, he insisted that I should come directly. After considerable discussion we agreed that that I should clear my agenda so that I could meet him and his shift the next day. So we did. The next day the feelings had cooled down. In a meeting of an hour or so I explained how the criteria were applied, which positive points were

[115]   M.J. Verkerk, A.Peeters, and W. Ramakers, 'Evaluatie unitteam 'De loodgieters', 18-12-1995.

identified, and which improvement opportunities were present. However, we could not come to an agreement.

Several weeks after this incident the unit started the 9-step for the second time. As part of this program the employees discussed the judgement of their performance by management. Again, they did not agree. They judged the performance of the unit themselves and came to a total of 44 points (this means: 6 points higher than the judgement by management). The feelings started running high. It was decided that the differences between the evaluation by management and the self-evaluation by the unit would be discussed in a separate meeting.

Later on, the differences in judgement were discussed. I explained again how the evaluation process was conducted and why we had given a particular evaluation. After that, the unit explained why they did not agree with the evaluation by management. This gave rise to a lengthy debate about both the judgement (38 versus 44 points) and the phrasing of the overall evaluation. In the end, it was agreed that the judgement (38 points) would stay the same but that the phrasing of the overall evaluation would be adapted in order to prevent any negative connotations. The meeting was closed with a good atmosphere.[116]

Reflection. This story shows two things. Firstly, it shows that the whole mini-company process was taken very seriously. The employees identified themselves with the mini-company. They interpreted the evaluation by management as a negative appraisal. Therefore, they reacted furiously and 'ordered' me to come to the factory directly. Secondly, it shows something about the culture in the factory. The employees 'ordered' management to discuss the evaluation. The fact that the discussion took place in a good atmosphere, shows the mutual trust between management and employees.

Personally, I took pleasure from this incident. It showed that the employees were very involved in the mini-company process. It was a challenge for me to handle this kind of 'confrontation' without losing their commitment. I intentionally stuck to the original evaluation because I wanted to highlight the improvement opportunities. In the course of the discussion the importance of the evaluation faded into the background and the discussion focused on the content of the evaluation. The proposal to stick to the points of the evaluation but to change the phrasing of the overall evaluation came from the employees.

The evaluation by management was an important tool to re-explain, to re-confirm, and to give meaning to the mini-company process.

2.4 Customer Day 1995

Several months after the start of the first mini-company the (third) customer day was organised (9th January 1995). The objective of this day was to communicate

---

[116]   One of the operators took the minutes of this meeting (RSB-20-96-YR002, dated 09-02-1996).

and to emphasise that 'understanding the needs of the customer, and bridging the gap between those needs and our performance, is critical to our future as a company and as individuals'.[117]

The morning of the customer day was used to listen to a presentation by the president of Philips (broadcast), the plant manager of Roermond, the business unit manager of Ceramic Multilayer Actuators, and a representative of our main customer. This representative explained the situation in the market with the title 'When it blows in the market, there is a storm in the factory'.

> *Reflection*. The management team invited a representative of our main customer to inform us about the situation in the market. During the preparation it was agreed that this representative would try to explain the position in the market, the consequences for the factory, and the consequences for the suppliers (and their factories). The main message was that every change in the market comes back in an amplified way in the factory. The motivation for this invitation was that it is more convincing when the customer himself or herself explains the policy and the requirements than when management itself does this.

The afternoon of the customer day was used to discuss the results of the Employee Motivation Survey.

> *Reflection*. The Employee Motivation Survey was a company-wide activity. Customer Day 1995 was also a company-wide activity. The management team decided to discuss the results of the Employee Motivation Survey during Customer Day 1995. The attitude of the management team with respect to these obligatory activities was 'if we have to do it, let's do it well'. It was believed that these activities could contribute to the improvement of the performance of our organisation.

Management linked the questions of this survey to the five values of the Philips group[118]. These values are:

> Shared values of the Philips group:
> 1. We delight customers
> 2. We value people as our greatest resource
> 3. We deliver quality and excellence in all actions
> 4. We achieve premium return on equity
> 5. We encourage entrepreneurial behaviour.

The results of the survey were discussed in the following way. For every Philips value two questions were selected with a (relatively) high score and two questions with a (relatively) low score. For the questions with a high score the following sub-questions had to be answered:

---

[117] 'Guide for Customer Day Managers', p3.
[118] This linkage was somewhat artificial because the twelve categories of the Employee Motivation Survey do not unambiguously cover these five values.

o   What can I do to maintain this high score?
o   What can my unit do to maintain this high score?
o   What can my unit leader or factory manager do to maintain this high score?

For the questions with a low score the following sub-questions had to be answered:

o   What can I do to improve this score?
o   What can my unit do to improve this score?
o   What can my unit leader or factory manager do to improve this score?

For example, for the value 'We delight customers' the following questions were selected[119].

> "Questions with a high score:
> H-1: I have a good understanding of the requirements of my internal and external customers.
> H-2: The people I work with are willing to help each other.
>
> Questions with a lower score:
> L-1: I have enough flexibility in my job to do what is necessary to provide good service to our customers.
> L-2: It is easy to get the required information and support from other departments or organisations".

And for the value 'We value people as our greatest resource', the following questions were selected[120]:

> "Questions with a high score:
> H-3: Management at my location does an excellent job of keeping us informed about matters affecting us.
> H-4: Morale in my department is generally high.
>
> Questions with a lower score:
> L-3: Philips deals appropriately with employees who perform poorly.
> L-4: My immediate boss usually gives me regular feedback on my performance".

These questions were discussed in groups of six to nine persons. Every group discussed the questions relating to one value. The assignment was to formulate one action point per sub-question. The objective was to elaborate and implement these action points after the customer day. In practice, a small number of action points were agreed.

For example, with respect to the value 'We value people as our greatest resource' the following remarks were made[121]:

---

[119] 'Customer Day 1995' Booklet, RSB-46-94 MV407, 16-12-1994, p9.
[120] 'Customer Day 1995' Booklet, RSB-46-94 MV407, 16-12-1994, p9.

Question H-3:

o   employees have to read the logbook and the information boards;

o   employees have to participate in the mini-company meetings where the management gives information about the state of play;

o   management should be regularly on the shop floor to listen to employees and to tell them about current affairs;

Question H-4:

o   employees have to be open to criticism;

o   employees have to behave as a good colleague;

o   employees have to respect the opinions of others;

o   employees have to discuss differences of opinion in the unit;

o   management has to express their trust in their employees;

o   management has to express their appreciation of the work done;

Question L-3:

o   when operators perform poorly it has to be made a subject of discussion;

Question L-4:

o   employees have to tell each other when the activities are going well;

o   management has to give good feedback to the employees.

Group 3 remarked that the questions H-3, H-4, L-3, and L-4 should be discussed in the mini-companies. They added that the mini-companies should adhere strictly to remarks that are made.

All the groups' reports were collated and summarised in a booklet that was distributed amongst all employees.[122]

> *Reflection.* Why was this set-up chosen? The actuator factory had obtained high scores in the survey (higher that the other factories in the plant). My objective in the design of this part of the customer day was to make the employees of the factory aware of these high values. On the one hand, by discussing how to maintain the well-designed processes at a high level. On the other hand by discussing how to improve the processes that are not yet running at such a high level. From my point of view, the awareness was more important than the execution of improvements because awareness of a high score will support the development of feelings of ownership and pride. Furthermore, by linking the Philips values to the survey, these values were translated into concrete activities for employees.

---

[121]   'Evaluation of Customer Day 1995' Booklet, RSB-46-95 MV522, 12-06-1995, p5, 6.

[122]   'Evaluation of Customer Day 1995' Booklet, RSB-46-95 MV522, 12-06-1995.

2.5 Investigations by the University of Twente

In May 1995, the University of Twente[123] started researching the actuator factory. The objective of this research was to study the contribution of semi-autonomous work groups to product and process innovation. Both the market situation and the mini-company process made the actuator factory an interesting case.

> *Reflection.* I had two reasons to take my chances with the University of Twente. Firstly, I had a lot of questions about the ins and outs of mini-companies and I expected the investigator could function as a scientific confidant. Secondly, I was quite sure that the investigations would reveal the advantages and disadvantages of the mini company approach. I could use this as a further justification of this approach. I wanted to prevent the mini-company process from being stopped.

The Roermond factory was investigated using qualitative methods such as document analysis, participative observation, in depth interviews, and one quantitative method in the form of a survey. The methodology is described elsewhere.[124] The objective of the investigations was to map the contribution of the shop floor to the innovation process. To realise this goal the structural and socio-dynamic characteristics of the actuator factory had to be investigated in-depth.

It has to be noted that these investigations were done in a period in which three mini-companies had been started up fully (Foil Casting, Screen-printing, and Dicing), one mini-company was in the starting-up process (Sintering), and two mini-companies had not yet started (End Terminations and Packing).

The investigations revealed a clear picture of the contribution of operators to the product and process innovation process. Further, they also gave a good insight into the quality of the mini-company process. Some findings are briefly reported in the next section. Details of these investigations are described and discussed elsewhere.[125] The results of these investigations were presented to and discussed by the management team.

> *Reflection.* The research by Twente University confirmed that the mini-company philosophy contributed strongly to the business. After this presentation, I intentionally used these results to give meaning to the mini-company process and to justify my approach.
>
> Although the management team supported the mini-company approach, I continuously felt the need to justify my approach. For example, during the last budget discussions I was asked to decrease the costs incurred by the mini-companies. A reference to the positive contribution of the mini-company process to the business (as confirmed by the investigations by Mr. De Leede) was enough to resist the pressure to decrease the costs. I later tried to prevent any reduction in the financial means allocated to the mini-companies by stating in informal discussions – as a signal to the

---

[123] The investigator was Mr. Jan de Leede.
[124] De Leede (1997, p73 ff.).
[125] De Leede (1997).

whole organisation – that I could realise a five percent increase in efficiency by stopping the mini-company process. I followed by saying that the price of this decision would be a decrease in yield of about ten percent, in which case, I said with a smiling face, they would also have to look for another factory manager.

At the start of the research, I had promised the crew that the results of these investigations would be presented. This promise was redeemed on Customer Day 1996.

2.6 Customer Day 1996

The objective of Customer Day 1996 (15th January 1996) was 'to build on what had been achieved' since the last customer day and 'to reinforce initiatives to give employees the confidence and capabilities to make their own decisions about the way they work'.[126]

The customer day was split into two parts. The first part consisted of four presentations: a video presentation by the president of Philips, a video presentation by the plant manager of Roermond, a live presentation by the business manager of Ceramic Multilayer Actuators, and a live presentation by myself. The initial idea was that the second part would consist of a number of prescribed formats to facilitate the group discussions. However, it was decided that the factory would not use these formats but would instead realise the objective of customer day by discussing the results of the research by the University of Twente.

> *Reflection.* There was a lot of freedom regarding the organisation of customer day. From the beginning, the actuator factory was strongly focused on the needs and wishes of the customer. Therefore, in discussing the results of the investigations of the University of Twente the objective of customer day would be well met. Furthermore, these results were so encouraging that I realised I could use them to strengthen the development of the factory organisation.

The investigator of the University of Twente summarised the research findings within the following topics[127]:

1. the influence of operators upon the work in the unit;
2. the importance of cooperation within the unit;
3. the role of management;
4. relationships with (internal) customers and (internal) suppliers;
5. responsibility for and satisfaction with the results and the work.

These topics were discussed in groups of six to nine persons. Per topic the following questions had to be answered by the group:

---

[126] Foreword by Mr. J.D. Timmer in 'The Customer Day 1996 Guide for Management Teams'.
[127] 'Customer Day 1996' booklet, RSB-20-96 MV001, 04-01-1996.

o   Do you acknowledge the results of the investigations?
o   What would you like to improve?
o   How important is this topic for the pleasure in your daily work?

Each group chose two or three topics, discussed the questions, and made a small report. The reports of all groups were summarised in a booklet.[128]

The influence of operators upon the work in the unit

The investigator reported on the influence of different hierarchical levels in the factory upon the work in the unit as perceived by operators and first operators.[129] The investigator focused on this influence upon general matters, workload, organisation of the work, and improvement and innovation. Figure 2.13 presents this data of the different areas of influence in a so called control graph.[130] This graph shows that operators have a lot of influence upon the work in the unit.

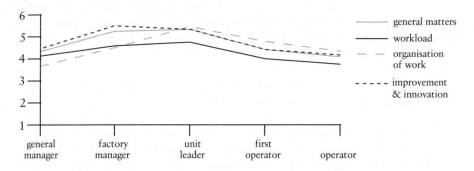

Figure 2.13 The influence of different hierarchical levels as perceived by the operators and the first operators (N=102; 1 = very little influence, 6 = a lot of influence)

In addition, the influence of the operators upon the work in the unit was also measured by asking about their contribution to the improvement and innovation process. This contribution was measured in terms of small improvements, big improvements, and innovations.[131] Operators and first operators reported a high contribution to small improvements, a medium contribution to big improvements, and a low contribution to innovations.

These results were generally acknowledged by the groups. For example, the Shift 1 report by the End Terminations unit read[132]:

---

[128]   'Evaluatie Customer Day 1996' booklet, RSB-20-96 MV120, 30-05-1996.
[129]   See also De Leede (1997, p282, 284).
[130]   Tannenbaum (1968).
[131]   Improvements are changes within the existing processes. Innovations are changes resulting in new processes.
[132]   Booklet 'Evaluatie Customer Day 1996', RSB-20-96 MV120, 30-05-1996, p10.

"The results are acknowledged by everybody. The meetings of the improvement teams and the monthly unit meeting are especially important. Improvements are made possible by intense communication and continuous feedback. Operators need to have a lot of influence upon the work in the unit".

One group reported that they had no influence upon their workload; this group also stated that this influence is very important regarding the pleasure they take in their daily work.[133]

The importance of cooperation within the unit

The investigator reported that cooperation in the actuator factory becomes more and more important.[134] The survey showed that the internal relationships are characterised as good, mutual acceptance is experienced as being on a high level, and mutual correction happens if necessary. He presented the following data:

Internal relations:
o   93 % of employees are willing to take over each others' work;
o   83 % of employees stimulate each other in working as a team;
     However:
o   53 % of employees state that the helpfulness of their colleagues could be better;
o   44 % of employees report internal frictions.
Mutual acceptance:
o   96 % of employees get on well with their colleagues and feel accepted.
Mutual correction:
o   90 % of employees remind each other to agreements;
o   92 % of employees correct each other if necessary.

Nearly all groups discussed this topic. The Sintering unit and the Dicing unit groups made the following comments[135]:

"We acknowledge the results of the survey. However, the aspects of helpfulness and internal frictions are better in our unit. As an improvement we propose that frictions are discussed and solved within the unit. The shift changeover has to be improved (…) Another item is the communication between the Sintering unit (the supplier, MJV) and the Dicing unit (the customer, MJV). This communication has to be improved. Better communication is important to have fun in work and to get good results".

"At this moment the internal frictions are much smaller, however, they have not yet disappeared. These frictions are especially present between different shifts, e.g. during the shift changeover. Especially, if you remind somebody to the agreements,

---

[133]   'Evaluatie Customer Day 1996' booklet, RSB-20-96 MV120, 30-05-1996, p6.
[134]   See also De Leede (1997, p280, 281).
[135]   'Evaluatie Customer Day 1996' booklet, RSB-20-96 MV120, 30-05-1996, p7, 9.

the acceptance is low. A possible improvement is – and this remark is often made – to listen to each other better and to interpret feedback positively".

The End Terminations unit also noted that they did not experience internal frictions.[136] Most groups also reported that cooperation is very important for fun in work.

The role of management

The investigator reported that employees of the actuator factory experience active support from management and have confidence in management.[137] The survey shows:

> Experience of support by management:
> ▪ 86 % experience support in their daily activities;
> o 88 % experience support in improvement activities.
> Trust in management:
> o 85 % of employees trusts management;
> o 90 % of employees trusts management with respect to improvement activities.

Many groups discussed this topic. Regarding trust in and support from management, a group from the End Terminations unit remarked[138]:

> "The support of and the trust in management is present. However, management can also improve further. They continuously have to support the operators in their work. Pats on the back will open doors. Respect the opinion of employees, even when management does not agree. This determines the fun in work. Less fun in work will result in less effort and lower quality".

Relationships with (internal) customers and (internal) suppliers

The investigator reported that the operators of the actuator factory have more contacts with internal and external customers and suppliers.[139] The survey shows:

> o 60 % of the operators have contacts with internal customers and suppliers;
> o 15 % of the operators have contacts with external customers and suppliers;
> o 70 % of the operators have contacts with internal specialists (engineers and so on);
> o 10 % of the operators have contacts with external specialists (engineers and so on);

Two groups discussed this topic. They were rather satisfied with their contacts.[140]

---

[136] 'Evaluatie Customer Day 1996' booklet, RSB-20-96 MV120, 30-05-1996, p12.
[137] See also De Leede (1997, p280, 281).
[138] 'Evaluatie Customer Day 1996' booklet, RSB-20-96 MV120, 30-05-1996, p10.
[139] See also De Leede (1997, p280, 281).
[140] 'Evaluatie Customer Day 1996' booklet, RSB-20-96 MV120, 30-05-1996, p11, 17.

Responsibility for and satisfaction with results and work

The investigator reported that the operators of the actuator factory bear more responsibility and are satisfied with the results and the work.[141] The survey shows:

> Feelings of responsibility:
> o 98 % of employees feel responsible for the results of the unit;
> o 97 % of employees feel responsible for the shift changeover.
>
> Satisfaction with the results:
> o financial results of the unit: 30 % of employees is not satisfied, 38 % is satisfied, and 31 % has no opinion;
> o financial results of the business unit: 25 % of employees is not satisfied, 42 % is satisfied, and 33 % has no opinion.
>
> General satisfaction:
> o 81 % of operators report that the working conditions in the unit are attractive;
> o 88 % of operators report that the work in the unit is interesting;
> o 3 % of employees would have chosen another unit if they could have done.

The Sintering and the Dicing units made the following comments[142]:

> "These results are acknowledged. It is remarked that the availability of auxiliary materials often are an annoyance. Housekeeping has to be improved. We also wonder whether the rejects and broken ceramics could be expressed in Dutch guilders. This would make the employees more conscious of the amount of money involved."

> "(...) The responsibility for the production results is large. This is can be seen in the attitude of colleagues. This is very important for the fun in work; if you get more responsibility, work is more interesting and it gives you more pleasure (...)."

Evaluation

The intention of the management was to use the findings of the University of Twente as a 'tool' to create awareness, to reconfirm the basic values behind the mini-company process, and to stimulate further improvements. The set-up of the discussion was decided in such a way that both the creation of awareness and the reconfirmation of the basic values were realised in a participative approach. The lively discussions and the content of the reports show that these objectives were fully realised. During this customer day nearly no concrete actions points were agreed upon. We did not regret this as management. After all, our main objective was to discuss the results. Moreover, a lot of action points would mean a lot of work for us.

> *Reflection.* The findings of these investigations were rather exceptional (this was also the view of the researcher of the University of Twente). Let us briefly summarise the

---

[141] De Leede (1997, p280, 281).
[142] 'Evaluatie Customer Day 1996' booklet, RSB-20-96 MV120, 30-05-1996, p7, 11.

results. The operators reported a high level of influence, good cooperation with colleagues, support of management, trust in management, many contacts with internal customers and suppliers, a high sense of responsibility, and satisfaction with their work. These positive results were also confirmed by in-depth interviews conducted by the researcher. And finally, all groups reported that they acknowledged the results. The only exceptions were the statistics on the helpfulness of colleagues and the number of internal frictions. In their opinion the results reported were too negative.

Personally, I had expected the results of the investigations to be positive. However, I had never expected the results would be so positive. The 'dream list' of attitudes and characteristics as outlined by Suzaki[143] had actually come true. At the time, I had only one explanation. Namely, that we had implemented the mini-company philosophy according to the spirit of the concept. We had particularly made it clear to the whole organisation that people really were the centre of the shop floor.

2.7 Start of the second cycle of the mini-company process

At the end of 1995 and the beginning of 1996, I evaluated the mini-company process with the personnel officer, unit leaders and factory engineers. The following considerations were brought up discussion. Firstly, unit leaders and factory engineers brought up the fact that the mini-company process had a positive influence on their own job. It was especially mentioned that the culture of continuous improvement and the high level of commitment of the operators made their life 'easier'. It was also noted that this process resulted in good working relationships. Only one disadvantage was mentioned: the mini-company process required a lot of effort. Secondly, management evaluations (as described in section 2.3.5) showed that the mini-company process met our expectations. At that time, two mini-companies (Foil Casting and Screen-printing) had finalised the whole cycle. Management evaluated both mini-companies and the results were positive. Finally, the investigations of the University of Twente had revealed that the mini-company process contributed strongly to the quality of working life and the performance of the business unit.

At this point, one outcome of the investigations of the University of Twente has to be highlighted. The research confirmed that the mini-company process was an excellent 'tool' for agreeing on and getting commitment for the objectives of the mini-company[144]:

Objectives:
o   96 % of the operators is well informed about the objectives of the unit;
o   95 % of the operators report that the objectives of the unit are clear to them;
o   99 % of the operators believe that the objectives of the unit are valuable for the business unit;

---

[143]   See section 6.3 of Chapter 2.
[144]   De Leede (1997, p280).

o   96 % of the operators agree with the objectives of the unit;
o   92 % of the operators believe that the objectives of the unit can be realised.

It was decided that the mini-company process would be continued in the same spirit. The practical consequence of this decision was that the units that had finished the 9-step would start this cycle again, i.e. for the second time.

The management evaluation of the mini-company process had revealed some lack of clarity. Therefore, a new set of overhead sheets was made to summarise and to highlight the essentials of the mini-company process.[145] I presented this set of sheets – which was named 'Let's make things better' – during the start of the second cycle.[146] In this set of sheets the responsibilities of the mini-company were clearly defined:

"*The unit is responsible for:*
o   the mission statement
o   relations with the internal customer
o   relations with the internal supplier
o   the results of the unit
o   continuous improvement
o   communication."

All these areas of responsibility were characterised with three words. For example:

"*The mission statement:*
o   formulate
o   execute
o   evaluate

Relations with the internal customer:
o   how do you measure quality?
o   how do you handle complaints?
o   is there regular consultation?

Continuous improvement:
o   everybody contributes
o   small improvements
o   use the workbook."

The objective of the three-word characterisation was to operationalise the different areas of responsibility.

---

[145]   The slides of this presentation were collated in a booklet that was distributed amongst all employees of the factory (RSB-46-94 MV401, 26-01-1996).
[146]   In spring 1995 Philips launched a worldwide campaign under the slogan 'Let's make things better'. This slogan was regularly used in 'internal campaigns'.

2.8 The Philips Quality Award process

In the nineties Philips started an important quality drive under the name 'The Philips Quality Award for process management in the nineties' (PQA-90). The aim of this program was "to stimulate organisations to engage in a regular and systematic evaluation of their improvement activities and results through self-evaluation, peer audit and management assessment".[147] The program sets a reference for assessing the performance of the organisation in quality improvement. The organisation is judged against six categories: Role of Management, Improvement Process, Quality System, Relationship with Customers, Relationship with Suppliers, and Results.

In mild 1996 the management team started to judge the actuator organisation against the standards of the Philips Quality Award. The objective of this judgement was to identify weaknesses and opportunities for improvement. The management finalised a first round of analysis. However, due to the business circumstances (see below), this process was not continued.

2.9. Closure of the actuator factory

In mid 1996, our business circumstances drastically changed. One of the competitors of our biggest customer launched a new inkjet printer. This printer appeared to be very successful in the market. Our customers' sales drastically decreased. As a consequence, our production was more than halved. Several months later, our customer decided to change the printer head technology in order to meet the competition. The actuator contained in the new design of the printer head was quite different. From a business point of view, it was not viable to develop and to produce this type of actuator in Roermond.

The management team made a plan to adapt its strategy and to reorganise the business unit. This plan was rejected. In November 1996, the management of the Passive Components Business Group decided to stop production. In spring 1997, the factory was closed down.

> *Reflection.* The closure of the actuator factory was a heavy blow for all employees. It was not 'just' the closure of a factory. It was the breakdown of a highly motivated unit. Permission to make all employees redundant (including the management of the business unit) was applied for and was granted. From mid 1996 on, management informed the crew in detail about the problems in the market, contacts with new customers, possible new strategic directions, the state of play of the discussions with the management of Philips, the consequences of the closure, and so on. Management allotted a lot of time to the organisation: to explain the background, to refute rumours, to share the worries, and to discuss the future. In this difficult period, employees kept confidence in the management of the business unit.

---

[147]   *PQA-90 Auditors' Scorebook*, Philips Corporate Quality Bureau, 1995, p3.

Personal comment. In my managerial career I have closed down several factories. I have built up a lot of know-how about the do's and don'ts of the closing-down process. However, I never got used to it. In all cases I was informed beforehand about the potential closure. In all cases I was actively involved in investigating alternatives. And in all cases I participated in drawing up the plan for closure. This also applied to the closure of the actuator factory. Nevertheless, the formal announcement to close the actuator factory was a blow for me. I was shocked. I was flustered. I could not concentrate. I sat in my office and stared blankly into space. I aimlessly walked around. Rationally, I agreed with the decision to close the actuator factory. Mentally, I had not really come to terms with it.

Sometimes, I was overcome with anger. Not because of the decision as such. I understood the decision and I agreed with it. I was angrier about the behaviour of higher management (I do not have not my direct boss in mind; he did a very good job in this period). For example, the closure was announced formally to the crew in several meetings. The day after these meetings, I was asked to meet a member of higher management. He asked me how the crew reacted to the announcement. I started to tell him about it. After two minutes he interrupted me. He changed the subject and offered me a job in another factory. The quick change in subject showed me that he was not interested in the reactions of the crew, and only wanted to solve his own problem (i.e. filling a vacancy). I succeeded in keeping my temper. However, I was furious. I swore to myself that I would never work under this manager. Several days later, I prepared a firm letter to refuse the offer. On my boss' advice I changed the phrasing. The result was a polite refusal.

In the first few days after the announcement I spent a lot of time on the shop floor. I talked with the operators about the background of the closure, improvements that were realised, the building-up of the organisation, cooperation between management and employees, the sorrow of the closure, and the uncertain future (compare this with the story 'Closing the factory' in section 2.5 of Chapter 1).

Personal comment. How did I personally come to terms with the closure? For me, this decision meant something like the 'end of a life's work'. I had played a key role in the building-up of the factory. I had taken the lead in the mini-company process. I was really proud of the achievements. In the first few days after the announcement I talked a lot about it; with my colleagues of the management team, with unit leaders and factory engineers, with technicians and operators. I also talked about it with family and friends. In addition, I laid my soul bare to my heavenly Father. I prayed for myself. I prayed for my colleagues and subordinates. I asked Him to give me wisdom to manage this closure process. Sometimes I could entrust in the hands of God. Sometimes I could not. Still, my confidence in the Lord was not broken. I settled down and got the strength to do my job.

After the announcement all our energy was directed to finding new jobs for the employees of the business unit. The employees were divided into two groups. The first group consisted of employees who had a chance on the labour market. This group was supported by an external agency. The second group consisted of employees who had no chance of finding a job outside. These employees had to be transferred internally. The personnel department supported this group.

> *Third group.* There was in fact a third group of about 5 employees. This group consisted of employees who had high absence through illness. For example, one employee had been absent for more than one year due to a brain operation. For several months, he had resumed his work on a 'therapeutic' basis. Now he worked part-time. Another employee had been absent for more than one year due to psychological problems (the consequences of incest). A therapist supported her. The health progress was quite good. It was expected that it would be very difficult to find other positions for this group.
>
> The employees of this group had one thing in common: they had a positive working attitude and had never 'caused any problems'. Therefore, it was decided to make a special arrangement. I explained the situation of these employees to my colleagues (the factory managers at the plant). I told them that I was absolutely sure about their positive working attitudes. I offered my colleagues the opportunity to take on these employees for free for a trial period of half a year. Their performance would be evaluated every month. If their performance was good, they would be transferred, and if their performance was unsatisfactory, they would be returned to me. These employees were intensively supported. All of them got a new position!

About six months after the announcement, one of the factories on the plant expanded unexpectedly, so many employees of the actuator factory were offered a new position there. In the end, all employees found another job; most of them within Philips and some outside Philips.

2.10 Evaluation

The process of developing the actuator organisation was very challenging. The orientation to the market and the mobilisation of the capabilities of all employees gave the organisation an immense spirit. It has to be noted that the Roermond case took place *before* paradoxes on the shop floor, short cuts by management, and the implementation of new production concepts in modern factories were problematised. Also, large parts of this case were already described *before* the research questions of this study were formulated.

2.10.1 The process of organisational development
In retrospect, the Roermond case might be interpreted as a well-controlled managerial activity in which all steps were planned carefully, in which technical and social aspects were balanced by design, and in which management resolutely chose the right direction. However, this interpretation would be incorrect. It was a process of trial and error. In the start-up period of the actuator factory, there was no blueprint for the development of the organisation. In the Roermond plant there

was some experience with the Dutch approach of the Socio-Technical Systems Design.[148] In the management team of the business unit I was the only one who had been trained intensively in this approach. I also only had very rough ideas about labour and organisation.[149]

In the introduction of the case description three red threads were identified: four-way communication, participation, and continuous improvement. In all fairness, it has to be said that these red threads were identified afterwards. Looking back, these red threads guided the whole process of organisational development. However, I experienced the process as such as trial and error. I often felt intense tension about this process. Therefore, I communicated intensively about my intentions and evaluated every step carefully. In addition, I urged myself to confirm and to reconfirm the basic philosophy. The result of this was that I was consistently convinced by the appropriateness of the new direction.

There were many 'accidental' steps in the whole process. For example, the President of the Philips group started up customer days. Every factory had to join in these activities.[150] I used this obligatory activity to support the process of organisational development. Another example is the research by the University of Twente. Mr. De Leede, a Ph.D student at this university, heard by accident – via a joint acquaintance – about the mini-company experiments in Roermond. In his opinion, an investigation of these experiments would fit very well in his program. I used this accidental 'intervention' to confirm and to reconfirm the basic philosophy of the mini-company process.

In conclusion, the development of the organisation in Roermond was not the result of a well-planned project that was designed in the start-up phase of the factory and was implemented with a firm managerial hand. On the contrary, it was a long development process of small steps and small organisational improvements. Three red threads guided this development process: four-way communication, participation, and continuous improvement. At the same time, the steps taken were evaluated and where necessary corrected. Furthermore, the philosophy behind the red threads was continuously confirmed and reconfirmed.

2.10.2 Structure of the organisation

In accordance with the philosophy of the Components Division of the Philips Group, the responsibilities for the business were assigned as low as possible in the organisation. This meant that a business team was formed in Roermond in which all relevant functions were present (marketing, development, and production).[151]

---

[148] In the preceding years, resistor and capacitor factories in the Roermond plant were organised according to these principles.

[149] See also section 1.2 of this chapter.

[150] In practice, there were considerable differences in compliance with the set-up of the customer days. In some organisations these days appeared to be an incident without a permanent influence. In other organisations these days were used to initiate fundamental improvements.

[151] Formally, the sales representatives were part of the sales organisations of the Passive Components Business Group. The sales organisations reported hierarchically to the

As indicated before, the actuator factory was designed according to the principles of the Dutch approach to Socio-Technical Systems Design.[152] The primary production process was divided into relating segments and the authority to control the processes within these segments was given to the employees involved. However, the Dutch approach did not offer a set of tools and techniques to develop a participative organisation and to support continuous improvement. The mini-company approach of Kiyoshi Suzaki[153] and the improvement philosophy of Maasaki Imai were chosen to fill this gap.[154]

The structural basis of the mini-company is comparable with the socio-technical view on primary work groups. In primary work groups, employees have a comparable level of authority and autonomy. However, the mini-company is much more oriented to the customer and the market. This has implications for the design and management of these primary work groups. The mini-company has four characteristics that make it distinct from socio-technical primary work groups:

1.   The mini-company has a name and a mission statement. The mini-company formulates both itself. This means the employees have an influence on the objectives of their work.
2.   The mini-company identifies its (internal) customers and (internal) suppliers and is responsible for managing these relationships. This means that the mini-company is not only oriented towards internal affairs, but is   actively involved in external relations.
3.   The mini-company is responsible for its own improvement programme. Based on its contacts with customers, suppliers and management, the mini-company is able to identify the main issues that have to be improved. These issues can be in the field of quality, costs, deliveries, safety and environment, motivation or morale, and housekeeping.
4.   The mini-company presents its name, mission, members, customers, suppliers, improvement programme and results on whiteboards. This has been called 'glass wall management'. Everyone, including a stranger, must be able to see and understand the process and the actual state of play. This means that transparency in organisational processes and performance is realised.

The mini-company process is a continuous cycle. Every time the cycle is started the requirements of the (internal or external) customers and suppliers are made visible. These requirements are the inputs for the improvement programme. In fact, every cycle is an evaluation of the functioning of the mini-company on the basis of market requirements.

The mini-company process appeared to be very successful. It resulted in a highly motivated crew, a customer-oriented organisation, and a continuously im-

---

Chief Executive Officer of Passive Components. In practice, the Ceramic Multilayer Actuators business unit had its 'own' salesmen in the sales organisation.
[152]   This approach is described in section 3.4. of Chapter II.
[153]   This approach is described in section 6. of Chapter II.
[154]   Imai (1986).

proving factory. By means of the mini-company process, the manufacturing activity contributed significantly to the competitive position of the business unit.[155]

2.10.3 Responsibility and Accountability

In the actuator factory the concepts of 'responsibility' and 'accountability' were never explicitly problematised (as was the case in the Aachen case study; see section 3 of this chapter). Instead, the practical implications of these ideas were learned step by step. The start-up of the new factory – with equipment and processes still under development – required continuous improvement in order to get the manufacturing process under control. The root cause of every problem had to be found. A suitable solution to every problem had to be implemented The story below shows that the drive for continuous improvement accelerated the learning process.

> *Story.* Every morning in the Roermond factory we had a so-called morning prayer. In this morning prayer the unit leaders, factory engineers, maintenance engineer, quality engineer and myself discussed the production results of the last day. Attention was paid to the number of products produced, quality problems, process problems, equipment breakdowns, and rejected batches. The question was regularly asked which operator caused the problems. The background to this question was the view that most of the problems were caused by the operators. After some time, it became clear that this question was irrelevant. After all, the majority of the problems was *not* caused by the operators but originated in *failing conditions*. For example, the process was not stable, the incoming goods were contaminated, the jig was not adjusted, the operator was not trained, the right information was not given, the standard was not set, and so on. In other words, the majority of the problems could be traced back to failing conditions. And, failing conditions is the responsibility of management. I tallied with these problems for some weeks. It appeared that about 80 % of the problems were due to failing conditions and about 20 % due to blameworthy behaviour of the operators. [156] From that time on, we focused our attention on failing conditions.

> *Reflection.* The change in focus (from failing operator to failing conditions) started with a change in language. The 'who' question was not allowed anymore. Only the 'why' question was asked. If necessary, this question was asked five times till the root cause was found. This change in language resulted in a change in behaviour: the members of the morning prayer could no longer 'solve' a problem by mentioning the name of a 'failing' operator, instead they had to look for failing conditions. This change in language also induced a change in mindset: the operator was no longer

---

[155]   Compare Wheelright and Hayes (1985). See also section 3.3 of Chapter I.
[156]   Later on, this experience was confirmed by literature (I don't have the reference anymore). In a book on quality management the so-called 85/15 rule was given. This rule states that operators can solve 85 % of the problems on the shop floor with the help of the management or engineering, and that operators can solve 15 % of the problems alone.

seen as the cause of the failure, instead the members of the morning prayer themselves were called to account (because they had to fulfil the conditions).

The high quality requirements of the (Japanese) customer also required the development of a learning organisation. Several times, the actuator factory had caused a production stop at the customer due to quality problems. Generally, a customer understands that a supplier has to learn to manufacture a new product. As a consequence, a customer will 'accept' failures or mistakes. However, a customer *never* understands that the same failure or mistake is made for a second time. This is especially the case for Japanese customers. Therefore, the whole organisation was focused on the identification and prevention of quality problems. For example, every employee knew that s/he had the authority to stop the machine in the case of quality problems. Everybody knew that it was better to stop the machine unnecessarily than to produce potentially defective products.

> *Reflection.* I personally passed on the message to the whole factory that it was better to stop the machine unnecessarily than to produce potentially defective products. I continuously repeated this statement. Generally, employees who stopped the machine because they doubted the quality were praised by (middle) management; employees who stopped the machine unnecessarily were explained the 'why' of the wrong decision. This procedure also confirmed the message that it was not acceptable to continue production if the conditions were not met.

Continuous improvement cannot be taken for granted. A learning organisation does not develop spontaneously. Both the start-up of a new factory and the high quality requirements of the Japanese customer 'pressed' the actuator factory to fulfil the conditions for continuous improvement and organisational learning. The Roermond case suggests that four-way communication, participation, and continuous improvement are the prerequisites for responsibility and accountability on the shop floor.

The investigations of the University of Twente have confirmed that the mini-company process is a very effective learning process. These investigations also suggest that a well-balanced division of influence and power drive organisation learning over the various hierarchical levels. Further it is made plausible that organisational learning is embedded in a culture of respect and trust. These items will be discussed extensively in the next chapter.

2.10.4 Conclusion
In the Roermond case the factory organisation has been developed in a process of trial and error. The socio-technical approach in combination with the mini-company concept has resulted in an organisation that is characterised by intensive cooperation between employees, a high sense of responsibility of employees, fun in work, and trust in management. Both the case description and the investigations of the University of Twente show the exceptional character of this case.

The most essential points in the development of the actuator factory were:

- three red threads could be identified: four-way communication, participation, and continuous improvement. These ideas appeared to be the driving forces behind the development of the actuator factory;
- the production structure has been designed according to the Dutch approach to Socio-Technical Systems Design;
- the control structure has been designed according to the Dutch approach to Socio-Technical Systems Design and to the Mini-Company Concept;
- the improvement structure has been designed according to the Mini-Company Concept and the improvement approach of Maasaki Imai;
- the philosophy of continuous improvement led to a factory organisation with a balanced division of influence and power between different hierarchical levels;
- the development of the organisation combined with the participative style of management initiated a high level of trust on the shop floor.

The Roermond case produces strong evidence that a careful design of the production structure, control structure, and improvement structure of a factory are prerequisites for responsibility and accountability of employees on the shop floor. Moreover, it shows that these conditions will only thrive in an organisation with a well-balanced division of influence and power, and in a culture which is characterised by mutual respect and trust.

> *Reflection.* While I was at Roermond I believed that the mini-company process was the 'one best way' to organise a factory. I am still convinced that the mini-company concept is very strong. The 'rhetoric' of the 'new hype' also proved to be very powerful.[157] Nevertheless, it has to be admitted that more roads lead to Rome.[158]

---

[157] Eccles and Nohria (1992).
[158] Compare Gustavsen (1992), Emery (1993), and Purser and Cabana (1998).

3 Case study: The Aachen Glass Factory

In April 1997, I joined the Aachen Glass Factory as factory manager. The glass factory employed more than one thousand employees. About 800 employees worked in the manufacturing division. In the Aachen Glass Factory screens and cones were manufactured for the television industry. The most important customers were tube factories in France and Germany (Philips factories). A small percentage of products (less than 5 %) were delivered to external customers.

I was informed beforehand that the glass factory was a 'difficult' factory. Both the quality of the technical processes and the quality of the organisation had to be greatly improved. The decision to assign me as factory manager in the glass factory was motivated by my experience in manufacturing excellence and my participative management style. It was my intention to develop the glass factory to become world class.

The 'Future' project was launched several months before I joined the Aachen Glass Factory. The objective of this project was to secure the long term future of the glass factory. Two aims were identified to realise this objective. Firstly, both the workforce and the costs needed to be reduced. Secondly, the basic processes of the organisation needed to be redesigned.

I spent my training period on the shop floor. It appeared that many processes were not transparent and not under control. In addition, I experienced a lot of frustration and mistrust on the shop floor and at middle management level. A world-class manufacturing program was designed based on my experiences during my training period.

The 'Future' project, as well as the world-class manufacturing programme, showed that change processes in the Aachen Glass Factory did not run smoothly. It appeared to be very difficult to get all employees to work in the same direction and to implement proposals quickly.

In April 1998, the current plant manager left and a new plant manager took his place. This manager restarted the Philips Quality Award process. The objective of this company-wide process was to improve the performance of the organisation. The peer audit in December 1998 showed that the basic processes of the glass factory had greatly improved in the last two years. A lot of progress had especially been reported in the improvement process, the quality system, and in relationships with customers.

The new plant manager had a marked hierarchical style. Important decisions were no longer taken by the management team but by the plant manager alone. Furthermore, fear developed in the organisation. It was difficult for me to handle the hierarchical style of the new plant manager. In fact, I was urged to change my style from participative to hierarchical. In April 1999, I left the Aachen Glass Factory on request of the plant manager. The official reasons were: 'insufficient improvement in customer satisfaction' and 'inappropiate (participative) management style'.

The Aachen Glass Factory was part of Philips Electronics N.V. The Philips group has a divisional structure. In 1997, the main divisions were PolyGram, Business Electronics, Components, Sound & Vision, Semiconductors, Lighting, Medical Systems, and Domestic Appliances and Personal Care. Each division consists of different Business Groups. In 1997, the main Business Groups of the Components division were Display Components, Passive Components, Optical Storage, and Flat Display Systems. The Aachen Glass Factory was part of the Display Components Business Group.

The Display Components Business Group delivers tubes to set makers. The business group is highly vertically integrated. Most components are made in-house, e.g. deflection units, guns, glass bases, metal parts, phosphors, and glass screens and glass cones. Internal suppliers deliver up to one hundred percent of supplies. The business group's vertical integration was gradually reduced. The business group focuses more and more on its core activity: the development and production of tubes.

The main elements in the industrial chain of television production are component makers, tube makers and set makers. At that time, an overcapacity of about 25 % was present along the whole industrial chain. This overcapacity resulted in a strong price pressure.

The Display Components Business Group had four glass factories. They were located in Brazil, England, Germany and Taiwan. This case focuses on the factory in Germany: The Aachen Glass Factory.

I joined the Aachen Glass Factory as factory manager on April 1st 1997 (just after the closure of the actuator factory). At that time, the reorganisation project entitled 'Future' had just started. Several months after I started, I initiated the world-class manufacturing program. In April 1999, I left the Aachen Glass Factory.

In Philips Electronics several company-wide programs were running in order to improve the performance of the whole organisation. [159] These programs had an obligatory character. In the Aachen case one of these programs – the Philips Quality Award process – will be described.

Two red threads can be identified in the Aachen case. The first one is the creation of a transparent organisation. The second one is the improvement of the processes on the shop floor. The first red thread is specifically present in the 'Future' project and the second one in the world-class manufacturing program. The Philips Quality Award process played a role in both these initiatives.

The case description has the following set-up: a short introduction to the Aachen Glass Factory (3.1), the 'Future' project (3.2), the world-class manufacturing program (3.3), the Philips Quality Award process (3.4), the notions of 'responsibility' and 'accountability' (3.5), the change process in the tool shop (3.6), and evaluation of the main themes of the case (3.7). Figure 3.1 gives an overview of the main activities and milestones in the Aachen case.

---

[159] De Weerd (2001) has given an extensive description of the quality policy of the Philips organisation.

AACHEN

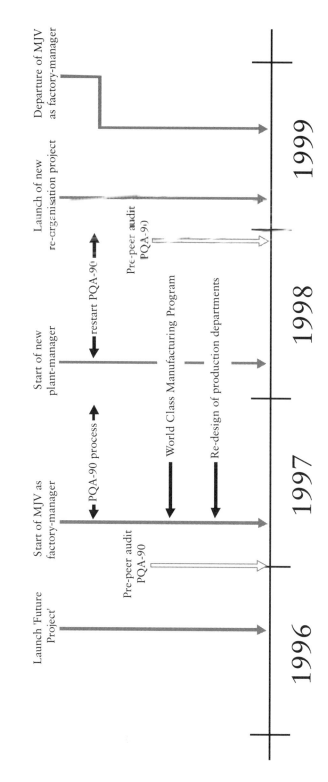

Figure 3.1 Main activities and milestones in the Aachen case

3.1 Introduction

3.1.1 History

Philips started its glass-making activities in Germany in 1928 with the taking-over of the 'Glasfabrik Weisswasser'. This factory was located in the eastern part of Germany. In 1948, the manufacturing of glass for the production of light bulbs was started up in Aachen. In 1954, the first industrial production of television glass was embarked upon: raw glass parts were finished. In 1956, the first glass tank for television glass was built (cone glass, tank A). Five years later the second tank for television glass was built (screen glass, tank B). In 1967, the production of glass for colour television was started up (cones and screens). In 1971, tank A was stopped and tank D was built. In 1984, the third tank was built (screen glass, tank C). In 1986, a great milestone was celebrated: 100 million sets of glass components. Tanks B and D were overhauled in 1986/1987. Their capacity was also increased. In 1992/1993, tank C was overhauled, in 1994 the capacity of tank B was increased, and in 1996 tank D was overhauled. In 1997, another milestone was reached: 150 million sets of glass components were produced.

In 1990, an important organisational change took place. The international development group, which was based in Eindhoven, was reorganised. Basic development stayed in Eindhoven; applied development was transferred to Aachen. The manufacturing activity in Aachen, the applied development in Aachen and the basic development in Eindhoven were brought under one umbrella: the Aachen Competence Centre was born. This centre also became responsible for the worldwide co-ordination of the glass business. The Aachen Competence Centre was certified in 1992 for ISO 9002, in 1993 for ISO 9001, and in 1997 for ISO 14001.

3.1.2 Market and products

In the nineties, three large players dominated the market for television glass. These players had a market share of about 70 %. There were also a large number of small players. Philips was one of them. The Aachen Glass Factory delivered the majority (> 95 %) of its products internally. The main customers were tube factories in Germany and France. In 1997 the following screen types were produced: 59 FS, 66 FS, 25 SF, 29 SF, 24 WS, and 28 WS. The following cone types were produced: 51 FS, 59 FS, 66 FS, 80 FS, 25 SF, 29 SF, 24 WS, and 28 WS. In 1998 the first product of the real flat family for screens and cones was introduced: 28 WS RF.

3.1.3 Process and operator activities

The process of manufacturing screens for television tubes consists of three distinctive process steps:

1. *Formation of a molten gob of glass.* This process step consists of the following sub-processes: mixing of raw materials, melting of these materials into a homogeneous glass, and formation of a molten gob of glass with specified properties. These sub-processes are done in the Mixing & Melting department.
2. *Formation of a raw screen.* This process step consists of the following sub-processes: pressing of the hot gob to a screen, inserting of the pins, automatic

244

measuring of dimensions, and a visual inspection. These sub-processes are done in the Screen Pressing department.

3. *Formation of a finished screen.* This process step consists of the following sub-processes: polishing of the screen surface and seal-edge, a visual inspection, transferring to a conveyor of a customer or packing on a pallet board. These sub-processes are done in the Screen Finishing department.

Generally, the operators operate the equipment, execute the quality measurements, take action in the case of deviations, enter data in the electronic data system, and repair the equipment. The following actions are carried out within each step of the process:

1. *Formation of a molten gob of glass.* The main task of the operator is to monitor the process. In the control room a number of monitors are present in which the furnace is schematically depicted and key parameters are indicated. The operator checks the key process parameters, e.g. temperature at the bottom of the tank. In addition, the operator receives data about the quality of the glass (data from downstream: visual inspection) via the computer system. Both the process data and the quality data are input for the operator to decide about interventions in the melting process. Several times during the shift the operator has to control the feeders and other parts of the glass tank. Operating a glass tank requires a lot of training and experience.

2. *Formation of a raw screen.* This process step is divided into two sets of activities. The first set of activities is the pressing of the hot gob to a screen and the insertion of the pins. The main tasks of the operator are monitoring the process, smearing the pressing jigs, executing quality measurements, adjusting the press and insertion equipment, and repairing the equipment. The operator checks some key process parameters on a regular basis, e.g. temperature of the gob. Glass screens are taken out at a fixed frequency and visually inspected. In addition, the operator receives data about the quality of the glass (data from downstream: visual inspection) via the computer system. All this data is used by the operator to decide about an intervention in the process, e.g. to replace one of the moulds. If the process is under control, the operator spends a large part of his time in the control room. If the process is not under control, he is outside the control room to adjust the press or the insertion equipment. The operators who perform these activities have a mechanical background. The second set of activities is the measuring of dimensions and the visual inspection of all screens. Every screen is visually inspected. It takes about 30 to 60 seconds per screen. The measurement of the dimensions is done automatically. The location of this equipment is close to the visual inspection. If the dimensions are out of control the operator has to take action, i.e. to warn the press operators. Part of the screens is transported to the finishing area via the conveyor and part of the screens is packed. This packing operation is done manually. It takes about 15 seconds per screen. The packing operation is integrated in the Screen Finishing department (see the description below). Most operators were

trained either for executing the press or for doing the visual inspection. Only some operators could execute both activities.

3. *Formation of a finished screen.* This process step consists of several sets of activities. The first set of activities is transporting and unpacking. As part of the screens is supplied from the warehouse, this leads to transporting and unpacking activities. Transporting one pallet of screens takes 3 to 5 minutes. Unpacking takes about 15 seconds per screen. Part of the screens was supplied directly from the press. In the case of a full buffer — which could be caused by equipment breakdown in the polishing area — the overflow of screens also had to be packed. Some of the operators handled both transporting and packing/unpacking. The second set of activities is the polishing of the screen surface and seal edge. This set of activities consists of different mechanical operations. The operator controls the process by physical measurements, by visually inspecting a sample, and by analysing the data of the visual inspection (next step). In addition, the operator replaces tools, repairs the equipment, and overhauls the equipment (together with technicians of the Technical Department). Most operators in this department have a mechanical background, some have an electrical background. The third set of activities is visual inspection. The operator takes the product from the conveyor, inspects the inside and outside of the screen, and places it back on the conveyor. Good products, repaired products, and rejected products have different positions in the conveyor. Handling and inspection takes one minute per screen. An empty position in the conveyor implies a one-minute break for the operator. The last set of activities involves transferring the (good) products to the conveyor of the customer (a tube factory was located on the plant), packing the (good) products on a pallet, and transporting the pallets to the warehouse. Both the transfer and packing activities take about 15 seconds per screen. Transporting the products takes about 5 minutes per pallet. Some of the operators performed both transfer/packing and transport tasks. The flexibility of the whole department was limited. Some of the operators executed both packing /unpacking/transferring activities and transport activities. A few of the operators performed both inspection and transport activities. The operators of the polishing department did not execute any activities other than polishing.

The process of manufacturing cones for television tubes consists of three distinctive process steps:

1. *Formation of a molten gob of glass.* This process step consists of the following sub-processes: mixing of raw materials, melting of these materials into a homogeneous glass, and formation of a molten gob of glass with specified properties. These sub-processes are done in the Mixing & Melting department.

2. *Formation of a raw cone.* This process step consists of the following sub-processes: pressing of the hot gob to a cone, inserting of the anode, automatic measuring of dimensions, a visual inspection, and packing on a pallet board. These sub-processes are done in the Cone Pressing department.

3.   *Formation of a finished cone.* This process step consists of the following sub-processes: polishing of the seal-edge, a visual inspection, transferring to a conveyor of the customer or packing on a pallet board. These sub-processes are done in the Cone Finishing department.

The operator activities in these departments are comparable to the activities described above for screen production. Therefore, an extensive description will be omitted.

3.1.4 Organisation

Figure 3.2 presents the organisation chart of the Aachen Glass Factory as of 01-01-1997. The plant manager, staff, and development department have local and international responsibilities. The production, personnel department, and controlling department have mainly local responsibilities. At the beginning of 1997, the Aachen Glass Factory had about 1050 employees.

Figure 3.2 also presents the organisation chart as of 01-01-1999. This chart will be discussed in the next section (section 3.2 of this chapter).

AACHEN GLASS FACTORY

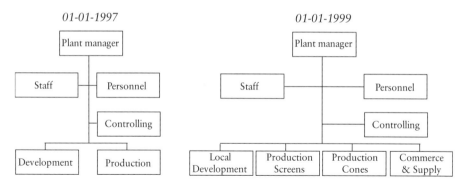

Figure 3.2 Organisation chart of the Aachen Glass Factory before and after the 'Future' project

Figure 3.3 shows the organisation chart of the production department as of 01-01-1997. The production department consisted of six operational groups: five production departments and one support department.

PRODUCTION DEPARTMENT

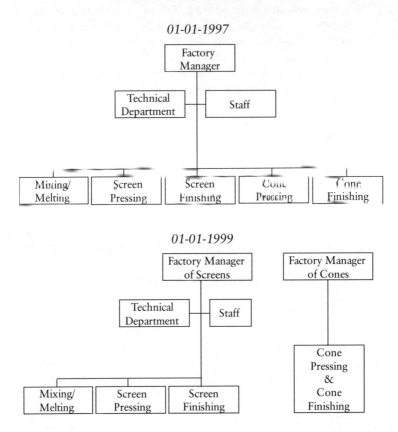

Figure 3.3 Organisation chart of the production department before and after the redesign process.

Mixing & Melting, Screen Pressing, Screen Finishing, Cone Pressing, and Cone Finishing are production departments. The Technical Department is a support department. At the beginning of 1997, about 800 employees worked in the production departments. About 600 employees were directly involved in production activities and about 200 employees were involved in maintenance, technical and management activities. The organisation charts of the production departments and the Technical Department are presented below (Figures 3.5 to 3.9).

Figure 3.3 also shows the organisation chart of the production department as of 01-01-1999. The development of the production organisation will be described in the next section (see section 3.2 of this chapter).

A glass factory is a round-the-clock process industry. A four-shift system is used in all production departments. If the production level is low, the Finishing Cones department returns to a three-shift system. About one third of the employees of the Technical Department are working within the four shift system. The others are working in day shifts.

3.1.5 Case description

The case description is focused on the period in which I worked at the Aachen Glass Factory: April 1ˢᵗ 1997 to April 1ˢᵗ 1999. The first draft of the case was written in the period between June and October 1999. The member checks were done in the period between November 1999 and June 2000. The first draft of the case description was finalised in September 2000.

The name 'Aachen Glass Factory' will be used to indicate the manufacturing and development activities in Aachen and the development activities in Eindhoven, the name 'Aachen plant' to indicate the manufacturing and development activities in Aachen, and the words 'production' and 'factory' to indicate the manufacturing activities at the Aachen plant.

The title 'plant manager' will be used to indicate the manager who is responsible for the Aachen Glass Factory, the title 'factory manager' to indicate the manager who is responsible for the manufacturing activities of the Aachen plant, and the title 'middle management' is used for the managers who operate one or two levels below the factory manager.

The terms 'reengineering', 'redesign' and 'reorganisation' will be used as synonyms for each other.

3.2 The 'Future' project

The financial performance of the Aachen Glass Factory had been below budget for years on end. In 1994, a new plant manager was appointed. He got two assignments. The first one was to bring the Aachen Glass Factory into the black. The second one was to reposition the glass business within the Display Components Business Group. The first assignment was indicated as a condition for realising the second one.

In 1996, the 'Future' project was launched. The objective of this project was to turn around the Aachen Glass Factory and to secure its future.[160] The following aspects are described: motive (3.2.1), organisation of the project (3.2.2), approach to reengineer the factory (3.2.3), reengineering of the Technical Department (3.2.4), reengineering of the production departments (3.2.5), and review of the project (3.2.6).

3.2.1 Motive

In 1995, the plant manager conducted an extensive analysis of the glass business and the current situation of the Aachen Glass Factory. He came to the following conclusions.[161] The first was that the television glass business is a mature business. This means that the growth of the market will be small. The second was that the financial results had been poor for many years. This performance threatened the long term existence of the factory. The third was that the Display Components

---

[160] At the same time, the 'yield improvement' project was started. This project will not be described.

[161] 'BG Display Components TV Glass' presentation, 1996.

Business Group had mixed feelings about the glass business. On the one hand, there was the feeling that the Business Group was not really in the glass business. On the other hand, there was the feeling that the Business Group needed a secure supply of glass.

The plant manager saw two major challenges. The first one was to create a television glass business which is integrated in the business group and which really supports the tube business. The second one was to greatly improve the financial results. Three important conditions were identified to realise these challenges. The first one was to decrease the costs of the manufacturing operation in Aachen. The second one was to change the mindset of the whole organisation to achieve a better performance. The third one was to safeguard the skills and know-how in television glass technology.

> *Reflection.* What was wrong with the mindset of the whole organisation? In the original presentation of the plant manager this statement was not elaborated on. In informal discussions, he mentioned three items. Firstly, the belief that Philips needed glass, which led to the belief that the Aachen Glass Factory would never be closed down. Secondly, the belief that the Aachen Glass Factory products could handle competition from their biggest competitor. Thirdly, the belief that the processes in the Aachen Glass Factory could handle competition from their biggest competitor – both in quality and in efficiency.

3.2.2 Organisation of the project
The management team of the Aachen Glass Factory designed the 'Future' project. Department managers and representatives of the workers council were involved. An internal and several external consultants guided the design process. Two objectives were identified. Firstly, the workforce and the costs needed to be reduced. Secondly, transparent processes needed to be designed so that the performance of the organisation could be improved. The following projects were defined:

1. overhead value analysis of all staff departments;
2. reorganisation of the development group;
3. improvement of the communication within the glass factory;
4. effective coaching of middle management and employees;
5. investigation of a five-shift system for production;
6. new payment system for shift employees;
7. reduction of costs in repair & maintenance;
8. reduction in manual handling of products during production;
9. optimisation of the planning of the production;
10. reduction in handling and transport of products;
11. increase in the efficiency of the sorting of products;
12. reduction in the number of technicians;
13. reorganisation of the operational groups.

Measurable targets were defined for all projects.

Reflection. The design of the reengineering project was done in autumn/winter 1996 – several months before I joined the Aachen factory. In my initial period in the Aachen factory I had the following impressions.

1. The project appeared to be very important. The internal and external consultants spent a lot of time on telling me about the set-up of the project. The management team and the department managers talked seriously about the project.
2. The department managers never criticised the set-up of the projects. They agreed with the chosen projects. They also told me that they were well involved.
3. The representatives of the workers council never criticised the design. They told me that they were involved in the whole project. They also said that they had left their mark on it. Basically, they also accepted the target of the project.
4. Finally, there was no spirit. The project was 'managed'. In the management team meetings the project was discussed seriously. The urgency of this project was expressed verbally by everybody. However, I did not feel enthusiasm or emotional involvement. In the factory management team, on the other hand, I sensed a stronger emotional involvement.

Reflection. The words 'reengineering', 'transparent processes' and 'lean management' were used regularly in Aachen. I took it for granted therefore that everyone understood what these words meant. I later found out, however, that there was no collective understanding of what these words meant. The plant manager had a clear view on these words. They originated from Business Process Reengineering and Lean Production. However, the other members of the management team and the department managers of the factory did not have such a clear view.

In the second part of 1996 the reengineering project was launched under the name 'Future' ('Zukunft'). The objective of the 'Future' project was summarised in the slogan 'the seven-hundred-employee factory'.[162] This slogan indicated that a reduction of the total work force to seven hundred employees would be necessary to secure the future of the Aachen Glass Factory. This objective had to be realised at the beginning of 1999. The project was presented to the whole workforce in two meetings. Project teams were put together. Official project start-ups were done.

A steering group reviewed the projects. This group consisted of the members of the management team, an internal consultant, an external consultant, and a representative of the workers council. The projects that involved a reduction in costs and personnel were reviewed regularly, other projects were reviewed once, and a few not at all.

The 'Future' project had its own logo: a ship that was heading towards a marvellous island. This logo is depicted in Figure 3.4. The ship symbolised the Aachen Glass Factory. The sails represented the employees, processes and resources. The island had a sandy beach and some palm trees and there were some mountains in the background. On the island, the words 'customers', 'profits' and 'certainty' were written. This logo was present everywhere in the factory.

---

[162]   The objective was later changed to the 'costs of a seven-hundred-employee factory'.

Figure 3.4 Logo of the 'Future' project

The plant manager who launched the 'Future' project left Aachen in the beginning of 1998 to take on another assignment within the Philips group. His successor continued the project. Some projects were completed and new ones agreed upon.

In the autumn of 1998 it became clear that the market situation would become worse. Cost reductions had to be realised at a much higher speed. The management team took the lead in redefining projects that were running and in defining new projects. At the beginning of 1999 a new reengineering project was launched. In this new project the outsourcing of activities was planned.

3.2.3 The approach to reengineering the factory
Reengineering the factory was an important project. The factory manager and the department managers managed this project. One internal and two external consultants coached this project.

> *Workshops.* The reengineering activities were carried out in so-called 'workshops'. These workshops were held at a place outside the plant. The length of the workshops varied between one and three days. Attendance was obligatory. The idea behind the workshops was that a concentrated effort was necessary in order to realise breakthroughs. Internal and/or external consultants always guided the workshops. The

workshops were focused on the reengineering process. A limited amount of time was spent on explaining the (theoretical) background of the reengineering process.

These workshops were very valuable. There was enough time to explain concepts, to share ideas, and to collectively develop a view with respect to reengineering the factory. However, a lack of confidence in management, the presence of mistrust and frustration, and the fact that the department managers were not a team, hampered this process (see below).

At the beginning of 1997, a workshop was organised to start-up the project. The following steps were performed: defining the mission of the department, defining the design rules for the organisation of the department, analysing the activities in the department, analysing the overlap with other departments, making a listing of the required functions, manning the positions, and finally, outlining the savings. In the second workshop the department managers presented the mission of their department, a proposal for the design rules, and an initial analysis of activities. The overlap with other departments was roughly sketched out. New organisational set-ups were proposed. In this workshop it became clear that there was a considerable overlap between the Technical Department and the production departments. The decision was taken to start with the analysis of this overlap, to redefine responsibilities and activities, and to reengineer the Technical Department. After that – and partly parallel to it – the production departments would be redesigned.

3.2.4 The redesign of the Technical Department

The third workshop was held in April 1997.[163] In this workshop the analysis of the overlap between the Technical Department and the production departments was started. This process took about half a year. The discussion was closed in the sixth workshop (October 1997).

I started the third workshop with two guidelines. The first guideline was that 'glass wall management' had to be applied. This meant that the different responsibilities of the Technical Department on the one hand, and the production departments on the other hand, had to be transparent for everybody. Secondly, a customer-supplier relationship had to be developed between the Technical Department and the production departments. Such a relationship is a condition for continuous improvement.

Figure 3.5 presents the organisation chart of the Technical Department before and after its redesign. Before the redesign, the Technical Department consisted of seven (sub-) departments: the Mechanical Department, the Electrical Department, Maintenance Planning, the Mechanical Parts Store, the Tool Shop (Presses), the Building Department, and Factory Engineering.

---

[163]   In April 1997, I started my job as factory manager in the Aachen Glass Factory. This workshop was the first one that I attended.

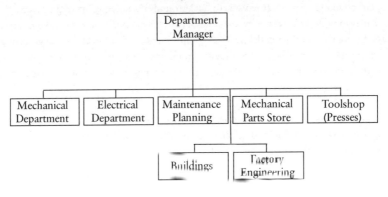

Technical Department 01-01-97

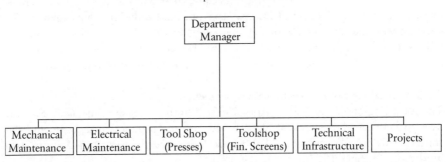

Technical Department 01-01-99

Figure 3.5 Organisation chart of the Technical Department before and after the redesign process

The analysis of the overlap between the Technical Department and the production departments was carried out as follows. First, the functions that were involved in the various activities of the Technical Department were listed in detail. After that, the functions in the production departments that were involved in these activities were listed too. This analysis resulted in a description of the 'ist' situation. A strong overlap in activities and responsibilities was identified.

> *Example.* It was found that the process of adapting pressing tools to meet the changing conditions was not transparent. Three departments played a role in this process: the production departments, Technical Department (the tool shop) and development department. The responsibility of every department in this process was well described. However, the chain was too complicated. Nobody really owned the process. Communication errors arose, The delivery of tools was regularly delayed and expensive mistakes were made.

254

Example. The responsibility for (planned) repair and maintenance activities was unclear. In one production department, the responsibility for these activities was borne by an engineer of the department itself. In another production department, the responsibility for these activities was borne by an engineer of the Technical Department. In practice, the lack of clarity was compensated by informal communication. However, this informal communication appeared to be insufficient. Reserve parts were regularly not ordered or (some of) the activities were not planned. This resulted in either a lot of additional work in order to realise the original planning or in a delay of the activities. It also caused friction between employees.

After that, the 'soll' situation was defined. First, some general criteria were formulated. The red thread was that the production departments would be responsible for their own business, including the management of tools and equipment. In addition, the Technical Department would deliver clearly defined services that could be measured with a performance indicator.

Reflection. The process of analysing the overlap between the Technical Department and the production departments took quite a long time. The discussions in the workshops were lengthy. Despite all the preparations, the whole process did not run smoothly. I have questioned the root cause of this phenomenon many times. Was it resistance? Was it mistrust? Was it unfamiliarity with the process? I have discussed this problem several times with the external consultant who supported the workshops. In my view, the pace of the process was too slow. However, I did not know how to increase the pace. The consultant did not believe that resistance was the main cause. In his/her view, we had to continue the present process. His/her view was dictated by the belief that commitment from the department managers was a basic condition for the implementation of the agreed actions. S/he was convinced that a (hierarchically steered) quick solution would result in political games. I followed the advice of the consultant. We continued the process at its own speed. (Note: This process was partly guided by a male consultant and partly by a female consultant. To prevent identification I have used 's/he' and 'his/her'.)

Later, I got more insight into the 'why' of the difficulties in the change process. In another workshop (one and a half years later) this phenomenon also rose to the surface. The external consultant who guided the workshop made this theme the subject of discussion. (Note: it was different consultant to the one who had guided the reengineering process). The main reason appeared to be mistrust. The department managers had a deep-rooted mistrust of the members of the management team. In their view, this mistrust was confirmed every day, every week and every month. In my opinion, the mistrust was so high that they missed any positive feedback. Another reason for the difficulties in the change process appeared to be the unfamiliarity with reengineering processes. Most department managers were 'hands-on' managers. They had neither know-how nor experience with change processes.

In conclusion, the execution of the 'Future' project was significantly hindered by mistrust. This phenomenon was insufficiently acknowledged. In addition, management and middle management were not well trained in reengineering techniques. This point was also insufficiently acknowledged.

In the fifth workshop, decisions about the activities and responsibilities of the Technical Department were taken. Five coherent clusters of activities – or five different 'products' - were identified:

1. maintenance and repair
2. technical infrastructure
3. pressing tools
4. polishing tools
5. projects

It has to be emphasised that the agreement between the participants grew step by step during the workshops, which meant that the decisions could be taken in consensus.

> *Reflection.* In the redesign process the identification of these five products was crucial. In the words of the Dutch approach to Socio-Technical Systems Design, the identification of these five products has to be characterised as 'parallelisation of the production structure'. In the redesign process I used the design theory and design methodology implicitly. The reason for that was that no one except myself was trained in this approach.

The technical infrastructure, pressing tools, polishing tools, and projects 'products' were analysed in more detail. It was decided that these 'products' would be allocated to separate departments.

At this point, two departments carried out maintenance and repair activities: a mechanical department and an electrical department. This division was brought up for discussion. The integration of the electrical and mechanical department was suggested. A customer-oriented division was also proposed. The various options were evaluated by analysing the activities and their interdependencies in detail. It was found that the electrical and mechanical activities were to a great extent mutually independent. A customer-oriented division was rejected in order to guarantee flexibility and to safeguard specialist knowledge. It was decided that the maintenance and repair 'product' would continue to be 'produced' by two departments: the electrical department and the mechanical department.

The identification of different 'products' and the allocation of these products to separate departments was more than 'merely' a redefinition of department boundaries. It was also the confirmation of a new philosophy: every department had its own product and every department had to continuously improve its product to satisfy the customers.[164] The organisation structure after the redesign has also been depicted in Figure 3.5.

The redesign of the Technical Department was agreed in a review meeting with the steering committee of the 'Future' project in August 1997.

---

[164] In the third workshop – the first one that I attended – I had emphasised the importance of customer-supplier relations. The overhead sheet with this philosophy was used regularly during the workshops.

Reflection. The review was well prepared. The conditions for the implementation of the redesign were made explicit. The management team was asked to support both the reductions in personnel and changes in management. The message was clear that if the decisions were blocked – due to opposition from the workers council, for example – the redesign would fail. The management team promised all the necessary support. The department managers reacted in a resigned way. They doubted the promise.

I asked the department managers why they doubted the support promised by the management team. They told me that in the past, the personnel department – which played a leading role in the negotiations with the workers council – never supported the department managers but always took the side of the workers council. They also gave several examples of this.

In the following months, the discussions sparked off. The support given by the personnel department did not meet expectations (the personnel manager was later replaced because of his passive attitude). An intervention by the plant manager appeared to be necessary to keep the promise. By the end of the year, the reduction in personnel and the changes in management were realised according to the original proposal.

The department managers expressed their surprise about this result. In their view, this was one of the few cases in which the management team fully supported the reengineering process of the factory. I regularly used this positive result to confirm the intention of the management team to support the reengineering process.

The next step in the redesign of the Technical Department was the organisational development of the different 'sub-departments'. The first step was for every department to develop a performance indicator together with its customers to measure the quality of the service it provided. The second step was for every department to start housekeeping according to the 5S-approach (see section 3.3.5). The third step was to start-up a formal mini-company program.

Reflection. The rationale behind these activities is as follows. Firstly, in the reengineering process the importance of customer-supplier relations was continuously stressed. A performance indicator that covers the main aspects of this relation is a good tool for describing the state of play and for identifying areas for improvement. In the glass factory there were already several examples of performance indicators between departments. These indicators covered the following items: information exchange, quantity of delivered products, and quality of delivered products. In practice, the development and implementation of performance indicators improved both the performance of the supplier and the relationship between customer and supplier.

Secondly, the housekeeping is one of the most sensitive thermometers of attitude and culture in a department. In practice, a low level of housekeeping goes hand in hand with wastage of materials, sloppy operation of equipment, ignorance of process instruction cards, and low awareness of quality. Housekeeping does not only have an instrumental meaning, i.e. a clean working environment. Housekeeping also has a social meaning. It reflects respect for the individual; it expresses the idea that everyone has the right to work in a clean environment. It also reflects a manufacturing philosophy. After all, a clean environment is a condition for continuous improvement. The 5S-approach is discussed in section 3.3.5 of this chapter.

Thirdly, the mini-company process includes four-way communication, participation, and continuous improvement (see section 2 of this chapter).

In the period from October 1997 to March 1999 the following progress was made. The service of the pressing tools and polishing tools departments – which had already developed a performance indicator with their customers – improved step by step (see section 3.6.7 for the pressing tools). The electrical and the mechanical departments developed a performance indicator. The housekeeping program was started up in most departments. The polishing tools department ended their housekeeping program at the end of 1998 with a management audit. The pressing tools department passed the management audit in March 1999 (see section 3.6.4). The electrical and mechanical departments started the housekeeping program at the end of 1998. A management audit was planned for mid-1999. The program for starting up the mini-company process had been designed for the polishing tools and pressing tools departments in the second part of 1998. The plan was to execute this program at the beginning of 1999. Due to the announcement of a new reengineering project (see section 3.2.2), this program was postponed.

In conclusion, the redesign of the Technical Department resulted in six 'subdepartments'. Each department had its own product and its own customers. It was agreed that these departments would be developed into mini-companies. The first steps were taken.

> *Reflection.* The Technical Department had definitively blazed the new trail. The decisive condition for the change process was the conviction of the department manager. He was convinced that the new direction was a good one. His style of management (listening, participative, personal commitment, honesty) was in accordance with the character of this change process.
>
> One of the external consultants and myself had intensively coached the department manager. We had deliberately agreed on different roles. The external consultant supported the design of the change process and tried to strengthen the self-confidence of the department manager. For myself, I focused on the planning and the content of the change process.
>
> I regularly discussed the new direction informally with the department manager. In these discussions I confirmed the chosen direction. The main objective of these informal discussions was to give meaning to the change process and to express confidence in him.

3.2.5 Redesign of the production departments
The redesign of the production departments was an important part of the 'Future' project. Every department had received a target with respect to the indirect head count. The first proposal had to be presented in the review of the steering committee of August 1997. In the period April 1997 - August 1997 several informal discussions took place. These discussions focused on two questions. The first was:

do we organise the departments according to a functional or a line structure? The second was: do we need middle management to work in shifts or is it possible that they work on day shift. However, at the moment of the review an in-depth discussion about the organisation of the production departments had not taken place. The department managers presented some preliminary proposals that went a long way to meeting the required reduction in head count.

Process of redesign

In the period between April 1997 and December 1998 a lot of informal discussions took place about the organisation of the production departments. In this period, a benchmark of two factories in England was also done: a tube factory in Durham and a glass factory in Simonstone.[165] In addition, the department managers discussed the redesign of their department several times with the internal and external consultant.

A fundamental discussion about the organisation of the production departments started in the seventh workshop that took place in December 1997. The external consultant guided this workshop. I started the meeting with a review of the different organisational models that were present in the factory. I identified the pros and the cons of the various approaches. I then proposed an 'ideal' picture: to split up the production departments into several 'mini-companies'. A mini-company is a technical, logistical and organisational entity. This entity has to include all shifts and has to be managed by one middle manager working within a day shift. In an ideal situation, the mini-company consists of one production line. The ideal size of a mini-company is between 30 and 50 employees.

The presentation was discussed intensively. Attention was especially paid to the feasibility of the proposed model. Some department managers did not believe in it. In their view, middle management is needed on shift in order to solve technical problems, to settle logistical issues, and to protect the customer against quality problems. Some department managers said that the 'ideal' model presented could be implemented. A prerequisite is the control of our technical and logistical processes. The responsibilities of the indirect crew also have to be defined. Another important question was: How to go from 'ist' to 'soll'? By the end of the workshop, there was total agreement about the necessity to control technical, logistical and organisational processes in our factory. It was acknowledged that these processes had to reach a certain level of control before we could change the organisation. However, there was no agreement about the feasibility of the presented model.

This discussion about the organisation of the production departments continued in the eighth workshop that took place in June 1998. An internal consultant

---

[165] The tube factory in Durham had reached a high level of excellence in all expects of manufacturing. Its sister factory in Simonstone had greatly improved its housekeeping. The main objective of this visit can be summarised in the slogan 'seeing is believing'.

guided this workshop.[166] Two presentations were given. I firstly presented the idea of reengineering based on the thoughts of Michael Hammer and James Champy in their book *Reengineering the Corporation*. Secondly, one of the department managers gave an overview of the papers presented at a national congress about the future of production in Germany. At this congress several authors discussed the organisational set-up of manufacturing organisations. These presentations were used to evaluate the reengineering process. Three conclusions were drawn: (1) fundamental reengineering had been achieved in the Technical Department , (2) some production departments had been fundamentally reengineered; others not at all, and (3) a lot of non-added value activities were still present in the manufacturing process. Agreements to continue the reengineering process were made.

Redesign of the Mixing & Melting department

The Mixing & Melting department is responsible for the production of glass. The 'product' of this department is a gob of molten glass with specified properties. This gob is delivered to the Screen Pressing and Cone Pressing departments. Three furnaces were in operation.

Figure 3.6 shows the organisation chart of the Mixing & Melting department before and after the redesign.

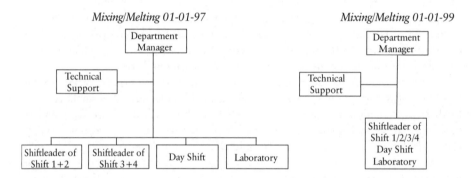

Figure 3.6 Organisation chart of the Mixing & Melting department before and after the redesign process

About 45 employees worked in the Mixing & Melting department before the redesign. Shift 1 and 2 were managed by a middle manager on day shift. Shift 3 and 4 were managed by another middle manager on day shift. Both middle managers supervised the operators on day shift. The laboratory, which carried out standard measurements, was managed by a middle manager. This was a part-time job

---

[166] In January 1998 the plant manager decided to end all external consultancy for the reengineering process. The main reason was to save money. Also, some management team members questioned the quality of the consultants.

(50 %). Technical support consisted of one material technologist, two equipment technologists and three process technologists.

Figure 3.6 also shows the organisation chart of the department after the reengineering process. The main difference is that one line manager (one of the middle managers) managed all operators (four shifts and day shift). The operators were extensively trained in cooperation and continuous improvement. They began to act as a group more and more. The employees of the laboratory were also trained in cooperation and continuous improvement. The same line manager managed them. As a result of the reengineering, the line manager was integrally responsible for all production activities. The technical support was unchanged.

> *Reflection.* Gradually, the technical and social processes were improved in this department. My role in the change process was explaining and re-explaining the basic principles of participation and continuous improvement, supporting initiatives for improvements, and giving meaning to realised improvements. The conviction of the department manager and middle manager in the path chosen was decisive in the change process.

The reengineering process in the Mixing & Melting department resulted in a reduction in middle management. In addition, a redesign of the controlling activities of the furnaces was planned, which would result in a reduction in operators. A budget to realise this redesign was applied for.

Redesign of the Screen Pressing department

The Screen Pressing department is responsible for the pressing of screens. The 'product' of this department is a raw screen with specified properties. This screen is delivered to the Screen Finishing department. A line consists of one press, pin insertion units, measuring equipment and a visual inspection station. Three lines are present in the department. Figure 3.7 shows the organisation chart of the department before and after the redesign process. About 175 employees worked in the Screen Pressing department before the redesign process. One shift leader was present in every shift. The shift leader was hierarchically responsible for the operators on shift. The manager of a line was responsible for the technical aspects of the production of one line (a press with a visual inspection station). Technical support consisted of two equipment technologists and a quality engineer.

Figure 3.7 also shows the organisation chart of the department after the redesign process. The main difference is that a line manager has the integral responsibility for the whole line. The function of the shift leader was disbanded. Technical support consisted of an equipment technologist, a quality engineer, an engineer for training and an engineer for coaching the visual inspection.

> *Reflection.* The department manager of Screen Pressing was convinced that the responsibility to manage a line had to be put in the hands of one manager. This conviction guided his actions. The change from the 'old' organisation to the 'new' one was done step by step. My role in this change process was to confirm and reconfirm

that the chosen direction was the right one. In addition, I stimulated that training activities and so on would support the implementation of the new organisation.

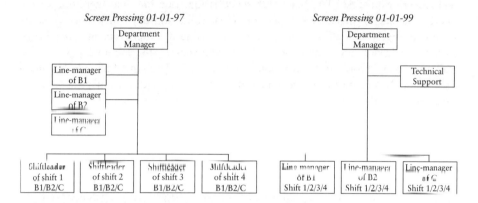

Figure 3.7 Organisation chart of Screen Pressing before and after the redesign process

The reengineering process in Screen Pressing resulted in a reduction in middle management. In addition, an improvement in process control, a reorganisation of activities, and an increase in flexibility, resulted in a big reduction in operators. At the beginning of 1999, about 125 employees were active in this department.

> *Member check.* One department manager remarked that a reduction of personnel in this department could be realised because the control of the technical processes was improved. In his view, the reorganisation was done without any theoretical concept.

> *Reflection.* In the perspective of all reengineering workshops the remark that 'the reorganisation was done without any theoretical concept' is incredible. How to understand such a remark? Firstly, in the course of the time I had sensed a certain tension between a few of the department managers. In my opinion, this remark has to be understood against the background of this tension. Secondly, it also shows that there was still no common opinion about the essence of the reengineering process. Some department managers believed that the Screen Pressing department had been reengineered successfully. Others did not. Obviously, during the whole reengineering process an unequivocal meaning about the redesign of this department had not been developed.

Redesign of Screen Finishing
The Screen Finishing department is responsible for the finishing of screens. The 'product' of this department is a finished screen with specified properties. A finished screen is transferred to the conveyor of the customer located at the site or packed for other customers. A line consists of an unpacking station, pre-grinding equipment, grinding equipment, high gloss equipment, visual inspection stations,

transference stations and packing stations. This department has six lines. The processes of lines 1 to 5 are functionally grouped together. The activities are spread over two buildings. Line 6 was an integrated line: all equipment was grouped in one line and all activities were in one room. At the end of 1996, about 240 employees were active in this department.

Figure 3.8 shows the organisation chart of the department before and after the redesign process.

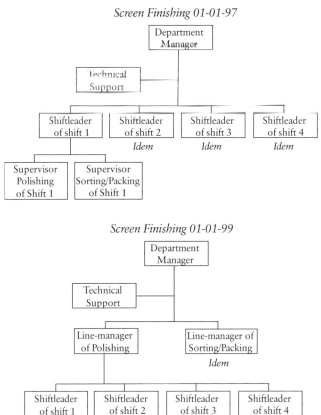

Figure 3.8 The organisation chart at the time and the agreed proposal for Screen Finishing

A shift leader managed the shifts. The shift leader led two supervisors, one for the polishing area and one for the sorting/packing area. The supervisors directed the operators. The technical support consisted of two equipment technologists and four process technologists.

Figure 3.8 also shows the new organisation chart of the department. This chart was agreed on with the plant manager at the end of 1998. Its implementation was meant to form part of the reengineering project that was launched in the beginning of 1999. The main features in the new organisation were the following. First, an increased efficiency of lines 1 to 5 would in theory have made it possible to close (the less efficient) line 6. Secondly, a line manager manages the polishing depart-ment. Thirdly, a line manager also manages the sorting/packing department. Fourthly, the line managers have the integral responsibility for the line; this means: technical, logistical, organisational and personnel responsibility. Fifthly, the line managers lead the supervisors on shift. And lastly, the technical support consists of two equipment technologists, one engineer for coaching the visual inspection, and two process technologists.

Reflection. The redesign of this department was really a 'disaster'. In my opinion only 'wrong choices' were made. Firstly, a change in the (functional) production structure of lines 1 to 5 was out of the question due to the high amount of investments involved. Parallellisation was not possible. Segmentation was determined by the present technical boundaries (polishing, visual inspection, transport) This meant that the whole production structure had to be considered as fixed. Because of this, the degree of freedom with which the control structure could be designed was very limited. Secondly, the possibilities for social contact between the employees in lines 1 to 5 were very limited. In the polishing area the distances were large and the high noise level required ear protection. In the inspection area every employee was inspecting a product in its own inspection cabinet. Improvements in this field were also out of the question due to the investments involved. Thirdly, an advantage of the proposal was that one line manager managed all polishing shifts. The same holds for all visual inspection shifts. As a consequence, the production losses caused by both poor handover between shifts and by frictions between shifts could be tackled more easily. A disadvantage of the proposal was a further loosening of the organisa-tional links. The technical and error linkage of polishing and inspecting is very high (Schumacher analysis, see section 2.2.1 of this chapter). Therefore, the integration of these activities in one department is recommended. The functional production struc-ture, spatial division, and time-consuming transport via the conveyors, resulted in a loose coupling between polishing and visual inspection. This loose coupling was fur-ther confirmed by assigning different line managers for these processes. Finally, line 6 was the only integrated line. From a socio-technical point of view it was the best line. However, the efficiency of this line was lower than that of the other lines. Therefore, this line had to be closed.

Reflection. Why was line 6 less efficient? Firstly, the capacities of the various machines in this line were not well adjusted. Therefore, the capacity of the line was lower than that of the other lines. Secondly, this line was not connected to conveyors that came from the Screen Pressing department. Therefore, additional packing, un-packing and transport activities were required. The consequence of these design deci-sions was that the technical and social advantages of the line concept disappeared.

The reengineering process in Screen Finishing had to result in a reduction of indi-rect and direct personnel. It was expected that after the reengineering about 200 people would be active in this department.

Redesign of Cone Pressing and Cone Finishing

The Cone Pressing department is responsible for the pressing of cones. The 'product' of this department is a raw cone with specified properties. This product is delivered as a semi-manufactured product to customers or as a semi-manufactured product to the Finishing Cones department. The production is carried out using two presses. The pressing activities are located on the second floor and the inspection and packing activities on the first floor. At the end of 1996, about 130 employees were active in this department.

Figure 3.9 on the next page shows the organisation chart of the Cone Pressing department before and after the redesign process.

Before the redesign process, a shift leader managed the different shifts. The shift leader was hierarchically responsible for the operators on shift. The line manager was responsible for the technical aspects of the production of one line (a press with a visual inspection station). Technical support consisted of two equipment technologists and two quality engineers.

After the redesign process, a line manager managed every pressing line. This line manager had the integral responsibility for that line; this means technical, logistical, organisational, and personnel responsibility. To manage the technical processes a shift leader was present in every shift. This means the 'dual' management structure was still present (line manager versus shift leader). However, *within* the dual structure the line manager had the first say. In addition, the Cone Pressing and Cone Finishing departments were integrated (see below).

> *Reflection*. During the redesign process the dual structure was discussed intensively. It appeared that a further improvement of the performance of this department required a better link between different shifts. For example, every shift had more or less its own 'ideal' process parameters. As a consequence, every shift started its job by turning the knobs till the 'right' process parameters were achieved. These adjustments always resulted in additional losses. These types of problems could be tackled better by giving the line manager the integral responsibility for the line. At the same time, it was acknowledged that shift leaders were still required because the organisational and technical processes were not yet under control.

The Cone Finishing department is responsible for the finishing of cones. The 'product' of this department is a finished cone with specified properties. The finished cone is transferred to the conveyor of the customer located at the site or packed for other customers. A line consists of an unpacking station, equipment to add a neck, grinding equipment, and a visual inspection/packing station or a visual inspection/transference station. This department has five lines. The different processes are functionally grouped together. At the end of 1996, about 90 employees were active in this department.

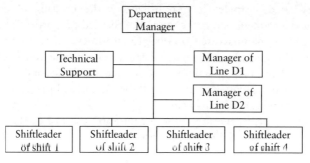

Cone Pressing 01-01-97

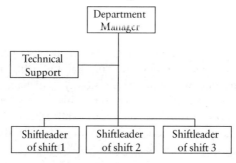

Cone Finishing 01-01-97

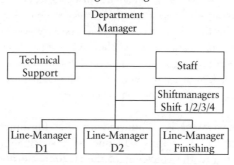

Cone Pressing/Finishing 01-01-99

Figure 3.9 Organisation chart of Cone Pressing and Cone Finishing before and after the redesign

Figure 3.9 shows the organisation chart of the Cone Finishing department. A shift leader managed the operators on shift. The technical support consisted of two equipment technologists. The Cone Finishing department was – apart from its integration with the Cone Pressing department – not redesigned. The only change was that a line manager replaced the department manager. The shift leaders were still present.

> *Reflection.* The same holds for the Cone Finishing department as for the Screen Finishing department. The (functional) production structure only could be changed with high investments. Therefore, the production structure had to be accepted as a given. Also, the possibilities for social contact between the employees were limited. In the polishing area the high noise level required ear protection. In the inspection area every employee was inspecting a product in its own cabinet. The distances between the polishing area and the inspection area were rather short so direct feedback was possible.

Figure 3.9 shows the Cone Pressing and Cone Finishing departments after re-design. These departments were brought under one department manager. Three line managers manage the unit: one line manager for each press (including visual inspection and packing), and one line manager for the finishing (including visual inspection and packing). One shift leader manages the operators in the cone pressing area and cone finishing area. At that time, shift leaders were still required due to the instability of the technical and logistical processes. The technical support was reduced to two equipment technologists and two quality engineers.

> *Reflection.* The decision to integrate the Cone Pressing and Cone Finishing departments was taken after I was discharged from my responsibility for these departments. Personally, I was not so happy with the decision to integrate them, especially because the problems *within* these departments were bigger than the problems *between* these departments.

The reengineering process in Cone Pressing and Cone Finishing resulted in a reduction in middle management. In addition, an improvement in process control, a reorganisation of activities, and an increase in flexibility, resulted in a reduction of operators. At the beginning of 1999, about 200 employees were active in this department.[167] A further reduction in personnel was planned.

Division of production into two lines: a screen line and a cone line
At the end of 1998, the (new) plant manager decided to split up the production into two lines: a screen line and a cone line. The Mixing & Melting, Pressing Screens and Finishing Screens departments, and the Technical Department were allocated to the screen line. The Pressing Cones and Finishing Cones departments were allocated to the cone line. The screen line was assigned to myself. The plant manager himself managed the cone line as acting manager.

> *Reflection.* The plant manager asked my opinion about the division of the production into a screen line and a cone line. I told him the advantages and the disadvantages. I

---

[167] The reduction in direct personnel was achieved partly by a reduction in the production level of finishing cones and partly by the reengineering activities.

hinted carefully that I was not an advocate of his proposal, especially as the intended organisational clarity (a screen line and a cone line) was blurred by the fact that the Mixing & Melting department and the Technical Department (which had to serve both lines) were assigned to one line (the screen line). I told one of my colleagues in the management team about the possible change in the organisation. He wrote an extensive e-mail to the plant manager. He explained the background of the factory organisation, pointed out several drawbacks of the proposal, and advised him to discuss the proposal in the management team. (Note: An e-mail was written because he left the plant for a business trip).

The proposal to split the production up into two lines was not discussed with department managers and not discussed in the management team. The plant manager took the decision alone.

Why were the lines split up? The formal arguments were a concentration of management effort to solve the problems in both lines and a strengthening of the 'voice' of the production in the management team. In my opinion, the most important motivation was dissatisfaction with the progress in the cone line. The plant manager and I had different opinions about the yield problems in the cone line. He believed that incapable management caused these problems, whereas I believed that fundamental process problems played a role.

Why did the plant manager not discuss his proposal with the management team or the department managers? I can only guess. I believe that he did not expect a lot of support.

The management team was asked to support the implementation of the decision.

3.2.6 Review of the project
In November 1997 the management team reviewed the whole project. The plant manager opened the meeting with some conclusions. The first was that the financial results were on track. Second, the reduction in the costs of materials and services were on track. Third, the personnel costs were off track. In his view the speed of the project was too slow. He also remarked that he was not sure about the commitment of the management team. He also asked us some questions:

o   where do the problems lie in us as management?
o   where are the problems in the organisation?
o   which problems do we have to focus on?
o   how can we design our management processes so that we reach our goals?

The objective of the plant manager was to discuss these questions together, to get everyone heading in the same direction and to continue the process at a higher speed.

An external consultant gave the second presentation. He emphasised five points. Firstly, that the project was too comprehensive. For that reason, it was difficult to make people accountable. Secondly, that the climate in the management team was not supportive. The following observations were mentioned: it is 'not the done thing' to criticise each other constructively; most of the critics can be heard outside the meeting; team members feel responsible for their own department but not for the whole business; and finally, they do not help each other. Thirdly, that the culture in the plant was determined by some 'unwritten rules'.[168] These rules were counterproductive with respect to the reengineering process. Fourthly, that the service level of the staff departments had to be clearly defined. Additionally, an improvement in performance was required. And finally, that the room for the bottom-up process had to be increased.

> *Reflection.* The external consultant gave a scathing judgement of the management team. In fact, he concluded that the management team was not capable of managing the reengineering project. This consultant was not 'just' anybody. He had guided the 'Future' project from its conception. One could expect his judgement to raise a lot of criticism. However, nothing happened. Why did nobody react? Did the silence confirm the judgement? Did the silence confirm the tension between the external consultant and the (German) members of the management team? After the meeting, the presentation of the consultant was criticised sharply in the corridors by some members of the management team.

After this review of the whole project, the individual projects were reviewed.[169] Attention was paid to the projects entitled 'overhead value analysis of all staff department' (no 1); 'reduction of costs in repair & maintenance' (no 7), 'reduction in manual handling' (no 8), 'reduction in handling and transport' (no 10), 'sorting of products' (no 11), 'reduction in the number of technicians' (no 12), 'reorganisation of the operational groups (the production departments and the Technical Department)' (no 13). Projects (1), (7), (10) and (13) were more or less on target. Projects (8), (11) and (12) were off target. Additionally, it was noted that in the budget of 1998 some savings were incorporated for which the plans were not yet available.

The questions asked by the plant manager in his opening speech about the commitment and the functioning of the management team were briefly discussed at the end of the review. It was concluded that a follow-up would be necessary. No concrete actions were agreed.

> *Reflection.* In fact, it is unbelievable that the questions asked by the plant manager about the commitment and the functioning of the management team were discussed only briefly at the end of the review. It is especially so because his questions were to a great extent answered by the external consultant. I have no explanation for this.

In April 1998, a new plant manager started in the Aachen Glass Factory. He reviewed the 'Future' project in May 1998. This review was focused on the head count target: the 'seven-hundred-employee factory'. It was concluded that the number of employees on board was much higher than the target. This conclusion

---

[168] The consultant referred indirectly to the book *The Unwritten Rules of the Game* (1994) by Scott-Morgan.
[169] A complete list of the projects is given in section 3.2.2 of this chapter.

was in accordance with the review of November 1997. It was also concluded that the present plans were not good enough to realise the target at the end of 1999. New actions were agreed upon.

In August 1998, the head count target was reviewed again. The state of play in every department was analysed. It appeared that some projects had been successfully concluded, some had partially realised their targets, and again some had failed. It was concluded again that the head count targets could not be met. The situation appeared to be more severe than forecasted in the review of November 1997. Several causes were identified. Firstly, necessary investments had not been released. Consequently, the targets of projects (10), (12) and (13) could not be met.[170] Secondly, the lack of process control made it impossible to reduce the head count. This was especially related to projects (11) and (12). Thirdly, there was a lack of good plans. No plans were available for some savings that had been incorporated in the budget of 1998. Also, no replacement projects were identified for the projects that did not meet their targets. In the review, extensive brainstorming was done and new projects were selected and priorities agreed. It was decided that in two departments external consultants would carry out an investigation to investigate possible savings.

In October and November 1998 the new projects were reviewed again. In this period, higher management foresaw additional price reductions in the market. New targets with respect to the head count were given. A new plan to realise the 'seven-hundred-employee factory' was developed. In this plan, outsourcing of activities was an important theme. This plan was presented to the workforce in January 1999.

> *Reflection.* In retrospect, the 'Future' project was a chain of making plans and reviewing plans. Between 'making plans' and 'reviewing plans' workshops were held to realise the targets. Why did so many plans fail? Why were so many new actions agreed upon? Here, I want to point to an important paradox. Despite all the workshops and reviews, a joint language with a coherent pattern of meaning did not develop. Consequently, no coherent pattern of cooperation developed to execute plans, to solve unexpected problems, and to develop new plans. In the evaluation, the root cause of this paradox will be discussed in detail (section 3.7).
>
> I have to make one remark about the content of the projects. In my last few months at Aachen, I had an extensive discussion with the internal consultant. We discovered that several problems were defined at the wrong level. For example, the reduction in the manual handling of products was investigated at the level of the individual departments. In our opinion, such a reduction could only be realised if the planning process at management team level (or even at business unit level) was improved.

---

[170] A complete list of the projects is given in section 3.2.2 of this chapter.

270

3.3 The world-class manufacturing program

In April 1997 I started my job at the Aachen Glass Factory. I spent the first three weeks on the shop floor. I spent about 6 hours in every shift of each production department. The objective was to meet the crew, to learn about the process, and to determine the state of play with respect to world-class manufacturing. These experiences led to the 'world-class manufacturing' program.

Assignment. My assignment was to bring the glass factory up to a world class level. In my job description the following subjects were specified: housekeeping, waste reduction, the mini-company concept, glass wall management, statistical process control, failure mode and effect analysis, control loops, and the design of experiments. I knew that Aachen was a 'difficult' factory. However, I was confident that I had enough experience to implement these methods in the glass factory.

Why world-class? The plant manager believed that Aachen suffered from non-transparent and uncontrolled processes. In his view, world-class techniques (like the ones mentioned in my job description) would help the organisation to make processes transparent and controllable.

3.3.1 Status quo

I spent the first three weeks of my work in Aachen on the shop floor. I gathered information through my own observations, informal interviews with employees on the shop floor, informal and structured interviews with middle management, and written information about improvement programs. This information was summarised in a presentation. The following topics were brought up for discussion:

Future. Employees worry about the future of the Aachen plant. A strong sense of urgency is expressed in some employees' worries. Others believe that the plant will never be closed.

Management. Members of the management team are not visible on the shop floor. Only the plant manager visits the shop floor regularly. Employees say that the management team does not know what happens on the shop floor.

Employees on the shop floor. Many employees have a lot of knowledge about their job. They feel ownership of their work. However, many employees report that a smaller part of the crew is not enthusiastic about their job. This part of the crew tries to earn as much as possible with a minimum amount of effort. They cut corners. This raises the question: why does the Aachen Glass Factory accept such behaviour?

Culture. The employees believe that numbers are more important than quality. They report that blocked batches are regularly delivered to the customer. The discipline on the shop floor with respect to standard operating procedures and safety instructions has slipped away. Improvements are made in an ad hoc way.

Logistics. The logistics are determined by the transport system in the factory. In the conveyor many empty places are present, indicating a lack of process control. Many non-added-value processes are present, i.e. packing and unpacking of products.

Organisation (1). Middle management do not experience the staff departments as a support. Middle management do not trust the development group. Failures were emphasises and successes were hardly reported.

Organisation (2). The organisation of the production in departments (production departments and Technical Department) is transparent. There is a customer-supplier relation between some departments. Between others not. Within the departments there is an overlap in responsibilities, especially between the shift leaders and line managers. Additionally, shift leaders take over a part of the responsibilities of the operators.

Organisation (3). In several departments a start has been made with respect to team-work or mini-companies. Good examples of improvement are present. However, these examples are not spread over the whole factory. Also, the philosophy behind the teamwork or mini companies has not taken a definitive shape.

Statistical Process Control. Several control charts are present in the factory. These charts are not always used. The charts are focused on product parameters and not on process parameters. Several processes are not under control. For difficult processes every shift has its 'own' settings. Failure Mode and Effect Analysis is rarely done in the factory. In the release of new products, new processes and new equipment, statistical process control and Failure Mode and Effect Analysis are not used in a standard way.

Housekeeping. In some areas the housekeeping is acceptable. In other areas the situation is unacceptable.

Safety. The safety instructions are not always complied with. For example, safety glasses, ear protection and hand gloves are often not worn in the required areas.

3.3.2 Process

I discussed these observations at first with the plant manager. An intensive discussion about the shop floor, support of the management, and relation to the staff departments came about. In conclusion, the plant manager agreed with the overall picture.

After that, the observations were presented to the production management team. There was agreement about the status quo. The discussion focused on the question: 'How to view the state of play?' Does Aachen follow industrial practice? Is Aachen behind the competition? Has Aachen reached world-class level? It was decided to discuss these questions in a separate workshop.

The observations were also presented to the management team of the Aachen Glass Factory. There was agreement about the status quo. There was – more or less – agreement that Aachen should reach world-class level.

Finally, the observations were presented to the workers council. In this meeting, there was also agreement about the status quo and the necessity to improve.

After these discussions, I concluded that my observations were acknowledged by the organisation and that there was enough support to start a change process.

Reflection. During my presentation to the management team I did not get the impression that everybody was really concerned about the state of play. I shared my feeling with the plant manager. In his view, I could not expect a lot of support from the

272

management team. He advised me to focus my efforts on the management team of the factory. Looking back, I made a big mistake here. Firstly, I expected that the management team would be familiar with the concepts of world class manufacturing. I drew this conclusion from the discussions in the management team about total quality management. However, it appeared that the management team knew the 'words' but was not familiar with the 'content'. Secondly, I underestimated the resistance of the management team to the world-class manufacturing program. I was of the opinion that the management team would at least tolerate this program; and I hoped that they would give it some support. Especially, because my approach was in accordance with the Philips Quality Award process (this obligatory program was also running in Aachen) However, my expectations appeared to be wrong. Some months before I left Aachen I was informed via several sources about underground resistance from the management team to the world-class manufacturing program. I was told that some members had expressed their doubts about this program in informal discussions with some of their faithful followers. They had even ridiculed some parts of the program. And ... I did not know this. I heard about it more than eighteen months after I started in Aachen. My conclusion that there was enough agreement to start the world-class manufacturing program appeared to be wrong.

It was decided that the world-class manufacturing program would focus on six topics: safety, personnel, housekeeping, mini-companies, process control and maintenance. Together with an external consultant, the change program was designed. The most important technical, political and cultural factors were mapped out. The main topics of this program were discussed at first with the plant manager. He promised all his support to realise this program. After that, the change program was discussed with the department managers individually. I interpreted the constructive atmosphere during these discussions as a sign of agreement and commitment.

The discussion about the observations and comments was continued in a workshop with the production management team. This workshop took place in the beginning of July 1997. An external consultant facilitated the meeting. A lot of questions arose. The discussion centred around three questions: (1) What is world class manufacturing? (2) Will the management team of the plant really support a world-class manufacturing program? And (3) Do we want to execute such a program as a team?

The discussion of these questions took a lot of time. Definitive answers could not be formulated. The workshop continued with the world-class manufacturing program. The topics of 'safety', 'personnel', 'housekeeping', 'mini-companies', 'process control' and 'maintenance' were brought up for discussion. The department managers proposed to continue the discussion after everybody was back from their holidays, which meant in October or November (3 to 4 months later!). I did not accept this proposal. It was decided to continue the discussion about the program in the next meeting of the production management team.

Reflection. Afterwards, I evaluated the workshop with the external consultant. In his view, the three questions were indicative of the state of play. The first question reflected their internal orientation and their lack of theoretical background. The second question reflected the mistrust with respect to the management team of the Aachen Glass Factory. And the third question showed that the management team of production was not really a team. In his view, these questions had to stay up for discussion. Furthermore, the proposal to delay the discussion to October or November had to be seen as an attempt to wriggle out of this theme. He advised me to continue steadily but carefully.

The discussion about the change program was continued in a meeting of the production management team. It was decided to start immediately with the topics of safety and personnel. Furthermore, it was agreed that the different aspects of world-class manufacturing would be discussed in a weekly meeting of one and a half hours (the world-class manufacturing meeting). Occasionally, half a day would be reserved to discuss a specific item in more detail.

> *Reflection.* It was a joint decision to start with the topics of 'safety' and 'personnel'. In my opinion, it was a good choice. Firstly, as factory manager I could not accept that legal regulations with respect to safety were so heavily violated. Secondly, enforcing compliance with the safety regulations is a good vehicle for teaching an organisation discipline. Thirdly, 'black sheep' constitute poison in an organisation. This poison has to be solved as quickly as possible (Note: 'black sheep' were defined as people who were capable of doing a good job but who seriously cut corners). Finally, (middle) management has to learn not to accept bad behaviour. In my opinion, 'safety' and 'black sheep' were good vehicles to improve managerial capabilities.

The topics of 'safety' and 'personnel' will be described in more detail. Other topics discussed in the world-class manufacturing meeting will be touched upon.

3.3.3 Safety
The responsibilities of management and employees with respect to safety are legally defined. An important part of this responsibility is the annual safety instruction. Managers have to instruct their employees about the safety regulations that are applicable to their workplace. After this instruction, the employee has to sign an official document stating that he or she has been taught. Additionally, in the production area the main safety regulations are indicated with a sign. Despite these procedures, the safety regulations were regularly not complied with.

In the management team meeting of the factory it was decided that two department managers and myself would tackle this problem. In addition, this topic was discussed with the workers council and the personnel department. Two causes were identified. In the first place, only part of the crew (about one third) was instructed intensively. The safety regulations were explained to these employees in a discussion of about one hour, after which the employee signed the official document. Most employees were instructed about the regulations in a three-minute discussion. The employee was asked whether he knew the instructions and whether he had any questions. Generally, the first question was answered affirmatively and the second one negatively. After that, the employee signed the official document.

Management tolerated this practice. In a discussion the personnel manager remarked:

> "Safety instructions are very important. However, the whole point is that the employee signs the document."

Line management also tolerated this practice. Line management rarely checked compliance with the safety regulations. Employees were rarely held accountable for breaking these regulations.

The following procedure was proposed. All employees would be instructed using a three-page guide.[171] This guide had to be prepared by the department manager and the safety engineer. The workers council also had to be involved. The official instruction had to be done in a meeting of thirty to sixty minutes. After that, management would check the state of play on the shop floor. The management team of production agreed with this proposal. It was decided to carry out the coming instruction round, which was due to take place in August-October 1997, according to this procedure. A schedule was agreed. Before the end of the year all employees had to be instructed according to the new procedure.

At the beginning of October, I instructed my own management team about safety. Three months later, the progress in the departments was reviewed. In some departments the old procedure had been used. The department manager in question indicated 'miscommunication' as the cause for neglecting the new procedure. For these departments it was agreed that the safety instruction would be repeated according to the new procedure. However, time slipped by. In the end, the decision was taken to skip the re-instruction because the next instruction round was in sight.

In other departments the employees were instructed according to the new procedure. Together with a representative of the workers council, I interviewed the crew of these departments about the quality of the instruction. It appeared that about fifty percent of the employees were instructed according to the new procedure. The others employees were instructed in a three-minute instruction. The department manager and his shift leaders were called to account. After that, the latter employees were instructed according the new procedure.

> *Reflection*. I took it for granted that agreements had been kept to. The reason I checked this was that I want to show both the crew and the workers council that I was serious about safety. At that time, I did not take bad faith into account.

In June 1998, the procedure for the safety instruction was discussed and reconfirmed. At the end of June I instructed my own management team again. Particular attention was paid to the behaviour of the management. It was agreed that after the safety instruction the department managers would inspect whether the employees worked according to the regulations. At the end of November all the safety instruc-

---

[171]   Such a guide was in use in the Technical Department. This guide served as example for the other departments.

tions had been done. Again, together with a representative of the workers council, I interviewed the operators about the quality of the instruction. It appeared that in all departments more that ninety percent of the employees had been instructed according to the new procedure (the remaining ten percent were absent during the instruction). However, despite the instruction, discipline with respect to using safety glasses and gloves was bad. I discussed the violations with the department managers responsible and ordered them to check all shifts. Also, if necessary, official warnings had to be given to employees who continued to refuse to follow the regulations. It appeared that in some areas the regulations were not quite clear. It took two months to clarify the regulations. After this, the department managers started to check compliance with the regulations and to call individual employees to account. From that time on, the employees complied with the safety rules.

> Reflection. This study is characteristic of the culture in Aachen. A lot of managerial attention was necessary to change the behaviour of department managers and their crew. Explaining the issue was not enough. Making agreements was also not enough. The agreements had to be checked and the threat of an official warning was required to realise compliance with the regulations. In the evaluation (section 3.7) the background of this behaviour will be discussed.

3.3.4 Personnel

The second topic that was discussed briefly after the workshop was 'personnel'. Obviously, a small number of the crew cut corners. Their performance was minimal and their behaviour was not acceptable. During my training period many employees (operators and middle management) complained about these 'black sheep' to me. It was decided that two department managers and myself would analyse this topic. I also discussed this point with the personnel manager and the chairman of the workers council.

> *Analysis.* Our analysis was as follows. The interaction between line management, the personnel department, and the workers council had resulted in a culture in which the bad behaviour of employees was accepted. The different parties had made themselves powerless. Line management did not built up cases about poorly performing employees. In their opinion, building up cases was not fruitful because the personnel department did not support any disciplinary measures. They had the feeling that the personnel department and the workers council 'conspired' against them. The personnel department did not support line management because they did not built up cases. Additionally, the personnel department preferred to maintain a good relationship with the workers council. In addition, the workers council protected all employees. They saw it as their job to protect the employees. They could protect the employees because no cases were built up. Management eventually sanctioned this 'game'. The department managers confirmed this analysis.

A constructive approach was chosen to get out of this vicious circle. This means the objective of the approach was for every employee to change his behaviour in a positive way. The following procedure was proposed:

1. Two to three 'black sheep' would be identified in every production department.
2. The department manager would arrange a discussion with each of these employees. The manager had to express his expectations clearly and to indicate where the employee had to improve. He also had to raise the question of whether there were any problems, which made the employee unable to perform well. A written report had to be made on the basis of this discussion.
3. The performance of the employee had to be evaluated in intervals of one to two months. These evaluations had to be recorded in a report. If the employee had changed his behaviour in a positive way, the procedure could be wrapped up. If the employee had not changed his behaviour in a positive way, a dismissal procedure had to be started. The role of the personnel department and the workers council in this procedure was still open.

I discussed the proposal with the personnel manager in private. After a long discussion, he agreed with the proposal under certain conditions. In his view, it was not necessary to involve the workers council. It was decided that an open discussion with the department managers and the staff of the personnel department would be organised.

In October a joint meeting between the management team of production and the staff of the personnel department took place. The proposal was explained. The personnel department made the following comments:

1. The personnel department had to be involved from the first step of the procedure.
2. The department manager had to indicate clearly why an employee did not function well.
3. The discussions had to be written down in a report.
4. During the procedure continuous communication had to take place between the department manager and the personnel department.

The department managers asked only one question: if we start the procedure, and if we take your comments into account, will you follow the procedure to the last step?

The discussion focused on two points. The staff of the personnel department questioned whether the department managers were willing to indicate the bad performance of an employee in a quantitative way, i.e. number of minutes too late for work. They were afraid of favouritism. The department managers doubted the willingness of the staff of the personnel department to follow the whole procedure. Would the personnel department stick to the procedure if the workers council put up strong resistance? Would the personnel department back the department managers if they had to go to court for dismissal? The discussion on these two points was laborious. In fact, both 'parties' questioned the willingness and reliability of the other. After a long discussion, it was accepted that the poor performance of employees could not always be easily expressed in exact numbers. However, it was accepted that it is always possible to specify poor performance in words and to elucidate it with examples. Further, it was agreed that the personnel department would be involved from the beginning of the procedure. And it was agreed that they would support the line management to the end.

> *Reflection.* The relation between the personnel department and the department managers was characterised by miscommunication and mistrust. In such an atmosphere cooperation is doomed to fail. The 'long discussions' were required to dismantle arguments and prejudices. However, these 'long discussions' did not change their attitudes about each other. At best, they gave each other a chance. At worst, they played a game.

The agreed procedure was implemented. About 15 employees were identified as 'black sheep'. In the period that followed the rest of the procedure was applied. Line management and the personnel department regularly discussed the progress in a joint meeting. Difficulties were deliberated. Misunderstandings were cleared up. Decisions were taken. Half a year later, about half of the 'black sheep' had improved their behaviour. The other half had decided to leave the company with a 'golden handshake' (by a 'golden handshake' a lawsuit was prevented).

> *Reflection.* During the execution of the agreed procedure I had to regularly intervene. Firstly, I often had to remind both parties of the agreed procedure. Secondly, I called into question the interpretation of the other parties' behaviour. For example, mistakes were often interpreted as a deliberate violation of the agreement. In this period, the cooperation between the department managers and the personnel department improved slightly. This 'learning experience' was not enough to change their attitudes about each other. A negative interpretation of the other parties' behaviour dominated the cooperation.

3.3.5 Other topics
In the world-class manufacturing meeting the following topics were discussed: housekeeping, self-managing teams or mini-companies, process control, total preventive maintenance, training of employees, voice of the customer, discipline on the shop floor, and aspects of the Philips Quality Award for the nineties. Generally, the following procedure was applied. Firstly, the opinion was formed by benchmarking another factory, by inviting an external specialist, or by a presentation of the factory manager or one of the department managers. Secondly, the pros and cons were discussed extensively. Especially the question of how professional methods could be successfully implemented in the Aachen plant was raised. Thirdly, the decision was taken on how to proceed. Generally, decisions were taken in consensus.

Housekeeping

It was decided that the 5S-approach would be applied. This approach was developed in Japan. It consists of five steps, which have to applied in the following order[172]:

> *5S-approach.* The '5S' stands for five Japanese 'S' words: *seiri, seiton, seiso, seiketsu,* and *shitsuke.* These words can be translated as: Organisation, Orderliness, Cleanliness, Standardised Cleanup, and Discipline.
>
> o   Organisation: clearly distinguish between the items (tools, materials, and so on) which are needed on the shop floor from the items that are not needed; and eliminate the latter ones,
>
> o   Orderliness: keep the items that are needed in the correct place to allow for easy and immediate retrieval.
>
> o   Cleanliness: keep the shop floor swept and clean (e.g. by checklists and schedules).
>
> o   Standardised Cleanup: organise 'Organisation', 'Orderliness', and 'Cleanliness' in such a way that cleaning becomes a habit (e.g. by assigning the responsibilities for cleaning, integration of cleaning in the daily work, and regular evaluation).
>
> o   Discipline: develop the discipline in the whole organisation (e.g. by making the '5S' visible, correcting others, training, company-wide promotion, and using promotion tools).

A training program was designed and a workbook was made. The factory manager trained his management team. The department managers trained their crew. The question of 'How to implement the 5S-approach in Aachen?' was discussed extensively. It was agreed that a pilot in two departments would be started. Additionally, two factories in England were benchmarked. The factory manager, three department managers, and a representative of the workers council visited a glass factory in Simonstone and a tube factory in Durham. In both factories the housekeeping process was management driven. In one factory the whole crew also supported the process.

The experiences of the pilots in Aachen and the benchmark studies were discussed. It was concluded that (1) all employees have to be trained, (2) all employees have to apply the principles to their own workplace, (3) all employees will be responsible for the housekeeping of their own workplace, and (4) employees who do not work according to the housekeeping principles will be held accountable. If necessary, disciplinary measures will be taken.

At the end of 1998, more than 90 % of the employees in production had been trained in the 5S-principles. At the beginning of 1999, the first departments had implemented the 5S-approach successfully (see section 3.2.4 and 3.6.4). The

---

[172]   Hirano (1995).

implementation of the approach in the other departments was planned through the year.

Self-managing teams or mini-companies

The initiative to introduce self-managing teams was taken by the workers council. After extensive discussions, an official agreement between the management team and the workers council about the principle and implementation was made mid-1994. In 1995, self-managing teams were implemented in the Pressing Screens department. At first, all employees were trained in a two-day course in the principles of self-managing teams. A lot of attention was especially paid to problem solving, decision making, and social skills. An external consultant did the training. After that, the implementation was carried out under the guidance of a member of a staff department.[173] In 1996 the crew of the Pressing Cones department was trained. No follow-up was given. It was not until the beginning of 1998, that a discussion about implementation of self-managing teams started. In 1997, the crew of the Mixing & Melting department was trained. After the training, some aspects of self-managing teams were implemented immediately. For example, every shift planned their own activities, organised a regular meeting, and started to solve their own problems. In 1998, part of the crew of the Finishing Screens department was trained. Some aspects of self-managing teams were also implemented immediately. For example, the shifts planned their own activities and organised a regular meeting to discuss the progress. Furthermore, a list of improvement actions – which were defined during the training – was completed step by step. Agreements for further implementation were made.

In the period between September 1997 and March 1999 the progress of the self-managing teams in the different departments was evaluated with the relevant department manager, an external consultant, and myself. The principles of self-managing teams were also discussed several times in the world-class manufacturing meeting. The following conclusions were drawn. First, the implementation of self-managing teams had led to an improvement of the processes on the shop floor. Second, the implementation of self-managing teams appeared to be much more difficult than expected. Power structures on the shop floor hindered changes in behaviour. Support was not sufficient. Members of staff department who had no experience in this field and who did not know the shop floor guided the implementation. Third, a fundamental problem appeared. Originally, the autonomy of the teams was emphasised strongly. In practice, teams and middle management drifted apart. Each 'party' had its own program: the teams focused their attention on working conditions and middle management on technical problems. As a result, the impact of self-managing teams was not very positive. This evaluation led to improvements in the functioning of self-managing teams.

---

[173]   Financial considerations determined the choice for a member of a staff department.

Process control

In 1995, the plant manager started a drive to improve the control of technical processes. Some process and product parameters were brought under statistical control. In 1997, I intensified this approach. In production, more and more failure mode and effect analysis was done. Out-of-control procedures were also implemented. Attention was especially paid to a regular review of yield, product control and process control data. From mid 1998, this data was reviewed on a monthly basis in all departments. In addition, development projects were reviewed with respect to process control.

Total preventive maintenance

In mid 1998, some specialists from Technical University of Aachen gave a presentation about total preventive maintenance. The objective was to form an opinion about the use of total preventive maintenance for the glass factory. The management team of production decided to take total preventive maintenance as the leading approach to increase the uptime of the equipment. In the second half of 1998, every department did a self-assessment. Two department managers prepared a workshop for the engineers of the production departments and the Technical Department. This workshop was planned for spring 1999.

Training of employees

The formal training of operators was focused on the general principles of technical systems. This training was rounded off with an examination. Specific technical training was done informally 'on the job'. Colleagues trained a newcomer. In practice, the specific know-how of operators on the shop floor appeared to be too low. It was concluded that more attention had to be paid to the specific technical training of employees. During benchmarking of an English factory a workable system for training and certification was discovered. In the course of 1998 this system was worked out in detail for the Aachen factory. In 1999, this system was used for the design of the training program.

The voice of the customer

Higher management regularly insisted that the voice of the customer had to be present in the production areas. During the world-class manufacturing meeting the importance of the voice of the customer was discussed. It was agreed that customer-related data would be discussed in the meetings of the self-managing teams. It was also agreed to make whiteboards. The management team of the factory regularly looked at the various whiteboards and discussed the information displayed. In practice, the white boards were often not up to date.

> *Reflection.* Generally, the existence of whiteboards with essential information about the customers is seen as clear evidence of customer orientation – especially if these boards are designed and up-dated by the operators and/or middle management. The existence of such boards gives a good impression to visiting customers and auditing higher management. Furthermore, in most quality programs – this also holds for the Philips Quality Award – the existence of such boards is an important criterion for

meeting the standards. Therefore, the management team decided that every depart-ment had to make such a board. In addition, the information displayed had to be dis-cussed regularly with the crew. However, the top-down approach did not provoke a bottom-up process. The boards were kept up-to-date as long as management checked them. Further, the boards were also updated just before a customer visit or manage-ment audit. The whiteboards were not 'alive'; operators and middle management did not own them. This story clearly illustrates the limitations of a top-down approach in the Aachen Glass Factory. It was nearly impossible to implement an improvement in a top-down process. A management-induced improvement lasted as long as the man-agement checks were done. In Aachen, however, an improvement could only be im-plemented effectively if the employees were convinced; without conviction it was doomed to fail.

Discipline on the shop floor

The discipline of employees on the shop floor left a lot to be desired. The standard operating procedures were often not followed and out-of-control action plans were seldom applied. Shortcomings were regularly observed during audits.

In the world-class manufacturing meetings in autumn 1998 this item was discussed intensively. Every department manager explained how he checked and controlled discipline. A 'best practice' was analysed in more detail. It appeared that a daily check of the working methods of the operators was crucial. This daily check had to be done both by middle management and engineers. Most departments did not have a daily check. Non-conformant methods of working were more or less accepted. Easily, middle management and engineers 'understood' that the employ-ees had no time to work according to the agreed procedures.

The discussion about discipline resulted in a description of the expected behav-iour of middle management and engineers. It was decided that department manag-ers would audit each other with respect to this point. In January 1999 the first department was audited. A schedule for other departments was made.

> *Reflection*. In this anecdote a basic paradox in the Aachen culture comes to the fore. On the one hand, everybody knew that it was essential to work according to the standard operating procedures and the out-of-control action plans. On the other hand, everybody knew that the employees often ignored the procedures and action plans. However, the shift leaders, line managers and department managers took this for granted. They did not take any action. In this way they endorsed this non-compliance. In other words, everybody pussyfooted around each other.
>
> Time after time, I ran into this problem. I regularly carried out checks myself. In case of deviations I took action. This type of actions did not result in a lot of pro-gress. I have to point out that I did not use any threat of disciplinary measures because I was afraid that such a threat would lead to 'window dressing' and to hold-ing back information. Therefore, I decided to problematise this paradox in the world-class manufacturing meeting. I hoped that the department managers would be convinced that a daily check would be an essential step in improving performance. Internal audits were agreed to learn from each other. In a production environment the existence of such a paradox is fatal. It hampers every improvement. Why does

everybody beat around the bush? Why were my initial checks not enough to convince department managers? Why were internal audits   necessary? These questions will be addressed in the evaluation (section 3.7).

Elements of the Philips Quality Award
In the introduction to this case I have discussed company-wide programs to improve the performance of the whole organisation. One of these obligatory programs was the Philips Quality Award process. In the world-class manufacturing meeting several elements of the Philips Quality Award for process management in the nineties were worked out. This program is described in section 3.4 of this chapter.

3.3.6 Further progress
In 1999 the world class manufacturing program was further deployed and formalised. Every production department (including the Technical Department) defined their own program. Targets were agreed. The progress was reviewed bi-monthly by myself. In this review the 'top 7' of the department were present (department manager, line managers, quality manager, and technologists).

3.4 The Philips Quality Award program

In the nineties, Philips started an important quality drive under the name 'Philips Quality Award for process management in the nineties' (PQA-90). The aim of this program was 'to stimulate organisations to engage in a regular and systematic evaluation of their improvement activities and results through self-evaluation, peer audit and management assessment'.[174] The program set a reference for assessing the performance of the organisation in quality improvement. Every Philips organisation had to participate in this program.

In the Philips Quality Award process the organisation is judged against six categories: (1) Role of Management, (2) Improvement Process, (3) Quality System, (4) Relationship with Customers, (5) Relationship with Suppliers, and (6) Results. For example, in the 'Role of Management' category, the following elements have to be scored in the cluster 'Provide leadership and set conditions':

1. Management team members guide the planning and control of improvement activities and lead quality improvement teams.
2. Achievement of improvement objectives is taken into account in the performance appraisal.
3. Every employee is given the opportunity and encouraged to participate in organised quality improvement activities.
4. Management acknowledges the accomplishments of teams and/or individuals in achieving significant results in quality improvement.

---

[174] *PQA-90 Auditors' Scorebook*, Philips Corporate Quality Bureau, 1995, p3.

5.	Employees report that the recognition process is visible, helpful and effective.
6.	The Philips Quality Policy is communicated to all employees. Employees are familiar with it and understand the intent of the Policy.
7.	The progress of team activities is regularly reported through bulletin boards, newsletters, team minutes, etc.

Two different types of scoring are used.[175] The first type of scoring is element scoring. In element scoring the individual elements are scored in three values: red, yellow and green. The scoring of all elements is summarised. This summary provides a measure of the level of achievement relative to the standard. The second type of scoring is cluster scoring. A cluster of elements is judged as a total against the perspectives 'approach' and 'deployment'. 'Approach' is defined as 'how the auditee has planned and tried to implement the requirement' and 'deployment' as 'how widely and pervasively the principles have been applied throughout the organisation'.[176] The two different types of scoring are used to assist the process of forming an opinion, making a balance, and passing a judgement.

Managers were trained to apply the audit procedure in a consistent manner. In addition, managers were expected to participate in peer audits.

3.4.1 Pre-peer audit
The management team of the Aachen Glass Factory decided to ask for a pre-peer audit to determine the current state of play. This audit was done in January 1997. The results of the element scoring are presented in Figure 3.10. The results were below target in all categories. The scoring on the 'Role of Management' and 'Results' categories was especially low. This result meant that all processes within the organisation (management processes, improvement processes, quality processes, and so on) were not clearly defined and managed.

	pre-peer audit 1997			peer audit 1998		
Category	red	Yellow	green	red	yellow	green
Role of Management	7 %	60 %	33 %	0 %	26 %	74 %
Improvement Process	3 %	36 %	61 %	0 %	26 %	74 %
Quality System	7 %	40 %	53 %	0 %	7 %	93 %
Relationship with Customers	0 %	25 %	75 %	0 %	4 %	96 %
Relationship with Suppliers	0 %	45 %	55 %	0 %	21 %	79 %
Results	15 %	62 %	23 %	0 %	50 %	50 %
Total	5 %	43 %	52 %	0 %	21 %	79 %
Standard	<5 %		>80 %	<5 %		>80 %

Figure 3.10: Results of PQA-90 audits (element scoring)

---

[175]	For details see PQA-90 Auditors' Scorebook, Philips Corporate Quality Bureau, 1995, p7-12.
[176]	PQA-90 Auditors' Scorebook, Philips Corporate Quality Bureau, 1995, p10.

In February 1997, multi-disciplinary and multi-level teams[177] were set up to improve the processes underlying the categories (1) to (5). These teams also covered the corresponding issues of category (6). In October 1997, it was decided to focus all efforts on the improvement of the yield in the factory and on the quality of the products delivered to the customer. All teams were dissolved.

Reflection. In my opinion, the multi-disciplinary and multi-level teams were not very fruitful. First, these teams did not contribute to a change in mindset. Most members of these teams showed up because they had to show up. They were not convinced that this process would help the glass factory. In the corridors a staff member said to me: "Why do we continue this foolishness? It does not help the financial results of the organisation". However, in the official meetings of these teams such type of criticism was not expressed. Second, these teams did not contribute to an improvement in the quality of the organisation. There was no structure to deploy proposals of the team in the whole organisation.

Reflection. This experience confirms the paradox identified in section 3.2.6. Despite all discussions, a joint language with a coherent pattern of meaning about the Philips Quality Award process did not develop. In the teams many items were discussed but a real dialogue did not take place. The absence of a coherent pattern of meaning paralysed the whole organisation. In fact, there was no breeding ground for such a program.

3.4.2 Peer audit

The management team of production decided in February 1998 to restart the Philips Quality Award process for the factory. In four months time all categories had been worked through. In the weak areas some improvement actions were defined and implemented.

Reflection. The reasons to start the PQA-90 process in the management team of the factory were three-fold. Firstly, in this team, the managers of all production departments (including the Technical Department) were present. The drive to use the PQA-90 standard to improve the factory had to come from them. They had to develop the right mindset. They had to enforce changes in their departments. Secondly, I hoped that by using the PQA-standard, weak areas in the factory could be identified and improvement actions could be implemented. Thirdly, I expected that in due time the PQA-90 process would be started up again. Taking the initiative, I wanted to prevent (unrealistic) targets from the management team. Finally, it was a signal to the management team that the factory took the Philips Quality Award process seriously. Or − negatively formulated − it would protect the factory against any reproaches from the management team that quality issues were not being given the right attention.

---

[177] A multi-disciplinary and multi-level team means that representatives of different disciplines (e.g. management, engineering, and the workers council) and different levels (e.g. plant manager, department manager, shift leader and operator) were present.

In June 1998, the (new) plant manager restarted the Philips Quality Award process for the whole plant. A half-day workshop was organised. In this workshop the management team and the department managers were present. The original target was reconfirmed: to pass the peer audit in December 1998. A self-evaluation was done. New category teams were installed.

In addition, just after the first workshop, the management team of production decided to discuss all Philips Quality Award activities in the world-class manufacturing meeting.[178] In this meeting, the action points defined by the different category teams were discussed and implemented in the production departments.

In November 1998 a second half-day workshop was organised. In this workshop the progress was discussed. Also the peer audit was prepared.

> *Reflection.* The team that was chaired by the plant manager did not meet. The plant manager – together with a staff member (ironically, the same one who had questioned the preceding year the 'foolishness' of the whole PQA-process, see above) – prepared a list of improvements which had to be implemented. In the following meeting of the management team these action points were allocated to the different members. The action points were worked out. Some of them were implemented before the peer audit. Others were planned shortly after the audit. However, the implementation of these improvements was short lived. Half a year after the audit they had come to a dead end. The story of this list of improvements shows – again – the difficulty of implementing improvements in Aachen in a purely hierarchical way.

In December 1998 a team of six peers audited the Aachen Glass Factory.[179] The audit took three days. The results of the element scoring are also presented in Figure 3.10. Great improvements were realised in all categories. However, the results for the 'Role of Management" and 'Results' categories were again relatively weak. The total score was 0 % in red, 21 % in yellow, and 79 % in green. The audit team identified the following strengths:

o   "Members of the management team are really guiding and leading improvement actions;
o   The use of professional improvement tools is evident at all levels;
o   A change from product-related to process-related control is visible;
o   A broad participation of employees in all levels and in all shifts is evident."

The following opportunities for improvement were identified:

---

178   For political reasons, the name of the meeting was changed from 'world-class manufacturing meeting' to 'Philips Quality Award/world-class manufacturing meeting'.
179   The pre-peer audit of January 1997 covered production, development and staff departments. The peer audit of December 1998 covered the production and the staff departments. The lead auditor was the plant manager of a tube factory, one of our most important customers.

o   "The targets of the management team are not realistic;
o   Technical processes are not completely under control;
o   Six out of eight key processes are not described in detail."

The score for the greens was slightly below standard. Taking into account the speed of the improvement process, the audit team decided that the Aachen Glass Factory passed the requirements for the peer audit. They expressed their confidence that the weak areas would be improved in the short-term, which would mean that the organisation could apply for a management audit.

Reflection. The auditors had a friendly approach. They asked for examples of improvements in the different categories. The manufacturing organisation 'sold' itself well. It showed a lot of examples that met the requirements. We had a bit of luck with the interviews. The auditors interviewed employees with a positive mindset. (I am quite sure – although I have no hard evidence – that the department managers did some 'preliminary work' to prevent the auditors from meeting operators with a negative mindset). In my opinion, the audit result clearly showed that the approach of the factory to improve the quality of the organisation was quite professional. However, with respect to the deployment the picture was too flattering.

3.5 Problematising responsibility and accountability

In the course of my assignment as factory manager it became more and more clear that the processes on the shop floor had to be significantly improved.

Reflection. In January 1998 I discussed the Aachen case with Professor Den Hertog and Professor Schuurman. I explained to them the existence of paradoxes and managerial short cuts on the shop floor and the difficulties to improve the performance of the organisation. I complained about the lack of clarity in the processes on the shop floor and about the powerlessness of the whole organisation. I mentioned the frustration and mistrust of the employees. I also told them about my search to find the 'key' to solve these problems.

The debate concentrated on the ideas about paradoxes, responsibility, power, domination, hierarchy, and morality. It was suggested that the core of this issue was the relation between responsibility and accountability. Apparently, in the Aachen factory, responsibility was reduced to accountability. This means that employees were held accountable for their performance even though management had not fulfilled the necessary conditions. As a result, employees tried to protect themselves against the reproaches from management by creating a lack of clarity and by inducing non-transparency. It was suggested that the observed phenomena were inherent to a culture that is characterised by domination, mistrust and hierarchy.

I experienced this discussion as an 'Aha Erlebnis'. I had the feeling that the concepts of 'responsibility' and 'accountability' could be helpful in understanding the observed phenomena. Furthermore, these ideas could also function as the key to tackling the problems of the glass factory.

It was decided that my study had to be focused on phenomena on the shop floor, the processes of responsibility and accountability, and new production concepts. I especially had to focus on the structural and cultural conditions that have to be fulfilled by management so that employees can bear responsibility and can be held accountable.

From that point on, I intentionally changed my use of words. I practised the words 'responsibility' and 'accountability' to characterise the problems on the shop floor. I asked middle management about the conditions needed for employees to bear responsibility. I asked them about the lack of clarity and non-transparency. I also asked them how and when they held employees accountable. At the same time, I brought the style of management up for discussion.

The words 'responsibility' and 'accountability' slowly became part of the daily vocabulary. They were used in informal discussions, the world-class manufacturing meeting, the meeting of the management team of the glass factory, and in workshops.

3.5.1 Problematising in the production departments

The concepts of 'responsibility' and 'accountability' were made operational for the first time in a workshop with the department manager, technicians and the shift leaders of the tool shop. They accepted the detailed elaboration of these concepts. The background of the workshop, discussions about responsibility and accountability, and the follow-up is described in section 3.6 of this chapter.

I used the results of this workshop to structure the discussion about 'responsibility' and 'accountability' with other department managers. In the Pressing Screens department the discussion about the responsibility and accountability of operators was raised during the redesign process of the organisation. A workshop was organised to prepare the crew to run the factory without shift leaders. For this workshop the activities, responsibilities and authority of employees were described. In the Finishing Screens department the topic 'responsibility' and 'accountability' was raised two times.

> *Example.* The topic of 'responsibility' and 'accountability' was raised during a discussion about the quality of the sorting process. It appeared that there were too many reject products slipping through to the customer. The problem was analysed in detail. It was found that the performance of the individual sorters was known (by sampling the flow of products delivered to the customer). However, this data was not discussed with the sorters and was kept in a drawer. In other words, the sorters were not held accountable for their performance. It was decided that this information would be discussed on a regular basis with the individual employees. At the same time, improvement targets were agreed with employees with a below-average performance. The results were amazing. Only by giving feedback – i.e. holding employees accountable – the slip through of reject products to the customer decreased by a factor of more than two.

Example. The topic of 'responsibility' and 'accountability' was raised during a discussion about quality. It was found that the quality of the slurry for the polishing process was not controlled by the employees. In practice, this part of the process was neglected. I decided to give the first version of the tool shop case study (as described in section 3.6) to the department manager. I later discussed the meaning of the concepts of 'responsibility' and 'accountability' with him. It was concluded that an important condition for responsibility was not realised, namely training. It was decided that all employees of the polishing department had to be trained in technology used. Employees were trained in five sessions of two hours. The program was closed with a presentation by the department manager about responsibility and accountability. In addition, the behaviour of middle management was brought up for discussion. The technicians and shift leaders were coached intensively by the department manager.

In the Pressing Cones department I discussed the ideas of 'responsibility' and 'accountability' intensively with the department manager and line managers. The atmosphere on the shop floor was bad and the processes were not transparent. It was very difficult to find out why things went wrong. Every employee had his 'own' machine settings to operate the equipment. Standard operating procedures were often not used. Employees did not cooperate well. The department manager decided to organise a workshop for the entire crew of this department (in total eight workshops). A committee consisting of operators, shift leaders, technicians, representatives of the workers council and the department manager, prepared the workshop. I was asked to present my view about responsibility and accountability in these sessions. I used the same sheets as presented in the workshop of the tool shop (see section 3.6). After that, this view was made concrete by discussing a number of practical questions. The committee prepared these questions and their preferred solutions in advance. After the workshop, I formally discussed the follow-up with the department manager. In addition, I guided the engineers in the implementation of three out-of-control actions plans. In this process, the ideas of 'responsibility' and 'accountability' were also made concrete. I also kept up-to-date with the progress by informal discussions with the crew. Finally, in the period between September 1998 and January 1999 the ideas of 'responsibility' and 'accountability' were discussed intensively during several meetings of the management team of production in order to elucidate the meaning of these ideas.

3.5.2 Problematising in the management team of the Aachen Glass Factory
I problematised the ideas of 'responsibility' and 'accountability' for the first time in the management team meeting in November 1998. Then, an intensive discussion arose about the quality of the products delivered to the customers. It was proposed to organise a workshop about quality management with the department managers, (quality) engineers, and the management team. I proposed that in this workshop the style of management had to be discussed. I suggested that a concrete elaboration of the ideas of 'responsibility' and 'accountability' would be very helpful in changing the behaviour of middle management, engineers and operators with

respect to quality. My proposal was accepted. To prepare the workshop, I gave a shortened version of the tool shop case study to the plant manager.

> *Reflection*. I have used the tool shop case study several times to explain the phenomena in the glass factory and to give a helping hand in improvement ('management by storytelling'). Politically, it is also advisable to use 'best cases' from the own organisation.

> *Important detail*. I asked the department manager's permission before I handed over the case description to the (new) plant manager. The department manager visibly hesitated. He was afraid that he would be held accountable for the mistakes made during the improvement process. Therefore, it was agreed that I would hand over a version in which all mistakes had been taken out.

The workshop was scheduled in the first quarter of 1999. In this quarter a new engineering project was launched (see section 3.4.1) For that reason, it was decided to shift the workshop to the second quarter.[180]

3.6 The change process in the tool shop

The tool shop is a sub-department of the Technical Department. The shop delivers press tools to the Pressing Screens and Pressing Cones departments. In 1998 about 35 people were working in the tool shop: one manager, three technicians, three operators in the day shift, and four shifts consisting of one shift leader and six operators. In April 1997 the state of play in the tool shop was as follows:

o   the performance was acceptable;
o   sometimes expensive mistakes were made;
o   the rate of improvement was low;
o   no statistical process control was used;
o   many standard operating procedures were not up-to-date;
o   the housekeeping was bad;
o   two shift leaders were not performing well;
o   some employees' behaviour was unacceptable;
o   there was no annual appraisal for employees.

The events, which stimulated the change process, will be chronologically described.

---

[180] I do not know whether this workshop was held (because I left the Aachen Glass Factory on April 1st 1999). I offered my help to prepare the theme of 'responsibility and accountability'. No use was made of this offer.

3.6.1 Acceleration of the change process

In 1994 more than 40 people were working in the tool shop. At that time, several initiatives were started to improve the performance of the shop. The most important initiatives were:

o   the number of employees was reduced. Particularly those employees who had performed badly left the company;

o   the activities of the department were analysed and re-organised. Two different 'work cycles' (chain of activities) were defined: a short-term cycle and a long-term cycle. It was decided that the activities of the short-term cycle should take place in the tool shop and the activities of the long-term cycle should be partly done by an external supplier and partly by the tool shop itself;

o   a computer system to manage the data of the tools was developed. This system supported the employees in judging the quality of the tools;

o   a project to improve the lifetime of the tools was started. This project was managed by the development department;

o   the results of a company-wide survey were discussed with the crew (the Employee Motivation Survey).

All these actions contributed to a change in the mindset of the department. The department believed more and more that the state of play should not be taken as a given but that the department was capable of improving.

In 1997 several important events took place which accelerated the change process in the tool shop. The first event was the decision of the management team to start the 'Future' project (see section 3.2). One of the objectives of this project was to improve organisational processes and to reduce costs. Therefore, the processes in the tool shop came under investigation. Firstly, the activities of the tool shop were analysed. It was shown that there was some overlap with the production departments. Responsibilities were redefined. Activities were rearranged. Secondly, the process of changing the specifications of the tools was analysed. It appeared that this process was not transparent. Several parties 'owned' it: the tool shop, the development group and an outside supplier. Wrong tools were regularly made due to communication problems between the different players. The process of changing the specification of the tools was redesigned. It was decided that the tool shop should be the owner. The transfer of an employee from the development group to the tool shop accompanied this decision. Also, some hardware and software was transferred. Thirdly, two new shift leaders were appointed. In the reengineering process, the 'how' of the reduction of indirect personnel was extensively discussed. It was agreed that the performance of the employees would play an important role in this process. For that reason, it was decided to 'do away with' the shift leaders of the tool shop who did not perform well. New shift leaders were selected from the employees who were redundant in the Technical Department. These changed were finalised in the first quarter of 1998. The change in shift leaders had two effects. In the first place, better leaders were available on the shift, resulting in a better working atmosphere and a better quality of the tools. In the second place, by replacing shift leaders a signal was given to the organisation that management was willing to intervene and that poor performance was not accepted. During the change process, management continuously gave meaning to these dismissals (see below).

The second event to accelerate the change process in the tool shop was the development of a performance indicator. For many years, the communication between the tool shop and its customers had been informal. Every morning the current situation was discussed. Agreements were made verbally. No minutes were made. In the second part of 1997 it was agreed that the performance of the tool shop would be improved. As a tool a performance indicator was developed. The performance indicator contained the following points: the availability of the tools, the quality of the tools and the information exchange. In a weekly meeting the customers gave a mark to the tool shop and agreements were made about improvements.

The third event to accelerate the change process was a presentation by management to the workforce of the tool shop. The management team had decided to inform all employees of the glass factory about the results of 1997 and to deploy the plans for 1998. This presentation took place in the beginning of 1998. Every member of the management team had to lead several meetings. It was my task to inform the tool shop. Four meetings were held: one meeting for every shift. After the presentation there was time for discussion. The atmosphere in these four meetings was quite different. Two shifts asked constructive questions resulting in a lively discussion about the plans for the coming year. The two other shifts vented a lot of criticism; criticism about colleagues and about management; criticism about the equipment and the working environment. After the last meeting, a discussion arose about the atmosphere in these meetings, especially regarding the meetings in which there was a lot of criticism. The manager of the tool shop said that the operators who aired a lot of criticism were the 'black sheep' of the department. He said they had a negative influence on the atmosphere in their shift and that their performance was not very good. The manager was asked how the problem of the 'black sheep' was managed. He said that no special agreements had been made.

The last event to accelerate the change process was the start of the housekeeping program. In the beginning of 1998 the housekeeping in the tool shop was discussed. As previously mentioned, the housekeeping was bad. Tools lay around everywhere. The production area was dirty. No regular cleaning was done. A program to improve the housekeeping was proposed. In this discussion the key question was asked. What was the best way to implement this program? How to realise a change in behaviour? It was acknowledged that 'only' training was not enough.

The definitive push for a change program was given in an informal discussion between the manager of the tool shop and myself.

Reflection. I am used to discussing critical subjects at first in an informal discussion. Therefore, I sought the opportunity to discuss the events mentioned above with the manager of the tool shop. I met him in his office and a discussion arose about management, the way the tool shop was managed, and the way the shift leaders managed the operators. I asked him a lot of questions. Why do you accept bad behaviour?

Why do you accept that employees do not clean their workplace? Why do you accept that employees do not stick to the instructions? Why do you not give regular feedback on performance? The tool shop manager acknowledged that a lot of improvements were possible. However, in his opinion the situation in the tool shop was not that bad. He also made the remark that it is very difficult to change the behaviour of employees because the management has no means to enforce a change in behaviour. The arguments given by the manager of the tool shop sounded familiar. In fact, they reflected the mindset of the glass factory: 'We are good' and 'We cannot change the behaviour of our people'.

After these explanations, I concluded by saying: "you don't know how to manage and your shift leaders either." The manager was shocked by my statement. We started an intensive discussion. About management. About the responsibility of management. About the responsibility of employees on the shop floor. These points were discussed using the housekeeping program as a tool. In this discussion a lot of (rhetorical) questions were asked. How to expect improvement when the employees are not trained? How to expect commitment when the employees are not involved in the program? How to expect cleaning activities if management does not check regularly? How to change behaviour if management does not give feedback? How to improve if management does accept bad behaviour? A breakthrough was required, and this breakthrough had to start with management.

We agreed to organise a workshop to discuss these topics.

3.6.2 The first workshop

The manager of the tool shop, the manager of the Technical Department, and an external consultant prepared the workshop (the same consultant who had supported the reengineering process in the Technical Department). It was agreed that I would open the workshop with a presentation about the theme 'Responsibility and Accountability'. I discussed the set-up and the first version of the sheets with the manager of the tool shop and the manager of the Technical Department.

The workshop was held in April 1988 in a simple restaurant in the suburbs of Aachen. The manager of the Technical Department, manager of the tool shop, technicians and shift leaders were present. The consultant was also there. I gave my presentation, see Figure 3.11. Some questions were asked during the presentation. After the last sheet, a lively discussion came about. As previously mentioned, a program to improve the housekeeping had been started. During the presentation many references were made to this program to show the practical importance and

Responsibility	Giving responsibility
The supervisor gives the employee responsibility 1	The supervisor has to create the conditions so that the employee can bear responsibility 2

Conditions for bearing responsibility	
- technical training (incl. examination) - standard operating procedures, out-of-control action plans, and so on - technical tools - training in discipline, safety, and housekeeping - procedures and checklists for discipline, safety and housekeeping - communication - feedback about the results - continuous improvement 3	**Conditions for bearing responsibility** After realising the conditions: the employee can take his or her responsibility 4

Accountability

The supervisor holds his or her employee accountable for the results

5

Conditions for accountability	Accountability
Individual discussion: - if the employee has done a good job: appraisal - if the employee has done a bad job: discuss the problem and take improvement actions Group discussion: - if the group has done a good job: appraisal - if the group has done a bad job: discuss the problem and take improvement actions 7	The supervisor has to create the conditions so that the employee can be held accountable 6
	Conditions for accountability
	When the supervisor has created the conditions, the employee can be held accountable 8

Consequences

Good performance:
- recognition
Bad performance:
- improvement actions, e.g. training
- if no improvement: warning
- if no improvement: dismissal

9

Figure 3.11 Sheets of the presentation: 'Responsibility and Accountability'

294

to elucidate the ideas. Generally, there was no discussion about the basics of responsibility and accountability. Everybody agreed that the presented approach was practical. Everybody agreed that line management had to work according to this approach. The main question was: how to best implement this program in Aachen? The background to this question was the mindset, which has been referred to above: 'We cannot change the behaviour of our people'. Rather quickly, the discussion centred on the questions of accountability and its consequences. I was told that it was not possible to threaten employees with disciplinary measures because of the juridical position of the employee. For that reason, it was very difficult to hold an employee accountable. I was also told that it was not possible to threaten employees with disciplinary measures because in the past the way of acting of management in case of labour disputes was weak. I emphasised that the process of 'holding employees accountable' has to start with friendly discussions about the performance of the employee, the expectations of management, and agreement about improvements. I also said to them that threatening employees with disciplinary measures is seldom necessary. Finally, I told them that in the case of very stubborn employees – who did not change their behaviour after several discussions and official reprimands in written form – I was prepared to go to court. I reminded the people present of the last reorganisation of the Technical Department, in which employees who had performed badly left the company. I closed the discussion with the words:

> "I have given you a presentation. I have discussed the problems with you. I will come back to this issue. Then I will ask you: What did you do with my presentation? How far are you with the implementation? If you have any problems, please call for help."

After these words, I left the workshop.

> *Reflection.* I left the workshop with the feeling that not all the people were convinced that changes could be implemented in the glass factory. I had the feeling that doubt still dominated.

> *Comments from the external consultant.* Before the workshop, I had asked the external consultant to make observations during my presentation, during the discussion and after my leaving. He told me afterwards: "The management and the technicians listened with an active attitude. They regularly nodded their head to approve your comments (...) In my opinion, they understood your message about responsibility and accountability. Basically, they agreed about it. The discussion after your presentation was critical. However, the atmosphere was quite constructive. They did not question the content of your presentation but questioned the implementation. They had a lot of doubts about the support of higher management (...) During dinner the discussion also circled around the problem of implementation. The shift leaders were not convinced that they would be backed by management (...) In these discussions the manager of the tool shop referred several times to the reengineering process in the Technical Department. He emphasised that the management took the lead, resulting in the dismissal of the two shift leaders. The manager of the tool shop had got some

confidence in the process. However, doubt was still there (...) My conclusion is that the change process really has been started. You have to take the doubts of shift leaders and the technicians seriously. Continue to give messages to the crew that bad behaviour will not be accepted. And, ... walk your talk!"

3.6.3 Follow-up of the workshop

Several weeks after the workshop, I had an official review with the manager of the tool shop. I asked him about his feelings about the workshop, his beliefs in the change process, and the deployment of the policy. I asked him: Do you understand the sheets? Do you fulfil the conditions? Do you behave accordingly? The answer of the tool shop manager was clear:

> "I do understand the sheets presented (...) I do agree with the contents (...) Not all the boundary conditions are met. We especially have to improve the standard operating procedures, the training of the employees, and the communication and the improvement cycle."

The following agreements were made:

o   the discussion and the agreed actions would be recorded in a report;
o   the tool shop manager would carry out the same type of review with his technicians and shift leaders. This review would also be recorded;
o   the tool shop manager would discuss the topic of 'Responsibility and Accountability' with the employees of the shop floor;
o   after two months these agreements would be evaluated.

After about four weeks, I received the reports of the reviews of the tool shop manager with the technicians and the shift leaders. These reports showed that the tool shop manager had reviewed the workshop in exactly the same way as I had done with him.

Two months later, I again had a formal discussion with the tool shop manager. The actions of the previous discussion were reviewed. These actions had been accomplished. The current situation was discussed. I asked him the following questions. Do the technicians, the shift leaders and the employees understand that it is serious? Do they understand that bad behaviour will not be accepted? Are the conditions realised? Are the standard operating procedures up-to-date? What about the training? What about the communication? What about the improvement process? These questions were discussed using the housekeeping improvement process as a vehicle (see below). The conclusion was that the discussion about responsibility and accountability with the employees had to be intensified. It was agreed that the shift leaders would have an individual discussion with every employee. It was also agreed that the personnel department had to be involved in this process. From this discussion a report was made.

> *Reflection.* A remark has to be made. Up until that point, the personnel department was not involved in the change process. The reason for that was as follows. This

296

department focused their activities on personnel administration. They had no experience with organisational development. I did not expect any positive contribution from them in the first phase of the change process. In my view, the time was now ripe to involve this department.

I later had an informal discussion with the manager of the tool shop about the follow-up. In his opinion, it was the right time to have a second workshop. The objective of this workshop should be the evaluation of the change process in the tool shop. The policy that had been deployed in the first workshop had to be reviewed formally.

3.6.4 The housekeeping program

At the same time, a project to improve the housekeeping in the tool shop had been started. It was decided that the so called 5S-approach (see section 3.5.5) would be applied. First, the whole crew would be trained in the principles of this approach. After that, every employee would become a member of an improvement team to bring these principles into practice in their own workplace. The management would coach the housekeeping teams.

As a result of a misunderstanding, only half the crew of the tool shop was trained. The tool shop manager decided to continue with the 5S-program and to train the other half in the future. Several improvement teams were started. However, these teams made no progress. There was opposition in the department. Several weeks later, there was a formal review. I was informed that the improvement teams had made no progress. It took a long discussion to get to the root cause of the problem. The tool shop manager told me about the opposition to the 5S-program. It appeared that the employees, who were not trained, obstructed the cleaning work of their colleagues. They laughed at them. They backed out of the cleaning activities. The management of the tool shop 'accepted' this behaviour and did not intervene.

The mechanisms behind these problems were extensively discussed. The decision was taken to restart the housekeeping process. The other half of the crew was trained. Every employee became a member of an improvement team. The manager of the tool shop, shift leaders and technicians were instructed on how to handle opposition. I decided to support the housekeeping process by visiting the shop floor. In one week, I visited the tool shop every day. I spoke with the employees of every shift. I asked them about the 5S-training, improvement teams and activities already done. Some employees reacted sceptically. They said that they did not expect a big improvement. Other employees were positive. They had the feeling that something was changing. And, ... they had a say in it! I used these discussions on the shop floor to reconfirm the policy. In an informal way I told the employees that housekeeping was very important to me. I told them that I expected everybody would cooperate. And, between the lines, I conveyed the message that I would not accept any opposition.

During these visits I was told that everyone was pulling together. In one shift I heard a nice story. One employee was refusing to do any housekeeping activities (as he had done in the past). His colleagues discussed this problem with one of the technicians. The technician took the employee aside and talked with him. Surprisingly, the employee did his share in the housekeeping activities from that point on. Several days later, I met this technician in the canteen. I asked him what had happened. He told me that he had said to the unwilling employee that the manager of the tool shop and the factory manager had approved the housekeeping program. This meant that if he refused to do his part, he had to deal with the consequences.

Additionally, management gave a strong signal to the crew that the housekeeping program was serious. One of the improvement teams had asked for some racks to store the tools and materials in a proper way. These racks were quite costly. I arranged for the budget to be approved within several days.

The housekeeping program was quite successful. The progress was evaluated in the second workshop (see below). At that point, the housekeeping program was halfway through the program. In March 1999, the tool shop passed the management audit. A member of the management team presented a certificate. Every employee got a souvenir: a watch with a logo symbolising the 5S program and the Aachen Glass Factory.

> *Reflection.* During the execution of the housekeeping program I visited the shop floor regularly. I got the feeling that the employees were not convinced about the program. Many of them expected it to blow over. For that reason, between the lines I conveyed the message that I would not accept any opposition. Later, the tool shop manager told me how my message got across: "Your message was interpreted as a threat. And quite as an empty threat. They saw you as another manager who threatened them (...) However, after some time your message was taken seriously. Two events contributed to that: the dismissal of the two shift leaders and the discussion between the technician and the operator who refused to take part in the cleaning. These events were interpreted as: 'It's serious now'."

> *Reflection.* My intention was to indirectly convey the message: 'it's serious'. However, this message was interpreted as a threat. I did not realise that. I also did not expect it. I am quite sure that I have made a lot of similar misinterpretations in Aachen. Looking back, I did not sufficiently take into account the meaning such messages could hold in a culture characterised by mistrust and frustration.

> *Reflection.* The resistance to the housekeeping program shows a well-known paradox. In a culture characterised by mistrust and frustration, management will never convince all employees of the necessity of the change. This means that at a certain moment management has to use its power to enforce changes. However, the use of power usually reinforces mistrust and frustration. Management has to operate very carefully to tackle this paradox. Generally, this paradox can only be overcome by using managerial power at the point at which most of the employees are convinced that the change is also in their personal interest. In the case of housekeeping that is not so difficult.

3.6.5 The second workshop

The second workshop took place in December 1998 in the same restaurant in the suburbs of Aachen. The manager of the Technical Department, the manager of the tool shop, and the shift leaders and technicians of the tool shop were present. The attendants used the first part of the day to evaluate the state of play and to agree on the next steps to be taken. The second part of the day was used for a formal review.

Later in the day, I joined the workshop. After showing the common courtesy, I reminded the people present of my closing words of the first workshop: that I would come back to ask them what they had done with my message. I summarised the key points of my earlier presentation by using the original overhead sheets.

The first key point, which was discussed, was housekeeping. The progress in the various improvement teams was reported. More than half of the work was done. It was expected that the program would be finalised within two months. I asked the shift leaders individually whether all employees cooperated wholeheartedly. Two shift leaders reported that there were no problems. The program was accepted. Two shift leaders reported that some employees performed the assigned tasks reluctantly. However, they said they did not need any help with this and that they would handle it themselves.

The second key point was responsibility and accountability. The conditions necessary for employees to bear responsibility and to be held accountable were discussed. The first item was the standard operating procedures. These procedures had been up-dated. A schedule to review the procedures had been agreed. The second item was the compliance with the standard operating procedures – especially regarding the procedures for the production of tools and the procedures with respect to safety and the environment. I asked every shift leader whether his crew stuck to the procedures and whether he needed any support. Improvements were reported – especially, in the shifts with the new leaders. The importance of the procedures was understood. The 'black sheep' had reconciled themselves with the situation: they 'were making the best of a bad job'. The third item was training. Until that point, the employees were trained functionally, which means they were trained in the execution of tasks using certain machines. It was acknowledged that employees had to be trained in a process-oriented way, which means executing all the tasks necessary to finish a tool. The general structure of the training program had been designed. A more detailed program was being prepared. The fourth item was communication on the shop floor. Some processes were functioning quite well. The shift change took place smoothly. The 'Bumerang' had been explained to the employees.[181] Other processes had to be improved. Daily communication was ad hoc.

Finally, the communication in the tool shop was discussed. As a result of the first workshop, the manager of the tool shop, technicians and the shift leader

---

[181] The 'Bumerang' was a leaflet with information on the glass factory from management. This leaflet was distributed monthly. Middle management had to explain the content verbally to the employees. If there was important information an extra 'Bumerang' was distributed.

present met each other every morning at eight o'clock – the so-called 'morning prayer'. Technical problems were discussed and alterations in the planning agreed. The topics and agreements of these meetings were recorded, so that the leaders of the afternoon and the night shift were also informed.

I closed the workshop. I complimented the attendants on the progress made. I told them that the progress was clearly visible on the shop floor. I expressed my confidence in the implementation of all elements of the policy.

> *Reflection.* The workshop was closed with a beer and dinner. While we were drinking our beer, I told the manager of the tool shop that I had noticed quite a big change in atmosphere. The first workshop was characterized by doubts. The second workshop radiated confidence. He commented: "Maybe, your impression of the first workshop was too negative. But, you are right. There is a big change." I asked him about the 'why' of this change. He answered: "During the housekeeping training we told the employees that it was serious. After some time, we started having talks with individual employees who showed unacceptable behaviour. We told them that if they did not change, they had to deal with the consequences. These talks made it clear to the people that what management was saying was serious. That's the key."

During the change process one employee decided to leave the tool shop. In his view, the requirements of management had become too high. Other employees changed their behaviour to an acceptable level. It was not necessary to take any disciplinary measures.

3.6.6 Other improvements
Parallel to the workshops and the housekeeping process the following improvements took place:

o   the continuation of improvements for the internal customer;
o   the starting up of statistical process control under the guidance of an external consultant;
o   a program to start up the mini-company process was being prepared.

3.6.7 Performance of the tool shop
The performance of the tool shop gradually improved. Firstly, the number of press tools that were rejected within one hour after mounting, decreased steadily, see Figure 3.12. Secondly, customer satisfaction increased. The performance of the tool shop was measured on a weekly basis. In the period between mid-1997 and the beginning of 1999 a steady increase in customer satisfaction was reported, as can be seen from Figure 3.13 and Figure 3.14.

Zero Hour reject plungers

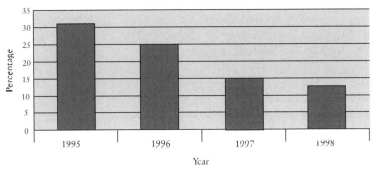

Figure 3.12 Zero hour rejects per year in the Pressing Screens Department

Performance Indicator of the Tool Shop
with respect to Pressing Screens

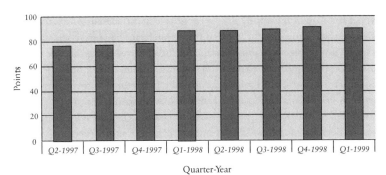

Figure 3.13 Performance indicator of the tool shop with respect to the Pressing
Screens department

Performance Indicator of the Tool Shop
with respect to Pressing Cones

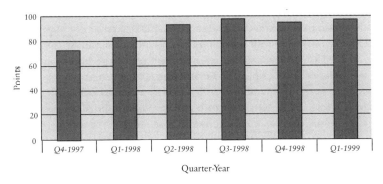

Figure 3.14 Performance indicator of the tool shop with respect to the Pressing
Cones department

301

3.6.8 Member check

In March 1999, I asked the manager of the tool shop to read the case description of the change process in his department. An appointment was made. An intensive discussion followed. The manager of the tool shop explained his intentions, expressed his feelings and reinterpreted the case:

"When you told me about the case description, I felt uneasy. Why did you use my department as a guinea pig? I was a bit angry. However, when reading the case, my irritation rapidly disappeared. For me, it was very helpful to go through the different parts of the change process once again (...) I started as a manager in the tool shop in 1994. I found this department in a poor condition. The technical processes were not under control. Data processing was not automated. The employees were poorly trained, neglected the procedures, and needed a lot of support. Also the motivation of the crew was low (...) I started very enthusiastically. My objective was to change the tool shop into a professional organisation. In my view, the control of the technical processes and the processing of the technical data were the first priorities. We started several improvement projects. These projects have been completed and implemented (...) In my experience, it is rather easy to implement new technologies in the tool shop. However, it is very difficult to change the behaviour of the people (...) In the discussions with you, I got the feeling that you saw me as a weak manager who could not implement changes on the shop floor. That's not true. From the beginning, I did not like the behaviour and the motivation of the employees on the shop floor. However, I could not change it (...) My experience was that I did not have enough power. Despite my hierarchical position, I could not enforce a change in the behaviour of employees and an improvement in the organisation (...) The position of the workers council was very strong. They always backed the employees. The personnel department always sided with the workers council. This means that in every discussion about personnel the score was three to one: the employee, the workers council and the personnel department on one side and myself on the other side. Every manager has had this experience. Every manager has lost these types of discussions. For that reason, my power to change the behaviour of employees was very limited (...) The workers council regularly refused permission to implement organisational improvements. Also, the personnel department did not me give enough support to realise these improvements (...) In one year, the situation has been changed. Life of management has become much easier. The workers council is more constructive. The personnel department is supporting us more and more. The behaviour and performance of employees can be discussed. The dismissal of two shift leaders has been interpreted by the crew that it is now serious. We focus on the real problems. We do not spend any time on problems created by employees[182] (...) The

---

[182] The expression 'creating a problem' has a specific background. In the Aachen Glass Factory a lot of agreements were made between the workers council and management about the working conditions. Most agreements described an 'ideal' situation. In practice, management did not adhere strictly to these agreements. Firstly, because everyday practice was more complicated than the 'ideal' situation described in the agreement. This means the acceptance of such agreements automatically implied a

housekeeping program had a positive influence on the motivation of the employees. They had influence on the organisation of their own workplace. They could celebrate this success".

Reflection. The member check as such speaks for itself. I would like to make two comments. Firstly, this member check shows the importance of storytelling ('it was very helpful to go through the different parts of the change process again'). Secondly, it shows that my words were interpreted differently to how I intended them ('I got the feeling that you saw me as a weak manager'). This phenomenon has also been reported in a reflection in section 3.6.4.

3.6.9 Conclusion

The change process in the tool shop was quite successful. Some elements of this process were planned, others happened by chance. Different actors played a role. The result was a change in culture and a breakthrough in performance. Key factors in this change process were the right people, a participative approach, a growth in trust, and consistency in management.

The notions of 'responsibility' and 'accountability' appeared to be a valuable key to focus the attention on the conditions that have to be fulfilled by the management so that employees on the shop floor can bear responsibility and can be held accountable. During the change process in the tool shop many improvements were realised. In fact, these improvements can be characterised as creating the conditions for responsibility. In addition, management was taught the 'how' and the 'what' of holding somebody accountable. It was especially shown that holding somebody accountable was only possible if the management had fulfilled the necessary conditions.

3.7 Evaluation

The change process in the Aachen Glass Factory was a difficult process. The organisation offered a lot of resistance. Mechanisms to neutralise management

---

violation of it. Secondly, the agreement tied the hands of the department managers. This means it was difficult for them to react in a flexible way to changing circumstances. Often, violation of the agreement was the easiest way to solve the problems. Now I come to the expression 'creating a problem'. In normal situations everybody accepted (small) violations of the agreements. However, in the case of differing opinions between a manager and an operator the latter could 'create a problem' by insisting that the management stuck to the relevant agreement in every detail. Then, the operator could 'create a problem' as a diversionary tactic to prevent any discussion about his behaviour or to prevent any disciplinary measures. In such a case the department manager had no choice: if he persisted, the workers council or even the court would overrule him. The main reason why such situations could occur was that the personnel department made agreements about the working conditions without any involvement of the department managers!

initiatives were well developed. All initiatives – the 'Future' project, the world-class manufacturing program, and the Philips Quality Award process – suffered from time delays, window dressing, failing plans and a lack of commitment. The change process did not run smoothly. Nevertheless, a lot of progress has been made. The financial results improved considerably. The quality of the whole organisation greatly improved.

3.7.1 Results of the turn-around process

The objective of the reorganisations in the period between 1994 and 1999 was to realise a complete turnaround to secure the future of the Aachen plant. What did all these reorganisations bring? Let us have a look from different perspectives.

Strategic perspective. In 1995 the plant manager formulated the challenge to create a television glass business that would be integrated in the Display Component Business Group. In the period in question (between 1994 and 1999) the strategic position of the glass business was discussed intensively. It was concluded that the production of glass components did not belong to the core of the business group. More specifically, it was concluded that the glass factories had to generate the cash to fund the development of new products. This conclusion had severe consequences – especially because high investments were necessary to overhaul the glass furnaces and to renew the technical infrastructure. Two options were left. The first option was to sell the whole glass business. The second option was to enter into a joint venture with a strong financial partner. The uncertainty of the strategic position negatively influenced the turnaround process.[183]

Financial perspective. Another challenge was to improve the financial performance of the factory. In 1997, the Aachen Glass Factory realised considerable profits for the first time in its history. The Philips standard with respect to the return on net assets was nearly met. Good profits were also realised in 1998. The main contributors to the profits were the improvement of the yield, reduction in the workforce, reduction in costs, the absence of a calamity and a loaded factory. Good financial results were expected for 1999 and onwards.

'Head count' perspective. A clear target for the reduction in the workforce was formulated in the 'Future' project. This target was summarised in the slogan the 'seven-hundred-employee factory'. In the reviews in the second half of 1998 it was concluded that this objective had not been met. About 50 % of the planned reductions had been realised. The main contributors to this failure were lack of investment, lack of transparency in production processes, lack of process control, poor logistics, and lack of management involvement. New plans to realise the original target were under development.

---

[183] The discussions about the strategic position of the Aachen plant were highly confidential. Generally, no information leaked out to the organisation. However, there were a lot of rumours about the future of the Aachen plant. These rumours were fuelled by the following facts. Firstly, most of the budget applications for capital investments were not approved by the headquarters (in Eindhoven). Secondly, the crew was told that the headquarters had not (yet) confirmed the overhauling of the glass furnaces. Everybody knew that not doing the overhaul would mean the closure of the factory.

Organisational perspective. Another objective of the 'Future' project was the design of a transparent organisation. In the period between 1996 and 1999 all departments had been or were being reengineered. In the production departments and in the Technical Department clearly defined responsibilities was developed.[184] For the glass factory as a whole, the transparency in key processes had to be improved further.[185]

The world-class manufacturing perspective. From mid 1997 on, a lot of attention was paid to bringing the production organisation up to world-class standards. The policy was clearly defined. The approach to implement this policy was agreed. Good examples were present in the organisation itself. The progress in this field was acknowledged by the auditors of the Philips Quality Award. The developed policy had to be implemented in all departments.

Conclusion. In the period between 1995 and 1999 a lot of changes took place in the Aachen Glass Factory. The question about the success of the turnaround process cannot be unambiguously answered. On the one hand, successes have to be reported. On the other hand, targets were not met.

3.7.2 Two 'languages'

Language is a central element in managerial work. Language is used to give orders, to communicate, to convince, to seek support and to give meaning. Language is a key to understanding the culture of an organisation. In the Aachen factory two 'languages' were spoken.[186] The first language was a financial language. This language can be characterised by the words 'yield', 'cost reduction', 'head count reduction' and 'reorganisation'. The second language was the total quality management language. This language can be characterised by the words 'quality', 'customer orientation', 'coaching' and 'empowerment'. The first language was embodied in the 'Future' project, and the second one in the world-class manufacturing program and the Philips Quality Award process. These two languages were not the 'only' languages. Every language expressed a specific perspective on man and organisation, and had a system of meanings, values and norms. At the same time, every language forced the organisation into taking certain actions.

---

[184] The last change – the division of the production into a screen line and a cone line – was intended to further increase the organisational transparency. However, this was not the case.

[185] The following key processes were defined: 'developing new customers', 'order fulfilment', 'suppliers relationship', 'yield improvement', 'world class manufacturing', 'product/process development', 'planning to win', and the 'hoshin review process'. During the Philips Quality Award peer audit it was found that only two key processes were described in detail: 'yield improvement' and 'world class manufacturing'.

[186] Watson (1994) presents a case study of a large electronics company in his book *In Search of Management*. He reports the existence of a formal language and an informal language. In the Aachen plant both languages were formal.

The financial language

The Aachen Glass Factory was originally a bureaucratic organisation. The factory had been managed for many years in a hierarchical and bureaucratic way. For that reason, the financial language was closely connected to a culture of hierarchy and bureaucracy. In the last decade, successive plant managers showed a more participative style of management. Also, on middle management level some changes in style could be observed. The coming of the new plant manager in April 1998 meant a return to hierarchy. The historical connection between the financial language and hierarchy was reinforced.

New plant managers usually used the financial language to give a 'shock' to the organisation. The plant manager who started his job in 1994 described to me his 'maiden speech' as follows (March 1998):

> "When I came to Aachen the idea dominated that the Aachen Glass Factory would exist forever. I intentionally gave the organisation a 'shock', I threatened the organisation that the factory would be transferred to a plant in Russia if the results did not improve. The objective of this shock was that the costs would decrease and the output would increase (...) The threat ended in an emotional response: fear. The objective of the 'Future' program was to take away the fear and to paint a future perspective for the Aachen factory."

In April 1998 a new plant manager started. In his first speech for the 'top 40' of the Aachen factory he indicated the main problem areas of the plant and presented his view. His presentation was received negatively. Afterwards, he motivated his behaviour as follows:

> "I had to give a shock to the organisation."

The approach of successive plant managers was criticised sharply by the chairman of the workers council. In a discussion in March 1999 he said to me:

> "For twenty three years in a row I have heard that the Aachen factory has to be reorganised. Every year is the same. Every year announcements are made about a reduction in the head count. And nothing happens. The employees do not believe in it anymore (...)."

He also criticised the dominance of the financial perspective:

> "The threat to transfer the factory to Russia appeared to be empty. Half a year ago Philips sold that plant because of severe losses (...) Management forgets that a factory is in fact a body, a body that reacts to interventions and threats. Employees cannot work peacefully. They have the question 'When will I be dismissed?' in the back of their minds (...) The Aachen Glass Factory is characterised by lifeless ideas and inhuman thought. Management does not think of employees. The only thing that counts is the financial result. By trampling over the employees we work for the shareholders."

In the vocabulary of the financial language the term 'taking out heads' was used regularly. The implications for the employees were seldom discussed.

> *Example.* In one meeting of the management team the ethical question of reorganisation was discussed explicitly. It was proposed to outsource some non-core activities. One of these non-core activities was a daytime operation. The employees who performed this activity were employees who were not allowed to work in shifts for medical reasons. The outsourcing of these activities would imply the dismissal of these employees. A member of the management team, an old hand in the factory, remarked that in his experience the ethical responsibility of management is determined by legal regulations. With this remark he intended not to give a normative statement, but a description of the practice in the Aachen plant. In addition, he confirmed this practice: the ethical question was not discussed and the members focused on juridical possibilities and financial consequences.

The employees of the Aachen factory also very much understood the financial language. I would like to give one example. Over the years a culture had grown in which employees used the existing regulations to maximise their income. For example, the production of glass products has to continue during Christian and national holidays because a glass furnace cannot be stopped. The employees are compensated by an additional payment (one hundred to two hundred percent). Part of these payments was tax-free. It was the intention to run the factory at minimal manpower. However, on these days nearly the whole crew was present. Some employees even interrupted their holidays to 'enjoy' these days in the factory.

The total quality management language
The total quality management language was stimulated by three initiatives: the agreement to employ self-managing teams, the Philips Quality Award program, and the world-class manufacturing program.

The first initiative was an agreement between the workers council and the management team about 'self-managing teams' that was signed in August 1994.[187] This agreement described the philosophy, organisation and method of working. The philosophy was formulated as follows:

> "Self-managing teams have to be understood as organisational units, which practice the planning, control, implementation, coordination and checks of their activities in self-responsibility (...) Self-managing teams as a principle of the organisation of labour, have to be organised in such a way that facilitates enlarged elbow room and an increase in the independence of the employee."

The agreement also specified a change in the style of middle management. Coaching of employees by management behaviour was explicitly described.

---

[187] Betriebsvereinbarung 'Gruppenarbeit', Nr 2/94, August 26th 1994.

The second initiative was the Philips Quality Award. In the period between 1996 and 1998 many teams were formed to improve the quality of the organisation in order to comply with the Philips Quality Award. The key ideas of the Philips Quality Award are the role of management, style of management, quality of procedures, quality of processes, training of employees, and participation of the whole crew. This process is described in section 3.4.

The third initiative was the world-class manufacturing program, which was started in mid 1997. The key points were safety, personnel, housekeeping, self-managing teams, process control, total preventive maintenance, the training of employees, voice of the customer, and discipline on the shop floor. This program is described in section 3.3.

The total quality management language was a new language. This language reflected a different view on man and organisation. The organisation had to learn the new language and this appeared to be very difficult. Let me give two examples of this.

> *Example.* The first example has to do with the implementation of self-managing teams. The employees of the Pressing Cones department were trained in the principles of self-management in a two-day course. Middle management and the engineers received a short training. However, the introduction of self-managing teams failed. This was basically because the management and the engineers of the department did not understand the new language. They did not support the change process. Moreover, the staff department that supported the introduction of self-managing teams did not have the required skills and know-how.[188]
>
> The second example has to do with the functioning of self-managing teams. In the agreement between the workers council and management on self-managing teams, the roles of the various functions were described in detail. The function of foreman was abolished. An elected team leader would lead the team. Often the team chose the former foreman as their leader. Additionally, the shift leader was not defined as being part of the team. His role was to coach the team from a distance. In practice, two phenomena could be observed. Firstly, the team and the shift leader drifted apart. The team used their autonomy to push the coach away. In turn, the coach kept a distance from the team. However, the elected team leader who often acted in a hierarchical way filled the power vacuum that arose. Secondly, some shift leaders did not change their behaviour. They did not accept self-managing teams and their role as coach. They continued to manage their shift in a hierarchical way. In both phenomena, the original philosophy of self-management was violated and the hierarchical principles persisted in the organisation.

The challenge of the total quality management language came to the fore in the implementation of the world-class manufacturing program and the difficulties of the Philips Quality Award process. Firstly, management and middle management

---

[188] An external consultancy bureau did the training for self-managing teams. Due to financial reasons, it was decided to support the introduction of self-managing teams by an internal staff department. This staff department had no experience in change processes.

were not really trained in the principles of manufacturing excellence. Only some of them had gained experience in it in another job. The theories behind manufacturing excellence were not well known. Benchmarking was seldom done. Secondly, total quality management language presupposes openness and trust. These characteristics were absent. Mistrust and frustration governed. Stories about grievous wrongs suffered were told. The employees on the shop floor did not trust management. Therefore, they resisted the change programs. Middle management did not trust the management team of the plant. Therefore, they did not believe that management would really support them in the implementation of the world-class manufacturing program (see section 3.3.2). Finally, the financial language drowned the total quality management language. Consequently, the impact of the total quality management language appeared to be limited. The dominance of the financial language came very strongly to the fore in the member check.

> *Member check.* The 'Future' project had two objectives. Firstly, reductions in the workforce and in costs. Secondly, the design of a transparent process in order to improve the performance of the organisation. During the member check a department manager – that is: a key actor who participated in the project from the beginning – remarked that he did not know that the design of transparent processes was one of the objectives of the reengineering project. In his opinion, reductions in the workforce and in costs were the only objective. This remark showed that – although the second objective (transparent processes) was discussed many times – the financial language had left a deep mark on this manager: he did not even 'hear' the total quality management language.

In all departments – despite the resistance to the total quality management language – changes could be observed. In some cases, even breakthroughs could be reported. An example is the improvement process in the tool shop, see section 3.6. Another example is the improvement process in the 'finishing tools' shop:

> *Example.* Many 'failures' worked in the 'finishing tools' sub-department of the Technical Department; employees who for one reason or another could not keep up in their original job. The reputation of this small department was bad. The middle manager understood the principles of self-managing very well. He started a housekeeping program. The employees rearranged their own workplace. They ordered some new equipment and greatly improved the working conditions. They even came back in their own time to paint their working room. The department passed the management audit for housekeeping. At the same time, the employees took a lot of initiatives to improve performance. For example, they solved the delivery problems during the (long) weekends, and improved the quality of the tools. As a result of all these changes, the morale and the atmosphere improved every day. Within half a year the department was ready for the next step in self-management.

Unwritten rules

In the evaluation of the 'Future' project in November 1997 the external consultant reported the existence of 'unwritten rules'.[189] Unwritten rules are the informal rules that really drive the day-to-day behaviour of employees in an organisation. The consultant established that management had formally emphasised an increase in the output, an improvement of the quality and a focus on the customers. However, critical questions had to be asked. What behaviour had been rewarded? What behaviour had been criticised publicly? What behaviour had a blind eye been turned to? The consultant concluded that the management team had to dismantle the unwritten rules by changing their own behaviour. In the meeting the remarks of the consultant were touched on lightly. The plant manager concluded that in the future more attention should be given to team forming. There was no follow-up to this conclusion. Four months later the plant manager left the Aachen factory.

In my opinion, many unwritten rules originated from the conflict between the financial language and the total quality management language. The organisation had learned that there was only one priority: the financial results of the factory. The output on the one side and the costs on the other side determined this result. The improvement of quality and customer orientation was secondary.[190] The most important unwritten rule was: 'if your output and financial results are okay, you are not troubled by quality'. The behaviour of management and middle management can be understood from this rule. I would like to give an example of this:

> *Example.* Customers regularly complained about the quality of the products they received. In their opinion, the level of quality of the normal production was too low. They also criticised the recurring incidents in which a larger number of sub-standard products were delivered. In the glass factory several measures were taken to guarantee the quality level of normal production and to prevent incidents. In the pressing area and in the finishing area quality inspectors were present who had to take samples from the conveyor. These samples were inspected in detail. The sampling frequency was described in a procedure. In the second half of 1997 several quality problems arose. These problems were discussed in the management team of production. The quality manager remarked that it was difficult to understand why the quality inspectors did not report these problems. The presence of the inspectors at the line was discussed. The department managers assured us that the inspectors were always present. They questioned whether the deviations reported by the customer could be easily identified. After the meeting, the quality manager told me that he had checked the presence of the quality inspectors at the line: they were often not present. In his opinion, the department managers deliberately lied about the state of

---

[189]   The existence of unwritten rules in the Aachen organisation was identified in an informal discussion between the external consultant and myself. It was agreed that the external consultant would elaborate on this concept for the review of the management team. The expression 'unwritten rule' is from Scott-Morgan (1994).

[190]   At that point, the customers were only partly compensated for the rejects caused by glass parts. Above a certain reject level, the costs of the lost glass parts were paid. Later, the Aachen Glass Factory also had to pay the costs of added value.

play. I decided to personally check the presence of the inspectors at the line. I went to the inspectors and interviewed them about their work. It was found that the quality inspectors were regularly not present or that a lower sampling frequency was applied – especially during the evenings and at night. Then, the inspectors carried out normal production tasks in order to guarantee the output. Further, there were strong indications that the absence of the inspectors at the line led to a decrease in the quality of the sorting process (see also section 3.7.4). I discussed these findings with the department managers concerned. In their view, the absence of inspectors as observed by myself was not normal and was caused by an 'unfortunate series of events'. It was later confirmed that inspectors were used structurally for normal production work. Why was this? The use of quality inspectors for normal production led to higher efficiency. Besides that, the (expected) increase in the slip through of reject products to the customer was 'welcomed' because it led to a higher output. The organisation tacitly consented to this type of behaviour.

Another unwritten rule was that 'management initiatives, which do not contribute immediately to the output or financial results, have to be resisted'. This unwritten rule especially affected the world-class manufacturing program and the Philips Quality Award program. From the beginning, these programs suffered from time delays and failing implementations. In the opinion of the organisation, every minute spent on these programs was at the expense of the financial results of the department. Therefore, various techniques were applied to cope with these types of initiatives. 'Saying yes and doing no' was one technique, 'misunderstandings' was another one, and 'window dressing' was the third one. Through time, this behaviour weakened slowly. The importance of the world-class manufacturing program and the Philips Quality Award program for the Aachen factory was acknowledged more and more. Essential elements of this program and this process were implemented. The progress on the shop floor of the factory was widely acknowledged. However, this unwritten rule remained dormant in the background. I would like to give a striking example.

Example. In June 1998 the (new) plant manager restarted the Philips Quality Award process (see section 3.4). A workshop was organised. New teams were set up. The management team of the factory discussed how to handle the proposals from these teams. The fear was expressed that more ideas would be proposed than could be implemented. At the same time, it was believed that the plant manager would not except any delay in implementation. In the discussion the dilemma was stated as follows: "We have the capacity to implement ten proposals or to window dress fifty proposals. How to handle this 'paradox'?" The department managers proposed that we accept all improvement ideas of the teams and apply window dressing. They guaranteed that during the Philips Quality Award audit no problems would arise. The employees present would be instructed to give the right answers to the questions of the auditors. If necessary, some fake material would be prepared. I asked the departments managers why they chose for window dressing – especially as window dressing does not help the Aachen factory on its way to becoming world-class. It appeared that the proposal to window dress was inspired by fear. Nobody dared risk a confrontation with the plant manager. Everybody preferred the 'survival mode'. I said that I did not accept this proposal. I proposed that all energy had to be focused on the realisation of real improvements. I promised the department managers that I would handle the number of proposals to be implemented. In the following months it appeared that the number of proposals to be implemented in the production was acceptable. No (or nearly no) window dressing was applied.

Member check

The member check with respect to this topic was very lively. The members acknowledged the phenomena. They gave a lot of comments. The case description functioned as an eye-opener. A member of the management team of the Aachen Glass Factory remarked:

> During the first reading of this section I acknowledged the existence of the two languages. During the second reading I became aware of the importance of the split between these languages (...) In my opinion, these languages did not exclude each other because a total quality management approach will lead to a more stable production. However, in Aachen these languages did exclude each other (...) Management of the glass factory never succeeded in connecting the financial and the total quality management language. The financial language stayed dominant."

A member of the management team of the factory remarked:

> "The former plant manager set an example with respect to the total quality management approach. He took the time to discuss quality themes with us (...) However, other members of the management team did not set an example. I doubt whether all members of the management team wanted to connect both languages. In fact, some of them used the existence of two languages for their own advantage (...) The new plant manager speaks the financial language. He only pays attention to quality if it is required from a financial point of view (...) Certainly, there are two languages, and the financial one is the strongest."

An external consultant remarked:

> "The Aachen case shows that total quality management 'works'. The conditions in Aachen were bad. Nevertheless, this approach resulted in a lot of improvements (...) It was the intention of the (former) plant manager to connect the two languages in the 'Future' project. However, this attempt has failed (...) We started with a team that was not team. We started with a team that could not connect both languages. The internal relationships were bad. The ideas about world-class manufacturing were different (...) The (former) factory manager made a treaty with the department managers: if the numbers are okay, it is not necessary to pay attention to total quality management or to the sub-projects of the 'Future' project (...) The integration of the financial and total quality management language failed."

Conclusion

In conclusion, in the Aachen plant two languages were spoken: the financial language and the total quality management language. Management failed to connect these different languages. The financial language stayed dominant and determined the behaviour in the organisation.

3.7.3 Management

In every change process the role of management is crucial. Does the management really understand what happens in the organisation? Does the management balance the top-down and the bottom-up movements in the design of the reengineering process? Does the management walk its talk?

Visibility, trust and control

In the Aachen factory, the management team as a whole was not visible. For many years in a row, the factory had been managed hierarchically. A large distance between the employees and the management team was present.

The plant manager who started his job in 1994 was visible in the factory. He visited the shop floor regularly. He discussed technical and non-technical issues with the employees. Operators and middle managers mentioned his presence on the shop floor. Stories were also told about his visits:

> *Story.* The plant manager often visited the factory on a Saturday morning. When he entered the factory, phone calls were made to all production departments 'The boss is coming'. Irregularities were corrected. Employees who did not want to meet the boss, disappeared. So, the plant manager came into an artificial environment.

The new plant manager seldom visited the factory. He did not visit the shop floor. He did not speak to the people. He was only present in the production departments for official audits and for the presentations of improvement teams. I made a tour every day. I visited one or two departments and talked to the people about technical and non-technical issues. Other members of the management team seldom visited the shop floor. And when they visited, they focused on the job they had to do and did not talk a lot with the crew. The logistics manager checked the progress of the production. The quality manager did formal audits on the shop floor. The development manager checked the implementation of new products and technologies. The financial controller and the head of the personnel department never visited the shop floor.

> *Background.* In the German culture, 'visiting the shop floor' means shaking hands with the employees. This means it is more than a quick visit. An exchange of words will always take place.

The invisibility of management had two effects. Firstly, it led to a low level of trust. The employees interpreted the invisibility of the management negatively. In their opinion, management did not know what happened on the shop floor. For that reason, they could not be trusted. The low level of trust in the management is clear from the Employee Motivation Survey of 1996. This survey showed that a minority of the employees trusted the management of the location.[191] The same survey showed that a minority of the employees believed the statements of the management team.[192] The distance between management and organisation also was expressed in daily language. The management was often referred to as 'them from WC'.[193] A new plant manager and the announcement of new reorganisation led to a further decrease in trust. A department manager said in February 1999:

> "The employees have no trust in the management. The former plant manager visited the shop floor regularly. The employees knew him. He talked with them. The new plant manager never visits the shop floor. They don't know him. They don't see him They don't trust him."

A member of the workers council made the following comment:

> "The employees have no trust in the (new) plant manager. He does not speak German. He does not visit the people on the shop floor. The employees do not believe that the plant manager fights for them and for their future." Note: the new plant manager was an expatriate."

The decrease in trust was confirmed by the survey that was held in the beginning of 1999.[194]

The invisibility of the management had a second effect: the management team did not know what really happened on the shop floor. A department manager remarked:

> "Management does not know what happens on the shop floor. Therefore, management cannot control the organisation."

In quality procedures and efficiency calculations the processes on the shop floor were described in detail. However, these formal descriptions did not reflect the reality. On the one hand, big deviations were present due to variations in processes and equipment. On the other hand, the employees developed their own method of working. Many processes on the shop floor were not transparent. For example, in production small calamities occurred regularly with the result that some tens, hun-

---

[191] Employee Motivation Survey of 1996: 36 % of the employees trusted the management and 40 % of the employees did not trust the management.

[192] Employee Motivation Survey of 1996: 29 % of the employees did believe in what the management of the plant said and 54 % did not believe in what the management said.

[193] The management team, including the staff, had their office in a separate building called WC. Only the factory manager and the logistics manager had their office in one of the production buildings.

[194] The Employee Motivation Survey in 1999 was done about one month after the announcement of the reorganisation. This survey showed a further decrease in the trust in management: 16 % of the employees trusted management and 64 % did not.

dreds or thousands of screens or cones had to be rejected. In practice, it appeared to be difficult to find out what happened just before the production became out of control. Consequently, the cause of these calamities was often not identified. Analysis of the rejects often showed that the calamity was induced in one or another way by an operator. Details about who and what remained hidden. This phenomenon is understandable. In addition to mistrust, fear was also present on the shop floor. The employees were really afraid of making mistakes. For that reason, operators and shifts had an interest in keeping processes non-transparent, with the result that the organisation as a whole did not learn from failures.

Employees also developed their own method of working to create freedom of movement. This method was often not known by higher management.

> *Example.* In the Finishing Screens department the sorting of screens was an equipment-bounded activity. The operator had to take a screen from the conveyor, inspect the screen on the inside and on the outside, and finally put it on another conveyor. The total cycle was determined by the speed of the conveyor. Generally, every minute a new screen arrived. Earlier investigations had shown that one minute was the minimum time needed to handle the screen and to inspect both sides. In the night shifts and in the weekend shifts, one operator regularly inspected two screens a minute, so that his colleague could spent more time drinking coffee, reading the paper, or making private telephone calls. After some time, the former employee left his working place and the latter one took for two. Middle management knew about this method of working. They regularly made use of it. They asked the employees to work in this way in order to guarantee the numbers during the breaks. It goes without saying that this method of working had a negative influence on the quality of the sorting process. The actual inspecting time was more than halved. In this example, both operators and middle management had an interest in keeping this method hidden.

In conclusion, many processes on the shop floor were not transparent. Management did not know the processes on the shop floor. Therefore, they could not control them. This phenomenon was observed sharply by the auditors of the Philips Quality Award. First, they found that most of the key processes were not described in detail. Second, they criticised the management because the targets of the organisation were not realistic.[195] The non-transparency of basic processes was one of the causes of the difficulties of the reengineering process. The challenge of the 'Future' project was to get a detailed insight into the processes on the shop floor and to reengineer these processes. Without doubt, management underestimated the difficulties of making the basic processes transparent. Without doubt, management underestimated the power of the organisation to resist the efforts of management. Too many parties had an interest in non-transparency. In the reengineering process all parties spoke the financial language. However, the interests of the management and the workforce did not align. Therefore, the total quality man-

---

[195] The (new) plant manager did not accept this criticism. In his view, the targets were 'realistic', but 'we have to manage better'.

agement language, which is a prerequisite for making all processes transparent, did not penetrate the shop floor.

In my view, the management team as a whole did not know the basic processes in the organisation in detail. Management lived in their own world, a world that consisted of budgets, efficiency data and improvement plans. From this world, a lot of initiatives were disseminated into the production. On the one hand, these initiatives led to a lot of directed improvement actions. On the other hand, the world of management did not always connect to the reality of the shop floor. The result was that the initiatives of management missed the mark.

Management as a team

A turnaround process demands the extreme from management. These types of processes require a strong personnel commitment. These types of processes require that the management team as a whole can make their commitment clear to the organisation. However, in the management team of the glass factory a clique was present. This clique consisted of the old guard. They had gone through good and bad times. They had 'suffered' from the initiatives from new plant managers. They met each other outside working hours. Their wives also had good relationships with each other. The old guard knew how to survive. They expected newcomers to work according to their 'rules'. One of these rules was not to criticise each other.[196] On the face of it, the management team was a team. In practice, the team consisted of individuals fighting for their own future.

> *Reflection.* The decision to appoint me as factory manager in the Aachen Glass Factory was partially motivated by my style of management. In the yearly appraisals (and in the management development discussions) my style had been characterised as follows: making problems explicit, building up relationships, focused on cooperation, and refusal to play political games. Before I started my job I was informed about the atmosphere in the management team. Looking back, the results of my approach were ambiguous. On the one hand, I got the confidence of some members of the management team and the cooperation with their departments did improve. On the other hand, I did not react adequately to 'political games' resulting in a weakening of my position. For example, five months after I started a member of a staff department questioned me about my commitment to the 'Future' project. He told me that my boss had received some signals from the management team that I had struck a bargain with my department managers with respect to the reengineering program. I made a telephone call to my boss (he was at home). He confirmed that he had received some signals. I informed him about the state of play. He was satisfied with my information. I interpreted this event as an once-only event. Much later, I realised that I had made a big mistake. I should have discussed the source of the signals with my boss. I should have said to my colleagues not to play any games with me in the

---

[196] A staff member told me a striking example. During a meeting of the management team he had criticised the members of the management team. After the meeting, he was taken aside by one of the members of the old guard. He was told that it was not customary to criticise each other openly in the management team.

future. I should have …. It was not an once-only event. It was a game to weaken my position. I too often did not see what others were up to.

Generally, it can be said that newcomers had a difficult period in Aachen. A member of a staff department told me the following story:

Story. In the corridors he heard two members of the management team criticise the decision of a new colleague. The tune of the discussion made him suspicious. He asked them why they damaged the image of their new colleague. No answer was given. He told me that he got angry because he was convinced that they tried to damage their colleague. At the same time, I got several signals out of other parts of the organisation about the 'weakness' of the new colleague

The issue of 'management as a team' was discussed once. The plant manager questioned the role of the management team during the evaluation of the 'Future' project in November 1997. He concluded that this issue had to be discussed in separate meeting. However, he left the Aachen Glass Factory about four months after the evaluation.

The new plant manager also raised the issue of 'management as a team'. Under the guidance of an external consultant a one-day workshop was organised in September 1998. Every member of the management team prepared a paper in which the 'whys' of the successes and the failures of the Aachen Glass Factory were discussed. One of the goals of the workshop was to improve cooperation and to build confidence and trust. The plant manager started the workshop with a presentation about the policy of the Display Components Business Group and the position of the Aachen Glass Factory. He explained his views about management and formulated his expectations of the management team. This presentation was received well. After that, the written contributions of the members of the management team were discussed. In these contributions the limitations of the organisation were identified and the weaknesses of the management team analysed. Also, the hierarchical style of the plant manager was criticised. An open discussion followed. By the end of the day, half of the contributions of the members had been discussed in detail. Several topics had not even been touched upon. It was agreed to organise a follow-up in order to carry out analyses, to identify relevant topics, and to agree on a change process. In the next few weeks, the plant manager decided not to continue the workshop. No justification was given.

Reflection. I was very sceptical about this workshop. I told the external consultant that I did not have any confidence in it. The constructive opening of the workshop by the plant manager surprised me. Members of the management team – including the old guard – surprised me by frankly criticising the hierarchical style of the plant manager. At the end of the workshop, I told the plant manager that I appreciated his attitude during the workshop. I really believed that he would continue the workshop.

I did not question the decision of the plant manager not to continue the workshop. I interpreted his decision as a conscious choice not to invest in the management

317

as a team; and... I had learned that it would be fruitless to make an attempt to change his mind.

Reflection. This workshop shows very clearly one of the main paradoxes in the Aachen Glass Factory. On the one hand, great efforts are put into consultation, dialogue, and consensus. On the other hand, joint action, cooperation and trust did not develop.

At the beginning of 1999 I interviewed a member of the old guard informally about the management team and the change process. He made the following comments:

"In the meetings of the reengineering 'Future' project the targets were set. Every member of the management team focused on the reengineering of his own department (...) The largest part of the 'Future' project had to take place in production. However, the management team was not involved in the reengineering projects in production. The management team did not support these projects. The factory manager had to manage it on his own. He asked several times for help. However, he did not get any help. The members of the management team did not help each other (...) The organisation (department managers, middle management, engineering and operators, MJV) felt that the management team was not really committed to the 'Future' project. The organisation felt that the management team was not fully involved. In this way, a negative signal was sent out (...) Management did not set an example with respect to the agreed priorities. There were always new plans and always new priorities. One loses the overview (...) We did not give the department managers in production enough room to make decisions. We gave them conflicting targets. For example, we expected a higher yield and a lower slip through of rejects to the customer. In the short term, these objectives are conflicting. If we have priorities, we have to accept the consequences. However, we did not do that (...) The heart of the problems in Aachen is the management team. It is not a team. They do not support each other."

The interview left an ambiguous impression. On the one hand, the interviewee felt responsible for the state of play in Aachen. On the other hand, he felt a victim of the culture of the organisation. On the one hand, he chose his words carefully. On the other hand, he spoke from his heart.

Reflection. I have often questioned how to handle the unwritten rules in the factory (section 3.7.2), especially, in relation to the department managers. Did I have to dismantle these rules by taking disciplinary measures? Did I have to dismantle them in a process of dialogue and consensus? Something in my heart said that the former option was not the good one. In practice, I used the latter one. This interview made me aware of a paradox that underlies these questions. On the one hand, management can be seen as responsible actors. On the other hand, they can be seen as victims of the past.

318

In an informal discussion about the glass factory a member of the workers council said to me:

> "The management team is not a team. It is a group of people who are fighting for themselves (...) The members of the management team dig pitfalls for each other. They stab each other in the back (...) Your world-class manufacturing program has been attacked by other members of the management team. They have used their connections to make this program laughable. They gave signals to the production organisation that this policy was wrong and was not supported by the management team (...)."

The Employee Motivation Survey in 1996 showed that a minority of the employees of the Aachen Glass Factory believed that management worked as a team.[197] In the survey of 1999 this minority was even smaller?[198]

> *Reflection.* In fact, it is a bitter paradox to do an Employee Motivation Survey in a factory that is characterised by mistrust and frustration. This paradox can only be understood by the fact that the Employee Motivation Survey was a company wide survey: every organisation had to join.

Style of management

In the last decade, successive plant managers had managed the organisation in a more participative style. The start of the new plant manager in April 1998 meant a return to a hierarchical style of management. At the same time, fear developed in the organisation.

The plant manager took decisions alone. Some decisions were made after consultation with the management team. Some decisions were made without consultation with the management team. The character of the meetings of the management team drastically changed. The discussions disappeared. The corridors were full of complaints about decisions taken. In March 1999, a member of the management team said in an informal discussion to me:

> "He (the plant manager) is not open. He does not respect me. He is not interested in what I am saying. His body language says that he is not interested in the opinion of other people. He radiates that he does not want to have a relationship with his team. He does not trust us (...) I have no home in the management team. I cannot be open (...) He discusses all problems in private conversations. There is no discussion in the management team. I do not know his policy. Where is the thread? The department managers also do not know what happens. They do not see the thread."

---

[197] The Employee Motivation Survey in 1996: 21 % of the employees believed that the management worked as a team and 37 % did not believe that the management worked as a team.

[198] The Employee Motivation Survey in 1999: 13 % of the employees believed that the management worked as a team and 56 % did not believe that the management worked as a team.

In a meeting of the management team of the factory a decision of the plant manager was discussed critically. One of the members proposed to stop the discussion:

"Keep your mouth shut. We have wife and children."

In other words, beware of the consequences.

In March 1999 I appraised one of my department managers. As part of the appraisal the next job in the Aachen organisation was discussed. The department manager questioned his future:

"There is no openness in the Aachen Glass Factory anymore. Everybody is careful. I often do not know why people make certain remarks. Are there ulterior motives? (...) The management style of the new plant manager is quite different. He is managing quite hierarchically. He does not consider the ideas of middle management (...) What do I get out of hierarchy? Only critics from the workers council? I have to convince the crew. I have to get them on my side (...) What kind of management do they want? Only managers who agree with everything? You say that I have a good future in Aachen. How do they judge me? As somebody who always says 'yes'?"

The change in management style greatly influenced the behaviour of management and middle management. Openness and trust disappeared. The game of 'how to survive' became the favourite game amongst managers and middle management.

Member check
The sections about trust, the management team, and style of management led to lively discussions. In these discussions, a lot of mistrust and frustration came to the fore. A member of the management team of the Aachen Glass Factory remarked:

"In the German culture, it is not usual for management to know the processes on the shop floor in detail. This is also the case in Aachen. Management do not know what happens on the shop floor. In fact, they do not know their job (...) Once we acted as a team. However, that was only once. Acting as a team does not come easily to us (...) Some members of the management team made deals with middle management or workers. They protect each other."

An external consultant said that:

"The management team did not know what happened on the shop floor (...). The management team lived in a little world of its own. This world is more or less separated from everyday practice. The management had its own view about what was wrong in the factory, and this view was not supported by the middle management and the shop floor (...). The members of the management team did not manage as a team. In every situation they ask: 'Which risk do I run?' They act out of self-interest."

During the last member check (which was done nine months after I left the glass factory, i.e. in December 1999) the change in the management culture was clearly indicated. A department manager remarked:

> "After you left ('you' is MJV) the world-class manufacturing program and the Philips Quality Award program were stopped. The management team did not support these programs anymore. It was impossible to continue. It was even dangerous to continue. (...) They (members of the management team, MJV) try other ways, ways without a concept. They tell us what to do. They require quick-thinkers and quick-doers. There is no time for discussion. Asking questions or making proposals are perceived as hampering the progress, as not being innovative. Thinking is not required. We have to execute the orders."

Another department manager fully supported the comments of his colleague. He added that:

> "The management team did not require any activities in the field of world-class manufacturing or the Philips Quality Award. Therefore, I did not do anything. At this moment, I spend my energy in a lot of separate issues but do not work with a guiding concept (...) In my opinion, it is fast going downhill."

Both department managers expressed a lot of frustration. They also told me that they had reduced their working hours to eight hours a day, whereas in the past they worked ten to fourteen hours a day.

Staff departments

In the production departments many complaints could be heard about the staff departments. In their opinion the staff departments did not understand what happened on the shop floor and did not really support the production. Some individual members of staff departments were strongly production oriented. Their efforts were acknowledged. However, the overall judgement of the staff departments was negative.

The negative judgement of the staff departments had a long history. Let me tell you two stories that were regularly told.

> *Story.* I will first start with a story about the financial department. It was said that this department was totally ignorant with respect to the production processes. Every time a mistake was made by this department, the old stories were 'confirmed' again. For example, one of the financial controllers signalled that in one of the production departments the costs had greatly increased, especially the cost of a certain component. This overspending was discussed with the department manager. It was found that a mistake was made in entering the data: a decimal point was placed wrongly. As a consequence, the cost of this component was too high by a factor of ten. The department manager interpreted the mistake as ignorance of the production. After all, the financial controller had to see that the costs of that component were much too high. During the reviews of the reengineering of the controlling department (the

'Future' project) this ignorance was acknowledged. It was emphasised that the employees of this department had to become more familiar with the production processes. However, this never happened. The negative judgement did not change.

Secondly, stories were told about the personnel department. It was said that this department did not support the production departments and that this department would make a deal with the workers council. Every department manager could give examples in which the personnel department 'opposed' the wishes and the expectations of production. The old stories were continuously 'confirmed'. Agreements were regularly made between the personnel department and the workers council without or with the limited involvement of the production departments. At the same time, internal and external reasons hampered the personnel department in solving problems in the production quickly. Altogether, the negative judgement did not change.

In September 1998 it was agreed that members of the staff departments would join the meetings of the management of production. The objective was to improve communication and to prepare joint proposals. However, it regularly appeared that the staff department concerned did not adopt these joint proposals. In a private discussion, a member of a staff department led off steam to me:

"I do not get any support for my ideas. When I present a joint proposal everybody tells me why the proposal cannot be implemented. Nobody gives an alternative (...) They (the members of the staff department, MJV) focus on their own processes. They do not ask what the customer wants."

This member of the staff department really supported production. His/her efforts were acknowledged by the department heads. After some time, he/she left the company.

The other side of this coin was that the staff had nearly no influence on the production. This led, in turn, to a lot of bitterness and frustration in the staff departments.

The workers council
Historically, the workers council had a strong position in the Aachen plant. The workers council and the personnel department often made deals and presented them to management as a 'fait accompli', resulting in a loss of power of the management team. The plant manager who started in Aachen in 1994, looked back to this alliance in the beginning of 1998 in the following way:

"When I started my job in Aachen, the personnel department and the workers council formed a strong axis. I had to break the power of this axis. Nowadays, the management team has its power back."

The 'management team has its power back' judgement has to be qualified. On the one hand, the axis between the personnel department and the workers council was indeed broken. The influence of both departments was reduced. Management controlled the organisation better. On the other hand, informal connections were still present. Via these connections confidential information was leaked and negotiations between management and the workers council were influenced.

The workers council was involved in the 'Future' project. The chairman of this council jointed the meetings of the steering group. He clearly declared which proposals could be acceptable and which ones were not acceptable at all. He mercilessly exposed the weaknesses of the management team. He took care of the interests of the employees. At the same time, he defended, within his political boundaries, the 'Future' project in the workers council. The involvement of the workers council in this project improved the relationship between them and management. Additionally, the feasibility of various sub-projects increased. In the beginning of 1999, the management team launched a new reengineering project. The workers council reacted furiously. This reaction has to be understood partly from the content of the proposals, partly because the council was not involved in the design of this project.

In Germany, details of working conditions are agreed locally between the management and the workers council. I would like to point to three aspects of that. In the first place, these official agreements gave the workers council a lot of power. In many aspects of management, personnel affairs and working conditions, the workers council had to give permission to management or has the right of veto, e.g. in working overtime. In critical situations – for example during the negotiations about a reengineering project or an important agreement – the workers council refused permission in order to strengthen their position in the negotiations. They did this even if this refusal resulted in (severe) financial losses.[199]

In the second place, agreements were often concluded without or with limited consultation with line management. Therefore, the practical applicability left a lot to be desired. Middle management did not always adhere strictly to these agreements because the details of these agreements did not reflect the reality on the shop floor. The agreements were often violated in normal operations. In addition, middle management intentionally violated these agreements to solve unexpected problems. Generally, everybody accepted (small) violations of the agreements. In critical situations, however, the workers council showed their power in demanding the strict observance of the agreement.[200] Management was regularly threatened with lawsuits.

---

[199] For example, in order to shorten the change-over time of the presses from one type to another type, middle management had to ask permission to shift the working hours or for employees to work overtime. The workers council regularly refused permission to strengthen their own position in negotiations.

[200] For example, the working hours of middle management were laid down in an agreement. In practice, it was difficult to comply with the wording of this agreement. Once, the workers council asked the employees working in production to report at which time the department managers arrived in the morning and at which time they left in the afternoon. Additional visits by the department managers to the factory in the evening and in the weekends also had to be reported. Some days later, management was confronted with the violations of the department managers with respect to the working

In the third place, in some agreements the wording was ambiguous. Sometimes, an ambiguity crept in by accident. Sometimes, it was the result of the negotiation process to overcome differences of opinion. Generally, these ambiguities did not influence the daily affairs. In daily practice, the organisation did not take any notice of the agreements and did its own thing. However, in critical situations a discussion kindled about the interpretation of the agreement. Such discussions significantly hampered the implementation of decisions.[201]

3.7.4 Responsibility and accountability

The organisational foundations for responsibility and accountability on the shop floor were laid with the redesign of the production departments. The plant manager who started the 'Future' project phrased his original objectives in beginning of 1998 as follows:

> "It was my objective to create a transparent organisation. The responsibilities and powers of employees have to be clear. The employees have to be managed better."

In the period from January 1997 to January 1999, the organisational structure of the departments has been significantly changed. The boundaries between the Technical Department and the production departments have been redefined. The organisation of the Technical Department was simplified by the parallelisation of activities (five 'products'). The organisation of the production departments was simplified by the introduction of the line concept. The relations between the different departments were defined as customer-supplier relationships. Finally, the reporting structure was designed in a business-oriented way. In summary, a more transparent organisation has been developed. The responsibilities of middle management were clearly defined. In most departments one manager managed the employees on the shop floor.

The cultural or socio-dynamic foundations for responsibility and accountability on the shop floor were laid in the world-class manufacturing program and in the

---

hours. The workers council used this data to strengthen their position in negotiations with management.

[201] For example, in the agreement on self-managing teams it was laid down that 'during the implementation of self-managing teams and the resulting group dynamics' no economically founded dismissals would be allowed. In the case of conflict between management and the workers council about a reengineering project, the interpretation of this clause was focused on the words 'the implementation of'. This meant that during the implementtation of a self-managing team it was not allowed to dismiss employees, and after the implementation it was allowed. In the case of conflict about self-managing teams, the interpretation was focused on the words 'the resulting group dynamics' (this expression refers to changes in the number of employees or the composition of the group after the training and after the formal implementation of the self-managing team). This meant that after the training and after the formal implementation of a self-managing team, it was not allowed to dismiss employees if this dismissal had to do in one way or another with the self-managing team (e.g. if the team had contributed to the implementation of more efficient working methods).

Philips Quality Award process. In the period from January 1997 to January 1999 many processes on the shop floor were improved. These improvements were acknowledged by the auditors in December 1998 (the Philips Quality Award). The improvement of the processes on the shop floor was significantly hampered by the existence of two languages in the organisation: a financial language and a total quality management language. This improvement was also hampered by the invisibility of management and by the style of management. Both phenomena worked against making the processes on the shop floor transparent, controllable, and manageable. Furthermore, the side effects of these phenomena could be observed: paradoxes, managerial short cuts, power structures, game playing, covering up problems, mistrust and so on.

The Aachen case shows that the notions of 'responsibility' and 'accountability' are not self-evident. On the one hand, the conditions for bearing responsibility were often not fulfilled. For example, the processes on the shop floor were not transparent and not under control, the training was not sufficient, and the employees did not feel responsible for their performance. On the other hand, employees were often not held accountable. For example, poor performance was accepted. The following stories illustrate some aspects of the notions 'responsibility' and 'accountability', i.e. the feelings of employees, the importance of internal motivation, and the necessity of holding somebody accountable:

> *Story.* During a workshop a department manager discussed the activities, responsibilities and powers of the employees. These workshops were organised in order to prepare the crew for the organisational changes. During this discussion an employee said: "I am sorting the products, but I am not responsible for it." And several colleagues took his side!

> *Story.* In a department all operators had been trained in the principles of housekeeping. After the training, some operators visited a sister factory. It took several months before the housekeeping really improved. I asked an employee why it took so much time before progress was made. He answered: "Everybody has to be convinced internally (...) The training in the principles of housekeeping was valuable. However, training does not stimulate people. At that moment, not everybody was convinced. If people are not convinced, then they don't do anything (...) Management pressure does not help. Employees have to be convinced. Otherwise, nothing happens (...) At this moment, everybody is convinced. Now we do make progress."

> *Story.* In the Finishing Screens department it was decided to improve the quality of sorting. The first step was to confront the individual operators with their own performance; in other words, the operators were called to account. The second step was to agree an improvement program with each individual operator. This decision led to an increase in the quality of the sorting process. I asked a sorter about this improvement. He made the following comments. "If you tell the crew that they have to improve the sorting quality, they will listen to you, they will believe you. However, there must be pressure. Without pressure nobody improves (...) Now the employees

know that it is serious. They get feedback. They are measured. You can compare it with the speed cameras on the motorway. Everybody knows that speeding is not allowed. If the camera is in use, every driver will respect the speed limits. If the camera is broken, every driver will speed. Exactly the same thing happens with sorting. If an inspector takes a sample, and if the results of these samples are fed back, then the employees will improve. Otherwise not."

The stories in this case show two types of paradoxes with respect to 'responsibility' and 'accountability'. The first type of paradox arises when the conditions for responsibility are not fulfilled and the employees are still held accountable. Then the operator finds himself in an impossible position. This paradox leads to frustration and mistrust. The only way an operator can handle this paradox is by making (or keeping) the processes on the shop floor non-transparent. The second type of paradox arises when the conditions for responsibility are fulfilled and in spite of this the employees are not held accountable. Then the operators get the impression that his labour is not important. In other words, this paradox leads to a loss of meaning. In practice, the result is that the operator goes his own way and the conditions for responsibility are undermined from within.

3.7.5 Leaving the glass factory
After two years, in April 1999, I left the Aachen Glass Factory. It was a leave 'on request' of the plant manager. The official reasons were 'insufficient improvement of customer satisfaction' and 'inadequacy of the (participative) management style'. I would like to give some personnel comments and some reactions.

> *Reflection.* The request to leave the glass factory was made during the annual evaluation. On the one hand, the request to leave the glass factory was a surprise to me. Several months before I had discussed my contract informally with the plant manager. Then, it was agreed that my contract would be lengthened by one year, i.e. until April 1st, 2000. On the other hand, this request did not really come as a surprise. There were big differences in style between the plant manager and myself. The plant manager had a marked hierarchical style and I had a marked participative style. Sooner or later, these differences had to clash with each other.
>
> Nevertheless, the request to leave the glass factory came as a heavy blow. The first hours after the request, I walked around stupefied. I had heard the words. I had understood the words. However, I did not feel a lot. It was as if my emotions did not come through. Afterwards, my 'stupefied' state gradually disappeared. At the same time, feelings of grief and anger started to develop. I felt unjustly treated. I did not believe that there had been insufficient improvement in customer satisfaction (the peer audit had shown the contrary). I was angry about the remark of the inadequacy of my participative management style. After all, this style was one of the arguments for assigning me to the glass factory (again, the peer audit had shown many improvements). I was also angry that I had been taken out of the loop – in my view – without any coaching from my boss.
>
> Several days after the request a director at Product Division advised me not to spend any energy in fighting with my boss about this request. I accepted this advice. I

wrote my boss a letter in which I explained my view. I then used all my energy to find a new job. Seven weeks later I started as a factory manager in another Philips plant.

Reactions. The reactions to my leaving were contradictory. Some people agreed with the request of the plant manager:
o 'you were too weak' (staff member);
o 'you were too soft' (member of management team);
o 'you were too intellectual' (member of management team);
o 'you were unable to intervene toughly' (department head);
o 'incompatibilité des humeurs' with the new plant manager' (director at Product Division level).
Others disagreed:
o 'it's a pity, you were a team player, and we need team players' (member of the management team);
o 'the wrong people leave Aachen' (operator);
o 'you were the only customer-oriented member of the management team' (purchasing manager of an internal customer);
o 'if you have to go, I have to go' (department head);
o 'I have never advised the plant manager to replace you, as I did with other members of the management team' (chairman of the workers council).

Reflection. I left Aachen with mixed feelings. On the one hand, I was angry and felt grieved. On the other hand, I was happy to leave behind the high level of stress and the bad atmosphere in the management team. On the one hand, I had the feeling that I had failed. On the other hand, a lot of progress in the quality of the organisation could be reported. On the one hand, I had lost a lot of self-confidence On the other hand, I was glad that I had not changed my style of management to suit my boss.

Reflection. I had never managed an organisation that was characterised by frustration and mistrust. Therefore, Aachen asked for the extreme of my management capabilities. Many times, I have asked myself whether I had taken the right position. Many times, I have asked myself whether I had chosen the right approach. I would like to comment on these questions both in relation to the prevailing culture and the new plant manager.

In the first place, I would like to describe my approach to the prevailing culture. The decision to assign me as factory manager in the glass factory was inspired as much by my experience in manufacturing excellence as by my participative management style. This means from the beginning that it was clear for both parties (my boss and myself) that I would approach the problems in the glass factory in a participative way. Therefore, I tried to convince the middle management about the change process. Therefore, I preferred a participative process with decision taking in consensus above a (quick) hierarchical decision process. However, it took a long time before I acknowledged the weak points of this approach. I took good faith for granted. I took keeping an appointment for granted. I took open communication for granted. And, ... I took mutual trust for granted. In a process of trial and error I learned the 'unwritten' rules of the organisation. In this learning process, I have questioned myself many times how to handle these types of 'unwritten' rules: using my hierarchical power or using a process of persuasion. I doubted whether a hierarchical approach would result in a dismantling of the 'unwritten' rules. I was afraid that a hierarchical approach would initiate more window dressing and political games. Therefore, I decided to use the latter approach. Additionally, I was aware that a dismantling of the 'unwritten' rules required the support of the whole management team; the discussion about these rules had only just been started (see sections 3.2.6 and 3.7.2). In retrospect, I am not quite sure whether I took the right balance between the use of power and the process of persuasion in this change process. Maybe I should have used my power within the participative process more subtly. Anyway, the leaving of the 'old' plant manager and the coming of the 'new' one changed the scene completely.

In the second place, I would like to comment on my relation to the new plant manager. As previously mentioned, there were big differences in management style between the plant manager and myself. At that moment, I believed that I could manage these differences to some extent. In retrospect, I have to admit that I was too optimistic. A clash was inevitable. The old guards in the factory had learned 'to bow with the wind'. I was not familiar with that strategy. The first few months after the new plant manager started, it was difficult for me to cope with my new boss. I felt uncertain. I am used to giving my opinion. I am used to asking questions. I am used to decisions being taken in a participative process. However, all that changed in a couple of weeks. More than once, I expressed my dissatisfaction with these changes. I am also convinced that my displeasure could be read on my face. The way the new plant manager behaved initiated a lot of fear in the organisation. Sometimes, I also felt scared. After some months, I had the feeling that I had developed the right mode of cooperation with my boss. This means I had changed my language (I presented my opinions as 'suggestions'), I tried to prevent disagreements with my boss (I did not succeed in that completely), and I did implement the decisions of my boss as best as I could (some window dressing was inevitable). However, I did not change my style of management in the factory.

Note: The timing of the start of the new plant manager was unfortunate. At that point in time, we had three serious quality problems with our customers. My new boss blamed me for these problems. Three months after he started, my daughter became seriously ill. She spent several months in hospital. After that, a long period of treatment was required. This meant an additional burden for me.

3.7.6 Conclusion

The Aachen Glass Factory had made a loss for many years in a row. In 1996 the 'Future' project was launched to realise a complete turn-around to secure the future of the factory. In addition, a world-class manufacturing program and the Philips Quality Award process was started. It was widely believed that – despite the financial losses – the Aachen Glass Factory would never be closed. Successive plant managers who threatened that the factory would be closed in losses continued, fed this belief. However, these threats always appeared to be empty. It was further believed that the Aachen Glass Factory could stand competition from its biggest competitor. However, this belief was not confirmed by benchmarking.

The organisational culture in the glass factory had an ambiguous character. On the one hand, employees (operators, middle management, management, staff, engineering, and the workers council) worked hard and were dedicated. On the other hand, they were full of frustration and mistrust. As a consequence, the different parties did not cooperate smoothly. Often, they pussyfooted around without solving the problems.

The shop floor in the Aachen Glass Factory was characterised by a low level of housekeeping, bad discipline with respect to the process instruction cards, and a low awareness of quality. In addition, the processes on the shop floor were not transparent.

The following are the most important points in the organisational development of the glass factory:

o   In the Aachen case two red threads were identified: the creation of a transparent organisation and the improvement of the processes on the shop floor. The first red thread is specifically present in the 'Future' project and the second one in the world-class manufacturing program. The Philips Quality Award process plays a role in both red threads.

o   As part of the 'Future' project, the organisational structure of the production departments was redesigned by parallelisation and segmentation. This means that these departments were split up into small organisational lines or units. Each line or unit manufactured a concrete (semi-finished) product. One manager managed the line or unit. The performance of the production departments was measured with performance indicators.

o   As part of the 'Future' project, the organisational structure of the Technical Department was redesigned by parallelisation. Five different 'products' were identified. These products were allocated to separate departments. The service level of the Technical Department was measured with performance indicators.

o   In the world-class manufacturing program some basic tools and concepts were discussed and implemented, e.g. continuous improvement, housekeeping, self-managing teams, process control, total preventive maintenance, and the training of employees. One of my roles was to confirm and to reconfirm this program and to give meaning to it.

In the change process of the glass factory several paradoxes came to the surface:

o   The financial situation of the glass factory required a high-speed turnaround process. However, this change process did not run smoothly.

o   Despite all the dialogues in workshops, project meetings, and review meetings, a joint language with respect to the change process did not develop.

o   Despite the large number of workshops, project meetings, and review meetings, the whole organisation did not work as one to solve the problems.

329

o   Two different languages were identified: a financial language and a total quality management language. These languages did not correspond with each other. The financial language was dominant and determined the behaviour in the organisation.

o   As a result of these different languages, a set of informal rules developed which did not correspond with the formal rules.

o   Most parties (e.g. management and the workers council) had a lot of formal power. However, these parties often felt powerless to solve the problems.

o   On the shop floor the following paradox arose. On the one hand, everybody knew that it was essential to work according to the standard operating procedures and the out-of-control action plans. On the other hand, everybody knew that the employees often ignored the procedures and action plans, and it was taken for granted.

o   A manager needs hierarchical power to change an organisation that is immobilised by frustration and mistrust. However, use of hierarchical power strengthens feelings of frustration and mistrust.

Two types of paradoxes were identified with respect to the notions of 'responsibility' and 'accountability':

o   A paradox arises if the necessary conditions for employees to take responsibility are not fulfilled and still the employees are held accountable.

o   A paradox arises if the necessary conditions for employees to take responsibility are fulfilled and in spite of that the employees are not held accountable.

Many actors were active in the paradoxes described above, e.g. employees, middle management, management, engineering, and the workers council. Maybe the biggest paradox is that these actors can be seen from two conflicting perspectives: as 'wrong doers' and as 'victims'. Wrong doers in that they were responsible for the situation and victims in that they were part of the system.

4 Comparison of the Roermond and Aachen cases

The cases described in this chapter are quite different. The Roermond case was related to a new product in a new factory, and the Aachen case to a mature product in an existing factory. The Roermond case was characterised by high-trust relations and the Aachen case by low-trust relations. In both cases I was one of the key actors: the factory manager. Both cases have left deep impressions on me and have enabled me to gradually develop my views about man, labour, and organisation. I focused my attention more and more on the conditions that have to be fulfilled by management so that the employees on the shop floor can act in a responsible way. As a consequence, the observation of the shop floor and the interpretation of the phenomena also developed gradually. In other words, the 'tool' of the investigations – in an ethnographic study the researcher is his or her own tool – was not fixed but was influenced by the experiences in the organisation under study.

Roermond and Aachen: two quite different cases. In Roermond the organisation developed itself in close cooperation with the customer. Cross-level and cross-functional cooperation were taken for granted. Pro-active product development and concurrent engineering emerged 'naturally'. Continuous improvement was quite obvious. However, after experiencing serious adversities in the market the curtain dropped: the business unit was closed.

The Aachen case was almost in the opposite direction. The organisation was strongly internally oriented. The main objective was to improve the financial performance of the factory. The interests of the customer were of less importance. The culture of the glass factory had an ambiguous character. On the one hand, the employees worked hard and were dedicated. On the other hand, they were full of frustration and mistrust. The result was that cross-level and cross-functional cooperation was an uphill battle. Therefore, it was not obvious that processes were continuously improved, that the customer satisfaction was a top priority, and that pressing problems were really solved. Nevertheless, the glass factory still exists.

In this section the Roermond case and the Aachen case will be compared on the basis of key variables. The objective is to identify variables that are decisive for employees on the shop floor in terms of the processes of assuming responsibility and accountability.

4.1 Business orientation

The Roermond plant was intended to be the birthplace of new businesses based on multilayer products. One of these babies was the Ceramic Multilayer Actuators business unit. The Aachen Glass Factory was a competence centre. In this centre new products and new processes were developed.

The actuator factory in Roermond was strongly externally oriented and the glass factory in Aachen internally oriented. The root of these differences lies in the historical background of both factories. The actuator factory was a new factory.

From the start, this factory was strongly customer oriented. Everybody knew that not keeping up with the changing demands of the customers would mean the end of the factory. In other words, a strong external orientation developed. The glass factory was a fifty-year old factory. From the start, this factory delivered all its products to internal customers. Around 1995 the current plant manager started a process to change the organisation's focus from internal to external. The internal reporting was changed to a kind of business reporting. Projects were started to deliver products to external customers. Despite all initiatives, a strong internal orientation dominated. The data are summarised in Figure 4.1.

Topic	Roermond case	Aachen case
1. Objective of plant	Birthplace of new businesses.	Competence centre for present factories.
2. Historical background of the factory	No history. Start up of new factory.	Fifty-year old factory.
3. Customers	External customers.	Internal customers.
4. Orientation	Strongly external.	Strongly internal. Process to change business orientation from internal to external was started.

Figure 4.1 Business orientation of the actuator factory in Roermond and the glass factory in Aachen

The consequences of these differences will be discussed in the following sections.

4.2 The production structure

The actuator factory in Roermond and the glass factory in Aachen were both high-tech operations. The production structures of these factories are comparable. An overview of the production structure is given in Figure 4.2.

The production structure of the Roermond factory was designed according to socio-technical principles. The production line was split up into six segments. The processes within these segments formed a coherent whole. Generally, long cycle times were present. The production structure of the Aachen factory was divided into five production departments. The Technical Department supported these departments. This division can be described as a result of a parallelisation and segmentation process. Parallelisation and segmentation further simplified the production departments and the Technical Department. In some departments the boundaries of the parallelisation and segmentation process were fully determined by the (fixed) production structure. In the glass factory workplaces with both long and short cycle times were present. The details of the production structures are summarised in Figure 4.3.

It has been shown that the design of the production structure is of the utmost importance in organising the processes of responsibility and accountability on the shop floor (Chapter 2). The actuator factory and the glass factory were both designed in accordance with the principles of the Dutch approach to Socio-Technical Systems Design. For that reason, the significant differences between the Roermond case and the Aachen case cannot be explained through the production structure.

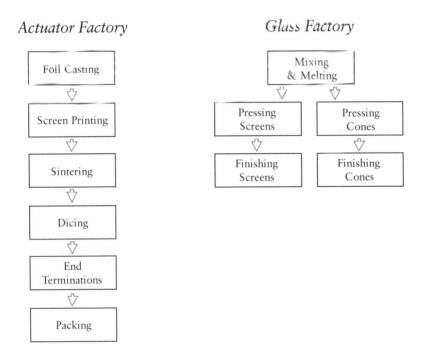

Figure 4.2 Schematic overview of the production structure in the actuator factory in Roermond and the glass factory in Aachen

Topic	Roermond case	Aachen case
1. Production structure at macro level	The production line was split up into six segments. The different segments formed a socio-technical unit. The size of the segments varied from 6 to 35 employees.	The production organisation was split up into five production departments. The Technical Department supported these departments. The production departments and the Technical department formed socio-technical units. The size of these departments varied from 35 to 240 employees.
2. Production structure at meso level	The different processes in a unit were integrated in a production cell structure. Generally, the processes of the unit were located in the same area.	The production departments were split up into smaller units by parallelisation and segmentation. Generally, the different processes in a unit were integrated in a production cell structure and were located in the same area. The Technical Department was split up into five units by parallelisation.
3. Production structure at micro level	Workplaces with long cycle times.	Some workplaces with short cycle times. Other workplaces with long cycle times.

Figure 4.3 The production structures of the actuator factory in Roermond and the glass factory in Aachen

4.3 The control and information structure

The control and information structures of the actuator factory and the glass factory are comparable. The control and information structure of the Roermond factory was designed according to socio-technical principles. First, the control structure was designed in a bottom-up process. After that, the information structure was designed. The members of the 'whole task' group were responsible for the control functions (quality, logistics, and low-level maintenance activities). The control and information structure in the Aachen factory changed significantly over the course of the years. The organisation originally had a functional structure with no integration of functions. Step by step, the control functions were allocated as low as possible in the organisation. For example, the operators who were operating the equipment carried out most of the quality checks and repair and maintenance activities. At several workplaces the production structure did not allow a full integration of functions, e.g. the quality check was done in the next segment. A summary of the control and information structure is given in Figure 4.4.

Topic	Roermond case	Aachen case
1. Control structure at macro level	Factory manager responsible for production, factory engineering, and repair and maintenance.	Factory manager responsible for production, factory engineering, and Technical Department.
2. Control structure at meso level	Control of quantity, quality, and logistics within the unit. Engineering and maintenance functions controlled at factory level.	Control of quantity, quality, and logistics within the production departments. Engineering and maintenance functions within the production department.
3. Control structure at micro level	At the workplace control of quality and logistics.	Control of quality in some workplaces. No control of quality in other workplaces.
4. Information structure	Main data available at the workplace and at management level.	Main data available at the workplace and at management level.
5. Discipline	High	Low to moderate

Figure 4.4 Control and information structures of the actuator factory in Roermond and the glass factory in Aachen

It has been shown that the design of the control and information structures is of the utmost importance in managing the processes of responsibility and accountability on the shop floor (Chapter 2). The control and information structures of the actuator factory and the glass factory were (more or less) designed in accordance with the principles of the Dutch approach. Therefore, the significant differences between the Roermond case and the Aachen case cannot be explained by these structures as such. However, there was a significant difference in the discipline with which employees executed the procedures inherent in these structures. The background and the influence of this difference will be discussed further in Chapter 4 (Evaluation).

4.4 The improvement structure

The characteristics of the improvement structures in the Roermond and the Aachen factory are comparable – especially in relation to company-wide quality programs. Both factories followed the same certification programs, the same Phillips Quality Award process, and a comparable manufacturing excellence program. Generally, the improvement programs were more widely deployed in Roermond than in Aachen. It has to be remarked that the smaller size of the Roermond factory made the deployment of an improvement structure much easier. A summary is given in Figure 4.5.

Characteristics	Roermond case	Aachen case
1. Certification	ISO 9001	ISO 9001
2. Certification	ISO 14001 in planning	ISO 14001
3. Philips Quality Award process	Philips Quality Award process started.	Philips Quality Award process guided continuous improvement process.
4. Manufacturing excellence programs	Continuous improvement. Statistical Process Control. Improvement teams. Housekeeping. Mini-company process. By the end of my period at Roermond these initiatives were in full operation.	Continuous improvement. Statistical Process Control. Improvement teams. Housekeeping. Total Preventive maintenance. Mini-company process. By the end of my period at Aachen these initiatives were partly in operation

Figure 4.5 Improvement structures of the actuator factory in Roermond and the glass factory in Aachen

It has been shown that the design of the improvement structure has a significant influence on the processes of responsibility and accountability on the shop floor (Chapter 2). The formal improvement structure in the actuator factory and in the glass factory was the same. However, there were three important differences.

Firstly, in Roermond the improvement structure was fully deployed and in Aachen partly deployed. Secondly, in Roermond the improvement structure was deeply embedded in the organisation and in Aachen shallowly embedded. Finally, in Roermond the process of continuous improvement was made possible by a high level of discipline whereas in Aachen the improvement process was significantly hampered by the low to moderate level of discipline. These differences will be discussed further in Chapter 4 (Evaluation).

4.5 Socio-dynamic or cultural factors

The socio-dynamic or cultural factors in the actuator factory and the glass factory were quite opposite. Figure 4.6 presents an overview of the differences in mindset, behaviour, distribution of power, discipline, perception of management, and relation with customers.

This data suggests that the significant differences between the Roermond case and the Aachen are related to the differences in socio-dynamic or cultural factors. These differences will be discussed further in Chapter 4 (Evaluation).

Topic	Roermond case	Aachen case
1. Mindset (basic beliefs)	Externally oriented. The factory is very vulnerable. The factory has to be better than the competition.	Internally oriented. The factory will never be closed down. The factory can handle the competition.
2. Behaviour	Intensive cooperation between operators, technicians, engineers, and line management.	Cooperation within departments, the management team, and between employees and management, was characterised by paradoxes, i.e. by making opposite demands.
3. Power	Balanced division of influence and power between different hierarchical levels.	Hierarchical distribution of power. Feelings of powerlessness regarding the solving of basic problems in the organisation.
4. Discipline	High.	Low to moderate.
5. Management	Highly visible. Perceived as a team. Mainly participative management style.	Partly visible. Not perceived as a team. Partly hierarchical and partly participative management style.
6. Trust	High-trust relations between management and employees	Low-trust relations between management and employees
7. Customers	High-trust relations with customers.	Low-trust relations with customers.

Figure 4.6 Socio-dynamic or cultural factors in the actuator factory in Roermond and the glass factory in Aachen

4.6 Responsibility and accountability

Analysis of the Roermond case and the Aachen case indicates that the design of the production structure, control structure, information structure, and improvement structure are prerequisites for operators to assume responsibility and accountability on the shop floor (as concluded in Chapter 2, section 7). However, these prerequisites are not enough. It is suggested that they will only thrive in an organisation with a well-balanced division of influence and power between hierarchical levels and with high-trust relations between management and employees.

In the Roermond case the notions of 'responsibility' and 'accountability' were never problematised. The practical meaning of these ideas was learned step by step. On the one hand, failing conditions for responsibility were identified and improvements were implemented. On the other hand, practical structures were developed to hold employees accountable. The key parameters in this learning process were four-way communication, participation, and continuous improvement.

In the Aachen case the notions of 'responsibility' and 'accountability' were problematised. On the shop floor, two types of paradoxes were identified. The first type arises if the necessary conditions for employees to assume responsibility are not fulfilled and still the employees are held accountable; the second one arises if the necessary conditions for employees to assume responsibility are fulfilled and in spite of that the employees are not held accountable.

The existence of paradoxes can be visualised by a 2 x 2 matrix of responsibility and accountability, see Figure 4.7.

Conditions for Responsibility

	Yes	No
Yes	I	II
No	III	IV

Calling to Account

Figure 4.7 2 x 2 matrix of responsibility and accountability

Quadrant I refers to a situation in which the conditions for assuming responsibility and accountability have been realised. This quadrant also refers to a situation in which developing paradoxes are identified and problematised. Especially, the act of 'calling account' will help the identification of paradoxes. Quadrant IV characterises a situation in which the conditions for assuming both responsibility and accountability not have been realised. Generally, for functional responsibilities this situation is not stable and the expectation is that it will evolve into quadrant II. However, for non-functional responsibilities such a situation can continue for a long period. The Aachen case shows many examples of these circumstances, e.g. safety aspects (section 3.3.3) and personnel (section 3.3.4). In the strict sense of the word such a state – despite its undesirable character – is not a paradox. If the organisation becomes aware of this situation, then it is expected that it will evolve into quadrant II. Paradoxes in the original meaning of the word arise in two quadrants: if the conditions for assuming responsibility are not fulfilled and the operators are held accountable (quadrant II) and if the conditions for assuming responsibility are fulfilled but the employees are not held accountable (quadrant III).

The relation between power and trust relations between managers and employees on the one hand and paradoxes on the shop floor on the other hand will be discussed in the next chapter (Chapter 4, section 4).

4.7 Personal reflection on management

I experienced the actuator factory and the glass factory quite differently. In Roermond I felt like a fish in water. I had a lot of influence and power. Cooperation went smoothly. The organisation developed gradually and the results were cause for much excitement. In Aachen I felt like a fish out of water. It was my intention to bring the factory organisation up to a world-class level. However, there was highly significant resistance to change. The organisation did not run smoothly. Paradoxes, mistrust and frustration had to be continuously fought against. Despite these problems, a lot of small victories could be reported. In addition, I have always experienced a lot of stress in the glass factory. In the first year, it was production problems that were the main cause of this stress. In the second year, the new plant manager, the atmosphere of mistrust, and the bad relationships in the management team were the main causes of this stress.

Management in Roermond
The actuator factory was more or less a green field operation. A new factory had to be built up. My boss focused on the development of the business. I could give all my attention to the development of the factory. In the starting phase, everybody was focused on the development of the process and the (fast) ramp-up of the production. From the beginning, the performance of the factory was quite good. Therefore, I had a lot of freedom. In a process of trial of error the organisation of the factory developed gradually. Especially, in a small organisation it is possible to 'experiment'. In Roermond I spent a lot of time on explaining my views, convincing employees, and asking for support from the management team. I seldom met serious resistance. Looking back, I have to say that communication was a daily pursuit. I regularly made tentative proposals to develop support for new ideas. In discussion, often better proposals developed. I also discussed many issues on the shop floor, especially improvements that had to be implemented. The main reason was to give meaning to the improvement process and to convince the operators that the management heard their 'voice'.

340

The philosophy of participation was such that everyone could give his/her opinion. Management decisions were reversed if there was insufficient support from the crew. As a consequence, window dressing was a deadly sin. The philosophy of continuous improvement made the organisation open to mistakes. It was allowed to make a mistake. However, it was not allowed to keep quiet about it. Not telling the truth was seen as a serious offence. I regularly carried out checks to support the implementation of new proposals. Extensive checks were not required because the crew knew why it was so important to work according to the procedures.

The management team supported the development of the factory organisation, including the mini-company process. My colleagues regularly gave me visible support, e.g. on the customer days, as an interviewee in the mini-company process, and in listening actively to a presentation of an improvement team. An improvement drive was never run down behind my back.

In summary, the development of the factory organisation ran – although it was a process of trial and error – smoothly. I had a lot of influence and power in this development process. Generally, the crew and the management team accepted my proposals – after a lot of discussions. As a result, I was used to it that ideas that were developed in a participative process were implemented. I was also used to people sticking to their agreements and no window dressing taking place. Finally, I was used to the management team giving me enough support.

Culture shock

In retrospect, I can see that I experienced a culture shock in the changeover from the actuator factory to the glass factory. However, at that point, I did not see it this way.

In the period between 1990 and 1992 I worked in Taiwan. Before going to Taiwan my wife and I attended a two-day workshop about the Taiwanese/Chinese culture. So I arrived in Taiwan well prepared. The first few weeks in the new country were exciting. However, after that questions came to the surface. I discussed a problem with my group and nobody made any comments. I made an agreement with somebody and nothing happened. My boss overruled one of my decisions and did not inform me. I came home angry many times: why do they behave in this way? I interpreted the words and the behaviour of my subordinates, my colleagues, and my boss within my own frame of reference. Repeatedly, my interpretation turned out to be wrong. In other words, I was experiencing culture shock. The two-day workshop (and all the books I had read about the Chinese culture) had not changed my frame of reference at all. However, I knew about the existence of culture shock. After some time, I took my notes from the workshop and compared my actual experiences with the predicted patterns. Furthermore, I discussed my experiences with other expatriates. Nevertheless, it took me about half a year to interpret the statements, agreements, and promises of my (Taiwanese) subordinates. And it took me more than one year to interpret the behaviour of my (Taiwanese) boss and to cope adequately with it.

Before joining the glass factory in Aachen I attended a one-day course about the German culture. A lot of do's and don'ts were explained. Special attention was paid to the focus of individual development (versus development of the group) and to the formal aspects of business relationships. Therefore, I was well prepared to work in a German company. In the first few months, I identified some phenomena in the glass factory that appeared to be typically German.[202] However, I did not recognise the patterns of behaviour, which are present in an organisation that is characterised by frustration and mistrust. I have to be careful in my choice of words here. Maybe it was more the case that I did not recognise the specific patterns of a culture in which (all) individual employees fight for their own life. On the surface, the glass factory looked to me like a typical western organisation. Therefore, I interpreted the words and deeds (excluding the phenomena that seemed to me to be typically German) of my German subordinates and my German colleagues within my own frame of reference. Therefore, I used a comparable approach in the development of the organisation to world class level as in Roermond.

In the previous section I summarised my experiences in the Roermond factory; I was used to having a lot of influence and power, I was used to it that ideas that were developed in a participative process were implemented, I was used to people sticking to their agreements, I was used to no window dressing taking place, and I was used to the management team giving me enough support. In retrospect, all these constituents of my frame of reference appeared to be problematic. All of them. And ... I did not know it ... I had to learn this by trial and error.

Understanding paradoxes

Six months after I started in Aachen somebody recommended that I read the book *The Unwritten Rules of the Game* by Scott Morgan. This advice was very helpful. After all, it is very difficult to understand social phenomena and organisational processes if you are in the midst of it. After reading this book I started to understand some of the phenomena which I had experienced. The idea that formal and informal rules could conflict became clearer and clearer to me. Further, I began to understand that aligning formal and informal rules would require the support and commitment of the whole management team. I also began to understand that an individual manager could not accomplish that much. However, I did not understand the full meaning of the paradoxes and the resulting behaviour until I started writing of the draft of the case study.

Management in Aachen

How can we handle mistrust? How can we align formal and informal rules? How can we weaken a paradox? At that time – without understanding these phenomena in detail – I tried the method of participation and persuasion. First, this method suits my personality. Second, I did not believe that these phenomena could be 'managed' in a hierarchical way.

---

[202] The Glass Factory in Aachen is not a typical German organisation. The reasons for this lie in the influence of the more easy-going local culture (Noordrijn-Westfalen) and the influence of the Dutch mother company.

In the previous section (section 3.7.6) I have identified the following paradox. A manager needs hierarchical power to change an organisation that is immobilised by frustration and mistrust. However, the use of hierarchical power will strengthen these feelings of frustration and mistrust. Without any doubt, to weaken this paradox requires participation and persuasion. Furthermore, a certain use of power is required. In retrospect, I am still not sure whether I used the right balance between participation/persuasion and hierarchical power to dismantle this paradox. At any rate, the Aachen case has clearly shown that a hierarchical style as such is not suitable for managing the phenomena of mistrust, formal/informal rules, and paradoxes. The way the new plant manager behaved – who had a marked hierarchical style – increased the mistrust, increased the differences between the formal and informal rules, and increased the paradoxes.

Roermond and Aachen revisited

Fons Trompenaars gives the following definition of culture in his book *Riding the Waves of Culture. Understanding Cultural Diversity in Business*[203]:

> "Culture is the way in which a group of people solves problems."

This definition clearly highlights the differences between Roermond and Aachen. In Roermond different hierarchical levels and disciplines worked together to solve the problems of the customers. In Aachen it was very difficult for different hierarchical levels and disciplines to cooperate together. Widespread mistrust had led to a culture in which many problems were not adequately tackled. Furthermore, specific German characteristics like the focus on individual development also played a role.[204]

In Roermond I took the way the problems were solved for granted. During my Aachen period I believed that Roermond was a 'normal' case and that Aachen was an 'abnormal' case. Both case descriptions have been written from this perspective. However, reflection on the cases, recent experiences in management, and disciplinary literature, has called this perspective into question. I looked at it from the opposite direction; i.e. could it be that Roermond was an 'abnormal' case and Aachen a 'normal' case? This reflection points to a major characteristic of the manager as ethnographer; namely that the tool of the investigation – i.e. the manager/ethnographer – is not an objective or stable tool, but is strongly influenced by previous experiences. This tentative conclusion shows that the order in which cases are experienced can have a significant influence on the case descriptions. This means if I had managed the glass factory in Aachen before the actuator factory in Roermond, then the case descriptions would have been quite different. This holds especially for the content of the 'reflection' sections of the case descriptions.

---

[203] Trompenaars (1993, p6).
[204] See also Womack and Jones (1997, p214-218, 282-283).

CHAPTER 4
Evaluation

Societal developments have urged modern industries to abandon classical manufacturing methods and to introduce new production concepts. These new concepts promise a 'new world of work' that combines technical superiority with social innovation. In practice, new production concepts fall short in preventing the development of paradoxes and managerial short cuts. Additionally, the promise of a 'new world of work' is often not realised.

To understand the failure of new production concepts an integrative analysis on three levels is necessary. These levels consist of concrete phenomena on the shop floor, the basics of organisational design theory, and the philosophy of organisation. For each level, a research question has been formulated. These questions are:

> *How do paradoxes evolve on the shop floor?*

> *Why do new production concepts fail in many modern factories?*

> *How can employees on the shop floor act in a responsible way?*

In Chapter 2 an in-depth study of the new production concepts in modern factories has been done. The focus was on the design of the workplace, the responsibility of employees, and the implementation strategy.

In Chapter 3 these research questions were investigated on the basis of two ethnographic case studies in manufacturing that have been written from the perspective of a factory manager as 'reflective practitioner'. The first case concerns the set-up of a new factory in Roermond (The Netherlands) and the second one the turn-around of a factory in Aachen (Germany).

In this chapter, lines of reasoning that have been developed in the previous chapters will be evaluated, integrated, and further explored to answer the research questions of this study. This chapter is structured in the following way. Section 1 is a recapitulation of the preceding chapters. Section 2 explicitly outlines the basic beliefs, intellectual tradition, and social criticism that underlie this study. Section 3 evaluates the research strategy of a manager as ethnographer. Section 4 discusses the cultural or socio-dynamic conditions necessary for assuming responsibility and accountability. Section 5 presents a philosophical analysis of industrial organisations to elucidate the multi-dimensional and normative character of the processes of assuming responsibility and accountability. Section 6 summarises the previous sections in a liberating perspective for the design and development of responsible organisations.

1 Recapitulation

The Prologue introduced the subject of this study with an everyday story about the shop floor. This story shows a clear paradox. Employees are made responsible for the production of electronic components. However, the conditions necessary for employees to execute this task are not fulfilled because the process is not under control. Therefore, they cannot produce the components with the required quality. Nevertheless, the employees are held accountable. The result of the paradox is that the employees are caught an impossible position. They are held accountable for a task they cannot execute; and that is not fair. The problem of this paradox is not its existence as such, but how easily it can come about.

The key person in this paradox is the manager. S/he has to fulfil the conditions necessary for employees bear responsibility and be held accountable. If s/he fails, then a paradox arises. In fact, the manager takes a 'short cut'. S/he calls the employee to account without checking that the conditions are fulfilled. S/he reduces 'responsibility' to 'accountability'.

This story was related to the technical aspects of a production process. However, these types of paradoxes also occur within non-technical aspects in manufacturing organisations, e.g. safety aspects, environmental regulations, social intercourse, moral issues, and so on. The mechanism behind the paradox is essentially the same. In these areas, employees have certain responsibilities. However, they cannot bear this responsibility due to failing conditions. Again, a short cut by management will lead to employees behaving irresponsibly. Generally, in these areas the paradox and short cut are even less visible due to the technological focus of industrial organisations.

In Chapter 1, paradoxes on the shop floor have been investigated in greater detail. The development of these paradoxes has been placed in the context of (the implementation of) new production concepts. It has been indicated that these new concepts fail in many factories. To understand this failure an integrative analysis on three levels was proposed. These levels consist of the phenomena on the shop floor, organisational design theory, and the philosophy of organisation.

Through stories about the shop floor it has been shown that the notions of 'responsibility' and 'accountability' have quite a problematic character. To understand the background to these concepts the history of industrial development has been sketched out. The path from Scientific Management, to the Human Relations movement, to new production concepts has been described. In addition, a philosophical account of the processes of responsibility and accountability on the shop floor has been given. It is made plausible that the manager's basic beliefs about man, labour, and organisation play an important role. It has been emphasised that the factory manager has to use his or her authority to create conditions for self-development and freedom for employees.

Based on the considerations given above the research questions on the different levels have been formulated as follows:

How do paradoxes evolve on the shop floor?

Why do new production concepts fail in many modern factories?

How can employees on the shop floor act in a responsible way?

These research questions have been studied from the perspective of a factory manager as 'reflective practitioner'. They focus on the structural and cultural conditions that have to be fulfilled by a factory manager so that operators on the shop floor can bear responsibility and can be held accountable for their performance.

In Chapter 2 the research questions of this study have been investigated from the point of view of new production concepts. These new concepts claim to offer a more efficient, more effective, or more human approach than Scientific Management. To understand this claim the principles of Scientific Management as developed by the American engineer Frederick Taylor have been discussed.

Taylor states that the interests of employers and employees are basically the same. He calls for harmonious cooperation so that maximum prosperity for both parties can be secured. In his opinion, this objective can be realised by a scientific approach to the organisation of production. In his *Principles of Scientific Management* book he identifies four principles for management. The first principle states that every production step has to be analysed in detail so that 'one best way' and 'one best implement' can be defined. The second principle states that the workmen have to be selected and to be trained scientifically. The third principle states that a heartily cooperation between management and workmen has to be present. The last principle states that management has to do its own job (thinking and controlling) and that the workmen have to do their own job (execution of standardised tasks). These four principles imply a division of work into its elementary parts, standardisation in tools and methods, and a separation between thinking (management) and doing (workmen). There is an inherent contradiction in Taylor's thinking. His system is based on two pillars: (1) a complete mental revolution and (2) scientific control of the manufacturing process. However, these pillars are incompatible with each other. In the Tayloristic approach the second pillar – scientific control – dominated. The Tayloristic mode of production has two major shortcomings. Firstly, it results in high absenteeism, low morale, worker dissatisfaction, and industrial conflicts. Secondly, it cannot cope with the requirements of a dynamic business environment. The new production concepts claim to give an alternative to Taylorism.

Socio-Technical Systems Design fundamentally attacks the Tayloristic principles of mass production. Socio-Technical Systems Design calls for a fundamental redesign of the production organisation. The Dutch school has developed a detailed design theory and design methodology. A key principle in this approach is the reduction of complexity in the factory by the parallelisation and segmentation of the production structure. A second principle is an increase in the control capacity of employees. The application of these principles leads to an organisation with 'self-managing' or 'whole task' groups. Such group is responsible for the produc-

348

tion of a module, a semi-finished product, or a whole product. This responsibility includes non-technical aspects such as logistical planning, quality measurements, repair and maintenance activities, and so on. The Australian and Scandinavian variants of Socio-Technical Systems Design emphasise the participative and communication processes, respectively.

Lean Production is based on the Tayloristic principles of division of work, standardisation, and hierarchical control. These principles are refined and extended by the development of a number of sophisticated production technologies. Lean Production finds its origin in the Toyota Production System. This system is characterised by a continuous drive to eliminate waste. The system is built on two pillars, 'just-in-time' and 'autonomation'. Just-in-time is a logistic concept to realise a continuous flow in the factory. Autonomation is a technological concept to prevent the production of defective parts. Lean Production deviates from Taylorism in its emphasis on continuous improvement and the participation of employees.

Business Process Reengineering focuses on a redesign of business processes. In the book *Reengineering the Corporation. A manifesto for Business Revolution*, Hammer and Champy attribute the poor performance of the American companies to their Tayloristic background. They state that companies should not be built around simple tasks but around business processes. They advocate a process-oriented approach. Hammer and Champy describe *what* they want: the rethinking of business strategies, the creation of a new organisation, the emergence of a new world of work, and a change in the behaviour of employees and managers. However, they do not describe *how* these objectives can be realised.

Kiyoshi Suzaki has developed the Mini-Company Concept. He emphasises that a factory has to be human-centred or human-oriented. This means that both technical and organisational structures have to be designed in such a way that 'people can make it happen'. Suzaki emphasises the importance of the production structure. He proposes the design of parallel production lines with a continuous flow. Suzaki promotes the idea of a 'company within a company'. This means that the employees who work in such a parallel production line form a group or mini-company. They are responsible for all aspects of the production, including planning, quality, safety and environment, social relations, and morality. Finally, Suzaki stresses the importance of continuous improvement and the participation of all employees.

In conclusion, Socio-Technical Systems Design, Lean Production, Business Process Reengineering, and the Mini-Company Concept offer different alternatives to Taylorism. Particularly, Socio-Technical Systems Design in combination with the Mini-Company Concept offer a structural approach to the design and development of organisations in which employees on the shop floor can bear true responsibility and really be held accountable for their performance.

In Chapter 3 the research questions of this study have been investigated in two cases studies. The first case study took place in Ceramic Multilayer Actuators Roermond (The Netherlands) and the second in the Aachen Glass Factory (Germany). Both organisations were designed according to the principles of Socio-

Technical Systems Design and in both organisations formal programs were present to implement the Mini-Company Concept.

The methodological approach was discussed first. It has been shown that an ethnographic case study is a suitable strategy to investigate the research questions of this study. Especially because the partial perspective of a factory manager is of the utmost importance in mapping out the phenomenon of paradoxes and understanding the 'deep structure' of processes of responsibility and accountability.

The Roermond case study describes the set-up of a new actuator factory for the printer industry. To meet the requirements of this industry a short time-to-market, a high volume and a high mix flexibility was required. The factory organisation was developed in a process of trial and error. This process was guided by the Dutch approach to Socio Technical Systems Design, the Mini-Company Concept, and the improvement philosophy of Maasaki Imai. In the course of time, an organisation characterised by intensive cooperation between all functions and all levels, a high sense of responsibility in employees, high satisfaction with work, and high trust in management was developed. Three red threads were identified: four-way communication, participation, and continuous improvement. The Roermond case study shows that a careful design of the production structure, control structure, and improvement structure are prerequisites for the enabling of responsibility and accountability on the shop floor. These prerequisites will only thrive in a culture that is characterised by a well-balanced division of power and high-trust relations.

The Aachen case study centres on the turn-around of a glass factory. The objective of this turn-around was to put an end to loss-making to secure the future of this factory. In this case study two red threads were identified: the creation of a transparent organisation and the improvement of the processes on the shop floor. The first red thread was especially present in the 'Future' project and the second one in the world-class manufacturing program. The turn-around process was significantly hampered by two phenomena. The first phenomenon was the existence of two (partly) conflicting languages: a financial language and a total quality management language. The second phenomenon was the existence of low-trust relations that hindered constructive cooperation between different parties. These obstacles led to severe paradoxes in the organisation. The case study strongly suggests that paradoxes thrive in a culture that is characterised by deep-rooted mistrust and widespread feelings of powerlessness.

A comparison between the Roermond and the Aachen cases shows significant differences in the embedding of the improvement process and socio-dynamic or cultural factors.

2 Basic beliefs, social criticism, and intellectual tradition

In Chapter 2 of this study, Scientific Management, Socio-Technical Systems Design, Lean Management, Business Process Reengineering, and the Mini-Company Concept have been investigated. These different concepts encompass certain views about man, organisation, and society. These views are determined to a large extent by the basic beliefs, social background, and professional education of their founding fathers.

In the previous chapters I have briefly touched upon my religious and philosophical background. For a clear understanding of the ideas developed in this chapter it is worthwhile making my views about man, organisation, and society more explicit.

2.1 Basic beliefs

The question of 'What is man?' is at the centre of this study. I have been raised in the Calvinistic tradition. This tradition has its own specific views about man and labour. I would like to summarise my interpretation of these views with four key words: *dignity, vocation, compassion,* and *shalom*. The key word 'dignity' refers to the basic nature of man, 'vocation' to the fundamental character of labour, 'compassion' to the painful aspects of labour and its appeal to management, and 'shalom' to an eschatological perspective of labour and labour relations.

> *Reflection.* The key words 'dignity' and 'vocation' belonged to my 'vocabulary' from my college days onwards (see Ch. 3, section 1.2). However, the importance of the words 'compassion' and 'shalom' were made clear to me in the glass factory in Aachen. Every morning I made my rounds on the shop floor of the factory. I shook hands with operators – a local custom – and exchanged a few words with them. Twice a week I visited the inspection area. In this area a number of 'black boxes' were present within which operators visually inspected the polished screens. The cycle time of this inspection was 60 seconds: 10 seconds for taking the screen from the conveyor, 15 seconds for inspecting the outside, 10 seconds for turning, 15 seconds for inspecting the inside, and 10 seconds for putting the screen back onto the conveyor. Most operators performed these actions hour after hour, day after day, and year after year. In this area I shook hand 'between two screens' and exchanged a few words 'during inspection'. Every time, I had to exercise a lot of will power to go there, to shake hands, and to say a few words. I felt uneasy about this short-cycled labour. I felt ashamed that deep-rooted mistrust made this monotonous work even more difficult. And ... I was responsible for it. And ... I could not change it. The only thing I could do was to continue my visits – which were appreciated by the crew ... There I experienced the pain of labour. There I was challenged to show compassion. There I learned ... the necessity and the comfort of an eschatological perspective (shalom).

Dignity

The Bible reveals some basic ideas about human beings. The author of the book *Genesis* writes that God has created man in his own image.[1] The poet of *The Psalms* sings that God has made man a little lower than God himself.[2] How can we interpret these expressions? What does it mean to be 'created in God's image' and to be 'a little lower than God'? In theology there is a lot of discussion about the precise meaning of these words.[3] It is not relevant to review the different positions in this discussion. It is enough to note that there is a total agreement that these words express the *dignity* of human beings. Somehow or other, man is related to God: ... in the image of God ... and ... a little lower than God.

The idea of dignity is the key to understanding the vocation of man. The nature of vocation is summarised in the 'first and greatest commandment' to 'love the Lord your God with all your heart and with all your soul and with all your mind' and in the 'second like it' to 'love your neighbour as yourself'.[4] This vocation is expressed in a quite different way in the two fold assignment (see below).

The idea of dignity is of major importance. First, it says something about myself as manager. It shows that I am not 'just' a creature. It shows that I am related to God: I look like God and I reflect His glory and honour. Second, it says something about my fellow men. They are also related to God. They are also created 'in the image of God'. They are also 'a little lower than God'.

The idea of dignity urges managers to rethink the basics of their organisations. This gives rise to many questions. Does the organisation respect the dignity of its employees? Is the quality of labour in accordance with the humanity of man? Can employees develop their unique gifts and talents? Does the style of management bring out the best in the employees? Is there room to employ one's creativity? All these questions challenge managers to develop their organisation in a way which respects the dignity of people.

Vocation

The vocation of man is directly related to his or her divine status. The first chapter of *Genesis* tells us that God created the male and female man in his own image. Then the text states that God blessed the first couple and gave them an assignment.[5] The assignment was two-fold. First, they had to reproduce themselves and to fill the earth. Second, they had to develop nature and to rule over the earth. The second chapter of Genesis describes this part of the assignment with the words 'to work' and 'to take care of'.[6]

The vocation to develop nature and to take care of the earth is embodied in the phrase 'cultural mandate' and the position of the male and female man in the

---

[1] Genesis 1 : 26, 27.
[2] Psalms 8 : 5.
[3] Berkouwer (1962), Berkhof (1985) and Van de Beek 1996. See also Verkerk and Vegter (1990).
[4] Matthew 23 : 37-39.
[5] Genesis 1 : 28-30.
[6] Genesis 2 : 15.

352

word 'stewardship'. In Christian thought, the implications these ideas have for our attitude towards labour and society have been discussed intensively. The Bible portrays man as a responsible being, characterises labour as a divine vocation, and stresses service to fellow men and to God.[7] In addition, it has to be noted that the idea of vocation is very important to experience, to understand, and to reflect upon the meaning ('Sinn') of labour.

The idea of vocation gives managers a handle to judge the quality of labour. It can be used as a standard to discuss whether labour in Western industry is in accordance with the dignity of man. Stewardship implies that employees are deployed as responsible beings. This can be expressed in the authority given to employees to make decisions about their own job and in the integral character of the responsibility of employees. Stewardship implies that employees can take care of the earth. This can be expressed for example in the participation of employees in reducing environmental pollution and in reducing the use of raw materials. Stewardship also implies that employees can serve the interests of fellow men and society. That means they have to know the ins and outs of the product and have to contribute to customer satisfaction. Finally, stewardship implies that labour has to be done in the honour of God. This means that the whole corporation has to behave in accordance with the norms and standards of the Bible.[8]

Compassion

In the New Testament it can be read several times that Jesus – seeing the needs of the crowds – had compassion with them. Compassion is a deep human emotion. Compassion is feeling for people who suffer. This orientation is quite important in the world of labour. In the previous paragraphs I have summarised the biblical teaching about human dignity and human vocation. However, the Bible reveals more. It also tells about the fall, about the rebellion of man against the Creator, and about the judgement of God.[9] One of the consequences of the fall is that the cultural mandate – working and taking care of the earth – became a painful activity. The author of the book *Genesis* speaks of 'painful toil', 'thorns and thistles', and 'sweat'.[10] A comparable characterisation is found in the letters of the apostle Paul who writes that the creation is subjected to 'frustration'.[11]

Karl Marx was one of the first authors who described the painful aspects of labour in full in his book *Das Kapital* (1867). Many organisational sociologists have followed in his footsteps and shown that dehumanisation and alienation are inherent to the Western method of mass production.[12] Despite all initiatives to improve the quality of labour the spectre of Taylorism still roams in many indus-

---

[7]   Berkhouwer (1962), Berkhof (1969, 1985), Douma (1974), Schilder (1977), Mulders (1991), Geertsema (1992), Van de Beek (1996), Verkerk (1997), and Boersema (1999).

[8]   See also Van Riessen (1953, 1962, 1971).

[9]   Genesis 3.

[10] Genesis 3 : 17-19.

[11] Romans 8 : 20.

[12] For example Walker and Guest (1952), Blauner (1964), Karasek and Theorell (1979), and De Sitter (1981).

trial organisations.[13] As a consequence, the phenomena of dehumanisation and alienation still persist.

Compassion is of the utmost importance. It is a prerequisite for caring. Compassion appeals to the manager as human being. It requires a manager to think about the suffering of employees, to consider the phenomena of paradoxes, short-cuts, dehumanisation, and alienation in his or her own organisation, to reflect on the manufacturing process, organisational structure, and style of management. It also requires a manager to be receptive to new ideas to improve the existing situation. Compassion is only possible when a manager makes an effort to build a personal relationship with his or her employees. It is only possible when a manager is present on the shop floor, knows the processes, discusses the vicissitudes of working life, understands the employees' point of view, and confronts him or herself with the pain of labour.

Compassion cannot be taken for granted. In the famous Sermon on the Mount, Jesus proclaimed the coming of the kingdom of heaven. In this new kingdom the old order of distress, domination, and humiliation is replaced by peace, love, and justice.[14] In the nightly discussion with the Pharisee Nicodemus, Jesus emphasised that this kingdom cannot break through unless man is 'born again' or 'born of water and the Spirit'.[15] Jesus was refering to a spiritual rebirth based on his own suffering and dying on the cross. It is my deepest conviction that compassion has to be rooted in the reconciliation with Christ and that renewal of labour and labour relations will be based on the renewal of the Spirit.[16]

Shalom

The Old Testament word 'shalom' has a much broader meaning than what we express with the word 'peace'. It means completeness, soundness, and welfare. It refers to material circumstances as well as to spiritual well being. It is used when one asks or prays for the welfare of another person, another city or another country.

Shalom is one of the most important words of the Old Testament messianism. Shalom symbolises the salvation of God. The prophet Isaiah closely relates shalom to the coming of Jesus Christ. He emphasises that Christ will reign the earth and that his shalom will never end.[17] In the Old Testament prophecies the word 'shalom' is also related to the fruits of labour. The prophet Micah promises that in the kingdom of peace 'every man will sit under his own vine and under his own fig tree'.[18] The prophet Zechariah sees a vision about the justification of the high priest Joshua. In this vision the prophet is told that one day the Lord will return and will remove all sin in a single day. That day, every man in Israel 'will invite his

---

[13]   Pruyt (1996).

[14]   Matthew 5-7.

[15]   John 3 : 1-21.

[16]   In Galations 5 : 22, 23, Paul states that the fruit of the Spirit is love, joy, peace, patience, kindness, goodness, faithfulness, gentleness, and self-control.

[17]   Isaiah 9 : 6, 7.

[18]   Micah 4 : 4.

neighbour to sit under his vine and fig tree'.[19] It is remarkable that the Old Testament prophecies do not focus on labour, but focus on enjoying the fruits of the earth. Grapes and figs are symbols of peace and well being.

The New Testament meaning of the word 'shalom' is two-fold. On the one hand, it is emphasised that the Old Testament promises are fulfilled in Christ.[20] In one of his teachings Jesus himself says his disciples will have peace in him.[21] The apostle Paul writes that peace is a fruit of the Spirit.[22] On the other hand, the New Testament is pervaded with the thought that the shalom will be complete and endless by the Second Coming of Christ. The book *Revelations* tells us that in the New Jerusalem there will be 'no more death or mourning or crying or pain' for the 'old order of things has passed'.[23] This book also speaks about the fruits of the earth. A river flows through the New Jerusalem. On both sides of the river is a tree of life. These trees bear new fruit every month, and the leaves of these trees are for the healing of the nations.[24]

The idea of shalom places the value of labour in an eschatological perspective. First, it stimulates the believer to make one's work faithful and to contribute to the coming of the new order. Secondly, it shows that one day an end will come to painful labour, dehumanisation and alienation. One day we will sit under our own vine and fig tree. One day, we will pick the fruit of the trees in the New Jerusalem.

2.2 Social criticism

I was brought up on social criticism. At home we debated political questions. At the students' union we questioned the order of western society. One of the first books I read about this subject was *Techniek en Toekomst* (1972) by Egbert Schuurman. This book came out in the English language under the title *Technology and the Future: A Philosophical Challenge* (1980). Another book that has strongly influenced my thinking was *Kapitalisme en Vooruitgang* (1976) by Bob Goudzwaard. This book came out in the English language under the title *Capitalism and Progress. A diagnosis of Western Society* (1979). Both books resulted – to phrase it figuratively – in a loss of my virginity with respect to the roles of technology and the economy in Western society. I would like to consider the key ideas of these studies.

> *Reflection.* In my college days, I often wondered whether the analyses of Schuurman and Goudzwaard were too pessimistic. I doubted the fundamental character of the technological and economic mechanisms that they said threaten human freedom. Now, reflecting upon fifteen years of industrial experience, I believe that the impor-

---

[19] Zechariah 3 : 10.
[20] E.g. Luke 2 : 14, Ephesians 2 : 14, and Romans 5 : 1.
[21] John 16 : 33.
[22] Galatians 5 : 22.
[23] Revelation 21 : 4.
[24] Revelation 22 : 2.

tance of these analyses cannot be underestimated. Fortunately, many employees – from chief execute officers to operators – fight against the techonological and economic domination of human responsibility. Nevertheless, mechanisms described by Schuurman and Goudzwaard still persist and dominate the development of western industry. Their call for a normative development of technology and the economy is just as relevant as in the seventies and eighties.

Technology and the Future. A Philosophical Challenge

Technology and the Future deals with a number of contemporary thinkers who have occupied themselves with the relation between technology and culture, the future of technology, and the meaning ('Sinn') of technology. It pays particular attention to the implicit or explicit motives that pervade and unify their views.

The first group of philosophers that are discussed are the so-called transcendentalists (Jünger, Heidegger, Ellul, and Meyer). This group of philosophers emphasise the freedom of man. They consider technology as an autonomous power that threatens the human subject and its freedom. For that reason, they judge technological development negatively. The second group of philosophers that are discussed are the so-called positivists (Wiener, Steinbuch, and Klaus). This group of philosophers emphasise the blessings of modern technology. They believe that the methods of science and technology can control the development of man and society. The reward of such control is welfare and prosperity; the price is a future that is determined by science and technology, and not by human freedom.

Schuurman shows that the transcendentalists make human freedom absolute with the result that they come to a negative judgement of technology. The positivists, however, make the scientific and technological absolute with the result that they clash on the problem of freedom. Schuurman wonders whether it is possible to find a way out of these difficulties. He argues that the origin of the tensions within the thought of the transcendentalists and positivists is the idea of 'human autonomy'. The transcendentalists emphasise human autonomy as expressed in human freedom and the positivists stress human autonomy as expressed in mastering the development of society.

Schuurman holds that every form of human autonomy has to be rejected. He proposes a philosophy that is based on the confession that reality is a creation of God. This view implies that man – as partner of God – has been endowed with freedom and has been given the responsibility to advance history. In this view, man has to develop technology in agreement with the meaning ('Sinn') character of reality. This means that technology has to match perfectly with the natural environment and human culture. In other words, man has to recognise that his destiny is to serve God and to serve fellow man. As a consequence, technological power and freedom will no longer live in a tensional relation but man will be able to live out his freedom within technology.

Capitalism and Progress. A diagnosis of Western Society

Capitalism and Progress deals with the background of western society. The relation between belief in progress and the growth of capitalism is investigated. Goudzwaard shows that the Enlightenment paved the way for a triumphal procession of the human ratio. Science, technology, and the economy were considered the sources of human progress. Not only sources, but also the guides in the development of western society. Goudzwaard argues that the dominant role of science, technology and the economy has made western society very vulnerable. The natural environment is strongly contaminated. The whole economic and political system appears to be very unstable. Man has adapted himself more and more to the economic-technological system. Especially in the field of labour. Finally, Goudzwaard concludes that the belief in progress has resulted in an enormous tension in our society; he believes that the idea of scientific control threatens the freedom of man.

Is there a way out? Goudzwaard calls for a 'difficult' way out. He argues that western society has to be disclosed under influence of the norms; not only technology and economy, but also the norms of justice and ethics. He calls for a simultaneous realisation of these different types of norms. Goudzwaard recognises that this direction is a very difficult one. It implies nothing less than a mental and spiritual revolution:

o   to bring the unassailable position of technology and the economy into discussion;
o   to take care that technology and the economy do not determine the standards of society but the other way around;
o   to bring back the responsibility for normative development back to the commercial enterprise;
o   to break down the utilitarian view on man, labour, and society.

Goudzwaard emphasises that this revolution requires shared norms and standards. He recognises that this is a problem in a pluralistic society. Speaking out of his own belief, he refers to God the Creator who has given norms and standards to make freedom possible.

Schuurman and Goudzwaard have a lot in common. First, they identify the idea of the autonomy of human beings as one of the main causes of the problems in our society. Second, they argue that the development of technology and the economy is bound to certain norms and standards. Finally, they call for a normative disclosure of western society based on norms of technology, economics, justice, ethics, and love.

2.3 Intellectual tradition

I came into contact with reformational philosophy in my student days. For a number of years I followed the lectures of the professors Klaas J. Popma and Jan D. Dengerink. In my fourth year I participated in a seminar in which *A New Critique of Theoretical Thought* by Herman Dooyeweerd was studied. Dooyeweerd is one of the founding fathers of reformational philosophy and the '*New Critique*' is considered to be his main work. My confrontation with reformational philosophy has been decisive for my intellectual development.[25]

> *Reflection*. In the third and fourth year of my study at the University of Utrecht I followed some lectures about the 'idea of truth'. These lectures made me very confused. I lost sight of the difference between 'scientific truth' and 'religious truth'. Intensive discussions with fellow students and reformational philosophers helped me to understand the different characters of science and religion.

Dooyeweerd observes that communication between different philosophical schools not very smooth. He notes that these schools are on different wavelengths, misunderstand each other, and are unable to fathom each other's motives. He questions why a debate on philosophical problems appears to be so difficult.[26]

Dooyeweerd suggests that the root cause of these difficulties lies in different opinions about the character of philosophical thought itself. He shows that different philosophical schools have different starting points; especially regarding nature and the character of human thinking. The crux is that every school takes its own view about the human ratio for granted. As a consequence, this view is not brought up for discussion. In fact, it is believed that every philosophical school can 'lay its own foundation' for theoretical thinking. However, the different schools are not aware that their starting points are different. This greatly impedes a real debate about philosophical problems.

Dooyeweerd does not believe that philosophical thinking can 'lay its own foundation'. In his view, such an undertaking can be compared with a farmer who pushes his barge along a canal by placing his pole in the barge itself or with the miracle of Baron Von Münchhausen who succeeded in pulling himself out of the swamp by his own wig.[27] Dooyeweerd makes plausible that the starting points of theoretical thinking cannot be founded on a rational basis. He states that these starting points precede theoretical thinking. More than that, they make theoretical thinking possible. Therefore, they are characterised as 'pre-scientific', 'supra-theoretical', or 'religious' presuppositions.

Dooyeweerd labels the idea that philosophical thought can 'lay its own foundations' as the 'dogma of the autonomy of philosophical thought'. In his opinion, one of the tasks of philosophy is to make this dogma into a *critical problem*. He takes the view that a 'new critique' of theoretical thought is necessary to unmask this

---

[25] Since that time, I have applied this philosophy in a number of studies to understand complex phenomena and to interpret changes in the climate of thought. See for example Verkerk (1989) and Verkerk (1997).

[26] Dooyeweerd has elaborated on his line of thought in his opus magnum *A New Critique of Theoretical Thought*. This work is not very reader-friendly due to its specific vocabulary and complex sentences. The best introductions to his 'new critique' are the papers 'Calvinistische wijsbegeerte' in Dooyeweerd (1967) and 'The Pretended Autonomy of Philosophical Thought' in Dooyeweerd (1975).

[27] Kalsbeek (1975).

dogma and to trace its religious presuppositions. Later, he uses the term 'transcendental critique'.

The aim of Dooyeweerd's 'transcendental critique' is two-fold. Firstly, he wants to develop a radical Christian philosophy. This means a philosophy that respects the sovereignty of God. Secondly, he wants to pave the way for a real discussion between the philosophers of different schools. He believes that a transcendental critique should make it possible to penetrate each other's supra-theoretical presuppositions.

I would like to focus on three elements of the transcendental critique of Herman Dooyeweerd: first, his statement that all theoretical thinking has a religious root, second, his view about the diversity, the coherence, and the unity of reality, and third, his analysis of the character of theoretical thought.

The religious root of theoretical thinking

In the foreword to *A New Critique of Theoretical Thought* Herman Dooyeweerd states that the great turning point in his thinking was 'marked by the discovery of the religious root of thought itself'.[28] He takes two different routes to make this statement plausible.[29] The kernel of these routes is that the process of acquiring

---

[28] Dooyeweerd (1969, I, pv). In the earlier Dutch edition the same remark can be found (Dooyeweerd, 1935, I, pv).

[29] The first way (Dooyeweerd, 1969, I, p3 ff.) is based on the idea that philosophy has to focus its attention on the 'totality of meaning' of our temporal cosmos. It is argued that taking a position outside or above this temporal cosmos is necessary to investigate this totality. The choice of such a position – an Archimedian point – is a religious act that can not be justified theoretically. The first way is also described extensively in the original Dutch version of '*A New Critique*' (Dooyeweerd, 1935, I, p5 ff.). The second way (Dooyeweerd, 1969, I, p34 ff.) is based on an analysis of the character of theoretical thought. This analysis is done in three steps. Firstly, it is argued that theoretical thought is based on dissociation and abstraction. In normal life we experience reality as a totality. However, in theoretical thought the many-sidedness or multi-dimensionality of reality is dissociated in different aspects or dimensions, e.g. physical, psychological, social, economic, juridical, or religious. These different aspects or dimensions are investigated analytically by the different sciences. Dooyeweerd characterises this analytical investigation as an antithesis: the logical aspect of our thought is opposed to the non-logical aspects of investigation. Secondly, this antithetical relation raises the question of how these opposed aspects can be synthesised in order to acquire knowledge. Dooyeweerd states that such a synthesis can only be done from a position above the opposed aspects. In other words, a synthesis requires a supra-theoretical position. In the view of Dooyeweerd that position is the human I-ness. After all, thinking is a human acivity: *I do think*. The 'I' does is not wrap up in theoretical thinking, but thinking is a function of me. In conclusion, Dooyeweerd locates the Archimedian point for the synthesis in the human I-ness. Thirdly, the question 'What is man?' is raised. Dooyeweerd states, in accordance with Calvin and Augustine, that our self-knowledge is dependent upon the knowledge of God. The implication of this statement is that the human I-ness has a religious character.

theoretical knowledge is not an act of an autonomous ratio but an act of a living human being.[30] He stresses that this living human being has a religious character. Therefore, differences in religious views will result in differences in starting points of theoretical thought.

Dooyeweerd characterises the religious view of human being on reality with the term 'religious ground motive'. This ground motive drives his or her thinking and acting.[31] It consists of basic ideas about the diversity and coherence of reality, the unity or totality of reality, and the Origin of reality.[32] Dooyeweerd distinguishes four religious ground motives in the history of Western civilisation. The first is the Greek form-matter motive, the second is the biblical motive of creation, fall, and redemption, the third is the scholastic motive of nature and grace, and the fourth is the Humanistic motive of nature and freedom.[33]

What is the importance of the idea of a religious root of theoretical thinking for organisational science and business ethics? In the first place, in organisational science technological and economic imperatives are still dominant. These imperatives are often presented as axioms that need no further justification. The idea of a religious root of theoretical thinking helps us to trace the hidden presuppositions about man, labour and organisation behind these imperatives; presuppositions that have a pre-scientific or religious origin. In the second place, in organisational science and business ethics different schools and trends are present. The communication between these schools and trends leave a lot to be desired. With the result that the kernel of a certain approach is not really understood, discussion and criticism remains too superficial, and learning within the scientific community does not take place.[34] In my opinion, it is very fruitful to penetrate each other's approaches up until the ultimate (pre-scientific or religious) starting points have been identified. Making starting-points explicit opens the possibility to discuss them from within, to analyse their internal consistency, and to confront them with daily experience.

The diversity, coherence, and unity of reality
The transcendental critique of Dooyeweerd implies an ontology or cosmology.[35] That means it presents a view about the character of reality. Dooyeweerd distin-

---

In summary, Dooyeweerd presents two ways to show that the dogma of the autonomy of philosophical thought does not stand up against critical analysis. Both ways shows that theoretical thought has a (hidden) religious root.

The transcendental analysis of Dooyeweerd is not undisputed. An overview of the criticism is given by Geertsema (in Griffioen and Balk, 1995, p11 ff.), Woudenberg (in Woudenberg et al., 1996, p21 ff.), and Vos (in Brink et al., 1997, p9 ff.).

[30] The idea that knowledge is *human knowledge* has been elaborated on by Geertsema (1992).

[31] Dooyeweerd (1975, p32).

[32] Dooyeweerd (1969, I, p69).

[33] Dooyeweerd (1969, I, p61 ff.) and (1975, p35 ff.).

[34] A striking example is the communication between the different schools within Socio-Technical Systems Design, see Van Eijnatten (1993).

[35] Dooyeweerd (1969, I, p38 ff.; 1975, p1-60).

360

guishes between the 'what' and 'how' of reality. The 'what' refers to concrete things, distinct structures, specific events, individual living beings, or certain social processes. The 'how' refers to the different aspects or dimensions of these things, structures, events, beings, or processes.

Dooyeweerd points out that every object, phenomenon, or living being functions in a lot of different aspects or dimensions. Dooyeweerd uses the example of a prism to elucidate this. A prism refracts white light into a diversity of beautiful colours. In the same way, a scientific analysis 'refracts' our experiential reality into a rich diversity of different aspects or dimensions.[36] In total, Dooyeweerd identifies a set of fifteen different aspects or dimensions: arithmetic, spatial, kinematic, physical, biotic, sensitive (psychic), logical (analytic), historical (power), lingual (meaning ('Bedeutung')), social, economic, aesthetic, juridical, moral, and faith (belief, trust). Every object, phenomenon, or living being functions in all these different aspects or dimensions.

Every mode or dimension is characterised by its own 'kernel'. This kernel cannot be reduced to one of the other dimensions. For example, the sensitive or psychic dimension is characterised by the moment of 'feeling'. This moment is unique. The juridical dimension is characterised by the moment of 'justice'. This moment is also unique. The idea of uniqueness raises the question about the relation between the different aspects or dimensions. Dooyeweerd stresses that the different aspects or dimensions are closely related: they refer to each other. Every aspect refers to the other aspects: to the ones that precede this aspect and the ones that succeed this aspect. In fact, a series of so-called analogical moments is present. For example, the sensitive or psychic modal aspect refers backward to the spatial aspect (sensation of spatiality) and refers forward to the aesthetic aspect (aesthetic feeling). In both cases the phenomenon is still characterised by the modal moment of 'feeling'. In other words, within a certain aspect or dimension all others come back via references. These references show the coherence of the different modes of experience.

The metaphor of the refraction of light also illustrates the idea of unity. Unrefracted light is split up into a number of different colours. These colours owe their existence to their source: the original white light. The same holds for our reality. Our 'unrefracted' reality is split up into a number of different aspects or dimensions. The different aspects or dimensions of our experience owe their existence to their source: the original whole reality. In turn, this whole reality is based on the act of creation of God. This means that the unity of reality rests upon the unity of divine law. This unity is expressed in the central command of love: to love the Lord and our fellow-creatures with all our heart, all our soul and all our mind.[37]

What is the significance of these ideas for the theory and practice of organising? Most important, Dooyeweerd's approach offers a cosmology of created reality. This cosmology functions as a basis for an all-embracing ethical theory. The cornerstone of this theory is the idea of multi-dimensional normativity: that different kinds of norms have to be realised simultaneously. I would like to specify these

---

[36]   Dooyeweerd (1969, I, p101, 102).
[37]   Dooyeweerd (1969, I, p101, 102).

general statements with a view to organisational science. Firstly, a number of new production concepts claim to offer an integral or holistic approach. Dooyeweerd's theory lends a helping hand to discuss such claims and to investigate a new approach. Secondly, a lot of questions are asked by organisation scientists about the relationships between technical, social, economic and moral considerations. Dooyeweerd's theory shows that these different dimensions (a) have their own character and own normativity, and (b) are strongly related. In addition, ignoring these normativities and relations is done at the expense of the human character of the organisation. Finally, the close connection between the unity of the multi-dimensional reality and the central command of love contains the promise that an integral and human design of technical organisations is possible. It is a challenge to cash in such a promise.

The character of theoretical thought

The transcendental critique of Dooyeweerd also has an epistemological meaning.[38] Dooyeweerd argues that theoretical thought is based on separation and abstraction. That means that in the scientific approach empirical reality is investigated by separating it into its different modal aspects. This act of separation entails that one modal aspect is abstracted from the unity of reality. In other words, the scientific method implies that the many-sided or multi-dimensional reality is broken up; one aspect or dimension is set apart and this aspect or dimension is studied in detail. For example, in psychological investigations the researcher tries to separate the psychological mechanism from other mechanisms, e.g. social or economic. Such a separation is often realised by doing a laboratory experiment with test subjects. In such a context, the coherence with other aspects or dimensions is broken in order to investigate the 'pure' mechanism.

The theoretical attitude of thought easily leads to the lapse that the investigated aspect or dimension is made absolute. For example, economic investigators often believe that in the end all human behaviour can be explained in economic terms. A comparable lapse is found in management circles in which employees are only described in terms of costs.

2.4 Conclusion

Basic beliefs, schools of social criticism, and intellectual traditions form core 'schemes of interpretation' (Weick). These cores influence my observations as ethnographer, my actions as manager and my reflections as scientist. Sometimes they function as a standard, sometimes they give direction, and sometimes their influence is not that clear.

---

[38] Dooyeweerd (1969, I, p38 ff.; 1975, p1-60).

3 The manager as ethnographer

In the Introduction to Chapter 1 it has been argued that an ethnographical research strategy would be very suitable for mapping out the context in which paradoxes arise and new production concepts fail to meet expectations.

The manager as ethnographer? It sounds like a contradiction in terms. A manager acts and an ethnographer observes. A manager is under constant pressure and an ethnographer works at his or her own leisure. A manager has no time to think and an ethnographer has abundant time to reflect. At first glance, the role of a manager seems to have nothing in common with the role of an ethnographer. This especially holds for factory management. This conclusion appears to be confirmed by literature because ethnographical studies by factory managers are entirely absent. Nevertheless, the main strategy chosen in this thesis is the ethnographical case study. This choice asks for a critical evaluation. First, the main arguments for an ethnographical study will be recapitulated. After that, the ethnographical method will be evaluated from an epistemological and methodological point of view.

3.1 Why organisational ethnography?[39]

In recent decades a number of authors have pleaded to use organisational ethnography. It is argued that an ethnographical method is very suitable 'to get as close as possible to the world of managers'.[40] Dalton criticises the theoretical approach in management science and states that an ethnographical method is necessary 'to interpret this world and its problems from the inside'.[41] Graham distinguishes between the 'rational mind' and the 'transactional mind'. The rational mind is about what we think, and the transactional mind is about what we do. He states that what is actually *done* in an organisation cannot be revealed by interviews and surveys but has to be investigated by participative observation.[42] Dyer and Wilkinson also call for an ethnographical approach. In their opinion, such an approach may provide a 'rich description of the social scene' and will reveal the 'deep structure of social behaviour'.[43] Roosen takes the view that the ethnographical method is the only method that gives a deeper insight into the relation between the behaviour of a group and the attached meaning system ('Bedeutung').[44] Watson argues that the 'ethnographer's hand' is required to understand the basic organisational activities and processes in which managers are involved.[45] Scott-Morgan states that

---

[39] This question has been discussed extensively in Chapter 3, section 1.4.
[40] Dalton (1959, p1).
[41] Dalton (1959, p1).
[42] Graham (1984, p528-530).
[43] Dyer and Wilkins (1991, p615).
[44] Roosen (1991, p12).
[45] Watson (1994, p1-8).

managers have to align the formal and the informal rules in an organisation. To identify and to understand informal rules an ethnographical method is required.[46] Finally, Bate argues that anthropology is about the detailed social processes of everyday life. Therefore, there is 'no other way to study process and change' in organisations.[47]

In summary, a number of studies point out that organisational ethnography is very valuable in getting insight into the basic processes of an organisation. In the words of Graham, organisational ethnography reveals the 'way we operate around here'.[48]

Roosen emphasises that every ethnographical study presents a 'partial perspective'.[49] In concrete terms, this study presents the partial perspective of a factory manager. Figure 3.1 gives an overview of the advantages and disadvantages of this perspective.[50]

Author	Advantages of factory manager as ethnographer
Dalton (1964); Roosen (1991)	Accessibility to (nearly) all information and presence in confidential meetings
Dalton (1964); Roosen (1991)	Development of relationships of mutual trust with informants
Dalton (1964); Bate (1997)	Long stay on the shop floor
Rooen (1991)	High level of working knowledge
This study (both cases)	First order description of the feelings, intentions and beliefs of a factory manager
This study (both cases)	Highest degree of participation with respect to the research question
This study (Roermond case)	Possibility 'to experiment'

Figure 3.1a Overview of advantages of a factory manager as ethnographer

---

[46] Scott-Morgan (1994).
[47] Bate (1997, p1165).
[48] Graham (1984, p529).
[49] Roosen (1991, p2).
[50] See also Chapter 3, section 1.4.3.

Author	Disadvantages of factory manager as ethnographer
Dalton (1964)	Presence of the factory manager may disturb the environment being investigated
Roosen (1991)	Interference between the role of the manager and the role of ethnographer
Author of this study (both cases)	Managerial bias: positive bias with respect to his or her own behaviour
Author of this study (Roermond case)	Managerial bias: positive bias with respect to results
Author of study (later experience)	Managerial bias: 'four-in-a-row effect'

Figure 3.1b Overview of disadvantages of a factory manager as ethnographer

3.2 Methodological evaluation

How did the ethnographical method function in practice? Were all the predicted advantages experienced? Were the predicted disadvantages avoided? First, the advantages of the role of the factory manager as ethnographer will be evaluated.

First order description of the feelings, intentions, and beliefs of a factory manager. A factory manager feels the tension of the factory in his or her own body. S/he is subjected to the continuous pressure to deliver products, the everlasting obligation to decrease costs, and the monthly battle to show profits. S/he is personally responsible for the organisational processes in the factory. For that reason, s/he can never visit the shop floor unmoved. A factory manager is also part of a change process. S/he feels the excitement of realising organisational innovation. S/he feels the pain of closing a factory. Therefore, a first order description is invaluable in understanding how a manager experiences critical phases and change processes. In addition, every organisation has its own 'language'. This means that managers have to found their ideas and proposals with arguments from the accepted 'discourse' of the organisation.[51] This discourse is generally dominated by technological and economic imperatives. As a result, the intentions and basic beliefs of a manager remain hidden. For that reason, a first order description is very important in understanding the intentions and basic beliefs of a factory manager.

High level of working knowledge. A factory manager has a high level of working knowledge. To observe and to interpret processes on the shop floor requires a detailed knowledge about technical, logistical, and organisational processes. As mentioned before, it takes a new manager at least two to three years to understand these processes in detail. Participating in improvement teams significantly increases this working knowledge. Usually, in such teams the participants get to the bottom of the issues and organisational failures are mercilessly laid bare. At the same time, a detailed insight is obtained into the behaviour of members of the organisation.

---

[51] Compare Nijhof (1999, p171 ff.).

The design and implementation of an improvement also significantly increases the working knowledge of a manager. Generally speaking, an 'external' ethnographer can never reach the same level of working knowledge as a factory manager.

Highest degree of participation with respect to the research questions. The research questions of this study are investigated from the perspective of the factory manager. By definition, the choice of this perspective implies that the factory manager has the highest degree of participation with respect to the topic of this study. In addition, s/he is a key actor in the design and execution of change processes. His or her behaviour will give meaning ('Bedeutung') to these change processes. Undoubtedly, the partial perspective of the factory manager is necessary to investigate the relation between paradoxes, change processes, style of management, and patterns of meaning.

Possibility 'to experiment'. The factory manager is one of the key actors in the process of organisational development. This gives him or her the possibility to intervene in a knowledgeable and well-timed fashion. In other words, this gives him or her the possibility 'to experiment'. The Roermond organisation has been developed in a process of trial and error. In retrospect, this process can be characterised as a lengthy experiment to answer the research questions of this study. The development of the Aachen organisation also had an experimental character. The basic ideas about the responsibility and accountability of operators on the shop floor had already been crystallised. Every step in the development was intended to realise these basic ideas. The possibility to experiment is a unique opportunity of a manager/ethnographer.

Long stay on the shop floor. The factory manager will generally hold his or her position for a long period of time. A period of two years – as in the Aachen case – is considered to be short. A period of five years – as in the Roermond case – is regarded as normal. That means that a manager/ethnographer can intensively observe the development of an organisation over a number of years. It especially enables an in-depth investigation of the long-term results of the actions of a manager. In the Roermond case study the influence of the participative approach could be observed over a period of five years. In this period I spent from half an hour to two hours a day on the shop floor! Such a long presence is impossible for 'external' ethnographers.

The development of relationships of mutual trust with informants. In the Roermond factory I knew all the employees from the beginning on. I had developed a relationship of mutual trust with many of them. Especially with employees with whom I had participated in a Process Inventory Team or improvement team. During the whole period these employees functioned as a reliable informant. In the Aachen factory I developed a relationship of mutual trust with some employees. Especially with employees who I had met during my training period. These employees also functioned as a reliable informant. Generally, in a culture of continuous improvement a factory manager can 'easily' develop relationships of mutual trust with informants because s/he can earn this by giving influence to the operators and by solving the problems of the shop floor.

Accessibility to (nearly) all information and presence in confidential meetings. Both in Roermond and Aachen I had access to (nearly) all official information. I was also present in (nearly) all confidential meetings. There were some exceptions. For example, I was not present in the meetings about the strategic position of the Aachen Glass Factory (i.e. to sell the whole business or to form a strategic alliance). However, even with these types of exceptions I heard (or could find out) the most essential information. This accessibility and presence is a significant advantage for a factory manager as ethnographer.

All the potential advantages that have been listed above may vanish into thin air if the disadvantages that have also been listed appear to be highly significant. The disadvantages may function as a negative sign in a multiplication whereby every advantage is turned into a disadvantage. Therefore, a critical evaluation of the problems and pitfalls of the manager as ethnographer is required.

The presence of the factory manager may disturb the environment being investigated. This can result in the observed phenomena being related to a distorted setting and not to an original setting. In all factories there are formal rules and informal rules. The formal rules are the rules that are written down in instructions and procedures. The informal rules relate to the actual behaviour of (groups of) employees. The presence of the factory manager will disturb the environment if there is a difference between the formal and the informal rules. In Roermond I observed several times that employees changed their behaviour when I came in. This especially relates to matters of discipline, e.g. taking a longer break, eating in the factory, and using industrial clothing incorrectly. Sooner or later, I was informed about such breaches in detail via an informant. In the course of time, the discipline in the factory increased and the differences between the formal and informal rules vanished. In other matters I did not observe that employees changed their behaviour when I came in. Observation by third parties also revealed that this was not an issue.

In Aachen I often observed that my presence changed the behaviour of employees. For example, when I entered a department I saw that people quickly put on their safety gloves. I also observed that people started doing quality checks when I came in. Furthermore, I heard via informants that especially at night and at the weekends formal rules were applied 'creatively'. In Aachen it was a public secret that formal and informal rules deviated from each other. It was also observed in checks and audits. However, management did not know all the deviations and informants did not tell management everything.

Some additional remarks have to be made. Firstly, the observation that employees change their behaviour when a manager comes in is an important observation. It indicates differences between formal and informal rules. It may also indicate the existence of low-trust relations. That means from a methodological point of view, the question is not whether employees change their behaviour when the manager comes in; the question is whether the manager/ethnographer observes employees change their behaviour when s/he comes in or whether the manager/ethnographer receives information about this change in behaviour via other channels (e.g. informants or members of an improvement team). Secondly, in all organisations there are deviations between formal rules and informal rules. And in all organisations new deviations also develop slowly. In an improvement culture all kind of deviations between formal and informal rules sooner or later come to the surface. Then actions can be taken to align them (either by changing the formal rule or by correcting the actual behaviour). In Roermond an improvement culture was present. In the course of time, the formal and informal rules corresponded increasingly. In Aachen an improvement culture was in development. In departments where concepts of manufacturing excellence were implemented the deviation between formal and informal rules decreased gradually, e.g. in the tool shop.[52] Thirdly, informal checks and formal audits are necessary to detect deviations from the formal procedures, to show that working according to the formal procedures is important, and to identify improvement opportunities. In Roermond this practice was fully operational and in Aachen it was partly operational. As a consequence, the differences between formal and informal rules were small in Roermond and considerable in Aachen. Finally, some deviations between formal and informal rules are so subtle that a manager will never observe a change in behaviour when s/he comes in. The only exception may be if s/he has done that job many years him- or herself. These kinds of deviations can only be tackled in organisations that are characterised by a well-trained and committed workforce (as in Roermond). The prerequisites for tackling these deviations are an improvement culture, a well-balanced division of influence and power, and mutual respect and trust.

Interference between the role of the manager and the role of ethnographer. In some cases, the role of manager and ethnographer do not interfere at all. For example, during a meeting of the management team it is easy to make notes, during a visit to the shop floor it is quite easy to ask questions, and during a meeting of an improvement team it is easy to ask questions and to make notes. In other cases, the role of manager and ethnographer do interfere. For example, during informal meetings it is often not possible to make notes because that would arouse suspicions. The interference between the different roles is partly counteracted by a long stay on the shop floor. Generally, 'a missed opportunity' will repeat itself after some time.[53]

Managerial bias: positive bias with respect to his or her own behaviour. A manager/ethnographer describes his or her own actions. By definition such a description is 'coloured' by a bias in observation and interpretation. The most obvious bias is that the manager/ethnographer him- or herself can interpret his or her effect on the behaviour of others too positively. In the case descriptions I have given several examples of this bias. Another bias is the expectation a manager/ethnographer has of his or her colleagues and subordinates. This expectation can easily lead to a wrong interpretation of behaviour. In the case descriptions I have also given examples of this bias.

Managerial bias: positive bias with respect to results. In the course of his or her career a manager learns that it is beneficial to interpret the results of his or her actions positively. This attitude can prevent – albeit temporarily – difficult ques-

---

[52] See Chapter 3, section 3.6.

[53] Bate (1997, p1164) states that such interference is inevitable. He argues that 'being there' is a quality of good ethnography. 'Being there' also implies that a blurring of roles takes place, i.e. the role of manager and the role of ethnographer.

tions from bosses, colleagues, and subordinates. At the same time, it can protect the manager – again albeit temporarily – from additional (time-consuming) actions. This managerial bias is especially present when the manager/ethnographer has 'to sell' the organisational improvements s/he is aiming for. Such sales pitching is not a once-only thing but has to be continued until the potential value of the organisational improvement is generally acknowledged. In conclusion, the manager/ethnographer has to be positively biased with respect to the results of his or her own actions. Such a positive bias can undoubtedly undermines the quality of the ethnographical observation.

Managerial bias: 'four-in-a-row effect'.[54] The manager may be so focused on his or her own position that s/he 'forgets' to make ethnographical observations. This happened to me during my position as factory manager of a multilayer factory (the position I held after leaving the Glass Factory in Aachen). My position came under threat due to a planned reorganisation. Several weeks afterwards a colleague shared some of his observations with me. Then I realised with a shock that I was so intently focused on my own problem that I had neglected to make ethnographical observations.

These pitfalls and disadvantages have to do with the *reliability* of social research in general and in particular the *quality* of a manager as ethnographer. In the description of the methodology a number of measures have been described to overcome these problems.[55] In both cases studies, the use of other observers resulted in comments about my own behaviour and in additional data. Examples of this have been given in the case descriptions. In both case studies I have made use of quantitative and semi-quantitative data gathered via questionnaires and audits. This data modified, refined, extended, corrected, or confirmed my own observations. Examples of this have also been given in the case descriptions. Finally, key people within the organisations reviewed both case descriptions (member checks).

Is playing the roles of manager and ethnographer a contradiction in terms? The above considerations show that playing the roles of manager and ethnographer has a number of specific advantages that cannot be realised by a 'normal' ethnographer. In the words of Bate: "insight always comes from the inside".[56] However, the above considerations have also pointed to a number of pitfalls and disadvantages. It is very difficult for a manager to reflect upon the reliability of his or her own observations and the quality of his or her reflections. It is also very difficult to judge whether or not all relevant phenomena have been covered. The problems inherent to a manager as ethnographer can be partly overcome by the use of other observers, quantitative and semi-quantitative data, and member check of the case

---

[54] I have named this effect after a game. 'Four-in-a-row' is a game for two players. Each player has a number of counters or tokens. In turn, the players place one counter or token on a two-dimensional or three-dimensional board. The first player who gets four counters or tokens in a row has won the game. Players are easily seduced into focusing on their own strategy and ignoring the moves of the other player.

[55] See Chapter 3, section 1.4.4.

[56] Bate (1997, p1161).

description by key figures within the organisation concerned. The conclusion forces itself upon us that ethnography by a manager can be compared with venture capital: the risks are great and if successful the benefits are enormous.

3.3 Epistemological evaluation

In the evaluation of the cases it has been remarked that the case descriptions were written from the perspective that Roermond was a 'normal' case and Aachen an 'abnormal' case.[57] This perspective was not questioned until the cases were compared explicitly. Then it was suggested that the opposite was true: that Roermond was an 'abnormal' case and Aachen a 'normal' case. This led to the thought that if the cases had been experienced in a reversed order – i.e. the Aachen case first and then the Roermond case – the case descriptions would have been quite different. This especially applies to the character and the content of the 'reflection' sections of the case descriptions. This begs serious questions about ethnographical investigations by a manager. How can a manager/ethnographer be judged from an epistemological point of view?

In a field study a manager/ethnographer is his or her own tool. That means s/he has to use his or her own senses to 'measure' the organisation under investigation. What is the character of this tool? How can it be 'calibrated'? How can it be 'sharpened'? I would like to investigate these questions based on the cases described in Chapter 3. First, I would like to mention four 'aha' experiences to explain the character of the manager/ethnographer as his or her own tool.

First, I have been trained in the Dutch approach to Socio-Technical Systems Design. This approach was used to design the lay-out of the Roermond factory in its start-up phase. Later, a benchmark was done and a consultant was called in to discuss the development of the organisation of the factory. A consultant advised to read the book *The New Shop Floor Management* by Kiyoshi Suzaki. I was very enthusiastic about this book. At that time, I did not know how to apply Suzaki's ideas in the actuator factory. Intellectually, I did not 'see' the relations between the socio-technical approach and the mini-company concept. Then I saw the light; I saw that the socio-technical working group was the most natural unit to apply the improvement philosophy of Suzaki to.[58] Obviously, my knowledge about socio-technical theory blocked my thinking about the improvement philosophy of Suzaki.

Second, in my training period in the Aachen Glass Factory I observed a number of phenomena. Especially phenomena relating to process control and continuous improvement.[59] Later on, I discovered my blind spot, i.e. political games on management level. That means the 'calibration' of the actuator experience made

---

[57] Chapter 3, section 4.7.
[58] Chapter 3, section 2.2.7.
[59] Chapter 3, section 3.3.1.

me very sensitive to phenomena on the shop floor but I was not 'tuned' to observe political phenomena. By trial and error I learned to see this type of phenomena.

Third, six months after joining the Aachen Glass Factory I read the book *The Unwritten Rules of the Game* by Scott Morgan. This book opened my eyes for a number of phenomena in the glass factory. I also had a name for it: 'written rules' and 'unwritten rules'.[60] I had a comparable experience when reading the book *In Search of Management* by Watson. This book opened my eyes to the existence of different languages. I could distinguish between a financial language and a total quality management language.[61] Evidently, the aforementioned books sharpened 'the ethnographical tool'.

Fourth, I discussed the Roermond and the Aachen cases extensively with my 'buddy' (Professor Den Hertog). Once he asked me: "Maarten, do you really believe that Roermond was a 'normal' case and Aachen an 'abnormal' case. Is it not the other way around?" This question was really an 'aha' experience. In my view the development of the factory organisation in Roermond was quite normal. From this perspective I judged the situation in Aachen as quite abnormal. However, the question of my buddy immediately switched my perspective around. The case descriptions were already finalised … but … a (hidden) presupposition was made explicit.[62] Suddenly, I had got a new 'pair of glasses' with which to read the case studies.

The above examples refer to step-wise changes in the ethnographical tool under influence of a well-defined event. However, other changes in the tool take place gradually. For example, with respect to the research questions of this study. The key ideas about responsibility and accountability were already present in the Roermond case. These ideas were made explicit in the improvement process in the tool shop. After that, they were used and refined in improvement processes in other departments of the glass factory. Finally, they were validated in another factory (the ceramic multilayer capacitor factory that I managed after leaving the Aachen Glass Factory). Over the years my insight into the processes of responsibility and accountability on the shop floor had gradually increased. As a consequence, the ethnographical tool also sharpened progressively.

The experiences described above show that the tool of a manager/ethnographer – the manager him- or herself – changes continuously. A step-wise change in the tool took place under the influence of intellectual reflection (relation between socio-technical approach and mini-company concept), trial and error (political games on management level), reading books (unwritten rules; existence of different languages) and discussions with a buddy (perspective to interpret the cases). A gradual change in the tool took place under a growing insight in processes on the shop floor (processes of responsibility and accountability). These step-like and gradual changes sharpened the tool of the manager/ethnographer so that the organisation could be 'measured' more adequately. Therefore, a man-

---

60   Chapter 3, section 3.7.2.
61   Chapter 3, section 3.7.2.
62   Chapter 3, section 4.7.

ager/ethnographer has to cherish intellectual reflection, to evaluate daily experience, and to seek external sources to intervene in his or her patterns of thinking
(e.g. books and buddies).

A step-like and continuous change of the ethnographical tool holds both for
manager/ethnographers and university ethnographers. However, a distinct difference comes to the fore. A manager/ethnographer uses the results of an ethnographical observation to get more insight in the concerned phenomena, to change
his or her behaviour, and to improve the improvement plans. Enhanced insight
makes more specific observations possible. A change in management behaviour
leads to a smoother change process. An improvement of plans results in a more
effective implementation. In this process there is continuous interaction between
action, the development of theory, ethnographical observation, and tuning of the
tool (manager/ethnographer). In other words, experimenting, theorising, observing, and tool-development go hand in hand. Such continuous interaction greatly
supports the formation of social theories. Glaser and Strauss emphasise the importance of empirical observations for the formulation of theories in social sciences.
They introduce the concept of 'grounded theory'. A grounded theory is discovered,
developed and verified through the systematic analysis of observations.[63] Due to
the fact that a manager/ethnographer combines the role of actor, experimenter,
observer, and theorist, s/he is in a good position to develop grounded theories. In
this study such a theory is developed with respect to the processes of responsibility
and accountability on the shop floor.

Watson focuses on the interaction between the manager and the organisation. He
introduces the concept of 'strategic exchange perspective' to indicate the
'exchanges' between a manager and his or her organisation. The adjective 'strategic' refers to the interests, purposes, and projects of those involved.[64] Rosen emphasises that an ethnographer interprets his or her observations against 'a tableau
of meaning structures'.[65] The experiences described above show that the exchange
process also holds for meaning structures. In other words, the interpretation of
phenomena by a manager/ethnographer is not a series of single events that 'only'
depends on the meaning structures of the ethnographer him- or herself. On the
contrary, it is an interactive and dynamic process in which many actors play a role.
Paradoxically, it is exactly these dynamics of the strategic exchange perspective
('many actors') that determines the success of a change process.

This study shows that the exchange of meaning structures is an interactive and
dynamic process between a manager/ethnographer and his or her organisation. In
addition, the exchange of meaning structures between a manager/ethnographer and
persons outside the organisation play a role. These findings are strongly supported
by the process approach as developed by the psychologist Karl Weick.

---

[63] Glaser and Strauss (1967).
[64] Watson (1994, p25).
[65] Rosen (1991, p17).

Weick interprets organisations as 'streams of materials, people, money, time, solutions, problems, and choices'.[66] These streams cannot be seen as a single homogeneous flow that moves at a constant rate. On the contrary, they have to be seen as multiple flows that are heterogeneous and that flow at variable rates. So the essence of management is to manage different, heterogeneous, and varying flows. In addition, Weick states that managers do not simply react to their environment but act in the light of their interpretation of their environment. In the words of Weick: they *enact* their environment. What does 'enacting their environment' mean for managers? What are the consequences of this statement for a manager/ethnographer? To answer these questions we have to understand the ideas of Weick in more detail.

The starting point in Weick's theory is the so called double interact.[67] An interact is when an action by actor A evokes a specific response in actor B. A double interact is when the specific response of actor B is then responded to by actor A. The double interact is the basic unit of an organisational process. Double interacts are made up into subassemblies, subassemblies are composed into processes, and processes are assembled into an organisation. The assembly (and disassembly) of subassemblies and processes occur according to certain assembly rules. These assembly rules can be seen as 'receipts' which are inferred from influential organisation members when they create a process.

Weick states that the assembly and disassembly of organising processes resemble processes that are involved in natural selection. He distinguishes four key elements in organising: ecological change, enactment, selection, and retention.[68] The first key element is *ecological change*. Normally, people are not aware of processes that run smoothly. However, when a change, difference, or discontinuity is observed, then people's attention becomes active. The idea of 'ecological change' refers to changes, differences, and discontinuities in a flow of experience that engage attention. The second key element is *enactment*. Enactment is closely connected to ecological change. When changes, differences, or discontinuities occur in a stream of experience, the actor (manager) may take action to isolate those changes for closer attention. The actor "puts part of the stream of experience between brackets in order to investigate it". The third key element is *selection*. The selection process is related to the selection of schemes of interpretation. Such schemes of interpretation are built up out of experiences in the past. The actor tries to reduce the equivocality of the bracketed part of the stream of experiences by using an appropriate scheme of interpretation. The fourth key element is *retention*. This process refers to the storage of a successful interpretation of the bracketed part of the stream of experiences. Stored interpretations can be applied in future selections.

---

[66]   Weick (1979, p42).
[67]   Weick (1979, p89 ff.)
[68]   Weick (1979, p130 ff.).

The key elements ecological change, enactment, selection, and retention are connected in a deviation-amplifying circuit. This circuit is presented in Figure 3.2.[69]

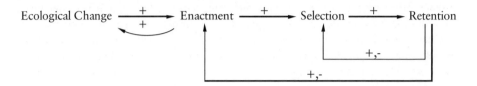

Figure 3.2 The relationships between the four processes of organising according to Weick

The following relations are present:

1.   ecological change and enactment are linked causally;
2.   enactment is linked to selection by a direct causal relationship;
3.   selection is linked to retention by a direct causal relationship;
4.   retention affects both selection and enactment, and these effects can be either direct or inverse, depending on whether the person decides to trust or to distrust his past experience.

This figure shows that ecological change, enactment, selection, and retention are closely connected and mutually dependent.

The theory developed by Karl Weick strongly supports the view that the exchange of meaning structures between a manager/ethnographer and his or her organisation is an interactive and dynamic process. Firstly, Weick's view that every process is composed of double interacts shows the interactive character of the exchange between a manager/ethnographer and his or her organisation. Secondly, Weick's view that enactment, selection, and retention are closely connected and mutually dependent shows that the processes of experimenting, theorising, observing and 'tool-development' in a manager/ethnographer are strongly interlaced. Finally, Weick's view that ecological changes influence the enactment process shows the importance of external interventions in the development of alternative schemes of interpretation.

3.4 The eye of the reflective practitioner

The first research question refers to phenomena on the shop floor. To investigate this question an ethnographical research strategy has been chosen. This study has shown the importance of organisational ethnography for management. It has been confirmed 'from the inside' that a manager does not simply react to his or her

---

[69]   Weick (1979, p132).

environment, but acts in the light of his or her interpretation of his or her environment. And ... that interpretation can be wrong. It appears to be risky for a manager to lead an organisation without reflection and without interventions by externals. An ethnographical attitude opens the eyes to surprises, forces one to dig deeper, urges one to falsify ideas that are generally accepted, invites one to develop new (grounded) theories, and even drives one to reinterpret a whole case. Most of all, organisational ethnography challenges a manager to question his or her interpretation of the environment and to question his or her reaction to ecological changes. This change in attitude might be one the most important benefits of organisational ethnography for management. These considerations also reveal one of the causes of the failure of new production concepts in many factories – our second research question; namely the interpretation of the environment by the factory manager.

4 Socio-dynamic conditions: Trust and Power

In the Introduction to Chapter 1 the failure of new production concepts in many modern factories has been questioned. Are these new concepts universally applicable? Do they have inherent shortcomings? Have we come to the limits of our design theories? These questions will be addressed in this section.

The cases described in this study are quite different. The Roermond case relates to a new product, a new process, and a new business unit. The factory organisation was developed in a process of trial and error. Step by step the processes on the shop floor were improved. Gradually, the necessary conditions for employees on the shop floor to assume responsibility and accountability were fulfilled. Paradoxes were identified and dismantled in a joint activity between management and employees.

The Aachen case relates to a mature product in an existing factory. The Aachen Glass Factory was originally a hierarchical and bureaucratic organisation. In the last decade the culture of the organisation gradually changed into a more demo-cratic one. This development was halted in April 1998 by the coming of a new plant manager. In many cases, the necessary conditions for employees on the shop floor to assume responsibility and accountability were not fulfilled. As a consequence, different types of paradoxes could be observed. The process of identifying and dismantling these paradoxes did not run smoothly.

In the last section of Chapter 3 the Roermond case and the Aachen case have been compared on the basis of key variables. It has been shown that both factories were designed according to socio-technical principles. That means that the structural characteristics of both organisations were comparable. However, it appeared that the cultural or socio-dynamic conditions of the two factories differed substantially. Roermond was characterised by an external orientation, a well-developed improvement structure, intense cooperation, a balanced division of power, and high-trust relations. Aachen was characterised by an internal orien-tation, a partly developed improvement structure, laborious cooperation, a hierar-chical division of power, and low-trust relations. Ultimately, the differences between the Roermond case and the Aachen case appear to be socio-dynamic: trust and power.

I have an anxious foreboding that the phenomena of trust and power are strongly related. In the Aachen case I observed that low-trust relations and organisational powerlessness went hand in hand. In addition, I experienced the effects of low-trust and powerlessness on my own body. It resulted in an under-current of fear, feelings of insecurity, a lot of stress, and periods in which problems were threats instead of challenges. Maybe these phenomena reinforce each other.

The Roermond case and the Aachen case will be re-interpreted from the perspective of trust and power. It is presupposed – referring to the research question of this study – that trust and power are the key conditions for enabling the responsible behaviour of employees on the shop floor. This re-interpretation will be done in the following steps: exploring the phenomena of trust and power (4.1), comparing the cases with respect to trust and power (4.2), analysing the relation between organisational design and the development of trust and power relations (4.3), describing the low-trust dynamic in Aachen (4.4), studying the high-trust dynamic in Roermond (4.5), and finally re-defining the idea of responsible organisations based on the relationship between trust, power, and organisational effectiveness (4.6). In the Appendix the multidimensional character of the phenomenon 'trust' is reviewed.

In the course of this study, the main research process shifted from 'participative observation', to 'the interpretation of the individual cases', and finally to 'the re-interpretation of both cases from a perspective of trust and power'. It has to be noted – both from a methodological and epistemological point of view – that these processes were closely interwoven. A complicating – but unavoidable – factor is that the one case (Roermond) preceded the other (Aachen).

4.1 Initial exploration

In the last decade a lot of effort has been made to try and understand the different characteristics of the phenomenon of 'trust' in organisations. It is becoming clearer and clearer that this phenomenon is quite complex. It has been shown that trust consists of different facets (e.g. psychological, social, economic, moral), depends on the organisational context (e.g. individual, group, firm, between firms), and develops itself in stages (e.g. from conditional to unconditional).[70] Such complexity is indicative of the importance of contextual factors. What is trust? The well-known study of Mayer et al. defines trust as[71]:

> "... the willingness of a party to be vulnerable to the actions of another party based on the expectation that the other will perform a particular action important to the trustor, irrespective of the ability to monitor or to control that other party."

This definition contains three main elements. The first is the existence of dependency between two parties. The second is the willingness to accept risk or uncertainty in this relation. The third is the belief that the other party will not take advantage from the vulnerability resulting from this willingness. Most definitions of trust share these three elements.[72] Mayer et al. do not specify the subject of the 'willingness' or 'expectation'. Rousseau et al. point out that economists tend to view trust as calculative behaviour, psychologists as personal attributions, and sociologists as a property of relationships.[73] Hosmer defines trust as an expectation

---

[70] Hosmer (1995), Mayer et al. (1995), Kramer and Tyler (1996), Bigley and Pearce (1998), Jones and George (1998), Lewicki et al. (1998), Rousseau et al. (1998), Sheppard and Sherman (1998), Whitener et al. (1998), Kramer (1999), Reina and Reina (1999), Reed (2001), Dirks and Ferrin (2001), Lane and Bachmann (2001), Williams (2001), and Nooteboom (2002).

[71] Mayer et al. (1995, p712).

[72] Lane in Lane and Bachman (2001, p3).

[73] Rousseau et al. (1998, p393).

about ethically just behaviour.[74] Burt and Knez believe that trust has mainly to do with organisational politics.[75] Finally, Nooteboom emphasises that trust has its own character or quality.[76]

It is widely acknowledged that the phenomenon of 'power' in organisations is also quite complex.[77] Kramer and Neale emphasise that an interdisciplinary approach is required to reveal the 'subtle psychological, social, and structural basis of power and influence in organisations'.[78] Tannenbaum, a psychologist, has shown that hierarchy, power and organisational effectiveness are strongly related.[79] In his view, control, power or influence refers to any process in which one party can change the behaviour of another party. He writes[80]:

> "It (control) is now commonly used in a broader sense synonymously with the notions of influence and power. We shall use the term in this way to refer to any process in which a person or group of persons or organisation of persons determines, that is, intentionally affects, the behaviour of another person, group, or organisation".

It is remarkable that this definition does not identify the character of power. It only speaks about 'any process in which ...'. Furthermore, it refers to a specific effect of power, namely a change in behaviour.

Tannenbaum has extensively investigated the relation between power and organisational effectiveness. He concludes that an increase in the total amount of power in an organisation has a positive influence on the effectiveness of that organisation. Van Haren and Van Oostrum have confirmed this conclusion.[81]

In Section 5 of this chapter a philosophical framework will be presented to understand the complex character of organisational reality. In advance of this analysis some preliminary remarks will be made. In reformational-philosophical thought a distinction is made between an entity and a modal dimension. An entity is a concrete thing, phenomenon, event, organisation, or individual person. A modal dimension refers to the different modes of existence of such an entity. For example, a chair is a concrete entity. This entity 'exists' in different ways: it is made of a particular material such as wood or metal (physical dimension), it is used in human meetings (social dimension), it has a certain value (economic dimension), it has an owner (juridical dimension), and it is ugly or beautiful (aesthetic dimension). In total, more than a dozen different dimensions are distinguished. Other

---

[74] Hosmer (1995, p398).
[75] Burt and Knez in Kramer and Tyler (1996, p70).
[76] Nooteboom (2002).
[77] Fox (1974), Van Haren (1984), Handy (1985, p118 ff.), Morgan (1986, p141 ff.), Van Oostrum (1989), Jermier et al. (1994), Kramer and Neale (1998), Boje and Rosile (2001).
[78] Kramer and Neale (1998, pix).
[79] Tannenbaum (1968) and Tannenbaum et al. (1974).
[80] Tannenbaum (1968, p5).
[81] Van Haren (1984) and Van Oostrum (1989).

important dimensions are power, morality, and faith or trust. I would like to emphasise that in reformational-philosophical thought *trust and power as modal dimensions have their own character or quality that cannot be reduced to a psychic, social, or economic mechanism.*[82]

The distinction between entities and modal dimensions is very helpful to clarify a widespread conceptual confusion. On the one hand, *trust and power are phenomena* that appear in all organisations. As concrete phenomena, trust and power function in different dimensions, e.g. psychic, power, social, economic, moral, and faith or trust. Depending on the specific context, some dimensions come to the fore and others remain in the background. For example, in a relationship based on mutual trust between two employees of the same group, psychological and social dimensions play an important role, but in a relationship based on mutual trust between an organisation and its customers particularly economic and juridical dimensions are notable. The context specificity of these phenomena is fundamentally related to their multidimensional character. On the other hand, *trust and power are modal dimensions* of everyday reality. As modal dimensions, trust and power come to the fore in every situation and every phenomenon. Therefore, it is not surprising that these dimensions are identified in a wide variety of organisational contexts. The dimensions of trust and power have their own character and have a complex structure of interrelations with other dimensions of our organisational reality. To understand the in-depth structure of organisational phenomena these interrelations – which are contextually determined – have to be analysed.

The thoughts above justify the conclusion that trust and power are complex phenomena. These phenomena have a complicated structure of interrelations with other modal dimensions of our organisational reality and with other phenomena in our organisational landscape. This conclusion saves us from reducing complex phenomena into simple mechanisms.

4.2 The Employee Motivation Survey

A more detailed comparison between the Roermond case and the Aachen case can be achieved by analysing the data of the Employee Motivation Survey. This survey has been held in both factories and contains a number of questions that relate to trust and power.

Interpreting and comparing this data has to be done with care. The following issues play a role:

o   *Population of survey:* The population of the survey differs between both cases. In the Roermond case the data relates to the *production department* (including management, repair and maintenance technicians, factory engi-

---

[82]   It has to be noted that literature often characterises trust as a psychological phenomenon, e.g. Rousseau et al. (1998) and Kramer (1999). This characterisation ignores the own character or own quality of the trust of belief.

neers, and quality engineers). In the Aachen case the data relates to the *whole organisation*, e.g. management, the production department, the development department, and staff and auxiliary departments;

o *Meaning of the word 'location':* The meaning of the word 'location' differs between both cases. In the Roermond case the word 'location' refers to the Roermond plant. The Roermond plant housed three business units. The Ceramic Multilayer Actuators Business Unit was the smallest one. In the Aachen case the word 'location' refers to the Aachen Glass Factory;

o *Perception versus reality:* A survey measures the perception of the respondents. There may be a difference between the perception of the respondents and the reality. Ethnographical observations can reveal such differences;

o *1999 Aachen survey:* The Aachen survey was done shortly after it was announced that another reorganisation would take place. Therefore it is probable that the results also reflect the feelings of the employees about this reorganisation.

Figures 4.1 and 4.2 summarise the main findings of the Employee Motivation Survey relating to trust and power.

The data presented in Figures 4.1 and 4.2 confirm substantial differences between the actuator factory and the glass factory with respect to trust and power.

Item	RMD 1994 N=110	RMD 1996 N=100	ACN 1996 N=755	ACN 1999 N=502
1. I feel I can trust the management at my location	83 %	80 %	36 %	16 %
2. I feel I can trust my immediate boss	91 %	88 %	66 %	64 %
3. I feel I can trust the people in my department	88 %	88 %	74 %	78 %
4. In my experience, my immediate boss trusts people at my level in the organisation	77 %	88 %	(*)	67 %
5. I usually believe what management at my location says	57 %	45 %	24 %	(#)
6. Management at my location works well together as a team	72 %	70 %	19 %	13 %
7. Management at my location does an excellent job of keeping us informed about matters affectting us	83 %	80 %	34 %	23 %
8. Management style at this location brings out the best in employees	58 %	52 %	32 %	21 %
9. Management at this location is interested in the well-being of employees	78 %	76 %	32 %	(#)
10. Our location has established a climate where employees can communicate openly with those above them without fear of reprisal	75 %	79 %	57 %	46 %
11. I think that management at my location will act on the problems identified through this survey	83 %	80 %	48 %	22 %

Figure 4.1.: Trust-related items of the Employee Motivation Survey. The percentage refers to the total favourable response to the item ('total favourable' is the sum of 'absolutely favourable' and 'tended to favour'). RMD = Roermond; ACN = Aachen; year is year of survey. The items below the blank line refer indirectly to trust.
(*) By accident this data was not present in my file.
(#) This question was not present in the 1999-survey.

382

Item	RMD 1994 N=110	RMD 1996 N=100	ACN 1996 N=755	ACN 1999 N=502
1. I have sufficient authority to do my job well	87 %	89 %	66 %	70 %
2. I have enough flexibility in my job to do what is necessary to provide good service to our customers	69 %	80 %	52%	56 %
3. Decisions are made at an appro priate level in this organisation	62 %	71 %	29 %	12 %
4. I have been in involved in improvement actions following customer day (*)	(#)	55 %	16 %	(#)
5. I have been involved in working in teams across my organisation (*)	(#)	31 %	14 %	(#)
6. I have the information I need to do my job well	86 %	97 %	66 %	64 %
7. I have the resources/tools I need to do my job well	82 %	83 %	70 %	69 %

Figure 4.2.: Power-related items of the Employee Motivation Survey. The percentage refers to the total favourable response to the item ('total favourable' is the sum of 'absolutely favourable' and 'tended to favour'). RMD = Roermond; ACN = Aachen; year is year of survey. The items below the blank line refer indirectly to power.

(*) This item was originally phrased as a question.

(#) This question was not present in the 1994- and 1999-survey respectively.

4.3 Organisational design and the development of trust and power relations

In Chapter 2 of this study it has been shown that manufacturing organisations can be designed in fundamentally different ways. It is tempting to conclude that every design shows its own trust and power patterns.

The relationship between power, trust, and organisational design has been discussed by Alan Fox in his book *Beyond Contract: Work, Power and Trust Relations.*[83] Fox shows that low-discretion jobs – a low-discretion job consists of tasks that are highly prescribed and that have a low discretionary content[84] – lead to low-trust relations between management and employees. He also shows that

---

[83] Fox (1974).
[84] Fox, 1974, p16 ff.

low-trust relations are in general accompanied by low-trust responses from the side of the employees such as absenteeism, high sickness, indifferent performance, high level of wastage, sabotage and so on.[85] Fox argues that the development of high-trust relations between management and employees – including the desired high-trust response of employees – is not possible without a change in job designs, authority relations, and control systems. With approval he quotes Tolfree who states that "so long as one section of the workforce is treated as second class Industrial citizens it is no use expecting from them a first class response".[86] Fox refers to socio-technical design as a possible organisational innovation leading to high-discretion jobs for employees.[87] [88]

To investigate the relationship between power, trust, and organisational design two opposite approaches will be compared: Taylorism versus Socio-Technical Systems Design / The Mini-Company Concept. These approaches have been discussed extensively in Chapter 2 of this study. In the Taylor system the responsibility of an operator is restricted to the execution of one short-cycled production step. The operator has to execute this step according to the instructions. The authority or power required for the execution of this step is very limited: it is restricted to the direct activities of that step. All other elements of this production step – the set-up of the equipment, repair and maintenance activities, judgement of the quality, planning and so on – are located at the next level in the organisation, i.e. the functional foremen. As a consequence, there is a strong division of power: a low-power position for the operator and a high-power position for the functional manager. Additionally, under the Taylor system the operator has a number of functional bosses to control his or her work. These different bosses were originally required to train and to guide the operators. However, in a hierarchical system with a high imbalance of power such an intention never materialises. On the contrary, the message of the whole system is that an operator 'cannot be trusted' and 'needs to be supervised'. Later developments in Scientific Management confirmed this message.[89] The mental revolution as advocated by Frederick Taylor did not take place. The scientific method – which was intended to be a neutral arbiter – could not solve the problem of the opposite interests between management and employees. The scientific method was a tool in the hands of management. As a consequence, this method further increased the mistrust between management and employees.[90] In conclusion, the Tayloristic design of an organisation implies a low-power position for an employee, expresses low-trust in an employee, and generally functions on the basis of a low-trust relation between management and employees.

---

[85] Fox (1974, p66-119).

[86] Fox (1974, p348).

[87] Fox (1974, p340). Note that Fox wrote his book in the early seventies – a period in which the socio-technical approach was still in development.

[88] Slater and Bennis (1964) and Collins (1997) use comparable arguments to show that democracy in industrial organisations is 'inevitably'.

[89] Braverman (1974) and Edwards (1979).

[90] Fox (1974), Tannenbaum et al. (1974) and Heisig and Littek (1995).

In a socio-technical design – especially in the Dutch approach – the situation is quite different. In this case the operator is responsible for the execution of a coherent part of the production process, a module, or a whole product. The operator is also responsible for all other controlling tasks that are inherent to the execution of these steps: the set-up of the machine, judgement of quality measurements, planning of the production and so on. This means the operator has the authority and the power to manage his or her own work. In the mini-company process this authority and power is extended to the formulation of a mission statement, the whole improvement process, and the external relations of the unit. In such a design the operator has a high-power position. The high-power position of an operator symbolises trust and can only function on the basis of trust.[91] In conclusion, the socio-technical design of an organisation implies a high-power position for an employee, expresses high-trust in an employee, and generally functions on the basis of high-trust relations between management and employees.

The thoughts given above could lead us to conclude that each organisational design would have specific trust and power patterns. Comparison of the Roermond case and the Aachen case – factories with a comparable organisational design but different trust and power relations – shows that the relationship between organisational design and the development of trust and power relations is quite complex. It is concluded that:

o   a socio-technical design (in combination with the Mini-Company Concept) is a necessary but not sufficient condition for employees to have a high-power position and for there to be high-trust relations between management and employees (conclusion 1).

4.4 Low-trust dynamics in Aachen

The dynamics of trust appears to be a key to understanding the differences between the Roermond case and the Aachen case. In this section, the low-trust dynamics in Aachen will be discussed. In next section, the high-trust dynamics in Roermond will be studied.

Alan Fox has studied low-trust phenomena in industrial organisations. In his book *Beyond Contract: Work, Power and Trust Relations* he states that highly prescribed and low-discretion work – as in Tayloristic designs – lead to the so-called low-discretion syndrome. This syndrome has the following characteristics[92]:

1.   the employee 'perceives superordinates as behaving as if they believe he cannot be trusted';
2.   'close supervision and bureaucratic rules generate a mutually reinforcing circle';
3.   'a close coordination' is required to coordinate the activities of the employee 'with those of others';

---

[91]   Deci et al. (1989), Heisig and Littek (1995) and Whitener et al. (1998).
[92]   Fox (1974, p25 ff.).

4. the assumption that failures in performance or inadequate performance result from 'careless indifference to job rules and organisational goals' and call for 'punishment and an intensification of supervision';

5. conflicts between employee and superior are handled through 'bargaining processes'.

In general, a low-discretion syndrome is accompanied by low-trust responses from the side of employees such as absenteeism, high sickness, indifferent performance, high rates of wastage, sabotage and so on.[93]

Niklaus Luhmann has investigated the functional effects of trust and power. He emphasises in his book *Trust and power* that trust and power are functionally equivalent.[94] This means that both phenomena are social mechanisms that reduce organisational complexity. In other words, trust and power increase the probability that employees will execute the assigned tasks. In Luhmann's view, managers can realise the objectives of the organisation either by trusting employees or by exerting power over them. In the case of low-trust relations, trust will not work and managers will have to resort to power in order to achieve their objectives.

Costa has shown that employees behave differently towards people they trust than to people they do not trust.[95] Towards people they do not trust they hold information back, decide what to tell, do not express problems or anxieties, become suspicious, and are alert.

The socio-dynamic phenomena of the Aachen Glass Factory show some similarities to the low-trust mechanism described by Fox, the use of power in the case of low-trust relations as predicted by Luhmann, and the behaviour described by Costa. Therefore, it is worthwhile to investigate the Aachen case in more detail.

Figure 4.1 presents an overview of the trust-related items in the Employee Motivation Survey (section 4.2). It shows that medium-to-high-trust relations are found *within* departments and low-trust relations are found *between* management and employees (see items 1 to 5). The low-trust relations between management and employees are accompanied by a lack of cooperation in the management team (item 6), inadequate information given to the crew (item 7), insufficient capitalisation of on the capabilities of the employees by management (item 8), a lack of interest in employees (item 9), the absence of an open climate (item 10), and disbelief that management will use the survey for improvement (item 11).

Figure 4.3 gives an overview of trust-related observations in the Aachen factory. Items 1 to 13 reflect the results of the Employee Motivation Survey and Items 14 and 15 are contrary to the results of the survey.

---

[93] Fox (1974, p66-119).
[94] Luhmann (1979).
[95] Costa (2000, p99-100).

1. existence of stories that management could not be trusted;
2. informally, middle management seldom expressed trust in the management team;
3. informally, middle management often expressed a deep mistrust with respect to the management team;
4. informally, employees regularly expressed mistrust of middle management and the management team;
5. invisibility of management on the shop floor led to mistrust by employees;
6. middle management did not believe that the management team would support difficult decisions in the redesign process;
7. middle management did not believe that the management team would support the world-class manufacturing program;
8. during a review the plant manager openly questioned the commitment of the management team;

9. existence of unwritten rules which contradicted the written ones;
10. employees remarked that managers did not know what happened on the shop floor;
11. an external consultant openly questioned the atmosphere and culture in the management team;
12. a lot of criticism was aired in the corridors instead of the meeting rooms;
13. existence of fear in the organisation;
14. management took great pains to inform the crew about reorganisations;
15. middle management was intensively involved in the 'Future' reorganisation project

Figure 4.3 Trust-related observations in the Aachen factory. The points below the blank line refer indirectly to trust

Figure 4.2 gives an overview of the power-related items in the Employee Motivation Survey (section 4.2). Employees reported that they had sufficient authority, enough information, and the necessary resources and tools to do their job (items 1, 6 and 7). However, they took the view that decisions were taken at the wrong level (item 3). Furthermore, they reported that they were hardly involved in improvement teams (items 4 and 5).

Figure 4.4 gives an overview of power-related observations in the Aachen factory. Items 1 to 3 illustrate the powerlessness of the organisation in solving problems whereas item 4 illustrates the power of the organisation in solving problems.

1. existence of stories of the powerlessness of line management;
2. power of the organisation to obstruct management decisions;
3. middle management and staff expressed feelings of powerlessness in solving critical problems;

4. the management team supported the decisions of middle management in the 'Future' project

Figure 4.4 Power-related observations in the Aachen factory. The item below the blank line refer indirectly to power

How can we understand the low-trust relations in Aachen? How can we understand the low-trust dynamics? How can we understand the powerlessness of the organisation in solving problems? How can we explain the apparent contradictions in the observations (items 1-13 versus items 14, 15 in Figure 4.3 and items 1-3 versus item 4 in Figure 4.4)? In order to do justice to the asymmetry of the employee-manager relationship, I would like to discuss these questions from two perspectives: that of the employee and that of the manager.

Perspective of the employee

To understand the low-trust relations in the glass factory I would like to point to two items. Firstly, we have to keep in mind that the Aachen factory had a hierarchical and bureaucratic background. In general, hierarchical and bureaucratic organisations suffer from mistrust, dissatisfaction, and a low sense of motivation and initiative.[96] In the Aachen factory mistrust and frustration were very deeply rooted. It is quite likely that this was developed in a long period of years. Secondly, the Aachen Glass Factory had made losses for many years in a row. Every new plant manager's brief was to make the factory profitable. Every new plant manager threatened the crew that the factory would be closed if the reorganisations were not successful. Furthermore, every new plant manager announced that there would be redundancies. These announcements were always received with cynicism, particularly as their meaning was ambiguous. On the one hand, the message was 'trust me, I will save the factory'. On the other hand, the message was 'maybe I will dismiss you (for the sake of the others)'.

The ambiguous messages induced a spiral of mistrust and fear. Mistrust stimulates low-trust responses. Fear paralyses an organisation. To compensate for these phenomena management tries to increase its grip on the organisation by hierarchical and bureaucratic measures. In turn, however, these measures increase mistrust and fear in the organisation. The increased level of mistrust and fear result in new low-trust responses and a further paralysis of the organisation. So, employees try to escape from the controlling activities of management in order to serve their own interests. To cope with that, management orders additional hier-

---

[96] Bendix (1956), Fox (1974), and Tannenbaum e.a. (1974).

archical and bureaucratic measures. Fox names this mechanism 'low-trust dynamics'.[97]

Recent research has identified different mechanisms that contribute to low-trust dynamics. Firstly, Kramer has shown that employees who have the lower position in a hierarchical relationship fear being exploited and are suspicious of being unfairly treated. As a consequence, they are more sensitive to false or exaggerated perceptions with respect to actions by management or organisational phenomena. They are also are more sensitive to violations of trust than to confirmations of trust.[98] Secondly, Williams has shown that group membership influences the development of trust. He states that it is especially difficult to develop trust and cooperation across group boundaries, because people often perceive the members of the other groups as potential adversaries.[99] Finally, Costa has shown that employees behave differently towards people they trust and to people they do not trust. Towards people they do not trust they hold information back, decide what to tell, do not express problems or anxieties, become suspicious, and are alert.[100] All these mechanisms were present in Aachen. Employees were very suspicious with respect to the actions and behaviour of management. They considered the management team as an out-group with conflicting goals.

Whitener et al. stress that it is the responsibility of management to initiate relationships based on trust.[101] However, the data presented above shows that the management team – instead of initiating trust and openness – boosted a spiral of mistrust and fear.

> *Reflection.* The management team of the glass factory was unfamiliar with the concept of low-trust dynamics. The mistrust and fear equilibrium was frequently disturbed by decisions of the management team. The behaviour of the management team frequently fuelled the spiral of mistrust and fear. And … I was I member of that team. And … I contributed to the dynamics of mistrust and fear.

> *Reflection.* When I started in the glass factory my starting point was that I would be able to earn the trust of the organisation step by step. In other words, I supposed that the phenomena were reversible, that the spiral could be turned into a direction of trust and openness. In literature, there are examples of low-trust dynamics being broken and being turned into high-trust dynamics.[102] In reflection, the conditions necessary to realise such a reversion were not present in Aachen. The combination of strategic uncertainty, the loss-making situation, and a management team that was no team, made it a 'mission impossible'.[103]

---

[97] Fox (1974, p102 ff.). See also Ashforth and Mael in Kramer and Neale (1998, p89 ff.).
[98] Kramer in Kramer and Tyler (1996, p216 ff.).
[99] Williams (2001).
[100] Da Costa (2000, p99-100).
[101] Whitener et. al. (1998).
[102] Fox (1974, p134 ff.).
[103] Den Hertog and Marie (2001).

Reflection. When I started in the Aachen factory I did not realise how deeply the mistrust and fear were rooted in the organisation. At the same time, I was not familiar with and had no experience of low-trust dynamics and the spiral of mistrust and fear. Furthermore, I was not familiar with the four processes of organising as presented by the psychologist Karl Weick (ecological change, enactment, selection, and retention).[104] As a consequence, I did not realise that my colleagues and subordinates *could only* interpret my words and my behaviour in terms of their 'schemes of interpretation' which were determined by mistrust and fear. On the contrary, I believed that my words and my behaviour would be interpreted the way I intended them to be interpreted. This mechanism also explains why middle management did not (or could not) see the positive actions of the management team (e.g. items 14 and 15 of Figure 4.3 and item 4 of Figure 4.4).

How can we understand the powerlessness of the organisation to solve problems? How can we understand that the change process in the glass factory did not flow smoothly? Is there any relation with mistrust? To answer these questions from the perspective of the employees I would like to refer to three phenomena: low-trust dynamics, organisational resistance, and organisational silence.

First, low-trust dynamics implies a continuous struggle of employees to resist and to escape management initiatives. This struggle has Darwinian characteristics: survival (keeping one's job). This struggle is aimed against all management initiatives – independent of the objective of these initiatives. Paranoid perceptions by normal individuals (Kramer), in-group-out-group phenomena (Williams), and adapted behaviour (Costa) contribute to it. As a consequence, management is continuously *de*-powered by the crew and problems are not solved.

Second, one of the most threatening low-trust responses in change processes is 'organisational resistance'. Organisational resistance refers to the resistance of parts of the organisation to a change process. Piderit strongly advocates that this phenolmenon should not only be considered from the perspective of the manager but also from the perspective of the employee. She especially stresses the ambivalent and multidimensional character of employees' resistance. For example, what some may perceive as unfounded opposition might also be motivated by individuals' ethical principles or by their desire to protect the organisation's best interests.[105] Ashforth and Mael point out that misinterpretation of resistance easily leads to the so-called 'resistance cycle', i.e. control induces resistance, resistance leads to counter control, counter control induces more resistance, and so on.[106] Collinson stresses the ambivalent character of resistance. He identifies two different strategies. By 'resistance through distance' the subordinates try to escape or avoid the demands of authority and by 'resistance through persistence' employees try to seek greater involvement in the organisation.[107] In summary, organisational resistance strongly hampers the implementation of management initiatives.

---

[104]   Weick (1979).
[105]   Piderit (2000).
[106]   Ashforth and Mael in Kramer and Neale (1998, p89 ff.).
[107]   Collinson in Jermier et al. (1994, p25 ff.).

Third, another threatening low-trust response is 'organisational silence'. Organisational silence refers to the phenomenon that most employees know the truth but do not dare to speak the truth to their superiors. Morrison and Milliken point out that a climate of organisational silence is based upon two beliefs. The first belief is that speaking up about problems in the organisation is not worth the effort. The second one is that voicing one's opinions and concerns is dangerous. Such a climate strongly impedes organisational change as it blocks the organisation's ability to detect and to correct errors. Furthermore, the manager may interpret silence as a signal of consensus and success. Finally, it feeds the feelings of the employees that their ideas and views are not valued, resulting in low commitment and low trust.[108] So, organisational silence strongly hinders problem solving and has serious side effects.

In conclusion, mistrust and fear lead to different responses in employees: low-trust dynamics, organisational resistance and organisational silence. In turn, these responses lead to change processes that do not run smoothly and to powerlessness at all levels of the organisation, i.e. *de*-powering of management by employees. A difficult change process and powerlessness elicits hierarchical measures and shows of strength from management, i.e. *de*-powering of employees by management. Hierarchical measures and shows of strength increase mistrust and fear. Again, the circle is round. A low-trust-low-power spiral evolves. In other words, low-trust dynamics induces low-power dynamics. The low-power dynamics consists of a continuous process in which management tries to *de*-power employees and employees try to *de*-power management. Consequently, the total amount of power in the organisation is low. In conclusion, low-power dynamics hampers the improvement of the internal processes and adaptation to the changes in the environment.[109]

Perspective of the manager

In the opening sentences of the paragraph 'Perspective of the employee' I referred to two characteristics of the glass factory: its hierarchical and bureaucratic background and loss-making situation. These characteristics left deep marks on management in terms of its beliefs, feelings, and cognitions. Kramer has shown that 'those on the top' suspect that the individuals for whom they are responsible are shirking their duties and are engaging in acts that might endanger the organisation.[110] Management in Aachen also believed that employees shirked their duties. They perceived the crew as an out-group with endangering interests. This perception hampered the development of trust and the cooperation between both groups (Williams).[111] Luhmann argues – from a functional perspective – that in the case of low-trust relations 'trust' will not work and a manager has to resort to power to realise his or her interests. In this line of thought, a manager will never empower

---

[108] Morrison and Milliken (2000).
[109] This conclusion is in agreement with the studies of Tannenbaum (1968), Tannenbaum et al. (1974), Van Haren (1984) and Van Oostrum (1989).
[110] Kramer in Kramer and Tyler (1996, p216 ff.).
[111] Williams (2001).

his or her employees in a low-trust culture but s/he will try to *de*-power them in order to safeguard the objectives of the organisation. However, every attempt by management to *de*-power employees will result in more distrust from the side of the employees. The accompanying low-trust responses of the employees 'confirm' the belief of managers that employees cannot be trusted. Thus, not only from the perspective of the employee but also from the perspective of the manager, low-trust dynamics (decreasing trust) induces low-power dynamics (continuous *de*-powering of employees by management and continuous *de*-powering of management by employees resulting in a decreasing amount of total power).[112]

It has to be emphasised that low-trust dynamics leads to a paradoxical situation. Management continuously *de*-powers employees (in reaction to the low trust responses of employees). Employees continuously *de*-power management (in reaction to the increased controlling activities of management). In other words, a low-trust-low-power dynamic results in a low-power position of both employees and management. As a result, the total amount of power in the organisation will be low. A low amount of power in the organisation will result in low effectiveness and a low efficiency of the organisation in solving problems.

The Aachen case shows a strong relation between the low-trust dynamic and the low-power dynamic. Based on this case it can be concluded that:

o   a low-trust dynamic induces a low-power dynamic. A key characteristic of a low-trust dynamic is a continuous struggle of management to control and to de-power employees. As a response, employees try to escape the controlling power of management in order to secure their own interests. Management, however, interprets the low-trust response of the employees as a confirmation that 'they' cannot be trusted. So, the low-trust-low-power spiral is fuelled (conclusion 2);

o   a low-trust-low-power dynamic results in an organisation with a low amount of total power. As a consequence, the effectiveness and efficiency of the organisation to solve problems, to make continuous improvements, and to adapt to the changing environment will be low (conclusion 3).

4.5 High-trust dynamics in Roermond

In the foregoing section (4.4) the low-trust dynamics in Aachen has been discussed. In this section the high-trust dynamics in Roermond will be evaluated.

Alan Fox has explored high-trust phenomena in industrial organisations. In his book *Beyond Contract: Work, Power and Trust Relations* he concludes that jobs with a high-discretionary content easily lead to the so-called high-discretion syndrome[113]:

---

[112]   Compare Kramer in Kramer and Neale (1996, p216 ff.) and Williams (2001).
[113]   Fox (1974, p30 ff.).

1. the employees are 'deemed to have commitment to and moral involvement in' organisational goals and values;
2. the belief that 'close supervision and/or detailed regulation by im-personal rules would be inappropriate';
3. 'problem solving relations' of an employee with his or her colleagues;
4. in case of failures or inadequacies the loyalty, support and goodwill of the employee are still taken for granted;
5. conflicts between employee and superior are handled in a 'problem-solving' way.

Generally, a high-discretion syndrome stands for high-trust relations. Fox suggests that the high-discretion syndrome would be an appropriate model for the working practices of senior managers, functional specialists, doctors in hospitals, and so on.[114]

Jones and George have proposed a model for the evolution of trust. In their view, the most common form of trust existing in organisations is conditional trust. *Conditional trust* is 'a state of trust in which both parties are willing to transact with each other, as long as each behaves appropriately'.[115] In conditional trust the 'attitudes of one party towards the other are favourable enough to support future interactions; sufficient positive affect and a relatively lack of negative affect reinforce these attitudes'.[116] *Unconditional trust*, however, characterises "an experience of trust" where "shared values now structure the social situation and become the primary vehicle through which those individuals experience trust."[117] [118] With unconditional trust "each party's trustworthiness is assured, based on the confidence in the other's values that is backed up by empirical evidence derived from repeated behavioural interactions".[119] Jones and George remark that with conditional trust parties are "less likely to cooperate in ways that entail considerable personal costs" whereas unconditional trust "can fundamentally change the quality of the exchange relationship and convert a group into a team."[120] [121]

Costa has shown that employees behave differently towards people they trust and to people they do not trust. Towards people they trust they are willing to be vulnerable, are more open to ideas and suggestions, do not hold information back, and are not careful about what they say.[122]

---

[114] Fox (1974, p36 ff.).
[115] Jones and George (1998, p536).
[116] Jones and George (1998, p536).
[117] Jones and George (1998, p536).
[118] Reina and Reina (1999) have also investigated the development of trust. They indicate the phenomenon 'unconditional trust' with the term 'transactional trust'.
[119] Jones and George (1998, p536, 537).
[120] Jones and George (1998, p539).
[121] A comparable model is developed by McAllister (1995) and Lewicki and Bunker in Kramer and Neale (1996, p114 ff.). See also Nooteboom (2002).
[122] Da Costa (2000, p99-100).

There were some similarities between the socio-dynamics of the actuator factory in Roermond and the high-discretion syndrome proposed by Fox, the model of the evolution of trust developed by Jones and George, and the behaviour described by Costa. Therefore, it is worthwhile investigating the Roermond case in more detail.

Figure 4.1 presents an overview of the trust-related items in the Employee Motivation Survey (section 4.2). The trust of employees in the management of the plant was quite high and in the immediate boss even higher (items 1 and 2). The trust in the people in the department is also high (item 3). In addition, the employees feel that their boss trusts them (item 4). High-trust relations between management and employees are accompanied by good cooperation in the management team (item 6), enough information being given to the crew (item 7), interest of management in well being of employees (item 9), an open climate (item 10), and the belief that management will act upon the outcome of the survey (item 11). This data seems to conflict with the rather low score with respect to the employees' belief in what management says (item 5). The actions of management to bring out the best in employees is also scored much lower (item 8).

Figure 4.5 presents an overview of the trust-related items of the survey by Twente University. High trust in management is reported (items 1 and 2). High trust is accompanied by management support of employees in their daily work (item 3), management support of employees who are involved in improvements and innovation (item 4), information about the business unit (item 5) and attention to problems (item 6). Figure 4.6 summarises the main observations in the actuator factory with respect to trust. The data of the Twente survey (Figure 4.5) and the ethnographical observations (Figure 4.6) are in accordance with the data reported by the Employee Motivation Survey (Figure 4.1). All this data supports the conclusion that high-trust relations were present in the actuator factory.

Item	percentage
1. I have full trust in the management of our business unit	85 %
2. I have full trust in the management of our business unit with respect to improvements and innovations	90 %
3. Management supports us in our daily work and in our teamwork	85 %
4. Management supports the employees who are involved in improvements and in innovations	88 %
5. We are informed about the most important issues of our business unit	75 %
6. Management pays enough attention to our problems	77 %

Figure 4.5 Trust-related items of the Twente survey. The percentage refers to the total favourable response to the item ('total favourable' is the sum of 'absolutely favourable' and 'very favourable' and 'favourable'). The items below the blank line refer indirectly to trust. N = 102

1. in informal discussions trust in colleagues and management was regularly expressed;
2. in informal discussions mistrust in colleagues and management was seldom expressed;
3. employees believed the information given by management;
4. during the discussions about the closure of the business unit the employees believed the information given by management;

5. employees and management easily admitted to failures;
6. improvement teams were allowed to implement their own proposals;
7. mini-companies were allowed to define their own mission statement and improvement program.

Figure 4.6 Trust related observations in the Roermond factory. The items below the blank line refer indirectly to trust

Figure 4.2 gives an overview of the power-related items in the Employee Motivation Survey (section 4.2). This table shows that employees have enough authority and flexibility to do their job (item 1 and 2). Most employees believe that decisions are made at an appropriate level in the organisation (item 3). Employees also report that they have enough information to do their job (item 6) and also have the required resources and tools (item 7).

Figure 4.7 gives an overview of the power-related items of the survey by the University of Twente. Operators report that they have reasonably much influence about general matters, workload, organisation of the work, and improvement and innovation. Figure 4.8 summarises the main observations in the actuator factory with respect to power. The data of the Twente survey (Figure 4.7) and the ethnographical observations (Figure 4.8) are in accordance with the data reported by the Employee Motivation Survey (Figure 4.2). All this data supports the conclusion that a high level of power was present in all levels in the actuator factory.

Item	GM	FM	UL	1st Op.	Op.
1. The influence of different persons/groups on general matters	4.4	5.0	5.1	4.3	3.8
2. The influence of different persons/groups on workload	4.1	4.6	4.9	4.1	3.7
3. The influence of different persons/groups on the organisation of work	3.6	4.5	5.3	4.7	4.1
4. The influence of different persons/groups on improvement and innovation	4.6	5.4	5.2	4.3	3.9

Figure 4.7: Power-related items of the Twente survey. The level of influence of all hierarchical levels as perceived by the (first) operators. This data represents the mean values on a six-point scale (1 = very little influence, 6 = significant influence). GM = general manager; FM = factory manager; UL = unit leader; 1st Op. = first operator; Op. = operator. N = 102

1. mini-companies had the authority to define their own mission statement and improvement program;
2. mini-companies had the authority to execute the improvement program;
3. improvement teams and Customer Day teams had the authority to implement proposals;

4. employees regularly confronted management with statements like: this is the problem, that is the solution, and the decision you have to take is so and so;
5. employees more and more expressed their disapproval if decisions were taken without their involvement;

Figure 4.8 Power-related observations in the Roermond factory. The items below the blank line refer indirectly to power

The power-related items in the Twente survey (Figure 4.7) show two striking characteristics. Firstly, the perceived influence is rather high for all hierarchical levels. This indicates, in the words of Tannenbaum, a significant total amount of control, which is an indicator of the effectiveness of the organisation. The reason is that high levels of influence indicate significant amounts of consultation and information exchange between hierarchical levels.[123] Secondly, the differences in the influence of the various hierarchical levels are rather small. In other words, the operators perceive their own amount of control to be almost on a par with that of management. This finding was confirmed by interviews with operators.[124] They

---

[123] Tannenbaum (1968), Tannenbaum et al. (1974), Van Haren (1984) and Van Oostrum (1989).
[124] De Leede (1997, p175 ff.).

indicated that 'nowadays' management listened to their arguments and 'nowadays' they were allowed to improve their own working situation. These findings might have important implications for the research question of this study. The first characteristic suggests that such an organisation will be effective in implementing responsible behaviour; and the second characteristic suggests that employees indeed have the power to work in a responsible way. These implications will be discussed in more detail in the following sections.

How can we understand the high-trust relations in Roermond? How can we understand the development of intense cooperation? How can we understand the evolution of a balanced division of power? These high-trust relations will be discussed in four steps. Firstly, it will be stressed that the factory had 'no history'. Secondly, it will be shown that the empowerment of employees generates trusting relationships. Thirdly, it will be made plausible that a growth in trust involves an evolution in the character of trust. Finally, it will be argued that the evolution of trust and the dynamic of high-power relations are strongly intertwined. Note: in this section the perspectives of the manager and the perspectives of the employee will be discussed simultaneously.

First, the actuator factory in Roermond had 'no history'. A new business was started up. There were no shared experiences. There were no successes or failures that had left their mark on the organisation. There were no shared values, beliefs, and presuppositions. There were also no stories. On the contrary, a new culture had to be built up.[125]

Second, the empowerment of employees generates trusting relationships. The culture in the actuator factory is in good accordance with the characteristics of the high-discretion syndrome as presented by Alan Fox. He suggests that a high-discretion syndrome would be an appropriate model for the working practice of senior managers, functional specialists, doctors in hospitals and so on.[126] However, the operators in the actuator factory were not senior managers, functional specialists or doctors. How can we explain the existence of a high-discretion syndrome in operators on the shop floor?

In my opinion, the existence of the high-discretion syndrome on the shop floor has to be understood from the high-discretion and high-power position of all employees. Let us first review the main structural aspects. The socio-technical design of the actuator factory implies that the employee has the authority and power to manage his or her own workplace. In the mini-company process this employee's authority and power is extended to the external relations of the unit and the whole improvement process. The Employee Motivation Survey (Figure 4.2), the Twente survey (Figure 4.7), and the ethnographical observations (Figure 4.8) confirm that the operators of the actuator factory indeed had the authority and power to manage their workplace as intended by the socio-technical design and mini-company process.

---

[125] Compare Schein (1999).
[126] Fox (1974, p36 ff.).

In addition, the whole mini-company process requires intensive cooperation and extensive communication between management, technical specialists, and operators. Mutual consultation, mutual information exchange, and mutual support are the cornerstone of the whole improvement process. In an improvement culture the intensity and the quality of consultation, information exchange, and support is high. A high intensity and high quality of interactions is required to develop trusting relationships.[127] In a manner of speaking, every successful consultation, information exchange, and support increases the trust of management in the employees and vice versa. And, negatively formulated, without a high intensity and high quality of interactions trust cannot develop because these interactions are a condition for the development of trust. These conclusions are supported by literature where the positive influence of participation and empowerment on the development of trusting relationships is reported.[128]

The symbolic meaning of the socio-technical design and the mini-company process cannot be underestimated. When managers design an organisation in a socio-technical way, they show respect for employees. When managers develop the mini-company process, they demonstrate trust in employees. Socio-technical design and the mini-company process symbolise trust that employees will use their authority and power to satisfy the needs of different stakeholders of the organisation, e.g. customers, management, colleagues, and themselves. And – remembering that the proof is in the eating of the pudding – when managers accept the mission statement of the mini-company process and visibly support the execution of the improvement program, they prove that trust is not a 'word' but a reality. Conver-sely, when in critical moments managers do not part with power, trust will not develop.

In many studies, the practice of empowerment is criticised.[129] Moreover, it is shown that new concepts and initiatives are used to increase control over employees instead of empowering the employee.[130] The weak point in the whole empowerment movement is management. Company-wide empowerment programs lead to political correctness. The language managers use expresses the need for empowered employees, but the behaviour of managers tells the opposite message. Managers love empowerment in theory, but use the command-and-control model in practice. Managers often take up empowerment instrumentally – especially in technical organisations. Sooner or later they will fall short because subtleties in their behaviour will show their real intentions.

Third, a growth in trust involves evolution in the character of trust. There is no doubt that the start-up phase of the actuator factory was characterised by conditional trust. All parties were willing to cooperate. There was a positive attitude and a lack of negative feelings. The three red threads of the development of the factory organisation – four-way communication, participation of all

---

[127]   Blau (1964).
[128]   Tannenbaum (1968), Fox (1974), Tannenbaum et al. (1974), Driscoll (1978), Deci et al. (1989), Whitener et al. (1998), and Costa (2000).
[129]   E.g. Argyris (1998), and Boje and Rosil (2001).
[130]   E.g. Rothschild and Ollilainen (1999).

employees, and continuous improvement – created a lot of shared 'experiences of trust'. These experiences were confirmed and reconfirmed by the formalisation of these red threads in the mini-company process. Perceptions of management about operators and vice versa changed gradually.[131] Failures and short falls in performance were no longer seen as a lack of loyalty or a breach of confidence, but were marked as a mistake or the result of failing conditions. Step by step, behaviour became embodied by shared values. A culture developed which was characterised by open and honest communication, the free airing of criticism, help-seeking behaviour, the subjugation of personal needs, high involvement, and high confidence in others (Costa). In other words, conditional trust evolved into unconditional trust (Jones and George).

Finally, the evolution of trust and high-power dynamics are strongly intertwined. The levels of trust and power in the actuator factory are high in comparison to cases reported in the literature.[132] [133] The explanation of these high levels has to be sought in the interaction between trust and power: a high-trust-high-power spiral. Employees of the actuator factory participated in the improvement process from the beginning on. This participation contributed strongly to the development of trusting relationships, which made the next step in participation possible, i.e. the mini-company process. In this process, increasing the power and influence of employees was agreed with management and structured in the 7-jump and 9-jump. The mini-company process facilitated a further growth in trust.[134] On the one hand, the implementation of proposals of an improvement team or mini-company strengthens the trust of employees in management because their proposals are accepted. On the other hand, a successful implementation of a proposal of an improvement team or mini-company strengthens the trust of management in employees because they use their power and influence to solve a problem in the organisation. Trust fuels empowerment. Successful empowerment fuels trust. An upward spiral of trust and power develops. It has to be emphasised that such an upward spiral only evolves when both parties – management and employees – experience the development of trusting relationships and experience empowerment. With respect to the latter: employees are empowered by management (authority to solve problems on the shop floor and authority to implement solutions) and management is empowered by employees (open information exchange, problem-solving capability of organisation, priority setting in open communication process and so on).

---

[131] See also Kramer in Kramer and Tyler (1996, 216 ff.).

[132] Tannenbaum (1968), Tannenbaum et al. (1974), Van Haren (1984), Van Oostrom (1989), and De Leede (1997).

[133] An unpublished study by Beteor (1996) has shown that the scores of the Employee Motivation Survey for the actuator factory were also considerably higher with respect to trust and power than for comparable factories within Philips.

[134] Nooteboom (2002) stresses that an increase in trust means a widening of the window of trust.

Reflection. I have experienced the high-trust-high-power spiral personally. My trust in employees of a mini-company considerably increased when they presented a challenging mission statement and a well thought-out improvement program. At the same time, their trust in me as a factory manager increased strongly when I – after an open discussion – accepted the proposals of the unit. The same holds for the completion of an improvement team. When an improvement team gave a presentation about the analysis of a problem, investigation of the root cause, and implementation of the solution, mutual trust also grew.

From the perspective of management – which underlies the research question of this study – the high trust-high-power spiral can be structured as follows:

1. a manager has to take the initiative in handing over power to employees, e.g. to solve a problem on the shop floor; such an initiative is a prerequisite for the development of the trust employees have in management;
2. if the initiative of a manager is 'rewarded' by employees – that means, the employees show that they have used this power to solve problems in the organisation – then his or her trust in employees increases;
3. an increase in the trust of a manager in his or her employees enables a manager to 'hand over' more power to employees;
4. if this initiative of a manager is 'rewarded' again by employees then his or her trust in employees increases further;
5. this spiral implies an increase in the problem solving capacity of the manager. Formulated paradoxically, management in *em*-powered through *em*-powering the organisation.

It has to be noted that the trust-power spiral can also start with an initiative from the side of the employee. The basic mechanisms are the same.

It has to be emphasised that the trust-power spiral is fuelled by a significant amount of micro-exchanges between management and employees. Some of these micro-exchanges directly serve the technical-economic interests of the organisation. Other micro-exchanges directly serve the social interests of the employees. And other ones are 'just human' and do not serve any interest at first sight. These thoughts also show why an instrumental view of trust and power does not 'work' (or will 'work' only temporally). An instrumental view is always determined by the technical-economic perspective of management. Such a perspective does not value the broader perspective of a human organisation. Sooner or later, employees will discover that it is all about the interests of the manager. This discovery means that the developing trust-power spiral will collapse.

Reflection. As a subordinate, I always sensed when a boss was interested in my well being or when he was interested 'in motivating me'. The same holds for operators on the shop floor as shown by the following quotes: "They are only on the shop floor when there is a problem" or 'They only talk to you when they want to know something". Note the word 'they'.

400

Reflection. Management books suggest that management is about 'sketching the main lines'. However, these books forget to tell the reader that these main lines receive meaning in 'patterns of subtleties' in behaviour of management. If these patterns express a deep respect for employees, customers and other stakeholders, then the main lines will be received with respect. If these patterns reflect the interests of management, then the same main lines will be received with distrust. It is tempting to conclude that most change programs and improvement programs do not fail on 'main lines' but fail on 'patterns of subtleties'. Change programs and improvement programs require professional skills. Subtleties in behaviour require authenticity in management and a sense of deep human values.

The high-trust-high-power spiral has a positive influence on the effectiveness of the organisation.[135] In this context high-power means a high level of total power. Power and influence strongly stimulates identification with, commitment to, and loyalty to the organisation.[136] This results in a greater conformity towards instructions, procedures and norms. In turn, this conformity leads to a higher uniformity in behaviour. In addition, the high-power-high-trust spiral significantly increases the problem-solving capacity of the organisation because people communicate openly and do not hold information back (Costa), there is less 'organisational resistance' (Piderit), no 'organisational silence' (Morrison and Milliken), and there are no 'dangerous truths' (Simmons) that can block the improvement of the situation.[137]

The Roermond case gives more insight into trust dynamics and power relationships. It can be concluded that:

o   the empowerment of employees supports the development of trusting relationships. Socio-Technical Systems Design and the Mini-Company Concept give an organisational form to realise empowerment (conclusion 4);

o   the evolution of trust has its own dynamics. With increasing trust the character of trust changes from conditional (behaviour-oriented) to unconditional (values-oriented) (conclusion 5);

o   the evolution of trust and power relations are strongly intertwined. Trust makes empowerment possible. Successful empowerment supports the development of trust. In other words, an upward spiral of trust and power will develop (conclusion 6);

o   high-trust dynamics supports the development of a high-power position for all hierarchical levels in the organisation (conclusion 7);

o   high-trust-high-power dynamics results in an organisation with a high level of total power. As a consequence, the effectiveness of the organisation will be high (conclusion 8).

---

[135]   Tannenbaum (1968), Van Haren (1984), Van Oostrom (1989) and Costa (2000).
[136]   Tyler and Degoey in Kramer and Neale (1996, p331 ff.) and Dirks and Ferrin (2001).
[137]   Pederit (2000), Morrison and Milliken (2000), and Simmons (1999).

4.6 Trust, power, responsible behaviour, and a 'new world of work'

In the previous sections the Roermond case and Aachen case have been re-interpreted from the point of view of trust and power. Several basic mechanisms have been identified. Figure 4.9 presents a 2 x 2 matrix of power and trust. Figure 4.10 presents a summary of the conclusions drawn in the previous sections.

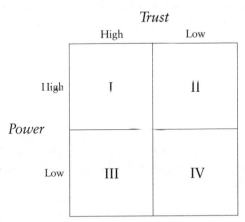

Figure 4.9 2 x 2 matrix of trust and power

Quadrant I is characterised by high-trust and high-power relations. A socio-technical design (in combination with the Mini-Company Concept) is a necessary but not sufficient condition to develop high-trust and high-power relations (conclusion 1). The empowerment of employees supports the development of trusting relationships (conclusion 4). With increasing trust the character of trust changes from conditional (behaviour-oriented) to unconditional (values-oriented) (conclusion 5). The evolution of trust and power relations is strongly intertwined. Trust makes empowerment possible. Successful empowerment supports the development of trust. An upward spiral of trust and power will develop (conclusion 6). High-trust dynamics supports the development of a high-power position for all hierarchical levels in the organisation (conclusion 7). Finally, high-trust-high-power dynamics results in an organisation with a high level of total power. As a consequence, the effectiveness of the organisation to solve problems and to improve will be high (conclusion 8).

Quadrant II is characterised by low-trust and high-power relations. To my knowledge, no cases are reported showing these characteristics. Such an organisation will be unstable. Most probably, it will disintegrate and move into Quadrant IV.

Quadrant III is characterised by high-trust and low-power relations. These characteristics can be found in hierarchical organisations with shared goals in a stable environment.[138] In a democratic society or changing business environment such an organisation will be unstable. Most probably, it will move into Quadrant IV.

number	section	conclusion
1	4.3	A socio-technical design (in combination with the Mini-Company Concept) is a necessary but not sufficient condition for a high-power position of employees and high-trust relations between management and employees.
2	4.4	A low-trust dynamic induces a low-power dynamic. A key characteristic of a low-trust dynamic is a continuous struggle of management to control and to de-power employees. As a response, employees try to escape the controlling power of management in order to secure their own interests. Management, however, interprets the low-trust response of the employees as a confirmation that 'they' cannot be trusted. So, the low-trust-low-power spiral is fuelled.
3	4.4	A low-trust-low-power dynamics results in an organisation with a low amount of total power. As a consequence, the effectiveness of the organisation to solve problems, to continuously improve, and to adapt to the changing environment will be low.
4	4.5	The empowerment of employees supports the development of trusting relationships. Socio-Technical Systems Design and the Mini-Company Concept give an organisational form to realise empowerment.
5	4.5	The evolution of trust has its own dynamics. With increasing trust the character of trust changes from conditional (behaviour-oriented) to unconditional (values-oriented).
6	4.5	The evolution of trust and power relations are strongly intertwined. Trust makes empowerment possible. Successful empowerment supports the development of trust. In other words, an upward spiral of trust and power will develop.
7	4.5	High-trust dynamics supports the development of a high-power position for all hierarchical levels in the organisation.
8	4.5	High-trust-high-power dynamics results in an organisation with a high level of total power. As a consequence, the effectiveness of the organisation will be high.

Figure 4.10 Overview of conclusions drawn in sections 4.3 to 4.5

Quadrant IV is characterised by low-trust and low-power relations. A low-trust dynamic induces a low-power dynamic. A key characteristic of a low-trust dynamic

---

[138] Fox (1974, p99) states that imbalances in reciprocity in relationships only can be maintained in the presence of compensatory mechanism. For example, low-power relation ships imply a unbalance in power between managers and employees. Such an imbalance can be maintained if shared values are present.

403

is a continuous struggle of management to control and to de-power employees. As a response, employees try to escape the controlling power of management in order to secure their own interests. Management, however, interprets the low-trust response of the employees as a confirmation that 'they' cannot be trusted. So, the low-trust-low-power spiral is fuelled (conclusion 2). A low-trust-low-power dynamic results in an organisation with a low amount of total power. As a consequence, the effectiveness of the organisation to solve problems, to continuously improve, and to adapt to the changing environment will be low (conclusion 3).

The first research question refers to phenomena on the shop floor. To investigate these phenomena an ethnographical case study has been done in two factories. To compare the Roermond case and the Aachen case a 2 x 2 matrix of responsibility and accountability has presented (Ch. 3, section 4.6). This matrix visualises the appearance of paradoxes on the shop floor. The first type of paradox arises when the necessary conditions for employees to assume responsibility are not fulfilled and still the employees are held accountable. The second type arises when the necessary conditions for employees to assume responsibility are fulfilled and in spite of this the employees are not held accountable. In addition, a situation has been identified in which both the necessary conditions for employees to assume responsibility as well as accountability are not fulfilled. Reinterpretation of the Roermond case and the Aachen case clearly shows that these paradoxes are related to trust and power. In a culture determined by high-trust-high-power relations paradoxes will be easily identified and dismantled collectively. In a culture determined by low-trust-low-power relations paradoxes are not identified and not dismantled. In addition, in a culture of high-trust-high-power relations the act of 'giving responsibility' indeed involves empowerment of employees with respect to their own workplace. In such a culture 'calling employees to account' contributes to the development of trusting relationships. In a culture of low-trust-low-power relations the opposite mechanisms are in place: 'giving responsibility' means limiting empowerment to a minimum and 'calling employees to account' means clearing one's own street.

The second research question focuses on the failure of new production concepts in many modern factories. This study shows that organisational processes on the shop floor have their own dynamics. Top-down approaches in the implementation of new production concepts – as in Lean Management and Business Process Reengineering – ignore the specific social context and do not cope with the deep structures of human behaviour. In addition, Lean Management neglects the organisational design aspects of trust and power. As a consequence, these approaches inherently run the risk of failure in implementation.

Participative approaches – like Socio-Technical Systems Design and the Mini-Company Concept – have the inherent ability to adapt to the dynamics of the organisational processes on the shop floor. Ethnography and reflection by the factory manager will strengthen this ability (section 3). In addition, these approaches honour the organisational design aspects of trust and power.

Therefore, these approaches have inherently more promise in terms of realising technical superiority and a 'new world of work'.

The phenomena of 'high-trust-high-power dynamics' and 'low-trust-low-power dynamics' have important implications for the answering of the second research question. It shows that power and influence is not a 'fixed pie' but that the total amount of power in an organisation can be increased. However, this increase in the total amount of power is only possible in an organisation with high-trust relations. This conclusion is of the utmost importance for the development of responsible organisations. Responsible behaviour requires the authority to make decisions. Conclusion 3 states that low-trust-low-power dynamics results in an organisation with a low amount of total power. This low amount of total power is unequally divided: a (relatively) high-power position for the manager and a (relatively) low-power position for the employee. The consequence of the low amount of total power is that the capability of the organisation to show responsible behaviour (effectiveness of the organisation) will be limited. This limited capability is present in all elements of the organisation; in both functional aspects (e.g. technical and economic) and also non-functional aspects (e.g. social and moral). Conclusion 8 states that high-trust-high-power dynamics results in an organisation with a high amount of total power. This high amount of power is more or less equally divided: a high-power position for the manager and a high-power position for the employee. As a consequence, the capability of the organisation (effectiveness of the organisation) to show responsible behaviour will be great. In principle, this capability will be present in all elements of the organisation; in both functional aspects (e.g. technical and economic) and also non-functional aspects (e.g. social and moral).

Ethnographic observations and the above reasoning lead to the following propositions[139]:

Proposition 1:
A factory manager has to develop the necessary organisational conditions through socio-technical design, the mini-company process, continuous improvement and style of management, so that trusting relationships can develop and balanced-power relationships can evolve.

Proposition 2:
High-trust and high-power relations are the key conditions for realising the promise of new production concepts, i.e. technical superiority and a 'new world of work'.

Proposition 3:
High-trust and high-power relations are the key conditions for ensuring that employees on the shop floor (and the organisation as a whole) can act responsibly.

---

[139] Strauss and Corbin (1990).

Appendix: Trust: a review

In this appendix a philosophical evaluation of the notion of 'trust' will be presented. In a recent discussion Handy stated that[140]:

> "Trust is the heart of the matter".

In an article about high-performance teams Kets de Vries concludes [141]:

> "The moral in all of this is that if we want teams to work, we need to build trust and mutual respect among team members. If such feelings are not present, other factors conductive to effective team behaviour become irrelevant".

These statements by Handy and Kets de Vries are fully supported by the Roermond case and the Aachen case.

In section 4.1 of this chapter some preliminary philosophical statements about trust have been presented. It has been argued that the word 'trust' has a double meaning. First, it refers to a multidimensional phenomenon. Second, it refers to a modal dimension of experience. The distinction between 'trust as phenomenon' and 'trust as modal dimension' is a very helpful tool to understand the complex character of 'trust'.

Trust as a multidimensional phenomenon

In the case descriptions several dimensions of the phenomenon of trust came to the fore. In the Roermond case it has been shown that psychological, power, social, and moral dimensions play an important role. The employees of the actuator factory identified themselves with the business unit. This identification process – which has a psychological background – strongly stimulates trust.[142] Both the socio-technical design and the mini-company process meant that the employees had a high level of power. This high level of power also increased the level of trust.[143] The employees of the actuator factory were a team. They cooperated with each other and with the management team. This type of cooperation – which has a social character – strongly supports the development of trust.[144] Finally, the quality of working life in the actuator factory was high. In a process of continuous improvement the quality of working life was further improved. Paying attention to the interests of employees – which has a moral character – was 'rewarded' by trust.[145]

---

[140] Quoted from Whitener et al. (1998, p524).
[141] Kets de Vries (1999, p69).
[142] Whitener et al. (1998) and Pierce et al. (2001).
[143] Fox (1974) and Whitener et al. (1998).
[144] Blau (1964), Kramer et al. in Kramer and Neale (1996, p357 ff.), and Williams (2001).
[145] Tyler and Degoey in Kramer and Neale (1996, p331 ff.), Hosmer (1995) and Whitener et al. (1998).

The Aachen case shows that mistrust has a strong negative influence on an organisation. Its effects were not limited to psychological or social dimensions, but extended to power, symbolic meaning, economic, and moral dimensions.

Trust as a modal dimension

I would like to make several comments about this subject. Firstly, Dooyeweerd identifies faith or trust as a separate dimension of the human experience.[146] This means that in every concrete situation or every organisational context, faith or trust plays a role. Sometimes, faith or trust is explicitly expressed. For example, when a manager says that s/he believes in the organisation, or when employees say that they trust management. Sometimes, faith or trust plays a role 'underneath the surface'. For example, when a manager gives an employee the authority to solve a problem, or when an employee openly tells his or her boss about abuses on the shop floor. In other words, faith or trust is a modal dimension of human experience. This modal dimension has its own 'character' or 'quality'. Dooyeweerd describes the essence of this dimension as 'transcendental certainty' and Dengerink as 'trustworthiness', 'credibility', or 'certainty'.[147] The identification of faith or trust as a separate modal dimension of the empirical reality is very significant. It recognises that faith or trust has its own character. It shows that faith or trust cannot be reduced to a psychic state, a power relation, social behaviour, or a moral attitude. In accordance with the language of this field of investigation, the word 'trust' will be used in the following paragraphs and not the word 'faith'.

Secondly, the different modal functions or dimensions are not scattered in 'a sort of chaotic disorder' but are arranged in a 'cosmic succession of prior and posterior'.[148] In this succession the dimension of 'trust' takes up the last position. The order of 'prior' and 'posterior' describes the relation between the different dimensions. Namely, the earlier modal dimensions are foundational for the later ones. In other words, the earlier modal dimensions make the functioning of the later ones possible. Trust holds the last position in the modal order. Therefore, trust is founded in all earlier modal dimensions. To be concrete, trust can only function on the basis of psychic feelings, the existence of power relations, symbolic meaning, social behaviour, economic exchanges, juridical agreements and moral standards. This foundational relation can easily lead to a misinterpretation of the character of trust. For example, the fact that trust is embedded in social relations does not mean that trust has to be qualified as a social phenomenon. The fact that trust can only function within a mutually dependant relationship does not mean that trust is a kind of power. Finally, the fact that the development of trust is strongly stimulated by morally just behaviour does not mean that trust is merely part of morality. In conclusion, foundational relations show that trust has a complex micro-structure without ignoring its own character (meaning kernel).[149]

---

146   Dooyeweerd (1969, II, p303).
147   Dooyeweerd (1969, II, p304), Dengerink (1986, p223).
148   Dooyeweerd (1969, II, p50).
149   This microstructure reflects the 'universality of the aspects within their own spheres' in the foundational direction (Dooyeweerd, 1969, II, p54). As a 'terminal sphere' trust

Thirdly, the order of 'prior' and 'posterior' modal dimensions in the cosmic order also implies that the earlier modal dimensions are opened and deepened by the later ones.[150] In other words, the earlier modal dimensions can develop a rich microstructure under the guidance of a later one. As previously mentioned, trust holds the last position in the modal order. That means under guidance of the modal dimension 'trust' all earlier dimensions will be opened and deepened. For example, in an organisation that is characterised by high-trust relations a number of social structures are developed to wield power; structures that are not present (or do not function) in organisations characterised by low-trust reactions. An example of such a social structure is the mini-company process as described in the Roermond case. In this example the social dimension is opened and deepened by trust (trust of management in their employees and the trust of employees in management) so that employees can exert power of influence. This type of opened structure is not characterised by the opening dimension (i.e. trust) but is still characterised by its original meanings (i.e. social). In conclusion, the opening relations show that under guidance of trust the earlier dimensions develop a complex microstructure without ignoring their own character.[151]

Finally, the dynamics of foundational dimensions and opening and deepening by the trust dimension helps us to understand the trust and power dynamics. Increased levels of trust opens new social structures to exert power. Successful new social structures to exert power found a higher level of trust. This type of dynamics is not only present between trust and power, but also between trust and care, trust and justice, and so on.

---

only shows 'retrocipations' to the earlier modal dimensions. The foundational process is much more complicated than is described here. See Dooyeweerd (1969, II, p163 ff.).

[150] Dooyeweerd (1969, II, p170 ff., p181 ff.).

[151] This microstructure reflects the 'universality of the aspects within their own spheres' in the transcendental direction (Dooyeweerd, 1969, II, p54). The social sphere (earlier dimension) shows anticipation to the faith/trust dimension (later dimension). The opening process is much more complicated than is described here. See Dooyeweerd (1969, II, p163 ff.).

5 Philosophical analysis of industrial organisations

The history of industrial organisations is characterised by dehumanisation and alienation. It is widely acknowledged that these characteristics have been caused by the one-sided scientific or technological approach of Taylorism. A number of new production concepts have attempted to overcome this one-sidedness. These concepts claim to present a 'more human' alternative. They claim to offer an 'integral' approach. However, in the Introduction to Chapter 1 it has been shown that in many modern factories the 'old problems' are still present. It has been argued that we have to dig deeper to understand the underlying views of new production concepts about man and organisation.

What is a 'more human' alternative? What is an 'integral' approach? These questions will be addressed in this section. De Sitter states that thinking about these questions requires a 'vision of the whole'.[152] In organisational science such a vision of the whole is not present. More importantly, there is a lot of confusion about the nature of and the relationship between the different dimensions of industrial organisations. However, this does not alter the fact that a 'vision of the whole' is required to fundamentally understand dehumanisation and alienation and to sketch the contours of a liberating perspective.[153]

The cosmology as developed by Herman Dooyeweerd offers a philosophical 'vision of the whole'. There are two reasons why I chose this approach. Firstly, I have been raised in the socio-technical tradition. This tradition has a normative approach to industrial organisations. It is challenging to relate Dooyeweerd's view about normativity to the basic principles of the socio-technical approach. Secondly, Dooyeweerd's view on man is in accordance with my basic beliefs. I expected his approach to support my efforts 'to apply' the notions of *dignity* and *vocation* in organisational practice.

The topic of this chapter lies in the field of the philosophy of organisation. I am fully convinced that a philosophical enquiry is necessary to give a theoretical basis for the idea of a human organisation, to explore the normative structure of industrial practice, and to design and to develop responsible organisations.

5.1 Basic distinctions

To facilitate the analysis of industrial organisations some basic ideas will be introduced. In the coming sections these ideas will be elaborated on in more detail and illustrated with examples from organisational practice.

---

[152] De Sitter et al. (1997, p505). See also De Sitter in Van Eijnatten (1993, p158-184).
[153] Schuurman (2002, p18) shows that contemporary philosophical thought on technology suffers from a cosmological deficit and from an ethical deficit. This characterisation also holds for contemporary thought on industrial organisations.

Whole or entity versus dimension or function

Reality consists of a great number of different wholes or entities. For example, living organisms (plants, animals, human beings), societal forms (states, churches, companies, and families), technical objects (washing machines, televisions, cars and computers) and cultural objects (paintings, literature, music, and architecture). These wholes express themselves in a great number of dimensions or functions. For example, a human being digests food (biological dimension), experiences feelings (psychic dimension), lives together with other human beings (social dimension), enjoys a work of art (aesthetic dimension), and prays to God (religious dimension). A commercial company wants to make a profit (economic dimension), has to abide by the law (juridical dimension), and has to behave in a morally responsible way (moral dimension). In total, more than a dozen dimensions or functions can be distinguished. Every whole expresses itself in all these different dimensions However, whole is more than the sum of its functions, it has its own individuality.

Subject function versus object function

Wholes or entities function in different ways. Let us compare for example a human being to a technical tool. A human being functions in all dimensions as a subject. For example, s/he takes up space, is subject to physical laws, experiences injustice, and trusts in God. On the contrary, a technical tool does not function in all these dimensions as a subject. It takes up space and is subject to physical laws, but it cannot experience injustice and cannot trust in God. In the latter dimensions it can only function as an object. That means it can be an object of a juridical investigation, or an object that is trusted by its users. In reformational-philosophical terminology, a technical tool functions as subject in spatial and physical dimensions and as object in juridical and faith dimensions.

Whole versus part

The words 'whole' and 'parts' are often used to describe a relationship. It appears that quite different types of interdependencies lie hidden behind these words. In this chapter, the words 'whole' and 'parts' will be used for a specific type of interdependency.

A whole has its own identity. Let us take for example a lawn mower. A lawn mower is a whole with its own identity. It is characterised by its technical function: to mow the lawn. The lawn mower consists of a number of different parts: motor, knives, wheels, handle and so on. These parts have no independent identity: they are entirely dependent on the whole. That means the function and construction of these parts can only be understood in terms of the function and the construction of the whole, i.e. the lawn mower.

Another example is a tree. A tree is a whole with its own identity. It is characterised by its biological function: it grows, sprouts, blossoms, and bears fruit. A tree consists of a number of parts: roots, trunk, branches, twigs, and leaves. These parts have no independent identity: they are entirely dependent on the whole. That means the function and structure of these parts can only be understood in terms of the biological function of the whole.

In Dooyeweerdian terminology, a whole has an 'independent leading function'. The independent leading function of a lawn mower is the power dimension. The parts of the lawn mower have no independent leading function but have to be understood in terms of the power dimension of lawn mower. The same holds for a tree that is characterised by a biological dimension. A whole also has its own 'internal structural principle'. In other words, a whole has its own design principle or characteristic structure. The design of a technical object like a lawn mower is quite different to the design of a voltmeter or computer. The characteristic structure of a biological object like a tree is quite different to the structure of a bush or plant. The parts of a lawn mower and a tree have no independent internal structural principle but have to be understood in terms of the internal principles of the whole. In summary, a part is fully dependent on the whole. Therefore, it lacks an independent leading function and an internal structural principle of its own

Enkaptic interlacement

A quite different type of interdependency is present in the so-called 'enkaptic interlacement'. Take for example the relationship between the calc-shell and the living organism of the molluse. The calc-shell and the living organism undoubtedly form a whole. If the shell and organism are separated, the whole (the molluse) will die. However, this relationship cannot be characterised as a whole-part relationship as described above. This is because the calc-shell and the living organism both have their own 'independent leading function' and their own 'internal structural principle'. The calc-shell is characterised by the physical-chemical dimension and the living organism by the psychic-sensory dimension. The calc-shell has its own 'internal structural principle' and the living organism also has its own 'internal structural principle'. Such a relationship is called an *enkaptic interlacement*.

Another type of enkaptic interlacement is found between different structures in society. Take for example, the state, an enterprise, and a church. The relationship between society and these structures cannot be characterised as a whole-part relationship because these structures each have a different leading function. The state is characterised by the juridical dimension, the enterprise by the economic dimension, and the church by the religious dimension. On the one hand, these structures have their own identity; on the other hand they depend strongly upon each other. In Dooyeweerdian terminology, in society, the state, the enterprise and the church are interlaced enkaptically.

Yet another type of enkaptic interlacement is found between molecules and living cells. Molecules in a living cell are characterised by their physical-chemical dimension. The cell is characterised by its biological dimension. This means that molecules and cell have different leading functions. However, a living cell can only exist because the molecules are able to support the different functions of this cell. The cell is 'indissolubly bound' to the nature and character of the different molecules. In other words, a cell is 'irreversibly founded' in chemical processes. In Dooyeweerdian terminology, a *foundational enkaptic interlacement* is present.

Values, norm principles, and norms
Values refer to wholes. They constitute the religious or ideological meaning of wholes. We can talk, for example, about the value of human beings, family life, an economic enterprise, and the church. Norm principles refer to dimensions. They constitute the basic principles of the normative structure of a certain dimension. For example, in our capitalistic society the profit principle is very important. This principle refers to the economic dimension of the enterprise and can be described as a norm principle. This general principle is elaborated in a system of concrete norms to realise profit. Another example is equality. Equality is very important in western society. This principle has been laid down in the constitution and refers to the juridical dimension of western society. This general principle is elaborated on in a number of concrete norms in different sections of the law.

5.2 The multidimensional character of an industrial organisation

In the socio-technical tradition different dimensions of organisational practice are highlighted. The Dutch approach emphasises that technical, social, and economic aspects have to be designed integrally. The Australian approach stresses the psychic and social aspects of participation. The Scandinavian approach focuses on democratic dialogue as a form of organisational power. The Mini-Company approach combines technical, social, psychic, economic and moral dimensions.

The Roermond case has shown that the mini-company process resulted in balanced-power relations between management and employees. Furthermore, high-trust relations developed. The Aachen case has shown that mistrust determined the whole culture in the glass factory.

Neither Socio-Technical Systems Design nor the Mini-Company Concept provide a theoretical explanation for the diversity of dimensions that are distinguished and for the relationships between these dimensions. In addition, these models do not give a fundamental account of the trust-power dynamics observed in the cases.

Which dimensions can be distinguished? In the case descriptions we discovered at least the following: physical (e.g. the chemicals being transformed), biological (the reduction of waste materials that polluted the environment of the plant, ergonomic aspects of equipment), psychic (the identification of the operators with their work and group, their motivation and satisfaction), power and influence (authority of operators, the mini-company process, improvement teams), lingual (sharing of information, communication patterns), social (cooperation of operators within a group, informal contacts between management and employees), economic (reduction of cost prices, competition in the market), juridical (safety and environmental laws), moral (care for individual employees, quality of labour), and trust (between management and employees).

The reformational philosopher Herman Dooyeweerd has presented an extensive analysis of created reality. His cosmology is based on the (naive, daily) experience. Therefore, it is not surprising that most of the dimensions indicated above come back in this analysis. Dooyeweerd has distinguished fifteen different aspects or dimensions: arithmetic, spatial, kinematic, physical, biological, sensitive (psychic), logical, historical (power), lingual (symbolic meaning), social, economic, aesthetic, juridical, moral and pistic (trust, faith).[154] Comparison of this list with the dimensions discovered in the cases gives the impression that Dooyeweerd's list is more complete.

Dooyeweerd argues extensively that every thing, event or phenomenon expresses itself in all these fifteen different dimensions. Depending on the context, some dimensions will come to the fore and others will be more 'hidden'. For example, the economic dimension of an enterprise is clearly visible whereas the dimension of faith is more hidden. In a church it is just the other way around, i.e. the dimension of faith is clearly present whereas the economic aspect is more hidden. However, a closer look reveals that these more hidden dimensions are still important. Trusting relationships with customers and suppliers to a great extent determine the success of an enterprise. A healthy financial basis is a prerequisite for a church to function in our society.

By means of everyday examples Dooyeweerd makes it plausible that every thing, event of phenomenon indeed functions in all these fifteen dimensions. I would like to illustrate this with a technical example: a production line. A production line consists of a number of machines (arithmetic), the machines are located in the line (spatial), the product flows along the line (kinematic), the processes transform properties of materials (physical), and the line is designed in accordance with ergonomic standards (biological). In addition, an operator identifies him- or herself with the line (psychic), distinguishes different critical settings (logical), has the authority to stop production in the case of quality problems (power), and acts on the basis of technical information (lingual, symbolic meaning). Moreover, the line enables social contact due to its low noise characteristics (social), is very efficient (economic), consists of balanced capacities (esthetical, harmony), satisfies safety standards (juridical), is designed to ensure the quality of working life (moral), and operates reliably (trust). A comparable analysis of the control structure and the information structure of this production line will also reveal the fifteen different dimensions.

The analysis of Dooyeweerd implies that the integral design and integral development of an industrial organisation has to cover all dimensions. What is more, that the ignorance of one or more dimensions will have a negative influence on the performance of the organisation. In other words, no one dimension can be ignored. I would like to illustrate this with some examples. In a manufacturing company the technical and economic dimensions are the dimensions most clearly visible. The efficiency of the production process and the operating costs of the line play a key role in the success of a manufacturing company. However, other dimensions cannot be ignored. For example, ignorance of the social dimension (e.g. the machine makes so much noise that communication is not possible) will have a negative influence on employee satisfaction. The result of this is that operators will

---

[154] Dooyeweerd (1969, II).

not devote themselves fully to the job and will not perform at maximal efficiency. Ignorance of the power dimension (e.g. minimisation of the influence of the operator) will contribute to organisational silence which will lead to operators not telling management about the fundamental causes of problems. This will cause the effectiveness of the organisation to decrease. Finally, ignorance of the moral dimension (e.g. the quality of working life) will result in high absenteeism and low motivation. This will without any doubt have a negative influence on the economic performance of the factory. These examples show that the more hidden dimensions cannot be ignored in favour of the technical and economic dimensions. Positively speaking, these examples show that technical and economic dimensions will flourish in an organisation in which the more hidden dimensions are explicitly addressed. This observation is indicative of a more fundamental phenomenon. Different dimensions of organisational reality are closely connected. Therefore, a one sided approach will always have negative repercussions on the whole organisation. In the same way, an integral approach will always have a positive influence on all dimensions of industrial organisations, including the economic one.

This analysis clarifies several issues mentioned in this study. Firstly, it shows why the Tayloristic method of production leads to dehumanisation and alienation. The methods of Scientific Management are totally focused on the technical and economic dimensions of the manufacturing process. The employee is subjected to technical and economic imperatives without taking into account other dimensions of human beings. Ignorance of, for example, psychic, power, social, moral and trust dimensions in organisations will 'automatically' result in dehumanisation and alienation. To put it bluntly, you get what you design.

Secondly, this analysis gives us an in-depth insight into the similarities and differences between the different approaches in Socio-Technical Systems Design. The Dutch approach offers a detailed design theory and design methodology. In the design of the production structure, control structure and information structure, the multidimensionality of reality – and with that the multidimensionality of humanity – is recognised. Particularly technical, social, economic, juridical and moral dimensions are addressed. The Dutch approach also offers a participative change strategy. In this process psychic, power, lingual (meaning), social and trust (faith) dimensions are developed. The Australian and the Scandinavian approaches emphasise democracy and participation. In this process psychic, power, lingual (meaning), social and trust (faith) dimensions are recognised. Due to the absence of a design theory and design methodology the multidimensionality of the production structure is not as well developed, which also has consequences for the other structures.

Thirdly, this analysis also gives us a (partial) explanation for the success of the Roermond case. The actuator factory was designed according to the Dutch approach of Socio-Technical Systems Design and was further developed using the mini-company process. The combination of these two approaches does justice to the multidimensionality of an industrial organisation. Not only technical and economic dimensions are addressed, but also psychic, power, lingual, social, juridical, moral and trust. The aesthetic dimension comes back in the harmonic relations between management and employees.

Finally, this analysis helps us to understand the relationships between a (mini-) company and its environment. This relationship is also multi-dimensional. This will be elaborated on in the following sections.

Every dimension is unique. It has its own character or quality. In the wording of Dooyeweerd: its own meaning-kernel.[155] For example, the power dimension is characterised by 'formative power', the lingual dimension by 'symbolic meaning', the social dimension by 'social intercourse', the economic dimension by 'frugality in managing scarce goods', the aesthetic dimension by 'harmony', the juridical dimension by 'retribution' or 'recompensing', the moral dimension by 'love in temporal relationships', and the pistic dimension in 'faith' or 'firm assurance'.[156] The 'character' or 'quality' of each dimension cannot be analysed further. It can only be experienced and intuitively understood. For example, to really know what power is you must have exerted power and been ruled over for a long period of time. To really understand what morality is you must have cared for somebody and been cared for in different situations.[157] To really grasp what trust means you must have worked in an organisation with high-trust relations and in an organisation with low-trust relations.

The uniqueness of these dimensions implies that every dimension has its own patterns, mechanisms, order, and normativity. These patterns and mechanisms have to be respected. This order and normativity has to be complied with. In organisational practice, respect for the quality of every dimension and compliance with its normative implications cannot be taken for granted. Scientific Management has trained many generations of managers to view industrial organisations from technical and economic points of view. The present business climate – which is caught by the terror of the Stock Exchange – strongly stimulates these points of view. The consequence is that the relevance and uniqueness of other dimensions is ignored.

> *Reflection.* Why do managers ignore non-technical and non-economic aspects? I have
> asked myself this question many times. In my career I have met a number of
> managers who only focused on technical and economic aspects. I know from expe-
> rience that these managers could not even be convinced by organisational studies that
> show the importance of social or moral aspects. Why do they stick to technical and
> economic dimensions? In my opinion, it is not a matter of unwillingness but a matter
> of impotence. Their 'frames of reference' (Weick) only consist of technical and eco-
> nomic categories. They do not 'see' other categories. They suppress their own

---

[155] Dooyeweerd (1969, II, p74 ff.).
[156] Dooyeweerd (1969, II, p107 ff.).
[157] Dooyeweerd defines 'love' as the meaning-kernel of the moral dimension. I would like to propose 'care' as the meaning-kernel.

feelings and beliefs.[158] Battaglia and Tarant call these types of managers 'professional eunuchs'.[159]

A consequence of the uniqueness of every dimension is that is cannot be reduced to another one. In organisational science – as in other sciences – there is the inclination to reduce complex phenomena into one or two dimensions. For example, a lot of studies have investigated the phenomenon of 'trust' in organisational contexts. Some authors believe that 'trust' has to be understood as a psychic propensity, others point out that 'trust' functions within social relations, and again others define 'trust' as a kind of power. The 'truth' of these reductions is that trust is strongly related to psychic propensities, social relations, and the exertion of power. However, the 'untruth' of these studies is that the own character of trust is not recognised. A comparable reduction often takes place with respect to justice and morality. These dimensions are easily referred to as social or economic phenomena. In this way, the unique character of these dimensions in organisational life is ignored.

This analysis shows that the multidimensional structure of the company is not an accidental phenomenon but hints at or is an expression of a meaningful order. In reformational philosophy it is presupposed that this meaningful order is a *given* order. This order has a normative character in which each dimension constitutes a set of specific norms or standards. These specific norms or standards are constitutive for an industrial organisation. At the same time, this normativity appeals to human responsibility.

It is concluded that every organisational structure or phenomenon is multidimensional. Depending on the context, one or more dimensions come explicitly to the fore and others are more 'hidden'. The more 'hidden' dimensions are still present and still important. Each dimension has its own character or quality. Each dimension also has its own normative structure.

5.3 Coherence of a multidimensional industrial organisation

The different dimensions of reality are closely connected. For example, in Socio-Technical Systems Design a strong coherence between the technical system, economic system and social system is presupposed. In the Mini-Company Concept a strong coherence between continuous improvement, economic performance and humanity is assumed. The Roermond case shows a strong relationship between high-power relations and high-trust relations. The Aachen case shows that mistrust and fear can paralyse a whole organisation. How can we understand the coherence between different dimensions?

The multidimensionality of organisational life shows a complicated structure.[160] This structure is related to the order of the different dimensions. These

---

[158] Kets de Vries (1993).
[159] Quoted in Solomon (1993, p242).

dimensions are arranged in an order of prior and posterior[161]: arithmetic, spatial, kinematic, physical, biological, sensitive (psychic), logical, historical (power), lingual (meaning), social, economic, aesthetic (harmony), juridical, moral (care) and pistic (trust, faith). I would like to illustrate this complicated structure with several examples.

Firstly, every dimension refers forward to the later ones. For example, in the design of a production line it is very important to take ergonomic aspects into account, to stimulate the development of feelings of ownership, to enable social intercourse, and to respect the quality of working life. How are these different issues related? More specifically, how are the physical or technical dimensions of the production line related to the biological (ergonomic), psychic (feelings of ownership), and social (social intercourse) dimensions? The production line has to meet certain ergonomic standards. The working height has to be adaptable to the height of the employee, repetitive movements have to be prevented, and regular relaxation has to be integrated. The engineer has to design the line in such a way that the ergonomics of the human body are respected. That means the line has to be designed to respect the biological laws of the human being. In other words, an ergonomically designed production line refers forward to the biological dimension. The production line has to meet certain psychic standards. To prevent boredom, the activities on and around the line must be sufficiently varied, to keep the employee attentive, the pace of the activities must not be too low, and to support feelings of ownership, the employee has to participate in cleaning, repair and maintenance. The engineer also has to design the line in such a way that the psychology of the operator is respected. Specific technical features are necessary to meet these requirements. Also here, although the technical features as such have a purely physical character, they refer to psychological well being. The production line also has to meet social standards. A conveyor-like structure makes social intercourse between different employees rather difficult. A cell-like structure strongly facilitates social contacts between colleagues. Especially the Dutch approach to Socio-Technical Systems Design has emphasised the social aspects of a production line. Again, this line remains a technical object. However, this object is designed in such a way that social life on the shop floor is enabled. In summary, these examples show that a production line can be designed in such a way that biological, psychic and social standards are honoured. In other words, in the technical design all kind of references to later dimensions are present. These references are named 'anticipations'.

Secondly, every dimension refers backward to the earlier ones. For example, morality penetrates the whole organisation. The use of power is highly morally charged. The use of power to force compliance with the safety regulations is morally required, whereas the use of power to serve self-interest is morally objectionable. In social behaviour morality plays an important role. To behave respectfully to an operator is seen as morally just behaviour, whereas ignoring employees of lower levels in the organisation is seen as morally unjust behaviour.

---

[160] Dooyeweerd (1969, II, p55 ff., p163 ff., p181 ff.).
[161] Dooyeweerd (1969, II, p50).

Finally, in economic transactions between supplier and customer morality plays an important role. To keep an agreement – also when it is to one's own detriment – will be morally welcomed. On the contrary, forcing a supplier to accept loss-making orders – when a supplier is highly dependent on the customer – is generally morally condemned. In all these examples morality is at stake. However, the specific 'tint' of this morality depends on the context: use of power, social behaviour and economic transactions. In summary, these examples show that morality shows a different 'tint' depending on the context. In other words, in the world of morality different references to earlier dimensions are present. These references are named 'retrocipations'.

Thirdly, every dimension refers to other ones. Combining anticipations and retrocipations shows that every dimension refers to other dimensions without losing its own quality of character. In these references the original dimension becomes 'tinted' by the dimension to which it refers. This phenomenon – Dooyeweerd names it 'universality within its own sphere' – shows both the coherence of reality and the complexity of reality.[162]

Finally, it has to be remarked that the existence of retrocipations and anticipations (universality within its own sphere) makes it very tempting to reduce multidimensional reality to one or two dimensions. For example, in many studies trust is described as a psychological phenomenon. Trust has without any doubt a positive influence on the psychological development of an employee (anticipatory moment of the psychic dimension) and psychological health makes trust development possible (retrocipatory moment of trust dimension). However, this complex relationship between the psychical and trust dimensions does not allow a researcher to reduce trust to a psychological phenomenon and to ignore the individual character of trust.

The coherence of the different dimensions can be discussed from two directions: from the first dimension to the last one (foundational direction), and from the last dimension to the first one (transcendental direction).[163] The direction from the first dimension (arithmetic) to the last one (pistic) is the so-called foundational direction. That means the earlier dimensions found or form the basis of the later dimensions. In other words, the later dimensions can only 'function' well if the earlier dimensions are well developed. For example, an industrial organisation functions in the market as an economic entity. From an internal point of view, an economic organisation will only function well if the employees are motivated and committed (psychic dimension), have the authority to take necessary decisions (power dimension), and cooperate with each other to serve the customer (social dimension). Negatively formulated, an economic organisation perform badly if employees are de-motivated and not committed, if the employees have no authority to take decisions, and if cooperation within the organisation is bad.

The direction from the last dimension (pistic) to the first one (arithmetic) is the so-called transcendental direction. That means the earlier dimensions are opened

---

[162]   Dooyeweerd (1969, II, p331 ff.).
[163]   Dooyeweerd (1969, II, p53, 54).

or deepened by the later dimensions. In other words, the latently present anti-cipations of a certain dimension are realised. This deepening process can be illus-trated well by the example given above. An economic organisation will be well developed (deepened) if the economic interests of all stakeholders are protected by contractual agreements (juridical dimension), if the economic transactions of the stakeholders are embedded in a set of human-oriented norms and values (moral dimension), and if the relationships with the stakeholders are based on trust (pistic dimension). The importance of deepening process clearly comes to the fore in its negative consequences. A company that does not write down important agreements will be summoned up sooner or later. A company that knowingly delivers low quality products to its customers will lose market share. Finally, a company that cannot trust their employees has to implement a number of costly checks to prevent misuse and to secure high productivity.

The idea of coherence in a multidimensional industrial organisation is of the utmost importance for the topic of this study. I would like to make three remarks about this. Firstly, it shows that the different dimensions of an organisation have to be designed and developed in close connection. In this process the normativity of every dimension has to be respected.

Secondly, it shows that the design and development of a responsible organisation implies a full opening or complete disclosure of the earlier dimensions by the later dimensions. This opening or disclosure has to respect the normativity of the concerned dimension and has to be oriented normatively at the quality or character of the opening or disclosing dimension.

Finally, it shows the importance of the moral as the latest dimension but one and the faith dimensions as the latest one. These dimensions open up and deepen all foregoing dimensions. In this way, high-care and high-trust relations within an organisation and between an organisation and its stakeholders can develop. At the same time, the specific position of these two dimensions show the importance of Christian ethics and Christian belief for the development of a responsible organi-sation. So, not surprisingly, Dooyeweerd characterises Christian faith as the 'open-ed window' through which the 'light of God's eternity' should shine onto the 'whole temporal coherence of the world'.[164]

It is concluded that the different dimensions of industrial organisations are not independent in the sense of being self-sufficient; rather, they mutually refer to one another in a meaningful, coherent, and integral order of reality. Further, the different dimensions are arranged in an order of prior and posterior. The earlier dimensions found the later ones; the later dimensions open up the earlier ones.

---

[164] Dooyeweerd (1969, I, p302).

5.4 The socio-technical unit or mini-company as interlaced structure[165]

The actuator factory in Roermond and the glass factory in Aachen have been designed according to the Dutch approach to Socio-Technical Systems Design. This approach offers a detailed design theory and design methodology (section 3.3 of Chapter 2). Three different structures are distinguished: the production structure, control structure and information structure. These three structures have their own specific quality as will be discussed below. The mini-company process and the improvement structure can be seen as a part of the control structure and the relevant information flows as a part of the information structure.

The three structures – production structure, control structure, and information structure – have different 'individuality structures'.[166] Dooyeweerd uses the term 'individuality structure' to indicate the typical identity of a thing, social relationship or organisation. This term expresses that a thing, social relationship, or organisation is more than the sum of its different dimensions: it has its own individuality. Two dimensions with a special status express the typical identity of an individuality structure: the foundational dimension and the qualifying dimension.[167]

The *foundational dimension* refers to the 'basis of existence' of the individuality structure.[168] For example, organisations are the result of the shaping activities of people. That means it requires (formative) power to establish and to maintain an organisation. As a result, the foundational dimension of an organisation is human power.

The *qualifying dimension* is the 'characteristic leading' or 'guiding dimension' of an individuality structure.[169] The qualifying dimension shapes the way in which the other dimensions of the individuality structure are developed. For example, the objective of every industrial company is to produce goods or services for customers in an efficient way. These goods and products have to be sold with a reasonable profit so that the continuity of the company is secured. For that reason, the qualifying function of an industrial company as a whole is the economic dimension. All other (normative) dimensions of the industrial organisation get their specific 'tint' under the guidance of this leading economic dimension.

The concepts of 'foundational dimension' and 'qualifying dimension' will be used to analyse the individuality structures of a manufacturing organisation.

Production structure. The production structure encompasses all aspects of the production line (equipment, processes, tools, and layout). The production structure is the result of a human design process. Therefore, the foundational function of

---

[165]   In this section I will limit myself to an analysis of the manufacturing department. For a philosophical analysis of the whole business unit I would like to refer the reader to Verkerk and Zijlstra (2003).

[166]   Dooyeweerd (1969, III).

[167]   Dooyeweerd (1969, III, p90 ff.).

[168]   Dooyeweerd (1969, III, p90 ff.).

[169]   Dooyeweerd (1969, III, p58 ff.).

this structure is the (human) power dimension. In the production line materials are transformed in a number of steps into a product. In other words, the product is the result of a technical formative process. For that reason the qualifying function is also the (technical) power dimension.[170]

Control structure. The control structure encompasses all actions and controls that are done by employees to control the production line (including management, technical functions, and auxiliary functions). The control structure is the result of a human design process. For that reason, the foundational dimension of this structure is the (human) power dimension. The control of a production line cannot be done by one person but is the result of the coordinated action of all employees: operators, management, technicians, engineers, and others. In other words, the control structure is characterised by human action and human cooperation. For this reason, the social dimension is proposed as the qualifying function of the control-structure.

Information structure. The information structure encompasses all information that is required to operate the production line (including the storage, processing, and communication of information). The information structure is also the result of a human design process. For that reason, the foundational dimension of this structure is the (human) power dimension. Information to operate a production line does not refer to simple 'data' but to data with a specific meaning. Every datum has a certain meaning. This meaning is crucial for operating the line. For that reason, the qualifying dimension of the information structure is the lingual dimension (symbolic meaning).

The concepts of foundational and qualifying dimension put the design process in a new light. Firstly, the fact that the production structure, control structure, and information structure are all founded in human formative power, stresses that these structures are not a 'technological fate' but belong to the area of human responsibility. Secondly, the fact that the production structure, control structure, and information structure have different qualifying dimensions shows that the character of these structures is quite different. The design process of the production structure has to be primarily guided by physical or technical standards, the design process of the control structure primarily by social norms, and the design process of the information structure primarily by lingual norms. As a consequence, the production structure, control structure, and information structure show different types of normativity. These differences have to be recognised and acknowledged.

How are these three individuality structures (production structure, control structure, and information structure) related? In reformational philosophy such an interlacement of individuality structures is conceptualised by the term 'enkapsis' or

---

[170] Human beings function in all dimensions as a subject. A production line functions in the dimensions arithmetic up to physical as a subject. The formative power of a production line is – in Dooyeweerdian terminology – an anticipation of the physical dimension to the power dimension. The term 'technical power' will be used to distinguish between human power and an anticipation of the physical dimension to the power dimension.

'enkaptic interlacement'.[171] Dooyeweerd derived this term from biology and transformed it in such a way that it could be applied to things, biological phenomena, and social communities. The theory of enkaptic interlacements helps us to investigate the characteristics of a socio-technical unit or mini-company as an enkaptic whole. Especially the relation between the technical 'aspect system' and the social 'aspect system' can be clarified.

Firstly, the most important criterion for an enkaptic interlacement of individuality structures is that they have different qualifying functions.[172] As shown above, the production structure, control structure, and information structure have indeed different qualifying functions. In an enkaptic whole these individuality structures influence each other without losing their own character or qualification. That means in the socio-technical unit or mini company the qualifying function of the production structure remains technical power, the qualifying function of the control structure remains social, and the qualifying structure of the information structure remains lingual. This statement cannot be taken for granted. For example, in Tayloristic and neo-Tayloristic thinking the technical power character of the production system is widely acknowledged. However, the social character of the control structure and the lingual character of the information structure are not acknowledged. In these traditions the control structure and information structure are moulded according to standards of technical power with the result that their original character or qualification is strongly distorted. More sharply phrased: dehumanised.

Secondly, in the Dutch approach these three individuality structures build upon one another. That means first the production structure is designed, after that the control structure, and finally the information structure. In other words, these individuality structures are 'hierarchically' organised. Such a hierarchical intertwinement of different individuality-structures is named in reformational philosophy as a foundational enkapsis. The concept of 'foundational enkapsis' reveals two normative features.[173]

The first normative feature of the concept of 'foundational enkapsis' is the idea of opening or disclosure. The (hierarchical) lower structure has not a total or fully autonomous character and is not independent from the (hierarchical) higher structure. In concrete, the production structure is not autonomous with respect to and is not independent from the control structure. The same holds for the relationship between the control structure and the information structure. The idea of opening or disclosure implies that the (hierarchical) lower structure has to be opened or disclosed by the (hierarchical) higher structure. In concrete, the control

---

[171]   Dooyeweerd (1969, III, p109 ff. and p627 ff.). Dooyeweerd (1969, III, p695) defines an enkaptic structural whole as follows. "We shall speak of a genuine enkaptic structural whole when an interlacement between structures of a different radical- or genotype is realised in one and the same typically qualified form-totality embracing all the interwoven structures in a real enkaptic unity without encroaching upon their inner sphere-sovereignty."

[172]   Dooyeweerd (1969, III, p634 ff.).

[173]   Dooyeweerd (1969, III, p640 ff.).

structure, which is socially qualified, has to open or disclose the production structure in such a way that employees can function as human beings. This opening or disclosure process has a normative character: it is leaded by the norms of the social dimension. The same holds for the relationship between the information structure and the control structure. The information structure, which is lingually qualified, has to open or disclose the control structure in such a way that relevant information is well interpreted and well communicated. This opening or disclosure process has a normative character: it is leaded by the norms of the lingual dimension (symbolic meaning). The idea of opening or disclosure cannot be taken for granted. In Tayloristic and neo-Tayloristic traditions it is believed that the production structure has to be designed according to the norms and standards of technical power without acknowledging the opening by the socially qualified control structure. Additionally, the specific disclosure of the control structure by the lingual qualified information structure is ignored. Only De Sitter (Dutch school of Socio-Technical Systems Design) has elaborated on the idea of opening or disclosure in detail. His design theory recognises that it is all about the production structure. Again and again, he emphasises that the problems of the Tayloristic method of mass production (dehumanisation and alienation) have to be attacked at its root: the production structure. That means the production structure has to be designed in such a way that employees can function as social beings. In this starting point, the professional background of De Sitter comes fully to the fore: he was a sociologist. Furthermore, De Sitter recognises that the control structure has to be designed in such a way that the employees at different levels of the organisation have the right information to do their job.

The second normative feature of the concept of 'foundational enkapsis' is the idea of the 'irreversible foundational relationship' between the different structures. The relation between the production structure, control structure, and information structure is not arbitrary. The chosen production structure strongly limits the design options of the control structure. The chosen production structure and control structure strongly limits the design options of the information structure. This normative feature is fully recognised by De Sitter. He states that the design of the different individuality structures has to be done in a certain order: production structure > control structure > information structure. In many organisations this normative feature is not recognised. Especially modern information technologies can easily lead to an integration of the production and information structure with the result that the control structure can no longer be developed according to its unique (social) characteristics.

The analysis of the microstructure of the socio-technical unit or mini-company can be summarised in the following conclusions.

Firstly, a socio-technical unit or mini-company is the interlaced structure of a production structure, control structure and information structure. On the one hand, these structures have their own quality and their own autonomy. The production structure is qualified by technical power, the control structure by social intercourse, and the information structure by symbolic meaning. On the other hand, these structures are strongly dependent on each other and strongly influence each other. To put it more sharply: they are bound into an encompassing organisational structure or enkaptic whole that we identify as the socio-technical unit or mini-company.

Secondly, the concept of the socio-technical unit or mini-company as an 'enkaptic whole' reveals two normative features. Firstly, the opening or disclosure of the production structure (qualified by technical power) by the control structure (qualified by social intercourse), and of the control structure by the information structure (qualified by symbolic meaning). Secondly, the irreversible foundational relationship between the production structure, control structure, and information structure.

Finally, misunderstanding of the unique character of the different structures – or rejection of the relationships between these different structures – leads to dehumanisation in industrial organisations.

5.5. The socio-technical unit or mini-company and its environment

This section presents the key elements of the relation between a socio-technical unit or mini-company and its environment. The analysis will be limited to four different relations: internal customer, external customer, local government, and natural environment.[174]

In the preceding section the socio-technical unit or mini-company has been characterised as an interlaced structure or enkaptic structural whole. A structural analysis of the external customer, local government, and natural environment will show that these 'entities' can also be characterised as interlaced structures or enkaptic structural wholes.[175] To describe the relationships between these types of structures it is important to extend our analysis one step more. How can we characterise an enkaptic structural whole?

Dooyeweerd argues that enkaptic structural wholes are characterised by an 'independent internal leading function' or an 'internal structural principle'.[176] A closer analysis shows that the structural wholes mentioned above have different internal leading functions. In a socio-technical unit or mini-company materials are transformed into a semi-finished product, semi-finished products into other semi-finished products, and semi-finished products into end products. Such types of transformations are characteristic of a socio-technical unit or mini-company. Therefore, the internal leading function of an internal customer (the next production unit) is technical power. The external customer is an economic enterprise. An economic enterprise functions in the open market. Such an enterprise is part of the whole business chain. It purchases materials and components, and it

---

[174] A socio-technical unit or mini-company usually has no relationships with external parties. In practice, the marketing and sales department represent the relation with the external customer. Staff departments represent the relation with the local government and the natural environment. However, this does not affect the core of this analysis.

[175] This analysis will not be given here. See Dooyeweerd (1969, III, p653 ff.).

[176] Dooyeweerd (1969, III, p637).

sells modules or complete products. Therefore, the internal leading function of an external customer is the economic dimension.[177] The local government is part of the national state. The western state is basically a constitutional state. As a consequence, the internal leading function of the local government is the juridical dimension.[178] Finally, the natural environment can be described as a structural whole that is characterised by the biological/ecological dimension.[179]

In conclusion, it is plausible that an internal customer (the next production unit), external customer, local government, and natural environment are enkaptic structural wholes that are characterised by different qualifying functions: formative power, economic dimension, juridical dimension, and biological/ecological dimension. How can we characterise the relationship between the socio-technical unit or mini-company and its environment? In this case, it is absolutely out of the question to characterise these relationships as a hierarchical one, e.g. the foundational enkapsis. On the contrary, it is a relationship of mutual dependence. Such a relationship is named a 'correlative enkapsis'.[180] [181] The ideas of 'internal leading function' and 'mutual dependence' are helpful in analysing the relationship between a socio-technical unit or mini-company and its environment.

Relation with the internal customer
The relationship between a socio-technical unit or mini-company and its internal customer (the next production unit) has the following characteristics:

o   The relationship between a socio-technical unit or mini-company and its internal customer is primarily characterised by technical power as qualifying functions. Both parties are focused on the transformation of materials via semi-finished products, into end products.
o   The relationship between a socio-technical unit or mini-company and an internal customer is an equal relationship. It is really a matter of *mutual* dependence and *mutual* influence. The solving of a problem can mean an improvement in the formative processes of one party or the other. The equality of this relationship is guaranteed by the interests of the mother company which surpass the interests of the socio-technical unit or mini-company. In a customer-oriented environment the wishes of the internal customer will strongly influence – in philosophical terminology: will open or disclose – the production structure, control structure and information structure of the socio-technical unit or mini-company.

---

[177]   Dooyeweerd (1969, III, p574).
[178]   Dooyeweerd (1969, III, p437).
[179]   Dooyeweerd (1969, III, p630 ff.).
[180]   Dooyeweerd (1969, III, p648).
[181]   A refined analysis shows that the relation between a socio-technical unit or mini-company and its internal customer (the next production unit) is a whole-part relationship. In addition, the relation between a socio-technical unit and the local government is a territorial enkapsis. See Verkerk and Zijlstra (2003). To facilitate the reading of this section these relations are also considered as a correlative enkapsis.

o   In the mini-company process as described in the Roermond case the *mutual* dependence and *mutual* influence of a socio-technical unit or mini-company and an internal customer is structured and formalised.

Relation with the external customer
The relationship between a socio-technical unit or mini-company and its external customer has the following characteristics:

o   The relationship between a socio-technical unit or mini-company and its external customer is primarily characterised by technical power and economic scarcity as qualifying functions, respectively. One party is focused on the transformation of materials into end products and the other one on the economic aspects of the business transaction.

o   The relationship between a socio-technical unit or mini-company and its external customer is an equal relationship. A customer is free to choose a supplier and a supplier can refuse to deliver to a certain customer. It is a matter of *mutual* dependence and *mutual* influence. Improvement is focused on the formative processes of the socio-technical unit or mini-company and the economic processes of the external customer. In a customer-oriented environment the wishes of the external customer will strongly influence – in philosophical terminology: will open or disclose – the production structure, control structure and information structure of the socio-technical unit or mini-company.

o   In the mini-company process as described in the Roermond case the *mutual* dependence and *mutual* influence between a socio-technical unit or mini-company and its external customer is structured and formalised.

Relation with the local government
The relationship between a socio-technical unit or mini-company and the local government customer has the following characteristics:

o   The relationship between a socio-technical unit or mini-company and the local government is primarily characterised by technical power and juridical recompensing as qualifying functions, respectively. One party is focused on the transformation process of materials into end products and the other one on the upholding of legal regulations.

o   The relationship between a socio-technical unit or mini-company and the local government is an unequal relationship. From a global point of view, economic and public organisations strongly depend on each other. From a local and national point of view, it is not a matter of *mutual* dependence and *mutual* influence but primarily a matter of *one-sided* dependence and *one-sided* influence. Especially because a local and national government has the power to enforce compliance with legal regulations. The legal regulations have a strong influence on the technical choices made in a factory. Especially safety and environmental regulations play an important role. In philosophical terminology: the formative processes are opened or disclosed

428

by the legal regulations. In practice, the relationship with the local government is much more complex. However, this complexity does not alter the
normative requirement that the production structure, control structure and
information structure have to be opened or disclosed by legal regulations.

o In the mini-company process as described in the Roermond case the legal
regulations were explicitly brought up for discussion. Especially health,
safety, and environmental regulations. In this way, compliance with these
regulations is strongly promoted. Furthermore, dangerous violations of the
regulations will be identified more quickly.

Relation with the natural environment
The relationship between a socio-technical unit or mini-company with the natural
environment has the following characteristics:

o The relationship between a socio-technical unit or mini-company and the
natural environment is primarily characterised by technical power and
biological/ecological life as qualifying functions, respectively. One party is
focused on the transformation process of materials into end products and
the other 'party' on maintaining its own biological quality.

o The relationship between a socio-technical unit or mini-company and the
natural environment is an unequal relationship. Basically, human organisations and the natural environment strongly depend on each other. However, the natural environment is not a real 'party' that can enforce its own
interests.[182] The natural environment has no power and has no voice. As a
consequence, the idea of *mutual* dependence and *mutual* influence is fully
dependent on the benevolence of human organisations. In most western
countries the interests of the natural environment are legally protected. And
... this protection is required to prevent technical and economic interests
from coming first. Biological/ecological standards have a strong influence on
the technical choices made in a factory. In philosophical terminology: the
formative processes have to be opened or disclosed by the biologi-
cal/ecological standards.

o In the mini-company process as described in the Roermond case environmental interests were explicitly brought up for discussion. Additionally, the
reduction of waste and decreasing the pollution of the natural environment
was promoted. This approach strongly stimulated the environmental consciousness of management and employees.

In summary, the (simplified[183]) analysis given above shows that the relationships
between a socio-technical unit or mini-company and its environment are quite
complex. They are characterised by different sets of standards and norms and

---

[182] Green organisations and action groups voice the interests of the natural environment.
This complication will not be further discussed.
[183] The opening process is much more complicated than described in this section. See
Dooyeweerd (1969, II, p170 ff. and p181 ff.).

standards, e.g. technical power, economic scarcity, juridical recompensing, and biological/ecological life. In principle, the relationships with other parties are characterised by mutual dependence and mutual influence. However, the features of this mutual dependence and mutual influence are strongly dependent on the character or the character or quality of the party concerned. An external orientation of the socio-technical unit or mini-company promotes that its production structure, control structure and information structure are opened or disclosed by the different parties in the environment. Two conclusions can be drawn:

Firstly, the relation between a socio-technical unit or mini-company and its environment can be described as a relationship of mutual dependency. In philosophical terms, a correlative enkapsis exists between a socio-technical unit or mini-company and its different relations ('stakeholders').

Secondly, the character or quality of the relationship between a socio-technical unit or mini-company and its environment strongly depends on the character or quality of the relation concerned ('stakeholder'). The specific character or quality of this relation ('stakeholder') also has to shape the production structure, control structure, and information structure of the socio-technical unit or mini-company.

5.6 Position of an employee in an industrial organisation

The concept of enkaptic interlacement is also very helpful in reflecting on the position of human beings in the socio-technical unit or mini-company. This topic requires an extensive philosophical analysis but can only be briefly touched upon here.

How can we understand the position of an employee in an industrial organisation? What happens to an operator the moment that s/he enters the factory? Does s/he use his or her unique know-how, capabilities, and basic beliefs to shape the ideals of the organisation? Does s/he become a source of organisational renewal? Or does s/he become a 'company man'? Does s/he leave his or her values and norms at the door in favour of the prevailing standards?

First and foremost, organisations are human communities. Unique human beings shape the ideals of the organisation. Unique human beings develop new products, manufacture consumer goods, and sell new designs. A company – to use the words of Arie de Geus[184] – is a living company. It depends on the specific capabilities, skills, know-how, and working experience of its crew. Despite standardisation, the execution of the primary process is still a human-controlled process. In other words, people make and break a company. This also holds for operators on the shop floor. They cannot be considered as cogs in the company machine that can be exchanged in accordance with the whims of management.

I would like to underline this statement from a normative point of view. The ideas of 'dignity' and 'vocation' have two consequences. Firstly, an employee is a unique person with specific know-how, particular capabilities, and certain basic

---

[184]   De Geus (1997).

beliefs. In the design and development of the organisation the uniqueness of the employees has to be respected. Secondly, the unique know-how and capabilities of every employee have to be developed and deployed in the organisation. The design and development of the organisation has to make this possible. It is the responsibility of the factory manager that the unique qualities of the employees are developed and that deadening or depersonalisation is prevented.

In reformational-philosophical terminology, employees are enkaptically interwoven in an industrial organisation.[185] That means both employees and the organisation have their own specific individuality. These specific individualities are (have to be) maintained in the interweaving process. However, the relation between employee and organisation is not symmetric. The type of enkaptic interweaving is that of an *irreversible foundational relation*.[186] [187] As they say, an organisation exists by the grace of people and not the other way around. That means in the interweaving process, the capabilities of human being are disclosed – not modelled – to shape the ideals and to realise the goals of the organisation. The difference between 'disclosure' and 'modelling' may be subtle but is fundamental. Disclosure makes the assumption of respect for the individual whereas modelling implies shaping of an object irrespective of its individuality. In organisational practice this subtle distinction is often not recognised resulting in the depersonalised 'company man'.

In conclusion, employees cannot be considered as 'parts' of the organisation. They are unique individuals that are enkaptically interlaced in an industrial organisation. The idea of irreversible foundational enkaptic interlacement highlights the dependency of an organisation on (the capabilities of) its employees.

5.7 The problem of evil

Evil is growing rampantly in all industrial organisations. Dehumanisation and alienation are everywhere. Injustice can be found in every nook and cranny. Some bosses tyrannise their crew. Some bosses are tyrannised by their crew. Pestering the life out of somebody is a widespread phenomenon.

Evil bewilders. Evil overwhelms. Evil makes us speechless. Is it possible to describe evil without changing its tearing character? Is it possible to analyse evil without weakening the bitter lamentation? The bewildering character of evil asks for modesty. Scientists cannot fathom the suffering of operators on the conveyor line. Philosophers cannot fathom the depths of organisational evil. At best,

---

[185] More specific: enkaptically interwoven in the production structure, controlling structure, and information structure.

[186] Dooyeweerd (1969, III, p653 ff.).

[187] In many ethical approaches employees are indicated as 'stakeholders'. Such a characterisation is very helpful to emphasise the interests of employees and to prevent an instrumental view of human beings. A possible disadvantage could be that the specific position of employees is not acknowledged because they are considered as (only) one of the many stakeholders.

managers can put their own experiences into words. Nevertheless, it is not allowed to neglect this problem. Rightly, the philosopher Johan van der Hoeven names the problem of evil the 'acid test for the authenticity of philosophising'.[188] And the philosopher Paul Ricoeur names the problem of evil a 'challenge to philosophy and theology'.[189]

Surprisingly, the problem of evil is widely acknowledged but is not an important theme in organisational investigations. Maybe, the rational-scientific background of organisational science causes this lack of attention. One of the presuppositions of the Enlightenment is that human beings are perfectible.[190] This presupposition invites scientists to work on the improvement of management and employees but this not ask them to investigate the problem of evil. A 'vision of the whole' as presented in this section gives a key to indicating the complex and fundamental character of evil. In this section I would like to draw some preliminary conclusions. An extensive inquiry of this problem requires a separate study.[191]

In the first place, an in-depth understanding of the multidimensionality of organisational reality is a prerequisite for investigating the problem of evil. It shows that the multidimensionality of reality has an ugly side. Namely, that evil is also multidimensional. For example, evil expresses itself in RSI-symptoms of employees (biological), apathy of employees (psychic), fear of management (psychic), misuse of authority by employees and employers (power), oppressing images about employees (symbolic meaning), tensions between operators in the group (social), unreliable payment of bills (economic), surpassing of safety laws (juridical), bad quality of working life (moral), and low-trust relations (faith). From a modal point of view, evil can be described as a-normative or anti-normative development of organisational structures. The idea of multidimensionality gives us in a manner of speaking different 'pairs of glasses' to investigate the modal complexity of the problem of evil.

In the second place, awareness of the complex character of the organisational reality helps us to understand the complex character of evil. The structural complexity of reality (anticipations, retrocipations, enkaptic structural wholes) has been described. Evil has a comparable complexity. The most obvious example is that a badly designed production structure penetrates the functioning of the whole organisation. Another example is that mistrust between management and employees restricts the development of the whole organisation. Evil is like a virus. It lodges in the fundamental structures of an organisation, becomes institutionalised in instructions and procedures, infects the whole culture and becomes self-replicating.

In the third place, both the idea of the multidimensionality and complexity of evil save us from believing that the problem of evil is a simple one that can be solved easily. From that point of view, the rhetoric of management about a bright future and promises of consultants to realise a 'committed organisation' in seven

---

[188] Van der Hoeven (1980, p168 ff.).
[189] Ricoeur (1985).
[190] Goudzwaard (1979).
[191] A detailed study of evil in human relations is given in Verkerk (1997, p133 ff.).

steps have to be distrusted beforehand. Evil can be compared with a many-headed chameleon. It is a monster that brings about harm once with the one head and once with the other head. It often uses several heads at the same time. The treachery is to be found in its adaptability: the monster adapts itself perfectly to the specific context of the organisational landscape.

In the fourth place, philosophical analysis can reveal the multidimensional and complex character of evil but can never answer the 'why' of evil. Therefore, science cannot solve the problem of evil. Rightly, Ricoeur has argued that 'only' thinking can show that the problem of evil is unsolvable.[192]

Finally, evil as suffering bears a fundamental character.[193] Evil penetrates all the nooks and crannies of human existence. Rightly, Popma speaks about a 'disturbed creation' and about the 'demonic character' of the reality.[194] The inclination to dominate is deeply rooted in human beings. The Bible reveals the tendency of the male to suppress the female.[195] This tendency is present in all human relations and is anchored and institutionalised in all types of organisations. In a discussion with the Pharisees, Jesus Christ emphasised that evil comes out of the heart of human beings.[196] Hannah Arendt has shown in her moving report about the Eichmann process in Jerusalem that the holocaust was carried out by 'normal people'.[197] Menachem Arnoni, a Polish Jew who survived Auschwitz, calls for people to identify the potential Eichmann in their own heart.[198] These thoughts show that evil does not only have an 'external cause' (e.g. capitalistic relationships, Tayloristic organisations) but also has an 'internal cause' (the human heart). The identification of the human heart as a source of evil reveals an existential dimension of evil: evil is also in *my* heart. The word of Christ declares *me* guilty. The conclusion of Arendt has to do with *myself*. The call of Arnoni is made to *myself*.

It is not my intention to describe the life of industrial organisations with only black chalk. It is also not my intention to compare a manager with the designers and executors of the holocaust. However, I would like to point out that evil has a fundamental character: it is present in the heart of every human being. Due to this presence evil is continuously institutionalised. Nobody can neglect the words of Jesus Christ, the observations of Hannah Arendt, and the call of Menachem Arnoni. The world of management and organisations is not a sinless oasis in a desert of evil. On the contrary, the practice of industrial organisations shows evil in all its different colours. And this practice does an appeal to every manager.

---

[192] Ricoeur (1985).
[193] See Verkerk (1997, p218 ff.).
[194] Popma (1977).
[195] Genesis 3 : 16.
[196] Marcus 7 : 20 - 23.
[197] Arendt (1965).
[198] Arnoni (1986).

5.8 Conclusions

The reformational-philosophical analysis presented in this section has shown that industrial organisations have a multidimensional character. The different dimensions are closely connected, refer to each other, and influence each other. Each of these dimensions has its own unique character and normativity. In addition, it has been shown that an industrial organisation has a complicated structure. Different types of structures – each with their own unique character and normativity – are interlaced with each other.

The reformational-philosophical analysis indicates that the dominating technological and economic perspective in western society is absolutely insufficient to understand phenomena on the shop floor of an industrial organisation. A scientific analysis has to cover all dimensions of organisational reality. In other words, the 'how' in the first research question refers not only to the technological and economic dimension of human behaviour, but also to psychic, power, lingual, social, juridical, moral and trust dimensions. All these dimensions have to be covered to understand the 'context in which events occur' and the 'deep structure of social behaviour' (Dyer and Wilkins[199]).

The reformational-philosophical analysis also supports us in analysing the underlying views of new production concepts. Managers who use a design theory and implementation strategy that ignore one or more of these dimensions will face serious problems during or after the implementation phase. Managers who turn a blind eye to the multi-dimensional character of the specific context of the shop floor will not realise the promise of new production concepts – technical superiority and a 'new world of work'. In other words, the 'why' of the second research question refers to the dominating technological, economic and hierarchical perspectives of manufacturing organisations and implementation strategies. As discussed before, in Lean Management the technical, economic, and hierarchical perspectives dominate both the fundamentals of the organisation and the implementation strategy of improvements. In Business Process Reengineering the hierarchical perspective dominates the implementation strategy.

Finally, the reformational-philosophical analysis has shown that industrial organisations have a complicated structure that consists of interlaced sub-structures, each with its own character and normativity. The 'how' in the third research question refers to normative design and development of these different interlaced structures. Socio-Technical Systems Design and the Mini-Company Concept to a great extent both honour the unique character and normativity of the different organisational structures, both in its fundamentals and in its implementation strategy.

---

[199]   Dyer and Wilkins (1991).

434

6 The design and development of a responsible industrial organisation

In the foregoing section it has been argued that a 'vision of the whole' is required to sketch the contours of a human organisation. This means an industrial organisation in which the humanity of employees is taken as a starting point in design and development.

It has been argued that the existence of human organisations cannot be taken for granted. The history of industrialisation seems to be inextricably bound up with dehumanisation and alienation. The Faustian Pact (Kanigel) – in which prosperity is exchanged for humanity and freedom – seems to have industrial companies in a firm grip. Again and again, social and moral values seem to lose out to technical and economic standards. Even successful organisational innovations seem to be vulnerable. In a moment of depression one asks oneself in despair whether the fight against dehumanisation and alienation stands a chance from the very start.

In the foregoing section it has also been shown that organisations have a multidimensional character, that different dimensions are strongly connected, and that each dimension is characterised by its own normative structure. In addition, it has been proposed that the design and development of human organisations requires a simultaneous development of the normative structure of all these different dimensions. Furthermore, it is plausible that – due to the coherence between different dimensions – an integral or multidimensional approach also has a positive effect on the performance of the whole organisation.

This line of thought will be developed further in this section. I would like to show that dehumanisation and alienation do not have to be taken for granted. On the contrary, I would like to present a *liberating perspective*. A perspective in which the *dignity of man* is respected and the *vocation of the employee* is supported; a perspective that is characterised by a *normative approach* to industrial organisations. I realise that the presentation of a normative perspective expresses a lot of *idealism*; an idealism that (too) often *gets crushed* by organisational reality; an idealism that is at odds with the *postmodern spirit of the times*. On the other hand, it is impossible to spend many hours on the shop floor without being moved by *the other*. It is impossible to be a human leader without showing *compassion* in seeing pains of labour. It is impossible – to my deepest belief – to be a Christian manager without fighting for *shalom* in labour relations and without struggling for *grapes* and *figs* (old testament symbols of peace and well-being). In other words, I would like to discuss the third research question of this study.

6.1 Closed or restricted development

Why is (neo-)Taylorism so problematic? Why does Scientific Management lead to dehumanisation and alienation? These questions have to be answered in detail to understand the field under discussion. (Neo-)Taylorism can be characterised as a fruit of the Enlightenment. Key elements are the postulate of autonomy of the human individual, belief in the liberating powers of science and technology, and the idea of progress. Dominance of the principles of Scientific Management in western industry has resulted in a *closed* or *restricted* development. Industrial organisations are designed and developed according to technological, economic and hierarchical imperatives.[200] [201] The multidimensional normativity of organisations – as outlined in section 5 – is ignored, which manifests itself in all organisational structures and processes.[202]

First, in Scientific Management the design of a production line – including both the design of equipment and the grouping of the equipment in a line – is determined by technological, economic, and hierarchical standards. As a consequence, a production line is not designed according to typical human aspects such as power or influence, social intercourse, and trust. In other words, dehumanisation and alienation start at the beginning: with the design of the production line. Furthermore, symptoms of dehumanisation and alienation (e.g. absence, high sickness, lack of interest, cutting corners, not complying with instructions and procedures) are often controlled by technological adaptations and hierarchical measures in order to safeguard economic interests.

Second, in Scientific Management technological, economic and hierarchical standards dominate the design and development of the organisation. As a consequence, the character of the control structure and information structure is misunderstood. The ideas of an organisation as social community and as meaningful or symbolic community are closed by the straitjacket of technological and economic values and are restricted by a hierarchical culture.[203] Closure occurs at the expense of the humanity of the organisation. In addition, employee responses are controlled by hierarchical measures, which further restrict the human organisation.

Third, in Scientific Management trust and power are not developed. The Tayloristic approach opts for low-trust-low-power relations. This means that trust and power – as modal dimensions and as integral phenomena – are closed or restricted. Low-trust-low-power relations contribute strongly to dehumanisation and alienation.

Fourth, in Scientific Management the relationships with stakeholders are partly closed and very restricted. (a) In a closed development of the organisation, technological, economic, and hierarchical interests dominate the different structures. As a consequence, the multidimensional normativity of these structures is strongly

---

[200] Edwards (1979), Goudzwaard (1979), Schuurman (1980, 2002) and Schuurman in Griffioen and Balk (1995, p185-200).

[201] Technological, economic, and hierarchical imperatives also have *each other* in a firm grip. As a consequence, even technological, economic and hierarchical developments are closed or restricted. See for example Schuurman in Griffioen and Balk (1995, p185-200) and Goudzwaard in Boersma et al. (2002, p202-213).

[202] Morgan (1986) has discussed several 'images of organisations'. He clearly shows – in my interpretation – that the one-sided development of organisations always means closure and restriction.

[203] De Geus (1997) emphasises the social dimension of organisations and Weick (1979, 1995) the lingual dimension (sensemaking, symbolic meaning).

frustrated or seriously neglected. In the long term, this will have a negative influence on the (multi-dimensional) interests of all stakeholders. (b) In a restricted development, the interests of powerful stakeholders such as shareholders and management have priority. The result is that the justified interests of powerless stakeholders are ignored (so far these interests are not protected by legal regulations). (c) In a closed development, the interests of the weak stakeholders are reduced and limited. On the one hand, the technological, economic, and hierarchical interests of these weak stakeholders are viewed from the perspective of the interests of the powerful stakeholders. On the other hand, other dimensions such as power, morality, and trust interests of these weak stakeholders are not honoured and often not acknowledged at all.

Generally, *closed* or *restricted* managers guide *closed* or *restricted* developments. The tradition of the Enlightenment and Scientific Management is deeply rooted in industrial organisations. The belief in human autonomy, the idea of progress, and the rejection of the religious sources has reproduced itself in many generations of closed managers. In a restricted development the employment relation is strongly instrumentalised. In addition, the asymmetry of this relation is blown up out of all proportion. In 1923 a manager wrote in the *American Management Review*[204]:

> "As a matter of fact, we all know that the great majority of executives have 'fallen down' in the human organisation of their plants (…) There has been in some cases, it is true, lack of tact, lack of good sense and lack of understanding of modern democratic tendencies. *The real difficulty, however, has been one of neglect* – the fact that in spite of our capacity for handling human beings when we put our mind to it, *we executives have treated the question of human organisation in our plants as a minor instead of as a major problem.*"

Bendix concludes that in the initial period of the Human Relations Movement rhetoric about the worker as a 'human being' already dominated the industrial discourse[205]:

> "(…) the bulk of the verbal imagery deals with the 'search for expression and growth' [of the employees, MJV], the bulk of managerial effort is no doubt directed toward the more or less efficient operation of economic enterprises."

The spectre of Scientific Management is still present in western organisations.[206] Control of and domination over employees is central; the right of the manager to control and to dominate is undisputed. From that point of view, it does not come

---

[204] Quoted from Bendix (1956, p299) (italics by MJV).
[205] Bendix (1956, p297).
[206] E.g. Pruyt (1996). Huys et al. (1999) have investigated four industrial sectors in Belgium. Their data suggests a neo-Tayloristic rather than a post-Tayloristic or post-Fordist concept. Rothschild and Ollilainen (1999) state that modern techniques like Total Quality Management does not reduce managerial control but obscures it.

as a surprise that Braverman identifies capitalism as the origin of the degradation of work in the twentieth century.[207] It also does not come as a surprise that Edwards identifies hierarchy as the biggest obstacle to the democratisation of a company.[208] Dooyeweerd has described the religious ground motive of the Enlightenment with the terms 'nature' and 'freedom'.[209] He has shown that this ground motive hides an enormous tension because the tendency to rule over nature and to control destiny is always at the expense of human freedom. In industrial practice this tension comes to the fore in the asymmetry of the employment relation: closed freedom for the manager and control and domination for the employee.

6.2 An ethics of responsibility

In philosophical ethics a number of different theories have been developed. For example, virtue ethics, deontological ethics, utilitarian ethics, discourse ethics, and the ethics of care.[210] All these approaches have their own specific perspective. They can only be understood against the specific social, political, and cultural background of the age in which they have been developed. They are based – explicitly or implicitly – on a certain pattern of values and norms. They express different views on morality and different status's for moral judgements.[211] Appendix 1 gives a summary.

The approaches mentioned above are all used in business ethics. For example, Robert C. Solomon presents a virtue ethics approach in his impressive book *Ethics and Excellence. Cooperation and Integrity*.[212] Ronald M. Green and Norman E. Bowie propose a deontological approach in their books *The Ethical Manager. A New Method for Business Ethics* and *Business Ethics: A Kantian Perspective*.[213] Milton Friedman takes a utilitarian view in his famous article 'The Social Responsibility of Business Is to Increase Its Profits'.[214] Horst Steinmann and Albert Löhr offer a dialogue ethics approach in their article 'Unternehmensethik - eine "realistische Idee"' ('Business Ethics - a "realistic view"').[215] André Nijhoff advocates an ethics of care approach in his thesis *Met zorg besluiten. Een studie naar morele afwegingen van leidinggevenden bij ingrijpende organisatieveranderingen* (*Deciding by care. A study of the moral considerations of major organisational changes*). In

---

[207] Braverman (1974).
[208] Edwards (1979).
[209] Dooyeweerd (1975, p45 ff.).
[210] Strictly speaking, the ethics of care originates in feminist thinking.
[211] MacIntyre (1998).
[212] Solomon (1993).
[213] Green (1994) and Bowie (1999).
[214] Friedman (1970).
[215] Steinmann and Lohr (1988).

addition, a lot of authors propose the use of different approaches depending on the moral question and the specific context.[216]

The application of philosophical ethics in business ethics has been very fruitful. It has significantly contributed to the development of the whole field: both to give a theoretical basis for business ethics and to apply business ethics in concrete situations. There is another side to this, however. Philosophical ethics as a primary perspective implies that *specific organisational characteristics are brought up for discussion as a secondary consideration*.[217] As a consequence, it cannot be taken for granted that typical organisational aspects of business ethics are identified. Also, it cannot be taken for granted that solutions proposed by business ethics can be implemented fruitfully. The description of the closed or restricted development of industrial organisations in section 6.1. strongly supports the case that business ethics has a blind spot. Especially ethical aspects of the design of organisations are ignored.[218] Also, the influence of typical organisational phenomena such as trust and power on responsible behaviour is not recognised. To prevent such a blind spot business ethics has to take the *inherent normativity of organisations* as a starting point. Such an approach implies the *anchoring of business ethics in organisational theory*. At the same time, it implies a *normative reinterpretation of organisational theory*.

Concern about societal developments has led a number of authors to call for an *ethics of responsibility*.[219] Such an ethics expresses the *fundamental responsibility of the human actor with respect to fellow man, society, and the natural environment.* It transcends thinking in terms of virtues, means, and ends. An ethics of responsibility starts with the *deepest motive* or *ethos* of a human actor.[220] *Deepest motive* or *ethos* refers to a religious-ethical motivation for human activities. It refers to a fundamental motivation in individuals to make certain choices and to act accordingly. In western culture two main motives can be distinguished: enlightened humanism and Christian belief. As described before, the deepest motive or ethos that underlies this study is Christian belief.   An ethics of responsibility stresses the importance of *values, norm principles*, and *norms*.[221] *Values* refer to the intrinsic meaning of wholes or entities, e.g. the value of the natural environment, human beings, and human organisations. *Norm principles* are the functional or dimensional expressions of a certain value. For example, in an industrial environment the

---

216   Jochemsen and Glas (1997), Willigenburg et al. (1998), Treviño and Nelson (1999), Jeurissen et al. (2000), Beauchamp and Bowie (2001), and Kaptein and Wempe (2002).

217   Verkerk (2002a, b).

218   Exceptions are Löhr and Bickle (1996) and Collins (1997).

219   Weber introduced this term in 1918 (Weber in Gerth and Mills (1970, p77-128). Jonas (1984) has emphasised human responsibility in technological society. In reformational-philosophical tradition Goudzwaard (1979), Schuurman (1980, 2002), and Jochemsen and Glas (1997) have elaborated on an ethics of responsibility for the eonomic, technical and medical sciences respectively.

220   Troost (1993).

221   See also section 5.1. of this chapter.

value of 'respect for human dignity' implies authority for employees on their own workplace (power), respectful behaviour between employees and between employees and management (social intercourse), legal measures protect the workers against (unjustified) dismissals (juridical), the design of ergonomic and safe equipment (moral responsibility), and the development of trusting relationships within the organisation (trust). *Norms* are the specification of norm principles in a specific context. For example, in a production line the authority employees have with regard to their own workplace has to be detailed with respect to equipment settings, quality measurements, the planning of labour, decisions about logistics, organisational procedures, and so on.

A liberating perspective for industrial organisations opens up when it is understood that fundamental values about human being, fellow man, society and the natural environment have to lead the design and development of organisations. A liberating perspective implies that management respects the dignity of human being and that the organisation supports the vocation of human being. A liberating perspective means that employees on the shop floor can really bear responsibility and really be held accountable. Not only with respect to the functional aspects of their jobs but also with respect to the non-functional aspects. Taking into account the widespread presence of the closed or restricted development of organisations it means nothing less than *transformation of organisational practice*.[222]

In this section I will sketch the contours of an ethics of responsibility from the perspective of a factory manager as key actor in the organisational process. Three lines of thought are integrated:

1. a fundamental line summarised by the key words *dignity* and *vocation* (see section 2);
2. an organisational line summarised by the words *trust* and *power* (see section 4);
3. a philosophical line summarised by the words *multidimensional normativity* and the *normative development of organisational structures* (see section 5).

An ethics of responsibility begins with the recognition that organisations are not neutral but are subject to normative principles. It begins with the recognition that managers are not autonomous individuals but that they serve customers and employees. It begins with the recognition that the objective of an enterprise is not profit making but contributing to human society.

An ethics of responsibility means that management takes the responsibility for the normative development of all organisational structures, processes, and relationships. A normative unfolding implies that these structures are opened, disclosed or

---

[222] Dooyeweerd's entire work was devoted to an inner reformation of philosophy and science through a transcendental critique of theoretical thought and a dialogue with modern secularised culture (Geertsema in Griffioen and Balk (1995, p11-28)). Jacob Klapwijk has emphasised that Christian scientists have 'to transform' humanistic thinking (Klap-wijk, 1995). Transformation implies 'borrowing' and 'purifying' ideas. In this case, the term 'transformation' is more suitable than 'reformation'.

developed not only in accordance with norms derived from technology, the economy, and the organisational hierarchy, but also in accordance with norms from the following dimensions: ecology, psychology, power, symbolic meaning, social intercourse, harmony, justice, morality, and trust. Fundamentally, a normative disclosure expresses a deep respect for employees as *created* human beings and an industrial organisation as *created* reality. If fact, it expresses a deep respect for God as the *Creator*.

Normative development relates to the whole organisation.[223] In Chapter 2 it has been argued that Socio-Technical Systems Design in combination with the Mini-Company Concept have good credentials for the design and development of a responsible organisation. This conclusion has been confirmed by the Roermond case. For that reason, Socio-Technical Systems Design and the Mini-Company Concept will be taken as a starting point to illustrate and to develop a liberating perspective. The normative development of organisations will be discussed from a reformational-philosophical point of view. Therefore, this section can be considered as a reinterpretation of Socio-Technical Systems Design and the Mini-Company Concept.[224] In addition, it has to be remarked that a normative approach to business ethics that takes its starting point in organisation science, 'speaks' the language of the organisation and can be 'easily' applied.

In the following paragraphs the normative development of the structures and processes of industrial organisations will be discussed. It will be elaborated by analysing some examples of the normative development of a production structure, control structure, information structure, and relationships with stakeholders. A more detailed description is given in Appendix 2.

The normative development of the production structure

Generally, the production structure of a factory is seen as 'just' an accumulation of technical objects. In other words, it is seen as technical objects that perform a technical function: the transformation of materials or components into a product. Accordingly, a production structure has to fulfil technical standards so that the end product will satisfy the agreed specifications. A production line also has to fulfil certain economic standards so that the end product will fulfil cost price requirements. In this approach equipment and employees are connected to each other from a purely technical and economic point of view. This means an operator executes actions that cannot yet be automated. In this view, the contribution of an operator is defined negatively; in management vocabulary: costs.

In a liberating perspective the production structure is approached from a normative point of view. It is not 'just' an accumulation of technical objects but is an

---

[223] In this section the word 'development' is used to indicate both processes of foundation and disclosure. I have decided to give up precise reformational-philosophical terminology in order to highlight the basic ideas.

[224] In my opinion, this reinterpretation greatly honours the intentions of the fathers of Socio-Technical Systems Design and the Mini-Company Concept. Especially because these approaches have a normative character.

essential 'part' of the whole factory organisation.[225] It is a technical 'part' that is developed by multi-dimensional normativity. For example, in the socio-technical approach, the design of the production structure respects technical, economic, and social dimensions. The technical and economic dimensions have been discussed above. But the social dimension has to be explained. In the socio-technical approach the equipment is designed and grouped in such a way that a group of operators can produce a well identified part of the process, a semi-manufactured product, or a whole product. The design of the production line supports cooperation and social contact. In a socio-technical approach operators also have the authority to take decisions about their own workplace. As a consequence, equipment has to be designed in such a way that an employee can indeed measure the quality of his or her performance and if necessary can adjust the equipment or can even stop the production. In other words, the equipment has to be constructed in such a way that employees can exert power. A participative approach as proposed in the mini-company process strongly develops the psychological dimension of a production line. By allowing a group of operators to implement ergonomic, safety, or efficiency improvements in the production line their psychological attachment will increase.

These illustrations clearly show the meaning of the word 'normative development' with respect to the production line. It shows that the technically quailfied production structure is designed in such a way that the psychological, power and social dimensions of employees are supported and respected. In reformational-philosophical vocabulary, the later dimensions disclose the object functions of the production structure normatively. In addition, also the lingual (symbolic meaning), aesthetic (harmony), juridical, and pistic (trust) dimensions of the production structure have to be disclosed in design requirements and organisational processes.

In this context I speak of *normative* development because the *dignity of man* and *vocation of the human being* requires all dimensions of the production structure *to be* developed ('ought'). Successfully meeting this requirement is what makes or breaks the humanity of industrial organisations. It is the responsibility of the factory manager to design the production line in such a way that this 'ought' can be realised. As discussed extensively in this study, Socio-Technical Systems Design and the Mini-Company Concept offer suitable organisational concepts to develop later dimensions of a production line normatively.

The normative development of the control structure
In the control structure an industrial organisation as a community of labour comes to the fore. It shows the organisation of a group of employees who cooperate to realise certain goals. It has been argued that in hierarchical organisations social intercourse is determined by the asymmetry of the employment relation. The main objective of (closed or restricted) managers is to control and to dominate the workforce in order to realise their own objectives. Especially the vocation of employees

---

[225] The word 'part' is set in quotation marks because it is not a part but an enkaptically bound individuality structure (section 5.4).

to contribute to a human organisation is ignored. Control and domination have their price: hierarchical organisations are characterised by all the kind of low-trust responses that are symptomatic of depersonalisation and dehumanisation.

In a liberating perspective the control structure is developed from a normative point of view. It is not 'just' cooperation to realise certain goals. It is the cooperation of dignified human beings who want to contribute to a responsible organisation. It is a group of dignified human beings who have the vocation to give shape to corporate social responsibility. The control structure embraces all actions and interactions to control the production. In the socio-technical approach the control structure is built up in a bottom-up process implying that the employees have the authority to manage their own workplace. In the mini-company process the control structure is extended by the formulation of a mission statement, management of the relationships with stakeholders, and authority to decide about the improvement program.

In the normative development of the control structure power and trust plays an important role. Development of the power dimension of the control structure means that training programs, organisation of meetings, and cooperation patterns are designed in such a way that all employees indeed have the know-how, skills, and authority to take decisions about their own workplace and to manage their mini-company. In section 4 of this chapter it has been shown that power and trust are strongly related. Successful empowerment supports the development of trust. The development of trust stimulates the development of social structures in which further empowerment can be realised.

In the normative development of the control structure the moral dimension also plays a role. Development of the moral dimension of the control structure means that all kinds of social processes such as daily interaction, organisation of meetings, safety training, management audits, and improvement programs are designed in such a way that the well-being of employees is strongly supported. For example, safety and the environment were part of the standard agenda of the mini-company meeting. In addition, in the mini-company process safety, environment, and morale of the group, were identified as areas of improvement. Furthermore, every three months a member of the management team and a specialist audited the factory with respect to safety and the environment.

Management plays a key role in the normative development of the control structure. In the first place, by confirming and reconfirming social values by showing model behaviour. In the second place, by creating the conditions so that employees can develop the required structures, processes and the relevant behaviour.

These illustrations show that the socially qualified control structure is developed by power, moral, and trust dimensions. In other words, justified power, moral and trust 'interests' of employees have to be integrated within all kinds of formal and informal social processes in the organisation. Here it is also a matter of *normative* development. *Dignity of man* requires all dimensions of the social structure *to be* developed ('ought'). *Vocation of man* requires all employees to be able to use their know-how, skills, and creativity so that they can contribute valuably to a responsible organisation. It is the responsibility of the factory manager to design and to develop the control structure in such a way that this 'ought' can be realised. The Roermond case is an example of the successful development of a control structure.

Finally, it has to be remarked that both virtue ethics and the ethics of care constitute an important contribution to the normative development of the control structure.

The normative development of the information structure

In organisations, which have a low-trust-low-power spiral, information is never reliable. Both the information told by management to employees and the other way around cannot be trusted. Typical examples are given in the Aachen case.

In a liberating perspective the information structure has to be developed from a normative point of view. All employees have to get information to be able to take decisions about their own workplace and to manage their mini-company. For example, information about planning, quality data, safety, and the environment, has to be available. Especially the information structure has to be disclosed by juridical, moral, and trust dimensions. This means the information structure has to be developed in such a way that the information fulfils juridical requirements, covers important moral issues, and is reliable.

These illustrations show that the information structure, which is qualified by symbolic meaning, has to be developed by other dimensions. Here it is also a matter of *normative* development. In other words, we are talking about an 'ought'.

The normative development of a manufacturing organisation as a whole

In section 5.4 of this chapter it has been argued that the production structure, control structure, and information structure are interlaced in an enkaptic whole. The idea of an enkaptic whole emphasises the strong coherence between these structures. Negatively speaking, the sins of the Tayloristic design of a production structure cannot be 'repaired' by some human-friendly measures in the control structure. Positively speaking, the normative development of the production structure such as that proposed by the Dutch approach to Socio-Technical Systems Design strongly supports the normative development of the control and information structures.

The normative development of relationships with stakeholders

Nowadays, the interests of different stakeholders are widely acknowledged. Managing stakeholders is becoming more and more important. Seriously neglecting the interests of stakeholders can result in a loss of image, financial losses, and even the existence of the company being threatened. In a liberating perspective the normative development of relationships with different stakeholders implies that the multidimensional interests of these stakeholders will be met from scratch. Such a development does not only symbolise respect for the stakeholders concerned, but also symbolises respect for the vocation of employees with respect to these stakeholders.

To illustrate this approach I would like to present two examples. The first example has to do with the development of the production structure to look after the juridical interests of the customer. In the components business it is very important for the customer that the products manufactured on the production line meet safety and environmental regulations. Development of the production line to comply with safety regulations means that the materials and components purchased meet certain specifications, that critical parameters are measured during manufacturing, and that safety features are measured during final testing. In other words, technical measures have to be applied in the production structure so that the safety regulations are met. Development of the production line to comply with environmental regulations means that no materials from the so-called 'black list' are used, that exhaust gases are treated in an afterburner, and that wastewater is cleaned by mechanical or chemical methods. In other words, technical measures are taken so that environmental regulations are met. This example clearly shows the meaning of the word 'development'. The production line that is qualified by technical power is designed (or adapted) in such a way that juridical qualified interests of customers are met.

The second example has to do with the development of the information structure to meet the economic and trust interests of shareholders. It is very important that transparent and reliable information is given about the economic situation, financial risks and business opportunities of a company. Development of the information structure to meet economic and trust interests occurs through clear financial processes, transparent accounting, unambiguous reporting, independent auditing, business risk assessments, and so on. In this example the information structure has to be developed in such a way that the economic and trust interests of shareholders are secured.

These examples show that the relationships with stakeholders have to be developed in a normative way. The justified interests of these stakeholders have to be 'translated' into technical measures in the production structure, into social processses in the control structure, and into meaningful data in the information structure. Here it is also a matter of *normative* development affecting both employees of the organisation and the different stakeholders. Here it is also a question of 'ought'.

In this section the responsibility of the manager in the design and development of industrial organisations has been emphasised. S/he is a key actor. His or her work orientation (Watson), religious ground motive (Dooyeweerd), or basic beliefs (this study) play a decisive role. Does s/he orientate him- or herself to the multi-dimensional normativity of reality? Does s/he respect the dignity of employees on the shop floor? Does s/he support the vocation of operators and technicians? These questions urge a manager to do critical soul-searching. Can s/he answer these questions positively? Or does s/he function as an enlightened manager who shapes the organisation to his or her own ends? Or does s/he function as a postmodern manager who is driven by a continuous drive to shape and reshape him- or herself in a continuously changing organisation?

My deepest conviction and belief is that a liberating perspective can only be founded in the belief of God the Creator who has revealed himself in the Bible. In my deepest belief this God has revealed himself in the coming of Jesus Christ. One of the most radical sermons by Jesus is the Sermon on the Mount. In this sermon he contrasts the order of society with the order of his Kingdom. The Beatitudes do not addresses the great of the earth such as kings and emperors, they address the 'poor in spirit', those 'who mourn', the 'meek', and those 'who hunger and thirst for righteousness'. The Beatitudes do not bless the powerful, they bless the 'merciful', the 'pure in heart', the 'peacemakers', and those who are 'persecuted because of righteousness'. After that, Jesus criticises the formal and juridical approach to the law and proposes the application of divine norms within a frame of love. The teachings of Jesus Christ have not lost any of their relevance. They appeal to the 'great of industrial life' to reject the idea of profit as the highest go(o)d, to overthrow the ideas of control and domination, and to aim for justice and love. The way shown by Christ is not the easiest one. In the same sermon, Jesus speaks about a 'small gate' and a 'narrow road'. It is a way that is characterised by the recognition that evil is rooted in the heart of every manager. Existentially formulated: in *my* heart. It is a way that is based on the renewal of life by submission to the order of the Kingdom. Existentially formulated: renewal of *my* life by the Spirit. The teachings of Christ urge managers *to act in this world* and *to reform organisational practices to the law of the New Kingdom*. This kingdom can only be realised – paradoxically – by submitting to Him who has shown that the secret of humanity is not in exerting power but in serving.

Appendix 1: Philosophical ethics: diversity, strengths, and limitations

The origin of all classical approaches to ethics is in Greek thinking. *Virtue ethics* was developed by Hellenistic thinkers such as Plato and Aristotle. It addresses character traits and styles of life that are necessary to realise the (highest) good. A *deontological approach* was already advocated by the Stoics. According to them, man is a part of cosmic nature and the law that governs the cosmos also provides the standard for human actions. *Utilitarian theories* go back to sophist thought. Sophists were not concerned with finding out the absolute truth about the world, but with teaching the practicalities of life in city-states. According to Protagoras the question is not whether one ethical view is true and another false; the question is whether one view is more useful than another.[226] A number of (post-) modern ethical approaches to ethics have been developed.[227] Particular attention will be paid to *discourse ethics* and *ethics of care*.

Virtue ethics

The origin of virtue ethics lies in classical antiquity. The Greek word *arete* means both 'virtue' as well as 'excellence'. It refers to making one's ability or character perfect in order to realise a specific goal, aim, or purpose. Aristotle calls something 'good' when it is desirable or strived for. A 'good' that is always chosen for its own sake and that in itself is sufficient is called 'the highest good' or '*the* good'. Aristotle calls the highest good '*eudaemonia*'. Eudaemonia is often translated into *happiness*. However, this translation is inadequate because it does not express the idea of prosperity. In Greek society eudaemonia encompasses both the notion of behaving well (well-doing) and the notion of faring well (well-being). Eudaemonia can only be attained by living a virtuous life. Thus, in virtue ethics a concrete style of life is linked up with the goal or *telos* of that style. In other words, means and ends are closely connected.

Aristotle did not consider virtue as a feeling or an innate capacity but rather as a trait or disposition that could be developed through proper training and intensive exercise. In his view, people acquire virtues in the same way as they learn skills. This means that people 'become' just by behaving in a just way and integer by behaving in an integer way. According to Aristotle the internal motivation of the actor is important. A just person does not only behave in a fair way but also has a moral desire to do so. In other words, an action can only be virtuous if performed with the right motive. Aristotle indicates that moral virtues as such provide little hold to make concrete choices. He introduces the idea of 'prudentia' or 'practical wisdom'. Prudentia is to know how to apply general principles in particular situations. Practical wisdom guides a person in a specific situation to choose the right ends and to attain these ends in the right way.

---

[226] For an extensive account of philosophical ethics see for example Schrey (1977), Beauchamp (1991), and MacIntyre (1998).

[227] Widdershoven (2000) gives a valuable overview.

Moral thinking was dominated by virtue ethics up to the Middle Ages. From the Renaissance onwards virtue ethics gradually lost ground. Alisdair MacIntyre has recently rekindled interest in virtue ethics with his book *After Virtue*.[228]

Deontological approaches

The father of the deontological approach is Immanuel Kant (1724-1804). Kant is a typical representative of the Enlightenment. He states that the goal of philosophical ethics is to establish the ultimate basis for validity of moral rules. He tries to show that this ultimate basis has to lie in pure reason and not in intuition, personal experience, or expected utility. In his view, philosophical ethics has to provide a rational framework of moral principles and rules that guide all people, independent of their personal interests, individual preferences or situations. This approach holds that moral laws cannot be deduced from nature or based on an external authority; on the contrary, that morality is a part of human being

The approach of Kant is based on respect for the autonomy of the individual. This respect is required because human beings possess a moral dignity. Respect for the individual is manifested in never treating people as a pure 'means' but considering them as a valuable 'end'. In Kant's view the motive for peoples' actions is important. People must not only act *in accordance with* moral obligations, but also *for the sake of* moral obligations. This means the moral action has to be internally motivated In addition, a person has to act irrespective of the consequences. This moral obligation has a universal character. This means no rational agent can reject it. "Act as if the maxim of your action were to become by your will a universal law of nature". Kant called this principle the *categorical imperative*. It is 'categorical' because there are no exceptions and it is an 'imperative' because it is my duty to obey.

Nowadays, deontological approaches appear especially in the form of contractarian and rights-based theories. John Rawls' *A Theory of Justice* is often classified as a deontological approach.[229]

Utilitarian theories

The first ethicist – since the sophists – who judged actions solely in terms of their consequences was Machiavelli. He takes the view that moral rules are technical rules to realise the ends of social and political life, i.e. the maintenance of political order and general prosperity. Since Machiavelli, utilitarian thinking has regularly cropped up. Utilitarian theories state that the moral value of actions or practices is determined solely by its consequences. This means that an action or practice is morally right if it leads to something that people prefer and is morally wrong if it leads to something that people do not prefer. In a more complex situation it is about the balancing the good consequences over the bad consequences. Utilitarians believe that the objective of an ethical theory is to promote human welfare by minimising harm and evil and by maximising the good. The fathers of the utilitarian approach are Jeremy Bentham (1748-1832) and John Stuart Mill (1806-

---

[228] MacIntyre (1984).
[229] Rawls (1971).

1873). They propose the 'greatest happiness principle' as the foundation of a utilitarian theory. This principle implies that everybody has to act in such a way that the greatest amount of happiness is created for the greatest number of people.

Utilitarianism has three main features. Firstly, it is based on the idea that an intrinsic good exists that can serve as a criterion for evaluating actions. Secondly, it is believed that the good can be measured, different types of good can be compared, and the common good can be summed up. Thirdly, it asserts that society has to act in such a way that negative values are minimised and positive values are maximised. In other words, the common good is used as a criterion for action.

Since Bentham and Mill utilitarian theories have never abandoned western culture. Industrialisation and free trade have stimulated economic ends to become dominant.

Discourse ethics
Discourse ethics or dialogue ethics is based on the work of the German philosopher Jürgen Habermas. Discourse ethics focuses on reaching consensus between different parties through a rational and open dialogue. In this dialogue the perspectives of all people concerned have to be brought forward, irrespective of the status or power of the participants. This means dialogue ethics does not primarily focus on the *content* of moral reasoning but on the *process* of moral reasoning. It is believed that moral problems can be solved by a rational discussion about presuppositions that underlie differences in perspectives of the people involved. Formal procedural rules have to be defined in order to guide the efforts to make a concrete moral judgement in a specific situation. Discourse ethics rejects the idea of universal norms that have to and can be applied in a concrete situation. It rejects this idea primarily because our world is too complex to cover all ethical problems with a couple of universal norms and because universal moral norms often cause dilemmas in practical situations.

In a 'practical' discourse the normative presuppositions upon which a certain practice is based are brought into discussion. Discourse ethics has some appealing points. Firstly, its starting point is in concrete situations. Therefore, it can be expected that moral reasoning really is related to everyday practice. Secondly, it calls for a dialogue between participants. This means that the perspectives of the people concerned in a specific situation are brought into discussion. The role of the expert is to support and to structure dialogue. Finally, a dialogue between all participants irrespective of their hierarchical position appeals. This should prevent differences in power determining the dialogue rather than the quality of the argumentation process.

Ethics of care

The ethics of care originates in feminist theory. Carol Gilligan is named as the 'founding mother' of this approach. Gilligan argues that men and women speak different moral languages. Men tend to speak and act in the language of justice and rights. This is the language of traditional ethical theories. Women, on the other hand, speak and act in the language of caring and responsibility. They have a 'different voice'. This 'different voice' should be reflected in a feminist theory.

Traditionalist approaches in ethics are based on the view that human beings can be considered as individuals. In addition, they are based on the view that knowledge is abstract, universal, impartial and rational. Feminist theory has different assumptions. It is based on the idea that people are essentially relational. As they say, there is no 'I' unless there is a 'you'. The idea of 'relatedness' leads to the notion of caring. Gilligan emphasises that women have to recognise both their own needs and the needs of those with whom they have a relationship. In other words, women have to care for themselves as well as for others.

Ethics of care has three interrelated aspects. Firstly, attention is given to particular persons. This means each person is seen as a unique human being. Secondly, contextual and narrative aspects are recognised. The previous history and the context of the moral problem are taken into account. Finally, communication is emphasised. Moral deliberations require a process of talking and listening to each other.

Evaluation

The approaches described above can only be understood against the specific social, political, and cultural background of the age in which they have been developed. They are based – explicitly or implicitly – on a certain pattern of values and norms. In addition, they specify a different view on morality and a different status of moral judgements.[230] These conclusions urge us to proceed with caution. Firstly, the current application of one of these approaches will easily introduce a change in the meaning of the basic concepts of that approach. Secondly, the application of one of these approaches can only be done on the basis of an – explicitly or implicitly present – pattern of values and norms.

> *Example.* Aristotelian ethics specifies virtues for citizens in the Greek polis. It is without doubt that the application of virtue ethics in business requires a specification of virtues to be aimed for. Competitiveness and toughness? Or cooperation and care? A choice between these alternatives can only be made on the basis of a coherent pattern of values and norms – which in turn is determined by the manager's portrayal of man.

It is emphasised that each of the classical approaches has its own perspective. Virtue ethics focuses on the moral quality of the actor, deontological approaches on the moral quality of the act, and utilitarian theories on the moral quality of the

---

[230] MacIntyre (1998).

450

attained utility. In addition, discourse ethics and ethics of care also have a specific perspective. Discourse ethics focuses on the quality of the moral dialogue and ethics of care on the specific responsibilities of actors in human relationships. In other words, it is not fruitful to oppose these approaches to each other; it is fruitful to use them in a complementary way.[231] In addition, each of these approaches has its own problems. For example, virtue ethics pays too little attention to the moral quality of acts, deontological approaches do not give a solution in the case of conflicting obligations, utilitarian theories do not pass judgement on the distribution of costs and benefits of a certain pleasure (problem of justice), discourse ethics does not describe which norms or standards have to be taken into consideration, and ethics of care has difficulties in relating contextuality and normative principles.[232] In the introduction to this section it has been remarked that deontological and utilitarian approaches dominate organisational practice. In view of that, two additional problems have to be mentioned. Deontological approaches tend toward a legalistic attitude with the result that responsible behaviour in organisations is limited to the agreed rules.[233] Utilitarian approaches stimulate an attitude in which the end justifies the means. As a consequence, the morality of human acts is not brought up for discussion.

---

[231] Jochemsen and Glas (1997, p54 ff.) propose to integrate the classical approaches within a perspective of responsibility. Kaptein and Wempe (2002, p54 ff.) suggest integrating the classical approaches within a perspective of integrity.

[232] Schrey (1977), Beauchamp (1991), and MacIntyre (1998).

[233] Weaver et al. (1999).

451

Appendix 2: The normative development of the production structure, control structure, and information structure

In this Appendix the normative development of the different structures – containing both foundational and disclosing dimensions – is described. It is not the aim to create an exhaustive list.

The production structure covers all transformation functions that are required to manufacture products. It consists of tools, equipment, layout, and housing. The production structure is technically qualified. Employees and stakeholders have their own specific requirements with respect to the production structure of an organisation. Figure 6.1 presents an overview of employee/stakeholders, primary character of this relation, main dimensions of interest, and some examples.

The control structure covers all control functions that are required in order to manufacture the products. It consists of work instructions, short term planning, long term planning, business planning, maintenance scheduling, decision making, quality agreements, training of employees, monthly unit meetings, management meetings, and so on. The control structure is socially qualified. Employees and stakeholders have their own specific requirements with respect to the control structure of the organisation. Figure 6.2 presents an overview of this.

The information structure covers all aspects of information, communication, and symbolic meaning that are required to execute and to control manufacturing operations. It consists of all kinds of information systems and communication structures such as work instructions, planning information, log books, process control data, quality measurements, computer assisted manufacturing systems, morning prayers, unit meetings, quality releases, safety and environmental reports and so on. It also encompasses the symbolic meaning of all types of behaviour and rituals in an organisation. The information structure is lingually qualified. Employees and stakeholders each have their own specific requirements with respect to the information structure of the organisation. Figure 6.3 presents an overview of this.

Employee stakeholder	primary character	main dimensions	examples
employee	encompassing all dimensions	o biological	o production line meets ergonomic standards
			o working conditions (noise, heat, humidity) meet standards
		o psychic	o identification with production line is supported
			o boredom and apathy is prevented
			o possibility to intervene in the case of quality problems or calamities
		o power	o design of production line makes social contact possible
		o social	o design of production line streamlines social communication between employees
		o economic	o efficiency of production line makes salary payment now and in the future possible
		o moral	o quality of working life (humanity)
external customer	economic	o technical	o production line meets delivery flexibility
			o production line meets technical specifications of products
		o economic	o production line realises target prices
		o juridical	o production line makes products that meet safety and environmental regulations
		o moral	o production line makes products that are safe
			o production line and products are as 'green' as possible
shareholder	economic	o technical	o reduction of the probability of quality, safety or environmental calamities (prevention of financial claims)
		o economic	o efficiency of production line (relation with shareholder value)
local government	juridical	o economic	o efficiency of production line guarantees employment
		o juridical	o production line meets safety and environmental standards
natural environment	ecological	o ecological	o production line minimises the use of materials and energy
			o production line minimises the pollution of the natural environment (at least meets the legal regulations)

454

	economic	o amount of packing material is minimised
		o recycling of product after lifetime
		o efficiency of production line makes protective measures possible

Figure 6.1 Overview of the normative development of a production structure of a factory

employee / stakeholder	primary character	main dimensions	examples
employee	encompassing all dimensions	o psychic	o employees feel committed to the organisation
			o employees feel ownership of their workplace and are proud to work
			o employees feel that they are respected by management
		o power	o employees have the authority to manage their own workplace
			o employees have the authority to stop the line in the case of quality problems
			o employees have the authority to demand support from management or technical specialists in the case of (serious) problems
			o employees have a clear voice in the mission statement and improvement program of their own department
		o social	o control structures for the transfer of information, priority setting, planning agreements, feedback, training, and so on are well structured and well managed
			o social processes are in operation to develop the production unit as a labour community
		o economic	o organisational structures for cost control are in operation
			o cost awareness is stimulated by means of feedback and training
			o control structures stimulate employees to use their know-how, skills and creativity to contribute to the company
		o moral	o the well-being of employees and quality of working life is monitored, discussed and continuously improved

Category	Stakeholder	Aspect	
		faith/trust	o open culture to identify technical, logistical, social and moral problems o daily interaction between employees and between employees and management is characterised by respect o managers and employees are accountable for their (daily) activities o the mission of the company is well-understood by the whole crew o the mission of the company is specified for the manufacturing department o the mission of the company honours the justified interests of different stakeholders o a culture of mutual trust
economic	external customer	technical	o employees are aware of the critical quality parameters o procedures are in operation to identify potential quality problems o capability to implement new types of products in the short term o customer comes first
		symbolic meaning	
		economic	o an improvement program is in execution to follow price erosion
		moral	o procedures to safeguard the quality safety, and environmental aspects of products are followed in practice
economic	shareholder	technical	o adequate control structure to identify potential technical problems and to prevent quality, safety, and environmental calamities o organisational structures for cost control are in operation o programs to reduce costs are developed, executed and monitored o control structure is effective and efficient
		economic	
juridical	local government	economic	o mission and strategy of the organisation safeguards employment on the long term o mission and strategy of the organisation stimulates the economic development of the region

| natural environment | | o juridical | o control structures for safety and environmental regulations are in operation
o procedures to deal with calamities are present |
| | ecological | o ecological | o on a regular basis the whole materials / processes / energy chain of the manufacturing operation is analysed and new spearheads for improvement are identified and executed
o for every new material, process, machine, and product, ecological aspects are taken into account from the beginning
o control structures for environmental issues are in operation |

Figure 6.2 Overview of the normative development of a control structure of a factory

employee / stakeholder	primary character	main dimensions	examples
employee	encompassing all dimensions	psychic	o information presented to the employees supports the development of feelings of commitment, ownership and respect
		power	o employees have the required information to manage their own workplace
			o employees have the required information to stop the line in the case of quality problems
			o employees have the required information to contribute to the mission statement and the improvement program of their unit or mini-company
		social	o effective and efficient transfer of information in all kind of social contacts and social meetings
			o model behaviour by management
		economic	o financial information about the manufacturing organisation and whole company
			o financial information about material, tools, equipment, and products in the employees' unit
		moral	o information about indicators relating to the well-being of employees and quality of working life (illness rate, accidents, and so on)
			o management regularly transfers information about moral issues
			o open culture with respect to the identification and solution to moral issues
		faith/trust	o employees trust the information given to them by management
			o management trust the information given to them by employees
			o employees have access to relevant information to define the mission statement and improvement program of their own unit or mini-company
external customer	economic	technical	o quality reports about process control
			o quality reports about delivered products

		o moral	o information about deviating deliveries o certification according to international standards, e.g. QS9000 for control of product quality and ISO 14000 for meeting environmental regulations
		o faith/trust	o information is relevant and reliable
shareholder	economic	o technical	o information about technical risks and calamities
		o economic	o information about financial key performance indicators
		o faith/trust	o information is relevant and reliable
local government	juridical	o economic	o data about employment o data about the economic impact on the region
		o juridical	o data about safety conditions o data about environmental control o information about calamities
		o faith/trust	o information is relevant and reliable
natural environment	ecological	o ecological	o information about environmental issues with respect to the whole chain is present
		o faith/trust	o information is relevant and reliable

Figure 6.3 Overview of the normative development of an information structure of a factory

In the Prologue it has been shown that paradoxes exist on the shop floor of industrial organisations. Paradoxes have their own dynamics. In a low-trust-low-power culture, paradoxes induce irresponsible behaviour and feed frustration, mistrust, and apathy. In a high-trust-high-power culture, paradoxes are identified and dismantled. As a result, responsible behaviour is stimulated and enthusiasm, commitment, and trust grow. It is concluded that high-trust and high-power relations are the main conditions for inducing responsible behaviour in employees on the shop floor.

Some fundamental questions still remain, however. What is the meaning ('Sinn') of work? What is the meaning of the daily activities on the shop floor? What is the relation between trust, power, and meaning? There is a lot of embarrassment surrounding this subject as reflection on work and meaning does not belong to standard industrial discourse. Daily problems determine the agenda and fundamental questions are pushed aside. At best, the relation between work and meaning is discussed in the bar at the end of a long working day. In my opinion, managers cannot run away from this subject. Sooner or later, they are confronted with it. The development of postmodern society has resulted in a crisis of morality and a longing for meaning.[234] Such crises do not pass by industrial organisations. When meaning becomes questionable, labour loses its significance. Ironically, postmodern philosophers are pleading for a re-evaluation of organisations as workshops for constructing morality and experiencing meaning.[235] Although industrial managers cannot solve the crisis in the experience of meaning, what they can do is design and develop organisations that respect the dignity and humanity of human beings. In other words, a framework can be organised in which meaning can be experienced.[236]

The Jewish thinker Abraham Joshua Heshel (1907-1972) has emphasised that the question of meaning cannot be answered from the perspective of the individual human subject. In his view, this question has to be answered from the perspective of the other: Am I of value to someone else? He writes[237]:

> "Why be concerned with meaning? Why not be content with satisfaction of desires and needs? Life should be a perfect circle: desire ... pleasure ... desire ... pleasure ... To be concerned with meaning is to go off on a tangent leading to the infinite (...) Animals are content when their needs are satisfied; man insists not only on being satisfied but also on being able to satisfy, on being a need not simply on having needs. Personal needs come and go, but one anxiety remains: Am I needed? There is no

---

[234] See for example Burms and De Dijn (1990), De Dijn (1994) and Kunneman (1998).
[235] E.g. Kunneman (1998).
[236] De Sitter (1994) is one of the exceptions in the industrial discourse. He brings up the question of labour and meaning extensively.
[237] Heshel (1965, p57, 60).

461

human being who has not been moved by that anxiety. It is a most significant fact that man is not sufficient to himself, that life is not meaningful to him unless it is serving an end beyond itself, unless it is of value to someone else (...) Unlike all other needs, the need of being needed is a striving to give rather than to obtain satisfaction. It is a desire to satisfy a transcendent desire, a craving to satisfy a craving."

Heshel emphasises that meaning cannot be derived from the value for others[238]:

"Human existence cannot derive its ultimate meaning from society, because society itself is in need of meaning. It is as legitimate to ask: Is mankind needed? As it is to ask: Am I needed! (...) The secret of being human is care for meaning. Man is not his own meaning, and if the essence of being human is concern for transcendent meaning, then man's secret lies in openness to transcendence."

Am I needed? In light of the history of western industry – a history that is characterised by dehumanisation and alienation – this frightening question is highly relevant for employees on the shop floor. Is there a need for *me*? Is there a need for *my* labour? Does my colleague need *me*? Does my boss need *me*? Does the customer need *me*? Or – am I just a cog in the industrial system that can be easily replaced by *somebody else*?

Am I needed? The Scientific Management answer to this question is bewildering. Tayloristic enterprises are a typical fruit of the Enlightenment. Scientific managers are typical representatives of the enlightened man. Scientific managers control their organisations by technological, economic and hierarchical means, shape their factories according to the newest management fashions, and subject their crew to power and authority. And where does this leave the employees? They are controlled. They are shaped. They are subjected. The enlightened subject-object relationship is embodied fundamentally in the manager-organisation bipolarity. The enlightened masculinity is expressed essentially in technological and hierarchical power structures. The enlightened tension between freedom and domination is crystallised in (closed) freedom for managers and (total) domination of employees. The employees' existential 'Am I needed?' question appears to be a rhetorical one. In Scientific Management, the humanity and subjectivity of employees is not taken as a starting point. Employees are required because of their 'hands' and not because of their humanity. In addition, it is believed that employees cannot be trusted. The system is focused on controlling the 'hands' technically and economically and on disciplining operators organisationally and bureaucratically. Employees are shaped according to the needs of the production line and the economic requirements of the organisation, and subjected to the hierarchy of the manager. In Tayloristic designs, employees are cut off from their own personality, from colleagues, and from customers. That cuts them off from transcendence. In this context, meaning refers only – in a closed shape – to managers and not to employees on the shop floor. This creates a deeper dimension of alienation.

---

[238]   Heshel (1965, p59, 66).

Am I needed? Postmodernism has deeply changed western society. Postmodern thought has attacked the foundations of the Enlightenment: the central position of the rational subject has been given up; the idea that man can control reality has been rejected; organisations are described in terms of relations; networks have replaced hierarchical structures; power and control make space for change and adaptation; and aesthetics have superseded ethics. What is the implication of these changes for employees in organisations? Postmodern organisation theories have contributed to a deepened understanding of organisations.[239] They show that organising cannot be understood from the perspective of the scientific manager. They show that 'dissolution of organisational substance' and 'death of the myth of manager control' is required.[240] Postmodern organisation theory sees employees as individuals who shape their own life and manage their own career.[241] It sketches strong autonomous individuals that position and reposition themselves in changing networks. The ideal of the self-fashioning individual certainly applies for 'strong' and 'powerful' managers. Most employees, however, do not fit in this picture. Postmodern organisations throw employees upon their own resources. In a context of dependency and powerlessness, employees are left alone with their question of 'Am I needed?'.

Am I needed? The reformational philosopher Herman Dooyeweerd has approached questions of normativity and meaning from quite a different perspective. His starting point is the 'mode of existence' of created reality.[242] He links up meaning with the multidimensional, dependent and non-self-sufficient character of our world. He couples meaning with normativity. He connects meaning with the essence of being human. He emphasises that meaning is *given* in the createdness of our world. So how does this relate to the relation between labour, organisation, and meaning? In this thesis, responsible behaviour in industrial organisations has been studied from the perspective of a factory manager. A plea has been made for a normative design and normative development of organisational cultures. A plea has been made for industrial organisations to be designed not only according to technological and economic factors, but also to respect aspects of power, social relations, justice, morality, and trust. A plea has been made for a design and development of organisations in which human dignity is honoured, human vocation is supported, and interests of different stakeholders are recognised. It has been shown that Socio-Technical Systems Design in combination with the Mini-Company Concept offer a fruitful approach. In this line of thought, meaning has to do with a normative design and normative development of the production structure, control structure, information structure, and improvement structure. In this line of thought, meaning has to do with feelings of pride and ownership, power and authority on the shop floor, symbolic meaning of behaviour, development of social relations, focus on cost control and efficiency, complying with safety and environ-

---

[239] E.g. Hassard and Parker (1993) and Boje et al. (1996).
[240] Gephart in Boje et al. (1996, p44).
[241] E.g. Bridges (1994).
[242] Dooyeweerd (1969, I, p3-5).

mental regulations, quality of labour, and trusting relationships between employees and management.

Am I needed? This frightening question encapsulates the crisis of meaning in our society. This study has shown that high-trust and high-power relations in organisations are required for employees to feel of value to others. It has explained that a normative design and normative development of organisations are required to create openness to transcendental meaning. Finally, an appeal has been made to industrial managers to respect the dignity of human beings, to support the vocation of employees, and to serve the interests of all stakeholders.

VERTROUWEN EN MACHT OP DE WERKVLOER

Een etnografische, ethische en filosofische studie naar
verantwoordelijk gedrag in industriële organisaties

Samenvatting

Verantwoord ondernemen staat sterk in de belangstelling. Instellingen, ondernemingen en organisaties houden zich hier intensief mee bezig. Op universiteiten en hogescholen wordt fundamenteel onderzoek gedaan naar verschillende benaderingen om verantwoord ondernemen vorm te geven. In het onderwijs worden theorie en praktijk nauw op elkaar betrokken. De overheid stimuleert dat kennis over verantwoord ondernemen in de verschillende sectoren van onze maatschappij wordt opgebouwd. Verder bevordert zij dat de onderscheiden spelers in het veld met elkaar samenwerken en van elkaar leren. In het bedrijfsleven worden verschillende initiatieven genomen om verantwoord ondernemen in de praktijk van alledag te realiseren. Veel aandacht wordt gegeven aan de ontwikkeling van gedragscodes en training in ethische dilemma's. Al deze ontwikkelingen wijzen op een toenemend besef dat gedrag in organisaties een ethische dimensie heeft.

Het onderzoek naar verantwoord ondernemen vertoont een zekere eenzijdigheid. Er wordt veel aandacht gegeven aan de manier waarop managers in de directiekamer beslissingen nemen over bijzondere ethische vraagstukken, zoals het afzinken van de Brent Spar door Shell, het bouwen van een fabriek door Heineken in Birma en het ontwerpen van de Pinto door Ford. Maar er wordt veel minder aandacht gegeven aan de manier waarop medewerkers omgaan met alledaagse ethische problemen op de werkvloer, zoals het volgen van wettelijke procedures, het geven van juiste informatie aan klanten, het melden van fouten en vergissingen, de correcte omgang met elkaar, en het identificeren van problematische situaties.

Deze studie richt zich niet op grote ethische vraagstukken die in een bedrijf spelen maar, op de alledaagse ethische problemen die zich in een organisatie voordoen. Het gaat in dit onderzoek om verantwoordelijk gedrag van medewerkers op de werkvloer. Immers, een verantwoordelijke organisatie vraagt niet alleen om verantwoordelijke managers maar ook om verantwoordelijke medewerkers. Een verantwoordelijke organisatie richt zich niet uitsluitend op grote vraagstukken in de directiekamer, maar geeft ook aandacht aan de kleine problemen op de werkvloer. Tenslotte, een verantwoordelijke organisatie heeft niet alleen oog voor beslissingen van het management maar ook voor dagelijkse activiteiten van de medewerkers. De verandering van focus – van beslissingsprocessen in de directiekamer naar dagelijkse handelingen op de werkvloer – werpt een nieuw licht op de verantwoordelijkheid van het management. Ten eerste, zo'n verandering benadrukt het belang van het primaire proces. Het erkent dat verantwoord ondernemen allereerst naar voren komt in de uitvoering van het primaire proces door de medewerkers op de werkvloer. Ten tweede, zo'n verandering benadrukt de verantwoordelijkheid van het management om de condities scheppen die verantwoordelijk gedrag van medewerkers in de organisatie mogelijk maken.

Dit proefschrift is geschreven vanuit het perspectief van de manager als *reflective practitioner*. Het gaat om verantwoordelijk gedrag van medewerkers op de werkvloer van moderne fabrieken. Met name wordt aandacht gegeven aan de voorwaarden die een manager moet vervullen zodat medewerkers op verantwoorde wijze kunnen handelen. Een onderzoek naar verantwoord handelen van medewerkers aan de productielijn vraagt om een analyse op drie niveaus: fenomenen op de werkvloer, ontwerptheorieën in de organisatiekunde en filosofie van organisaties. De kernvraag die deze niveaus integreert luidt:

> *Hoe kunnen medewerkers op de werkvloer op verantwoorde wijze handelen?*

Deze kernvraag wordt bestudeerd door middel van een exploratief onderzoek in fabricage-organisaties. In een proces van zoeken en vinden worden paradoxen geïdentificeerd, bestaande inzichten bevestigd, onverwachte gegevens gerapporteerd, ideeën gefalsificeerd en theorieën geherinterpreteerd. In dit onderzoek wordt organisatie-etnografie als belangrijkste methode gebruikt. Gedurende het onderzoek heeft de auteur – in de etnografie is de onderzoeker zijn of haar eigen gereedschap – zich ontwikkeld tot organisatiesocioloog.

Deze studie staat op het kruispunt van twee verschillende tradities: een organisatiekundige en een filosofische traditie. De organisatiekundige traditie is de sociotechniek of participatieve democratie zoals deze is ontwikkeld door De Sitter, Dankbaar, Den Hertog, Van Eijnatten en anderen. In deze benadering staat de bevoegdheid van medewerkers om beslissingen te nemen over hun eigen werkplek en de participatie van medewerkers in de ontwikkeling van de organisatie centraal. De filosofische traditie is de reformatorische wijsbegeerte zoals deze is ontwikkeld door Dooyeweerd, Vollenhoven, Van Riessen, Schuurman, Goudzwaard en anderen. In deze benadering wordt een pleidooi gehouden voor een normatieve ontwikkeling van de westerse samenleving. Het gaat hierbij niet alleen om een ontwikkeling naar normen van techniek en economie, maar ook om een ontwikkeling naar normen van rechtvaardigheid, moraliteit en liefde.

In de Proloog wordt de kernvraag van deze studie geïntroduceerd aan de hand van een verhaal uit mijn eigen managementpraktijk. Dit verhaal laat een duidelijke *paradox* zien. In een fabriek krijgen medewerkers de verantwoordelijkheid voor de productie van elektronische componenten. Echter, het fabricageproces is niet stabiel. De ene keer loopt de productie soepel, de andere keer komt er geen goed product uit. Toch moeten de medewerkers verantwoording afleggen over de aantallen en de kwaliteit van de producten die zij maken. De paradox brengt de medewerkers op de werkvloer in een onmogelijke positie: zij worden ter verantwoording geroepen voor een taak die ze niet kunnen uitvoeren.

De sleutelfiguur in deze paradox is de fabricagemanager. Hij of zij moet de voorwaarden vervullen zodat medewerkers verantwoordelijkheid kunnen dragen en verantwoording kunnen afleggen. Als deze voorwaarden niet vervuld worden, dan treedt er een paradox op. In feite neemt de manager de 'binnenbocht'. Hij of zij roept medewerkers ter verantwoording zonder aandacht te geven aan de voorwaarden die hij of zij zélf had moeten vervullen. Eigenlijk wordt daarmee de verantwoordelijkheid van de medewerker gereduceerd tot het afleggen van rekenschap. De onderstaande figuur visualiseert deze binnenbocht.

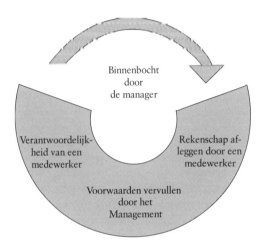

Dit soort paradoxen treedt niet alleen op voor technische aspecten van een productieproces maar ook voor allerlei niet-technische elementen, zoals het opvolgen van veiligheidsinstructies, het voldoen aan milieuvoorschriften, het bijdragen aan goede sociale verhoudingen in een groep, het werken volgens een gedragscode enz. Het mechanisme achter deze paradoxen is in essentie hetzelfde. Medewerkers worden verantwoordelijk gesteld voor bepaalde handelingen, terwijl de voorwaarden om deze verantwoordelijkheid te kunnen dragen niet vervuld zijn. Maar deze paradoxen zijn 'venijniger' door een 'dubbele reductie'. Allereerst wordt verantwoordelijkheid van de medewerker weer gereduceerd tot het afleggen van rekenschap. Maar daarnaast is er weinig oog voor het specifieke karakter van niet-technische verantwoordelijkheden. Vaak worden die verantwoordelijkheden voornamelijk gedefinieerd in technische termen. Met als gevolg dat de integrale verantwoordelijkheid van medewerkers op de werkvloer wordt gereduceerd tot technische verantwoordelijkheden.

Paradoxen komen elke dag voor op de werkvloer van een moderne fabriek. Het problematische is niet het bestaan van zulke paradoxen, maar de vanzelfsprekendheid waarmee managers een binnenbocht nemen. Managers roepen medewerkers ter verantwoording zonder zich de vraag te stellen of de randvoorwaarden – die zij hadden moeten vervullen – daadwerkelijk vervuld zijn. Paradoxen hebben een desastreus effect op gedrag in organisaties. Als managers een binnenbocht nemen, worden medewerkers – om aan hun onmogelijke positie te ontsnappen – gedwongen tot onverantwoordelijk gedrag, zoals het overtreden van veiligheidsinstructies, het negeren van milieuvoorschriften, het falsificeren van gegevens of het creëren van onduidelijkheid. Het behoeft geen betoog dat de aanwezigheid van paradoxen verantwoordelijk gedrag van medewerkers op de werkvloer danig belemmert.

In hoofdstuk 1 wordt deze paradoxen verder onderzocht. Allereerst worden deze paradoxen geplaatst in de context van (de implementatie van) nieuwe productie-concepten. Uit onderzoek blijkt dat deze nieuwe concepten in veel fabrieken niet tot de gewenste resultaten leiden. Om het falen van deze nieuwe benaderingen te begrijpen is een analyse op drie niveaus noodzakelijk: fenomenen op de werkvloer, ontwerptheorieën in de organisatiekunde en filosofie van organisaties. Uit verhalen over de werkvloer blijkt dat de begrippen verantwoordelijkheid en rekenschap een problematisch karakter hebben. Om de achtergrond van deze begrippen te begrijpen wordt eerst een historische schets gegeven van de ontwikkeling van de fabriek. De weg van *Scientific Management*, via de *Human Relations* beweging naar nieuwe productieconcepten wordt beschreven. Vervolgens wordt de vraag naar de verantwoordelijkheid van de mens in een technologisch tijdperk aan de order gesteld. De filosoof Hans Jonas benadrukt dat niet alleen aandacht gegeven moet worden aan normatieve principes voor menselijk gedrag, maar ook aan de moti-vatie van het individu om zich volgens deze principes te gedragen. De manier waarop managers met vragen rond verantwoordelijkheid en rekenschap omgaan, blijkt in hoge mate af te hangen van zijn of haar religieuze of ideologische visie op mens, arbeid en organisatie.

In deze studie wordt ethiek gedefinieerd als de leer van het verantwoordelijk handelen van de mens. De uitdrukking de 'morele dimensie' heeft betrekking op dát aspect van het handelen van de mens waarin de zorg voor de ander of voor de werkelijkheid tot uitdrukking wordt gebracht.

In hoofdstuk 2 wordt de kernvraag van deze studie onderzocht vanuit het gezichts-punt van de fabricagewetenschap. Aan het begin van de twintigste eeuw legde de Amerikaanse ingenieur Frederick Taylor het fundament voor de westerse massafabricage. In de loop van de tijd kwamen de beperkingen van deze benade-ring sterk naar voren. De eenvoudige, eentonige en weinig verantwoordelijke arbeid leidde tot apathie, demotivatie en vervreemding. Later bleek dat deze fa-brieken ook niet meer aan de eisen van de markt konden voldoen. De kwaliteit van de producten was te laag en het productieapparaat was niet flexibel genoeg. Na de Tweede Wereldoorlog werden verschillende nieuwe productieconcepten ontwik-keld om de genoemde beperkingen te kunnen ondervangen. Te weten: *Socio-Technical Systems Design*, *Lean Production*, *Business Process Reengineering*, en het *Mini-Company Concept*. Al deze concepten werden gepresenteerd als efficiënter, effectiever en menselijker alternatief.

Frederick Taylor stelt in zijn boeken dat een harmonieuze samenwerking tussen werkgevers en werknemers kan leiden tot een maximale welvaart voor beide partijen. In zijn visie kan zo'n harmonieuze samenwerking alleen gerealiseerd worden als de productieorganisatie op wetenschappelijke leest geschoeid wordt. In zijn boek *Principles of Scientific Management* identificeert hij vier basisprincipes. Het eerste principe formuleert dat elke productiestap wetenschappelijk geanalyseerd moet worden om de meeste efficiënte productiewijze te kunnen vaststellen. Het tweede principe stelt dat medewerkers op wetenschappelijke wijze geselecteerd en opgeleid moeten worden. Het derde principe benadrukt het belang van een hartelijke samenwerking tussen management en medewerkers. Het laatste principe beschrijft de onderscheiden taak van leidinggevenden en medewerkers. Managers moeten het denkwerk verrichten en controle uitoefenen en medewerkers moeten gestandaardiseerde taken uitvoeren. De opvattingen van Taylor dragen een onoplosbare spanning in zich. Zijn systeem is gebaseerd op twee uitgangspunten: (1) een mentale revolutie bij werkgevers en werknemers en (2) een wetenschappelijke beheersing van het gehele productieproces. Echter, deze twee uitgangspunten staan op gespannen voet met elkaar. In de praktijk blijkt de wetenschappelijke beheersing de boventoon te voeren.

Socio-Technical Systems Design – ook wel sociotechniek genoemd – heeft de Tayloristische basis van de massafabricage scherp aangevallen. De sociotechniek pleit voor een fundamenteel nieuw ontwerp van de organisatie. De Nederlandse variant van de sociotechniek heeft een gedetailleerde ontwerptheorie en ontwerpmethodologie ontwikkeld. Een sleutelprincipe is de reductie van complexiteit door het parallelliseren en segmenteren van de productiestructuur. Het tweede principe is een toename in het regelvermogen van medewerkers op de werkvloer. Toepassing van deze principes leidt tot een organisatie met 'zelfsturende teams' of 'hele taakgroepen'. Zo'n team of groep is geheel verantwoordelijk voor het vervaardigen van een halffabrikaat, een module of een compleet product; inclusief de logistieke planning, kwaliteitsmetingen, reparatie en onderhoud, enz. De Australische en Scandinavische varianten van de sociotechniek benadrukken respectievelijk het participatieve en het communicatieve aspect.

Lean Production is gebaseerd op de Tayloristische principes van arbeidsdeling, standaardisatie, en hiërarchische aansturing. Deze principes zijn verfijnd door de ontwikkeling van een aantal methoden en technieken. *Lean Production* vindt zijn oorsprong in het productiesysteem van Toyota. Dit systeem wordt gekenmerkt door een continue actie om verspilling te elimineren. Het systeem is gebaseerd op twee pilaren: 'just-in-time' en 'autonomation'. Just-in-time is een logistiek concept om een continue flow in de fabriek te realiseren. Autonomation is een technisch concept dat de productie van kwalitatief slechte producten voorkomt. *Lean Production* onderscheidt zich van Taylorisme door zijn nadruk op continu verbeteren en de participatie van medewerkers. Gezien de Tayloristische opzet van de productiestructuur en de productieorganisatie moet *Lean Production* gekarakteriseerd worden als neo-Taylorisme.

Business Process Reengineering richt zich op het hernieuwd ontwerpen van business processen. Hammer en Champy schrijven in hun boek *Reengineering the Corporation. A manifesto for Business Revolution* dat de slechte prestaties van Amerikaanse fabrieken toegeschreven moeten worden aan hun Tayloristische achtergrond. Zij stellen dat organisaties niet rond eenvoudige taken opgebouwd moeten worden, maar rond business processen. Zij pleiten dan ook voor een proces-georiënteerde benadering. Hammer en Champy beschrijven uitvoerig *wat* ze willen: het opnieuw doordenken van de business strategie, het creëren van een nieuwe organisatie, de ontwikkeling van een nieuw soort arbeid, en een verandering in gedrag van medewerkers en managers. Echter, zij vertellen niet *hoe* deze doelstelling gerealiseerd zou moeten worden.

Kioyoshi Suzaki heeft het *Mini-Company Concept* ontwikkeld. Hij benadrukt dat in elke organisatie mensen in het middelpunt moeten staan. Dat betekent voor een fabriek dat de productielijn en de organisatie zo ontworpen moeten zijn, dat mensen het 'waar kunnen maken'. Suzaki benadrukt het belang van een goede productiestructuur. Hij stelt voor om parallelle productielijnen te ontwerpen met een continue flow. De medewerkers die in zo'n lijn werken, vormen een groep of een mini company. Zij zijn verantwoordelijk voor alle aspecten van de productie, inclusief planning, kwaliteit, veiligheid en milieu, relaties met de klant, sociale verhoudingen in de groep, en het continue verbeteren daarvan. Het *Mini Company Concept* kan geïnterpreteerd worden als een sociotechnische benadering waarin klantgerichtheid, participatie en continu verbeteren structureel zijn verankerd.

Samenvattend, *Socio-Technical Systems Design*, *Lean Production*, *Business Process Reengineering*, en het *Mini-Company Concept* bieden verschillende benaderingen van de fabriek. *Socio-Technical Systems Design* in combinatie met het *Mini-Company Concept* bieden de meeste aanknopingspunten voor het ontwikkelen van verantwoordelijk gedrag van medewerkers op de werkvloer.

In hoofdstuk 3 wordt de kernvraag van dit proefschrift onderzocht aan de hand van twee case studies: case Roermond en case Aken. Beide fabrieken waren ontworpen op basis van de principes van *Socio-Technical Systems Design*. In beide fabrieken was de auteur van deze studie fabricagemanager.

Allereerst wordt de gebruikte methodologische benadering besproken. Aan de hand van de literatuur wordt aannemelijk gemaakt dat etnografisch onderzoek een geschikte benadering is om de kernvraag van deze studie te beantwoorden. Met name omdat het specifieke perspectief van een fabricagemanager als '*reflective practitioner*' van groot belang is om de 'dieptestructuur' van verantwoordelijk gedrag van medewerkers op de werkvloer te onderzoeken.

De case Roermond beschrijft de opstart van een actuator fabriek in Roermond (Nederland). Deze fabriek produceerde onderdelen voor de printer industrie. Om aan de eisen van de klant te kunnen voldoen was een fabriek nodig die snel op de veranderingen in de markt kon inspelen. Bijvoorbeeld, door de productie te verhogen of te verlagen en door snel op een ander type over te stappen. De organisatiestructuur van de fabriek was ontwikkeld in een proces van zoeken en vinden. Als richtsnoer voor dit proces werd de Nederlandse benadering van de sociotechniek, het *Mini-Company Concept* en de verbeterfilosofie van Maasaki Imai gebruikt. In de loop van de tijd werd een organisatie ontwikkeld die werd gekarakteriseerd door een intensieve samenwerking tussen alle functies, een groot verantwoordelijkheidsgevoel van de medewerkers, hoge tevredenheid met het werk, en veel vertrouwen in elkaar en in het management. In dit ontwikkelingsproces zijn drie rode draden geïdentificeerd: vier-weg communicatie, participatie en continu verbeteren. De case Roermond laat zien dat een zorgvuldige ontwerp van de productie-, regel- en informatiestructuur essentiële randvoorwaarden zijn voor verantwoordelijk gedrag van medewerkers op de werkvloer. Deze randvoorwaarden komen alleen tot hun recht in een cultuur die gekarakteriseerd wordt door een evenwichtige verdeling van macht en van een hoog niveau van vertrouwen tussen management en medewerkers.

De case Aken beschrijft de turn-around van een glasfabriek in Aken (Duitsland). De doelstelling van deze turn-around was het beëindigen van een verliesgevende situatie en het veilig stellen van de toekomst. In de case Aken kunnen twee rode draden onderkend worden: het creëren van een transparante organisatie en het verbeteren van de processen op de werkvloer. De eerste rode draad was met name aanwezig in het project Future en de tweede in het *world class manufacturing* programma. Het turn-around proces werd sterk gehinderd door twee fenomenen. Het eerste fenomeen was het bestaan van twee – deels conflicterende – talen: een financiële taal en een *total quality management* taal. Het tweede fenomeen was het bestaan van wantrouwen tussen management en medewerkers die een constructieve samenwerking verhinderde. Beide fenomenen droegen bij tot het ontstaan van paradoxen op de werkvloer. De case Aken laat zien dat paradoxen gedijen in een cultuur die wordt gekarakteriseerd door een diepgeworteld wantrouwen tussen management en medewerkers en wijdverspreide gevoelens van machteloosheid.

De case Roermond en de case Aken stemden overeen in de sociotechnische benadering en de aanpak van de kwaliteit door middel van formele programma's. Desondanks zijn er grote verschillen tussen de twee cases. Met name als het gaat om de fenomenen vertrouwen en macht.

In hoofdstuk 4 worden de nieuwe productieconcepten en de beide cases geëvalueerd met het oog op de beantwoording van de kernvraag van deze studie. In paragraaf 1 van dit hoofdstuk wordt een samenvatting gegeven van de voorgaande hoofdstukken.

In paragraaf 2 wordt geconstateerd dat elk productieconcept een visie op mens, organisatie en maatschappij vooronderstelt. Een visie die in hoge mate bepaald wordt door de intellectuele vorming, de sociale afkomst en de fundamentele over-tuigingen van haar grondleggers. En dat geldt natuurlijk ook voor de visie die in deze studie naar voren komt. Voor een goed begrip van deze visie wordt een korte beschrijving wordt gegeven van de wijsgerige, maatschappijkritische en levens-beschouwelijke achtergrond van de auteur.

In paragraaf 3 wordt de belangrijkste onderzoeksstrategie – organisatie-etnografie – geëvalueerd. Uit deze analyse blijkt dat de manager als etnograaf een aantal belangrijke voordelen meebrengt. Hierbij kunnen we denken aan een eerste-orde beschrijving van de gevoelens en intenties van een fabricagemanager, een hoog kennisniveau van de organisatie, de mogelijkheid om te experimenteren en een lange aanwezigheid op de werkvloer. Maar de manager als etnograaf heeft ook een aantal nadelen. Met name is het moeilijk zicht te krijgen op de betrouwbaarheid van zijn of haar eigen observaties. Dit nadeel kan grotendeels ondervangen worden door gebruik te maken van andere observators, het verzamelen van kwantitatieve en semi-kwantitatieve gegevens en het voorleggen van de case beschrijving aan enkele betrokkenen. Vanuit epistemologisch oogpunt is de manager als etnograaf bijzonder interessant omdat deze de rol van actor/experimentator en observator/theoreticus combineert, wat de ontwikkeling van 'grounded theories' bevordert.

In paragraaf 4 wordt nader ingegaan op de verschillen tussen de case Roermond en de case Aken. Deze verschillen zijn voornamelijk terug te voeren op twee fenomenen: vertrouwen en macht. De case Aken wordt gekarakteriseerd door een *low-trust* cultuur en een *low-power* dynamiek. In een *low-trust* cultuur is er weinig vertrouwen tussen management en medewerkers. Het management probeert het gedrag van medewerkers op hiërarchische wijze te beheersen. In reactie daarop proberen medewerkers zich op allerlei manieren aan de beheersingsmacht van het management te onttrekken met als doel om hun eigen belangen veilig te stellen. Het management interpreteert vervolgens de reactie van de medewerkers als bewijs dat 'ze' toch niet te vertrouwen zijn. Met als gevolg dat het management extra hiërarchische maatregelen afkondigt om het gedrag van medewerkers toch te kunnen beheersen. De medewerkers interpreteren deze extra maatregelen als het zoveelste bewijs dat het management toch niet vertrouwd kan worden en probeert zo veel mogelijk de nieuwe maatregelen te ontduiken. Het gevolg hier van is dat de uiteindelijke macht van het management en de medewerkers afneemt. Op deze manier ontstaat er een *low-trust-low-power* spiraal. Het gevolg van deze spiraal is dat paradoxen op de werkvloer niet ontmanteld worden en problemen in de fabriek niet opgelost worden waardoor de effectiviteit van de organisatie afneemt.

De case Roermond schetst juist de tegenovergestelde situatie. In deze case zijn de ontwikkeling van vertrouwen en macht op positieve wijze met elkaar verstrengeld. In het mini-company proces en door deelname aan verbeterteams krijgen medewerkers macht over en invloed op belangrijke aspecten van hun eigen werk. De medewerkers gebruiken deze macht om de problemen op de werkvloer op te lossen. Als deze problemen inderdaad opgelost worden, neemt het vertrouwen van het management in de medewerkers toe met als gevolg dat het management meer macht en invloed delegeert. De medewerkers interpreteren deze reactie van het management als bewijs van vertrouwen en zullen er van hun kant positief op reageren. Bijvoorbeeld door het management goede informatie te geven, paradoxen snel te identificeren en problemen op te lossen. Het management zal hier weer positief op reageren. Het gevolg hier van is dat de uiteindelijke macht van management en medewerkers toeneemt. Op deze manier ontwikkelt zich een *high-trust-high-power* spiraal. Een *high-trust-high-power* spiraal resulteert in een grote hoeveelheid macht waardoor de effectiviteit van de organisatie toeneemt. Vergelijking van de case Roermond en de case Aken laat zien dat high-trust en high-power relaties basisvoorwaarden zijn voor verantwoord gedrag van medewerkers op de werkvloer.

In paragraaf 5 wordt een filosofische analyse gegeven van industriële organisaties. Deze analyse geeft een scherp zicht op de verschillende soorten normen die een rol spelen in de industriële praktijk. Allereerst wordt duidelijk gemaakt dat elke industriële organisatie een multi-dimensioneel karakter heeft. Met name springen de technische dimensie, machtsdimensie, sociale dimensie, economische dimensie, juridische dimensie, morele dimensie en vertrouwensdimensie in het oog. Elke

472

dimensie heeft een eigen aard en karakter. Elke dimensie kent haar eigen patronen, wetten en normativiteit. Deze verschillende dimensies hangen op allerlei manieren met elkaar samen. Een gedetailleerde analyse laat zien dat in een fabriek een aantal vervlochten structuren te onderkennen zijn. Deze vervlochten structuren vertonen een complex karakter ten gevolge van allerlei relaties met de omgeving. Deze filosofische analyse verheldert en articuleert de complexe normativiteit van de fabriek als menselijke organisatie. Tegelijkertijd laat deze analyse zien dat het negeren van deze multi-dimensionele normativiteit leidt tot institutionalisering van kwaad, dehumanisatie van medewerkers, en vervreemding in technische organisaties.

In paragraaf 6 schetsen we een bevrijdend perspectief voor menselijke organisaties. Er wordt een pleidooi gevoerd voor een verantwoordelijkheidsethiek. Een verantwoordelijkheidsethiek benadrukt de fundamentele verantwoordelijkheid van de menselijke actor voor de medemens, de maatschappij en de natuurlijke omgeving. In deze benadering wordt het denken in termen van deugden, plichten en doelen overstegen. We laten zien dat recht gedaan moet worden aan de integrale normatieve structuur van een industriële organisatie. Dat betekent dat niet alleen aandacht gegeven moet worden aan de ontwikkeling van technologische, economische en hiërarchische dimensies van de organisatie – zoals dat in Tayloristische en neo-Tayloristische fabrieken gebeurt – maar ook aan de ontwikkeling van andere dimensies van een organisatie zoals macht, moraal (zorg) en vertrouwen.

In dit bevrijdende perspectief worden drie verschillende lijnen geïntegreerd:

1. een levensbeschouwelijke lijn die gekarakteriseerd wordt met de sleutelwoorden 'waardigheid van de mens' en 'roeping van de mens';
2. een organisatiekundige lijn die samengevat wordt met de woorden 'vertrouwen' en 'macht';
3. een filosofische lijn die gekenmerkt wordt door de begrippen 'multidimensionele normativiteit' en 'normatieve ontwikkeling van organisatiestructuren'.

Een verantwoordelijkheidsethiek begint met de erkenning dat organisaties niet neutraal zijn maar aan normatieve principes onderworpen zijn. Het begint met de erkenning dat het doel van de onderneming niet het maken van winst is, maar het leveren van een waardevolle bijdrage aan de maatschappij. Het begint met de erkenning dat het management niet autonoom is, maar ten dienste van klanten en medewerkers staat.

Hoe kan een medewerker op de werkvloer op verantwoordelijke wijze handelen? Een analyse van beide cases laat zien dat de ontwikkeling van *high-trust* en *high-power* relaties basisvoorwaarden zijn voor verantwoordelijk handelen van medewerkers op de werkvloer van een fabriek. Theoretische reflectie laat zien dat juist de Nederlandse variant van Socio-Technical Systems Design in combinatie met het Mini-Company Concept een kader geeft waarin *high-trust* en *high-power* relaties ontwikkeld kunnen worden. In de ontwikkeling van deze relaties is de fabricagemanager één van de belangrijkste actoren. Zijn of haar opvattingen over mens, arbeid en organisatie spelen een belangrijke rol. Zijn of haar stijl van leidinggeven is van doorslaggevende betekenis. Een multidimensionele normatieve ontwikkeling van industriële organisaties doet recht aan de waardigheid van de mens, ondersteunt de roeping van de individuele medewerker, leidt tot *high-trust* en *high-power* relaties en respecteert de morele belangen van andere stakeholders.

De keuze voor een normatieve ontwikkeling van organisaties is niet de gemakkelijkste weg. Deze keuze gaat in tegen het vigerende denken van de industriële wereld, dat gedomineerd wordt door technische, economische en hiërarchische normen. In deze keuze wordt een fabricagemanager teruggeworpen op zichzelf. Op zijn of haar eigen visie op mens, arbeid en organisatie; op zijn of haar eigen waarden en normen. En dan komen er – ik formuleer deze vragen bewust persoonlijk – kritische vragen naar boven. Zie ik het als mijn eerste roeping om mijn kennis, gaven, vaardigheden en macht te gebruiken voor de ander? Voor de waardigheid en de roeping van mijn medewerkers? Voor de wensen van mijn klanten? Voor de bescherming van het milieu? Of ben ik een verlichte manager die zijn organisatie vormt naar eigen doelstellingen? Een postmoderne manager die gedreven wordt door de neiging om zichzelf steeds weer opnieuw vorm te geven in een continue veranderende organisatie?

In dit kader wil ik wijzen op de Bergrede. In deze rede keert Christus zich op indrukwekkende wijze tegen de bestaande maatschappelijke orde. Zijn zaligsprekingen richten zich niet op koningen en keizers, maar op 'de armen die op God hopen', 'die verdriet hebben', 'die nederig zijn' en 'die ernaar hongeren en dorsten dat God recht doet'. Zijn zaligsprekingen richten zich niet op de machtigen van deze wereld, maar op mensen 'die met anderen medelijden hebben', 'die een zuiver hart hebben', 'die zich inzetten voor de vrede' en 'die vervolgd worden omdat ze recht doen'. Deze zaligsprekingen zijn nog steeds actueel. Ze doen een beroep op de 'groten van de industriële wereld' om de idee van winst als hoogste go(e)d te laten varen, om definitief te breken met de gedachte van hiërarchische beheersing van mens en organisatie, en zich actief in te zetten voor een rechtvaardige en duurzame samenleving. Naar mijn diepste overtuiging kan deze nieuwe orde – paradoxaal genoeg – alleen werkelijkheid worden in de weg van de overgave aan Hem die heeft laten zien dat niet in macht maar in dienstbaarheid het geheim van het menszijn is gelegen.

References

Adler, N., and Docherty, P., 1998, 'Bringing Business into Sociotechnical Theory and Practice', *Human Relations*, vol. 51, no 3, p319-345.

Adler, P.S., and Cole, R.E., 1993, 'Designed for Learning: A Tale of Two Auto Plants', *Sloan Management Review*, vol. 35, no 1, p85-94.

Alvesson, M., and Willmott, H., 1996, *Making Sense of Management. A Critical Introduction*, Sage, London

Alvesson, M., and Willmott, H. (eds.), 1999, 2nd ed. (1982, 1st ed.), *Critical Management Studies*, Sage, London.

Amelsvoort, P. van, 1992, 'Het 'Lean Production' concept: Japanse socio-techniek of neo-Taylorisme?', *Panta Rhei*, vol. 2, no 1, p6-9.

Arendt, H., 1965, *Eichmann in Jerusalem*, Viking Press, New York.

Argyris, C., 1991, 'Teaching Smart People How to Learn', *Harvard Business Review*, May-June, p99-109.

Argyris, C., 1998, 'Empowerment: The Emperor's New Clothes', *Harvard Business Review*, May-June, p98-105.

Arnoni, M.S., 1986, *De overlevenden tellen niet*, Meulenhoff, Amsterdam.

d'Aveni, R., 1994, *Hypercompetition, Managing the Dynamics of Strategic Manoeuvring*, The Free Press, New York.

d'Aveni, R., 1995, *Hypercompetition Rivalries, Competing in Highly Dynamic Environments*, The Free Press, New York.

Bate, S.P., 1997, 'Whatever Happened to Organisational Anthropology? A Review of the Field of Organisational Ethnography and Anthropological Studies', *Human Relations*, vol. 50, no 9, p1147-1175.

Beauchamp, T.L., 1991, 2nd ed. (1982, 1st ed.), *Philosophical Ethics. An Introduction to Moral Philosophy*, McGraw-Hill, New York.

Beauchamp, T.L., and Bowie, N.E., (eds.), 2001, 6th ed., (1979, 1st ed.), *Ethical Theory and Business*, Prentice Hall, New Jersey.

Beek, A. van de, 1996, *Schepping. De wereld als voorspel voor de eeuwigheid*, Callenbach, Baarn.

Beers, M.C., 1996, 'The Strategy That Wouldn't Travel', *Harvard Business Review*, November-December, p18-31.

Benders, J., 1996, 'Leaving Lean? Recent Changes in the Production Organisation of some Japanese Car Plants', *Economic and Industrial Democracy*, vol. 17, no 1, p9-38.

Bendix, R., 1956, *Work and Authority in Industry. Ideologies of Management in the Course of Industrialization*, Wiley, New York.

Berggren, C., 1993, 'Lean Production - The End of History?', *Work, Employment & Society*, vol. 7, no 2, p163-188.

Berkhof, H., 1969, 5th ed. (1960, 1st ed.), *De mens onderweg*, Boekencentrum, 's Gravenhage.

Berkhof, H., 1985, 5th ed. (1973, 1st ed.), *Christelijk geloof*, Callenbach, Nijkerk.

Berkouwer, G.C., 1962, *Man: The Image of God*, Eerdmans, Grand Rapids. Translation of *De mens het beeld Gods* (1957).

Besser, T.L., 1996, *Team Toyota. Transplanting the Toyota Culture to the Camry Plant in Kentucky*, State University of New York Press, New York.

Beteor, 1996, *Mini-companies*, paper HRM Components Conference 1996 (unpublished).

Bigley, G.A., and Pearce, J.L., 1998, 'Straining for Shared Meaning in Organisation Science: Problems of Trust and Mistrust', *Academy of Management Review*, vol. 23, no 3, p405-421.

Bird, F., and Waters, J., 1989, 'The Moral Muteness of Managers', *California Management Review*, vol. 32, no 1, p73-88.

Blau, P.M., 1964, *Exchange and power in social life*, John Wiley, New York.

Blauner, R., 1964, *Alienation and Freedom*, University of Chicago Press, Chicago.

Boersema, J., 1999, *Political-Economical Activity to the Honour of God*, Premier Publishing, Winnipeg.

Boersma, K., Stoep, J. van der, Verkerk, M.J., and Vlot, A. (eds), 2002, *Aan Babels stromen. Een bevrijdend perspectief op ethiek en techniek*, Buijten & Schipperheijn, Amsterdam.

Boje, D.M., Gephart, R.P., and Thatchenkery, T.J., (eds), 1996, *Postmodern Management and Organisation Theory*, Sage, London.

Boje, D.M., and Rosile, G.A., 2001, 'Where's the Power in Empowerment? Answers From Follett and Clegg', *The Journal of Applied Behavioral Science*, vol. 37, no 1, p90-117.

Bolwijn, P.T., and Kumpe, T., 1986, 'Towards the Factory of the Future', *McKinsey Quarterly*, Spring 1986, p40-50.

Bolwijn, P.T., and Kumpe, T., 1991, *Marktgericht ondernemen. Management van continuïteit en vernieuwing*, Van Gorkum, Assen/Maastricht.

Bos, A.P., 1987, *Wetenschap en zinervaring*, VU-uitgeverij, Amsterdam.

Bovens, M.A.P., 1990, *Verantwoordelijkheid en organisatie. Beschouwingen over aansprakelijkheid, institutioneel burgerschap en ambtelijke ongehoorzaamheid*, Tjeenk Willink, Zwolle.

Bowie, N.E., 1999, *Business Ethics: A Kantian Perspective*, Blackwell Publishers, Malden, Massachusetts.

Braithwaite, J., 1985, 'Taking responsibility seriously: Corporate compliance systems', in B. Fisse and P.A. Franch (eds), *Corrigible Corporations and Unruly Law*, San Antonio, p39-61.

Braverman, H., 1974, *Labor and Monopoly Capital. The Degradation of Work in the Twentieth Century*, Monthly Review Press, New York.

Breukelen, Q.A. van, Koolhaas, C.B., and Kumpe, T., 1998, *The Improvement Machine*, Addison, Wesley and Longman, Amsterdam.

Bridges, W., 1994, *Jobshift: how to prosper in a workplace without jobs*, Addison-Wesly, Massachusetts.

Brink, G. van den, et al., 1997, *Filosofie en theologie*, Buijten & Schipperheijn, Amsterdam.

Brüggeman, J.D., 1989, *Humanisering van de arbeid. Bijdrage tot de ontwikkeling van een humaniseringsprofiel*, thesis, University of Amsterdam, Amsterdam.

Burms, A., and Dijn, H. de, 1990, 3rd ed., *De rationaliteit en haar grenzen. Kritiek en deconstructie*, Van Gorkum, Assen.

Carter, H., 1998, 'Re-engineering in practice', *Work Study*, vol. 47, no 4, p135-140.

Champy, J., 1995, *Reengineering Management. The Mandate for New Leadership*, Harper Business, New York.

Cherns, A., 1987, 'Principles of Sociotechnical Design Revisited', *Human Relations*, vol. 40, no3, p153 162.

Clifford, J., and Marcus, G.E., (eds), 1986, *Writing culture*, University of California Press, Berkeley.

Collins, D., 1997, 'The Ethical Superiority and Inevitability of Participatory Management as an Organisational System', *Organizational Science*, vol. 8, no 5, p489-507.

Conti, R., and Warner, M., 1993, 'Taylorism, new technology and just-in-time systems in Japanese manufacturing', *New Technology, Work and Employment*, vol. 8, no 1, p31-42.

Costa, A.C., 2000, *A matter of trust, Effects on the performance and effectiveness of teams in organizations*, thesis Katholieke Universiteit Brabant.

Crozier, M., 1964, *The Bureaucratic Phenomenon*, University of Chicago Press, Chicago. Translation of *Le phénomène bureaucratique: Essai sur les ten dances bureaucratiques des systèmes d'organisations modernes et sur leur re- lations en France avec le système social et culturel* (1963).

Dalla Costa, J., 1998, *The Ethical Imperative. Why Moral Leadership Is Good Business*, Perseus, Massachusetts.

Dalton, M., 1959, *Men who Manage. Fusions of Feeling and Theory in Admini- stration*, Wiley & Sons, New York.

Dalton, M., 1964, 'Preconceptions and methods in *Men who Manage*', in P. Hammond (ed.), *Sociologists at Work*, Basic Books, New York.

Dankbaar, B., 1997, 'Lean Production: Denial, Confirmation or Extension of Sociotechnical Systems Design', *Human Relations*, vol. 50, no 5, p567-583.

Davenport, T.H., and Short, J.E., 1990, 'The New Industrial Engineering: In- formation Technology and Business Process Reengineering', *Sloan Manage- ment Review*, Summer 1990, p11-27.

Deci, E.L., Connell, J.P., and Ryan, R.M., 1989, 'Self-Determination in a Work Organization', *Journal of Applied Psychology*, vol. 74, no 4, p580-590.

Delbridge, R., 1998, *Life on the Line in Contemporary Manufacturing. The Workplace Experience of Lean Production and the 'Japanese' model*, Oxford University Press, Oxford.

Dengerink, J.D., 1986, *De zin van de werkelijkheid*, VU-uitgeverij, Amsterdam.

Dijn, H. de, 1994, *Hoe overleven we de vrijheid*, Kok, Kampen.

Dirks, K.T., and Ferrin, D.L., 2001, 'The role of trust in organizational settings', *Organization Science,* vol. 12, no 4, p450-467.

Dooyeweerd, H., 1935-1936, *De Wijsbegeerte der Wetsidee*, Paris, Amsterdam.

Dooyeweerd, H., 1963, 2nd ed., *Vernieuwing en Bezinning. Om het reformatorisch grondmotief*, Van den Brink, Zutphen.

Dooyeweerd, H., 1967, *Verkenningen in de wijsbegeerte, de sociologie en de rechtsgeschiedenis*, Buijten & Schipperheijn, Amsterdam.

Dooyeweerd, H., 1969, *A New Critique of Theoretical Thought*, Volume I, II, III, The Presbyterian and Reformed Publishing Company, USA.

Dooyeweerd, H., 1975, *In the Twilight of Western Thought. Studies in the Pretended Autonomy of Philosophical Thought*, The Craig Press, Nutley, New Jersey.

Douma, J., 1974, 2nd ed. (1966, 1st ed.), *Algemene genade. Uiteenzetting, vergelijking en beoordeling van de opvattingen van A. Kuyper, K. Schilder en John Calvijn over 'algemene genade'*, Oosterbaan & Lecointre, Goes.

Driscoll, J.W., 1978, 'Trust and Participation in Organizational Decision Making as Predictors of Satisfaction', *Academy of Management Journal*, vol 21, no 1, p44-56.

Dyer, W.G. and Wilkins, A.L., 1991, 'Better Stories, not better Constructs to Generate Better Theory: a Rejoinder to Eisenhardt', *Academy of Management Review*, vol. 16, no 3, p613-619.

Eccles, R.G., and Nohria, N., 1992, *Beyond the Hype. Rediscovering the Essence of Management*, Harvard Business School, Harvard.

Edwards, R., 1979, *Contested Terrain. The Transformation of the Workplace in the Twentieth Century*, Basic Books, New York.

Eijbergen, R. van, 1999, *De invoering en het effect van zelfsturende teams in organisaties*, Lemma, Utrecht.

Eijnatten, F.M. van, 1993, *The Paradigm that Changed the Work Place*, Van Gorkum, Assen.

Eijnatten, F.M. van (ed.), 1995, *Als het maar stroomt! Ulbo de Sitter. Laveren tussen simpel en complex*, Van Gorkum, Assen.

Eijnatten, F.M. van (ed.), 1996, *Sociotechnisch ontwerpen*, Lemma, Utrecht.

Eijnatten, F.M., van, and Zwaan, A.H. van der, 1998, 'The Dutch IOR Approach to Organisational Design: An Alternative to Business Process Reengineering?', *Human Relations*, vol. 51, no 3, p289-318.

Emery, M. (ed.), 1993, Revised ed. (1989, 1st ed.), *Participative Design for Participative Democracy*, Centre for Continuing Education, The Australian National University.

Ewijk-Hoevenaars, A.M. van, Jaarsveld J.C.M. van, and Hertog, J.F. den, 1995, *Naar eenvoud in organisatie. Werken met zelfsturende eenheden*, Kluwer, Deventer.

Forward, G.E., Beach, D.E., Gray, D.A., and Quick, J.C., 1991, 'Mentofacturing: a vision for American industrial excellence', *Academy of Management Executive*, vol. 5, no 3, p32-44.

Fox, A., 1974, *Beyond Contract: Work, Power and Trust Relations*, Faber and Faber Limited, London.

Friedman, M., 1970, 'The Social Responsibility of Business Is to Increase Its Profits', *New York Times Magazine*, September 13th. Reprinted in Beauchamp and Bowie (2001, p51 ff.).

Galan, C. de, Gils, M.R. van, and Strien P.J. van, (eds.), 1983, *Humanisering van de arbeid*, Van Gorkum, Assen.

Geertsema, H.G., 1992, *Het menselijk karakter van ons kennen*, Buijten & Schipperheijn, Amsterdam.

Gerth, H.H., and Wreight Mills, C., 1970, *From Max Weber: essays in sociology*, London.

Geus, A. de, 1997, *The living company. Habits for survival in a turbulent business environment*, HBS Press, Boston.

Gillespie, R., 1991, *Manufacturing Knowledge: A History of the Hawthorne Experiments*, Cambridge University Press, Cambridge.

Glaser, B., and Strauss, A., 1967, *The Discovery of Grounded Theory: Strategies of Qualitative Research*, Wiedenfeld & Nicholson, London.

Goldman S.L., and Nagel, R.N., 1993, 'Management, technology and agility: the emergence of a new era in manufacturing', *International Journal of Technology Management*, vol. 8, no 1/2, p18-38.

Goudzwaard, B., 1979, *Capitalism and Progress, A Diagnosis of Western Society*, Eerdmans, Grand Rapids, Michigan. Translation of *Kapitalisme en vooruitgang. Een eigentijdse maatschappijkritiek* (1976).

Gouldner, A.W., 1954, *Patterns of Industrial Bureaucracy*, The Free Press, New York.

Graham, R.J., 1984, 'Anthropology and OR: The Place of Observation in Management Science Process', *Journal of Operations Research*, vol. 35, no 6, p527-536.

Green, M.R., 1994, *The Ethical Manager. A New Method for Business Ethics*, Prentice Hall, New York.

Griffioen, S., and Balk, B.M. (eds), 1995, *Christian Philosophy at the Close of the Twentieth Century. Assessment and Perspective*, Kok, Kampen.

Guillén, M.F., 1994, *Models of Management. Work, Authority, and Organisation in a comparative perspective*, University of Chicago Press, Chicago.

Gustavsen, B., 1992, *Dialogue and Development*, Van Gorkum, Assen.

Hall, R.W., 1987, *Attaining Manufacturing Excellence*, Dow Jones-Irwin, Homewood, Illinois.

Hammer, M., 1990, 'Reenginering work: don't automate, obliterate', *Harvard Business Review*, July-August 1990, p104-112.

Hammer, M., 1996, *Beyond Reengineering. How the Process-Centred Organisation is Changing Our Work and Our Lives*, Harper Collins Publishers, London.

Hammer, M. and Champy, J., 1994, (1993, 1st ed.), *Reengineering the corporation: a manifesto for business revolution*, Harper Business, New York.

Hammer, M., and Stanton, S.A., 1995, *The Reengineering Revolution. A Handbook*, Harper Business, New York.

Handy, C.B., 1985, 3rd ed. (1976, 1st ed.), *Understanding Organisations*, Penguin, London.

Haren, T.H.C. van, 1984, *Macht in Organisaties*, proefschrift, Rijksuniversiteit Utrecht.

Hassard, J., and Parker, M., (eds), 1994, *Postmodernism and Organisations*, Sage, London.

Hayes, R.H., and Pisano, G.P., 1994, 'Beyond World-Class: The New Manufacturing Strategy', *Harvard Business Review*, January-February 1994, p77-86.

Hayes, R.H., Wheelwright, S.C., and Clark, K.B., 1988, *Dynamic Manufacturing. Creating the Learning Organisation*, The Free Press, New York.

Heisig, U., and Littek, W., 1995, 'Trust as a basis of work organisation', in Littek, W., and Charles, T., *The New Division of Labour. Emerging Forms of Work Organisation in International Perspective*, Walter de Gruyter, London.

Hennestad, B.W., 2000, 'Implementing Participative Management', *The Journal of Applied Behavioural Science*, vol. 36, no 3, p314-335.

Hertog, J.F. den, 1977, *Werkstructurering*, Wolters-Noordhoff, Groningen.

Hertog, J.F. den, and Marie, Ch., 2001, 'Management of Change & Human Resources. Transfer of Learning in the European Steel Industry', Report, Eurofer, Brussels.

Hertog, F.J. den, and Sluijs, F. van, 1995, *Onderzoek in organisatie. Een methologische reisgids*, Van Gorkum, Assen.

Herzberg, F., Mausner, B., and Snyderman, B.B., 1959, *The Motivation to Work*, Wiley, New York.

Heshel, A.J., 1965, *Who is Man?*, Stanford University Press, California.

Hinkelammert, F.J., 1986, *The ideological weapons of Death. A theological critique of Capitalism*, Orbis, New York.

Hirano, H., 1995, *5 Pillars of the Visual Workplace*, Productivity Press, Portland, Oregon.

Hoeven, J. van der, 1980, *Peilingen*, Buijten & Schipperheijn, Amsterdam.

Hofstede, G., 1980, *Culture's Consequences. International Differences in Work-Related Values*, Sage, London.

Hogenhuis, C.T., 1993, 'Beroepscodes en morele verantwoordelijkheid in technische en natuurwetenschappelijke beroepen; een inventariserend onderzoek', *publication of the Ministry of Education and Science*, MCKS, Den Haag.

Hooft, M.C.G. van (ed.), 1996, *Synergetisch produceren in praktijk. Toepassing van de structuurbouw in industrie en dienstverlening*, Van Gorkum, Assen.

Hoogland, J., 1998, *Hoezo bijzonder? Over de vraag hoe universeel een standpunt zijn kan*, Inaugural speech, University of Twente, Enschede.

Hosmer, L.T., 1995, 'Trust: The connecting link between organizational theory and philosophical ethics', *Academy of Management Review*, vol. 20, no 2, p379-403.

Huys, R., Sels, L., Hootegem, G. Van, Bundervoet, J., and Hendrickx, E., 1999, 'Toward Less Division of Labor? New Production Concepts in Automotive, Chemical, Clothing, and Machine Tool Industries, *Human Relations*, vol. 52, no 1, p67-93.

Imai, M., 1986, *Kaizen*, Random House Business Division, New York.

Jacques, R., 1996, *Manufacturing the Employee. Management Knowledge from the 19th to 21st Centuries*, Sage Publications, London.

Japan Human Relations Association (ed.), 1995, *The Improvement Machine. Creativity & Innovation through Employee Involvement*, Productivity Press, Portland.

Jermier, J.M., Knights, D., and Nord, W.R., 1994, *Resistance & Power in Organizations*, Routledge, London.

Jeurissen, R.J.M. (ed.), 2000, *Bedrijfsethiek. Een goede zaak*, Van Gorkum, Assen.

Jochemsen, H., and Glas, G., 1997, *Verantwoord medisch handelen. Proeve van een christelijke medische ethiek*, Buijten & Schipperheijn, Amsterdam.

Jonas, H., 1984, *The Imperative of Responsibility. In Search of an Ethics for the Technological Age*, University of Chicago Press, Chicago. Translation of *Das Prinzip Verantwortung: Versuch einer Ethik für die Technologische Zivilisation* (1979).

Jones, G.R., and George, J.M., 1998, 'The experience and evolution of trust: implications for cooperation and teamwork, *Academy of Management Review*, vol. 23, no 3, p531-546.

Kalsbeek, L., 1975, *Contours of a Christian Philosophy. An Introduction to Herman Dooyeweerd's Thought*, Wedge, Toronto. Translation of *De Wijsbegeerte der Wetsidee. Proeve van een christelijke filosofie* (1970).

Kamata, S., 1986, *Japan on the Passing Lane*, Pantheon Books, New York.

Kanigel, R., 1997, *The One Best Way. Frederick Winslow Taylor and the Enigma of efficiency*, Little, Brown and Company, London.

Kaptein, M., and Wempe, J., 2002, *The Balanced Company. A Theory of Corporate Integrity*, Oxford University Press, Oxford.

Karasek, R., and Theorell, T., 1979, *Healthy work: stress, productivity and the reconstruction of working life*, Basic Books, New York.

Kaulingfreks, R., 1996, *Gunstige vooruitzichten. Filosofische reflecties over organisaties en management*, Kok, Kampen.

Kets de Vries, M.F.R., 1993, *Leaders, Fools and Imposters: Essays on the psychology of leadership*, Jossey-Bass, San Francisco.

Kets de Vries, M.F.R., 1999, 'High-Performance Teams: Lessons from the Pygmies', *Organizational Dynamics*, winter, p66-77.

Kidd, P.T., 1994, *Agile Manufacturing. Forging New Frontiers*, Addison-Wesley, Wokingham, England.

Kieser, A., 1993, 'Die 'Zweite Revolution in der Autoindustrie' - Eine vergleichende Analyse und ihre Schwächen', in F. Meyer-Krahmer (ed.), *Innovationsökonomie und Technologiepolitik. Forschungsansätze und politischen Konsequenzen*, p103-134, Physica-Verlag, Heidelberg.

Klapwijk, J., 1995, *Transformationele filosofie. Cultuurpolitieke ideeën en de kracht van een inspiratie*, Kok, Kampen.

Kobayashi, I., 1995, *20 Keys to Workplace Improvement*, Productivity Press, Portland.

Kramer, R.M., 1999, 'Trust and distrust in organizations: Emerging Perspectives, Enduring Questions', *Annual Review Psychology*, vol. 50, p569-598.

Kramer, R.M., and Neale, M.A. (eds), 1998, *Power and Influence in Organizations*, Sage, London.

Kramer, R.M., and Tyler, T.R., 1996, *Trust in Organizations. Frontiers of Theory and Research*, Sage, London.

Kunneman, H., 1998, *Postmoderne moraliteit*, Boom, Meppel.

Lane, C, and Bachmann, R. (eds), 2001, *Trust Within and Between Organizations. Conceptual Issues and Empirical Applications,* Oxford University Press, Oxford.

Latour, B., 1987, *Science in Action. How to Follow Scientists and Engineers through Society*, Harvard University Press, Cambridge, Massachusetts.

Leede, J. de, 1997, *Innoveren van onderop. Over de bijdrage van taakgroepen aan product- en procesvernieuwing*, thesis, University of Twente, Enschede.

Leonard-Barton, D., 1992, 'The factory as a learning laboratory', *Sloan Management Review*, Fall 1992, p23-38.

Lewicki, R.J., McAllister, D.J., and Bies, R.J., 1998, Trust and distrust: new relationships and realities, *Academy of Management Review*, vol 23, no 3, p438-458.

Lier, M. van, 1998, *Nooit meer werken. Op zoek naar bezieling in je werk*, Spectrum, Utrecht.

Löhr, A., and Blickle, G., 'The Moral Dimension of Recent Organisation Concepts', 1996, *Éthique et Enterprises*, September, no 6, p43-51.

Looise, J.C., 1996, *Sociale innovatie moet, maar hoe?*, Inaugural speech, University of Twente, Enschede.

Luhmann, N., 1979, *Trust and Power*, Wiley, New York. Translation of *Vertrauen* (1973) and *Macht* (1975).

MacIntyre, A., 1984, 2nd ed. (1981, 1st ed.), *After Virtue*, University of Notre Dame Press, Indiana.

MacIntyre, A., 1998, 2nd ed. (1967, 1st ed.), *A Short History of Ethics*, Routledge, London.

Maslow, A., 1954, *Motivation and personality*, Harper & Row, New York.

Mayer, R.C., Davis, J.H., and Schoorman, F.D., 'An integrative model of organizational trust', *Academy of Management Review*, vol. 20, no 3, p709-734.

McAllister, D.J., 1995, 'Affect- and cognition based trust as foundations for inter personal cooperation in organizations', *Academy of Management Journal*, vol. 38, no 1, p24-59.

McGregor, D., 1985, 25th Anniversary Printing, *The Human Side of Enterprise*, McGraw-Hill, New York.

McIntire, C. (ed.), 1985, *The Legacy of Herman Dooyeweerd. Reflections on Critical Philosophy in the Christian Tradition*, University Press of America, Lanham.

Meek, C.B., 1999, '*Ganbatte:* Understanding the Japanese Employee', *Business Horizons*, January-February 1999, p27-36.

Milgram, 1992, 2nd ed. (1977, 1st ed.), *The Individual in a Social World. Essays and Experiments*, McGraw-Hill, New York.

Mishina, K., 1994, 'Seeing is Believing, Believing is Doing, and Doing is Learning: Lessons from Toyota Motor Manufacturing, USA', Paper GERPISA Conference, Paris.

Mok, A.L., 1994, 2nd ed., *Arbeid, bedrijf en maatschappij*, Stenfert Kroese.

Monden, Y., 1998, 3rd ed. (1983, 1st ed.), *Toyota Production System. An Integrated Approach to Just-In-Time*, Engineering & Management Press, Georgia.

Morgan, G., 1986, *Images of Organization*, Sage, London.

Morrison, E.W., and Milliken, F.J., 2000, 'Organizational silence: a barrier to change and development in a pluralistic world', *Academy of Management Review*, vol. 25, no 4, p706-725.

Mulders, P.J., 1991, *Arbeid om te leven en arbeidsleven*, Boekencentrum, 's Gravenhage.

Naschold, F., Cole, R.E., Gustavsen, B., Beinum, H. van, 1993, *Constructing the New Industrial Society*, Van Gorkum, Assen.

Nijhof, A., 1999, *Met zorg besluiten. Een studie naar morele afwegingen van leidinggevenden bij ingrijpende organisatieveranderingen.* Thesis, University of Twente, Enschede, The Netherlands.

Nooteboom. B., 2002, *Trust: forms, foundations, functions, failures and figures*, Edward Elgar, Cheltenham.

Ohno, T., 1988, *Toyota Production System. Beyond Large-Scale Production*, Productivity Press, Portland, Oregon.

Oostrum, J.G.M.P. van, 1989, *Macht en invloed inorganisaties vanuit een onzekerheidsreductieperspectief: een experimentele benadering*, proefschrift, Rijksuniversiteit Utrecht.

Pascale, R.T., and Athos A.G., 1981, *The Art of Japanese Management*, Simon & Schuster, New York.

Paine, L.S., 1994, 'Managing for Organisational Integrity', *Harvard Business Review*, March-April 1994, p106-117.

Peters, T., 1987, *Thriving on Chaos. Handbook for a Management Revolution*, Alfred A. Knopf, New York.

Pierce, J.L., Kostova, T., and Dirks, K.T., 2001, 'Toward a theory of psychological ownership in organizations', *Academy of Management Review*, vol. 26, no 2, p298-310.

Pfeffer, J., 1994, *Competitive Advantage through People*, Harvard Business School Press, Harvard.

Piderit, S.K., 2000, 'Rethinking resistance and recognizing ambivalence: a multidimensional view of attitudes toward an organizational change', *Academy of Management Review*, vol. 25, no 4, p783-794.

Popma, K.J., 1977, *Gestoorde wereld*, Benedictus, Hilversum.

Porter, M.E., 1980, *Competitive Strategy: Techniques for Analysing Industries and Competitors*, The Free Press, New York.

Porter, M.E., 1985, *Competitive Advantage, Creating and Sustaining Superior Performance*, The Free Press, New York.

Pruyt, H.D., 1996, *The Fight against Taylorism in Europe. Strategies, Achievements in Job Design and Technology, Setbacks, Obstacles, Changes for Upgrading Work*, Thesis, Erasmus University, Rotterdam, The Netherlands.

Pugh, D.S., and Hickson, D.J., 1996, 5th ed. (1964, 1st ed.), *Writers on Organisations*, Hutchinson, New York.

Purser, R.E., and Cabana, S., 1998, *The Self-Managing Organisation. How Leading Companies are Transforming the Work of Teams for Real Impact*, The Free Press, New York.

Quinn, J.B., 1992, *Intelligent Enterprise*, The Free Press, New York.

Rawls, J., 1971, *A Theory of Justice*, Harvard University Press, Cambridge.

Reed, M.I., 2001, 'Organization, trust and control: A realist analysis', *Organization Studies*, vol. 22, no 2, p201-228.

Reina, D.S., and Reina, M.L., 1999, *Trust and Betrayal in the Workplace. Building Effective Relationships in Your Organization*, Berrett-Koehler, San Francisco.

Ricoeur, P., 1986, *Le mal: un défi à la philosophie et à la théologie*, Labor et Fides, Genève.

Riessen, H. van, 1949, *Filosofie en Techniek*, Kok, Kampen.

Riessen, H. van, 1953, 3rd ed. (1953, 1st ed.), *De maatschappij der toekomst*, Wever, Franeker.

Riessen, H. van, 1962, *Mens en werk*, Buijten & Schipperheijn, Amsterdam.

Riessen, H. van, 1971, 3rd ed. (1967, 1st ed.), *Mondigheid en de machten*, Buijten & Schipperheijn, Amsterdam.

Rawls, J., 1971, *A Theory of Justice*, Harvard University Press, Cambridge.

Roberts, H.J.F., 1993, *Accountability and Responsibility*, Thesis, University of Maastricht, Maastricht, The Netherlands.

Roethlisberger, F.J., and Dickson W.J., 1967, (original ed. 1939), *Management and the Worker: An Account of a Research Program Conducted by the Western Electric Company, Hawthorne Works, Chicago*, Harvard University Press, Cambridge.

Rosen, M., 1985, 'Breakfast at Spiro's: Dramaturgy and Dominance', *Journal of Management*, vol. 11, no 2, p31-48.

Rosen, M., 1988, 'You Asked for It: Christmas at the Bosses' Expense', *Journal of Management Studies*, vol. 25, no 5, p463-480.

Rosen, M., 1991, 'Coming to terms with the field: understanding and doing organisational ethnography', *Journal of Management Studies*, vol. 28, no 1, p1- 24.

Rothschild, J., and Ollilainen, M., 1999, 'Obscuring But Not Reducing Managerial Control: Does TQM Measure up to Democratic Standards?', *Economic and Industrial Democracy*, vol. 20, no 4, p583-623.

Rousseau, D.M., Sitkin, S.B., Burt, R.S., and Camerer, C., 1998, 'Not so different after all: a cross-discipline view of trust', *Academy of Management Review*, vol. 23, no 3, p393-404.

Runcie, J.F., 1980, 'By days I make the cars', *Harvard Business Review*, May-June 1980, p106-114.

Sasaki, N., and Hutchins, D. (eds.), 1984, *The Japanese Approach to Product Quality. It's Applicability to the West*, Pergamon Press, Oxford.

Scandura, T.A., and Williams, E.A., 2000, 'Research methodology in management: current practices, trends, and implications for future research', *Academy of Management Research*, vol. 43, no 6, p1248-1264.

Schein, E., 1999, *The Corporate Culture Survival Guide: Sense and Nonsense About Cultural Change*, Jossey-Bass, San Francisco.

Schilder, K., 1977, *Christ and Culture*, Premier, Winnipeg. Translation of *Christus en cultuur* (1948).

Schipper, F., 1993, *Zin in organisatie. Een filosofische beschouwing over organisatiecultuur en rationaliteit*, Boom, Meppel.

Schonberger, R.J., 1982, *Japanese Manufacturing Techniques. Nine Hidden Lessons in Simplicity*. The Free Press, New York.

Schonberger, R.J., 1986, *World Class Manufacturing. The Lessons in Simplicity Applied*. The Free Press, New York.

Schonberger, R.J., 1996, *World Class Manufacturing: The Next Decade. Building Power, Strength, and Value*. The Free Press, New York.

Schrey, H.H., 1977, 2nd ed. (1972, 1st ed.), *Einführung in die Ethik*, Wissenschaftliche Buchgesellschaft, Darmstadt.

Schumacher, E.F., 1973, *Small is beautiful*, Blond & Briggs, London.

Schumacher, P.C., 1983, *Manufacturing System Design. the Schumacher Work Structuring Methods, steps I to VI*, training manual Philips Electronics, Surey/London.

Schuurman, E., 1980, *Technology and the Future: A Philosophical Challenge*, Wedge, Toronto. Translation of *Techniek en Toekomst. Confrontatie met wijsgerige beschouwingen* (1972).

Schuurman, E., 2002, *Bevrijding van het Technische Wereldbeeld. Uitdaging tot een andere ethiek*, farewell lecture, University of Delft.

Schwartz, Y., 1992, *Travail et Philosophie. Convocations mutuelles*, Octares, Toulouse.

Scott-Morgan, P., 1994, *The Unwritten Rules of the Game*, McGraw-Hill, New York.

Sheppard, B.H., and Sherman, D.M., 1998, 'The grammars of trust: a model and general implications', *Academy of Management Review*, vol. 23, no 3, p422-437.

Simmons, A., 1999, *A Safe Place for Dangerous Truths*, Amacom, New York.

Simonse, L., 1994, 'Business Process Reengineering: Sociotechnisch organisatie-herontwerp in een informatietechnologisch 'jasje'?', *Panta Rhei*, vol. 4, no 2, p9-15.

Sitter, L.U. de, 1981, *Op weg naar nieuwe fabrieken en kantoren*. Kluwer, Deventer.

Sitter, L.U. de, Vermeulen A.M.M., Amelsvoort, P. van, Geffen, L. van, Troost, P. van, and Verschuur, F.O., 1986, *Het flexibele bedrijf*, Kluwer, Deventer.

Sitter, L.U. de, 1993, 'A Socio-Technical Perspective', in Van Eijnatten (1993, p158-184).

Sitter, L.U. de, 1994, *Synergetisch produceren. Human Resources Mobilisation in de produktie: een inleiding in de structuurbouw*, Van Gorkum, Assen.

Sitter, L.U. de, Hertog, J.F. den, and Dankbaar, B., 1997, 'From Complex Organisations with Simple Jobs to Simple Organisations with Complex Jobs', *Human Relations*, vol. 50, no 5, p497-534.

Skinner, W., 1986, 'The productivity paradox', *Harvard Business Review*, July-August 1986, p55-59.

Skinner, W., 1988, 'What Matters to Manufacturing', *Harvard Business Review*, January-February 1988, p10-16.

Slater, P.E., and Dennis, W.G., 1964, 'Democracy in inevitable', *Harvard Business Review*, March-April 1964, p51-59.

485

Solomon, R.C., 1993, *Ethics and Excellence. Cooperation and integrity in business*, Oxford University Press, Oxford.

Spear, S., and Bowen, H.K., 1999, 'Decoding the DNA of the Toyota Production System', *Harvard Business Review*, September-October 1999, p97-106.

Stainer, A., and Stainer, L., 1995, 'Productivity, quality and ethics - a European viewpoint', *European Business Reveiw*, vol. 6, no 6, p3-11.

Steinmann, H., und Löhr, 1988, 'Unternehmensethik - eine "realistische Idee"', *Zeitschrift für betriebswirtschaftlicher Forschung*, vol. 40, p299-317.

Strauss, A, and Corbin, J., 1990, *Basics of Qualitative Research: Grounded Theory, Procedures and Techniques*, Sage, Newbury Park.

Suzaki, K., 1987, *The New Manufacturing Challenge. Techniques for Continuous Improvement*, Free Press, New York.

Suzaki, K., 1993, *The New Shop Floor Management; Empowering People for Continuous improvement*, The Free Press, New York.

Suzaki, K., 1996, *Reflection of my work with Philips*, Internal note.

Tannenbaum, A.S., 1968, *Control in Organizations*, Mc Graw-Hill, New York.

Tannenbaum, A.S., Kavcic, B., Rosner, M., Vianello, M., and Wieser, G., 1974, *Hierarchy in Organizations*, Jossey-Bass, San Francisco.

Taylor, F.W., 1903, *Shop Management*, reprinted in *Scientific Management*, Harper & Row (1947), London.

Taylor, F.W., 1911, *The Principles of Scientific Management*, reprinted in *Scientific Management*, Harper & Row (1947), London.

Taylor, F.W., 1912, *Taylor's Testimony Before the Special House Committee*, reprinted in *Scientific Management*, Harper & Row (1947), London.

Taylor, F.W., 1947, *Scientific Management*, Harper & Row, London.

Taylor, J.C., and Felten, D.F., 1993, *Performance by Design. Socio-technical Systems in North America*, Prentice Hall, New Jersey.

Teal, T., 1996, 'The Human Side of Management', *Harvard Business Review*, November-December 1996, p35-44.

Toyota, 1992, *Toyota Production System*, Toyota Motor Corporation, Tokyo.

Treviño, L.K., and Nelson, K.A., 1999, 2nd ed., *Managing Business Ethics. Straight Talk About How To Do It Right*, Wiley, New York.

Trist, E.L., and Bamforth, K.W., 1951, 'Some Social and Psychological Consequences of the Longwall Method of Coal-getting', *Human Relations*, vol. 4, no 1, p3-38.

Trist, E.L., and Murray H. (eds), 1993, *The Social Engagement of Social Science, Volume II: The Socio-Technical Perspective*, University of Pennsylvania Press, Philadelphia.

Trompenaars, F., 1993, *Riding the Waves of Culture. Understanding Cultural Diversity in Business*. Nicholas Brealy Publishing, London.

Troost, A., 1993, 'Toward a Reformational Theory of Action', *Philosophia Reformata*, vol. 58, no 2, p221-236.

Veldman, J., 1998, *Project bedrijfspastoraat. Een historisch en theologisch onderzoek naar een verantwoord spreken van de gelovige in de economie*, Kok, Kampen.

Velema, W.H., 1974, *Ethiek en pelgrimage*, Bolland, Amsterdam.

Verkerk, M.J., 1989, 'Gödel, Escher, Bach & Dooyeweerd', *Philosophia Reformata*, vol. 54, no 2, p111-146.

Verkerk, M.J., 1997, *Sekse als antwoord*, Buijten & Schipperheijn, Amsterdam.

Verkerk, M.J., 1998, 'Verantwoordelijkheid op de werkvloer? (I), *Beweging*, vol. 62, no 4, p8-12.

Verkerk, M.J., 2002a, 'Het ontwerpen en ontwikkelen van een verantwoorde onderneming (I), *Beweging*, vol. 66, no 2, p4-9.

Verkerk, M.J., 2002b, 'Het ontwerpen en ontwikkelen van een verantwoorde onderneming (II), *Beweging*, vol. 66, no 4, p10-14.

Verkerk, M.J., and Loode, J. de, 1997, 'Tussen beheersing en verantwoordelijkheid', *Filosofie in Bedrijf*, vol. 7, no 1, p9 21.

Verkerk, M.J., and Leede, J. de, 1999, 'Verantwoordelijkheid op de werkvloer? (II), *Beweging*, vol. 63, no 1, p7-11.

Verkerk, M.J., Leede, J. de, Tas, H.J. van der, 1997, *Marktgericht productiemanage-ment. Van taakgroep naar mini-company*, Kluwer, Deventer.

Verkerk, M.J., and Vegter, W., 1990, 'Het cultuurmandaat is geen zeepbel', *Radix*, vol. 16, no 1, p33-44.

Verkerk, M.J., and Zijlstra, A., 2003, 'Philosophical analysis of industrial organisations', *Philosophia Reformata*, vol. 68, no 2, p101-122.

Voss, C.A., 1988, 'Implementation: A Key Issue in Manufacturing Technology: The Need for a Field of Study', *Research Policy*, vol. 17, p55-63.

Walker, C.R., and Guest, R.H., 1952, *The man on the assembly line*, Harvard University Press, Cambridge, Massachusetts.

Warnecke, H.J., 1993, *The Fractal Company. A Revolution in Corporate Culture*, Springer-Verlag, Berlin.

Watson, T.J., 1994, *In Search of Management. Culture, Chaos & Control in Managerial Work*, Thomson Business Press, London.

Weaver, G.R., Treviño, L.K., and Cochran, P.L., 1999, 'Corporate Ethics Programs as Control Systems: Influences of Executive Commitment and Environmental Factors', *Academy of Management Journal*, vol. 42, no 1, 41-57.

Weerd, H. de, 2001, *Plezier in Werken. Zingevingsaspecten en Waarden op de Werkvloer*, thesis, Universiteit voor Humanistiek, Utrecht.

Weers, A.J.M. van, 1977, 'Het bevredigend antwoord. Een analyse van het begrip 'verantwoordelijkheid', *Tijdschrift voor Filosofie*, vol. 39, no 2, p207-245.

Weick, K.E., 1979, 2nd ed. (1969, 1st ed.), *The Social Psychology of Organising*, McGraw-Hill, New York.

Weick, K.E., 1995, *Sensemaking in Organisations*, Sage, London.

Wheelwright, S.C., and Hayes, R.H., 1985, 'Competing Through Manufacturing', *Harvard Business Review*, January-February 1985, p99-109.

Whitener, E.M., Brodt, S.E., Korsgaard, M.A., and Werner, J.M., 1998, 'Managers as initiators of trust: an exchange relationship framework for understanding managerial trustworthy behavior', *Academy of Management Review*, vol. 23, no 3, 513-530.

Widdershoven, G.A.M., 2000, *Ethiek in de kliniek. Hedendaagse benaderingen in de gezondheidsethiek*, Boom, Meppel.

Williams, K., Haslam, C., Williams, J., and Cutler, T., 1992, 'Against lean production', *Economy and Society*, vol. 21, no 3, p321-354.

Williams, M., 2001, 'In whom we trust: Group membership as an effective context for trust development', *Academy of Management Review*, vol. 26, no 3, p377-396.

Willigenburg, T. van, Beld, A. van den, Heeger, F.R., en Verweij, M.F., 1998, 2nd ed. (1993, 1st ed.), *Ethiek in de praktijk*, Van Gorkum, Assen.

Wolters, A.M., 1984, *Creation regained: biblical basics for a reformational world view*, Eerdmans, Grand Rapids, Michigan.

Wolterstorff, N., 1984, 2nd ed. (1976, 1st ed.), *Reason within the Bounds of Religion*, Eerdmans, Grand Rapids, Michigan.

Womack, J.P., Jones, D.T., and Roos, D., 1991, (original ed. 1990), *The Machine that Changed the World*, Harper Perennial, New York.

Womack, J.P., and Jones, D.T., 1997, (original ed. 1996), *Lean Thinking. Banish Waste and Create Wealth in Your Corporation*, Touchstone Books, London.

Woudenberg, R. van, 1996, *Kennis en werkelijkheid. Tweede inleiding tot een christelijke filosofie*, Buijten & Schipperheijn, Amsterdam.

Yin, R.K., 1994, 2nd ed. (1984, 1st ed.), *Case Study Research*, Sage, Beverly Hills.

Zuthem, H.J. van, 1993, *Verantwoord bestaan. Over de noodzaak en de grenzen van persoonlijke verantwoordelijkheid*, Kok, Kampen.

Acknowledgements

The writing of this thesis was a great adventure. In the very beginning it was obvious that I would investigate processes on the shop floor and would reflect on my own work as a factory manager. At that time, the approach, aim, and relevant theoretical perspectives were not yet defined. In the first draft of this study the words 'trust' and 'power' were not even present. At the start of the investigations it was decided that ethnography would be used as the main research method. It was not until the analysis of the case studies that the importance of the phenomena of 'trust' and 'power' came to the fore. I was really excited when I discovered that many phenomena in the factories that I had managed were related and could be interpreted in terms of *trust-power* dynamics. Especially when I could link these dynamics with my own experiences of trust and mistrust, power and powerlessness, relaxation and stress, and happiness and distress. In addition, I was enthusiastic when I discovered that trust and power were normative dimensions of manufacturing organisations that are crucial in enabling the processes of responsibility and accountability on the shop floor. Especially when I could develop an industrial ethics using the basic ideas of the socio-technical tradition and reformational philosophy.

Reflecting on my own work has been difficult. It required being open with my own emotions, being critical of my own intentions, and intensive soul searching. Above all, reflection requires peace and quiet. In manufacturing the pace of life is very fast. Therefore I had to tear myself away from the daily activity to create the conditions for reflection.

I am very thankful that I could finish this study. First of all, I would like to thank my heavenly Father who gave me the drive, capabilities and strength to write this thesis. He guided my family and me in times of difficulties and during reorganisations and dismissals. He cared for us like a shepherd who cares for his sheep (Psalm 23).

I would like to thank Friso den Hertog and Egbert Schuurman for supervising this study. It was very fruitful to have supervisors with different backgrounds, i.e. organisational science and philosophy. I was offered two different perspectives from which to analyse problems and investigate the research questions. At the same time, I was urged to manage the natural tension between disciplinary evaluation and philosophical reflection.

Egbert Schuurman gave me the final push to begin this study. He convinced me to complete my philosophical education by investigating human responsibility in manufacturing organisations. He insisted that this study should have a solid organisational basis to make ethical and philosophical reflection possible. He pointed out the importance of a fundamental analysis of technical organisations to discover the normative structure of organising. He strongly stimulated me by his prophetic view on the meaning of technology in relation to the Kingdom of God. I have enjoyed the regular visits to him and his wife very much.

Friso den Hertog strongly supported the idea of studying processes on the shop floor from the perspective of a factory manager. He forced me to open the 'box of management'. He questioned me about my style of management, my role in change processes, and my own emotions and intentions. He functioned as a buddy to interpret my ethnographical observations and to discover my own 'schemes of interpretation'. He changed my view several times by asking me only one or two questions. He especially challenged me to show the importance of Christian belief in the practice and theory of factory management. I have very good memories of our pleasant discussions during dinner and over a glass of wine.

I would like to thank my mother for her love and interest during this study. In writing this thesis my thoughts have regularly returned to my father who passed away in 1991. In his working life he was an inspector in the building industry. He set an example for me to do justice in labour relations and to interpret the rules creatively in order to protect the weak.

I would like to thank my wife Nienke for her devotion and support. I am very thankful that I could discuss the fundamental questions of this study with her. She regularly offered me a third perspective from her own discipline – psychology. I would like to thank my kids Remme and Femmie, Jaapjan, Marc and Marianne for their loving interest. Reflecting, reading and writing is also a way for me to relax from daily stress. Therefore I am grateful for the opportunity to retire in the study.

I would like to express my appreciation to my colleagues at Philips who functioned as the main characters in this book. I have told them about my interest in organisational processes and about my plans to publish a thesis about the shop floor. Some of them have read parts of this study in the form of a book or article. Others have read the first draft of the case descriptions. I have made their roles as anonymous as possible. In addition, I asked them permission to use their quotations in this study. I would like to thank Peter Franken for his permission to publish the Roermond case, Cor Saris for his permission to publish the Aachen case, and Bernt Mansfeld for his permission to use the photograph on the cover of this book. I would like to thank Erica van Riet, Jan de Leede and Henk van der Tas for their support in the development of the Mini-Company Concept in Roermond, Arthur Zijlstra for the numerous discussions about ethics, philosophy, and the development of western society, and Jan Westert for our talks about the quality of working life. I would especially like to thank all the operators who told me their stories, their feelings and emotions, and their views on the meaning of work.

I would like to thank Wouter Vuurboom for making the lay-out. I would like to express my appreciation to the Stichting Psyché Nikai and the Gereformeerd Maatschappelijk Verbond for their financial upport to publish this study.

Curriculum Vitae

Maarten Johannes Verkerk was born on 3 August 1953 in Ruwiel, The Nether-lands. In 1971 he finished secondary school (College Blaucapel in Utrecht). In 1977 he obtained his Master's (cum laude) degree in Chemistry. Between 1978 and 1981, he worked as a Junior Scientist at the Technical University of Twente. In 1982 he received his Ph. D. in the Technical Sciences with his thesis entitled *Electrical Conductivity and Interface Properties of Oxygen Ion Conducting Materials*. From 1982 to 1986 he worked as a Senior Scientist at Philips Natuurkundig Laboratorium in Eindhoven. In the period between 1986 and 2002 he worked as a Factory Manager in The Netherlands, Taiwan, and Germany. Within this position, he was responsible for the production of image intensifiers, multilayer actuators, television screens, and ceramic multilayer capacitors. In 2003 he took on the role of Manager in a psychiatric hospital in Maastricht. In January 1998, it was agreed that he would begin his second Ph. D. as a non-university member.